UNDERSTANDING AND RESPONDING TO TERRORISM

NATO Security through Science Series

This Series presents the results of scientific meetings supported under the NATO Programme for Security through Science (STS).

Meetings supported by the NATO STS Programme are in security-related priority areas of Defence Against Terrorism or Countering Other Threats to Security. The types of meeting supported are generally "Advanced Study Institutes" and "Advanced Research Workshops". The NATO STS Series collects together the results of these meetings. The meetings are co-organized by scientists from NATO countries and scientists from NATO's "Partner" or "Mediterranean Dialogue" countries. The observations and recommendations made at the meetings, as well as the contents of the volumes in the Series, reflect those of participants and contributors only; they should not necessarily be regarded as reflecting NATO views or policy.

Advanced Study Institutes (ASI) are high-level tutorial courses to convey the latest developments in a subject to an advanced-level audience.

Advanced Research Workshops (ARW) are expert meetings where an intense but informal exchange of views at the frontiers of a subject aims at identifying directions for future action.

Following a transformation of the programme in 2004 the Series has been re-named and re-organised. Recent volumes on topics not related to security, which result from meetings supported under the programme earlier, may be found in the NATO Science Series.

The Series is published by IOS Press, Amsterdam, and Springer Science and Business Media, Dordrecht, in conjunction with the NATO Public Diplomacy Division.

Sub-Series

A.	Chemistry and Biology	Springer Science and Business Media
B.	Physics and Biophysics	Springer Science and Business Media
C.	Environmental Security	Springer Science and Business Media
D.	Information and Communication Security	IOS Press
E.	Human and Societal Dynamics	IOS Press

http://www.nato.int/science
http://www.springer.com
http://www.iospress.nl

Sub-Series E: Human and Societal Dynamics – Vol. 19   ISSN: 1574-5597

Understanding and Responding to Terrorism

Edited by

Huseyin Durmaz
University of North Texas, USA
Police Major, Turkish National Police – Interpol-Europol-Sirene Department

Bilal Sevinc
Michigan State University, USA
Police Major, Turkish National Police – Anti-terrorism Department

Ahmet Sait Yayla
Police Major, Turkish National Police – Anti-terrorism Department

and

Sıddık Ekici
University of North Texas, USA
Police Major, Turkish National Police

Amsterdam • Berlin • Oxford • Tokyo • Washington, DC

Published in cooperation with NATO Public Diplomacy Division

Proceedings of the NATO Advanced Research Workshop on Policing Responses to Terrorist Operations
Washington, USA
8–9 September 2006

© 2007 IOS Press.

All rights reserved. No part of this book may be reproduced, stored in a retrieval system, or transmitted, in any form or by any means, without prior written permission from the publisher.

ISBN 978-1-58603-740-6
Library of Congress Control Number: 2007925114

Publisher
IOS Press
Nieuwe Hemweg 6B
1013 BG Amsterdam
Netherlands
fax: +31 20 687 0019
e-mail: order@iospress.nl

Distributor in the UK and Ireland
Gazelle Books Services Ltd.
White Cross Mills
Hightown
Lancaster LA1 4XS
United Kingdom
fax: +44 1524 63232
e-mail: sales@gazellebooks.co.uk

Distributor in the USA and Canada
IOS Press, Inc.
4502 Rachael Manor Drive
Fairfax, VA 22032
USA
fax: +1 703 323 3668
e-mail: iosbooks@iospress.com

LEGAL NOTICE

The publisher is not responsible for the use which might be made of the following information.

PRINTED IN THE NETHERLANDS

Preface

This book represents the proceedings from the North Atlantic Treaty Organization's 2006 Advanced Research Workshop on "Policing Responses to Terrorist Operations." This NATO Workshop was held in Washington D.C. on September 8–9, 2006, alongside of two complementary workshops on various aspects of terrorism organized on the general theme of *"Understanding and Responding to Terrorism: A Multi-dimensional Approach."* The event was planned and organized by the Turkish Institute for Police Studies (TIPS) with the excellent support from NATO and the Turkish National Police.

At the workshop, distinguished participants from academia and law enforcement came together to discuss how to advance cooperation levels and to explore workable ways to counter terrorism. A total of 69 participants made presentations in twelve sessions.

The workshop was organized around three main topics:

1. Dynamics of effective international cooperation against terrorism: Facilitators and barriers;
2. Law enforcement response to terrorism in different countries and regions; and
3. Emergency management lessons for Homeland Security.

On the first topic on the role of international organizations, the barriers for cooperation and their solutions were explored. With respect to the second topic, participants explained their respective country's legislative efforts against terrorism, the level of terrorism threat they experience, and how law enforcement agencies fight terrorism in their respective states. The third topic included evaluations of the response and recovery operations that are implemented after terrorist attacks in order to enhance emergency management and homeland security policies and procedures as well as the integration of crisis and consequence management activities.

Following the classification of the workshop topics, the articles in this book have been categorized in five parts:

1. International Police Cooperation
2. National Approaches to Terrorism
3. Responding to Terrorism
4. Terrorism Emergency Management
5. Closing Remarks

We hope this book will be a useful source to better understand and respond to the terrorism threat. Many thanks to the TIPS members who provided enormous help in making the event successful and to all participants for their contributions. We are also grateful to the NATO Science Programme for funding the workshop and this publication and to the Turkish National Police for their great support.

Mathieu Deflem and Huseyin Durmaz
March 2007

Principal Contributors

Mehmet Afacan
Ph.D. Candidate, Northeastern University, USA

Huseyin Akdogan
Ph.D. Candidate, Department of Public Administration, University of North Texas, USA

Arif Akgul
Ph.D. Candidate, Department of Political Science and Criminal Justice, Washington State University, USA

Giuli Alasania, Ph.D.
Professor, International Black Sea University, Georgia

Necati Alkan
Police Major, Psychologist, Counter Terrorism and Operation Department, Turkish National Police

Sudha Arlikatti, Ph.D.
Assistant Professor, Department of Public Administration, University of North Texas, USA

Suleyman Aydin, Ph.D.
Turkish National Police Academy

Abraham Benavides, Ph.D.
Assistant Professor, University of North Texas, USA

Huseyin Cinoglu
Ph.D. Candidate, Sociology Department, University of North Texas, USA

M. Cemil Citak
Police Major, Counter Terrorism and Operation Department, Turkish National Police

Mathieu Deflem, Ph.D.
Associate Professor, Department of Sociology, University of South Carolina, USA

Serhat Demir, Ph.D.
Political Science Department, Kent State University, USA

Huseyin Durmaz, Ph.D.
Information Science Department, University of North Texas, USA

Sıddık Ekici
Ph.D. Candidate, Department of Public Administration, University of North Texas, USA

Kubra Gultekin
Ph.D. Candidate, Information Science Department, University of North Texas, USA

Recep Gultekin, Ph.D.
Police Chief, Head of Foreign Relation Department, Turkish National Police

Sebahattin Gultekin
Ph.D. Candidate, Department of Public Administration, University of North Texas, USA

Cuneyt Gurer, Ph.D.
Political Science Department, Kent State University, USA

Jennifer Hurst
Assistant Director, Public Safety and Terrorism Sub-Directorate, Interpol General Secretariat, Lyon, France

Olena Ivaschenko
Major, Senior Desk Officer of international Relations Department, Ministry of Interior, Ukraine

Alican Kapti
Ph.D. Candidate, Department of Public Administration, University of North Texas, USA

Naim Kapucu, Ph.D.
Assistant Professor, Department of Public Administration, University of Central Florida, USA

Elnur Kazimli, Ph.D.
Instructor, Qafqaz University, Azerbaijan

James Kendra, Ph.D.
Assistant Professor, Emergency Administration and Planning Program, Department of Public Administration, University of North Texas, USA

Mykola Khaschevoi
General-Major, Deputy Head of Organized Crime Department, Ministry of Interior, Ukraine

Kambarali T. Kongantiev
Attorney General of Kyrgyz Republic

Michael K. Lindell, Ph.D.
Professor, Department of Landscape Architecture and Urban Planning, Texas A&M University, USA

Robyn R. Mace, Ph.D.
Specialist, Michigan State University, USA

Otwin Marenin, Ph.D.
Professor, Department of Political Science and Criminal Justice, Washington State University, USA

David A. McEntire, Ph.D.
Associate Professor, Department of Public Administration, University of North Texas, USA

Edmund F. McGarrell, Ph.D.
Professor, Director of School of Criminal Justice, Michigan State University, USA

Farhad Mehdiyev, Ph.D.
Acting Dean of Law Faculty, Qafqaz University, Azerbaijan

Ersin Oguz, M.D.
Gynecologist and Obsetrician, Turkey

Iskender Ormon Uulu, Ph.D.
International Ataturk-Alatoo University, Kyrgyzstan

Zeki Pamuk
Ph.D. Candidate, Criminal Justice Department, University of Cincinnati, USA

Carla S. Prater, Ph.D.
Associate Director, Hazard Reduction & Recovery Center Department of Landscape Architecture and Urban Planning, Texas A&M University, USA

Max-Peter Ratzel
Director of Europol, The Netherlands

Mitchel P. Roth, Ph.D.
Professor, College of Criminal Justice, Sam Houston State University, USA

Jack L. Rozdilsky, Ph.D.
Assistant Professor, Emergency Administration and Planning Program, Department of Public Administration, University of North Texas, USA

Ali Safak, Ph.D.
Professor, Faculty of Security Sciences, Turkish National Police Academy

Armen Sanoyan
Chief Specialist, Ministry of Justice, Republic of Armenia

Monica Schoch-Spana, Ph.D.
Senior Associate, Center for Biosecurity of the University of Pittsburgh Medical Center, USA

Murat Sever
Ph.D. Candidate, College of Criminal Justice, Sam Houston State University, USA

Stephen Sloan, Ph.D.
Professor and Fellow, Office of Global Perspectives, University of Central Florida, USA

Trpe Stojanovski, Ph.D.
Assistant Minister for European integration and international cooperation, Police Academy, University of St. Kliment Ohridski, Ministry of Internal Affairs of the Republic of Macedonia

Samih Teymur, Ph.D.
Police Major, Director of Turkish Institute for Police Studies
Information Science Department, University of North Texas, USA

Derin N. Ural, Ph.D.
Associate Professor, Civil Engineering, and Founding Director, Center of Excellence for Disaster Management, Istanbul Technical University, Turkey

Tricia Wachtendorf, Ph.D.
Disaster Research Center, Department of Sociology and Criminal Justice, University of Delaware, USA

M. Murat Yasar, Ph.D.
Police Major, Anti-Smuggling and Organized Crime Department, Turkish National Police

Ahmet Sait Yayla, **Ph.D.**
Police Major, Anti-terrorism Department, Turkish National Police

Selcuk Zengin, Ph.D.
Information Science Department, University of North Texas, USA

Contents

Preface   v
    Mathieu Deflem and Huseyin Durmaz

Principal Contributors   vii

Part 1. International Police Cooperation

Chapter 1. Interpol – Providing Support and Assistance to Combat International Terrorism   3
    Jennifer Hurst

Chapter 2. Europol in the Combat of International Terrorism   11
    Max-Peter Ratzel

Chapter 3. International Police Cooperation Against Terrorism: Interpol and Europol in Comparison   17
    Mathieu Deflem

Chapter 4. International Organizations and Non-Traditional Conflicts   26
    Cuneyt Gurer and Serhat Demir

Chapter 5. Barriers to International Police Cooperation in the Age of Terrorism   42
    Mitchel P. Roth and Murat Sever

Chapter 6. Employing Global Need-Based Information and Technology Sharing to Enhance Cooperation Among Law Enforcement Organizations   56
    Selcuk Zengin and M. Murat Yasar

Chapter 7. Extradition of Terror Suspects and Developments in Extradition Process   66
    Huseyin Durmaz

Chapter 8. Global Developments in Transnational Police Training: TADOC (Turkish International Academy Against Drugs and Organized Crime)   84
    Arif Akgul and Otwin Marenin

Chapter 9. Establishing the International Institute for Police Research and Training in Turkey   99
    Recep Gultekin, Samih Teymur, Selcuk Zengin, Huseyin Cinoglu and Kubra Gultekin

Part 2. Country Approaches to Terrorism

Chapter 10. Socio-Juridical Characteristics of Terrorism in the Laws of Azerbaijan   111
    Elnur Kazimli

Chapter 11. The Last Amendments to the Prevention of Terror Act of Turkey 117
Ali Safak

Chapter 12. Terrorist Activities in Kyrgyzstan and Precautionary Measures 129
Kambarali T. Kongantiev

Chapter 13. International Cooperation as a Strategy of Fighting and Prevention Terrorism in Georgia 138
Giuli Alasania

Chapter 14. Macedonia as a Leader in the South-East Europe's Cooperation in the Fight Against Organised Crime 153
Trpe Stojanovski

Chapter 15. Collaboration in the Field of Prevention to the Organized Crime and Terrorism 164
Mykola Khaschevoi and Olena Ivaschenko

Chapter 16. Initiatives Taken by the Republic of Armenia in the Fight Against Terror: Legislative Regulations and Intergovernmental Cooperation with the CIS States 173
Armen Sanoyan

Part 3. Responding to Terrorism

Chapter 17. Terrorism as a Social and Criminal Phenomenon: A Complete Model to Deal with Terrorism 185
Ahmet Sait Yayla

Chapter 18. Legal Policing Responses to Terrorist Operations 207
Farhad Mehdiyev

Chapter 19. Organizing to Combat Future Terrorist Threats: Policy and Operational Implications 217
Stephen Sloan

Chapter 20. Intelligence Led Policing as a Framework for Law Enforcement in the 21st Century 221
Edmund F. McGarrell

Chapter 21. Supply Chains, Illicit Markets, and Terrorism: Understanding Organizations and Strategies 236
Robyn R. Mace

Chapter 22. Money Laundering and Financing of Terrorism 242
Suleyman Aydin

Chapter 23. Local Policing: Using Community Policing Principles as a Tactic in the Time of Terror 252
Mehmet Afacan

Chapter 24. Local Values and Police 260
Iskender Ormon Uulu

Chapter 25. Family Case Approach in Understanding and Combating Crime in General and Specifically Terror — 271
Ersin Oguz

Chapter 26. Youth and Terrorism — 285
Necati Alkan and M. Cemil Citak

Part 4. Terrorism Emergency Management

Chapter 27. An Emerging Concept: 'Terrorism Emergency Management' — 307
Alican Kapti and Zeki Pamuk

Chapter 28. The Impacts of Catastrophic Events in Large Cities: Considerations for Coping with the Aftermath of Terrorism in Urban Settings — 314
Jack L. Rozdilsky

Chapter 29. Terrorism, Vulnerability and Assessment — 318
Huseyin Akdogan

Chapter 30. Improvisation, Creativity, and the Art of Emergency Management — 324
James Kendra and Tricia Wachtendorf

Chapter 31. Coordinated Response to Man-Made and Natural Disasters — 336
Naim Kapucu

Chapter 32. Reassessing FEMA and Its Role in Preparing the Nation: Recommendations to Respond Effectively to Disasters — 344
Sıddık Ekici and David A. McEntire

Chapter 33. Responding to Terrorist Attacks Within the Labyrinth of Independent Governments: Collaborating and Quarrelling — 352
Abraham Benavides and Sebahattin Gultekin

Chapter 34. Public Archetypes in U.S. Counter-Bioterrorist Policy — 364
Monica Schoch-Spana

Chapter 35. The Disaster Management Perspective of the November 20, 2003 Events in Istanbul, Turkey — 375
Derin N. Ural

Chapter 36. Building Trust Among Community Stakeholders — 383
Sudha Arlikatti, Michael K. Lindell and Carla S. Prater

Part 5. Closing Remarks

Closing Remarks — 395
Mathieu Deflem

Author Index — 399

Part 1

International Police Cooperation

Interpol - Providing Support and Assistance to Combat International Terrorism

Jennifer HURST
*Assistant Director, Public Safety and Terrorism Sub-Directorate,
Interpol General Secretariat, Lyon*

Abstract. This paper aims to provide a summary of the tools and services that Interpol has available to support and provide assistance to Interpol member countries to combat international terrorism.

Keywords. Interpol; International terrorism; Project Kalkan; Fusion taskforce; bioterrorism; Interpol Weapons and Electronic Tracing System (IWETS); Interpol Money Laundering Automated Search Service (IMLASS); Border security/stolen and lost travel documents (SLTD) database; Interpol notices; Incident Response Teams

Introduction

Interpol is the world's largest international police organization, with 184 member countries. It facilitates cross-border police co-operation, and supports and assists all organizations, authorities and services whose mission is to prevent or combat crime. To support this mission, Interpol has identified three core functions:

- a unique global police communications system,
- a range of criminal databases and analytical services,
- proactive support for police operations throughout the world.

This article aims to illustrate the scope of activities and resources that Interpol provides to member countries in supporting their efforts to fight terrorism. The projects being conducted at Interpol and the tools available or under development are only as good as the information shared and contributed by Interpol member countries.

1. Communication Network/Information Exchange

Each Interpol member country maintains a National Central Bureau (NCB), which acts as the central point of contact between the Interpol General Secretariat in Lyon, France, and the various law enforcement agencies in the country. In October 2004, Interpol established a liaison office at the United Nations in New York to facilitate closer co-operation between the two organizations, especially with Security Council committees dealing with terrorism issues.

In 2003, Interpol created I-24/7 (Interpol 24 hours a day, 7 days a week), a secure global police communications system which enables police around the world to exchange information and access instantly Interpol's databases and other services. At the end of June 2006, 183 member countries were connected, plus 25 remote sites, including regional offices and other international organizations to which Interpol has granted access. The last remaining country should be connected before the end of the year. More than nine million messages were exchanged through I-24/7 in 2005.

Many member countries have extended the use of I-24/7 beyond the NCB, with direct access now available to border control and special investigation units.

The staff of the Command and Co-ordination Centre at the Interpol General Secretariat monitor I-24/7 message traffic around the clock, ready to respond to requests from member countries in any of the organization's four official languages: Arabic, English, French, and Spanish.

2. Terrorism Secure Website

The terrorism secure website is accessible through I-24/7 after access has been granted by the General Secretariat and the user has been issued an individual password. The site contains information and presentations from Interpol terrorism working group meetings, analytical reports based on information received by Interpol, lists of suspected or wanted terrorists, and recent notices issued on suspected or wanted terrorists.

3. Interpol Public Safety and Terrorism Sub-Directorate (PST)

The PST Sub-Directorate manages all terrorism-related projects and encompasses the Fusion Task Force (terrorism projects) and the bioterrorism unit. PST also manages a firearms-tracking programme (IWETS) and an environmental and wildlife crime project.

3.1. Fusion Task Force

Terrorism is one of Interpol's priority crime areas, along with drugs and criminal organizations, fugitives, financial and high-tech crime, and trafficking in human beings. Created in September 2002, the aim of the Fusion Task Force is to initiate a proactive, multi-disciplinary approach to assist member countries in terrorism-related investigations. Its primary objectives are to:

- identify active terrorist groups and their membership,
- solicit, collect and share information and intelligence,
- provide analytical support, and
- enhance the capacity of member countries to address the threat of terrorism.

The task force's projects currently focus on the following regions:

- Project Baobab - Africa
- Project Pacific - Southeast Asia/Pacific
- Project Kalkan - Central Asia

- Project Amazon - Central and South America
- Project Southeast Europe
- Project Middle East

Each of the projects has an allocated project manager who is the primary point of contact for member countries in that region. They monitor message traffic related to their projects; provide support and assistance to member countries; and compile analytical information on the regions they are responsible for, noting trends, current issues or information that may be valuable to other member countries.

The project managers organize working group meetings for their projects each year, bringing together senior law enforcement officers working in terrorism to discuss and provide information on current terrorism issues or case studies in their countries. These working group meetings are also excellent opportunities for member countries to network and draw on each other's experience and knowledge.

3.2. Fusion Project Kalkan - Central Asia

Launched in 2004, Project Kalkan is one of the most successful and productive counter-terrorism projects conducted by Interpol. It is overseen by a senior police officer from Turkey with more than 20 years' experience in this field. Some of the strongest contributors of terrorism information to Interpol are the member countries involved in this project.

Kalkan is an excellent example of the results that can be achieved by the Fusion Task Force and the assistance that Interpol can provide when member countries share high-quality and timely information. In collaboration with anti-terrorism bodies in the Central Asian region and in neighboring and overseas countries, we have made a great deal of progress, as detailed below:

- The first of two operational working group meetings since the project was initiated was conducted in Almaty, Kazakhstan, in April 2005. During this meeting, a considerable amount of operational and intelligence information was shared and evaluated. The second meeting was held in Baku, Azerbaijan, in February 2006. The meeting focused on current issues and future trends, and covered briefings on terrorism and terrorism financing-related matters, including information on newly emerging terrorist groups. All of the data supplied during the meeting was entered into Interpol databases.
- Since this project was launched in 2004, the number of member countries in the Central Asia region that share information with Interpol has grown from five to more than 60, while the number of messages received by Interpol currently totals 2,237, up 433 per cent from 2002-2003.
- The names of 1,087 terrorists from this region were entered into Interpol databases between 2004 and 2005 compared to 15 in 2002 and 2003. Statistically speaking, 99 per cent of the data has been recorded since the project began. There has been an increase of 183 per cent in the number of terrorists arrested in connection with this project. Fourteen terrorist groups and movements in the Central Asian region have been profiled by this project.
- Since February 2006, more than 660 messages were received at Interpol, containing identity details of more than 130 terrorists and their modus operandi from the terrorist groups Hizb-ut Tahrir, the Islamic Party of Turkestan and Al Qaeda. More than 70 terrorists have been arrested in

connection with Project Kalkan. These terrorists were the subject of Interpol diffusions and/or Red Notices. Project Kalkan is currently working on the profiles of 169 terrorists belonging to Al Qaeda and its affiliates in Pakistan. Their identities have been confirmed with aliases and photographs.

The success of Kalkan bodes well for future Interpol Fusion projects in terms of the results that can be achieved when member countries are motivated and involved.

3.3. Bioterrorism

Interpol's Bioterrorism Prevention Training for Police programme was created in 2004 following the award of a grant of nearly one million dollars from the US Sloan Foundation. The project's aim is to educate the law enforcement community about the need to make preventing bioterrorism a priority. To officially launch the project, Interpol held the first-ever Global Conference on Preventing Bioterrorism in March 2005, which was attended by more than 500 participants from 155 countries; making it world's largest-ever police conference.

To date, three successful bioterrorism prevention workshops have been conducted by Interpol in Africa, Asia and the Americas. The workshops have focused on awareness, education and training, in addition to bridging the gap between law enforcement, public health, academia, science and research institutes.

Additional funding by the Sloan Foundation and the Canadian government has provided support for the next two years, and the project will now concentrate on expanding its activities in the following four areas:

1. Engaging the science, public health and development communities: During the first phase of this programme, Interpol established very strong partnerships with organizations such as the World Health Organization (WHO), public health agencies and the scientific community. In the second phase, Interpol will further develop relationships to expand the scope of capabilities and knowledge
2. Expanding the scope of programme participants: Interpol is reaching out to the regions that have not yet had the opportunity to participate in the regional workshops. The focus will now be to identify geographic areas that require education and awareness training
3. Enhancing training and preparedness: Interpol is introducing a 'train the trainer' programme to enhance member countries' capabilities and expand training to as many countries as possible
4. Assessment: 'Table top exercises' are being developed to assess national capabilities and preparedness in an effort to identify legal gaps, technical weaknesses and areas where further co-ordination or training is required.

September 2006 will also see the development of Interpol's bio-criminalization project, with initial funding from the US Department of State. It will focus on developing a database to track the progress of foreign governments in the enactment of domestic laws to criminalize or otherwise restrict biological weapons-related activities and other activities linked to the use of dangerous biological agents and toxins, as required by the Biological Weapons Convention (BWC) and the United Nations Security Council Resolution (UNSCR) 1540.

Phase 1 of this project will focus on collection, analysis and compilation of information on national legislation and assistance to countries. Phase 2 will involve a broader effort to assist countries in this area.

3.4. Project Geiger - Radiological Project

Project Geiger is a joint intelligence project funded by the US Department of Energy and the US Environmental Protection Agency on the theft of radiological materials that could be used for the manufacture of radiological dispersal devices (RDD). A database is being developed by Interpol to track radiological materials if a theft occurs.

3.5. Interpol Weapons and Electronic Tracing System (IWETS)

The IWeTS project was created to provide member countries with the capacity to trace illicit firearms seized through national law enforcement. The project will be linked to the Bureau of Alcohol, Tobacco, Firearms and Explosives (ATF) National Tracing Center in Martinsburg, West Virginia. The value of using ATF's Tracing Center is that it is the only US federal agency with the capability to trace firearms by using information from the manufacturer, wholesaler and dealer, so that complete and accurate details can be obtained regarding firearms recovered by law enforcement during investigations.

The project was created by Interpol to enable law enforcement officers in member countries to trace any firearms around the world via I-24/7. After receiving passwords, officers will simply need to enter the details of the recovered firearm. The trace request will be automatically routed to ATF through the NCB in Washington, which can then provide the trace result back to the requesting officer.

To enhance this system, law enforcement officers will also be able to use the Canadian Firearms Reference Table (CFRT) computer software created by the Royal Canadian Mounted Police (RCMP) in association with a private Canadian corporation, Forensic Technology Incorporate (FTI), which owns the distribution rights. The CFRT information will be automatically updated thorough I-24/7 in conjunction with Interpol and FTI.

Interpol is currently working with other countries with significant firearms databases and securing their agreement to connect these through the IWeTS system. It is envisaged that a pilot programme will commence before the end of the year to test the use of this electronic tracing system.

4. Interpol Money Laundering Automated Search Service (IMLASS)

Interpol is developing the Interpol Money Laundering Automated Search Service (IMLASS), which will automatically compare suspected money laundering and terrorism financing-related queries from financial intelligence units (FIUs) and anti-money laundering investigators against database records submitted by Interpol's 184 member countries.

Through this initiative, FIUs or police money laundering investigation units will be able to submit queries concerning targets, associates and suspicious transaction data directly to the IMLASS database at the General Secretariat via Interpol's I-24/7 global police communications system. These queries will automatically be searched against Interpol's criminal databases and IMLASS. They will also be stored so that future enquiries can be compared against existing entries.

The system will make it possible to establish links between the names of individuals and companies, addresses, phone numbers, identification document details such as passport numbers, etc. in Interpol databases. If there is a match, positive responses will be sent to the sender and all Interpol National Central Bureaus (NCB) involved.

I-24/7 enables law enforcement officers around the world to exchange information securely and rapidly, and provides access to databases of suspected terrorists, wanted persons, lost, stolen or fraudulent travel and identity documents and other data which can assist money laundering investigations. Unfortunately, most money laundering investigators do not have direct access to I-24/7 or ICIS, which Interpol is working to change. Where permission has been granted by the member country, FIUs and police money laundering investigation units will have direct access to I-24/7. A pilot programme will begin in January 2007.

5. Border Security/Stolen and Lost Travel Documents (SLTD) Database

The database was launched in June 2002 after Interpol and its member countries identified a clear link between terrorist activities and the use of lost or stolen travel documents.

Interpol has developed integrated solutions, FIND and MIND, which enable member countries' national servers to connect directly to databases on stolen or lost travel documents, stolen motor vehicles and wanted criminals, giving front-line law enforcement officers (border police, immigration) immediate access to accurate and up-to-date information.

- *FIND - Fixed Integrated Network Databases:* This provides access to Interpol databases through 'online' integration and allows communication between national servers and those at the General Secretariat via I-24/7.
- *MIND - Mobile Integrated Network Databases:* This provides 'offline' access to Interpol databases. Using I-24/7, the General Secretariat can provide member countries with a copy of the data in its databases, which can be accessed locally through connection between existing national servers and the local copy of the data. MIND is controlled and updated by the General Secretariat. Updates are automatic whenever new records are added.

The ability to verify suspect travel documents by front-line control/border officers will raise proportionately the number of lost/stolen travel documents being identified worldwide. There are currently around 12 million lost and stolen document records in the database, with the objective of more than 30 million records by the end of the three-year project.

For member countries with a national infrastructure in place, which means an existing central national database with connection to the front-line control officer, the recommended accessibility to Interpol's international databases will be through the national server. An application needs to be developed, on the national side, to enable a simultaneous query to both the national and Interpol databases. For those member countries that do not have a developed or existing national infrastructure in place, Interpol will offer short-term solutions while assisting in the development and implementation of long-term solutions.

Since 13 December 2005, FIND has been operating in Switzerland, providing instant access to Interpol's stolen/lost travel documents and stolen motor vehicles databases to 20,000 federal law enforcement officers throughout the country and at Swiss embassies and consulates. Switzerland now conducts far more passports checks than all other Interpol member countries combined and generates a proportional number of positive hits. During 2006, Switzerland conducted more than 744,000 searches against the stolen lost and travel document database, generating 278 positive 'hits.' This is in contrast to other Interpol member countries not connected to MIND or FIND, which, for the same period, generated just over 13,000 searches, with 138 positive hits. The Swiss example illustrates that the integrated solution is the way forward for first-line users.

Two other countries are now fully integrated and 13 more are currently in the process of connecting, with 20 other countries in discussions with Interpol in regards to implementing either MIND or FIND.

6. Interpol Databases

Complementing Interpol's I-24/7 communication system are its databases, all of which are accessible to NCBs and contain critical information on criminals and criminality provided by member countries. These databases include:

- Suspected terrorists - approximately 10,600 records
- Nominal data on criminals (name, photos, etc.)
- Fingerprints - over 48,000 records
- DNA profiles - approximately 56,000 records
- Stolen or lost travel documents - around 12 million records
- Child sexual abuse images
- Stolen works of art
- Stolen motor vehicles

7. Interpol Notices

One of Interpol's most important functions is to help police in member countries share critical crime-related information using the organization's system of international notices. The information concerns individuals wanted for serious crimes, missing persons, unidentified bodies, possible threats and criminals' modus operandi. In addition, notices are used by the United Nations to alert police of individuals subject to UN sanctions against Al Qaeda and the Taliban, and by the International Criminal Tribunals for the Former Yugoslavia and Rwanda to seek persons wanted for serious violations of international human rights laws.

Interpol's seven notices serve to alert law enforcement authorities of:

- Red Notice - wanted persons
- Blue Notice - individuals of interest in relation to a crime
- Green Notice - warnings and intelligence about serious criminals
- Yellow Notice - missing persons
- Black Notice - unidentified bodies
- Interpol-United Nations Security Council Special Notice - individuals associated with Al Qaeda and the Taliban, as listed by the 1267 Committee of the UN Security Council and subject to the freezing of assets, travel bans, and arms embargoes
- Orange Notice - potential threats from disguised weapons or other dangerous materials

As of 23 June 2006, 258 Interpol-UN Special notices have been published. Checks against the Interpol Criminal Information System (ICIS) showed 145 were already known to police, enabling additional identifying information to be included in the notices. Of those 145 individuals, 30 were the subject of Interpol Red Notices, 22 were the subject of Interpol diffusions (wanted for crimes committed at the national level), and two were the subject of Blue Notices.

UN Taliban List - Due to the fact that the Afghanistan and Taliban list is the weakest in terms of information, only 71 of the 142 names had sufficient identifiers to produce UN Special Notices. Interpol is liaising closely with the NCB in Kabul to obtain additional information. Al-Qaeda List - The UN monitoring team submitted to Interpol the names of 18 individuals from the Al-Qaeda section of the UN Consolidated List for whom notices had not been published, because there were insufficient identifiers. Interpol carried out searches of these names in its databases and determined matches on seven names or aliases.

Interpol has commenced the process of reviewing all of the information obtained in order to determine which information should be submitted to the 1267 Committee for possible inclusion on the UN Consolidated List.

8. Interpol Incident Response Teams (IRT)

Interpol's role is not to intervene in investigations, perform crime scene analysis or supersede national authorities with regard to crisis management. However, Interpol can provide effective support and assistance to member countries in the event of major incidents. Incident Response Teams (IRT) have been deployed to numerous terrorism incidents around the world and provided crucial assistance following the 2004 tsunami in Southeast Asia.

Whenever a major incident occurs anywhere in the world, Interpol will offer to send an IRT to assist the member country by facilitating the exchange of information, providing quick access to Interpol databases, supplying specific software or analytical assistance, and assisting with identifying international-level experts in ballistics, forensics, criminal investigations, disaster victim identification, etc.

The composition of an IRT varies in accordance with the needs of the country concerned. It may consist of a police officer, an assistant and an IT specialist. The IRT will arrive in the country with all of the IT equipment needed for direct, immediate access to I-24/7, databases and all General Secretariat support. It will set up at the NCB or, if necessary, closer to the incident site.

It should be noted that deploying IRTs also stimulates the use of Interpol's services for other cases, particularly with regard to the publication of Interpol notices, the sending of warning/wanted messages through I-24/7, or the transmission of fingerprints or data linked to crime investigations. IRTs have been deployed to support the investigations into the Bali suicide bombings in October 2005 and the bombing in Jordan in November 2005.

9. Conclusion

Interpol is active in supporting its member countries and, as indicated in this article, is always looking for ways to further assist law enforcement in terrorism-related matters. The tools developed by Interpol to assist in the fight against terrorism are invaluable but require awareness, support and use by member countries to reach their full potential.

Project Kalkan has been cited in this article as an example of the results which can be achieved through the involvement, commitment and support of member countries. Interpol is ready and willing to assist all member countries in the fight against terrorism - a united front is the only way to progress and achieve results in order to better protect the citizens of the world.

Europol in the Combat of International Terrorism

Max-Peter RATZEL
Director of Europol

Abstract. The fight against terrorism lies at the centre of the European Union's activities in the area of justice, freedom and security. It has been one of the most dynamically developing sectors of the European Union integration project in the recent years. The EU Member States have been creating this security network by a continuous harmonised approach in the area of intelligence and law enforcement cooperation. Europol is an important part of this network because it was established in response to the need to ensure protection to EU citizens against international threats. It is one of the main platforms used by the MS in this continuous cross border and multidimensional endeavour. Europol carries out its work through facilitating a smooth and secure information exchange between the MS and accredited third partners, by monitoring of terrorism related information, by providing operational support, ensuring analysis of criminal intelligence provided by MS and other sources and by conducting threat and risk assessments. Europol in close cooperation with the MS and its partners will accordingly improve its counterterrorism mechanisms and will adapt to new policy responses as elaborated by the EU political leadership.

Keywords. Europol, counterterrorism, security policy, EU justice, freedom and security, EU police cooperation, threat analysis, open source intelligence sharing and analysis

Introduction

From its very beginning the twenty-first century has been tainted by the rise in international terrorism at an unprecedented scale. The attacks in New York, Virginia and Pennsylvania on 9/11 demonstrated this fact in a monstrous and painful way. Although some Member States (MS) of the European Union (EU) had then already faced problems with both international and national terrorism, the mechanisms of effectively counteracting international terrorism in a coordinated multilateral approach had not yet been fully developed.

The attacks which followed in Madrid in 2004 and in London in 2005, as well as some recent thwarted attempts in e.g. Germany and the UK, proved what was already known and shared by the international community i.e. that no continent, no country is immune to terrorism. These attacks reinvigorated the efforts of the EU MS to improve common policies and mechanisms designed to prevent and combat terrorism.

1. Combating Terrorism in the European Union

The fight against terrorism lies at the centre of the EU's activities in the area of justice, freedom and security, and has been one of the most dynamically developing sectors of the EU integration project in the recent years. This constitutes the environment in which EU counterterrorist policies have been anchored.

It is necessary to have an international security network to aptly respond to the threats posed by the terrorist network. The EU MS have been creating this security network by a continuous harmonised approach in the area of law enforcement cooperation. Europol is one of the main platforms used by the MS in this continuous cross border and multidimensional endeavour.

The abortive London attacks of August 2006, following the successful counter-operation of the UK authorities, but also more widely, the success of EU counterterrorist efforts, showed that the concerted EU actions and counterterrorist policies proved to be effective when put to the test. This is some most recent success of EU counterterrorist efforts but a number of other terrorist cells have been dismantled throughout the EU and terrorist plans foiled as a direct result of the concerted EU actions and counterterrorist policies.

In light of this introduction, let me focus on the role of Europol, being one of the important actors within the EU, in preventing and combating international terrorism.

2. Role of Europol

From the inception of the European integration project of new MS, it was realised that while bilateral cross border cooperation in principle works very well, the sharing of sensitive information with more than two partners to ensure a good coverage of the global phenomenon is still difficult and can become problematic. This is especially valid for domains covered by analysing criminal intelligence, such as terrorism, but also for the areas covered by law enforcement such as fight against trans-national and organised crime.

Thus, from the beginning politicians ensured that a legal basis for the development of mechanisms and agencies whose mandate concerned the area of justice, freedom and security was established. The Treaty of the European Union of 1992, the Maastricht Treaty, states that it is the Union's objective to provide citizens with a high level of safety within an area of freedom, security and justice. Consequently this treaty called for the establishment of Europol even in the early 1990s.

Europol was established in response to the need to ensure protection to EU citizens against certain defined international threats. It evolved from what was previously known as the Europol Drugs Unit established in 1994, into a fully fledged law enforcement cooperation agency which in July 1999 assumed its full functions on the basis of the Europol Convention. Europol's first mandate included fighting international organised crime in the areas of drugs, terrorism, and forgery of money, money laundering, and illegal immigration, trafficking in human beings, trafficking in stolen vehicles and trafficking in nuclear and radioactive materials. Based on the first experiences and evaluations the original mandate was then extended in 2002 by decision of the Ministers of Justice and Internal Affairs to include also environmental and economic crimes, fraud, kidnapping, murder, and arms trafficking.

Europol's role is unique as it offers the only EU-wide secure platform for multilateral exchange and analysis of personal data in relation to organised crime (OC) and terrorism via a secure network which is subject to very strict regulations on handling of data based on specific handling codes. By using this secure network as well as by enforcing the rigid data protection and confidentiality regime, Europol guarantees the adequate handling of sensitive information. Both of these measures are the precondition for a trustworthy and secure cooperation and communication throughout the EU.

The Europol Headquarters in The Hague houses experts in all crime areas, as well as Counter Terrorism experts, analysts and liaison officers from the 25 EU MS and from some other non EU MS, notably from the USA, Columbia, Norway, Switzerland and Bulgaria and Romania. These officers come from different competent authorities in their countries. Some of them have law enforcement backgrounds such as the police, border control, customs and security services. They represent at least 20 official EU languages as well as some others.

This multinational, multiagency, multilingual and multicultural approach ensures a swift and efficient bilateral and multilateral information exchange between MS as well as between MS and Europol and vice versa. Through the 25 Europol National Units in the MS, Europol provides access to all law enforcement officers within the EU. This network is further expanded by the countries which cooperate with Europol on the basis of bilateral operational and strategic agreements. These are countries (so-called Third States) which are just about to enter the EU (Bulgaria and Romania) or which are in the European Economic Area (Iceland, Norway, Switzerland), but also includes partners which are geographically more distant, such as Croatia, Turkey and Russia in Europe or USA, Canada and Colombia outside of Europe. Europol also cooperates with EU agencies and institutions (such as Eurojust, Frontex, OLAF) and international organisations such as Interpol, the World Customs Organisation and the UN Office on Drugs and Crime. Other agreements are actually being negotiated or ratified. Once adopted they will expand the security network, which is hinged on Europol, to include countries outside of Europe, such as Australia, and Israel as well as European states, such as some Balkan states and Ukraine. Once expanded, this network will be even more expanded in its nature.

In speaking about dealing with terrorism in the area of the present EU one must mention some historical developments of relevance. One example of an early multinational network in the area of terrorism is the Police Working Group on Terrorism (PWGT). Founded in the late 1970s, the PWGT was an informal association of the BeNeLux countries, Germany and the UK for the purpose of exchanging information on Northern Irish terrorist groups. This network still exists today but has been enlarged to include all 25 EU MS plus Switzerland and Norway. Representatives meet twice a year to exchange general operational information. In *ad hoc* cases a secure communication network was established for enabling informal communication.

When it became obvious that multinational cooperation in this area is invaluable, a very important area was implemented into the Europol mandate at the beginning - that of counterterrorism. Whilst at the outset MS were reluctant to share counterterrorism related information, cooperation has evolved and the Europol counterterrorism unit is now running two specific data bases specifically designed for terrorism related information.

As mentioned previously, the terrorist attacks in the USA now known as '9/11', were one of the main triggers for further EU cooperation in the security area in general and the counterterrorism area in particular. In the wake of the attacks in the USA, a range of urgent measures was set out by the Justice and Home Affairs Council of 20 September 2001[1].

---

[1] The Council document of 25 September 2001 (12156/0 JAI 99).

They covered judicial cooperation, cooperation between police and intelligence services, financing of terrorism, measures at borders, and improved cooperation with the US.

This led to the creation of the original EU Action Plan on Terrorism of 21st September 2001[2], which is annually amended and updated. Other policy and legal responses included further instruments such as, the Framework Decision on Terrorism[3], the establishment of the European Arrest Warrant[4] and the facility of Joint Investigation Teams[5], as well as numerous Council Decisions applying specific measures in support of MS' fights against international terrorism.

The European counterterrorism measures and actions have developed efficiently and fast in the recent years. As part of this machinery Europol participated in the 'Evaluation of National Anti-terrorist Arrangements of Member States'[6]. Formal cooperation agreements have been set up with European partners like the EU Joint Situation Centre (SitCen) in Brussels, Eurojust in The Hague and others in order to allow better exchanges between law enforcement, the intelligence community and the justice sector. Beside this, Europol is closely cooperating with the Counterterrorism Coordinator of the EU, Gijs de Vries.

Europol's counterterrorist efforts cover the following mandated areas as laid down in the Europol Convention: terrorism, illicit trafficking in nuclear and radioactive substances, illicit trafficking in arms, ammunition and explosives as well as racism and xenophobia.

3. Functions of Europol

Europol carries out its work through the monitoring of terrorism related information, by providing operational support (i.e. supporting MS operational work, *not* conducting its own operations), by ensuring operational analysis of criminal intelligence provided by MS and other sources and by conducting threat and risk assessments in the format of strategic analysis.

3.1. Monitoring Information

Monitoring is an important ongoing process of checking the flow of information into Europol's databases, the contributions to the various projects and open sources. This process results in *ad hoc* information, briefing papers and periodical reports but also in complex analysis of open sources concerning current problems. This activity aims at keeping counterterrorism staff and other internal and external users of this information up to date. Monitoring, therefore, is carried out regardless of the feedback from MS and notwithstanding any possible duplication of work.

---

[2] The EU Action Plan on Terrorism (11882/06 JAI 384; latest update of 20 July 2006).
[3] The Council Framework Decision on combating terrorism of 13 June 2002 (2002/475/JHA).
[4] The Council Framework Decision on the European arrest warrant and the surrender procedures among the Member States (2002/584/JHA).
[5] Article 3 of the Europol Convention.
[6] Final report on the evaluation of national anti-terrorist arrangements: improving national machinery capabilities for the fight against terrorism (12168/3/05).

3.2. Providing Operational Support

Europol provides operational support to the MS in many ways. In 2005, 40 ongoing operations in the field of terrorism were supported in different MS. In addition Europol provides on request of the hosting MS, operational support to major sports events such as Olympics 2006 in Turin, FIFA World Cup 2006 in Germany and European Athletic Championships in Sweden.

3.3. Analysis of Data

The processing and analysis of the data related to terrorism is carried out by Europol specialised staff members, especially by analysts. A number of dedicated data bases called Analytical Work Files have been developed to deal with various aspects of international terrorism. Moreover, suspicious transactions dealing with the money flow which is inherently linked to the financing of terrorist activities are also in the focus of Europol experts.

3.4. Threat and Risk Assessments

Threat and risk assessments are increasingly requested by MS in relation to major events like sports championships or political gatherings. Europol's counter-terrorism involvement in educational activities has also increased within the recent two years. Requests for specific training on counterterrorism matters were received from MS as well as requests for general awareness training with a specific focus on Europol's counterterrorism activities from outside the EU, e.g. from the International Law Enforcement Academy (ILEA) run by the FBI and based in Budapest.

4. Counter Terrorism Task Force

One of Europol assets in the domain of preventing and fighting terrorism is the Counter Terrorism Task Force. The Council Decision of September 2001[7] called for the set-up of a Counter Terrorism Task Force (CTTF 1) at Europol. More than 20 members of law enforcement agencies and security services from different MS worked together for the first time in the history of the EU within one team on different projects. The CTTF 1 was disbanded by the end of 2002. Some of the projects carried out were finalised, other projects were transferred into ordinary activities of Europol's counterterrorism unit.

Subsequently following the events of 11th March 2004 in Madrid, the Justice and Home Affairs Council implemented a Revised Action Plan on 26th March 2004 which, among other decisions made, called for the reinstatement of the Counter Terrorism Task Force (CTTF 2) at Europol. Since October 2004, experts from MS, again both with law enforcement and security services backgrounds have been working on the tasks assigned by the European Council, such as the financing of terrorism, terrorist modus operandi including use of the Internet by Islamists groups, terrorist recruitment, and provision of threat assessments and strategic reports in these areas. A number of projects related to these tasks were launched and are currently being carried out.

---

[7] See 1.

Based on a review of the experiences made within the CTTF and the support provided to Spain and the UK after the Madrid and London bombings, Europol and representatives from the EU MS discussed and agreed to update the Europol Preparedness Programme in order to deliver enhanced assistance to future CTTFs should the need for them arise.

5. Open Source Intelligence

The most recent developments employed by Europol include the increasingly sophisticated use of open sources intelligence, upon which subsequently, Europol strategic analysis products are partially based.

Monitoring, collection and exploitation of open sources intelligence (OSINT) supports Europol in all counterterrorism activities. The collected information is organised and processed for further exploitation. For instance, the new Terrorism Event Database includes information on all terrorism-related events relevant from an EU point of view. The definition 'terrorism event' includes: terrorist threats, attacks and other activities, claims, statements and publications, arrests, house searches, investigations or other operations against terrorism suspects, judicial proceedings and decisions. Europol's Counter Terrorism OSINT activity includes also the production of finished intelligence products, namely the Europol Counterterrorism Monthly and Briefing Notes.

Europol is currently in the process of developing the new Terrorism Situation and Trend Report (TeSat) the first issue of which will be disseminated to the European Parliament by 31 March 2007. The new TeSat remains an unclassified document. However, in line with the Organised Crime Threat Assessment (OCTA) developments, it will become a Europol product and its data collection will be widened. It aims at assessing the phenomenon of terrorism from the point of view of the EU in order to support decision makers.

Terrorism is international in its nature and terrorists use globalisation and integration processes very effectively. This has influenced the approach of countries also in the sensitive areas of intelligence and law enforcement cooperation. Many countries have speeded up their contributions whose quality and quantity has been increasingly improving. There is a clear improvement from the previous 'need to know' approach towards the 'need to share' approach within the European counterterrorism community. Good intelligence and its sharing amongst partners based on common understanding and mutual trust is the best weapon against international terrorism. In fact, good intelligence can be defined as shared intelligence. Sharing of information is an ongoing process and the basis for a common approach.

6. Conclusion

Europol in close cooperation with the MS and its partners is trying to improve its counterterrorism mechanisms and will adapt to new policy responses as elaborated by the EU political leadership. This process will continue to concern Europol partners also who are an integral aspect of the EU network of security. In the current environment which is exposed to the omnipresent terrorist threat, there remains a need to share experiences and information, to apply concerted policies and to stand united in order to ensure security to our citizens and to eradicate the evil of terrorism.

International Police Cooperation against Terrorism: Interpol and Europol in Comparison

Mathieu DEFLEM
University of South Carolina, USA

Abstract. Since the events of September 11, many police institutions across the globe have reorganized and expanded their counter-terrorism strategies. In view of the international dimensions of contemporary forms of terrorism, international police organizations take a special place among these counter-terrorism efforts. In this paper, I analyze recent counter-terrorism efforts that have been undertaken by Interpol, the International Criminal Police Organization, and by Europol, the European Police Office. Both organizations offer specific models of international police cooperation against terrorism, with respective problems and prospects for an effective police cooperation in matters of international terrorism, which this paper discusses.

Keywords. Interpol, Europol, counter-terrorism, international police cooperation

Introduction

With increasing vigor since the events of September 11, police institutions across the globe have proliferated their counter-terrorism strategies, including participation in international police organizations. This paper discusses some of these developments on the basis of the theory of police bureaucratization. Specifically, this article analyzes the counter-terrorism efforts undertaken by the International Criminal Police Organization (Interpol) and the European Police Office (Europol).

The bureaucratization theory of international police cooperation predicts a high degree of autonomy of police institutions to determine the means and objectives of activities related to crime control and order maintenance [1, 2, 3]. Founded on the work of the sociologist Max Weber [4], the theory holds that police bureaucracies achieve institutional autonomy on the basis of a purposive-rational logic to employ the most efficient means (professional expertise) given certain objectives that are rationalized on the basis of professional systems of knowledge (official information). However, periods of societal upheaval are seen to affect the institutional autonomy of police institutions in functional and organizational ways. Three conditions are important in this context.

First, in order to accomplish cooperation across national borders, police institutions must have gained a position of relative independence from the dictates of the governments of their respective national states. Such a condition of institutional independence or formal bureaucratic autonomy allows public police institutions, though formally sanctioned by states, to autonomously plan and execute relevant strategies of crime control and order maintenance. Conversely, without a sufficient degree of detachment from the political centers of states, police institutions will not be in a position to engage in international cooperation on a broad multilateral scale beyond more limited cooperation among politically akin states. Early efforts to organize international police cooperation in Europe in the 19th century, for instance, were limited in scope and operations because they were politically motivated and planned by autocratic governments [1]. From these political efforts, however, police gradually developed more autonomously conceived cooperation efforts on the basis of professional expertise. Following Weber's rationalization theory, I maintain that police institutions have gained such a position of relative independence because the execution of their duties is increasingly guided by formal criteria of efficiency and an impersonal calculation of means, a trend towards instrumental rationalization which Weber equated with modernity itself. The reliance on technologically sophisticated means of criminal investigation is the most concrete expression of this development among police institutions.

Second, under conditions of formal bureaucratic autonomy, police agencies develop expert systems of knowledge that can be shared among fellow professionals across national boundaries. In the case of international cooperation, such knowledge systems will particularly concern expertise about the course of international crime, including crimes that traverse the boundaries of national jurisdictions, as well as criminal developments that affect several countries at once, such as the influence of economic modernization on criminal conditions across the world. When such systems of knowledge have developed, police agencies are also bureaucratized in operational respects and can effectively form international cooperation plans on a broad multilateral scale. In the context of counter-terrorism, such knowledge systems will be shared across the police of national states when there is a common understanding about the nature and development of international terrorism. Under such circumstances, police can define and respond to terrorism in a manner that is not limited by the ideologically divisive conceptions of terrorism that often dominate in the world of international politics.

Third, considering the form in which international cooperation will take place, it is noteworthy that international police work will primarily remain oriented at enforcement tasks that have a distinctly local or national significance. This national persistence is manifested in at least three ways [1, 3]. First, police institutions will prefer to engage in unilaterally enacted transnational activities, most typically through a system of international liaisons stationed in foreign countries. Unilaterally planned international operations are not always possible because police agencies may lack necessary personnel and means. The police institutions of more powerful nations are at a considerable advantage in this respect. Second, international cooperation among police will typically take place in a bilateral form, between the police of two nations, and will be maintained only on a temporary basis for a specific inquiry or investigation. Third, and finally, national persistence in international police work is revealed in the fact that multilateral cooperation among police is of a collaborative nature that does not involve the formation of a supranational police force. The idea of a supranational police force clashes with conceptions of both state sovereignty and police autonomy, whereas a collaborative network among police of different nations, for instance such as it currently exists among the 184 member agencies of Interpol, can bring about the advantages of international cooperation. Collaboration among police of different nations can be formalized by means of regular meetings, shared communication networks, and other institutions of cooperation, such as a central headquarters through which information can be routed. The police agencies of national states are thereby affirmed as the partners of cooperation.

Turning to the organization of international policing since the events of September 11, it can be noted that the function and organization of policing in many nations across the global as well as at the international level have changed very significantly. Among the most important external determinants of counter-terrorism policing are political pressures by means of new legislations and other forms of official policy. Yet, despite the renewal of political and legal efforts to control counter-terrorist policing, it also makes sense to expect that police institutions can resist such politicization attempts because the bureaucratization of modern police institutions is now at an unparalleled high level. Thus, police agencies remain focused on an efficiency-driven treatment and depoliticized conception of terrorism. In what follows, I will make this case by focusing on the counter-terrorism strategies of the international police organizations Interpol and Europol[1].

1. Interpol and Counter-Terrorism

Interpol is an international police organization that aims to provide and promote mutual assistance between criminal police authorities within the limits of national laws and the Universal Declaration of Human Rights. Originally formed in Vienna in 1923, the organization has steadily grown in membership but never substantially changed in form or objectives [1, 7]. Interpol is not a supranational police agency with investigative powers, nor an organization sanctioned by an international governing body such as the United Nations, but a cooperative network formed independently among police agencies in order to foster collaboration and provide assistance in police work across nations. To this end, Interpol links a central headquarters, located in Lyon, France, with specialized bureaus, the so-called National Central Bureaus (NCB), in the countries of participating police agencies. At present, Interpol counts 184 member agencies.

1.1. Interpol Policies against Terrorism

For several decades, Interpol has passed various resolutions to combat terrorism and terrorist-related activities. During the 1970s, Interpol passed resolutions that pertained to certain crimes that are typically associated with terrorist activities, such as criminal acts conducted against international civil aviation and the holding of hostages. Such terrorism-related resolutions were considered valid only within the context of a 1951 Interpol resolution that the organization would not concern itself with matters of a political, racial, or religious nature, a restriction that has since been adopted explicitly as Article 3 of the Interpol constitution. In 1984, an Interpol resolution passed concerning 'Violent Crime Commonly Referred to as Terrorism' to encourage member agencies to cooperate and combat terrorism within the context of their national laws. Following certain highly public-cized terrorist incidents during the 1990s (such as the World Trade Center bombing on Feb. 26, 1993) Interpol's commitment to combat international terrorism was explicitly confirmed in a 1998 'Declaration against Terrorism.' Accompanying this declaration, it was decided to break down terrorist incidents into their constituent parts, only the criminal elements of which can then be identified and subjected to investigations by the Interpol agencies.

---

[1] The following sections rely on materials summarized from [5] and [6].

A few weeks after the terrorist attacks in the US, the Interpol General Assembly passed Resolution AG-2001-RES-05 on the 'Terrorist Attack of 11 September 2001.' Condemning the attack as a crime against humanity, the Interpol leadership decided to implement new policies to tackle terrorism and organized crime more effectively. Since then, Interpol pays special attention to the financing of terrorist activities, because it is assumed that the frequency and seriousness of terrorist attacks are often proportionate to the amount of financing terrorists receive. Moreover, Interpol maintains liaisons with other international organizations to fight terrorism more effectively. In November 2001, for example, Interpol signed an agreement with Europol to foster cooperation in the policing of terrorism and other international crimes. Similarly, in March 2002, Interpol reached an agreement to cooperate closely with the Arab Interior Ministers' Council to facilitate the exchange of information with the Arab police community.

From a practical viewpoint, Interpol reorganized in several key respects after September 11. Most concretely, Interpol Secretary General Ronald K. Noble announced the creation of '11 September Task Force' at Interpol's Headquarters in Lyon, France. Also instituted was a General Secretariat Command and Co-ordination Center. In April 2002, Interpol announced the creation of an Interpol Terrorism Watch List to provide police access to information on fugitive and suspected terrorists who are subject to Interpol warrants. Also in 2002, a new global communications project was announced as Interpol's highest priority. This project involves the launching of a new internet-based Global Communications System (I-24/7) to provide for a more rapid and secure exchange of information.

1.2. Interpol and the Dynamics of Global Counter-Terrorism

The theory of bureaucratization suggests that structures and processes of international police cooperation rely on a high degree of institutional independence among police institutions on the basis of professional expertise and efficiency considerations. Interpol indeed places most emphasis on a smooth coordination of and direct contacts between the various participating police agencies. Therefore, the organization has managed to attract cooperation from police agencies representing nations that can be ideologically very diverse and not always on friendly terms in political respects. The diversity among Interpol's member agencies, however, can also hinder the organization to be effective in its missions, as members do not always trust one another. Especially in matters of international terrorism, it is important to note that police agencies from the US and other powerful nations prefer to conduct their international activities unilaterally rather than participate in an international organization.

The emphasis on efficiency in Interpol's counter-terrorist work reveals the relevance of formal rationalization processes which have been observed in many modern bureaucratic institutions. In terms of the objectives of social control, the bureaucratization of policing involves a de-politicization or criminalization of the target of counter-terrorism. This criminalization of terrorism is accomplished by defining terrorism very vaguely ('a crime against humanity') and/or by identifying and isolating the distinctly criminal elements (bombings, killings) from terrorist incidents. Therefore, also, cooperation among national police agencies engaged in counter-terrorism can take place irrespective of the similarities and/or differences among nations in political, legal, cultural, and other respects.

2. Europol and the Policing of International Terrorism

In Europe, the modern era of counter-terrorism policies can be traced to the 1970s, when the 'Terrorism, Radicalism, Extremism, and International Violence' group, or TREVI group, was formed in 1975 by European police officials to exchange information on terrorism and related international crimes [8]. In 1993, the TREVI Group and other European institutions of judicial, customs, and immigration issues were brought together under Title VI of the Treaty of European Union - EU concerning the compensatory measures following the removal of border controls between the member states of the EU [9]. In 1997, a counter-terrorism preparatory group was set up to determine Europol's role in matters of counter-terrorism and, thereafter, the Amsterdam Treaty approved an extension of Europol's mandate to specifically include counter-terrorism. Since January 1, 2002, the mandate of Europol has been expanded to deal with all serious forms of international crime.

2.1. Europol Programs against Terrorism

The establishment of Europol was first agreed upon on February 7, 1992 in the Treaty on European Union or the Maastricht Treaty [10, 11]. In 1994, Europol started limited operations in The Hague, The Netherlands, in the form of the Europol Drugs Unit. In 1995, the Europol Convention was drawn up in Brussels and, in 1998, the EU member states had ratified the convention. Europol commenced its full range of activities on July 1, 1999. Because Europol is the result of a decision by the political and legislative bodies of the EU, its activities are legally framed and bound to certain areas of investigation. Europol's operations are also supervised by the political representatives of the EU. Yet, I argue, Europol is nonetheless characterized by a degree of autonomy to determine the specific means and objectives of its policing and counter-terrorist programs and is oriented at an efficient sharing of information among police on the basis of professional standards of policing. Also, like Interpol, Europol is not a supranational police force but an international cooperative network that coordinates the activities of police in the EU member states (the Europol National Units) via a central headquarters. Additionally, there is a persistence of nationality and regionalism in that police and counter-terrorism objectives in Europol harmonize with distinctly European concerns over terrorism and, furthermore, that there exist national variations in counter-terrorism across the police units of the EU nations participating in the international police organization.

The events of 9/11 have served as an important catalyst in the development of new terrorism legislation in the EU [12] and a prioritization of counter-terrorism at Europol [13, 14, 15, 16, 17]. In November 2001, a specialized counter-terrorism unit, the Counter-Terrorism Task Force was instituted at the Europol headquarters. A year later, the Task Force was incorporated into Europol's Serious Crime Department, but after the terrorist bombings in Madrid on March 11, 2004, it was re-established as a separate entity. The events of 9/11 also influenced the EU's formal policies against terrorism. In 2002, the Council of the EU agreed upon several important framework decisions. These framework decisions define terrorist offences as various criminal activities, such as attacks upon a person's life, kidnappings, and the destruction of public facilities, that are committed with the aim of seriously intimidating a population, unduly compelling a government or international organization from performing or abstaining from any act, and/or seriously destabilizing or destroying the fundamental structures of a country or of an international organization. In matters of police cooperation, the framework decisions allow for the creation of joint investigation teams made up of the security forces of two or more EU member states. The 2002 framework decisions also allowed for an elaboration of Europol's counter-terrorism mandate and international cooperation activities. Europol can now maintain relations with police and security forces outside the EU, such as with Interpol and the police of non-EU states. Finally, a newly introduced European Arrest Warrant allows for the handing over of wanted persons directly from one member states' judicial authority to that of any other EU state.

2.2. The Dynamics of Europol's Counter-Terrorism

Although Europol is formally mandated by the EU and overseen by the regulatory bodies of the EU, the organization is also dependent in its activities on the police agencies of EU states and these agencies are highly bureaucratized in respect of the knowledge and know-how of their enforcement duties. Europol relies on the participation of existing police institutions in the EU for the staffing of the headquarters and the Europol National Units in the 25 member states. Personnel at the headquarters and in the National Units are typically made up of experts in international policing with prior experience participating in non-governmental international police organizations. Thus Europol operates within the context of an existing professional culture of policing that is highly bureaucratized.

Europol is guided by a formal set of documents that lays out the organization's functions, but the political decision-making process in the EU can be relatively ineffective in fostering police cooperation. In the aftermath of the terrorist bombings that hit Madrid in March 2004 and London in July 2005, for instance, the Council of the EU swiftly agreed to condemn these attacks, strengthen the European commitment to fight terrorism, and propose a new series of counter-terrorism measures, but not all of those measures have been implemented at the national level of the EU member states. However, while counter-terrorism cooperation at the political level sometimes remains an expression of goodwill with little consequences, police and security agencies can achieve cooperation in practical matters. A few days after the July 7 bombings in London, for example, a confidential meeting of police and intelligence officials was held at Scotland Yard that included participants from about 30 countries, including the US, Israel, Australia, Japan, and the EU states, as well as representatives from Interpol and Europol.

While the formal framework of the EU's governing bodies places limits on the autonomy of Europol, the organization also engages in cooperation agreements at an institutional and nation-state level. Europol maintains relations with countries outside the EU, such as Switzerland, Turkey, Colombia, and the US, and with other international police organizations [18, 19]. As such Europol can effectively broaden its mandate beyond the restraints of formal political decision-making. For instance, Europol cooperates with the Counter Terrorism Group (CTG) that was formed after 9/11 and which, unlike Europol, was formed at a professional level by the heads of the police and intelligence services in the EU on the basis of an informal memorandum of understanding. Europol entertains such agreements also with other police organizations that are marked by a high degree of bureaucratic autonomy, such as Interpol.

Europol's policing and counter-terrorism operations are organized in the rationalized terms of an efficient control of crime. Besides the creation of the Counter-Terrorism Task

Force as a specialized unit and the development of functional programs to combat terrorism, the relevance of instrumental rationality in Europol can also be observed in the organization's emphasis on efficiency in operations. As is the case in other international police organizations [3], an emphasis is placed in Europol's crime-fighting activities on establishing swift methods of communication and information exchange among the participating agencies. The agencies participating in Europol need not contact one another directly but can route information via The Hague by means of an 'Information Exchange System' (INFO-EX) that enables encrypted electronic messages. Similarly, Europol's liaison agreements with the police and intelligence services of non-EU nations functions to ease international cooperation across the boundaries of the EU.

It is to be noted that an emphasis on efficiency does not necessarily imply effectiveness. Among the obstacles Europol faces in its counter-terrorism activities is that terrorism is in some EU countries dealt with by police agencies while in other EU states intelligence agencies are responsible for counter-terrorism. Cooperation across intelligence and police agencies can be difficult because police institutions tend to be interested in specific information about suspects in order to make an arrest, whereas intelligence agencies are very broadly interested in general information without prosecutorial purposes. Also, the lack of knowledge of Arabic among Europe's police forces and resulting difficulties in penetrating underground groups of non-European origin are obvious and important concerns [20]. Police cooperation is further compounded by the linguistic, cultural, legal, and political diversity that exists across the countries of the EU [21].

Finally, a persistence of nationality in international policing is also shown in Europol's cooperation efforts. Europol's counter-terrorism focus has gone most centrally to 'Islamic extremist terrorism' or 'fundamentalist jihadist terrorism.' Although the police of EU nations generally agree on the relevance of these categories, there is cross-national variability as well and many EU police agencies remain concerned primarily with nationally defined enforcement tasks, even when these tasks involve criminal problems of an international nature. Thus, Europol concentrates its efforts on Islamic fundamentalist terrorist groups inasmuch as they are active in or relevant to Europe. Within the EU, indeed, some countries have been targeted by terrorist cells because of the countries' involvement in the wars in Iraq and Afghanistan. Other counter-terrorism work done by Europol is distinct to some of the EU's nation states, such as the various nationalist terrorist groups that operate in Spain and the UK.

3. Conclusion

Much like has been the case for police and criminal justice agencies in many countries across the world, counter-terrorism activities enacted by Interpol and Europol have increased considerably in scope and significance since the events of September 11. While Interpol is more global in approach, Europol's activities against international crime and terrorism focus on distinctly European problems or the European dimensions of more global concerns. Islamic extremist terrorism, particularly, is conceived by Europol as a global criminal concern that also affects security conditions in the EU. Interpol's member agencies see the problem similar in its relevance to their own respective nations. The emphasis on Islamic fundamentalist terrorism has in Europe met with little opposition. Strikingly, only a source from the Turkish press has criticized Europol's over concentration on Islamic-linked terrorist organizations [22].

Ideological and political sentiments on terrorism are very divided in the world of international politics and diplomacy. Yet, efforts at the level of police agencies and international police organizations, such as Interpol and its member agencies, can be based on a common ground surrounding terrorism through its treatment as a depoliticized crime. Terrorism is thereby fought in ways that are considered to be efficient, irrespective of normative concerns. As such, the bureaucratization of modern police institutions harmonizes with Weber's perspective of societal rationalization as having gone in the direction of an increasing reliance on principles of efficiency in terms of a calculation of means. It is under those conditions, Weber [4, pg. 570] argued, that the modern state bureaucracy becomes an "almost unbreakable formation," with little political control and democratic oversight.

It is important to recognize that the processes and structures of policing and other state activities are comprised of a multitude of dimensions and institutions which are not necessarily in tune with one another. For our theorizing of the rule of law, an important implication of the developments of bureaucratization at the level of policing is that we need to recognize a fundamental irony of the modern political state from its origins through its further evolution. The centrality of the state in any discussion on law and police needs no introduction, but it is also important to contemplate the evolution of the state and its functionally divided components, specifically the legal system and the forces of internal coercion. Developing a bureaucratic apparatus to fulfill the state's concentrated and growing arsenal of functions, the state's powers are dispersed across a multitude of institutions, the organization and activities of which the state can no longer carefully control. As the case of international police cooperation shows, the institutions that develop and multiply during the state's continued development cannot be assumed to always be carefully disciplined by the center of the state.

Not only does the evolution of the modern state bring about that the spontaneous collective attention of society is inevitably relaxed [23], the functionally divided state institutions that are created in response to the weakening influence of tradition also lead to a diversification of the objectives of state power. The expansion of state bureaucracies such as the police has ironic consequences for as the state grows, the relative power of its center weakens. There is no common end to the state, of course, but it also does not suffice to merely enumerate the state's multiple functions. What is particularly important is that the many functions of the state are not always neatly harmonized, for they each have their own instruments and institutions that develop in relative autonomy to one another and with respect to the center of the state. A state with many means will also have many ends. Therefore, whatever model that is suggested towards the adoption of constitutional-democratic principles at the global level of law and politics in order to decrease the chances of terrorism must also take into account the manner in which effective control of terrorism is currently accomplished by international cooperation among public police agencies.

References

[1] M. Deflem, *Policing world society: Historical foundations of international police cooperation.* Oxford; New York: Oxford University Press; 2002.
[2] M. Deflem, editor, *Terrorism and counter-terrorism: Criminological perspectives.* Oxford: Elsevier Science; 2004.

[3] M. Deflem, Social control and the policing of terrorism: Foundations for a sociology of counter-terrorism. *The American Sociologist* **35** (2004), 75-92.
[4] M. Weber, *Wirtschaft und gesellschaft: Grundriss der verstehenden soziologie.* Tübingen: J.C.B. Mohr (Paul Siebeck); [1922] 1980.
[5] M. Deflem, Global rule of law or global rule of law enforcement? International police cooperation and counter-terrorism. *The Annals of the American Academy of Political and Social Science* **603** (2006), 240-251.
[6] M. Deflem, Europol and the policing of international terrorism: Counter-terrorism in a global perspective. *Justice Quarterly* **23** (2006), 336-359.
[7] M. Deflem, Bureaucratization and social control: Historical foundations of international policing. *Law & Society Review* **34** (2000), 601-640.
[8] J. Peek, International police cooperation within justified political and judicial frameworks: Five theses on TREVI. In J. Monar, R. Morgan, editors. *The third pillar of the European Union.* Brussels: European Interuniversity Press; 1994, p 201-207.
[9] J. Benyon, The developing system of police cooperation in the European Union. In W.F. McDonald, editor. *Crime and law enforcement in the global village.* Cincinnati: Anderson Publishing Co.; 1997, p 103-122.
[10] E. Marotta, Europol's role in counter-terrorism policing. *Terrorism and Political Violence* **11/4** (1999), 15-18.
[11] J.D. Occhipinti, *The politics of EU police cooperation: Toward a European FBI?* Boulder: Lynne Rienner; 2003.
[12] K.L. Scheppele, Other people's PATRIOT acts: Europe's response to September 11. *Loyola Law Review* **50** (2004), 89-148.
[13] M. den Boer, J. Monar, 11 September and the challenge of global terrorism to the EU as a security actor. *Journal of Common Market Studies* **40** (2002), 11-28.
[14] C. Fijnaut, The attacks on 11 September 2001, and the immediate response of the European Union and the United States. In C. Fijnaut, J. Wouters, F. Naert, editors. *Legal instruments in the fight against international terrorism: A transatlantic dialogue.* Leiden, The Netherlands: Martinus Nijhoff Publishers; 2004, p 15-36.
[15] N. Lavranos, Europol and the fight against terrorism. *European Foreign Affairs Review* **8** (2003), 259-275.
[16] J. Monar, The problems of balance in EU Justice and Home Affairs and the impact of 11 September. In M. Anderson, J. Apap, editors. *Police and justice co-operation and the new European borders.* The Hague: Kluwer Law International; 2002, p 165-182.
[17] J. Wouters, The European Union and 'September 11.' *Indiana International & Comparative Law Review* **13** (2003), 719-775.
[18] V. Mitsilegas, The New EU-USA cooperation on extradition, mutual legal assistance and the exchange of police data. *European Foreign Affairs Review* **8** (2003), 515-536.
[19] T. Schalken, M. Pronk. On joint investigation teams, Europol and supervision of their joint actions. *European Journal of Crime, Criminal Law and Criminal Justice* **10/1** (2002), 70-82.
[20] R. Kupchinsky, Intelligence and police coordination in the EU. *RFE/RL Organized Crime and Terrorism Watch* **4/11** (2004). [Online] Available from: URL: http://www.rferl.org/reports/corruptionwatch/2004/04/11-210404.asp [2004, October 26]
[21] P.J.P. Tak, Bottlenecks in international police and judicial cooperation in the EU. *European Journal of Crime Criminal Law and Criminal Justice* **8** (2000), 343-360.
[22] Shallow fight against terrorism. [Online] Available from: URL: http://www.turkishpress.com/news.asp?id= 52120 [2005, July 12]
[23] E. Durkheim, *The division of labor in society.* New York: The Free Press; [1893] 1984.

International Organizations and Non-Traditional Conflicts

Cuneyt GURER and Serhat DEMIR
Kent State University, USA

Abstract. Latest developments in the world have shown that International Organizations (IO) have an important role in mediating conflicts and assisting states in their fight against terrorism. However, there is considerable literature in the field of international relations on the role of IOs and there is a debate as to the effects of IOs over states. While realists argue that states do not matter, liberalists argue that IOs are an important part of international relations. Both arguments hold at different stages of the life cycle of various IOs. In that sense, North Atlantic Treaty Organization (NATO), United Nations (UN) and European Union (EU) have been examined. While establishment of some IOs can be explained by realist explanations, the decision making procedures of some IOs are better explained by liberalist arguments.

Keywords. International organizations, realism, liberalism, non-traditional conflict

Introduction

The international fight against terrorism requires effective cooperation and collaboration facilitated by fast communication and mutual understandings. Most authors emphasize the importance of international cooperation as a response to terrorism [1]. IOs such as Interpol that specifically deal with security issues are very important agents that provide mutual cooperation towards the common interests of the member states [2]. IOs can also be very effective agents in terms of providing technical assistance to their member states [3].

In this study, we will first examine the assertions of different theories on the role of IOs within the international context. Major schools of thought, namely liberalism and realism, have highly distinct, even highly contradictory arguments on the role of IOs. However, there are times when all those arguments hold. We can see hints of realism in the creation of IOs and hints of liberalism in their decision making procedures. In that sense, in the second part of this study, we will examine the life cycles of several IOs in order to see how they survive and manage based on those schools of thought.

While organizational resources and funding are very crucial factors that enhance the ability of an IO to perform its duties, the effectiveness of an IO in terms of making its member states act the way the organization requires is the most important factor for an IO to run effectively [2, 4, 5, 6]. In fact, effective IOs are the ones that have effective measures to ensure compliance of the members with the rules and decisions of the organization. Otherwise an IO becomes just another bureaucracy or a mere instrument. We do not deny the importance of the wide range of functions of IOs here. Our main argument in this study is that dealing with non-traditional conflict on an international level requires more than just information sharing and mutual collaboration. Handling non-traditional conflict requires joint action whereby contracting parties stick together in terms of action and reaction. When IOs cannot promote collective action, they have minimal influence on state behavior, and thus hold little promise for promoting stability in the post-Cold War world [5].

There are numerous examples of IOs created by sovereign states to organize their relationships in the pursuit of their interests in the international arena. Theories of international regimes and international organizations have different and mostly contradictory views on the effectiveness of IOs in terms of making states obey their rules and abide by their decisions. There are opposing views among different schools of thoughts about the role these organizations play in the international system. While some believe in the effectiveness of IOs on states' behavior, others view IOs as mere puppets that act in the interest of powerful states with no mandate over states.

Emphasizing the particular institutional arrangements that organize international politics Abbott and Snidal [7] claim that the active and independent functions of IOs are above international regimes which generally include only norms and collective choice procedures. Regimes, according to Krasner [8, pg. 2] are "implicit or explicit principles, norms, rules and decision-making procedures around which actors' expectations converge in a given area of international relations." IOs are a problematic issue of international relations. Based on the considerable body of literature that favor IOs, it would not be easy to argue that IOs are insignificant for world politics but the difficulty to manage them and their incapability to achieve important issues are still causes of the debates for their existence and functionality.

1. Theoretical Approaches to International Organizations

1.1. Realist Argument

Realism holds a pessimistic view of how the world works and three main assumptions can be derived from the realist perspective about the international system:

1. The international system is anarchic. Anarchy is not conflict; it is an ordering principle. States are the main actors in this system of anarchy and there is no central authority above them. State sovereignty is central because there is no higher ruling body in the international system. There is no government over governments.
2. States holding the central authority in the international system are self-benefit maximizers and their basic motive is survival. They need to think strategically to survive in the international system.
3. There is a trust deficit among states because they can never be certain about the intention of other states.

No state can be certain another state will not use its offensive military capability against the other. They also potentially threaten each other. As they gain more material capabilities they increase their desire for weaker opponents. To survive and make sure that other states will not have bad intentions against them, states create alliances. Those alliances are not in the form of international organizations at the first step but those states can create organizations which will be considered as an extension of states which are willing to participate in the alliance. The most powerful states in the system create and shape institutions so that they can maintain their share of world power or even increase it. In this view institutions are essential arenas for acting out power relationships. In short, the balance of power is the main explanatory variable that explains war; institutions are merely intervening variables in the process. NATO is a classic example of this kind of argument. According to the realist claims NATO was created by the US during the Cold War era and other states jumped on the bandwagon to make sure about the consequences of cold war. Therefore, it is a left over organization from the Cold War era and should have dissolved after the Cold War, since the reason for its creation does not exist any more.

1.2. Liberalist Argument

Compared to realism, liberalism holds a more optimistic view of international relations. Liberalism rejects the realist argument of systemic anarchy and argues that even though there is not a world government, there are international organizations that serve some of the purposes of an international government. According to liberalist theory of international relations, good intentions of the states and cooperation among states are the main assumptions that run the world politics. At the state level where the realists do not care about individual state characteristics outside of power, liberals argue that other than power, regime type, bureaucracies, public opinion, individual characteristics of political leaders etc. might be important determinants of state behavior.

2. Theories and International Organizations

Theories of international relations and world politics explain the role and the significance of international organizations in different ways. The Realist approach considers international organizations as insignificant actors on the international arena [5], whereas liberals see IOs as important elements of world politics [6]. In other words, Realists argue that IOs do not constrain state behavior, and that states can simply disregard IOs if they do not serve the state interests. Realists maintain that institutions are basically a reflection of the distribution of power in the world. They are based on the self interested calculations of the great powers and they have no independent effect on state behavior. Realists therefore believe that institutions are not an important cause of peace. They matter only in the margins.

Liberals, who contend that IOs matter, view IOs as binding and as important tools for establishing and maintaining peace and cooperation among states. Neoconservatives, on the other hand, even go further in arguing that IOs constrain 'good' states, but not 'bad' states. Institutionalists argue that institutions can alter state preferences and therefore change state behavior. Whether IOs are significant elements of world politics or not, the fact remains that they are nearly at every level of international relations, and states act through the IOs. Given the reality that a variety of IOs operate in the international arena, the crucial question then is to what extent and how IOs constrain or enable state behavior, and whether they are effective in achieving their objectives.

From a rationalist-institutionalist standpoint, Abbott and Snidal [7, pg. 5] argue that rational states use or create formal IOs when the value of IOs' functions, such as "facilitating the negotiation and implementation of agreements, resolving disputes, managing conflicts, carrying out operational activities like technical assistance, elaborating norms, shaping international discourse," outweigh the costs, such as limits on unilateral actions of the states and obligation to obey rules of IOs even though theses rules are in contradiction with the interests of the states. And they also emphasize that in appropriate circumstances, IOs' two functional characteristics, centralization and independence, cause the states to prefer IOs to alternate forms of institutionalization.

On the other hand, Gallarotti [4] presents a counter argument about the foundations and the role of international organizations. He claims that "while international organizations are created to prevent conflicts among nations and to eliminate disorder by creating strategic structures, they often have the opposite effect of exacerbating existing problems or creating new ones" [4, pg. 184].

IOs' functions require substantive independence to maintain neutrality and enhance the efficiency and legitimacy of collective and individual actions. "Information created or verified by an independent and neutral IO is more reliable than that provided by states because it is free of national biases" [7, pg. 20]. UN peacekeeping operations are a very good example of IOs' trustee function. "UN forces patrol or even control territory of combatants, prevent conflict, and supervise negotiated cease-fires" (pg. 21).

Even though Abbott and Snidal [7] reveal the positive effects of the IOs on international cooperation, at some point they make arguments parallel to those of realists stating that "IO independence is highly constrained: member states, especially the powerful, can limit the autonomy of IOs, interfere with their operations, ignore their dictates, or restructure and dissolve them. But as in many transactions, participation by even partially autonomous, neutral actors increase efficiency and affect the legitimacy of individual and collective actions. This provides even powerful states with incentives to grant IOs substantial independence" [7, pg. 5].

In terms of support for state interactions, IOs allow for a fast response to sudden developments. Representation and voting rules define precise terms of state interaction, reflecting balances among states having different levels of power, interest, and knowledge. Although such structures constitute a disproportionate influence in favor of powerful states, it is noted that they may also constitute a base for the protection of weaker states by holding powerful states accountable to fixed rules and procedures. Abbott and Snidal [7] characterize the protection of weaker states as the price that powerful states have to pay for participating in such centralized arrangements. The Security Council and the EU Council are given as examples, where the most powerful states have veto powers, but, even if united, cannot approve actions without support from smaller states.

Abbott and Snidal [7] note that although centralization requires some degree of autonomy, many valuable functions of IOs require more substantive operational independence. They argue that the participation of an IO as an independent, neutral actor can transform relations among states, and enhance the efficiency and legitimacy of collective and individual actions. The authors also note that powerful states will not enter into an IO they cannot influence; however, too much interference will undermine the neutrality and the legitimacy of the organization, which will in turn undermine the effective functioning and the ability of the organization to achieve valued ends. Independence is a very essential aspect of an IO, since it provides an organization with third party neutrality power in pushing forward negotiations in case of interstate disputes and enhances intergovernmental organizations. They point out that these functions could have been implemented by the dominant states, but suspicion of bias would impede cooperation. Related to the neutral nature of IOs, the authors also note that direct assistance by powerful states -financial or technical- to weaker states may create dependence, reduce policy flexibility, and be domestically controversial. For that reason, weaker states are said to prefer the assistance through IOs in order to avoid such controversies. Authors aptly use the term 'laundering functions' to refer to those functions of IOs that enable the international and domestic legitimatization of a course of action taken by the IOs.

3. International Organizations and Their Role in Non-traditional Conflicts

In the second part of this study we will examine the role of international organizations in non-traditional conflict situations. Three major IOs will be selected as case studies and five main questions will be applied to all three cases in order to figure out their levels of independence from state influence and also to determine whether they could develop an independent decision making process. Their level of technical capacities to intervene in conflicts is also considered as an important indicator of acting independently from individual states.

Soros [9], in his most recent book, states that he is in favor of stronger international institutions to enforce the international law and pursue the collective interests of humanity such as peace, security, environment, social justice and stability of financial markets. To him, states by themselves are not capable of dealing with those collective interests.

We will not be discussing the role of the states within the IOs' context in this paper, since it is out of the scope of this study; however it is sufficient to say here that some of the issue areas such as counter terrorism require transnational responses of the states relayed through international institutions.

As we discussed in earlier parts of this study, international relations theories provide different explanations to the question of whether international organizations can effectively contribute to world peace as an independent actor from states. Assuming that previously explained theories of international relations and their look at IOs provide useful explanations at different levels of analysis (systemic, state/societal and individual) and in different time periods (Realism and the Cold War era, establishment of EEC after WWII and later integration etc.), we will look at three organizations and try to identify which theoretical approaches provide more insight about the their involvement in the non-traditional conflicts.

We picked the concept of non-traditional conflict instead of terrorism because the definition of terrorism is not clear cut and international organizations can be better assessed by looking at their role in other conflict situations. Our criteria to show whether those institutions are highly state dominated or have their own power to apply in any policy area, will be related to five different subjects; rules for entry, decision making procedures, financial contribution of states, technical capabilities and the main focus of the organization, the level of involvement in the 'war on terrorism.'

We are aware that all these organizations were established for different purposes and motivation of the states' participation differs for each organization. For example country A can decide to participate in NATO for security reasons and in the EU for economic and political reasons. However, above all, all those organizations at some point are directly or indirectly involved with the decisions about common problems such as 'war on terror' and other regional conflicts. Therefore, we will focus on the overall question of whether international organizations can make a difference to solve the non-traditional conflicts and terrorism in particular. We do not consider the IOs' position as a dichotomy of success and failure or effective -ineffective. Rather, they have a more complex role and they might be successful in one level of analysis and vain in another. In a direct military involvement an international organization such UN or NATO might be slow to act either because of the decision making process or the lack of military capabilities.

4. Evaluation Framework and Criteria for Theoretical Application

We developed five critical questions which, we believe, will help us to find the evidences of theoretical approaches to international organizations. For each question both realism and liberalism will have its own answers but we will seek for answers using objective criteria such as formal participation regulations, decision making procedures, budget and technical capacities.

4.1. Creation of IOs and Participation:

The first criteria will seek evidence to understand how the IO was planned and created by its founders. As realists argue, IOs are created by powerful countries to serve their interests. The second objective of this criterion is to identify the procedures which are applied to new members of the club. Our main concern will be whether any member country has dominance in deciding new members because of a privileged position in decision making. We collected information regarding their original foundation purposes and participation procedures for new countries from different resources.

The realist argument about the creation of IOs and participation of new members would state that IOs have been mainly created by the powerful state and new members are only accepted if they accept the rules created by the powerful state which holds the system.

Systemic level pressures and power relations among nations are important factors in creating international organizations. However, not every international or regional organization succeeds like the one supported financially and politically by powerful states.

The question of why countries want to join international organizations is central in Gruber's [10] book, where he analyzed the World Trade Organization (WTO), European Monetary Union (EMU) and North America Free Trade Agreement (NAFTA) in terms of their initial creation and the motivations of participating countries. Gruber argues that the 'losers' or states who have no power to set the rules and do not stand to gain from a new regime, 'acquiesce because they know that the winners are in a position to proceed without them.' When powerful states decide to create new international regimes, all other states face a difficult choice. They will have no say over whether or not a new regime is formed. The choice faced by weaker states is a simple one: whether they want to be 'in' or 'out' of the new club. To this extent Gruber's argument that international institutions are instruments of the powerful is a realist argument. However he also states that the powerful state which creates the rules of the club is not entirely unconstrained. Gruber also argues that the design of the international institutions will keep the ongoing support for powerful states and those rules will keep the weaker states in their commitments.

4.2. Decision Making

Zweifel [11, pg. 13] in his recent book argues that "international organizations suffer from democratic deficit and accountability deficit; therefore, it is generally acknowledged that international organizations lack democratic procedures and compare badly with democratic nation-states in this regard." He, then, proposes three possible reactions to the democratic deficit international organizations; be cautious in using them in the democratization of countries, abolish them, and reform them towards a more democratic institutional establishment. Although we accept the argument of democratic deficit in terms of their decision making procedure and the way they use the authority given to them, our examination does not focus on democracy explicitly, but the source of power in the decision making process and dominance of a state.

Under this topic we will examine the general decision making procedure of the organization and specifically evaluate their decision making procedures for involvement in non-traditional conflicts. The main focus will be whether or not any states have a privileged position in the decision making process.

4.3. Budget

Monitory contributions can be a power source to influence the decisions of international organizations. Our hypothesis is that as the amount of financial contribution in the form of country membership dues increases, a country will have more formal or informal power over the organization. Financial contribution is related with countries' economic power; rich countries contribute more than other countries to an IO budget.

4.4. Capacities

We will examine the level of independence in having technical capacities which includes military equipment, combat weapons, technological and technical materials to be used in their daily works. Not relying on powerful states for military equipment and other technical materials would mean less dependence on the states' decision for their contribution to any kind of intervention decisions.

4.5. Involvement in the Global War on Terrorism (GWOT)

Our last criterion is about the level of commitment and involvement of the organization to the global war on terror. Creating an objective measure of commitment requires looking at the changes of organizational behavior before and after the 9-11 terrorist attacks, and how they respond to the incident. It is also necessary to look at the policy level changes of the organizational objectives. We will rely mainly on information provided by the organizations and their open sources. We also need to look at whether the involvement is an output of an overall agreement of member states, or international organizations simply jump on the bandwagon of the global war on terror because of a dominant actor.

5. North Atlantic Treaty Organization (NATO)

5.1. Criteria for Participation for New Candidates and the Role of Member States in Participation Decision

In the history of NATO new members joined the club in five waves of enlargement that all were followed by major changes in world politics and international relations. Therefore enlargement and participation of new countries can be considered as a response to the structural changes in the international system. However it is widely accepted that NATO has been created in response to the uncertainties of the cold war era, and therefore it was an organization created by US dominance. NATO has an *open door policy* for new members;

however, membership requirements involve a series of technical procedures which are mainly designed to assist candidate countries to meet the criteria for membership. The Memberships Action Plan outlines the structure of accession process and the rules for entry.

Realism can provide a better explanation about the initial establishment of NATO and latter enlargement decisions. However, the realist prediction of the decline of NATO after the end of the Cold War is not happening; alternative explanations can be found in the liberalist approach saying that the cooperation among states justifies the continued existence of NATO as a security organization. We find some evidence for the liberal argument that the regime type of states matter in international relations, by looking at the participation of former Warsaw pact countries and Spain after regime changes in each country. Therefore we can argue that NATO was created by the initiative of the US, but participation is related to the changes both in the system and participants' regimes.

Table 1. NATO member countries and year of participation (Source: NATO web site)

1949-	**Foundation of NATO and 12 founder countries** Belgium, Canada, Denmark, France, Iceland, Italy, Luxembourg, the Netherlands, Norway, Portugal, the UK, the US.
1952 -	Greece and Turkey
1955 -	Federal Republic of Germany (After German reunification in 1990, the whole of Germany, including the territory of the former German Democratic Republic became NATO member)
1982 -	Spain
1999 -	The Czech Republic, Hungary and Poland (first former members of the Warsaw Pact to join NATO)
2004 -	Bulgaria, Estonia, Latvia, Lithuania, Romania, Slovakia and Slovenia.

5.2. The Decision Making Procedure for Involvement in Non-traditional Conflicts

This question basically refers to whether any of the member states have a privileged position in the decision making process and have influence over other states. When decisions have to be made in NATO, action is agreed upon on the basis of unanimity and common accord. There is no voting or decision by majority. Each nation represented at the Council table or on any of its subordinate committees retains complete sovereignty and responsibility for its own decisions.

5.3. Budget and State Contributions

2005 figures obtained from the NATO web site indicate that the US provides a significant amount of monetary and military (technical) contribution to the NATO alliance. Defense expenditure and GDP ratio of the US is the highest among other NATO and NRC states.

Table 2. Percentage cost shares of NATO member countries (civil and military budgets)
(Source: Financial and economic data relating to NATO defence, M-DPC-2(2000)107 published on 5.12.2000)

NATO Member Country	Civil Budget	Military Budget (Headquarters, Agencies and Programmes)		Military Budget (NATO Airborne Early Warning & Control Force)	
Participating Countries	"19"	"19"	"18"	"14"	"13"
Belgium	2.76	2.8	3.3	2.5869	3.2821
Canada	5.35	5.33	5.95	7.1994	9.1343
Czech Republic	0.9	0.9	1.08	0	0
Denmark	1.47	1.68	1.94	1.5282	1.9389
France	15.35	15.25	0	0	0
Germany	15.54	15.54	18.2	21.4886	27.2638
Greece	0.38	0.38	0.46	0.4728	0.5999
Hungary	0.65	0.65	0.78	0	0
Iceland	0.05	0.04	0.05	0	0
Italy	5.75	5.91	7.08	5.5485	7.0397
Luxembourg	0.08	0.08	0.1	0.0825	0.1045
Netherlands	2.75	2.84	3.28	2.8625	3.6317
Norway	1.11	1.16	1.36	1.1146	1.4142
Poland	2.48	2.48	2.97	0	0
Portugal	0.63	0.63	0.75	0.5323	0.6754
Spain	3.5	3.5	4.19	2.77	3.1
Turkey	1.59	1.59	1.9	1.2419	1.5757
UK	17.25	16.09	19.12	20.8558	0
US	22.41	23.15	27.49	31.716	40.2398
Total	**100**	**100**	**100**	**100**	**100**

5.4. Technical Capacities and Main Focus

NATO's technical capacities are mainly provided by the member states. Each country has a diplomatic and military presence at NATO headquarters. The costs of maintaining and staffing their national delegations and military missions are also a national responsibility, financed in accordance with the different accounting principles and practices of each country.

5.5. Involvement in the 'War on Terrorism'

NATO is very active in the global war on terror and on 12 September 2001, less than 24 hours after the terrorist attacks against the US, NATO declared the attacks to be an attack against all the 19 NATO member countries within the terms of Article 5 of the North Atlantic Treaty. NATO claims that it has been actively engaged in the campaign against terrorism on both the political and military fronts.[1]

---

[1] For further information see: NATO and the fight against terrorism, http://www.nato.int/issues/terrorism/index.html

6. United Nations (UN)

6.1. Criteria for Participation for New Candidates and the Role of Member States in Participation Decision

Any country can participate in the UN with the approval of the Security Council, although there are some procedural and technical requirements; the main decision to participate is political and not restricted to any geographical or conditional terms. Therefore it is a worldwide organization. The Security Council and its five permanent members -China, France, the Russian Federation, the UK and the US- has the power to block any decision; therefore, it is fair to claim that the Security Council has the power to accept new members.[2]

Provisional Rules of Procedure of the Security Council[3] (Rule 58) state that "Any State which desires to become a member of the UN shall submit an application to the Secretary-General...", the same document continues in the following articles as "The Security Council shall decide whether in its judgment the applicant is a peace-loving State and is able and willing to carry out the obligations contained in the Charter and, accordingly, whether to recommend the applicant State for membership. If the Security Council recommends the Applicant State for membership, it shall forward to the General Assembly the recommendation with a complete record of the discussion. If the Security Council does not recommend the Applicant State for membership or postpones the consideration of the application, it shall submit a special report to the General Assembly with a complete record of the discussion."

According to the Provisional Rules of Procedure of the Security Council, the Security Council has the power to decide which country will be a member of the UN. Although the Security Council sends the application to the General Assembly for the discussions, that is only a procedural requirement which does not effect the decision at all.

6.2. The Decision Making Procedure for Involvement in Non-traditional Conflicts

The main decision making body of the UN is the Security Council, which consists of 15 member states. Five of those states are permanent members of the Council. The ten non-permanent members are periodically elected by all Member States for a two-year term. Permanent members, namely China, France, the Russian Federation, the UK and the US, can block any proposal brought before the Council by casting a negative vote. Any permanent member state, thus, can leave out decisions that are clearly not in their interest. Therefore, national interests of the permanent member states play a significant role in the decision making process, which also fits into realist arguments.

6.3. Budget and State Contributions[4]

The budget of the UN is made of member states' annual contributions which are determined based on their level of economic development. In that sense the largest contribution to the budget should be given by the US; however, because of political reasons the US has not paid membership dues for the last couple of years. We would

---

[2] List of UN member states and their date of entrance can be obtained: http://www.un.org/Overview/unmember.html
[3] Provisional Rules of Procedure of the Security Council http://www.un.org/Docs/sc/scrules.htm
[4] For further information see: state contributions, UN Finance: http://www.globalpolicy.org/finance/tables/index.htm

assume that the biggest contributor would have the most influence in the policy making. However, non-payment of her dues does not deny the US the ability to exert power over the decision making process. In other words, the US still uses her power which we assumed was sourced by the amount of contributions as membership dues.

6.4. Technical Capacities and Main Focus

The UN is a multipurpose organization from peace keeping operations and crime prevention to environmental programs and energy issues. It has a huge bureaucratic apparatus and technical capabilities in various fields. Under joint operations the UN provides basic technical needs; however, depending on the operational type member states joining the operation, it may provide other related technical needs. The UN has the ability to generate basic technical military equipments, which are not heavy weapons for war, but mainly for peace keeping purposes. In that sense, as Doyle and Sambanis [12] state, while the UN can be very poor at implementing a settlement by force (war making), it can be very good at mediating and implementing peace through negotiations.

6.5. Involvement in the 'War on Terrorism'

The history of the UN involvement in the war on terror goes back years before the 9-11 terrorist events. The UN developed anti-terrorism strategies over the years and asked its members to implement those strategies. After the 9-11 attacks, however, UN passed a new strategy document to fight against terrorism and asked all members to implement its requirements.[5]

7. European Union (EU)

7.1. Criteria for Participation for New Candidates and the Role of Member States in Participation Decision

Initially founded after WWII as regional economic cooperation (EEC), in 1990s with the Maastricht treaty, it became the European Union (EU) and the political side of the Union was established. The role of the US in the first place is significant. For new members highly technical accession process and enlargements based on a decision after 1998, and the preparation for full membership takes between 6-10 years depending on the countries' economic and political conditions.

7.2. The Decision Making Procedure for Involvement in Non-traditional Conflicts

The Council is the EU's main decision-making body. Like the European Parliament, the Council was set up by the founding treaties in the 1950s. It represents the member states, and its meetings are attended by one minister from each of the EU's national governments. Which ministers attend which meeting depends on what subjects are on the agenda. If, for example, the

---

[5] For detailed information about the UN efforts please see : http://www.un.org/terrorism

Council is to discuss environmental issues, the meeting will be attended by the Environment Minister from each EU country, and it will be known as the 'Environment Council.'

Each minister in the Council is empowered to commit his or her government. In other words, the minister's signature is the signature of the whole government. Moreover, each minister in the Council is answerable to his or her national parliament and to the citizens that parliament represents. This ensures the democratic legitimacy of the Council's decisions.

Up to four times a year the presidents and/or prime ministers of the member states, together with the President of the European Commission, meet as the 'European Council.' These 'summit' meetings set overall EU policy and resolve issues that could not be settled at a lower level (i.e. by the ministers at normal Council meetings). Given the importance of European Council discussions, they often continue late into the night and attract a lot of media attention.

7.3. Budget and State Contributions

The EU receives most of its revenue from the member states in three different forms. Import duties on goods brought into are collected on behalf of the EU by the member states and they are allowed to keep a proportion of the revenue to cover administrative expenses. The second form of the income consists of the Value Added Taxes (VAT) generated from the EU citizens. The third one is direct payments by the member states. The EU budget is always balanced and cannot have deficit. Contributions of the states based on the Gross National Income (GNI) constitute the largest amount of income of the budget. Most of the budgetary process and collection of taxes are carried out by the member states and they all have the responsibility to protect the EU's budgetary interest. Therefore, although the amount of contribution changes based on the state's GNI, the decision making process is more harmonized in the EU in that the largest contributors cannot influence the process solely based on budgetary criteria.

7.4. Technical Capacities and Main Focus

The EU is an economic and political organization in that the main objective of the member states is economic and political integration so that the free movement of goods, capital and people can be achieved. In addition, the EU, after the Maastricht treaty, started to become involved in the social lives of the European citizens and expand its area of concern significantly. Foreign and security affairs are one of those areas which required new organizations and policies to deal with foreign relations. In terms of domestic security affairs, the EU established Europol to increase the level of cooperation in Justice and Home affairs among member states. However, none of those institutions are mature enough to deal with large scale conflicts.

7.5. Involvement in the 'War on Terrorism'

The EU has developed measures and policies against terrorism because it has suffered from terrorism from various sources for decades (e.g., ETA, IRA). One of the main aims, the policy of increased judicial co-operation between member states, had already been agreed as part of the Tampere Programme when the attack against the US took place in 2001. However, right after the 9-11 attacks, the EU prepared an anti-terrorism action plan, followed by a framework decision defining terrorist offences and aligning the level of sanctions between member states.

8. Conclusion

In this study, we attempt to understand the role of international organizations in transnational security concerns and their ability to contribute to the peace process and security by looking at the indicators of participation, budget, technical capacities, involvement in WOT and their decision making process. We applied the two major international relations theories to explain each of those concerns. We found a strong evidence for a realist explanation of the foundation of the organizations which is basically for the interest of world hegemony. However, each organization developed a unique participation procedure for new members.

- NATO - bandwagoning,
- UN - Security Council,
- EU - enlargement structural decision with Atlantic partnership, because it is also US's interest.

1. *Decision making:* NATO and the EU developed mechanisms to give equal say to each member; however, the UN Security Council did not; therefore, there is evidence for both realist and liberal explanations.
2. *Budget:* Powerful states contribute the most, except for the UN (the US does not pay dues because of some other concerns); however, the US still keeps its position in the Security Council.
3. *Technical capacities:* NATO relies on individual states and the US; the UN and EU mostly have their own capacities but not heavy military equipment.
4. *WOT:* NATO is highly involved; the UN has relevant bodies more in an involvement with peaceful solutions to root causes; the EU has regional capacity building through rules and regulations.

Overall, NATO's functioning presents positions which are very close to realist argument, UN and EU liberalist. However, EU has its own mechanism of developed relations with the US in world affairs, and despite some disagreements on different issue areas, it usually acts with the US.

In order to develop the argument we need to look at the bureaucratic politics of those organizations. There is also evidence for both theories in individual cases. Therefore, it is also necessary to look at the specific cases and issues of debates to understand the IOs' policy outcomes whether they act according to the interests of powerful states or actually a common ground for international cooperation.

We believe that IOs can only achieve their addressed issues when they are able to act free of influence from the interests of powerful states and when they have power to force states to obey fairly created rules rather than giving them advice, even though it seems less likely in the near feature. For instance, EU's achievement of harmonization and cooperation in Europe can lead to better global cooperation. In that sense, further studies should focus on how to make IOs function independently from the influence of the states' interests and how to create simple and effective management systems for IOs.

On the one hand, the centralized structure of IOs increases the efficiency of all the participating states; on the other hand, their independence provides some sort of protection for weaker states from the powerful states' arbitrary action [7]. Barnett and Coleman [2] view IOs as strategic actors and argue that IOs have three goals: the first is to further their mandate as defined by their professional training and expert knowledge, the second is to survive and be secure, and the last one is to be autonomous. For effective operation, IOs are dependent on states for symbolic and material resources. Getting these resources from others puts pressures on IOs to conform to external environments. Thus, IOs face the autonomy-resource trade-off. Barnett and Coleman's [2] emphasis on IOs' resource dependence on external environments suggests that resource dependence could limit the effectiveness and the autonomy of IOs. Barnett and Coleman [2] also suggest that IOs could reach a significant autonomy and enhance their effectiveness when there are no rival organizations that could threaten their relevance and organizational security.

Lepgold [13], on the other hand, points to a serious problem that could undermine the effectiveness of an IO, especially whenever pooling resources is required from member states. The problem is the collective action problem. He would suggest that first of all, the problems an IO is likely to confront should be diagnosed through the collective action theory lenses, and only then a viable solution could be produced. In that sense, IOs such as the UN should not aspire to be a substitute for states, but instead should focus on doing things that individual states, even the most powerful, may not be able to do. For example, it seems unlikely that the UN could develop an effective role in the use of force against terrorism (nor would it necessarily want to) but it could play a role in informing states about non-military options for ending terrorism [14].

Gallarotti [4] emphasizes the effect of IOs' management functions to their outcomes and asserts that since the management of complex relations is one of the goals of international organizations and because these complex systems are difficult to understand, managing those organizations becomes even harder. Failure in management can create problems that IOs themselves are not capable of solving. Also, IOs can be a source of destabilization when their solutions discourage nations from pursing more substantive long term resolutions to international problems.

Gallarotti [4] argues that traditionally IOs have been redundant in their managerial functions and has expended more managerial capital than necessary. States created IOs because they needed them in order to maintain cooperation. Citing from Edward Morse, Gallarotti [4] indicates that modernization increased the levels and types of interdependences among states, which require a high level of cooperation. Nevertheless, by their nature, they have gone so far astray that they became the sources of problems because of the complexity of managing those organizations and multipart interest of states on certain issue areas.

According to Gallarotti [4] the solution to avoid those problems is "limited international organization[s]" with restricted managerial capabilities focusing on providing expert knowledge and functions within the limits of their issue area. Gallorotti [4, pg. 220] asserts that "their specific roles, functions and goals should be dictated both by the nature or underlying strategic structures of the international problems and by the potential positive and negative effects of possible managed solutions."

Consequently, based on the literature we suggest that in order for IOs to be effective in the fight against terrorism, IOs should;

- be autonomous from state influence
- be able to force states to comply with its decisions
- have mechanisms of monitoring
- be able to adapt itself to changing international power dynamics
- have adequate resources independent of states

- be able to provide necessary incentives to states
- be able to provide expert knowledge
- should function within its limited sphere of expertise and issue area

Future research should focus on each of our proposals with a set of data to test the hypotheses presented in our study. Qualitative case study observation might be helpful to identify some of the key points considering our general question; however, statistical analysis of available data on the subject might tell us a different story. Therefore, to capture an adequate picture of the problem we should combine quantitative data analysis with qualitative analysis.

Table 3. Summary of the case studies

	Participation	Decision Making	Budget	Capacities	Involvement into WOT
NATO	'Open Door Policy', however enlargement decisions after major changes in the international structure	Unanimity, or common accord, but 'bandwagoning' is possible due to unbalanced power structure of member states	US provides the most contribution and technical input	Based on the countries' support	Highly involved
UN	Security Council	Security Council	Individual states, US did not pay dues, but has the most share in normal conditions	US has its own technical capacities, under military joint operations countries can provide some input	Highly involved
EU	European Council and Commission working together	EC	Members states	Some technical cap. Newly developed skills	Rules and regulations for states to adopt common polices

References

[1] J.W. Amos II, R.H.S. Stolfi, Controlling international terrorism: Alternatives palatable and unpalatable, *Annals of the American Academy of Political and Social Science* **463** (1982), 69-83.
[2] M. Barnett, L. Coleman, Designing police: Interpol and the study of change in international organizations. *International Studies Quarterly* **49** (2005), 593-619.
[3] C.A. Ward, Building capacity to combat international terrorism: The role of the United Nations Security Council. *Journal of Conflict & Security Law* **8** (2003), 289-305.
[4] G.M. Gallarotti, The limits of international organization: Systemic failure in the management of international relations. *International Organization* **45/2** (1991), 183-220.
[5] J.J. Mearsheimer, The false promise of international institutions. *International Security* **19** (1994), 5-49.
[6] C.A. Wallander, Institutional assets and adaptability: NATO after the Cold War. *International Organization* **54** (2000), 705-736.
[7] K.W. Abbott, D. Snidal, Why states act through formal international organizations. *The Journal of Conflict Resolution* **42** (1999), 3-32.
[8] S.D. Krasner, Structural causes and regime consequences: Regimes as intervening variables. In S.D. Krasner, editor. *International regimes*. Ithaca: Cornell University Press; 1983. p 1-22.
[9] G. Soros, *The age of fallibility: Consequences of the war on terror*. New York: Public Affairs; 2006.
[10] L. Gruber, *Ruling the world: Power politics and the rise of supranational institutions*. Princeton: Princeton University Press; 1964.
[11] T.D. Zweifel, *International organizations and democracy: Accountability, politics, and power*. Boulder: Lynne Rienner; 2006.

[12] M. Doyle, N. Sambanis, *Making war and building peace: United Nations peace operations.* Princeton: Princeton University Press; 2006.
[13] J. Lepgold, NATO's post-Cold War collective action problem. *International Security* **23/1** (1998), 78-106.
[14] M. Crenshaw, The causes of terrorism. In C. Besteman, editor. *Violence: A reader.* New York: Palgrave Macmillan; 2002. p 99-117.

Barriers to International Police Cooperation in the Age of Terrorism

Mitchel P. ROTH and Murat SEVER
Sam Houston State University, USA

Abstract. Terrorism is a common threat to most countries in the twenty-first century. Terrorism, like other crimes that transcend borders, creates a number of complications for law enforcement and is a potential challenge for police forces throughout the world. International cooperative ventures in policing have confronted a number of obstacles. Although international police cooperation is not a new area of study, as transnational crime and the concomitant increase in terrorist activities, the need for police services from different countries to cooperate effectively has become a paramount concern. This paper examines various barriers to international police cooperation engaged in fighting.

Keywords. Terrorism, international police cooperation, obstacles, barriers

Introduction

Transnational criminal matters have stimulated cooperation between international police agencies for more than one hundred years. However, it was only in the years following World War I that a true organizational apparatus was created to further police cooperation between nations with the creation of Interpol. However, as recently as 2004 one expert asserted that despite its international standing Interpol's "impact on terrorism and terrorists has been minimal" [1, pg. 154]. International cooperative ventures in policing have confronted a number of obstacles. Problems include financial constraints, geographic factors such as large porous borders, cultural and linguistic complexities, and the lack of internationally accepted professional police standards, often resulting in corruption.

Challenges to police cooperation can result from civil and internal disturbances that lead to the demise of civil society. Some countries lack laws relating to organized crime, extradition, passports, and other matters, often leading to distrust between police organizations. A major stumbling block to police cooperation has been the attempt to reconcile principles of national sovereignty with joint efforts at international police cooperation. Conflict arises when some countries become hesitant about ceding their sovereign authority to strengthen the collaborative fights against terrorism and transnational criminal activity. These concerns have led some countries to refrain from supporting diverse conventions, agreements, and protocols. As a result, bilateral and multilateral agreements are out of the question with these countries.

Barriers to International Police Cooperation

Terrorism is a common threat to most countries in the twenty-first century. Terrorism like other crimes that transcend borders creates a number of complications for law enforcement - a challenge to police services everywhere. As likely as not countries will disagree about the policies of partner states. Barriers to police international cooperation in counter-terrorism and related investigations are very similar to those faced when conducting traditional transnational crime investigations. In both instances, police are typically the first responders and must treat the scene, whether terrorist or run-of-the-mill criminality.

Policing terrorism in the current century is fraught with obstacles. International terrorism is a potential challenge for police forces throughout the world. Although international police cooperation is not a new area of study, as transnational crime and the concomitant increase in terrorist activities, the need for police services from different countries to cooperate effectively has become a paramount concern. Anytime criminal activity transcends borders it creates numerous complications for police. Variance in legal systems, languages, cultures, and police practices are but a few of the factors influencing current crime control issues.

New technologies including miniature explosive devices, the ease of immigration, and rapid and cheap transportation have all facilitated the transition of the world to a more complex and dangerous era. Policing terrorism in the 'information age' has led to new conceptions of policing. National boundaries are less marked and clear as security and secrecy concerns have become paramount concerns for police cooperation. The ubiquities of the Internet and global information networks that are both public and private have compounded concerns about sharing information between international police systems. Barriers to police coordination and cooperation come from every corner as more and more nations have less control over definitions of crime and punishment in their territories, as these issues become shared concerns for world's police organizations.

Defining Terrorism

Barriers to cooperation begin at the basic level - the legal definition of terrorism. Without a consensus as to which groups should be labeled terrorist groups little in the way of cooperation will go forward. An accepted definition is required when legislating against it on a bilateral or multilateral agreement. Just important is the fact that legislation and punishment needs to be defined to make terrorism distinct from other crimes. Therefore an internationally accepted definition is required before going forward. Although there are some regionally approved definitions, such as in the EU, there is still not an international consensus.

The tendency to paint terrorism with wide brush strokes often creates too broad a criminalization of certain activities. For many in the law enforcement community it can come down to the adage, "I know it [terrorism] when I see it."

A pioneer in terrorism research, in 1977, Walter Laqueur presciently wrote, "It can be predicted with confidence that disputes about a comprehensive, detailed definition of terrorism will continue for a long time, that they will not result in consensus and that they will make no noticeable contribution to the understanding of terrorism" [quoted in 1, pg. 142]. As far back as 1988 one source offered 109 definitions of terrorism obtained through a survey of leading academics in the field [2]. More recently, one authority asserts that the foresighted work was still relevant and that this survey demonstrated that "a minimum consensus definition of terrorism has become accepted among the international community of social scientists who study conflict" [3, pg. 27].

One expert suggests that the lack of an agreed upon definition in the 1970s hampered early attempts at international cooperation [1]. However, since 1999, when the UN approved the Convention for the Suppression of the Financing of Terrorism resolution there has been a much greater worldwide acceptance of a terrorism definition and what activities are related to it. Since 2002 the EU at least has agreed to a definition of 'terrorist offenses' and what is a terrorist group [1].

Language Barriers

More than four years ago, Deflem [4], made the connection between barriers that hampered the US in both the 'war on drugs' and the 'war on terror,' writing, "As in the global war on drugs, efficiency in policing" is the key, and investigations have been hindered by "Language barriers, poor inter-agency communications, aging equipment, and the fact that the Justice Department has made wiretapping slow and burdensome" (pg. 6). In 2002, for example, the anti-terror drill Euratox was held in France. This drill brought together two thousand participants from six EU countries. According to one report, "Great cooperation difficulties were experienced as the participants spoke different languages." Language facilitators are key ingredients in the war on terror. Any shortage of translators and interpreters can quickly hamper international investigations and create an insurmountable barrier to effective communication, timely interrogations, and timely translation of documents. Language barriers can also discourage or interfere with communication between nations and between interrogators and suspects.

Using the European Union (EU) as a microcosm for examining the language barrier issue explains this barrier on the regional level. The EU has twenty official languages for its more than two-dozen member states.[1] Of these only three are considered working languages - French, German, and English.[2] As a result, there is always the potential at any given time that hundreds of different interpretations might be required to translate all statements into all languages incorporated in the EU. For example, a meeting of the EU in eleven official languages would require 380 interpreters (www.2-2.se/en/3). Currently, the EU employs at least 4,000 interpreters. However, due to the exigencies of the language variations it can take up to a week for something to be translated into the languages of all the member states. This often involves the translation first across intermediate languages because of a lack of interpreters for some languages. This process, as it does elsewhere, has led to a loss of information and clarity, and even errors due to the inherent dangers of multiple language interpretations.[3] In one meeting a British document contained the words "airplanes flying by automatic pilot over nuclear power plants." The French interpreter translated this as "*les avions sans pilote qui prennent pour cibles les centrals nucleaires,*" or "pilotless airplanes whose targets are on nuclear power plants (www.2-2se/en/3)." Put this into the context of terrorism and one easily understands the perils of international communication in age of terror.

---

[1] EU official languages include Czech, Danish, Dutch, English, Estonian, Finnish, French, German, Greek, Hungarian, Italian, Lettish, Lithuanian, Maltese, Slovak, Slovene, Polish, Portuguese, Spanish, and Swedish. Although official EU documents are supposed to be published in all the languages, daily routine is dominated by English as the use of French is diminishing.
[2] By comparison, the United Nations uses 6 working languages.
[3] Suggestions have been made to make English the official language of the EU; or to make Esperanto a common second language.

In a country such as Estonia there exist several native languages. A country of 1.4 million people, 70% speak Estonian and 29% Russian. There are also a number of dialects. EU country Switzerland, with a population of 7.3 million, has 4.6 million German speakers, 1.4 million French, 500,000 Italian, and 35 Rheto-roman speakers. Both of the aforementioned countries then require a number of interpreters.

In 2004 ten of the acceding countries to the EU were able to meet the deadline for the translation of the EU's 85,000-page notebook into their native languages. As a result some of the laws of the EU could not be enforced in national courts since citizens could claim they did not understand them. Among the countries affected was Malta, 'due to a lack of Maltese translators.' But, even larger companies such as Poland are not able to translate the book on time [5].

One of the main arguments against using other languages besides a nation's common language as the official language is that much of the legislation produced in the EU has important implications for the populations of all member states; therefore, the average monolingual individual should not be impeded from accessing documents in their own language. If this tact were overlooked it would be understood that some countries were being favored over others.

Respecting Customs and National Sovereignty

Shortly before the American invasion of Iraq in 2003 television journalist Dan Rather interviewed Saddam Hussein. But, before the interview could take place Rather committed a grave error by sitting down with the bottom of his shoe facing the erstwhile dictator - a cardinal sin in Arabic culture, a gesture of insult and disrespect. This was not on purpose, but a faux pas that instantly got the interview off on the wrong foot (no pun intended). What seems like a minor issue to one country could end collaboration before it even gets started in similar circumstances during an investigation. It is therefore for a nation's representatives to be culturally sensitive toward a variety of issues, not the least being religion, ethnicity, ideology, cultural uniqueness, customs and culture, and national and political history.

In the EU the decision to use only twenty official languages has forced several nations to share a language. In reality, by doing this, it has required member countries to 'relinquish' its 'national sovereignty.'

Different Notions of Criminality/Variations in Legal Traditions

There is no common system of criminalization. Discrepancies among national substantive criminal laws can create almost insurmountable obstacles to mutual legal assistance and extradition. As its stands what might be considered a crime in one country might not be in another. For example, crimes such as blasphemy and apostasy are serious crimes under the Islamic legal tradition, the Sharia. This brings up the question, 'would a non-Islamic country be expected to extradite an individual for this offense?' which is not recognized as such at home. Obstacles often beckon when secular nations cooperate with more religious regimes. It is important that nations are sensitive to religion and ideology of countries at all levels, including law enforcement. With different histories, customs, and legal conditions among the world's nations there exists very different conceptions about what constitutes properly governed state justice. For example, the difference between common and civil legal traditions requires a commensurate reconciliation of disparate legal systems.

Immigration

With the rising tide of immigration over the past decade, most nations have new immigrant communities within their borders. Sometimes these communities act as transit points for traveling terrorists, particularly when there is tension between the immigrants and the nation state. In the early 1950s, the British military implemented a strategy, called a 'hearts and minds' campaign. The idea is relatively simple. A government cannot assume either way - whether the community is for or against promoting terrorism. It is, therefore, incumbent on the government to win the hearts and minds of the population. The second half of the twentieth century is littered with failed campaigns from Vietnam to Iraq. Therefore, it is essential that a police organization play its part in this strategy.

Different Political Systems

In Europe, attempts at cooperation are often hampered by the fact that some countries "have legal impediments to taking firm judicial action against suspected terrorists," usually due to "asylum laws, that afford loopholes, inadequate CT legislation, or standards of evidence that lack flexibility in permitting law enforcement authorities to rely on classified-source information in holding terrorist suspects" [6].

According to one official, the 9/11 hijackers "jurisdiction-shopped" to determine where to and how to pull off their attack on America [7, pg. 39]. By all accounts terrorists and others see Democratic states as more vulnerable and possessing more advantages as a potential terrorist target. Indeed countries with more civil liberties, more freedoms, more liberal immigration policies, and more liberal asylum policies are attractive targets to potential terrorists and other malefactors [7].

Political Instability

The absence of a strong central government often serves as an 'open invitation' for the relocation of international terrorists and criminal syndicates that see. It sends out signals much the way that 'broken windows' do in bereft communities in urban ghettos, that this is a place to conduct criminal enterprises. With the absence of a meaningful central authority there is little to prevent a terrorist organization from taking advantage of the opportunities presented them and in the end offers attractive bases for terrorist groups. One need look no further than failed governments in each hemisphere and on most continents to find regimes that have become home to evolving terrorist organizations. Here, unimpeded terrorist groups are free to build training camps, recruit new terrorists, conduct strategic planning meetings, and increase their base of support.

Extradition Treaties

Extradition should be considered a cornerstone of mutual legal cooperation in the fight against terrorism. Since terrorists frequently cross-national boundaries, any single nation's refusal to cooperate will weaken the chances of bringing them to justice. Among the barriers to efficient extradition practice, none has been more daunting than the ideological differences between nations that sometimes lead detractors to point to extradition's conflict with traditional policies of asylum and hospitality for oppressed newcomers.

Most countries belong to bilateral or multilateral international agreements regarding a variety of transnational crimes. But, "extradition for political offenses is often explicitly excluded, and the background of terrorism is always political" [8]. While this problem is improving, there are still cases where countries will not extradite individuals wanted for terrorism. Countries such as the US, Italy, and France have all been guilty of refraining from extraditing terrorists to other countries over the past three decades.

In some cases, individuals capture din various countries have been able to thumb their noses at powerful nations where they committed their original crimes. No event exemplifies the lack of extradition agreement than the 1985 aftermath of the Achille Lauro hijacking. In this case terrorists hijacked the Italian cruise ship and killed American hostage Leon Klinghoffer. The US government tried to capture the hijackers through military channels to bring them to justice. But the rescue plan failed because of intervention by the Italian government, within whose territory the capture was almost made. In this incident, the US government also filed formal criminal charges against the hijackers for violations of US criminal law and requested Italy to extradite them for prosecution. The Italian government refused to honor the request and instead prosecuted the hijackers under Italian law. This is considered the first time the US used the extradition process in a terrorism case [9]. Unlike other governments, the US lacks the legal authority to either extradite anyone in the absence of an extradition treaty or to prosecute anyone in the absence of an extradition treaty, or to prosecute anyone for acts committed abroad that violate foreign laws but not American laws. On the other hand, most other nations, especially those shaped by the civil law tradition, are bound by a different limitation, one that the US does not share - their laws and constitutions prohibit extradition, but make up for it in other ways - they can prosecute citizens for crimes committed abroad.

One critic of the current state of extradition treaties suggests there are double standards at work, noting:

"The consequences of any international terrorist act, which be definition is politically motivated and pursues political goals, are assessed by each state through the prism of its won national interests, which are not only different for different states, but may be diametrically opposite. Therefore, concrete terrorist attacks may simultaneously cause heavy damage to the security of some countries, make no difference to the interests of other countries and objectively play into the hands of third countries" [10, pg. 6].

Extradition is a tricky issue, particularly when it comes to death penalty statutes. The very existence of the death penalty in a country can, in the end, slow down or even prevent the extradition of terrorists - convicted or suspected. As it is today, even America's neighbors Canada and Mexico, are reluctant to turn over to the US suspects facing capital punishment. Since a number of wanted terrorists might face the death penalty if extradited to the US, this has become a major obstacle at times. Attempts were made to simplify the extradition process between the US and the EU in 2003. In two separate treaties the US agreed to EU demands that suspects extradited from the EU will not face the death penalty, which is banned in the EU. On the other hand, the US was forced to back down from its demand that this Mutual Legal Assistance treaty (MLA) guarantee the extradition of any EU national [11].

Another obstacle to international cooperation is the fact that many countries have different terrorist lists. What might be considered a terrorist group in one country is sometimes viewed as a legitimate political party or charity in another. Some EU countries have even resisted pressure to place Hamas and Hezbollah related charities on the common list.

Interrogation

Law enforcement styles vary widely. Some use interrogation techniques that violate what other nations would consider civil liberties, although these protections might not exist in both/all countries in a terrorism investigation.

Among the four major legal traditions there are a variety of different standards of acceptable interrogation procedures. Prosecution procedures vary widely as does the protocol for detaining suspected terrorists. More recently, America's rendition policies have led to a renewed criticism by its allies in the war on terror. The question as to, 'What constitutes torture?' and 'Is it ever appropriate to use torture?' has been replaced by outright admissions that various partners in the war on terror are actively using torture to obtain information. This has created a wide divide between international police organizations many of which are dead set against this as a human rights abuse. So, like other barriers a lack of consensus hamstrings potential cooperation between nations.

A number of issues arise when considering the objections to certain interrogation techniques. These are typically centered on Geneva Conventions, International law, and issues of state sovereignty. Acceptable standards for interrogation methods vary widely. National standards for interrogation are a byproduct of a complex national institutional process. As a result "interrogators in non-democratic states may use practices that are illegal in democratic states, including the use of torture" [7, pg. 39]. However, in the post-9/11 world, the demarcation between these tow two types of states has become increasingly obscured - just witness US treatment of detainees at Abu Ghraib and Guantanamo Bay and recent rendition cases and the debate over CIA prisons overseas.

Sharing Intelligence

Early in 2003, in a speech before the Council on Foreign Relations in Washington, D.C., then Attorney General John Ashcroft noted the importance of sharing vital information, "I have said often that in this global war on terror, the best friend of prevention is information, and the best friends of information are cooperation, coordination and collaboration." If only this was a reality. Any researcher need look no further than the non-cooperation between the FBI and the CIA that according allowed information between the two to fall into a void preventing them from communicate properly and "track two of the terrorists that flew a plane into the World Trade Center" [12, pg. 294]. One of the biggest shortcomings in the 'war on terrorism' has been the lack of information sharing, not just between nations, but also within the countries themselves. The sharing of intelligence has been the traditional Achilles heel of international policing. One criticism that had been directed at the US has been the inconsistency in how it shares information; that quite often there is a tendency to demand more information without giving much in return.

National sensitivities need to be considered due to fears that by sharing information with another country it could end up in the hands of a third party. Some countries separate their domestic intelligence, which is more prevention oriented, from the police organizations and law enforcement, which is considered more prosecution oriented. A number of countries even have to decide whether to share information with either the US FBI or CIA. By most accounts the CIA was the most likely choice for information exchange. According to one RAND researcher, "Countries may resist sharing information on terrorists with the FBI, preferring to work with the CIA in the hopes of receiving useful intelligence information in return" [7, pg. 39]. Another researcher also voiced European concerns that "the US expects intelligence from others, but does not readily share its own" [11, pg. 5].

One of the weaknesses in most international conventions and agreements is that they are more focused on judicial cooperation instead of police cooperation. Without sound systems for regulating the exchange of operational police information terrorist will continue to hold the upper hand. Until police share data on cross-border population movement of suspected terrorists, police will be handicapped at any attempt at intervention. In a speech in 2004, Interpol Secretary General Noble [13] gave an example of how critical this barrier is. He offered the example of the assassination of Zoran Djindic, the Prime Minister of Serbia, on March 12, 2003. When the assassin was apprehended he was in possession of a stolen Croatian passport, one of a hundred stolen four years earlier. Since then he traveled extensively on the passport - it was stamped 26 times. If there had been a global database that could be checked by border immigration officers - the suspect could have been arrested prior to the assassination -preventive policing rather than reactive.

Technology

When it comes to access to modern technology there is a major divide between the 'have' and 'have not' countries. It should be a high priority that these countries enter agreements allowing for the sharing of access to the most modern counter-terrorist technology. These disparities in technology can act as a shield for terrorist groups or are likely to take refuge in such states. Major problems also include the existence of obsolete technologies and the inability of one technology to interact with another. September 11, 2001 alone witnessed a tremendous example when the various phone technologies sued by firefighters, police officers, building security and headquarters failed to interact properly.

Corruption

Police corruption can occur on any level. However, when it occurs at the highest levels, it presents one of the greatest barriers to transnational police cooperation. Nations will be reticent to enter into cooperative ventures if they know a police force or government is corrupt. One of the foundations of modern American counter-terrorism policy is offering assistance to other countries in order to improve their civilian and military security services [14]. Hundreds of millions of dollars have been spent in this direction. While any country would be happy to receive this aid for training law enforcement and other agencies, how can the American government be sure that these investments are directed at threats that are in American interests? Therein lies the rub. Since CIA and FBI agents typically resist placing pressure on host regimes, the State Department must place pressure on countries so that the money is not directed toward unapproved programs. Even if the aid is directed at the desired goal, all efforts should be made to prevent the government for using the aid against 'legitimate opposition.'

Abuse of Diplomatic Immunity

Although this obstacle has not been a major concern of late, it has in the past. According to one authority "diplomatic protection has been exploited for the planning and commission of politically motivated crimes for many centuries" [15, pg. 39]. By most accounts the "terrorist abuse of diplomatic privileges and immunities" did not become a major issue until 1984 when a British police officer was shot and killed from the confines of the Libyan People's Bureau in London. The immunity of the assailants suggested the beginning of a "new era of vulnerability to terrorism" [15, pg. 40]. Between 1984 and 1986 similar incidents took place in Turkey, Germany, and again in Great Britain. It is doubtful that we will see a recrudescence of this type of activity since it was mostly identified with state sponsored terrorists rather than the nebulous groups of the modern era.

Time Zones

According to VOGON, a world leader in computer evidence services, promises, "Whenever you call, you will speak with a person, not a machine! No matter which time zone you are in." This is a rare promise in a world with numerous time zones that often prevents law enforcement from speaking with counterparts in distant time zones. For example, a representative from California has to deal with an eight- hour time difference with Scotland Yard. Such a variance in time serves as a barrier to cooperation because it might interfere with a timely response from the countries involved -particularly when time is of the essence. Internal workings of an organization can interfere as well, including when it comes to automation and manpower deployments.

It should be the goal of all police forces to be able to offer and receive critical information at real time 24/7. Achieving this goal will save considerable lives. In recent years Interpol's Secretary General asserted that "Every country should have a police office, staffed 24 hours a day 7 days a week that can immediately query international databases, respond to urgent information requests from police officers in the field and act on information, received from other countries, in real time" [13].

Borders and Border Control

There are a number of regions in the world where terrorist groups take advantage of porous borders and a lack of cooperation among law enforcement authorities, including such regions as the Caucasus, and central and Southeast Asia [14]. From a geographical perspective, nations with long borders punctuated by deserts, mountains, and water sources, are usually plagued by lack of manpower (witness the US border with Mexico). Ease of travel within Schengen visa countries has made Europe an attractive destination to terrorists. Since the breakup of the Soviet Union the elimination of numerous travel restrictions between the East and West has also reduced the levels of security and social control within and former Soviet bloc countries [16].

Problems of manning joint frontiers call into question the issue of responsibilities and accountability in law enforcement. What makes many terrorist groups and campaigns so successful is their ability to train in one country, develop a strategy in a second country, and then mount attacks in a third country. Poor border controls are the bane of every country with long borders. Porous border allow weapons and terrorists to spill over into contiguous countries. Terrorists are often able to take advantage of refugee movements by blending in with them as they overwhelm border checkpoints.

Simple Geography

It is relatively common for a nation's border to consist of some type of natural barrier-- a mountain range, long coastline, a river or some other type of natural border. The longer the border the more difficult it is to adequately protect it. Throw into the mix geographical barriers such as mountains or rivers and it becomes even tougher. One of the questions that often arise is 'Which country is doing the protecting?' For poor countries bordering wealthier countries, it often falls on the responsibility of the wealthier country since this is where immigrants and refuges frequently target. According to Interpol, geographical problems are a primary limitation for police cooperation and coordination [13]. More encompassing institutional agreements are needed. Currently, "most successful international legal initiatives are regionally based" or only involve a "limited number of countries on a bilateral or multilateral basis" [13]. Noble [13] suggests that it is not a realistic goal to create a worldwide accepted "Global arrest warrant."

Regional Conflict and Civil War

Throughout the past half century there has been some type of regional conflict of civil war in at least one region in the world. These conflicts, sometimes internecine, tribal, or ethnic often causes huge flows of refugees into surrounding regions, providing an excellent cover for mobile terrorists. These conflicts often divert law enforcement sources from other capacities. Recent examples include the Hezbollah-Israeli conflict in Lebanon, Hamas and Israel, the Balkan civil war, and current conflict in West Africa in Sierra Leone, Liberia, and the Republic of the Congo.

Police Organizational Culture

Police organization varies throughout the world. As a result one force is often unfamiliar with the organizational culture of counterparts in other parts of the world. Without knowing the difference between centralized and decentralized policing police officials from one country might not realize whom their counterparts in an unfamiliar country. This can include unfamiliarity with police organizational procedures, particularly in the realm of rank and decision-making. The nature of group dynamics in police decision-making protocol depends on whether the system is decentralized or centralized.

The different structures of police forces around the world makes it difficult for officers in one country to know which department and which rank in another country has the authority to deal with a particular terrorist or criminal case or even who shares information with whom.

Inter-organizational Coordination

More recently one RAND researcher has suggested that international counter-terrorism cooperation is practically impossible in the absence of inter-organizational coordination [17]. As a recent example he cited the May 3, 2003 bomb attacks in Riyadh, Saudi Arabia that resulted in the deaths of 26 expatriate residents. The US government claimed that it had warned Saudi Arabia of this specific threat (it took place at the residential compounds) two weeks earlier. This lack of coordination, according to Newsome, "bode ill for the joint investigation," that was to follow [17, pg. 77].

Attempts at Inter-organizational coordination are required on every level including police organizations. For example, countries that maintain public and private police organizations often experience poor coordination between the two sectors, sometimes due to the existence of competing objectives between the two as well as a lack of agreement on institutional objectives. In any case since most international agreements between police forces fall short of permitting police officers to maintain operational powers inside another country. As a result, the exchange of information has become the foundation for cooperation.

Deflem has suggested other barriers to inter-organizational cooperation, particularly North America, where he notes that American law enforcement has been troubled by the "lack of professionalism and cooperation," citing this as a reason why US police, "sometimes forego cooperation altogether and work abroad unilaterally" [18, pg. 78].

Data Protection

There are a number of differences between US and EU data protection standards, complicating closer cooperation between the two on border controls and travel security. For many law enforcement agencies it comes down to a reluctance to share information because of fears about compromising unrelated criminal investigations. As far back as 1990 England's House of Commons Home Affairs Committee expressed a concern that Interpol did not have "a secure communications system with regard to terrorism." In this critique the focus zoomed in on Article 3 of Interpol's constitution, which "had long been held to prevent it getting involved with terrorist acts, as being 'activities of a political, military, religious or racial character" [19, pg. 66]. Although Interpol has made a number of improvements in this arena over the past two decades and has moved "more directly into tackling terrorism" it is often difficult for partners to overcome certain perceptions about the organization. Again, the very nature of its very substantial worldwide membership has led some members to fear information and classified materials 'getting into the wrong hands.' It is difficult to beyond the past for some police organizations, which, like elephants have long memories. Particularly grating was a case in the early 1990s when Interpol was alleged to have held back information on a high-ranking Palestinian "guerilla chief" that flew to France for emergency medical care [19, pg. 67; 20].

More recently, steps have been taken by the US and the EU to improve police and judicial cooperation. However negotiations were hampered because of concerns by the EU that the US did not meet their data protection standards. On European Affairs specialist has noted that "The EU [in comparison with the US] considers the privacy of personal data a basic right, and EU regulations are written to keep such data out of the hands of law enforcement authorities as much as possible" [11, pg. 3].

Financial Barriers and Fiscal Limitations

For more than three decades, Western countries only had to contend with simple terrorist organizations, what one analyst describes as "mainly disorganized local entities in Europe, Middle-East and Asia, or state-sponsored entities such as Hezbollah" [21, pg. 2]. In the years surrounding September 11, 2001, it has become abundantly clear to counter-terrorist agencies that a number of organizations, particularly Al-Qaeda, have adapted by creating financial networks combining the most sophisticated tools of finance with the oldest transactional instruments [Hawala]. One expert noted that in "the financial area, the efforts [by law enforcement] have mainly failed to assess and combat the roots of Al-Qaeda [financing]" [21, pg. 21].

A fundamental stumbling block in the "war on terror" has been the fact that not all governments are enforcing terms of the financial coalition against terrorism; leading one critic to suggest that related measures have "not been implemented with the same enthusiasm with which they were adopted." Furthermore, according to reports by the United Nations and independent think tanks "governments around the world are not enforcing these measures, and that terrorists are still receiving and transferring" funds for terrorist activities [7, pg. 37]. There are a number of barriers to successfully addressing the financial support for terrorism. On one hand, there are legal obstacles, which law enforcement agencies cannot overcome, including "different criteria and regulations to fight terrorism financing, while state cooperation depends on political will." Many countries offer diplomatic and political reasons why they avoid the issue of terrorist funding, claiming risks to state interests. Transnational police cooperation is hampered by "the national approach culture of most law enforcement and prosecution bodies around the world." By most accounts various agencies are only interested in following up information on national based cells. This way they do not have to worry about sharing information with counterparts in other countries. This has resulted in neighboring countries not being aware of Al-Qaeda and others in their won territories.

Another major barrier is that although every state has its own justice system, there is no international body to date imbued with a "sanction mechanism to enforce decisions." Several years go at a conference called the Financial Action Task Force on Money Laundering, its director suggested dismissing uncooperative members states from the organization.

There are a number of fiscal limitations hampering international police cooperation against terrorism. The major issues surround traditional privacy issues in the financial world. For one thing it is difficult to distinguish terrorist customers from other patrons. In addition countries in many cases cannot even agree on which groups or financial accounts are "terrorist related." In recent years, the EU blocked the assets of only two out of 28 groups on the US list of terrorist groups. To make this obstacle more glaring the EU did not even freeze the assets of eleven European groups on the watch list.

In the end, financial barriers represent formidable obstacles. Taking into account that definitions of terrorist groups are often inconsistent from country to country, and financial regulations vary throughout the world, it is not surprising then that terrorist groups have been able to reroute financial transactions through countries less inclined to participate in the war against terrorism.

As Paul Pillar has made clear, "terrorism is cheap" and since funding through charities is notoriously difficult to detect, it is almost impossible to distinguish genuine charities from terrorist funding fronts [7, pg. 37; 22, pg. 94].

Conclusion

Terrorism in the twenty-first century is an international phenomenon. leading one expert to lament, "terrorist acts can affect any country, prosecution can occur in any country, and information for investigations, as well as evidence and alleged offenders, are to be found in a multitude of countries. Thus, the legal regime, to be effective, should be universal" [23]. Among the suggestions for remedying this problem is to rapidly increase the ratifications of the various conventions and the action of the UNODC, Terrorism Prevention Branch [23].

One of the biggest barriers to international cooperation in the war on terrorism has been the inability to arrive at a mutually accepted definition of terrorism. Terrorist groups mount attacks in different countries from a variety of settings - victims can be of different nationalities while organizations receive support from different ethnic communities - all of these requiring a solution that is an international solution. In order to create appropriate legislation and strategies, there needs to be an agreement of what terrorism is. As Ganor [8] noted, "Without answering the question of 'what is terrorism,' no responsibility can be imposed on countries supporting terrorism, nor can steps be taken to combat terrorist organizations and their allies" [8].

Lindsay Clutterbuck [1] has addressed the international strategic planning necessary to suppress terrorism from a law enforcement perspective. Writing from the perspective of the long-lived war between the IRA and Great Britain, Clutterbuck suggests that the UK was successful because it devised counter terrorism systems and structures "that were generic in their applicability, whatever the ultimate source of the terrorist threat" [1, pg. 143].

Recognizing the need for cooperation and coordination between countries in creating police strategies and developing appropriate tactics and policies, Clutterbuck [1, pg. 143] warns that without it, "organizational gaps, duplication of effort, and overlapping responsibilities are inevitable," and will surely "be exploited by terrorists."

Another goal that has hindered international police cooperation has been a lack of harmonization of national legislation. As Interpol Secretary General Noble [13] noted in 2004, "harmonizing national legislation is the best way for states to fight terrorism beyond their borders, as terrorists will be denied the means to exploit legal loopholes and countries will have the means to collectively act to disrupt terrorist groups" through the seizure of property and the arrest and extradition of terrorists.

Most importantly in the arduous task of achieving international police cooperation in the war against terrorists is overcoming a number of longstanding obstacles. These include various examples of countries with long and short-term enmities as well as rivalries between nation states. Also essential is a shared vision and perception of the terrorism threat as a real crime problem.

References

[1] L. Clutterbuck, Law enforcement. In A.K. Cronin, J.M. Ludes, editors. *Attacking terrorism: Elements of a grand strategy.* Washington, D.C.: Georgetown University Press; 2004. p 140-161.
[2] A.P. Schmidt, A.J. Jongman, *Political terrorism: A new guide to actors, authors, concepts, data bases, theories, and literature.* Amsterdam: Transaction Books; 1988.
[3] P. Wilkinson, Implications of the attacks of 9/11 for the future of terrorism. In M. Buckley, R. Fawn, editors. *Global responses to terrorism.* London: Routledge; 2003, p 25-36.
[4] M. Deflem, Law enforcement 9-11: Questioning the policing of international terrorism. *Pro Bono, Newsletter of the SSSP Law & Society Division* **9** (2002), 5-9.
[5] R. Davies, New EU member states will not meet rulebook translation deadline (2004, April 22). [Online] Available from: URL: http://www.maltamedia.com/cgi-bin/artman/exec/view.cgi?archive=1&num=1439 [2006, July 27]
[6] W.P. Pope, European cooperation with the United States in the global war on terrorism (September 14, 2004). Remarks to the House International Relations Committee, Subcommittee on Europe and on International Terrorism, Nonproliferation and Human Rights. [Online] Available from: URL: http://www.state.gov/s/ct/rls/rm/2004/36239.htm [2006, August 22]
[7] N. Bensahel, A coalition of coalitions: International cooperation against terrorism. *Studies in Conflict and Terrorism* **29** (2006), 35-49.
[8] B. Ganor, Defining terrorism: Is one man's terrorist another man's freedom fighter? [Online] Available from: URL: www.ict.org.il/aarticles/ditems/c1901.php [2006, August 22]
[9] M. Roth, Comparative overview of policing, courts, and corrections. In P. Reichel, editor. *Handbook of transnational crime and justice.* Thousand Oaks: Sage; 2005. p 235-254.
[10] B. Mylnikov, Problems of international cooperation in fighting terrorism. Third Annual Worldwide Security Conference, Brussels. 2006, February 21-23.

[11] K. Archick, Europe and counter terrorism: Strengthening police and judicial cooperation (2006). Congressional Research Service, CRS Report RL31509 updated January 24, 2006. [Online] Available from: URL: http://www.au.af.mil/au/awc/awcgate/crs/rl31509.pdf [2006, June 30]
[12] A.K. Cronin, J.M. Ludes, editors, *Attacking terrorism: Elements of a grand strategy*. Washington, D.C.: Georgetown University Press; 2004.
[13] R.K. Noble, Prosecuting terrorism: The global challenge, Interpol. (2004, June). [Online] Available from: URL: http://www.interpol.int/public/ICPO/speeches/SG20040604.asp [2006, July 15]
[14] M.A. Sheehan, Building police forces in a post-conflict environment (2004, April). Testimony for the Senate Foreign Relations Committee on April 21, 2004. [Online] Available from: URL: http://www.senate.gov/~foreign/testimony/2004/SheehanTestimony040421.pdf [2006, June 21]
[15] G.M. Levitt, *Democracies against terror: The western response to state-supported terrorism*. New York: Praeger; 1988.
[16] A.J. Balzer, International police cooperation: Opportunities and obstacles. In M. Pagon, editor. *Policing in Central and Eastern Europe: Comparing firsthand knowledge with experience from the West*. Slovenia: College of Police and Security Studies; 1996. [Online] Available from: URL: http://www.ncjrs.gov/policing/int63.htm [2006, August 23]
[17] B. Newsome, Expatriate games: Interorganizational coordination and international terrorism. *Studies in Conflict and Terrorism* **29** (2006), 75-89.
[18] M. Deflem, International police cooperation in North America: A review of practices, strategies, and goals in the United States, Mexico, and Canada. In D.J. Koenig, D.K. Das, editors. *International police cooperation: A world perspective*. Lanham: Lexington Books; 2001. p 71-98.
[19] B. Hebenton, T. Thomas, *Policing Europe: Co-operation, conflict and control*. New York: St. Martin's Press; 1995.
[20] L. Doyle, U.S. Police chiefs attack Interpol over Habash case. *The Independent*. (1992, November 12).
[21] J.C. Brisard, Written testimony before the Committee on Banking, Housing and Urban Affairs, (2003, October 22). [Online] Available from: URL: http://banking.senate.gov/_files/brisard.pdf [2006, August 15]
[22] P.R. Pillar, *Terrorism and U.S. foreign policy*. Washington, D.C.: Brookings Institution Press; 2001.
[23] G. Polimeni, Strengths and weaknesses of international cooperation provisions in the field of anti-terrorism, (2005, April). Presentation at Eleventh United Nations Congress on Crime Prevention and Criminal Justice, 2005, April 18-25. [Online] Available from: URL: http://www.unicri.it/wwk/speeches/050418dir.pdf [2006, August 10]

Employing Global Need-Based Information and Technology Sharing to Enhance Cooperation among Law Enforcement Organizations

Selcuk ZENGIN[a] and M. Murat YASAR[b]
[a] *University of North Texas, USA*
[b] *Turkish National Police, Anti-Smuggling and Organized Crime Department*

Abstract. Today, international law enforcement organizations are grappling with creating pathways to share necessary information to cope with the rise in transnational crimes. While it is important to recognize that sharing information crosses over geographical, cultural, and value-based differences, it is even more important to understand that this sharing can only happen if it includes technology and tech support for both gathering and disseminating the information. A review of recent research and current information-sharing protocols from international, national, and regional law enforcement agencies provides a list of barriers (legal, technical, political, organizational, and managerial), but emphasizes the advantages of creating a system for sharing information and technology between the developed and developing countries.

Keywords. Information & technology sharing, cooperation, law enforcement agencies, global information sharing, intelligence

Introduction

As General Alfred M.Gray of the US Marine Corps (USMC) stated, "Communication without intelligence is noise. Intelligence without communication is irrelevant" [1]. This has particular relevance to current concerns with global information sharing. The analogy is clear when we understand that communication in this case is the information that law enforcement organizations are trying to share internationally. The intelligence can be seen as the knowledge to understand the importance of the information joined with the technology necessary to utilize the information. Recently, the focus has been on encouraging law enforcement agencies to share information with colleagues from other countries. But, what has not been included in this discussion is the crucial role technology plays, and thus no framework has been established to share and utilize the information. Clearly, we agree that the information should be available globally as needed; what is also necessary is that the technology to support and share the information must be available as needed. What this means in practical terms is that the developed nations engaged in gathering and disseminating the information must also gather and disseminate the technology and tech support to the developing nations who need it but currently cannot access it.

In this context, we must understand that 'need-based' sharing transcends geographical, cultural, and value-based concerns. In practical terms, an action may not be considered a crime in one country but may be illegal in another country. All law enforcement organizations need to be aware that the potential for this situation exists and they need to be able to access any information pertaining to possible criminal activities if they choose to, since, as we know, criminals ignore the boundaries that we would like to set. Thus, we need to be able to think and act beyond the boundaries when necessary; global sharing of information and technology allows us to do this.

Therefore, we propose that today's international law enforcement agencies must consider not only the sharing of information globally, but also the creation of a framework to share the technology, and these agencies must also understand that needs go beyond individual, geographical, cultural, and legal boundaries as transnational crimes escalate.

1. Information Sharing among Law Enforcement Agencies Internationally

Since the US attacks on September 11th, 2001, information sharing has been discussed by many people in many sectors, including politicians, bureaucrats, academicians, and law enforcement officers. Almost everybody agrees that organizations should share their information with others. As Chu [2] asserted, if information sharing is implemented properly, this could be helpful to increase the ability of law enforcement officers to respond to incidents, provide assistance to all situations, both emergency and non-emergency, boost the number of criminals being identified, captured, and convicted, and lessen administration and operation costs.

Discussions continue over the advantages and disadvantages of a centralized law enforcement system, but after the 9/11 disaster happened, it is clear that there should be communication among the law enforcement agencies, both intra-and internationally. The US is one of the most decentralized and fragmented law enforcement systems. This can easily be seen in Table 1, which shows how many governmental organizations the US has. The American law enforcement system includes of thousands of agencies at the federal, state, and local levels. There are common concerns about a centralized system and a fear of an authoritarian rule. Some opponents argue that a centralized information and technology sharing system contradicts the American constitutional foundation of separation of powers (judicial, legislature, and executive) as well as federalism (states' rights): "The accumulation of all powers, legislative, executive, and judiciary in the same hand, whether of one, a few, or many, and whether hereditary, self-appointed, or elective, may justly be pronounced the very definition of tyranny" [3].

Proponents insist that sharing in fact strengthens each branch's ability to make informed decisions for the common good, and helps support states' rights and powers by keeping them informed.

Table 1. Number of independent governments within the states in the US (Source: US Census Bureau, 2002)

County Governments	3,034
Municipal Governments	19,429
Township Governments	16,504
Special District Governments	35,052
School District Governments	13,506

Although governments at different levels have changing degrees of law-making capabilities, every government has the right to enforce the laws within its own jurisdiction. In this context, it is not surprising to see that the number of law enforcement agencies in the US is not less abundant than the number of governments (Table 2).

Table 2. Number of law enforcement agencies in the US (Source: US Department of Justice, 2000)

All State and local	17784
Local police	12666
Sheriff	3070
Primary State	49
Special jurisdiction	1376
Texas Constable	623

One of the most significant consequences of the establishment and operation of this many agencies has been the creation of thousands of law enforcement information systems that were designed and are managed independently of each other. However, this fragmented structure has caused serious public safety problems. Consider the following examples:

Example 1
"In June 1999, Simon Gonzales of Castle Rock, Colorado, shot and killed his three young daughters with a 9 mm pistol he should never have been allowed to purchase. Gonzales later died in a shootout with police, after firing at a Castle Rock police station. In April 1999, when Gonzales purchased the gun, the Federal Bureau of Investigation (FBI) background check failed to turn up a restraining order taken out by his estranged wife. The restraining order would have disqualified Gonzales from buying the gun. At the time, because the state and federal databases were not integrated, most restraining orders had not been entered in the FBI system" [4, pg. 2].

Example 2
"On April 26, 2001, a sheriff in Broward County, Florida, stopped the vehicle of Mohamed Atta, one of the men suspected to be responsible for the terrorist attacks of September 11, 2001. The sheriff issued Atta a ticket for driving without a license and ordered him to appear in court. Authorities in Broward County never had access to information indicating that Atta was on a US government 'watch list' for terrorist activities. Shortly before his scheduled court date, Atta applied for and received a Florida driver's license. However, he failed to appear in court on May 28, and authorities issued a criminal bench warrant for his arrest. On September 11, Atta, despite having an outstanding warrant for his arrest and despite being on a government watch list, boarded a plane in Portland, Maine, using his recently issued Florida driver's license" [4, pg. 2].

As it is evident in example 2, the scope and the probable consequences of such an information disconnection were exposed after the September 11 attacks, the immediate damage of which included the destruction of the World Trade Center and a wing of the Pentagon, as well as the deaths of thousands of people. The disclosure of the so-called 'intelligence failure' in anticipating the attacks has had dramatic effects on the general understanding of how federal and local law enforcement agencies should operate. In the aftermath of the horrible incident, the Bush Administration, the US Justice Dep. and the US Congress have enacted a series of Executive Orders, regulations, and laws that are aimed at creating a unified approach against terrorism threats, despite alarming levels of concern related to the future of civil liberties and the checks and balances system that have been long viewed as essential to the structure of American democracy.

The poor coordination in sharing information between law enforcement agencies was a specific of Title VII, Sec. 701 of the Patriot Act, which refers to "Increased information sharing for critical infrastructure protection, expansion of regional information sharing systems to facilitate Federal-State-local law enforcement response related to terrorist attacks" (Electronic Privacy Information Center, 2001). Title VIII,

Subtitle I of Homeland Security Act of 2002, H.R.5005, is reserved for information sharing: "Procedures for sharing of homeland security information."

Changing government attitudes toward the traditional way of communication (or maybe miscommunication) of information between law enforcement agencies in the US can be found in the following paragraphs that are excerpted from the act:

"(1) Under procedures prescribed by the President, all appropriate agencies, including the intelligence community, shall, through information sharing systems, share homeland security information with Federal agencies and appropriate State and local personnel to the extent such information may be shared, as determined in accordance with subsection (a), together with assessments of the credibility of such information.
(2) Each information sharing system through which information is shared under paragraph (1) shall-
　(A) Have the capability to transmit unclassified or classified information, though the procedures and recipients for each capability may differ;
　(B) Have the capability to restrict delivery of information to specified subgroups by geographic location, type of organization, position of a recipient within an organization, or a recipient's need to know such information;
　(C) Be configured to allow the efficient and effective sharing of information; and
　(D) Be accessible to appropriate State and local personnel" [5, pg. 300].

This integration of information resources post 9/11 is exemplified by the creation of many new information sharing networks, including the Department of Homeland Security (DHS) Information Sharing Network and COPLINK.[1]

The National Commission on Terrorist Attacks upon the United States (9/11 Commission) suggested recommendations in its July 22, 2004, report to improve information sharing among the governmental organizations at all levels. "The types of information potentially within the scope of such sharing include raw data, which has undergone little or no assessment regarding its accuracy or implications; knowledge, which has been determined to have a high degree of reliability or validity; and intelligence, which has been carefully evaluated concerning its accuracy and significance, and may sometimes be credited in terms of its source" [6, pg. 2]. Based on these suggestions and thanks to DHS, FBI Dallas Emergency Response Network (FBI ERN) was created. FBI ERN achieved many successes in its daily and crisis use mode. This network provides intelligence sharing and dissemination among the agencies in a short time. Robert F. Decay, Director of Information Security Issues of HS, emphasized the importance of information sharing in his testimony to the House of Representatives. Decay asserted that "the success of homeland security relies on establishing effective systems and processes to facilitate information sharing among government entities and the private sector" [7, pg. 37]. He further stated that based on the National Strategy for HS:

"In the aftermath of the September 11th attacks, it became clear that vital watch list information stored in numerous and disparate databases were not available to the right people at the right time. In particular, federal agencies that maintained information about terrorists and other criminals had not consistently shared it. The strategy attributed these information sharing limitations to legal, cultural, and technical barriers that resulted in the watch lists being developed in different ways, for different purposes, and in isolation from one another. To address these limitations, the strategy provides for developing a consolidated watch list that would bring together the information on known or suspected terrorists contained in federal agencies' respective lists" [7, pg. 36].

All these cases show that information sharing among the governmental and private organizations is essential to create an effective system to deal with terrorist and criminal activities. As mentioned above, the US has one of the least centralized law enforcement systems. In contrast, Turkey has one of the most centralized law enforcement systems.

---

[1] See the website of the COPLINK: The COPLINK® team has extensive expertise in both knowledge management and law enforcement The mission of the COPLINK® team is to help you consolidate, share, and identify relationships within the most valuable source of criminal information you have - your online criminal records.

2. POL-NET (Police Network)

To facilitate communication and information sharing, Turkish National Police (TNP) has created an intranet which is called POL-NET. POL-NET was established by the Department of Information Technology in 1996.

"This department basically produces information systems' projects by working with the officers in the field so that the software and systems are developed appropriately for the needs of the field. It then makes those programs and systems available to the TNP. The Department of Information Technology established one of the largest closed computer network systems for the TNP, which is an organizational intranet with around 15,000 computers and over 30,000 users in every location where the TNP has jurisdiction, including TNP Headquarters, city police departments, police stations, airports, border gates, and other places where the TNP has infrastructures around the country. Currently, this network is one of the largest Microsoft-based networks in the world" [8, pg. 7].

POL-NET includes more than 25 different projects, such as border gate control, vehicle registration, traffic control, automatic finger identifications system (AFIS), public security, driver's licenses, passports, and so on. Yayla stated that "this network helped the TNP to obtain information considerably faster and to share information more appropriately" [8, pg. 7]. It was mentioned in his testimony that this information system helps to fight against terrorism "by developing special software packages that are designed by the officers who were working at anti-terrorism departments and by making those packages available to officers at other anti-terrorism departments" [8, pg. 7]. This does not mean that this system is limited to fighting terrorism; as mentioned above, POL-NET supports many projects. TNP is utilizing POL-NET for information-sharing purposes at the national level very successfully.

3. International Information and Technology Sharing

3.1. Integrated Border Enforcement Team (IBETs)

This program is not a multi-national program, but as a bi-national program, it serves as an example for this context of information and technology sharing among law enforcement agencies. The Integrated Border Enforcement Team program is defined as "a multi-faceted law enforcement initiative comprised of both Canadian and American partners" [9]. According to official RCMP website, "this bi-national partnership enables the five core law enforcement partners involved in IBETS to share information and work together daily with other local, state and provincial enforcement agencies on issues relating to national security, organized crime and other criminality transiting the Canada/US border between the Ports of Entry (POE)" [9].

This program could be called a 'force multiplier;' the personnel, technology, and intelligence are coming together from many different agencies. Canada and the US created a multi-disciplinary operational and intelligence team to strengthen border integrity and security, and to fight trans-border crime by sharing information and technology.

3.2. International Police Organization (Interpol)

"Interpol is the world's largest international police organization, with 186 member countries. Created in 1923, it facilitates cross-border police co-operation, and supports and assists all organizations, authorities and services whose mission is to prevent or combat international crime" [10].

Based on the official website information of Interpol, this organization "aims to facilitate international police co-operation even where diplomatic relations do not exist between particular countries. Action is taken within the limits of existing laws in different countries and in the spirit of the Universal Declaration of Human Rights. Interpol's constitution prohibits any intervention or activities of a political, military, religious or racial character" [10].

Interpol is sharing not just information but also technology among the member countries. They are facilitating the adoption and use of new technology by lesser developed and developing nations who could not have access to it otherwise.

4. Benefits and Obstacles of Information and Technology Sharing among Law Enforcement Agencies

4.1. The Benefits of Information Sharing Between Government Agencies

Solution of the complex social problems described above will require the collaboration and response of more than one agency. More effective government will require leveraging information [11]; integration of knowledge bases of law enforcement agencies should provide effectiveness. Interagency information systems reduce transaction costs, thus lowering costs and increasing participation [12]. It is also true that better access to information will allow governments to act faster and more effectively to identify problems and respond to them [13].

Information and technology sharing and coordination among law enforcement organizations are central to producing comprehensive and practical approaches and solutions to criminal threats. First, having information on threats and on actual incidents experienced by others can help an organization better understand the risks it faces and determine what preventative measures should be implemented. Second, more urgent, real-time warnings can help an organization take immediate steps to mitigate an imminent attack. Third, information sharing and coordination are important after an attack has occurred in order to facilitate criminal investigations, which may cross jurisdictional boundaries. Such after-the-fact coordination could also be useful in recovering from a devastating attack, should such an attack ever occur (US General Accounting Office, 2000).

Information sharing also avoids duplicate data collection, processing and storage and reduces paperwork, which should improve productivity and data processing costs of the agencies involved in sharing [12].

4.2. The Barriers to Information Sharing Between Government Agencies

General problems, as found in the literature, that prevent the communication of information between agencies that serve the public can be divided into:

- Legal and procedural obstacles,
- Technical issues, and
- Political, organizational and managerial barriers that discourage communication between the agencies.

4.3. Legal and Procedural Obstacles

From the beginning, public organizations have been equipped with enough power to function and also furnished with enormous internal and external controls to make sure that they do not abuse the power vested in them. "Public managers are given considerable resources and broad discretion for administering programs, but are subjected to an array of laws, procedures, and norms intended to closely control their behavior" [14, pg. 357]. The role of suspicion in this paradoxical environment can best be summarized in the statement that: "…they (American public) want government to do things for them, but not to them" [15, pg. 21]. This atmosphere forces bureaucrats to be extra careful in exercising their powers and remain within the limits that are drawn by the law for them.

In this sense, agencies cannot act outside the power delegated to them under their authorizing statutes. "Agencies cannot collect information outside of the subject delegated to them" [16, pg. 737]. An open question for most agencies is whether, and under what circumstances, information collected by one agency can be shared by another agency. Agencies that are hesitant to share information would prefer to have explicit statutory authority to share information. More proactive agencies view narrow statutory guidance as an encumbrance to their discretion [12].

There is certainly ambiguity in any statute and that invites abuses by either overzealous administrators or inaction by timid bureaucrats. This is clearly an area where a model code of law needs to be developed to help lawmakers and administrators.

4.4. Technical Issues

Incompatible hardware, software and wireless/wire line communication infrastructure creates a serious interoperability problem. On some level, most of these problems can always be solved, with the real question of how much cost will be involved [17]. However, even if these differences could be overcome, metadata problems will remain to be solved. Information sharing often is problematic due to conflicting data definitions [18]. The obvious answer is to create uniform standards, but because some procedures may be built on data definitions, changing standards might require changes to existing procedures.

4.5. Political Barriers

Each agency has a powerbase, the extent of which is shaped by the level of policymaking ability of the agency under focus. Meier [19] (cited in [12]) says that executive departments have become a fourth branch of government with powers to shape and influence policy quite independently from the chief executive, legislature, and judiciary. Sharing a critical asset such as information with outsiders would mean losing power in policy making and implementation. It should be kept in mind that information that is collected by an agency throughout the years, usually in a painful process, is generally seen like the property of the agency, not the property of people or any other institutions.

Turf is a major barrier to overcome, and it includes four major reasons organizations act defensively: to avoid the cost of change, reduce or control risk, preserve autonomy, and protect their position in a competitive and adversarial environment [20]. Information sharing would require a higher coordinating authority and bring shared decision making, which could lead to the collapse of the agency's control of its own operations and resources.

If it is probable that an agency's loss of power would benefit political or institutional adversaries, the agency will resist the information-sharing initiative more aggressively [20].

Beyond the difficult problem of actually putting appropriate information exchange systems in place, there needs to be a genuine feeling of trust and control by citizens before it becomes politically and operationally possible to have interoperable information systems [21]. Citizens expect to trust the government in exchange for putting their privacy at risk for the sake of general public safety. A carefully designed political campaign would be required to explain to the citizens that the government is not planning to create a 'big brother' type super database to spy on people, but only an information exchange structure to enhance the public safety.

4.6. Organizational Barriers

Organizations are similar to individuals in that they make a benefit/risk calculation before making a decision. Because the benefits of organizational cooperation are often indirect and difficult to measure [22], agencies will generally engage in cooperative action only when there is also some reasonable expectation of achieving self-interest goals [23]. It is probably unreasonable to expect an organization to share its information resources without an expectation that it will gain internal benefits, improve its public image, or expand its influence over others [12].

Before agencies can share information, they must develop mutual trust [24]. Much has been written about trust, though with little consensus on its meaning or role [25]. Child defines trust as the "confidence of a person, group, or organization relating or transacting with another under conditions of some uncertainty that the other's actions will be beneficial rather than detrimental to it" [21, pg. 243-244].

Trust does not require common belief, but obligation and expectation. Ferguson and Stoutland [26] relate to such expectation through four trust dimensions: (1) participant motives, not to exploit or betray purposes; (2) competency, possessing the knowledge and skills to do what is expected; (3) dependability, e.g., holding the necessary resources to act; and (4) collegiality, i.e., showing respect and fairness. Sabel [27] suggests that mutual obligation and expectation are keys: trust-based governance structures have rich, consultative institutional structures whose very existence belies the assumption that the agents expect their actions automatically to be harmonized by the confluence of belief. Operationally, Perrow [28] (cited in [29]), suggests several forces that build trust within small firm networks: sharing and discussing information; similarity in processing and techniques; experience in working with another firm; long-term relationships, even if contact is intermittent; similar size, power, or strategic position among firms; rotation of leadership; similar financial rewards; and economic advantages to support shared meaning. Experience in working with others beforehand is especially important, because lack of past experience in inter-organizational relationships may inhibit future experiences. According to Dawes [12], agencies incrementally increase their knowledge about the benefits and costs and the 'how' of information sharing, a process which leads them to feel less anxious about future initiatives of information exchange.

Intra-organizational problems with the information management may be another reason for low levels of information sharing for certain agencies. Good information resource management requires an inventory of an agency's information resources [30].

Financial shortcomings of agencies may be a problem in setting up systems for information sharing. It is not fair to expect an agency that hardly makes ends meet to develop interoperable systems, where the benefits are ill-defined and the costs are unclear and uncertain. As cited in Landsbergen and Wolken (2000), why should an agency expend its own scarce resources to make information available for the benefit of another agency when there are much more pressing and concrete information system needs? (Strategic Computing and Communications Program, 1998).

4.7. Managerial Barriers

The term 'networks' typically refers to multi-organizational arrangements for solving problems that can not be achieved, or achieved easily, by single organizations [29]. Application of classical management perspective, which is developed for intra-organizational settings, into inter-organizational forms can not lead to satisfactory results. "Relationships and interactions that result in achieving the network purpose - synthesis- are the aim of the network manager, and important management behaviors include facilitating and furthering interaction among participants, reducing complexity and uncertainty by promoting information exchange, changing incentives to cooperation, developing new rules and procedures of interaction, changing positions, relations, and roles of participants, helping the network to be self-organizing, and engendering effective communication among participants" [29, pg. 4].

One possible ingredient in the inter-organizational information flows that are necessary for developing groupware is social capital. Fountain (1998, p.104), as cited by Agranoff and McGuire [29] refers to social capital as the 'stock' that is created when a group of organizations develops the ability to work together for mutual productive gain. Like physical capital and human capital, tools and training that enhance individual productivity, social capital refers to features of social organization, such as networks, norms, and trust that facilitate coordination and cooperation for mutual benefit.

5. Conclusion

In the post 9/11 era, policymakers at all levels of government are trying to find ways to enhance emergency vigilance and pro-active responses to potential transnational criminal activities. The sharing of law enforcement information is a vital component of these efforts and of any comprehensive strategy to improve public safety. Just as any information systems project needs pre-planning, including a comprehensive survey of the potential users of the system, specifically of their information needs and attitudes towards the endeavor, so does setting up a law enforcement information system. At the global level, these needs include not just an integrated pathway to exchange information, but also the sharing of technological resources to identify, gather, and analyze potentially relevant information.

Through the review of relevant research and current cases of information-sharing protocols at the international, national, and regional levels, a list of barriers were compiled. However, to effectuate a global information and technology sharing network, the focus clearly needs to be two-fold: overcoming the organizational and cultural barriers, and creating a framework for dispersing the technological resources and technical support necessary to strengthen the system.

References

[1] M. Brunker, Feds: No warrants for Net wiretaps (2000, May 17) ISN-Information Security News. [Online] Available from: URL: http://seclists.org/isn/2000/May/0112.html [2006, November 21]
[2] J. Chu, *Law enforcement information technology: A managerial, operational, and practitioner guide.* Washington D.C.: CRC Press; 2001.
[3] C.R. Kesler, C. Rossiter, editors, *Federalist papers.* New York City: Penguin Books; 1999.
[4] NGA (National Governor's Association) Center for Best Practices, Issue Brief: Improving public safety through justice information sharing (2002, February 24). [Online] Available from: URL: http://www.nga.org/cda/files/JUSTICEINTEGRATIONIB.pdf [2006, November 1]
[5] FindLaw, Homeland Security Act of 2002 (2002). [Online] Available from: URL: http://news.findlaw.com/cnn/docs/terrorism/hsa2002.pdf [2006, November 18]
[6] H.C. Relyea, J.W. Seifert, Information sharing for homeland security: A brief overview (2005, January 10). [Online] Available from: URL: http://www.fas.org/sgp/crs/RL32597.pdf, [2006, November 18]
[7] R.F. Decay, Information sharing responsibilities, challenges, and key management issues (2003, September 17). [Online] Available from: URL: http://www.gao.gov/new.items/d031165t.pdf, [2006, November 18]
[8] A.S. Yayla, Turkish police force's response to terrorism at the local and the national level (2006). [Online] Available from: URL: http://homeland.house.gov/hearings/109_060921_LawEnforcement/ TestimonyYayla.pdf [2006, November 18]
[9] RCMP, Integrated Border Enforcement Teams (IBETs) (2006). [Online] Available from: URL: http://www.rcmp-grc.gc.ca/security/ibets_e.htm [2006, November 20]
[10] Interpol (2006). [Online] Available from: URL: http://www.interpol.int/default.asp [2006, November 20]
[11] K.L. Kraemer, J.L. King, Computing and public organizations. *Public Administration Review* **46** (1986), 488-497.
[12] S. Dawes, Interagency information sharing: Expected benefits, manageable risk. *Journal of Policy Analysis and Management* **15** (1996), 377-394.
[13] G.B. Reschenthaler, F. Thompson, The information revolution and the new public management. *Journal of Public Administration Research and Theory* **6** (1996), 125-144.
[14] J.W. Worton, J. Worthley, A perspective on the challenge of public management: Environmental paradox and organizational culture. *Academy of Management Review* **6** (1981), 357-361.
[15] S. Cohen, W. Eimicke, *The new effective public manager: Achieving success in a changing government.* San Francisco: Jossey-Bass Publishers; 1995.
[16] A.T. Aman, W.T. Mayton, *Administrative law.* St. Paul: West Publishing Co. Inc.; 1993.
[17] D. Hack, *Telecommunications and information standardization - Is America ready?* Washington, D.C.: The Library of Congress: Congressional Research Service; 1987.
[18] D.F. Andersen, S. Belardo, S. Dawes, Strategic information management: Conceptual frameworks for the public sector. *Public Productivity and Management Review* **17** (1994), 335-353.
[19] K. Meier, *Politics and bureaucracy: Policy making in the fourth branch of government.* North Scituate: Duxbury Press; 1979.
[20] A.M. Creswell, D.R. Connelly, Reconnaissance study: Developing a business case for the integration of criminal justice information (1999, September). Study conducted for Center of Technology in Government, University at Albany, SUNY. [Online] Available from: URL: http://www.ctg.albany.edu/publications/ reports/reconnaissance/reconnaissance.pdf [2006, November 13]
[21] J.K. Harmon, R.N. Cogar, *The protection of personal information in intergovernmental data-sharing programs.* Columbus: Ohio Supercomputer Center; 1998.
[22] A. Van de Ven, On the nature, formation and maintenance of relations among organizations. *American Management Review* **1** (1976), 24-36.
[23] A. Van de Ven, D. Ferry, *Measuring and assessing organizations.* New York: John Wiley & Sons Inc.; 1980.
[24] H.B. Thorelli, Networks: Between markets and hierarchies. *Strategic Management Journal* **7** (1986), 37-51.
[25] W. Creed, R. Miles, Trust in organizations: A conceptual framework linking organizational forms, managerial philosophies, and the opportunity costs of controls. In T.R. Tyler, R.M. Kramer, editors. *Trust in organizations: Frontiers of theory and research.* Thousand Oaks: Sage Publications; 1996. p 16-38.
[26] R.F. Ferguson, S.E. Stoutland, Reconceiving the community development field. In R.F. Ferguson, W.T. Dickens, editors. *Urban problems and community development.* Washington, D.C.: Brookings; 1999. p 33-76.
[27] C.F. Sabel, Study trust: Building new forms of cooperation in a volatile economy. *Human Relations* **46** (1993), 1133-1138.
[28] C. Perrow, Small firm networks. In N. Nohria, R.G. Eccles, editors. *Networks and organizations: Structure, form, and action.* Boston: Harvard Business School Press; 1992.
[29] R. Agranoff, M. McGuire, Big questions in public network management research. Paper presented at the Fifth National Public Management Research Conference, Texas A&M University; 1999, December.
[30] S. Caudle, Managing information resources in state government. *Public Administration Review* **50** (1990), 515-524.

Extradition of Terror Suspects and Developments in Extradition Process

Huseyin DURMAZ
University of North Texas, USA

Abstract. It is apparent today that terrorism requires a global response and a well-built international cooperation. Such response and cooperation may only be achieved by utilizing effective *legal* instruments, such as extradition, among states. It has become routine for people to hear diplomatic crises between states as a result of rejected extradition requests which sometimes lead to big public demonstrations. It is high time states considered ways to create workable extradition systems and thereby, advance the level of sincere cooperation.

Keywords. Terrorism, cooperation, extradition, European Arrest Warrant

Introduction

Terrorism is a heinous phenomenon constituting a global threat to democracy, peace, and security. Regardless of the religion, culture, and color of the people, terrorism poses a serious threat to all humanity, and it obviously warrants a global response. Even though the existing international treaties, declarations, institutions, and organizations serve to form a global response against terrorism and attempt to establish lasting peace worldwide, terrorism increasingly shakes the daily lives of people, and the world is far from being the world we are longing for.

Need for a global response to terrorism and a sincere cooperation has been underlined in many studies so far [1, 2]. One factor weakening global response to terrorism stems from the manner how states handle this threat. As Anderson [3] emphasizes "terrorism is not a homogeneous criminal threat which governments invariably have a common interest in repressing." She lists some factors, such as different colonial backgrounds, regional problems, autonomy struggles, extreme social tensions, and cultural cleavages, as the reasons for the lack of common interest in combating terrorism at the same level. National interests in international relations shape the actions of the states and their willingness to cooperate with other states to a great extent [3]. For example, some states may prefer -explicitly or implicitly- not to risk their national interests by detaining or extraditing individual terrorists for the sake of international cooperation against terrorism.

Turk [4] ranks the options the states hold to suppress international terrorists: monitoring, confiscation, extradition, extraction, assassination, and war. Among these options, extradition has a particular importance as a workable extradition procedure among the states and is a must for a successful global response to terrorism. Extradition is quite an old formal procedure between states and quicker, 'no place to hide' extradition conventions have always been desired and placed on the agenda of the international community. Any state can find loopholes in extradition conventions and various reasons to reject extradition requests. However, one could assume that a state's stance to grant extradition requests *particularly* for terror offenders is an indicator of that state's willingness and sincerity in cooperation with other states and combating international terrorism.

This article focuses on extradition, touches upon alternatives to extradition, and explores new developments in this process to figure out how international terrorists may be cornered and made to stand trial more swiftly through extradition.

1. Extradition

Extradition is an international judicial cooperation tool that *legally* enables states to bring back the fugitives before their competent courts or -if already convicted- to their prisons. Traditionally, the sovereign state holds the right as to whether or not to grant extradition to another state. Even if the relevant court approves its admissibility, all governments remain free to reject extradition [5]. Although extradition conventions impose a duty on contracting states to surrender criminals, it has been debated for decades among the law experts if extradition is a legal or only a moral obligation [6].

The roots of extradition may be traced back to medieval and even ancient societies where states used it as a matter of good will and courtesy. The earliest known extradition provision was placed in a peace treaty signed in 1280 B.C. between the Egyptian Pharaoh Ramses II and the Hittite King Hattusli III. This treaty had allowed for the return of common criminals between these kingdoms [7 (cited in 6)]. In Europe, the first arrangement concerning extradition was made between England and Scotland in 1174 A.D. [8 (cited in 6), 9]. There are a number of common rules that formulate extradition process.

1.1. Extradition Rules

1.1.1. Principle of Reciprocity

This principal espouses the right to equality and mutual respect between states in international law. One state has the obligation to handle another state's requests in a manner similar to how its requests have been handled. For instance, in the absence of treaty regulating extradition, countries may require a guarantee of reciprocity as a condition for the extradition of an accused person [6]. In other words, such a guarantee assures that extradition will work both ways [5]. If a treaty exists, states still take this principal into consideration, for example, for the reservations made to the treaty provisions. Indeed, the matters of reciprocity and mutuality are very important considerations that often influence the level of international cooperation.

1.1.2. Principle of Double Criminality

In order for an extradition to take place, the conduct under consideration must constitute an offence both in the requesting (the state which seeks extradition) and the requested parties (the state where the extradition request is submitted). In a case where the conduct is not a crime and not prosecuted in the requested state, such a situation is called 'lack of double criminality' and is sometimes used as grounds for a refusal to extradite [9]. For example, as to the criminality of abortion, euthanasia, and soft drug use, there is no world wide consensus. Therefore, an extradition request regarding such behaviors is most likely to be turned down.

1.1.3. Nature and Seriousness of Penalty

The offence subject to the extradition request must be serious enough to merit extradition. Seriousness is usually measured by the term of imprisonment attached to the offence. This term may vary in different extradition agreements. Some agreements, for instance, require offenses punishable for a maximum period of at least one year penalty. If the person has already been convicted then they require a penalty for a period of at least four months. Also extradition is only permissible for punishments that deprive human liberty.

1.1.4. Principle of Speciality

This principal prevents the requesting state from further prosecuting or punishing a person for criminal conduct other than for that which he was extradited for [10]. However, the requested state may give consent for a further trial or punishment after surrender. Also the person that is surrendered to a state is given an opportunity to leave the state within a certain time period following his prison term. If the person does not leave that territory within the determined period or returns there after leaving, then the rule of speciality does not apply. This rule is to protect the individual against prosecution and punishment on additional charges for offences committed prior to extradition and does not apply for offences committed after the extradition [9].

1.1.5. Ne bis in idem

Ne bis in idem, also known as double jeopardy, is a widely accepted international criminal law principle which literally translates into English as *'not twice for the same'* [11]. It states that a person cannot be prosecuted or tried more than once for the same act [12]. In order to protect suspects from double jeopardy, states reject extradition requests for offences that have already been concluded by other courts regardless of whether the decision was guilty or innocent.

1.1.6. Aut dedere aut judicare

This principal requires states either to extradite or to prosecute any person subject to an extradition request [9]. It is designed to prevent such persons from going unpunished and is used to counter balance the practice of non-extradition of nationals.

These rules are taken into account by the relevant bodies while preparing or handling extradition requests. Besides these rules, the following issues are considered as well in determining the acceptability of extradition requests.

1.2. Grounds for Refusal

There are some practical problems in the extradition process, which -according to Plachta-[13, pg. 178] "are almost as old as the extradition itself." A number of mandatory and/or optional grounds for refusal still exist in the traditional extradition conventions. These not only provide many refusal options to the judicial authorities but also open the door to political interference. Even though many of these refusals are done in accordance with the extradition conventions, they often weaken international cooperation and policing efforts. It is a fact that some exceptions to extradition are essential to ensure that the human rights of the wanted persons are respected. Despite this, there is always a high risk of political intervention and arbitrary decisions, particularly in sensitive requests. In addition to the basic extradition rules explained above, such as double criminality, ne bis in idem, and seriousness of crime, the following also form grounds upon which extradition maybe refused.

1.2.1. Political Offense

In many states a request for extradition for a political offense is itself grounds for refusal of extradition. Traditionally, this exception has also been used extensively to secure freedom of political and religious opinions. It protects the political offender from a potentially partial trial and helps one state avoid having to take sides in the internal affairs of another state [14]. It also recognizes the legitimacy of political dissent [10].

If an offence is directed at the State and is intended to affect only the structure of the State, it is almost always identified as a *'purely'* political crime and is rarely extraditable. On the other hand, the other category of *'relative'* political crime causes some confusion. Relative political crimes cannot be easily separated from political crimes as they combine political goals with ordinary crimes [15]. Some international treaties clearly excluded some serious offences such as aircraft hijackings and hostage-taking from being considered political crimes.

1.2.2. Nationality

Many states do not want to extradite their nationals due to their concerns with the protection of their own nationals or a distrust of the foreign state's criminal justice systems. There are many differences between the practices of different law systems. European countries, for example, tend to use nationality as a barrier to extradition. They only permit such extradition in exceptional cases. Anglo-Saxon countries, on the other hand, traditionally do not take into consideration nationality for purposes of extradition. In terms of jurisdiction, the civil law countries usually claim jurisdiction over crimes committed in their territories. They also claim jurisdiction over crimes committed by their nationals abroad. For that reason, they prefer often to decline extradition requests for their nationals [9]. This is not the case for the common law countries as they establish only territorial jurisdiction [16].

Non-extradition of nationals continues to endanger the efforts to fight international terrorism. If states do not extradite their citizens who commit crimes in other countries, they may easily become safe havens. Therefore, the multinational conventions encourage states to establish jurisdiction over cases when they refuse to extradite a fugitive (aut dedere aut judicare rule).

1.2.3. Death Penalty

States with no capital punishment tend to refuse extradition of criminals when the person faces the risk of being sentenced to death unless the requesting state agrees not to impose the death penalty or not to carry it out if it is imposed. The states that still have capital punishment in their legal systems are opposed to the death penalty exception. They assert that it interferes with the judicial discretion of the requesting state and in so doing violates the sovereignty of that state.

1.2.4. Judgments in Absentia

Refusal occurs when the person's extradition is sought in order to carry out a sentence or detention order that has been rendered against him or her in absentia. The requested state may reject the extradition if it considers that his or her defense rights have been violated during the trial process.

1.2.5. Discrimination

When the requested party establishes significant reasons for considering that the extradition request has been made because of the person's race, religion, citizenship or political opinion, it is refused outright. This matter is vulnerable to political intervention because there are no subjective criteria that define 'substantial grounds.'

1.2.6. Human Rights

The state turns down the extradition request when there is a real danger that the person wanted for extradition will be subjected to torture, brutal, inhuman, degrading treatment or punishment. However, this exception to extradition may easily be abused because there isn't any consensus concerning what causes a 'real risk.'

1.2.7. Lapse of Time

The person requested may become immune from prosecution or punishment if the statute of limitation expires in the law of either state.

1.2.8. Place of Commission

According to the requested state's law, if the offence is regarded as having been committed in its territory -in whole or in part- the request may be rejected. Also when the crime is committed out of the territory of the requesting state, the requested stated may refuse extradition on the condition that their law does not allow prosecution for such offences.

1.2.9. Insufficient Proof

The common law countries used to require extradition requests to be accompanied by proof of apparent guilt. This meant that the offender could be convicted in the requested state by considering the existing evidence. Comparatively, the civil law countries only ask for a minimum amount of evidence and a certified arrest warrant is usually good enough to meet this requirement. The insufficient proof obstacle seemed to have faded away as the UK abolished the 'prima facie - at first sight' standard in 1989 and adopted the civil law approach at least for non-commonwealth countries [6]. Likewise, according to Harris [16], the US is requiring 'probable cause' or just sufficient proof to issue a warrant of arrest rather than asking the complete evidence.

In addition to the explained grounds for refusal, some events and relationships in the international arena may also have profound impacts on states' extradition policies. For instance, McElrath [17] alleges that, for the last 150 years, the US was a safe haven for Irish people who were convicted in British courts. In the 1980s, Margaret Thatcher established a close friendship with Ronald Reagan and British air bases were opened to the US for bombing Libya. This alliance resulted in a significant change in the US extradition policy; the US revised its treaty with Britain in 1986, restricted the political offence exception to a great extent and ended a long history of providing refuge for Irish political offenders [18]. After examining many extradition cases after this policy change, Riley [19] concludes that rather than breaking the laws, the US bent them to appease a foreign ally.

In lieu of extradition, some states may prefer its alternatives to catch international fugitives.

1.3. Alternatives to Extradition

As the rules of extradition and grounds for refusal demonstrate, extradition involves many complicated administrative and judicial requirements. Moreover, most international criminals, particularly terror offenders, are clever enough to seek sanctuary in states sympathetic to their cause and which are more likely decline their request for extradition [14]. States' interests are also directly involved in the decision-making process and some states are notorious for their bad reputation in this matter from time to time. For instance, according to Hoffman and Morrison-Taw [20] terrorists located in Europe could find political refuge in France, East European countries and the Middle East in the 1970s and early 1980s. Anderson [3, pg. 234] also informs that "Until 1985, the French authorities were reluctant to extradite Basque terrorists; between 1986 and 1988, they seemed willing to bargain with Middle Eastern terrorist groups in return for the release of hostages; and in January 1994 they refused to extradite Iranians wanted for murders in Switzerland on grounds of national interest, despite the protest of the Swiss authorities."

Hundreds of examples can be listed here proving the existence of political concerns and pressure in handling extradition requests for terror offenders. The following cases are given just to name a few interesting cases where basic extradition rules seem to be disregarded; Abdel Osama al Somar (requested from Greece) [14], Abdullah Ocalan (requested from Italy), and Fehriye Erdal (requested from Belgium). Considering the failures in extradition requests, some conclude that extradition is of little use in stopping international terrorists [4].

While these problems led some states to consider facilitating and developing extradition procedure, some other states focused on other options, such as deportation, expulsion, abduction, foreign prosecution, revocation of passports, and even assassination of the fugitives, which result either in the return of the fugitive or limitations on the fugitive's ability to live or travel overseas. However, acts like abduction are taken as illegal or unethical means to apprehend fugitives abroad because such actions are mostly executed in another state's territory without permission, and thereby, constitute obvious violations of international law. Some states -like the US- seem to be practicing alternative ways -deportation, kidnapping- rather than extradition in the first place more often than other states to bring suspects to trial. According to Turk [4], the US government even authorized the Federal Bureau of Investigation to investigate cases anywhere in the world, and to apprehend and bring back suspects. Even though those countries may have domestic regulations to legitimize such actions, other sovereign states do not recognize any legal status of their agents [4]. On the face of these options, extradition is still accepted the most appropriate *'legal'* method to make sure that terrorist acts do not go unpunished [21].

2. Developments on Extradition after September 11

After the 9/11 terrorist attacks, international terrorism unsurprisingly became the number one concern of many nations and international organizations. Showing how successfully terrorist organizations can plan their attacks without regard to the national borders and how the security measures could be defeated, these attacks awakened the institutions responsible for security and combating terrorism.

On 28 September 2001, the UN declared a strong resolution emphasizing the need for a sincere global response to terrorism. In the Security Council Resolution[1] numbered 1373, all states are openly warned not to support any terrorist acts at all, deny safe haven to terrorists, and handle refugee requests with utmost care, which often are abused by terrorists to prevent extradition.

Besides the UN resolution, Interpol changed some of its policies on information circulation after the 9/11 attacks. Interpol utilizes a color-coded notice system to circulate the alerts and warnings worldwide. Interpol General Secretariat used to reject the requests from member states for the issuance of a red notice for individuals charged with being a member of a terrorist organization. Rather, involvement in a terrorist offense was a must in order for a red notice to be issued against a suspect. Since an increasing number of nations have tended to criminalize membership in a terrorist organization, Interpol, as of November 2003, also started to publish red notices for suspected members of a terrorist group [22]. Moreover, Interpol introduced two new international notices. Through new yellow notices, member states are warned about bombs, hidden weapons, or biological, chemical, and radiological threats [23]. The Interpol-UN Security Council Special Notice, the latest notice, is being published against the groups and persons affiliated with the Taliban and Al Qaeda. This special notice is supposed to assist the UN Security Council's 1267 Committee by asking member states to co-operate with Interpol and the UN through taking necessary measures regarding blocking of assets, travel interdictions and arms embargos for Al Qaeda members [24].

In the US, the office of Homeland Security was created by executive order of the President on October 8, 2001 in order to ensure interagency cooperation in the fight against terrorism. In November 2002, this office became a separate department bringing together many agencies such as US Customs Service, the Federal Emergency Management Agency (FEMA), the Secret Service, and the US Coast Guard [22]. The police powers against terrorism were considerably expanded with the Patriot Act (the Provide Appropriate Tools Required to Intercept and Obstruct Terrorism Act) which was approved just one month after the attacks [22]. On June 25, 2003, the US and the European Union (EU) signed an extradition agreement [25] in order to update the old treaties in force and to provide new tools to fight terrorism, organized crime, and other serious crimes.

---

[1] UN Security Council
2. *Decides also* that all States shall:
(a) Refrain from providing any form of support, active or passive, to entities or persons involved in terrorist acts, including by suppressing recruitment of members of terrorist groups and eliminating the supply of weapons to terrorists;
(c) Deny safe haven to those who finance, plan, support, or commit terrorist acts, or provide safe havens;
3. *Calls* upon all States to:
(c) Cooperate, particularly through bilateral and multilateral arrangements and agreements, to prevent and suppress terrorist attacks and take action against perpetrators of such acts;
(g) Ensure, in conformity with international law, that refugee status is not abused by the perpetrators, organizers or facilitators of terrorist acts, and that claims of political motivation are not recognized as grounds for refusing requests for the extradition of alleged terrorists;
4. *Notes* with concern the close connection between international terrorism and transnational organized crime, illicit drugs, money-laundering, illegal arms trafficking, and illegal movement of nuclear, chemical, biological, and other potentially deadly materials, and in this regard *emphasizes* the need to enhance coordination of efforts on national, sub-regional, regional and international levels in order to strengthen a global response to this serious challenge and threat to international security.

At the EU level, steps to determine terrorist offences and harmonize criminal laws were successfully taken in 2002. Up to date, the lack of a common definition of terrorism and terrorist offences has been mentioned by several scholars as one of the most important obstacles to combating terrorism. It is commonly believed to be a very difficult task to define terrorism because the interests of states are usually involved and may conflict [26]. In April 1937, the League of Nations created the first international legal instrument - Convention for the Prevention and Punishment of Terrorism- to fight terrorism; however, the outbreak of the Second World War impeded its entry into force [27]. The international community has been still trying to define terrorism and spent years to produce an international convention to combat terrorism. Even though no international definition of terrorist offences exists yet, some good steps have been achieved at the EU level.

On 13 June 2002, the Council of the European Union adopted Framework Decision on Combating Terrorism which entered force on 22 June 2002. Such framework decisions have a binding power over all EU member states equally and this particular one required the member states to approximate their domestic criminal laws to determine terrorist offences by 31 December 2002. The Council of the European Union also adopted another framework decision at the same time, Framework Decision on the European Arrest Warrant and the Surrender Procedures between Member States. At the EU Council meeting in Tampere in October 1999, it was decided to develop legal mechanisms for combating terrorism by such changes as abolishing the formal extradition procedures among the Member States [28]. Through recognizing the judicial decisions mutually, this simple surrender procedure was considered to replace traditional extradition procedure and speed up the process. When taking into consideration these two framework decisions, it can easily be seen that they are complementary in nature. Defining terrorism in a similar way and criminalizing the same acts as terrorist offences in national laws would enable the mutual recognition of legal decisions and verdicts among Member States and thereby, facilitate the creation of a common European warrant for arrest and extradition.

3. Main Extradition Conventions

In order to escape prosecution, criminals prefer living in states not a party to an extradition treaty with the countries where they commit their crimes. States generally act reluctantly to prosecute or punish individuals for crimes out of their jurisdiction or occurring beyond their borders but, at the same time, most of them do not want to become a safe heaven for criminals. Such situations compel states to establish international cooperation to ensure that fugitives are surrendered. Today there are several bilateral, regional, and multinational extradition conventions in which provisions and rules over extradition are more or less the same. Only those that are considered most helpful in understanding the emergence of the new extradition system in the EU have been explained in the next part.

3.1. European Convention on Extradition of 1957

In the 1950s, the Council of Europe, the oldest political organization in Europe, prepared a series of multilateral conventions on the main topics in international judicial cooperation: extradition of criminals, mutual assistance, transfer of prisoners, enforcement of sentences, transfer of proceedings, and confiscation of proceeds of crime. Among these conventions the European Convention on Extradition, which was signed on December 13, 1957, especially became popular in Europe [29, 30]. It has been ratified by 46 states and only two of them, Israel and South Africa are not members of the Council of Europe.

The European Convention on Extradition became so popular that it has served as a *'mother convention'* for all further developments concerning extradition [5, 31]. Two additional protocols were signed in 1975 and 1978 in order to exclude war crimes and crimes against humanity from the category of non-extraditable political offenses. Also, some provisions about fiscal offences, judgments in absentia and amnesty were supplemented. The members of the Council of Europe also signed the European Convention on the Suppression of Terrorism in 1977, which was designed to facilitate the extradition of persons who have committed terrorist crimes. The latter convention required that a series of offences such as unlawful seizure of an aircraft, hostage taking and offences involving an attack against the life of internationally protected persons would be kept out of the political offence exemption [5].

According to the 1957 Convention, the Contracting Parties undertake to surrender all persons to each other who are wanted for offences punishable under the laws of both the requesting and the requested states by deprivation of liberty for a maximum period of at least one year or when there is a sentence for a period of at least four months (Article 1 and 2/1). This provision entails the application of the double criminality principal as it states that the offence must be punishable by both states' laws. It first determines how serious the offence should be to warrant extradition and the thresholds -one year or four months- constitute mandatory grounds for refusal. Furthermore, in case the national laws of contracting states do not allow for extradition for certain offences, Article 2 allows for the opportunity to exclude such offences from the application and to instead apply the reciprocity principle for the excluded offences. Such reservations and declarations, which were commonly used by the Contracting states, ultimately encumbered the convention and as a result, this multinational convention became like a patchwork of bilateral conventions.

The 1957 Convention and its protocols provide the following mandatory grounds for refusal:

- Double criminality (Article 2/1),
- Seriousness of the offence (Article 2/1),
- Political offences and other offences connected with political offence (Article 3),
- Military offences (Article 4),
- Ne bis in idem principle: (a) When final judgment has been passed in the requested state (Article 9/1); (b) if the wanted person was acquitted in the final judgment rendered by a third state (Article 2/2 of First Additional Protocol); (c) following the final judgment rendered by a third state: (c1) the sentence was wholly executed, (c2) the offender was pardoned, (c3) the court convicted the person without imposing a sanction (Art. 2/2 of First Additional Protocol),
- Lapse of time: When prosecution or punishment become statute-barred according to the law of either the requesting or the requested states (Article 10),
- Discrimination concerns: When the requested state has substantial grounds for believing that the extradition request has been made to judge or punish a person for his race, religion, nationality, or political opinion (Article 3/2),
- Amnesty: If the requested state declares amnesty for the offence subject to the request provided that this state has competence to prosecute that offence (Article 4 of Second Additional Protocol).

The optional grounds for refusal provided in these extradition instruments are:

- Nationality (Article 6),
- Death penalty (Article 11): As mentioned earlier, 44 out of 46 contracting parties of the 1957 Convention are members of the Council of Europe and all have already abolished the death penalty except the Russian Federation, which introduced a moratorium on executions but still retains the death penalty as a part of its penal code [32].
- Place of commission (Article 7),
- Judgment in absentia (Article 3 of Second Additional Protocol),
- Ne bis in idem principle: (a) Offense for which decision not to institute or to terminate proceedings is made in requested state (Article 9/1); (b) final judgment has been rendered in a third state but the offence was committed in the requesting state against a person, an institution or any thing having public status, or the requested person has a public status in the requesting state (Article 2/3 of First Additional Protocol).

On the other hand, the 1957 Convention arranges time limits only for the delivery of extradition documents during the 'provisional arrest period' -the period between date of arrest with a view to extradition and date of surrender- and for the surrender date of persons. The requesting state should send the necessary documents through diplomatic channels within 18 days after the arrest or within 40 days provided that the requested state accepts the period extension (Article 16). Once the extradition is granted and the surrender date is established, the extradition should take place within 30 days after the appointed date (Article 18). Apart from these time limits, the relevant courts and administrative authorities are not limited to a certain time period in which to reach a decision on the extradition. There are no limits for provisional arrest periods and it has not been established how long the person can be kept in detention by the requested state after the extradition has been approved. Some of the worst examples of a lengthy extradition process can be found in the UK, where it used to take about 18 months to be extradited and in some cases, it can stretch out to 6 years [33].

In terms of principle of speciality, Article 14 restricts implementation of any judicial process (for example, initiating proceedings, sentencing or detaining) in the requesting state for the offences committed before the surrender except for which the person was extradited. That person may only be proceeded against if the requested state gives consent or if the extradited person, while having full opportunity, does not leave the territory of requesting state within 45 days of his final release or if he returns after leaving the state.

Indeed, the 1957 Convention provides a 'negative list' explaining the situations when the extradition should be refused. It allows the contracting states to make reservations to the articles. Moreover, various interpretations and loopholes existing in the Convention enable states to present interesting excuses for their refusals. In practice, even if all the requirements are met by the requesting state, unfortunately there is no mechanism to impose sanctions upon states that obviously fail to fulfill their responsibilities stemming from this Convention.

Extradition is a whole judicial process in nature; however, the existence of political intervention in the extradition process is an undeniable part of the process too. In a traditional extradition, the courts are supposed to assess the admissibility of the requests in legal terms and the final approval is usually given by administrative authorities. As a result, a legal process that is relatively smooth and swift for ordinary criminals can become a subject of long lasting discussions and hard bargaining for well known, top criminals. And at this point, the presence of political interference can become particularly evident. For instance, the politicians in the requested state will sometimes not allow the judicial authorities to make the final decision concerning the surrender of a terror organization leader. Therefore, on one hand the politicians support international cooperation efforts against criminals; on the other hand, they often prefer the legal instruments that allow for leeway in their maneuvering.

Though the 1957 Convention has filled an enormous gap in international cooperation, the problems arising from the Convention have become more evident day by day and this traditional extradition method is now considered to be slow, inefficient, problematic, and outdated by the contracting states.

3.2. The 1995 and 1996 EU Extradition Conventions

Interdependency resulting from geographic proximity and common crime problems has forced the EU members -with great pressure from Spain- to explore solutions to the problems that arise during the traditional extradition procedure [26]. According to Plachta [13, pg. 179] "The efforts undertaken so far to improve the situation by modernizing the procedure and updating the existing legal instruments, have achieved limited results." It was believed that controlling international crime may only be attained through regional agreements between close countries that share common tradition, culture, and values [13, 34].

In order to supplement and facilitate the 1957 European Convention on Extradition, two Conventions were prepared in the mid-1990s: the 1995 Convention on simplified extradition procedure between the EU Member States (1995 EU Extradition Convention) and the 1996 Convention relating to extradition between the EU Member States (1996 EU Extradition Convention) [9, 35, 36]. These EU conventions represent new trends that are more flexible and less rigid. Extradition procedures and requirements were simplified, and the political offence exception lost its importance by making all serious offences extraditable [15]. Since these conventions were negotiated in an intergovernmental framework, they have to be ratified by each EU member state. According to Plachta [13], the 1995 EU Convention was ratified by nine states while the 1996 EU Convention received only eight ratifications. None of these has entered into force yet [30].

3.3. European Arrest Warrant

Improvement attempts through the 1995 and 1996 EU Extradition Conventions showed that the EU member states were not satisfied with the level of cooperation in extradition matters. Spain, in particular, was experiencing problems with the extraditions of members of the terrorist group Euskadi ta Askatasuna (ETA - Basque Fatherland and Liberty) [37]. As a result, Spain signed a series of bilateral agreements with Italy, France, the UK, and Belgium in the late 1990s which were based on the mutual recognition of court judgments. This was a new principle in Europe. The Spanish government has continued to further its efforts at the EU level to establish the mutual recognition principal, in which states consider each other's legal and judicial systems trustworthy enough to recognize any request for extradition without applying the reservations. This new principal entails the abolition of traditional double criminality rule, thereby making the extradition possible even if the offense is not considered punishable by the requested state [5].

Politicians, being aware that the enlargement of the EU would only make the existing problems in extradition worse, have become increasingly focused on the future development of the extradition system within the EU. The first steps were taken at the Tampere meeting of the European Council in October 1999 [13]. During the meeting, it was emphasized that rather than using the formal extradition method, member states were to consider a simple transfer of the wanted persons. Upon the suggestions of the European Commission and the Spanish government, the member states approved the principle of mutual recognition as a basis for future judicial cooperation. At the meeting, representatives acknowledged that both the mutual recognition of judicial decisions and judgments and the approximation of legislation could ease and strengthen assistance between authorities and enhance the protection of individual rights. As a consequence, the approach followed thus far for the modernization of extradition was officially replaced by a revolutionary approach to build an area of freedom, security, and justice within the EU [12, 30].

After the events of September 11, 2001, the European Commission prepared a proposal for a Framework Decision establishing a European arrest warrant to replace the existing extradition procedure between member states. Such framework decisions are adopted by the Council of the EU in order to approximate the laws and regulations of the member states. Even though member states are free to select their form or methods, these decisions are binding in nature and the member states are expected to achieve the results [38]. June 13, 2002, marks a significant date in the modern history of extradition as the Council of the EU adopted the 'Framework Decision on the European arrest warrant and the surrender procedures between the Member States' (hereinafter Framework Decision). This Framework Decision naturally applies only to the EU member states and the existing bilateral and multilateral extradition agreements still utilized for the third (non-EU) countries.

It was commonly believed that the 9/11 attacks culminated in acceleration of the adoption of some legal instruments and the European Arrest Warrant (EAW) was the primary response of Europe to the 9/11 terror attacks [13, 30, 33, 36]. However, some people emphasized that the efforts to modernize the extradition procedure among EU members were already underway before the 9/11 attacks happened and the attacks might only have facilitated and sped up those efforts [21].

3.3.1. Why is the EAW a Revolution?

3.3.1.1. Mutual Recognition

The most visible feature of the Framework Decision is that the traditional requirement of double criminality, which has been the most prominent barrier to extradition and reflects skepticism towards any other state's legal order, has been abolished for certain crimes and replaced with the principle of mutual recognition of court judgments among the EU member states. The mutual recognition system necessitates that the decision of the issuing state (the member state issuing the arrest warrant) takes effect as such within the legal system of the executing state (the member state executing the arrest warrant). Therefore, the executing state loses some of its sovereign power over the full control of the enforcement of criminal decisions in its territory [5].

Contrary to the prior agreements, the Framework Decision contains a *'positive list'* of offence types for which the principle of dual criminality has been abolished across the EU for offences carrying at least a three year maximum sentence (Article 2/2). The list consists of 32 types of crimes including: participation in a criminal organization, terrorism, trafficking in human beings, sexual exploitation of children and child pornography, illicit trafficking in narcotic drugs and psychotropic substances, illicit trafficking in arms, ammunition and explosives, money laundering, murder, illicit trade in human organs and tissue, sabotage, racism and xenophobia, organized or armed robbery, illicit trafficking in cultural goods, illicit trafficking in nuclear or radioactive materials, trafficking in stolen vehicles, rape, and unlawful seizure of aircraft/ships.

In fact, the list contains more than thirty-two offences as some points cover more than one offence. Moreover, the Council of the EU is authorized to add other crimes to the list. It should be emphasized that the double criminality requirement still prevails for offences which are not on this list and which are below the 3 years' threshold.

3.3.1.2. No Political Involvement
In traditional extradition procedures, the final decision as to whether or not to surrender the person is a political decision. Though courts have been involved in this procedure, their role is usually "limited to rendering an opinion -which is not binding on the government in all cases- on the admissibility of extradition in legal terms" [13, pg. 184]. Courts have thus far been unable to prevent political intervention particularly in high profile cases. The Framework Decision is designed to terminate political safe heavens in the EU by abolishing the political stage of extradition. Article 1 of the Framework Decision says that "the European arrest warrant is a judicial decision…"

Likewise, Article 6 of the Framework Decision defines the issuing and executing judicial authorities and lays down "the executing judicial authority shall be the judicial authority of the executing Member State which is competent to execute the European arrest warrant by virtue of the law of that State." The judicial authorities are the only authorized bodies which can issue, and/or refuse the execution of the EAWs (Article 3 and 4). The extradition, thus, has become simply a judicial process which allows for direct communication between the issuing and the executing judicial authorities (Article 9). More importantly, it is up to the executing judicial authority to decide whether the person is to be surrendered or not (Article 15).

The Framework Decision only allows the designation of a central authority -an administrative body- to assist the competent judicial authorities in administrative transmission and reception of EAWs (Article 7).

3.3.1.3. Surrender of Nationals
The Framework Decision makes it impossible for any member state to decline to surrender one of its citizens who has committed a crime in another EU state solely on the grounds of nationality. This approach was rooted in the notion of 'EU citizenship.' On the other hand, in accordance with Article 5/3 of the Framework Decision, member states are able to apply conditions for the return of their nationals or residents -after being heard- back to the executing state to serve their sentence. It is considered that by imprisoning the citizens or residents in their own country, their reintegration to the society will be more easily facilitated.

3.3.1.4. Faster Procedure
The Framework Decision imposes short time limits not only for the execution of arrest warrants but also for the surrender of person requested. The states are required to give a final decision concerning the execution of the EAW within ten days if the requested person approves his surrender (a kind of simplified extradition procedure) or within 60 days in other cases (Article 17/2-3). In case the EAW cannot be carried out within these limits, the period may be extended by a further 30 days (Article 17/4). After the final decision, the requested person must be surrendered within a ten day period which can be prolonged ten more days due to circumstances beyond control (Article 23/2-3).

3.3.1.5. Simpler Procedure

The Framework Decision contributes to simplifying the process by providing for an alternative mechanism rather than relying on the traditional diplomatic channels. EAW can directly be sent by the issuing judicial authority to the executing judicial authority when the requested person's whereabouts is known. Also, telecommunications systems of the European Judicial Network may be used, or a Schengen Information System - SIS alert may be issued (Article 9-10). An Interpol channel may also be used as well to transmit an EAW in accordance with Article 10/3 when it is not possible to use SIS services. Europol has not been given any active role in this mechanism [13].

3.3.1.6. Political Offense

The political offence exception was eliminated in the 1996 EU Extradition Convention. That decision remains the same in the Framework Decision. The idea is based on the fact that the EU is established on common democratic ideas and any attack against the political order of any of their members is taken as an attack against all EU democratic values. In other words, any threat against the democratic structure of a single EU member state is considered a threat to the whole EU. So, political offenses are no longer exempted from extradition.

3.3.1.7. Human Rights

The Framework Decision appears to be different from traditional extradition agreements regarding human rights issues. At the beginning of the Framework Decision, it is said that "no person should be removed, expelled or extradited to a State where there is a serious risk that he or she would be subjected to the death penalty, torture or other inhuman or degrading treatment or punishment."

Convictions in absentia, though, are not classified as grounds for refusal in the Framework Decision. The executing states are allowed to ask for a guarantee from the issuing state that the convicted -after the surrender- will be given a chance to ask for a retrial of the case and to attend the judgment (Article 5/1).

Likewise, if the offence is punishable by a life sentence, the executing state may insist, as a condition of executing the arrest warrant, that if sentenced to life, the accused person will have a right to have his personal situation reconsidered upon request or at the latest after 20 years (Article 5/2). There is no mention of death penalty in the Framework Decision because it has already been abolished EU-wide.

To ensure that the arrested person's basic rights are guarded, the Framework Decision asks executing states to inform the arrested person of the content s of warrant and about the possibility of consenting to the surrender. Moreover, it clearly requires the executing states to provide legal counsel and, if need be, an interpreter for the person under arrest (Article 11).

3.3.1.8. Speciality Principle

As expressed by Platcha [13, pg. 189] "The Framework Decision represents yet another attempt to eliminate one of fundamental principles of extradition: the rule of speciality." In the Framework Decision, consent of the executing state is assumed to have been given for the prosecution of an offence committed prior to the surrender other than that for which the person was surrendered, unless otherwise stated by the executing state (Article 27). In other words, while the consent must be explicit in the traditional system, the Framework Decision suggests that the consent is implicit.

This new approach has been criticized for being open to abuses. An issuing state, for example, might request extradition for a serious offence and then drop those charges once extradition has been completed. The issuing state might charge that person with certain crimes which it could not have obtained extradition for, thereby circumventing any refusal to extradite on any grounds.

3.3.2. Grounds for non-execution of the EAW

According to Article 3 of the Framework Decision, the execution of the EAW should be refused in the following cases:

- Amnesty: When the offence is covered by amnesty in the executing state where that state had jurisdiction to prosecute the offence,
- Ne bis in idem principle: If the requested person has been finally judged and sentenced by a member state in respect of the same acts, and
- If the person may not be held criminally responsible owing to his age under the law of the executing state.

The grounds for optional refusal explained in Article 4 include:

- Double criminality: For acts that are not included in the list of 32 types of specific offences provided in Article 2/2 of the Framework Decision,
- Ne bis in idem principle: (a) If the person is prosecuted in the executing state for the same act; (b) if the judicial authorities of the executing state decided not to prosecute the same offence or to stop proceedings, or if the person is judged in a member state and this judgment prevents further proceedings; (c) if the person has been finally judged by a third state for the same act,
- Lapse of time: Where the prosecution or punishment is statute-barred under the law of the executing state,
- When there is a conviction for a national or a resident of the executing state and it undertakes to execute this conviction,
- Place of commission: (a) If an offence is accepted by the law of the executing state as having been committed in whole or in part in the territory of the executing state; (b) an offence has been committed outside the territory of the issuing state and the law of the executing state does not allow prosecution for the same offence when committed outside its territory.

In terms of the seriousness of the offence, an EAW may be issued for any act punishable in the issuing state by a period of at least twelve months or, where a sentence has already been passed, for at least four months (Article 2); however, there is no reference to the law of the executing state.

3.3.3. Application of Framework Decision

The adaptation process to the new system has been troublesome for many EU member states. Although the EAW was supposed to enter into force on January 1, 2004 among 15 EU member states (Article 31), seven of them failed to comply with the Framework Decision because of the transitional difficulties. Belgium, Denmark, Ireland, Finland, Spain, Sweden, Portugal and the UK were successful in the integration process. Likewise, only half of the newly acceded states implemented the EAW on time, by May 1, 2004. The Czech Republic and Germany joined the group after an almost eight month delay and the last EU member state, Italy, eventually applied the EAW on May 14, 2005.

Even if the transition period was problematic, the overall evaluations prove the efficiency of the Framework Decision. For example, the European Commission Report [39] dated February 23, 2005 confirms that the surrender process is totally judicial and has provided the provisional numbers for the first eight months to emphasize the effectiveness of the EAW. The numbers are as follows: 2,603 warrants issued, 653 persons arrested, and 104 persons surrendered.

As to the surrender of nationals, the Commission Report says that most member states, except Ireland, Slovakia, and the UK have preferred that the sentence should be carried out in their territory. Some states also refused the surrender on the grounds which are not even included in the Framework Decision. These have been things such as political reasons or national security concerns. Moreover, according to the Commission Report, the average time taken to execute a warrant has decreased from more than nine months to 43 days. The average time is 13 days where consent for surrender was given by the individual. It is concluded that although 10 member states are not applying the EAW sufficiently, its effectiveness and speed are favorable [39].

In his study, Durmaz [40] created Table 1 to display the differences between the traditional and new extradition systems. The innovations offered by the Framework Decision are likely to be a real panacea for the chronic extradition problems. This new extradition system, which is based on a high level of mutual trust, mutual recognition, and confidence between the EU member states, successfully eliminates most of the exceptions to extradition while keeping those which are vital to ensure human rights. The determined time limits as well as the direct communication and simplified extradition possibilities make the new process very fast, thereby, highly effective.

Table 1. Grounds for refusal and other differences

			1957 European Convention on Extradition	European Arrest Warrant
NEGATIVE Barriers to extradition	Double criminality		+	-**
	Political crime		+	-
	Military crime		+	-
	Nationality		+ (optional)	-
	Lapse of time		+	+ (optional)
	Seriousness of the crime (at least one year or if convicted, at least four months)	in requesting/issuing state	+	+
		in requested/executing state	+	-
POSITIVE Grounds for refusal	Ne bis in idem (double jeopardy)		+	+
	Discrimination on grounds of ethnic origin, race, sex, or status		+	+
	Death penalty		+ (optional)	+
	Life sentence		-	g
	Judgment in absentia		+ (optional)	g
OTHER DIFFERENCES	Political intervention		+	-
	Rule of speciality		+	-
	Direct communication between judicial authorities		-	+
	Simplified extradition		-	+
	Time limit for	extradition decision	-	+
		surrender	-	+
	Human rights concerns i.e. torture, degrading treatment		-	+

(+) Exists   (-) Non-exists   (g) Guarantee may be required
(**) For 32 crime types if offence is punishable in issuing state by at least three years

4. Conclusion

Even if the international cooperation mechanisms seem to work well today, the last word on the extradition request is often the final step in all levels of cooperation. Most of the international police and judicial cooperation efforts are simply rendered to trace and bring back the suspects to trial. Therefore, extradition is a vital tool in the fight against terrorism. This article has underlined the importance of extradition and pointed out the significant differences between the traditional and new extradition procedures.

It has to be emphasized here that international laws and extradition conventions are extremely important instruments for international cooperation but what is far more important is the practice and sincerity of the states in the fight against terrorism. Trust is a cornerstone and sine qua non in international relations. If one state's top police chief believes that one terrorist organization, which has caused more than 30,000 deaths in that country, is being financially, militarily and politically supported by neighboring and western countries that they consider allies [41], then it is impossible to fight international terrorism with legal instruments. It is believed that no state should consider terrorism as an instrument of foreign policy and a global response to terrorism can only be achieved when states act sincerely in accordance with the effective tools of international law and more importantly with morality.

For better cooperation and stronger global response to terrorism, first of all, workable extradition conventions, which disallow political intervention and are based on mutual trust, should spread to all regions and continents. The new EAW eliminates lasting barriers to extradition and offers a number of fundamental positive changes in some extradition rules; therefore, it sets a good example for other states. Secondly, each state should think about revising its domestic law to remove the issues that cause difficulties in extradition procedure. For instance, Turkey abolished death penalty in August 2002 and in June 2004, all State Security Courts were terminated (kind of special courts that hear defendants accused of crimes dealing with terrorism, gang-related crimes, drug smuggling, and membership in illegal organizations). In so doing, Turkey eliminated two important factors that used to endanger its extradition requests. Finally, some organizations -like the UN- should be enabled to impose sanctions on those states violating extradition conventions or disregarding their liabilities.

References

[1] I. Bal, Terrorism, liberal state and international co-operation. In: *Istanbul Conference on Democracy & Global Security*; 2005 June 9-11; Istanbul, Turkey. Ankara: Oncu Press, 2006. p 565-575.
[2] C. Cerrah, Istanbul bombings and a few important strategic issues related to struggling against religion-motivated terrorism-radicalism. In: *Istanbul Conference on Democracy & Global Security*; 2005 June 9-11; Istanbul, Turkey. Ankara: Oncu Press, 2006. p 238-240.
[3] M. Anderson, Counterterrorism as an objective of European police cooperation. In F. Reinares, editor. *European democracies against terrorism: Governmental policies and intergovernmental cooperation*. Burlington: Ashgate; 2000. p 227-243.
[4] A.T. Turk, Policing international terrorism: Options. *Police Practice and Research* **3** (2002), 279-286.
[5] W. Wagner, Building an internal security community: The democratic peace and the politics of extradition in Western Europe. *Journal of Peace Research* **40** (2003), 695-712.
[6] I.A. Shearer, *Extradition in international law*. Manchester: Manchester University Press; 1971.
[7] S. Langdon, A.H. Gardner, *Journal of Egyptian Archeology* (1920), 179.
[8] E.G. Clarke, *Treatise on the Law of Extradition*. Fourth ed. London: Steven and Haynes; 1903.
[9] G. Gilbert, *Transnational fugitive offenders in international law: Extradition and other mechanisms*. The Hague: Martinus Nijhoff Publishers; 1998.
[10] K.I. Rebane, Extradition and individual rights: The need for an international criminal court to safeguard individual rights. *Fordham International Law Journal* **19** (1996), 1636-1685.

[11] Wikipedia. [Online] Available from: URL: http://en.wikipedia.org/wiki/Ne_bis_in_idem [2006, October 12]
[12] M. Fletcher, Some developments to the ne bis in idem principle in the European Union: Criminal proceedings against Hüseyn Gözütok and Klaus Brügge. *The Modern Law Review* **66** (2003), 769-780.
[13] M. Plachta, European arrest warrant: Revolution in extradition? *European Journal of Crime, Criminal Law and Criminal Justice* **11** (2003), 178–194.
[14] S. Johnson, *Peace without justice: Hegemonic instability or international criminal law?* Burlington: Ashgate; 2003.
[15] J.A. Carberry, Terrorism: A global phenomenon mandating a unified international response. *Indiana Journal of Global Legal Studies* **6** (1999), 685-719.
[16] J.E. Harris, International cooperation in fighting transnational organized crime: Special emphasis on mutual legal assistance and extradition. In: *UNAFEI - Annual Report for 1999 and Resource Material Series No. 57*; Tokyo: UNAFEI, 2001. p 133-148.
[17] K. McElrath, *Unsafe haven: The United States, the IRA and political prisoners.* Sterling: Pluto Press; 2000.
[18] A.P. Dobson, *Anglo-American Relations in the Twentieth Century.* London: Routledge; 1995.
[19] J. Riley, Is US playing politics with extradition? *National Law Journal* (1986), 3-8.
[20] B. Hoffman, J. Morrison-Taw, A strategic framework for countering terrorism. In F. Reinares, editor. *European democracies against terrorism: Governmental policies and intergovernmental cooperation.* Burlington: Ashgate; 2000. p 3-29.
[21] P.J. Van Krieken, *Terrorism and the international legal order.* The Hague: T.M.C. Asser Press; 2002.
[22] M. Deflem, L.C. Maybin, Interpol and the policing of international terrorism: Developments and dynamics since September 11. In L.L. Snowden, B.C. Whitsel, editors. *Terrorism: Research, readings, and realities.* Upper Saddle River: Pearson; 2005. p 175-191.
[23] Interpol, Interpol fact sheet – COM/FS/2006-06/TE-01 (2006a). [Online] Available from: URL: http://www.interpol.int/Public/ICPO/FactSheets/TE01.pdf [2006, October 24]
[24] Interpol, Interpol fact sheet – COM/FS/2006-02/GI-02 (2006b). [Online] Available from: URL: http://www.interpol.int/Public/ICPO/FactSheets/GI02.pdf [2006, October 24]
[25] Agreement on extradition between the European Union and the United States of America. *EU Official Journal L* 181, 19/07/2003, p 0027–0033. [Online] Available from: URL: http://eur-lex.europa.eu/LexUriServ/LexUriServ.do?uri=CELEX:22003A0719(01):EN:IITML [2006, August 10]
[26] M. Den Boer, The fight against terrorism in the second and third pillars of the Maastricht Treaty: Complement or overlap? In F. Reinares, editor. *European democracies against terrorism: Governmental policies and intergovernmental cooperation.* Burlington: Ashgate; 2000. p 211-226.
[27] A. Mohsen, Challenges of the terrorist phenomenon in the twenty-first century. In D.K. Das, P.C. Kratcoski, editors. *Meeting the challenges of global terrorism: Prevention, control, and recovery.* Lanham: Lexington; 2003. p 117-129.
[28] B. Saul, International terrorism as a European crime: The policy rationale for criminalization. *European Journal of Crime, Criminal Law and Criminal Justice* **11** (2003), 323-349.
[29] C.D. Guymon, International legal mechanisms for combating transnational organized crime: The need for a multilateral convention. *Berkeley Journal of International Law* **18** (2000), 53-101.
[30] S. Peers, Mutual recognition and criminal law in the European Union: Has the Council got it wrong? *Common Market Law Review* **41** (2004), 5-36.
[31] W. Schomburg, Are we on the road to a European law-enforcement area? International cooperation in criminal matters. What place for justice? *European Journal of Crime, Criminal Law and Criminal Justice* **8** (2000), 51-60.
[32] S. Karaganov, On the death penalty, Russia and Europe. *Current Digest of the Post Soviet Press* **56** (2004), 8.
[33] J. Bennathan, Another act of poodledom? *New Statesman* **12** (2003, June). [Online] Available from: URL: http://www.findarticles.com/p/articles/mi_m0FQP/is_4641_132/ai_103415794 [2005, Feb. 10]
[34] D.K. Das, P.C. Kratcoski, International police co-operation: A world perspective. *An International Journal of Police Strategies & Management* **22** (1999), 214-241.
[35] P. Chalk, The third pillar on judicial and home affairs cooperation, anti terrorist collaboration and liberal democratic acceptability. In F. Reinares, editor. *European democracies against terrorism: Governmental policies and intergovernmental cooperation.* Burlington: Ashgate; 2000. p 175-210.
[36] M. Jimeno-Bulnes, European judicial cooperation in criminal matters. *European Law Journal* **9** (2003), 614-630.
[37] A.G. Bondia, Spain's European policy in relation to the accelerated extradition procedures establishment under the Aznar administrations (2004, December). [Online] Available from: URL: http://selene.uab.es/_cs_iuee/english/obs/working_ocasionals_ang_archivos/Spain_in_Europe/EE122004.pdf [2005, May 3]
[38] F. Gregory, Policing transition in Europe: The role of Europol and the problem of organized crime. *Innovation* **11** (1998), 287-305.
[39] European Commission, Report {COM(2005) 63 final} dated 02.23.2005 (2005). [Online] Available from: URL: http://europa.eu.int/comm/justice_home/doc_centre/criminal/doc/com_2005_063_en.pdf [2005, May 25]
[40] H. Durmaz, International police cooperation as a response to transnational organized crime in Europe: Improvements in extradition [MS thesis]. Denton (TX): University of North Texas; 2005.
[41] G. Aydiner, Terrorism in the world and in Turkey. In: *Istanbul Conference on Democracy & Global Security*; 2005 June 9-11; Istanbul, Turkey. Ankara: Oncu Press, 2006. p 1-6.

Global Developments in Transnational Police Training: TADOC (Turkish International Academy against Drugs and Organized Crime)

Arif AKGUL and Otwin MARENIN
Washington State University, USA

Abstract. International police training -training offered by the police of one country to the police of other countries- has a long history. A recent development is training offered by international police academies, such as the International Police Academies (ILEAs) created by the US in Hungary, Thailand, and Botswana; the Middle European Police Academy (MEPA) jointly created by Austria and Hungary; or the attempts by the European Union to start a common police academy for police in members states. The paper will examine the original, organization, policies, and training offered by TADOC (Turkish International Academy against Drugs and Organized Crime), place its creation within the larger context of international policing assistance efforts, and speculate on the likely impacts of training offered on the performance of participating police forces.

Keywords: International police training, international academies, Turkish International Academy against Drugs and Organized Crime - TADOC

Introduction

Police from one country training police from other countries has a long history. Police anywhere have always looked beyond the borders of their countries and have sought to work with other police on solving particular cases; help establish formal and informal liaisons with each other; participate in the large number of transnational police organizations which exist, ranging from professional umbrella groups (such as the IACP) to formal institutions which link police in a common effort (such as Interpol or Europol); assist other police in institutional and program developments (as during peace building operations or the changes required for accession countries who wish to join the European Union - EU); participate in visits and exchange programs; and set up formal teaching and training institutions and programs [1, 2, 3, 4, 5, 6, 7].

The focus of this paper is on the last category of transnational activities. We will describe earlier efforts to establish formal transnational teaching and training programs, but will focus on the recently established international police academy in Turkey - TADOC. We will describe the history, organization, policies and goals of TADOC. Ultimately, the questions to be asked about the performance and effectiveness of this international academy are the same which have been asked about prior training efforts.

- Does the program meet its stated goals, in the delivery of training and courses and the attendance goals set for foreign participants?
- What could be done to improve the performance of the academy, if improvements need to be made?
- What is the impact of transnational training on the performance of policing systems which have sent their officers to be trained outside the country?
- What are the unanticipated consequences (benefits and costs) of training?
- Will the emergence of a large number of transnational training programs and institutions -of which TADOC is only one example- lead to a convergence of policing ideologies and cultures among the countries which have participated in such training? Are these training programs the first step toward a universal, global police culture?
- Will these changes, such as have occurred, lead to more effective and fair transnational and domestic crime control?

1. Early Efforts in Transnational Training

Training has often been a major, if not the most important, aspect of police to police relations, either arranged directly from one police organization to another police or through national government programs.

Colonial powers have always created their own police forces, including the minimal training necessary to be called police and act like a police. The police forces of all former colonies have their origins in colonial policies and purposes and quite frequently the power of foundational ideologies and practices continues to exert a powerful influence on current policing. One such influence is the continuing practice of sending officer rank police for training and study to the command colleges of their former colonial powers which practice, of course, perpetuates foundational ideologies and organizational behaviors.

The US has basically created many of the constabulary police forces in Central America and the Caribbean as part of its foreign policy goal in the area. Assistance to police forces in that region has persisted throughout the 20th century [8]. Another example were the efforts by the victorious powers in the Second World War who sought to recreate the police of the defeated axis powers -especially Japan and Germany- in their own images. They established training programs for the new police in Japan and Germany (in the US occupation zone).

Many developed countries have created police training programs for other countries as part of their overall strategies of global development (delivered through foreign assistance offices and programs) and for the protection of perceived national interests. The Office of Public Safety (OPS) Program in the US, during the late 1960s and early 1970s sought to transform police forces in developing countries into the eyes and ears and allies of counter-insurgency policies pursued by the US to protect friendly regimes against internal subversions [9, 10]. Part of OPS was an International Law Enforcement Academy located in Washington, D.C. Officers from assisted countries came to the academy to learn how to think about threats and safety and to learn effective techniques for investigating, detecting, and deterring crime and criminal groups [11].

The EU, through its Phare program, sought to bring the criminal justice system and the police in potential accession countries up to European standards through technical and financial assistance and advice [12].

Under the aegis of the Stability Pact for SE Europe, the Regional Civilian Police Training Program in SE Europe has sought to develop police competencies by delivering courses to the former republics, now independent countries of Yugoslavia. The delivery of courses is based on the MEPA model, here called Central European Police Academy (CEPA), and is coordinated by CEPA and the Nordic Baltic Police Academy. A common curriculum has been developed and tested by the AEPC (Association of European Police Colleges), a consortium of 39 police academies in 32 European countries, and is delivered on a roaming based, instructors and students traveling to different countries rather than students coming together in one fixed location [13]. The program also delivers short technical and administrative/managerial training courses.

More generally, police from one country have routinely attended established domestic academies in another countries, such as international courses at the FBI academy or the Federal Law Enforcement Training Center in the US, or Bramshill College in the UK [14, 15]. Many countries and international organizations offer short training courses taught be foreign police or consultants to local police, to introduce them to new investigative techniques, legal requirements, human rights standards or managerial skills. The US Department of State hires consultants to teach, for example, a course on cyber crime in Kenya or Botswana; the UN Human Rights Offices sends experts to several countries to teach local police human rights standards, practices, and goals. There exists a vast and flourishing transnational trade in ideas and skills which is promoted, organized, staffed by non-local experts.

2. Training through Formal International or Transnational Academies

2.1. Examples

In recent years, establishing international academies has been a major focus of national government, professional groups, and regional and international agencies.

The Nordic-Baltic Police Academy[1] is a network of national police academies in the Nordic Countries (Denmark, Iceland, Finland, Norway, and Sweden) which allows officer rank police to come together in common training program and setting. The Nordic countries have also organized an exchange program (Nordcop) which allows new recruits from one country to attend the police academies of other Nordic countries.

Austria and Hungary, in 1992, agreed to establish the *Mitteleuropäische Polizeiakademie*[2] (Middle European Police Academy-MEPA; also called CEPA in the English translation -Central EPA), which now has grown to eight members countries. Training is organized as a traveling academy. Students travel for three months from member country to member country for short familiarization tours and information sessions in each. Students write a long terminal paper, some of which are published in the MEPA journal. The language of instruction is German, a deliberate policy by the two founding members to stress the Central European, or non-American, origins of MEPA (Interview in Austria, Otwin Marenin - OM). MEPA also organized short training courses in current topics and issues of importance to members, such as 'Special Course for Integrated Border Security'; these courses are delivered in one member country.

---

[1] More information about The Nordic-Baltic Police Academy can be reached at http://www.nbpa.net/
[2] More information about Middle European Police Academy can be reached at http://www.mepa.net/

The EU fulfilled a long standing ambition to create a European police command college with the creation of European Police College[3] (CEPOL), established in 2000 by a decision of the European Council of Ministers as a network of senior police, or command academies (now 25 after the accession of ten new members to the EU in 2005). The administrative headquarters is located at Bramshill, England. The basic goal of CEPOL is to create a 'harmonized European space for police education' and the development of a European approach to dealing with domestic and transnational crime control and law enforcement. To achieve this goal, CEPOL organizes general and technical courses, open to police from all members states, which are held at different national academies; organizes an annual Research and Science Conference to share ideas and knowledge; supports an European Police Learning Network to which police can post relevant information; and has established a group of national correspondents to act as liaisons between national police and CEPOL and add 'hidden national data' to the CEPOL database.

Basic police academies are essential elements in UN sanctioned peacekeeping and peace building operations and in regionally sponsored interventions and rebuilding efforts in post-conflict and failed states. The goal is to instill basic poling skills and attitudes in newly created or reorganized police, at first through short training courses to stand up a police service as quickly as possible, and later to train police through more lengthy police academy courses [16, 17]. The Police Academy in Kosovo, started under NATO auspices, was created to help train new police forces in Kosovo to European professional standards. Similar efforts to retrain existing police have been undertaken in conflicted societies (e.g., East Timor, Cambodia).

The Chapultepec Accords, which ended the civil war in El Salvador, included a detailed set of changes for recreating a new civil police, detached from military control, in El Salvador, including the percentages of former guerillas, national police (vetted for human rights violations) and new recruits which would comprise the new police. A new Academy and curriculum were developed and delivered by consultants and police experts from European and North and Latin American countries [18, 19, 20].

In Haiti, which did not have a police organization at all, the first international intervention led by the US and Canada trained new recruits, initially at an army base in the US and later in-country in Haiti, using curricula developed by US, Canadian, and Latin American experts.

The police in Iraq are currently being trained in a new academy in Jordan which is based on the model developed Kosovo, and headed by the same expert (former US police officer) who helped establish that academy.

Lastly, there are the International Law Enforcement Academies (ILEAs) established by the US in cooperation with other countries, the first in Hungary and the second and third in Thailand and Botswana. A planned academy in Costa Rica [21] did not get off the ground, and the US in cooperation with the government of El Salvador, opened an ILEA in San Salvador which will be drawing its students from police forces from all Central American and some Latin American countries [22]. In addition, a new International Academy was set up in New Mexico as a second tier academy which is attended by international police who were trained in one of the established four regional ILEAs. ILEAs are distinct from other training efforts in that they are created as regular police academies which are attended by police from catchments areas. For example, the Budapest ILEA draws on police from former Soviet Union satellites and republics - now independent countries. The Bangkok ILEA is open to the police from ASEAN member states. The Botswana academy initially selected police from member states of the Southern African Development Community but

---

[3] More information about European Police College can be reached at http://www.cepol.net/

recruitment has been expanded to include East African countries. Instruction is largely by US police with some participation from by local police and specialized courses offered by other police from other states or regional institutions (such as EUROPOL) [11, 21, 23, 24, 25] (also see ILEA websites[4]).

There is a great similarity in the structure, student composition, and curricula of these international academies, since they were developed using both national (US) and international police regime standards and widely shared professional experience and expertise. All include human rights and rule of law component but the substantive content of curricula are oriented towards conveying specific technical and managerial skills. The ultimate goals is to acquaint police who are presumed to be unfamiliar with notions of democratic policing with international police regime norms (as these can be found in international agreements and codes of conduct on police behavior), the treatment of alleged offenders, the use of force, technical skills largely focused on detecting and investigating crime, common principles of the effective management of large police organizations, or relations with communities [26, 27, 28, 29]. There is almost always a strong endorsement of community policing as the most effective form of democratic policing.

In short, academies attempt to create a police culture attuned to international professional, legal and human rights norms as well as a more effective capacity to deal with local and transnational crime.

3. The Impacts of Transnational Training

It is notoriously difficult to assess the consequences of educational policies on the thinking and practices of the police. So far, two types of evaluations have been conducted on the impacts of ILEAs and other transnational training programs. Most of these are in-house evaluations which focus on outputs and testimonials about how well the academies are doing. Students who attended the academies are typically asked about, at the end of their training periods, how they feel about the training, whether they found it useful, interesting, and the general experience of being at an academy rewarding. Responses to such surveys, or in debriefing sessions, tend to be uniformly positive and are used by the supporters and managers of academies as proof that the academies are doing a good job. Academies also publish output data -numbers of courses delivered, number of students from how many countries who attended, number of topics covered- to show that the academies are meeting their stated goals. Basically, these evaluations are either testimonials from attendees which typically are, not unexpectedly, quite positive, or implementation measures. They tell us little about impacts, whether short -or long- range.

The more difficult evaluation questions deal with the impact of training -that is the consequences of the training delivered- on the behavior, culture, and performance of agencies whose officers have attended academies. For one, such evaluations are complicated, expensive, take time (how long does one have to wait to see impacts?), and must deal with

---

[4] ILEA Bangkok at www.state.gov/p/inl/ilea/c11280.htm and at www.ileabangkok.com
ILEA Budapest at www.state.gov/p/inl/ilea/c11279.htm
ILEA Gaborone at www.state.gov/p/inl/ilea/c11283.htm
ILEA Latin America at www.state.gov/p/inl/ilea/c11286.htm
ILEA Roswell at www.state.gov/p/inl/ilea/c11285.htm
ILEA Student Output at www.state.gov/p/inl/ilea/c11287.htm
Program Overview at www.state.gov/p/inl/ilea/c11243.htm
Statement of Purpose at www.state.gov/p/inl/ilea/c11242.htm

a large number of confounding variables in assessing impacts. For example, how reasonable is it to assume that a few officers from a large national organization, once they return, will have an impact on the general culture and performance of their agencies? Evaluations will have sophisticated and fine tuned to arrive at even tentative conclusions.

For such practical and social scientific reasons, few systematic evaluations of the impact of training on the performance of police who attended the academies or on their home police organizations have been done; and if done are not published or easily available. The USA has commissioned evaluations of ILEAs but the results cannot be found in public documents but may be discerned in conversations with experts who have conducted these evaluations. An evaluation of the Budapest ILEA concluded that the impact of training on the organizational performance in home countries was minimal, that skills learned by police at the academy were not passed on to other police in home organizations, but that having attended ILEA enhanced the technical performance of officer, was beneficial for their career, and led to greater interactions with foreign police on transnational cases (Interview with evaluator, OM).

Interviews (conducted by OM) with US police at the Budapest ILEA and at federal police agencies in Washington, D.C. left the clear impression that the most important impact US police perceived and valued were the personal connections established between trainers and students, and among students, which could lead to greater familiarity with each others' crime problems and legal systems and could facilitate greater cooperation, on an informal rather than only a formal basis. In case of common transnational crime problem, rather than go through the mandatory legal channels at home or the time consuming and slow process of formal international information exchanges through international police agencies (e.g., Interpol), police officers could just pick up the phone and talk to someone they knew personally at the other end.

One recently published study [30] confirms these informal findings. Johnson et al. [30] studied the impacts of having taken a 4-6 week long Supervisor Criminal Investigation Course, divided into 32 training modules, on the 214 students who had participated in four courses in 2000 and 2001. A three wave design was used. Students took self-administered surveys and tests before beginning training, immediately after finishing the courses, and after a six months period (using a follow-up mail survey). Four outcome measures were developed and used: student satisfaction with the quality and usefulness of the course; changes in knowledge and commitment to using new ideas; effect on own on performance once back on the job; and information transfer to home agency or other domestic and international agencies. The overall results were these: student evaluations of the quality of training were highly positive; there was a "medium size increase" (pg. 210) improvement in cognitive knowledge but there was little short or long term increase in commitment to using that knowledge (but neither did commitment decrease from pre-training levels); the training did have an impact on individual job performance; but there was little to no transfer of knowledge or practices to other agency units. There were some differences in outcome measures by cohorts.

Answers to the six questions, and impact criteria stated in the introduction, hence, can only be tentative and best guesses.

- *Does the program meets its stated goals, in the delivery of training and courses and the attendance goals set for foreign participants?*

The answer is generally yes. Enough resources are poured into such program to make them perform as planned. Students are attracted, courses are delivered, welcoming and graduation speeches celebrate the goals and success of the academies. It has not been difficult to attract students as a stay at an international academy is a break from routine work, a chance to meet fellow officers and gossip about life and work, an opportunity to learn new skills which will raise one's prestige back home, and generally an interesting way to spend some time as both a student and a tourist. Courses tend to be delivered as planned. Trainers can spend some time in an interesting place as well as meet and establish relations with mid-level officers. As they rise and move up in the organization, these officers will continue to keep in touch with their trainers and fellow officers and be favorably disposed to work-related requests. (This phrase came up a number of times in interviews in Budapest and Washington, D.C., when ask whom ILEAs are trying to attract; OM)

- *What could be done to improve the performance of the academy, if improvements need to be made?*

The CEPOL website tells a little joke which may be appropriate here. John talks to James and says, "See my dog Tiger there. I have taught him how to whistle." James says, "No way. Dogs cannot whistle." John says "I'll show you," and repeatedly tell Tiger to whistle. But Tiger just sits there and looks bored. James says "I told you so." "Well," says John "I said I taught him how to whistle. I did not say he learned how to do it." The point of the CEPOL joke (which I am sure is an old one) is that teaching is less important than learning. But most teaching at academies stresses rote learning and competence testing; since that is what the trainer know how to explain. Less attention is paid to how students learn in order to adjust training to help students learn. Competence training is suitable for technical skills but is not likely to teach the attitudes and skills in exercising discretion and to produce a police culture attuned to democratic values [31]. As Das and Palmiotto [32] point out, based on their experiences with human rights training, of which especially Das does a lot, police do not easily accept human rights training since it does not fit into their dominant cultures, especially for police from countries which lack a human rights tradition in politics or policing. Training in cultural values needs to be congruent, to some degree, with the professional learning students attending academies have already experienced and to which environment they will return. Training and concepts have to make sense for their everyday work to be learned, and that is not done in a class room setting but by experiential learning.

- *What is the impact of transnational training on the performance of policing systems which have sent their officers to be trained outside the country?*

As far as one can tell from episodic information and stories one hears, very little. At best, technical training will have an impact on the performance of subunit of a police for which such training is appropriate -forensic skills, forged document identification, conducting an undercover operation, or personnel management- but the impact on overall performance or the culture of the home organization, quite reasonably, can only be slight. For one, only a tiny percentage of officers will attend the academy and the chances that, on their return, they can become trainers of trainers or, like yeast, become catalysts for change although those chances are very slight. Some observers will make the argument that even a few trained officers can make a big difference once they rise in the organization and become heads of units and managers, since in an organization which is structured along semi-military lines their words and wishes will have an impact and effect needed changes. There is very little evidence that this is happening.

- *What are the non-formal or unanticipated consequences (benefits and costs) of training?*

As noted earlier, the most important consequences for trainers are the personal relations established with officers in other countries, as well as knowledge gained of the legal environments in which other police work. Relations matter and make it easier to work together, especially on the large number of transnational crimes which now bedevil police organizations. Knowledge of legal constraints matters since laws and regulations have to be abided by if cases are taken to court. In an interview (OM), an FBI agent said, "I tell (officer in country xxx), if you bring me a case, and you have arrested someone, I have to ask you, how did you get the confession? Because when I take that person to court in the USA, the defense will ask about the confession, and if I have to say, 'well they beat it out of him,' the confession will be thrown out. So if you want to help me, you have to do it in a way that I can use." He thought that training at ILEA did familiarize police on what was mandated in other countries if they wanted to pursue a case in court.

- *Will the emergence of a large number of transnational training programs and institutions -of which TADOC is only one example- lead to a convergence of policing ideologies and cultures among the countries which have participated in such training? Are these training programs the first step toward a universal, global police culture?*

The answer is speculative, but a likely yes. It is not difficult to imagine that international exposure by police officers to other systems will have an impact on how they think about policing, at least as individuals. For one, the police are almost predisposed to see police in other countries as being like them and doing similar work. Professional journals spread the word; international regimes are at least known; personal exposure validates such often used phrases as 'we are all police', or 'there exists an international fraternity (still so) of the police,' or 'we know how to talk to each other since we are police.'

It may seem odd to argue that this change will happen when we argued earlier that there is little known impact of international training on police performance and the cultures of police organizations. But it is not. Officer exposed to international training will return to a societal and organizational environment in which their voices are but few among many. And their police organizations will be restricted by the political and cultural climates of their countries. The values internationally trained officers have learned may have little resonance within that environment. For both reasons, their experience will not have much of an impact on the performance or culture of their organization.

But a global police culture is evolving even if country organizations are not yet in tune with the values enshrined in it. And that global culture is not evolving only by the efforts the police but by the work and advocacy of an international policy community concerned with police improvement and reforms, a community which includes regional and international decision-makers on policing affairs, members of think tanks and NGOs, and scholars. The community shapes the language of reform, and the content of curricula, and sooner or later police who wish to be invited to attend international academies will have to at least learn and speak the language congruent with international policing regimes.

- *Will these changes, such as have occurred, lead to more effective and fair transnational and domestic crime control?*

This is unknown, since the comparison baseline would be the number of cases solved, how quickly and by what means, had no international training been offered. No such baseline exists or could be created. Right now, one can read about numerous cases of transnational and domestic crimes which have been solved by the cooperative work of different national police. The question is would these cases have been solved in the absence of training? Alternatively, could cases have been solved, which now are not, had international training be delivered? Both of these contingencies are unknowns.

It is reasonable to argue that specific types of cases which were solved -e.g., drug trafficking investigations, money laundering schemes- benefited from the skills gained through international training. That, probably, is the greatest impact of international training in that it provides skills which are directly linked to a capacity to solve specific types of transnational crimes. Yes training is not likely to increase a general police capacity to deal with transnational crimes.

4. The Turkish International Academy against Drugs and Organized Crime (TADOC)

4.1. Origins

The Turkish International Academy against Drugs and Organized Crime (TADOC) was established in June 26, 2000, which is also the International Day against Drug Abuse and Illicit Trafficking, a day that has been celebrated since December 7, 1987 based on UN resolution 42/112. The main goal in establishing an international academy in Turkey was not only to train Turkish and other law enforcement agencies in confronting drugs and organized crime at the national and international levels but also to conduct research relating to organized crime, drug trafficking and money laundering which are the main financial sources supporting terrorist activities [33, 34]. The basic goal of the TADOC project is to implement educational and training programs in the controlling drugs and organized crime for law enforcement agencies from Balkan, Central Asia, and Middle Eastern countries, improve police professionalism, capacity, and performance, and enhance cooperation and coordination among the police agencies in the region. Professionally and effectively trained law enforcement agencies should be able to manage drug and organized crime related problems more successfully. Specifically, TADOC seeks to meet the training needs of regional countries; develop experts in both Turkey and the region; conduct scientific research and develop new national and regional policies; assist national academies in the region in meeting their training needs; enhance cooperation among regional countries; and "establish a social and professional network of law enforcement officers engaged in the field of combating these crimes" [35].

Turkey, straddling the cross roads between Asia and Europe, occupies a strategic location in confronting and suppressing the "serious threats to economic and governmental stability and community safety posed by the activities of organized crime groups and others who are involved in the trafficking of narcotics, weapons and people and the associated crimes of violence, corruption and money laundering" [35]. It is a logical place for an international police academy.

The project began as a cooperative project between the United Nations Office on Drug and Crime (UNODC) (formerly UNDCP) and the Turkish Government (specifically the Turkish National Police) in the late 1990s. Turkish police managers also visited International Law Enforcement Academy (ILEA) in Budapest, Hungary to gather information on how to adapt the system of international training at the ILEAs to the needs and goals of TADOC. Unlike the ILEAs, which were developed by US federal law enforcement agencies in cooperation with host countries, TADOC was finally established by the Turkish Government in collaboration with UNODC [36, 37]. According to the final report delivered after an international conference in Greece [38] the projects of UNODC in the Balkans are mostly focused on drug trafficking and narcotics enforcement. In fact, TADOC is one of the most significant projects of the UN in the [Balkan] region.

During meetings between the Turkish Government and UNODC, the parties agreed that the restoration, renovation, and furnishing costs of the Academy would be covered by the Turkish Government, and that the cost of international training programs -including pay for instructors- would be supported by UNODC. The Turkish Government spent $2,831,800 for the restoration and furnishing of the Academy. UNODC, for its part, financed $300,000 for the international training costs during the first phase of the project [39]. According to *Turkish Daily News* [39], UNODC financial support would reach more than $2,150,000 by the end of 2005.

TADOC started as a three-phase project in June 2000. The first phase (which lasted 10 months) and the second period (from June 2002 until the end of 2004) have been completed. The third phase of TADOC was initiated in March 2005 and is expected to be completed by the end of 2007 [40]. Within the framework of phase III, plans are to:

- Finalize the standardization of the training curriculum of the Academy;
- Initiate the TADOC Computer Based Training Center (CBTC) to the countries of the region, and to provide specific training modules for those countries;
- Establish CBTCs, which have been activated in nine cities in Turkey and planned to reach a total of (15) centers;
- Temporarily assign the expert trainers of TADOC who have experience in both teaching and practice to the countries of the region;
- Research centers will be actively involved in preparing and implementing drugs and organized crime strategies for Turkey and other countries of the region.

4.2. Distance Training and Computer-Based System

The software for the training programs related to drugs and organized crime in CBT project has been completed and the center has been established in TADOC [40, 41]. Most of the courses cover basic skills in analyzing false documents and drugs, risk analysis, illegal immigration, and search and seizure techniques in policing.

Additionally, computer based training modules and courses, which are delivered by the CBT Center in TADOC, has been put into service in nine cities of Turkey, with financial support from UNODC. CBT center according the report [40] serves;

- To reduce the training costs;
- To train more trainees in a shorter time;
- To provide the trainees with the opportunity of self-training at any time;

- To deliver standard training programs to trainees simultaneously;
- To reach out to larger groups.

4.3. Research Units at TADOC

In addition to training and courses, four training and research centers were established at TADOC, which are Crime Prevention and Organized Crime Research Center, Drug Demand Reduction Research Center, Money Laundering Research Center, and I.T. Crimes Research Center, which are the important steps in analyzing and gathering data in drug and drug related areas.

The European Monitoring Centre for Drugs and Drug Addiction (EMCCDA), which was established in order to gather reliable and objective data to analyze drug use and abuse in all EU member countries, has decided that TADOC be designated as the National Focal Point of EMCDDA to fulfill the EU membership requirements [41, 42, 43]. National Focal Points are set up in all EU states including recent member states, Romania and Bulgaria as well as Turkey, as a candidate country. In fact, the Family Research Institute of Turkey used to be the Focal Point of EMCDDA; however, it was transferred to TADOC in 2004 due to its more experienced personnel and greater technical capabilities as well as its national and international connections.

In fact, EMCCDA is an EU-financed project, which Turkey has been supported, based on a partnership agreement between Turkish and Spanish government delegations [44]. This partnership is implemented through a 'twinning project', whose aim is to assist a candidate country to adopt and implement the project. Therefore, the European Community Budget has financed this project in TADOC with 1,200,000 Euro [44].

The project has three specific objectives [40]:

- To develop a comprehensive National Drug Strategy for Turkey which conform with EU legislation and programs,
- To set up a National Monitoring Center for Drugs,
- To develop a Drug Demand Reduction Strategy.

4.4. Drugs and Terrorism

Turkey has been a target of internal and external terrorist activities since the 1970s and 1980s. The country has spent enormous efforts to eliminate this threat. However, terrorism and organized crime as well as drug trafficking have been perceived as different activities and threats, and thus different policy initiatives have been pursued to counter them. Focusing on the linkages between the terrorism and organized crime has become a new perspective for all law enforcement agencies, including those in the US.

Pino Arlacchi, the former UN Deputy Secretary General, who delivered the opening address at TADOC, pointed out that law enforcement agencies now realize that there is a link between terrorist organizations and drug trafficking, including such terrorist organizations as the PKK (Kurdistan Workers' Party) [45]. In fact, the major funding resource of PKK is derived from drug smuggling. According to Hill and Ward [34], the PKK's annual budget is estimated to be more than $120 million. The British National Service of Criminal Intelligence (NSIC) reported that in early 1990s, PKK extorted 2.5 million pounds from Turkish immigrants and businesses. In addition, more than 50 million DM were obtained from drug smuggling [cited in 34]. Other terrorist organizations elsewhere, such as Al-Qaeda or paramilitary groups in Columbia, also finance their operations through drug production and distribution.

4.5. Organizational Structure

TADOC is located, for administrative purposes, under the Ministry of the Interior and the Turkish National Police. The Director of the Academy is advised by a Directorate comprised of members of Turkish security establishments. The yearly budget for running TADOC is part of the annual budget of Turkish National Police, supplemented by financial support from EU projects and the UNODC.

4.6. Facilities

TADOC's facilities, located in the center of Ankara, include a Main Training Center, the Tactical Training Center, and a Guest House for students and visiting trainers [43, 46]. The Main Training Center is equipped with 'state of the art' technology for class and distance training and includes a library, cafeteria, and meeting rooms. The Tactical Operation Center provides opportunities for hands-on training and includes interview rooms, a car and body search platform, and a Mock Bar and Discotheque [43].

4.7. Training

4.7.1. Instructors

Teachers are drawn mainly from the Department of Anti-smuggling and Organized Crime of the Turkish National Police, supported by operational experts from other Turkish law enforcement agencies, academicians and other criminal justice staff. For specialized courses, experts from other countries such as Canada, England and Germany may be invited as trainers.

4.7.2. Students

Students are drawn from national agencies, mainly the Turkish National Police, the Gendarmerie, and the Coast Guard [36, 41]. International training activities are offered to law enforcement officers from countries who are members of the Economic Cooperation Organization (Afghanistan, Azerbaijan, Iran, Kazakhstan, Kyrgyzstan, Pakistan, Tajikistan, Turkey, Turkmenistan, Uzbekistan), the Black Sea Economic Cooperation (Albania, Armenia, Azerbaijan, Bulgaria, Georgia, Greece, Moldavia, Romania, Russian Federation, Turkey, Ukraine), and Balkan countries (Albania, Bosnia, Herzegovina, Croatia, Macedonia, Romania, Slovenia) and from countries with which Turkey has signed bilateral cooperation agreements such as Nigeria, Sudan and Syria. So far, law enforcement officers from 38 countries have been trained at TADOC [41].

4.7.3. Curricula

The language of courses is Turkish, but simultaneous translation in four other languages (English, French, German, and Russian) as well as other languages such as Arabic and Pashto can be delivered if needed.

The basic courses are designed to teach to fundamental police tactics and analysis skills, and cover such topics as drugs and organized crime, crime intelligence analysis, illegal immigration and human trafficking, risk analysis and profiling, surveillance, money laundering and financing of terrorism among others.

The 2006-07 calendar of courses, most of which are between one to two weeks long, lists 94 specialized courses [35]. Most courses will be held at the Ankara; however, starting from 2006, some of the courses are delivered in other countries, such as Syria, Yemen, and Romania.

4.8. Performance Assessments

TADOC is one of the most modern training institutions, equipped with electronic and computerized technology as well as tactical training centers and a guesthouse, which compares well with the other international law enforcement academies around the world. Still, the evaluation of the program's impacts needs to be one of the main pillars of the academy's training efforts. Without proper evaluations, the strengths and weaknesses of the training and needed changes will neither be detected nor addressed.

The 'Underlying Principles' that guide the development and implementation of TADOC's training and research activities provide some outcome and implementation criteria against which the performance of TADOC can be judged. The TADOC principles suggest that all 'training should be evaluated.' In addition, the principles specify that training has to reach the right people; that it should improve the performance of participants once they return to their home agencies; that effective performance assessments need to be part of the training program to identify needed changes; and that proper selection (of students) processes are in place [35]. Translated into outcome and implementation measures, these principles suggest the following assessment criteria:

- Have appropriate trainee selection mechanisms been implemented leading to the 'right' students attending to the right courses?
- Have effective self-assessment mechanisms identifying needed changes been established?
- Is research to measure improvements in the capacities of participants to deal with drug and organized crime problems being planned and conducted?
- Is research to assess the impacts of training on the activities and performance of other police agencies being planned and conducted?

It may be too early to be able to assess the consequences of training except through outputs measures (e.g., the delivery of courses) or satisfaction expressed by participants about their experiences at the academy. Nonetheless, one can ask what is being done to be able to evaluate the training delivered by TADOC and its impacts in an objective and systematic manner. Do the administrators, managers and advisors who supervise TADOC take seriously the need for systematic impact evaluations or are they, as seems to be the case with many of the other international academies, satisfied to rely on subjective assessments and episodic reports of success achieved by former students?

5. Conclusion

The origins of TADOC reflect both international needs and the desire by the Turkish government and the National Police to be seen as an effective participant in the global struggle against transnational crime. A subsidiary consideration for Turkey is its desire to join the EU, which requires that Turkey establish it legitimacy as an effective partner in the protection of its own and of European interests. Having TADOC be successful and be seen as a success would help advance Turkey accession prospects. Turkey, hence, as a country has a stake in having TADOC achieve that recognition and success.

References

[1] P. Andreas, E. Nadelmann *Policing the globe: Criminalization and crime control in international relations*. New York: Oxford University Press; 2006.
[2] D.H. Bayley, *Changing the guard*. New York: Oxford University Press; 2006.
[3] C.T. Call, *Challenges in police reform: Promoting effectiveness and accountability*. New York: International Peace Academy, IPA Policy Report; 2003. [Online] Available from: URL: http://www.justiceinitiative.org/db/resource2?res_id=101709 [2007, January 30]
[4] M. Deflem, *Policing world society: Historical foundations of international police cooperation*. Oxford: Oxford University Press; 2003.
[5] D. Koenig, D. Dilip, editors. *International police cooperation*. Lanham: Lexington Books; 2001.
[6] O. Marenin, Restoring policing systems in conflict torn nations: Process, problems, prospects. Geneva: Geneva Centre for the Democratic Control of Armed Forces, Occasional Paper No. 8; 2005, June. [Online] Available from: URL: http://www.dcaf.ch/publications/kms/details.cfm?lng=en&id=18349&nav1=4 [2006, September 01]
[7] E.A. Nadelmann, *Cops across borders: The internationalization of U.S. criminal law enforcement*. University Park: Pennsylvania State University Press; 1993.
[8] M. Cottam, O. Marenin, Predicting the past: Reagan administration assistance to police forces in Central America. *Justice Quarterly* **6** (1989), 589-618.
[9] M.K. Huggins, *Political policing: The United States and Latin America*. Durham: Duke University Press: 1998.
[10] T.D. Lobe, *United States national security policy and aid to the Thailand police*. University of Denver, Graduate School of International Studies, Monograph Series in World Affairs; 1977.
[11] O. Marenin, From IPA to ILEA: Change and continuity in United States international police training programs. *Police Quarterly* **1/4** (1998), 93-126.
[12] J.D. Occnipinti, *The politics of EU police cooperation*. Boulder: Lynne Rienner Publishers; 2003.
[13] Association of European Police Colleges - AEPC, *Project Europol 118*. European Curriculum for Police Training in Central and Eastern European Countries, Groningen: AEPC; 2002.
[14] Drug Enforcement Administration - DEA, International Training. [Online] Available from: URL: http://www.usdoj.gov/dea/programs/training/part18.html [2007, January 15]
[15] Federal Law Enforcement Training Center - FLETC, 2000 Annual Report. [Online] Available from: URL: http://www.fletc.gov/pao/annual00/annual00_trg.htm [2004, June 01]
[16] R. Dwan, *Executive policing: Enforcing the law in peace operations*, Oxford: Oxford University Press, SIPRI Research Report No.16; 2002.
[17] G. Peake, *Policing the peace: Police reform experiences in Kosovo*. New York: International Peace Academy; 2004.
[18] R. Neild, Democratic police reforms in war-torn societies. *Conflict, Security and Development* **1** (2001), 21-43.
[19] W. Stanley, C.T. Call, Rebuilding a new civilian police force in El Salvador. In K. Kumar, editor. *Rebuilding societies after civil wars: Critical areas for international assistance*. Boulder: Lynne Rienner; 1996.
[20] Washington Office on Latin America – WOLA, *Themes and debates on public security reform: A manual for civil society*. Washington, D.C.: WOLA; 1999-2000.
[21] E. Green, Costa Rica to house law enforcement academy for the Americas (2002). [Online] Available from: URL: www.sanjose.usembassy.gov/ilea5.htm [2005, December 12]
[22] US Department of State, International Law Enforcement Academy (ILEA)-Latin America. [Online] Available from: URL: http://www.state.gov/p/inl/ilea/c11286.htm [2006, December 12]
[23] J. Fehérváry, International Law Enforcement Academy in Budapest (ILEA). *European Journal of*

Crime, Criminal Law and Criminal Justice **5/2** (1997), 165-169.
[24] E. Kovchok, Budapest bank scene of FBI robbery. *Law and Order* **48/10** (2000), 64-67.
[25] O. Marenin, The International Law Enforcement Academies (ILEAs) of the United States. In G.T. Kurian, editor. *World encyclopedia of police forces and correctional systems.* Farmington Hills: Thomson Gale; 2006.
[26] Independent Commission on Policing for Northern Ireland (Patten Commission), *A new beginning: Policing in Northern Ireland* (1999, Sep.). [Online] Available from: URL: www.belfast.org.uk/report.html [2006, August 05]
[27] P. Neyroud, A. Beckley, *Policing, ethics and human rights.* Cullompton: Willan Publishing; 2001.
[28] M. O'Rawe, L. Moore, *Human rights on duty: Principles for better policing - International lessons for Northern Ireland.* Belfast: Committee for the Administration of Justice; 1997.
[29] United Nations, *Human rights and law enforcement. A manual on human rights training for the police.* Professional Training Series No.5. Geneva: High Commissioner for Human Rights. Centre for Human Rights; 1997. [Online] Available from: URL: http://www.unhchr.ch/html/menu6/2/training.htm [2006, July 21]
[30] K.W. Johnson, L.Young, J.P. Foster, S.R. Shamblen, Law enforcement training in Southeast Asia: A theory driven evaluation. *Police Practice and Research* **7/3** (2006), 195-215.
[31] O. Marenin, A police training for democracy. *Police Practice and Research* **5/2** (2004), 107-123.
[32] D. Das, M. Palmiotto, International human rights standards: Guidelines for the world's police officers. *Police Quarterly* **5** (2002), 206-221.
[33] United Nations, Economic and Social Council - Commission on Narcotic Drugs, International assistance to the states most affected by the transit of drugs. Report of the Executive Director, Forty-fifth session, Vienna (2002, March 11-15). [Online] Available from: URL: http://www.unodc.org/pdf/document_2001-12-27_1.pdf [2006, July 02]
[34] S.D. Hill, R.H. Ward, *Extremist groups: An international compilation of terrorist organizations, violent political groups, and issue-oriented militant movements.* Huntsville: Sam Houston State University; 2002.
[35] Turkish International Academy against Drugs and Organized Crime - TADOC (2006). Website http://www.tadoc.gov.tr/
[36] Turkish National Police, Department of Anti-Smuggling and Organized Crime 2002 Report (2003). [Online] Available from: URL: http://www.kom.gov.tr/turkce/konu_detay.aspx?uid=91&sm=comp12 [2005, February 13]
[37] United Nations, International Drug Control Programme, Project of the Economic Cooperation Organization (ECO). Available from: URL: http://www.unodc.org/pdf/iran/programme/completed/ECO.pdf [2005, March 10]
[38] Andreas Papandreou Foundation, Report of the conference *"The Problem of Illegal Drugs in the Balkans"* held in Athens, Greece (2006, March 31). [Online] Available from: URL: http://www.agp.gr [2006, November 09]
[39] Turkish Daily News - TDN, (2001, May 15). [Online] Available from: URL: http://www.turkishdailynews.com.tr/ [2002, June 01]
[40] Turkish National Police, Department of Anti-Smuggling and Organized Crime 2005 Report (2006). [Online] Available from: URL: http://www.kom.gov.tr/turkce/konu_detay.aspx?uid=277&sm=comp12 [2006, September 13]
[41] Turkish National Police, Department of Anti-Smuggling and Organized Crime 2004 Report (2005). [Online] Available from: URL: http://www.kom.gov.tr/turkce/konu_detay.aspx?uid=256&sm=comp12 [2006, September 13]
[42] Commission of European Communities, 2002 Regular Report on Turkey's Progress towards Accession, Brussels, SEC(2002) 1412. (2002, October 9), [Online] Available from: URL: http://ekutup.dpt.gov.tr/ab/uyelik/progre02.pdf [2006, August 17]
[43] C. Bodur, The role of TADOC in law enforcement training in response to transnational organized crime. In: *Istanbul Conference on Democracy & Global Security*; 2005 June 9-11; Istanbul, Turkey. Ankara: Oncu Press, 2006. p 621-627.
[44] European Union Commission - EUC, Report (2004). [Online] Available from: URL: www.deltur.cec.eu.int [2006, May 15]
[45] BBC Monitoring European, 2000, June 27.
[46] Turkish National Police, Department of Anti-Smuggling and Organized Crime 2003 Report (2004). [Online] Available from: URL: http://www.kom.gov.tr/turkce/konu_detay.aspx?uid=92&sm=comp12 [2006, September 13]

Establishing the International Institute for Police Research and Training in Turkey

Recep GULTEKIN[a], Samih TEYMUR[b], Selcuk ZENGIN[c],
Huseyin CINOGLU[d], and Kubra GULTEKIN[e]
[a] *Head of Foreign Relation Department, Turkish National Police (TNP)*
[b] *Director of TIPS (Turkish Institute for Police Studies), Police Major, TNP*
[c] *Deputy Director of TIPS, Police Major, TNP*
[d] *Police Captain, TNP*
[e] *Police Lieutenant, TNP*

Abstract. Because of increasing technology, telecommunication, and transportation, crime activities have become borderless. Therefore, the needs of international cooperation and establishments are undeniable. However, the current state of international cooperation can be characterized as too formal and too limited due to so many barriers, such as technical and policy-related barriers and cultural barriers. To overcome these problems, it is proposed that of an International Institute for Police, Research, and Training (IPRT) be established in Turkey. The purpose of this article is to understand why international cooperation is necessary, the role of Turkish National Police (TNP) in the international arena, the role and structure of IPRT, and why this center should be instituted in Turkey.

Keywords. International cooperation, combating crime, Turkey, Turkish National Police (TNP), Turkish Institute for Police Studies (TIPS), IPRT

Introduction

Fighting against crime and criminals has become an important issue all over the world. In combating crime, the most important need is international cooperation between countries. Because of increasing technology, telecommunication, and transportation, crime activities have become borderless. It is obvious that minimum cooperation in the fight against newly emerged borderless crimes is not sufficient. Unfortunately, the current state of international cooperation can be characterized as too formal and too limited due to many barriers. In their efforts to coordinate law enforcement agencies, the existing international establishments are limited by technical and policy-related barriers; cultural barriers are also among the most difficult obstacles to overcome.

To overcome these problems, it is proposed that an International Institute for Police, Research, and Training (IPRT) be established in Turkey. IPRT will bring law enforcement personnel together to work, learn or teach, get to know each other, learn from each other, share information, and build not only formal but also informal networks with the members from neighboring or related countries. The purpose of this article is to understand why international cooperation is necessary, the role of Turkish National Police (TNP) in the international arena, the role and structure of IPRT, and why this center should be instituted in Turkey.

1. Needs of International Co-operation

Kappeler and Potter [1] and Walker [2] have shown the crime rate has decreased in the US. This trend is also backed by police reports. However, crime is still a big concern of countries throughout the world. In today's world, criminals use brand new technologies as well as law enforcement agencies, and crime has become transnational. Because of borderless and transnational crimes, such as terrorism, organized crimes, human trafficking, international fraud, the narcotics trade, and IT crime, global security has become the most important problem for all states, especially for their law enforcement agencies. Unlike in the past, the risk threatening countries' security is not coming from a state or legitimate government. The problems of terrorism, organized crime, corruption, and other types of transnational and international criminal activities have become major problems for states [3].

International crime pertains to any kind of criminal activity which crosses national borders [4]. Although some efforts by INTERPOL, EUROPOL, or other international law enforcement bodies have been made, it is not enough to share information among law enforcement agencies and prevent transnational crime. For example, the terrorist attacks on September 11th showed a disastrous result due to the lack of sharing information among state law enforcement agencies in the US and with other countries. It is still necessary to establish new grounds to get law enforcement personnel together.

Resolution 1373 [5], number 4, in the UN Security Council,

"notes with concern the close connection between international terrorism and transnational organized crime, illicit drugs, money laundering, illegal arms trafficking, and illegal movement of nuclear, chemical, biological and other potentially deadly materials, and in this regard emphasizes the need to enhance coordination of efforts on national, sub-regional, regional and international levels in order to strengthen a global response to this serious challenge and threat to international security."

UNDP administrator Kemal Dervis (2006), while touring the newly renovated police station commissariat in Tirana, Albania, said "We at the UN have learned that development is not just income -income is important- but that to feel free and secure in one's city, in one's country is one of the most important aspects of development."

2. Role of Turkish National Police (TNP)

Because of its unique location, Turkish law enforcement agencies have always been responding to criminal activities ranging from terrorism to organized crime, including drug trafficking and human trafficking.

Turkey has realized that cooperation with neighboring countries and other countries on criminal activities in addition to education of law enforcement personnel must be established. For those purposes, Turkey has long been training many countries' ranking police officers since the mid-1990s. The latest statistics show that as of 2005, the number of international police administrators who have graduated from the Turkish National Police Academy (TNPA) has reached 476. This number does not include those who come to get short in-service trainings from international and national institutions located in Turkey. Some of the countries who are sending their mid-level police officers to be trained on a regular basis are as follows: Albania, Azerbaijan, Bosnia-Herzegovina, Palestine, Georgia, Kazakhstan, Kyrgyzstan, Turkish Republic of Northern Cyprus, Mongolia, Turkmenistan, Moldova, Macedonia, Jordan, and Belarus. Turkey strengthens and maintains its ties with these countries through these graduates. Some of the graduates are working with the TNP on different projects to promote justice and increase security within their countries.

Moreover, the Turkish International Academy against Drugs and Organized Crime (TADOC), which was established with financial support from the UN, still trains academicians and practitioners from 54 different countries, including Canada, Iran, and Syria.

The TADOC mission is to;

- Identify and meet the training requirements of the law enforcement authorities in the countries of the region on smuggling and organized crimes,
- Meet the trained expert personnel needs of our country and the countries of the region,
- Conduct scientific research on the above crimes, develop new methodologies, and shape national and regional policies in that manner,
- Provide input to the national academies of the region with respect to modern training techniques,
- Contribute to the existing communication and cooperation between the operational institutions of our country and of the other countries in the region [6].

In addition to training facilities, TNP has 217 high-level and mid-level police officers working abroad under UN, European Union Police (EUPM), and Organization for Security and Co-operation in Europe (OSCE) missions, such as Liberia, Congo, Kosovo, and Georgia.

Besides training many countries' ranking police officers in Turkish education and training centers and working with international organizations, the TNP established a Turkish Institute for Police Studies (TIPS) in the US. TIPS has been housed at the University of North Texas for over five years. The goal of TIPS is to combine the practical experience of the TNP in policing areas (especially terrorism, organized crime, narcotics, administration, intelligence, and investigation) with the academic and theoretical foundation represented by masters and doctoral training in US universities. TIPS is the mechanism to create a nucleus of US -educated leaders who will shape the future of the TNP organization. TIPS acts as a bridge between the TNP and various law enforcement agencies in the US. Through TIPS, not only Turkey and the US but also other countries can share their experiences and approaches to cope with the overwhelming problems human beings have faced. TIPS also promotes peace and the dignity of the human being in other parts of the world [3].

TIPS coordinates the annual placement and monitoring of students in masters and doctoral programs in more than twenty-four universities in the US, such as University of North Texas, American University, Rutgers University, University of Maryland at College Park, Michigan State University, University of Cincinnati, John Jay College, Kent State University, Sam Houston State University, and University of Central Florida. Graduate Programs involve masters and Ph.D. degrees in criminal justice, information science, sociology, public administration, IT technologies, and political science.

Additionally, TIPS organizes and oversees professional training programs worldwide in the following areas, among others: police intelligence, human rights, community policing, police training, forensic sciences, cyber crime, terrorism, crime analysis, criminology, corruption, juvenile justice, and police administration. For example, 'Istanbul Conference on Democracy and Global Security,' which was held from June 9 to June 11,

2005 in Turkey, was one of the important achievements of TIPS. More than 60 countries attended this conference, whose aim was to bring together specialists from academia and law enforcement agencies. The second 'Istanbul Conference on Democracy and Global Security' is planned for 2007.

TIPS is also well-known for its history of supporting and contributing to the fight against crime. For example, currently TIPS is conducting a multidimensional project against terrorism which is funded and supported by NATO. In this project, both academicians from universities all over the world and practitioners are contributing to developing a universal approach against terrorism through international cooperation.

3. Institute for Police, Research, and Training (IPRT)

As mentioned above, the existing international establishments are not sufficient to overcome transnational crimes because, as Schlegel [7] states, the most significant problems facing law enforcement agencies are both the nature of transnational organized criminal activity and the structure of relationships between law enforcement agencies.

The aim of IPRT will be to educate neighboring countries by using the experience and knowledge of EU law enforcement agencies. It will increase coordination and cooperation between local countries. The efficiency of crime investigation and combating crime will increase. The Middle East, which is the center of international crime, will be more secure. TNP will share its knowledge with neighboring countries and use their knowledge to fight crime. This institute will establish a mutual culture between European and Asian law enforcement agencies.

IPRT will also be established to fulfill the hope to promote justice throughout the developing world. As UNDP Administrator Kemal Dervis rightly stated in one his interviews with TIPS members, "to ensure a stable future, we need to build institutions to strengthen international cooperation."

As the Secretary-General of the UN stated in his speech in the General Assembly on 27 April 2006, "the UN plays an important role in promoting good governance, the rule of law and human rights. I urge UNDP to scale up the good governance assistance it is already conducting to support economic and social development" [8] of developing countries.

With solid connections and support from almost 40 universities throughout the world, especially in the US, and with its almost 200 active members located within these universities, TIPS will provide any type of help possible to create and functionalize the IPRT. TIPS' connections are not limited to academic institutions. Additionally, TIPS has worked with numerous law enforcement agencies and international bodies, such as NATO. Moreover, due to prior cooperation and coordination on different projects, the Federal Bureau of Investigation (FBI), TNP, Drug Enforcement Agency (DEA), and US Marshals Service (USMS), and other local law enforcement departments have been critical in TIPS education and cooperative efforts.

3.1. Structure of IPRT

The institution will have two main branches: the Research and Training Branch and the Administrative Branch (Figure 1).

The centers under the first branch are as follows: Police Management Research and Training Center, Terrorism and Intelligence Research and Training Center, Transnational

Crime and Corruption Research and Training Center, Information Technology (IT) Research and Training Center, Crime Prevention Research and Training Center, Human Rights Research and Training Center.

The centers under the second branch are as follows: International Affairs Cooperation Office, Data Processing Center, Publication Center, Human Resources Center, and Budget Center.

3.1.1. Research and Training Branch Coordinator

3.1.1.1. Police Management Research and Training Center

In this center, ranking and non-ranking police officers will be educated and trained by experienced trainers. Special attention will be given to VIP protection unit training and SWAT training. In addition to these specialized areas, basic police training will be given.

3.1.1.2. Terrorism and Intelligence Research and Training Center

This center will deal with problematic aspects of international terrorism. Especially, the nature of the threat that is posed by terrorism will be scrutinized. Some of the major interests of this unit will center on the answers to the following questions: What types of measures need to be taken by police departments? What kinds of tactics and activities are appropriate during early interventions? How do concerned agencies employ intelligence activities during the fight against terrorism? Most importantly, while doing these, what types of human rights violation challenges might be faced?

3.1.1.3. Transnational Crime and Corruption Research and Training Center

Given the borderless nature of crime, especially organized crime, and issues related to corruption, this unit intends to develop cooperation among developing countries through education and training. In this way, international awareness will also be increased, which will help develop more unified counter-activities against crimes of this nature. Through this center, special attention will be given to the research and studies related to human trafficking; also, recommendations will be developed accordingly.

3.1.1.4. Information Technology (IT) Research and Training Center

One of the major aims of this center will be offering and providing assistance to developing countries' computerization and networking. To do that effectively, screening and assessing computer infrastructures of developing countries will be of utmost importance. Moreover, research and studies will be conducted to evaluate technology use in policing, and strategies to increase it will be developed. Also, this center will focus on some of the new types of IT crimes, such as ID theft, among other computer crimes.

3.1.1.5. Crime Prevention Research and Training Center

From this center, contemporary and classical approaches to fight against conventional and unconventional crimes will be evaluated. New strategies against crimes will be developed and training will be given. This center will spend considerable amounts of time and energy on youth delinquency, community policing, and trafficking, which are among the most significant problems of the developing countries.

3.1.1.6. Youth Delinquency

The problems associated with youth are becoming more and more important in developing countries. Not only are these people becoming perpetrators, but also they are victimized in unprecedented numbers. Due to this reality, the attitude of police towards these people has also changed significantly. Therefore, this center will train officers from developing countries to meet that end.

Additionally, due to numerous reasons, since community policing is a well known strategy to combat new types of crimes, this center will develop new strategies to develop and implement community policing philosophy in these countries.

3.1.1.7. Traffic

To most crime analysts, traffic has become one of the biggest problems of developing countries. This center will target this issue not only from an academician's perspective, but also from a practitioner's viewpoint as well. To achieve that, the experiences of developed nations will be utilized.

3.1.1.8. Human Rights Research and Training Center

Issues related to human rights are among the most important challenges of contemporary policing. Even a small deviation by police officers bears the potential risk to result in unexpected outcomes. Riots and violent protests are perfect examples of that fact. This center will conduct research to unearth underlying reasons and some of the contributing factors to these types of violations. Also, recommendations to solve human rights violations will be developed and published in reports. These reports are projected to be yearly and will provide invaluable information to the concerned researchers who are interested in this topic. Additionally, training opportunities will be offered to officers, especially to those coming from developing countries.

3.1.2. Administrative Branch Coordinator

3.1.2.1. International Affairs and Cooperation Center

The institute will develop its international relations with others through this office. Mostly, the initial contact with other countries' agencies will be made by this office. Within this contact, the institute and the concerned country will decide on the nature and type of the training needed. After that, this office will convey this information to the related center to continue with the project.

3.1.2.2. Data Processing Center

This office will assist other centers and offices in their research activities. One of its first and most important activities is going to be developing institutional-level standards that will be followed by each center.

3.1.2.3. Publication Center

This office will publish, distribute, and write the reports and outcomes of research available to anybody who requests them.

3.1.2.4. Human Resources Center

This office will deal with issues related to personnel management and allocation within the institution.

3.1.2.5. Budget Center

This office will be responsible for managing the yearly budget, and evaluate requests related to financial resources.

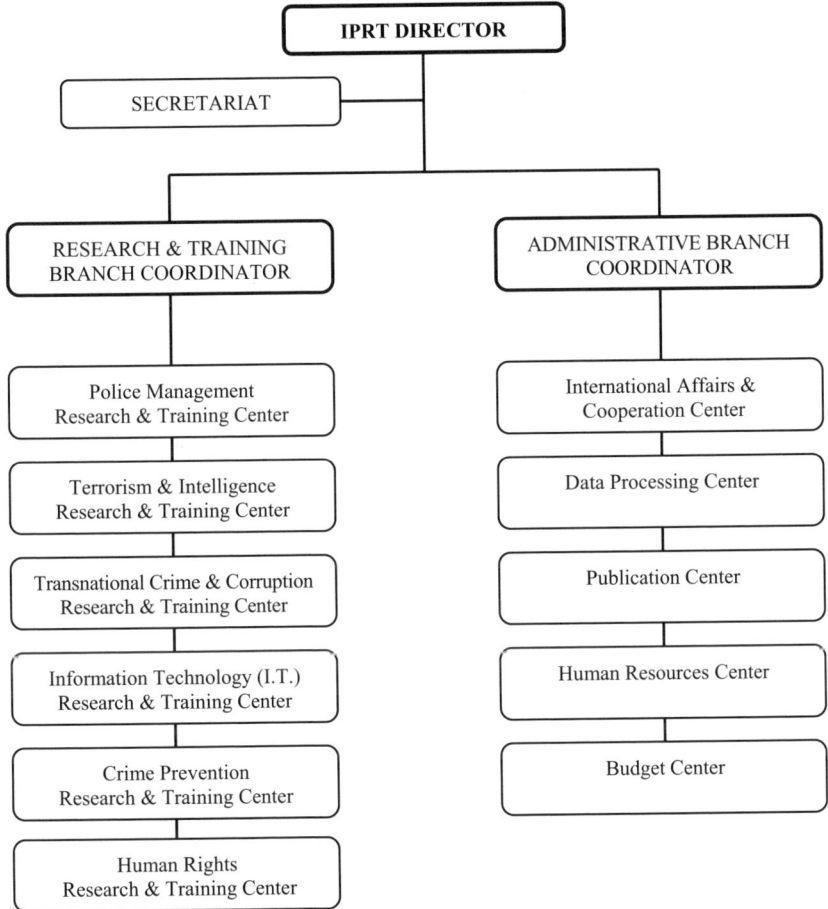

Figure 1. Structure of IPRT

3.2. The Budget

The budget of the project will not be financed by a single organization or country. Rather, due to its mission of developing international cooperation, the budget also will be internationally generated. However, since IPRT will be established in Turkey, it would be normal for this country to provide the seed money and the facilities required to start the institution. Moreover, the TNP would assign some of its internationally experienced trainers to that institution.

Turkish Cooperation and Development Agency (Türk İşbirliği ve Kalkınma İdaresi Başkanlığı-TİKA) is willing to provide IPRT with boarding/lodging expenses and travel costs of the officers who will come to that institution from the formerly mentioned developing countries. The Scientific and Technological Research Council of Turkey (Türkiye Bilimsel ve Teknolojik Araştırma Kurumu-TÜBİTAK) has unofficially agreed to contribute to the project. The amount will be settled once the project is accepted by UNDP. Along with the major part of the seed money to start the academy, the TNP (Emniyet Genel Müdürlüğü-EGM) have agreed to provide IPRT with facilities in Ankara, the capital city of Turkey, where IPRT will be located.

UN Development Program (UNDP) is expected to create contracted and/or seconded posts allocated to IPRT, and other types of contributions. According to UNDP Annual Report of 2006 [9]:

"UNDP works to strengthen the capacity of national partners to manage their own development effectively. This means empowering people and giving them tools to chart their own course and working to establish the larger institutional frameworks that will help to transform societies. UNDP is a leading member of the UN Development Group (UNDG), the coordinating umbrella for all UN funds, programs, and departments working on development issues, which is chaired by the UNDP Administrator."

4. Why Turkey?

Turkey is located in one of the most strategic areas in the world. Our country acts as a bridge between Europe, the Middle East, and the Far East. She also acts as a door of Turkish States to the world. Turkey is the east border of Europe with Asia and the west border of Asia with the European countries. Because of its unique location, Turkey has deep historical and cultural ties with the Balkans, Caucasus, and the Middle East.

In this project, geographically, three areas will be the focus: the Balkan countries, African countries, and Turkish Republics of Central Asia. Turkey, due to its strategic importance to the region, can play a central role to demonstrate and promote international cooperation among developing nations. Additionally, given its close relationship with these countries in terms of history, culture, and regional proximity, Turkey seems to be one of the best candidates. As a matter of fact, Turkey has long been training these countries ranking police officers since the mid-1990s.

Additionally, TNP has had experience in combating and reducing terrorist activities and related crimes, such as drug trafficking, human trafficking, and organized crime. Turkey has had many victims of terrorism since the 1990's. The victims were not only Turkish citizens but also foreign mission chiefs and officers.

TIPS also has 183 members who are studying for their master or doctorate degrees in many countries, mainly in the US. Their graduate programs are in criminal justice, information science, sociology, public administration, IT technologies and political science. All of the TIPS members are experts in their subjects. Table 1 shows how many TIPS members have been educated in different countries.

Table 1. Distribution of TIPS members according to countries

Country	Number of TIPS members
USA	154
Turkey	13
Great Britain	7
France	5
Germany	3
Russia	1
Total	183

In 2005, five TIPS members graduated from their universities with Ph.D. degrees. In 2006, eight TIPS members, and in 2007, sixty-five TIPS members are expected to graduate with Ph.D. degrees. Graduated TIPS members will educate participant countries' law enforcement agencies to achieve their goal in a more efficient way.

5. Conclusion

In the fight against crime, especially those which are transnational, such as terrorism, organized crime, and human trafficking, international cooperation is crucially important. That does not necessarily mean that current institutions do not perform and promote international solidarity against crime. However, in many areas, it became evident and was later proven that these bodies are not adequate, if not totally insufficient. The recent September 11, 2001 terrorist attacks targeting the US are perfect examples of that.

The IPRT aims to work within the formal rules and agreements between countries and hopes to build an increasing number of informal relationships between countries; in other words, the IPRT wants to establish a stronger network in order to better fight global crime. Actually, fulfilling this need will be one of the most central tasks for this project. The IPRT will aim to combine theoretical and practical experience of the international law enforcement community in policing areas. The ultimate goal will be not only to explore new approaches towards crime, but also to help developing countries adopt these new policies.

The goals of IPRT are:

- To research the needs of developing countries so that they can form an effective, responsive, transparent and accountable governance system and effective security forces.
- To ensure education for public administrators in order to promote effective government systems in developing countries.
- To ensure education and training for law enforcement agencies to be more effective in developing countries.

As was mentioned above, the institution will have two main branches, academic and administrative branches. The academic branch will mostly deal with strategies and tactics against some of the pressing issues and important crimes, while the administrative branch will handle more managerial tasks, such as budgeting, human resources, and publishing.

Turkey is a good candidate for hosting this institution, since the officials of this country unofficially accepted support of the project by agreeing to provide a campus, instructors, staff, and the seed money to start. Also, Turkey's experience in having and successfully operating international institutes is another reason. Moreover, Turkey has strong historical and cultural ties in addition to geographic proximity to the countries where cooperation is of the utmost importance in the fight against crime. Terrorism is another justification for establishing this institution in Turkey. Terrorism is a problem not only for Turkey but also for the whole world. The 9/11 terrorist attacks in the US and the bombings in Bali, Istanbul, and Madrid show that terrorism has no nationality, religion, color, race, and region. Turkey provides security and stability in her region with global power because Turkey is following the path of Mustafa Kemal Ataturk, founder of Turkey. His invaluable phrase, "Peace in the country, peace in the world," has inspired Turkish people to continue to pursue his goal.

In short, IPRT should not be seen as simply another institution. Furthermore, establishing it in Turkey should be recognized as an excellent opportunity to bring criminal justice agencies of the supporting countries together. There is no doubt that receiving their support is crucial in the fight against transnational crime. Through the IPRT, the UNDP and UN will find invaluable opportunities to share concerns, develop crucial partnerships, and build cooperation between developing countries in the fight against borderless crime.

References

[1] V.E. Kappeler, G.W. Potter, *The mythology of crime and criminal justice.* Long Grove: Waveland Press; 2005.
[2] S. Walker, *Sense and nonsense about crime and drugs: A policy guide.* Belmont: Wadsworth/Thomson Learning, Inc.; 2001.
[3] R. Gultekin, Cooperation among law enforcement agencies: TIPS. In: *Istanbul Conference on Democracy & Global Security*; 2005 June 9-11; Istanbul, Turkey. Ankara: Oncu Press, 2006. p 532-535.
[4] H. Moore, International crime and integration: The development of Europol (1996). [Online] Available from: URL: http://www.is.rhodes.edu/modus/96/Moore.html [2005, July 10]
[5] United Nations Security Council Resolution 1373 (2001, September 28). [Online] Available from: URL: http://www.unodc.org/images/resolution%201373.pdf [2005, July 10]
[6] TADOC, Introdroduction to TADOC (2000). [Online] Available from: URL: http://www.tadoc.gov.tr/flash/tadoctanitimeng.swf [2005, July 10]
[7] K. Schlegel, Transnational crime: Implications for local law enforcement. *Journal of Contemporary Criminal Justice* **16** (2000), 365-385.
[8] United Nations General Assembly, Uniting against terrorism: Recommendations for a global counter-terrorism strategy. Report of the Secretary-General (2006, April 27). [Online] Available from: URL: http://www.un.org/unitingagainstterrorism/sg-terrorism-2may06.pdf [2006, August 10]
[9] United Nations Development Programme, *Global partnership for development: Annual Report 2006.* New York: The Office of Communications United Nations Development Programme; 2006. [Online] Available from: URL: http://www.undp.org/publications/annualreport2006/english-report.pdf [2006, August 15]

Part 2

Country Approaches to Terrorism

Socio-Juridical Characteristics of Terrorism in the Laws of Azerbaijan

Elnur KAZIMLI
Qafqaz University, Azerbaijan

Abstract. Terrorism has a long history in humanity and the roots of terrorism lie not so much in psychology but in anomalies: political, territorial, ideological, religious. On the other hand, a state has to struggle with terrorism whether it has got such a complex structure or not. The lawful guarantee of anti-terrorist activity is the most important prerequisite of successful opposition both to domestic and international terrorism. We will try to give characteristics of terrorism in the laws of Azerbaijan.

Keywords. Terrorism, terrorism in laws of Azerbaijan

Introduction

Terrorism has become a constant scourge of humanity, acquiring ever more diverse forms and an increasingly threatening scale. Terrorist acts cause mass human victims, exert strong psychological pressure on large masses of people, destroy material and intellectual values, will sow hostility between states, and provoke wars, distrust and hatred between social and national groups. It is a politically significant phenomenon when separate groups in the society bring into question the legality and rights of the state and by these justify their terrorist acts. Different criminal groups perpetrate terrorist acts to frighten and destroy competitors and to attain the best conditions for their criminal activity. The level of terrorism and the concrete forms of its manifestation are indexed, from one side, to public morals, and from another, to the effectiveness of the efforts of society and the state to solve the most acute problems, in particular, preventive maintenance and suppression of terrorism itself.

Unfortunately, terrorism is a very efficient instrument to cause fear and destruction. Although terrorism is as old as the radically differing cultures that have suffered from it, in recent years the problem of terrorism has the steadily increased.

1. The Principal Causes Generating Terrorism

Terrorism appears when the society experiences deep crisis, first of all crisis of ideology and state - legal system. In such a society, there are various oppositional groups - political, social, national, religious, which doubt the legality of existing authority. Terrorism tends to grow in transition periods and stages of a life of a society when a certain emotional atmosphere is created and instability is the basic characteristic of base attitudes and social communications. It is a fertile field for the cultivation of violence and aggression in a society.

The problem of terrorism gains a special acuteness during social conflicts, which are the provoking factor of terrorist behaviour. In turn, the transition period, a basic change of the socio-political and economic structure of a society, causes more conflict [1].

The transition period burdened by a heavy economic crisis creates conditions of social opposition, generates a special condition of mass consciousness in which an inadequate grasp of reality is characteristic, and engenders a mood uncertainty, social fear, embitterment, and aggression. In these conditions extremist appeals to protest actions are easily perceived. Poverty, unemployment, hopelessness, extreme differentiation of the population on a level of incomes, weakness of the government, its inability to provide safety for persons and property - all these clear a road for the cult of violence, and the extremism in these conditions becomes an integral part of mentality of a society. Loss of confidence in the present and the future, destruction of all ideals of former Soviet societies, an atmosphere of violence reigning everywhere, and the cruelty cultivated by mass media create rather favourable conditions for the growth of criminality, and terrorism expands to the scale of a national disaster [2].

Economic crisis infringes upon interests of average layers of the population and thus can create political instability. Unemployed youths unite in groups, and the presence of plenty of free time leads them to participate in group activities. The personal qualities of a person (absence of diligence, desire quickly to grow rich, hunger for attention and popularity) can induce such a person to active terrorist activity.

Negative influences on the transition period include:

- Contradictions between democratic constitutional principles and real practice;
- Contradictions following from the process of political delimitation of a society, formation of social groups and layers with opposite political interests;
- Contradictions generated by estrangement between authority and the population;
- Contradictions caused by the lessening of social and economic and cultural communications between the centre and regions, and also between separate regions.

All social, economic, political, and other contradictions are supplemented with contradictions in the spiritual sphere, degrading the spiritual life of a society, destroying historical, cultural, and moral traditions, humanistic values, and giving rise to a cult of individualism, egoism, cruelty and violence, and to a disbelief in the ability of the state to protect its citizens. From such phenomena, criminal authorities, gangsters and terrorists emerge [3].

The roots of terrorism lie not so much in psychology as in political, economic, and other social attitudes. People are engaged in terrorist activity not by virtue of psychological anomalies (though this has been known to happen). The major reasons are instead political, territorial, ideological, and religious anomalies. Deep social, economic, spiritual and political crises cause an easing of law and order and generate new contradictions which trigger violence by terrorist individuals and organizations. Destroying and killing, terrorists pursue remote purposes, and murders and explosions are considered by them only as means to achieve their purposes. Terrorism in its broadest understanding combines diverse forms of motives and terrorist activities - from political, ideological, and religious motives come bloody actions, ranging from individual kidnapping and murder to actions that produce mass destruction. Although terrorists see themselves as involved in a struggle for survival, society as a whole view their actions as political or mercenary [4].

The considered preconditions and the reasons of terrorism, certainly, do not give a full picture of this complex phenomenon. There are many private, individual reasons and motives for terrorist activity, i.e. personal insults, envy, sadistic bents, emotional disorders, etc.

2. Lawful Aspect of Combating Terrorism in Azerbaijan

2.1. Normative Regulation of the Anti-Terrorist Activity

The lawful guarantee of anti-terrorist activity is the most important prerequisite of successful opposition both to domestic and international terrorism. The basic Azerbaijanian normative report is the Law about Combating Terrorism from June 18, 1999, which determines the lawful and organizational bases of combating terrorism in the Azerbaijan Republic.

Generally acknowledged as the major principles of combating terrorism are measures for preventing terrorism, the inevitability of the punishment of the guilty, the priority of protecting human rights, and measures to mitigate destruction and loss of life. These concepts are, of course, endangered by terrorist action, the minimum concessions to terrorists, etc.

The bringing of national legislation into line with international standards could prevent an increase in terrorism and contribute to a more successful fight against it. But since the discussion deals with the normative regulation of the fight with this phenomenon in Azerbaijan, the first necessity is to introduce some changes and additions into the criminal legislation, in which there are a number of gaps and deficiencies.

According to the Law about Combating Terrorism, the basic purposes of this activity are:

"1) the protection of persons, society and state from terrorism;
2) the suppression of terrorist activity and the minimization of its consequences;
3) development and the elimination of reasons and conditions which facilitate the realization of terrorist activity" [5].

There are some omissions in Chapter 2 of the Law about Combating Terrorism, which regulates anti-terrorist operations. The questions are connected with the control of counter-terrorist operations, the invitation of forces and facilities for these operations, the lawful regime in the zone of the operation, the organization for negotiating with the terrorists, the order of the propagation of information, and the end of a counter-terrorist operation. The law does not determine the maximum time interval for conducting counter-terrorist operations, and nothing is said about what is necessary to undertake such an operation or how to manage the scale of the operation.

2.2. The Criminal - Lawful Content of Terrorism and Criminal Responsibility for Terrorism

The specific object of the crime in question is public safety; the direct object of encroachment can be life and health of citizens, property, or the normal functioning of the organs of authority.

According to Article 214 of Criminal Code of the Azerbaijan Republic:

1. Terrorism, that is, the perpetration of an explosion, arson, or any other action endangering the lives of people, causing sizable property damage, or entailing other socially dangerous consequences, if these actions have been committed for the purpose of violating public security, frightening the population, or exerting influence on decision-making by governmental bodies, and also the threat of committing said actions for the same ends, shall be punishable by deprivation of liberty for a term of five to eight years.
2. The same deeds committed: a) by a group of persons in a preliminary conspiracy; b) repeatedly; c) with the use of firearms shall be punishable by deprivation of liberty for a term of seven to ten years.

3. Deeds stipulated in the first or second part of this Article, if they have been committed by an organized group or have involved by negligence the death of a person, or any other grave consequences.

Note: A person who has taken part in the preparation of an act of terrorism shall be released from criminal responsibility if he facilitated the prevention of the act of terrorism by timely warning to governmental bodies, or by any other method, unless the actions of this person contain a different composition of crime [5].

In the Law about Combating Terrorism, the concept of this phenomenon is represented in a broader sense. Thus, to the crimes of a terrorist nature, besides strictly the terrorism, the law adds the seizure of hostages, deliberate false communication about an act of terrorism, organization of an illegal armed unit or participation in it, endangerment of the life of a state or public worker, and an attack on the persons or the establishments, which have international protection.

There is also one shortage here. Concept of hostage in this law coincides with the concept given in article 215 of Criminal Code. Nevertheless, this concept is distorted, since in the law there is no indication of the threat of public safety, which determines the specific object of this crime. In Criminal Code this indication is absent, since article 215 is located in chapter by the name 'crimes against the public safety.'

Thus, the objective side of terrorism consists of the accomplishment of an explosion, arson or other actions, which create the danger in the loss of people, reason for the significant property damage to either the offensive of other publicly dangerous consequences, (for example, attempt on the objects of the subsistence of population by water, by heat, by electric power, seizure and the destruction of buildings, stations, the infection of the sources of water and food products, the radioactive, chemical, bacteriological contamination of locality) or in the threat of the accomplishment of the actions indicated. It is assumed that other 'actions' imply only the active form of the behavior of man, although the terrorist act sometimes can be realized via inaction. For example, the non-fulfillment of responsibility on timely turning off of production processes in power engineering, in the field of transportation, in the depletion industry.

The objective side of terrorism can be encountered not only in the single, single actions (arson, explosion, the destruction of building, area contamination), but also in the continued acts, which consist of a number of the interconnected encroachments of the life, health, property, united under the general idea and the purpose to intimidate population. For example, the pogroms, accompanied by murders and violence among the population, the group armed attacks and mass murders with the application of such instruments, means and methods, which are clearly intended for eliminating of inhabitants and excitation of panic.

It's no secret to anyone, what threat for entire humanity contains this comparatively new 'variety' of terrorism as nuclear terrorism. Let us note that until 1999 the objective side of terrorism did not include such actions as encroachments of the objects of the use of atomic energy and the use of nuclear materials, radioactive materials or the sources of radioactive radiation. This gap was not removed by the Criminal Code of Azerbaijan.

The subject of terrorism can be any responsible person, who is citizen Azerbaijan, foreigner or by face without the citizenship and reached fourteen year old age. This position is extremely important, since in the national and religious terrorism sufficiently many adolescents, who in view of their age easily fall under the influence of adult, participate.

The composition of terrorism contains indications of the special purposes (disturbance of public safety, the frightening of population, the rendering of action on decision making by the organs of authority); therefore, from the subjective side terrorist act can be accomplished only with the straight design: the guilty realizes the public danger of its behavior, will foresee possibility or inevitability of the offensive of publicly dangerous consequences it desires their offensive for achievement of its purposes. Emotions the experiences of the person, which accompany the preparation of crime and the process of its accomplishment, occupy special position in the subjective side of the crimes of terrorist directivity. Increasingly more frequent terrorist acts of steel to be accomplished when emotion prevail over the reason and they lead to the publicly dangerous manifestations of intolerance, extremism, political, nationalistic or religious fanaticism.

The second part article 214 of Criminal Code provides for responsibility for the accomplishment of the actions, with the presence of the qualifying circumstances, which testify about the larger public danger:

- By a group of persons in a preliminary conspiracy;
- Repeatedly;
- With the use of firearms.

Article 34 of Criminal Code of Azerbaijan provides for responsibility for the accomplishment of crime with the group of the persons on the preliminary agreement, who previously agreed themselves about the joint accomplishment of crime. This qualifying sign, as repeatedly, indicates repeatedly of the accomplishment of precisely terrorist, but not any other crimes. Repeatedly - this not into the first, but, as a minimum, second time.

The application of firearms during the accomplishment of terrorism is examined as one additional aggravating penal responsibility circumstance. This qualifying sign it will not be, if firearms adapted for the purpose to avoid detention after the accomplishment of act of terrorism. Such actions are qualified independently. Terrorist act can consider perfect the use of firearms, if it adapted for putting the solid damage or was demonstrated to others as the readiness of criminal to release him in the course. However, it is not entirely understandable, why legislator did not include in the number of aggravating fault circumstances the application of ammunition, explosives and explosive devices, which according to the destructive properties considerably exceed the destructive properties of firearms. According to the sense of law it turns out that the device of collapses either floods with the application of a firearms or the shooting of it at the building of station is more dangerous crime than the accomplishment of the same actions with the application of explosive devices or explosion on the station.

The third part article 214 of Criminal Code of Azerbaijan establishes penal responsibility for the acts, provided by the parts of the first and second present article, if they are perfected by the organized group either they entailed on carelessness death of man or other heavy consequences.

As to the organized group, the Criminal Code acknowledges the steady group of those, who were previously combined for the accomplishment of one or several crimes. It is important to note that the basic distinguishing features of criminal organization is the scale of its activity, the duration of functioning, the fixed mechanism of control, concealment, elusiveness, ability to influence the large social, political, economic solutions, close underground connection with the state, political, public, financial organizations.

In article 1 of the Law about Combating Terrorism, the concepts of terrorist group and terrorist organization are revealed. In the sense of the law indicated these concepts differ from each other only in terms of the fact that the organization assumes the presence of structural subdivisions and leading organs. It is necessary to correlate these determinations with the criminal - lawful concepts of the forms of participation, after refining that the terrorist group and terrorist organization - is the variety of criminal group and criminal organization in accordance with article 34 of Criminal Code of Azerbaijan.

The subjective side of the terrorism, which entailed on carelessness death of man or other heavy consequences, is characterized by the dual form of the fault: by straight design with respect to the terrorist actions and by carelessness (lightness or carelessness) with respect to the indicated in the third part article 214 of Criminal Code of Azerbaijan.

Financing terrorist activity from the private individuals, credit organizations and even states is a vital problem. There are somewhat incomplete in the Azerbaijan Criminal Code from this point of view. From one side, Law about Combating Terrorism considers financing terrorism as one of the functions of terrorist activity (article 1). From other side, according to the sense of Criminal Code, the person, who finances terrorism as the systematic accomplishment of the crimes of terrorist nature, it falls under not which of the forms of participants (214), since its action not they are directed on the accomplishment concrete crime. Therefore, in conclusion, it would be desirable to again focus attention on the need for as soon as possible developing the united concept of anti-terrorist activity under the contemporary conditions and bringing national legislation into correspondence with the international standards.

3. Conclusion

There are numerous deficiencies and omissions in the Azerbaijanian criminal legislation as it was already stated in this work. Such gaps not only they allow for terrorists and their 'sponsors' to avoid responsibility, but also weaken crime control as a whole. Lawful regulation - one of most important components of entire package of measures for combating of terrorism, it must have united clear concept, be clear and understood, capable of the effective application in practice, and also it must serve as guarantee from the arbitrariness of the subjects of anti-terrorist activity. It is moreover, necessary to bring national legislation into correspondence with the international, and also taking into account the tendencies of contemporary terrorism to modernize criminal and criminal procedure codes Azerbaijan, which will make it possible to enlarge the possibilities of law-enforcement agencies for development, intersection, disclosure and investigation of terrorist activity.

Important significance has an association of efforts in the opposition to the terrorism of all forces of state and society. This and the upper echelons of representative authority, legislators, special service, law-enforcement agencies, the media, religious and other public associations.

The combating of terrorism requires the integral approach, which must include the measures also of economic, and political, and social, and lawful nature. This is the long-range program, realization of which depends on many factors. But it's no secret to anyone, that decisive and effective measures are necessary already today.

References

[1] W. Paul, *Terrorism and the liberal state.* London: The Macmillan Press Ltd.; 1977.
[2] Terrorism: Psychological sources and legal assess. Moscow. *Authority and Law* **4** (1995), 25-26.
[3] L. Walter, *The age of terrorism.* Boston: Little Brown and Company; 1987.
[4] M.E. Erkal, *Social problems and social changes.* Ankara: Mayas Publications; 1984. (*in Turkish*)
[5] Azerbaijan Republic Law about Combating Terrorism, from June 18, 1999.

The Last Amendments to the Prevention of Terror Act of Turkey

Ali SAFAK
Professor, Turkish National Police Academy

Abstract. Terrorism is one of the main priorities of Turkey. By the means of separatist terrorism, Turkey has had many sorrowful experiences and lost more than thirty thousand people. As a democratic country, Turkey takes important measures to overcome this problem. Legal regulations are at the front line on these efforts. The first big step was the enactment of the Prevention of Terrorism Act (PTA) by the Turkish Parliament. In this article we try to give some details about major amenmendts done in 2006.

Keywords. Terrorism, Prevention of Terrorism Act

Introduction

Terrorism and terrorist movements have seriously affected Turkish social, political and economic development since 1970, as well as other neighboring countries, which have the same problems. The Turkish community had lived through bloodshed, among the extreme rightist and leftists groups, in the 1970s and has lived through separatist terrorist group and guerilla activities since 1980. There is no doubt that all sorts of terrorist separatist activities have been supported by some people or group in the land on one side, and by other countries having bad intentions towards the Turkish Republic on another side.

Actually, in our history the Ottomans had also come face to face with terrorism and particularly with separatist movements throughout last two centuries. Later on, the Ottoman Empire was collapsed and more than 40 states were established by opposition groups and by other European empires. A few states still show the same separatist desire against Turkey by supporting in several ways terrorist and separatist groups in Turkey. That is why the Turkish Parliament enacted the Prevention of Terrorism Act (PTA), Law no: 3713 of 12 Apr. 1991. The Turkish government has forcibly carried out this law since that year. The origins of this Act come from Spanish, British, and some other European countries which have the same kind of terrorist, separatist, and organized crime groups. Later on, this Act has, several times, been amended in terms of human and civil rights and public benefits. The last major amendment was done in 2006. We try to give some information and explanation about the Amending Act in this paper. Turkey has been criticized by her European allies for taking illegal action against the terrorist groups.

Should such a major amendment really be made or not? In my opinion, it should be because the Turkish Criminal Code (TCC), and the Criminal Procedure Act have completely been changed and State Security Courts have been abolished. For these legal reasons and arrangements, PTA should also completely be revised in terms of contents and measures to make it parallel with the above mentioned Acts.

1. General Problems of the Amendment in Brief

Terrorist movements are, generally speaking, big threats to civil rights and individual freedom. It is an important obstacle to social and commercial changes and development in every state. The main duty of a democratic administration is to realize a peaceful environment, where members of the society honorably live within a free environment and have all sorts of civil rights. As every body knows, the main principles of a legal administration are as follows:

- The right of living in peace and honor in the community,
- The right of individual immunity and respectfulness,
- The right of individual freedom and security and so on.

These legal rights and principles are denied and destroyed by terrorist groups. That is why terror crimes are committed; terrorists use force and violence to frighten innocent people for the terrorists' own purposes.

The meaning of the word 'terror' is not clear. That is why it is so difficult to find a clear definition of terror crimes or terrorism in international legal agreements upon preventing terror. However, some international declarations include a list of violations or events which are classified as terrorism. These actions are designed to change the principles of the state or its structure, or to create conflicts or threat of conflicts. These actions may be underrtaken by individuals or organizations.

The 'European Agreement upon Prevention of Terrorism,' dated 27th January 1977, could be mentioned as an example of a list of terrorist actions and of explaining the meaning of 'terror' (see Article 1, 2). The Amending Act of PTA refers mainly to the Turkish Criminal Code (TCC). Mainly, terrorist movements or crimes are mentioned in Article 3, and a few crimes of supposed terror, depending on intention and inclination of subjects, are mentioned in Article 4 of the TCC.

When does a crime become an act of terrorism? If an ordinary crime is systematically committed for a special purpose or by a crime organization, it might be terrorism. One of the more effective ways to prevent terrorism is to enact special investigation and judging procedures and to put into practice special rules concerning the execution of penalties.

Terrorism has been at the top of Turkey's agenda for a long time. Every single state has to struggle with terror. However, terrorism prevention policies cannot achieve intended results unless countries collaborate to fight terror and organized crimes. At the beginning, Turkey felt herself alone in the fight against terrorism; moreover, she was criticized while she was struggling with terrorism by other states, mostly by members of EU. When terrorist movements reached international levels, other states found Turkey was on the right road to prevent terrorism. In 1991, the Turkish Parliament enacted Act 3713, regarding preventing terror and organized crimes.

While struggling with terror, it is very important that balance should be established in the use of force against terrorist actions. There must be a balance between freedom on one hand and public security and law and order on the other. Nevertheless, individual freedom seems impossible before establishing public law and order in daily life. Wherever there is no public peace and security, there will be no individual freedom and civil rights. That is why public rules and regulations must be set up before anything else.

Of course, terrorism cannot be solved by passing a law. Struggling with terror must be done at both the national and international level. Every democratic country has to help the others in this field. For instance, criminals (particularly terrorists) should be extradited to the country where he/she committed a crime. Extradtion is unfortunately not so easy in practice. Look at O. Sabanci and Fehriye Erdal case. She is exactly a terrorist and a member of a crime organization, but she has still not been given back to Turkey by Belgium.

The last amendment to the Prevention of Terrorism Act is entirely done in the frame drawn by law. Government officials are required to obey basic principles of a democratic country while they combat either with a terrorist group or with any ordinary criminal. They should never cause personal damage or harm individual freedom and rights. To combat terrorism, people should have more freedom and more democracy in the society. An absolute deterrent does not help in solving social problems.

Security forces (i.e., policemen and soldiers) come first in preventing terror. From this point of view, the proposal for amending the act is not complete. It should contain something about cooperative efforts to combat terrorism, but it doesn't. The citizens might be informed about preventing terror. In this regard we must educate and train our children to be good citizens. The way to achieve is not by making a law but training them in a reasonable program in which they are taught in terms of moral, social, and ethical values.

In the case of of Turkey, the supporting sources of terrorism could not be prevented, from the beginning up to now, by any one, but only by herself. She needs to be supported at both the national and international level. There has been no change in the position of terrorist groups in spite of the Turkish army and police forces bombing some places where terrorist groups live. It shows us that terrorist groups find several sources of money, food, and personnel, and in finding national and international support in some ways. However, these sources of support could be eliminated by national and international solidarity.

Terror organizations wish to demolish the existing state and administration, but they are mostly subcontractors of alien powers either at the national or international level. Consequently, it is necessary to take care and pay attention to the methods of preventing terrorism.

The main problem is to train our children to be good citizens in this land. The number of unemployed in the young generation is too high, and it causes an undesirable effect for those who fight against terrorism. Generally speaking, this situation is a very important factor in social and economic life.

The terrorist movement has no racial aim and purpose, but it has a separatist aim and economic problem. All these negative conditions could be resolved by solving economicand regional problems. Counterterrorist actions are a kind of subsidiary means for solving and ending the terrorist problem.

The matter of terror does not mean the subject of violence but has different dimensions such as health, education, and economy. The PTA defines common and collective conditions of terror actions, which are compulsion, violence, and force. In addition to these common conditions, those crime actions are intentionally committed by a criminal or organized criminals. That is why the new amending act does not regard the one who helps or supports unintentionally a terror organization as a direct subject of terrorism and of crime.

2. Definition of Terror and Terror Criminals

The title of Article 1 was changed and its second and third paragraph were erased by the new amending act. The main text of Article 1 is:

"The Definition of Terror[1]: Article 1: Terror means that all sorts of following actions or behaviors are committed with special purposes by someone who is/are member of an organized crime committee, such as by using compulsion and violence to disrupt principles of the Republic, being defined in the Constitution; and to change political, legal, social, secular, economic regime through pressure, frightening, discouraging, assimilating or restriction; and to change unities of land and nation by using the above mentioned means; to bring the existence of the State and Republic into danger; to make weak the jurisdiction of or to destroy and to get in control of the public authority; and to demolish fundamental rights and freedoms of human beings; and to disorder the state security either at the national or international level, or the public order or general health ."

This definition of terrorism has been adopted from the TCC (Article 220) and from an international agreement accepted by the UN, which is called 'International Agreement Prevention of Organized Overbearing Crime' (Article 2/a).

2.1. Who Is the Terrorist or Who Are Terrorist Criminals?

There is no change in Article 2 of the Act which contains two paragraph Translation of the text follows:

"Whoever intentionally or freely commits an act to achieve special purposes, each of which is mentioned in the above article (i.e. Article 1) is considered a member of a crime organization, together with others or alone; moreover, if he/she does not directly commit the act but is a member of that organization, he/she is supposed/considered terrorist. Whoever is not a member of a crime organization but he/she promotes a terrorist intention of above mentioned crimes by using the organization's name, he/she will be considered a terrorist and will be punished with the same punishment."

2.2. What Is Terror Crime?

The answer to this question is found in Article 3 of Act 1. This article was completely changed, and does not contain any new act considered a terror crime, but some existing crimes in the basic TCC are considered terrorist crimes, depending on the criminal's intention to produce a result mentioned in Article 1. Article 3 includes only article numbers from TCC. However, the titles of the articles will be mentioned here in brief.

1. "To demolish the unitary structure of the state and the wholeness of the country" (TCC-Article 302). An attempt to place under the control and sovereignty of an alien state the whole of the land or some part of it, or to cause weakness of independency of the country or to demolish the social unity of the people, or to separate some part of the land from state control and administration - all those attempts are considered completely terror crimes.
2. To move together with foreign military services or in favor of them to demolish the national army and its bases. Such a kind crime is explained in Article 307 of TCC. A definition of the crime is briefly mentioned in paragraph 1.
3. "Violating the constitution" i.e., a crime against constitutional regime, which is explained in Article 309 of TCC. It is said in the first paragraph that

    "whoever commits a crime by using pressure or by coercion against constitutional law and order or by establishing another administrative system instead of the existing constitutional one, or preventing existing constitutional law and order is a terrorist."

4. "Crime contrary to lawmakers' power of the State" i.e. to the Parliament. This crime is basically described in TCC Article 311/1st paragraph as following:

---

[1] The Amending Act, Law no: 5532, of 29 June 2006. The edge title of Article was changed, and paragraph 2 and 3 were abrogated (Official Newspaper - 18/07/2006, issue nr.: 26232).

"whoever commits a crime by using pressure or by coercion against the Turkish Great National Assembly, or attempts to obstruct the whole performing its duty or partially is a terrorist."

5. Rebellion committed by using weapons against the executive power of the Turkish Republic. This crime is basically defined TCC Article 313/1st paragraph as following in brief:

"whoever provokes the people to rebel against Turkish Republic Government, or administrates a rebelling armed group against the government or participates in such a rebellion, he/she is supposed rebellious and is punished for this crime."

6. "Organizing an armed force";

"whoever organizes an armed group for committing crime, or administrates such a group, or whoever becomes a member of a crime organization, he/she is supposed a terrorist and is heavily punished compared with the ordinary situation of that crime."

7. To supply weapons to groups, described in TCC Article 315.

"Whoever tries intentionally to supply all sorts of weapon to terrorists or terror groups to be used in terrorist activities, or produces or buys or sells, smuggles, imports, transports, or stocks those weapons for a crime organization, he/she is accused and judged as a terrorist or a member of a terror organization."

8. To register soldiers for foreign military service or to find soldiers for foreign military service. These crimes are defined in TCC Article 320 as following:

"Whoever finds soldiers among the people for foreign military service, without getting official permission, or whoever registers persons for foreign military service, without getting official permission, he/she is guilty of a crime. When he/she commits that kind of crime with one of the purposes, mentioned in PTA Article 1, he/she is accused of a terror crime."

9. Assassination or assault against Head of the Turkish Republic. If this crime is committed with special purposes, mentioned in PTA Article 1, he/she is accused of a terrorist crime.

As it has been seen, Article 3 of the PTA has entirely been adapted to the new TCC, and the PTA never creates or provides a new crime.

2.3. Crimes Committed with Terrorist Purposes

The crimes mentioned above are supposed primary and essential terrorist crimes. Whoever commits with terrorist intention those crimes, his/her action is qualified as a terror action. But some other crimes are mentioned in PTA Article 4. If those crimes are committed with special purposes, they are supposed terrorist crimes; otherwise, they are qualified as ordinary crimes. However, the main criterion here is criminal intention and purpose. If the criminal's intention is changed, the judgment of the action should be changed. The briefs of Article 4 will be written down as following:

a. If the following crime actions, mentioned in TCC, are committed with terrorist purposes, they are qualified as terror crimes:
- To smuggle immigrants (Art.79), illegal commerce of human beings (Art.80),
- Intentional murder (Article 81), qualified murder (Article 82), to guide someone to suicide (Article 84).
- Intentional injury (Article 86), intentional qualified injury (Article 87), and persecution of the people (Article 96).
- Crimes against freedom, such as: threats against someone (Article 106), blackmail (Article 107), constraint (Article 108), illegal limitation of individual

freedom (Article 109), to block educational freedom (Article 112), to prevent activities of public institutions or semi-public institutions (Article 113), illegal limitation of political rights (Article 114), To block freedoms of belief, thought and opinion (Article 115), damage to a residence (Article 116), to block the freedom to work (Article 117), to block trade union activities (Article 118).
- Qualified theft (Article 142), burglary (Article 148), qualified burglary (Article 149), causing damage to things (Article 152).
- Intentionally causing a hazard to public security (Article 170), spreading radiation (Article 172), release of atomic energy (Article 173), keeping or supplying dangerous materials without permission (Article 174).
- Crimes concerning public health, such as mixing poisoned material in drinks and foods (Article 185), unofficially producing narcotics and stimulants, or trading them (Article 188).
- Crimes concerning public confidence, such as to forge official seals (Article 199), to obtain means and materials for the purpose of forging money or official seals (Article 200), falsifying all kinds of seals (Article 202), falsifying official documents (Article 204), and falsifying a document to appear official (Article 210).
- Crimes concerning public peace and confidence, such as threats to create fear or restlessness among people (Article 213), to provoke people to commit a crime (Article 214) and to praise crimes or criminals (Article 215).
- Crimes regarding transportation and vehicles and stable bases and platforms, such as stealing or preventing the use of transportation vehicles (Article 223) and occupying fixed platforms at the seaside or in the sea (Article 224).
- Crimes against data processing, such as illegally breaking into data processing (Article 243), illegally changing or interfering with a database (Article 244).
- Resistance to government officials doing their official jobs (Article 265).
- Crimes against justice, such as aiding an escape (Article 294).
- Disrespect for signs and symbols of state sovereignty (Article 300).
- Assassination of the Head of the Turkish State or deadly assault on him/her (Article 310/2) or conspiracy to commit such an act (Article 316).
- Illegal occupation of military bases (Art.317), demoralization of the military services (Art.318), and encouraging soldiers to disobedience (Art. 319).

b. Crimes described in Act 6136 (1953).
c. Intentionally causing forest fires, as mentioned in the Forestry Act, Law no: 6813 of 31 Aug. 1956, Article 110/paragraph 4 and 5.
d. Crimes described in the Prevention of Smuggling Act, Law: 4926, 10 July 2003.
e. Crimes in violation of Constitution Article 120.
f. Crimes described in the Act for Protecting Cultural and Natural Wealth, Law no: 2863 of 21 July 1983, Article 68.

2.4. Information on Article 4 of PTA

The above mentioned crimes could be considered as ordinary crimes punished in the frame of the TCC. However, if those crimes are committed with terrorist aims, they will be considered terrorist crimes and punished more severely. As mentioned before, intent and purpose are crucial in the classification of these crimes.

3. New Criteria concerning Penalties

It has been seen that no new crimes or punishments were enacted by the amendments. Crimes that are classified as terrorist crimes are more heavily punished, for terrorist crimes include hazards and risks that are more serious. That is why Article 5 is completely changed and regulated to the TCC and to other acts.

"Increasing the amount of punishments: Article 5[2]: Whoever commits a crime describes in Article 3 or 4 will be punished by the fine mentioned in the original text being increased by 50 percent. Thus the highest limit of punishment may be exceeded in the case of a terrorist crime. Prison sentences may also be increased in acccordance with the Article. At this time the amount of increase cannot be more than two thirds of the original punishment."

A brief justification of Article 5 is as following; firstly the amendment has made an adaptation of the article to the judgments of the TCC. The 2nd paragraph has been added to the article. The increase in the punishment is stipulated regarding to following crimes; crimes concerning public health such as mixing poisoned material in water and foods (Article 185), unofficially producing narcotics and stimulants, or trading them (Article 188). If those crimes or some others are committed under the control of a terror organization or in the frame its activities, they are considered terrorist crimes and the punishment will be increased according to Article 5.

4. Some Situations Arising by the way of Press and Speech Negatively Affecting the Prevention of Terror

Everyone knows that the role of the press is very important for people. But the freedom of the press is not absolute and unlimited. If public benefit and necessity lead to limitations on the press and free expression, it must be seen as a necessary evil, and everyone has to obey. Sometimes major damage can only be prevented by such means. This is a principle of the law. Accordingly, Article 6 has entirely been changed. The text in English follows:

"Expression and publication: Article 6[3]: (1) Whoever makes known or publishes the identity of public officials who are involved with preventing terror, or gives information about names or identity cards of the persons against whom terrorists could easily commit a crime, he/she will be punished by imprisonment ... (2) Whoever publishes or broadcast announcements or declarations of terror organizations, he/she will be punished. (3) Whoever declares or publishes identity cards of informers against terrorists, he/she will be punished. (4) If the actions mentioned above are committed by the press or broadcasting, the owners and responsible directors will be punished by a fine, if they do not participate in committing a crime. (5) If a periodical openly encourages terrorist actions. praises terrorists, or promotes a terror organization, it can be closed down stopped by the decision of a judge in normal times, or by the order of the public prosecutor in extraordinary times for a period of fifteen to thirty days. The order of the public prosecutor has to be reviewed by a judge in twenty-four hours. The judge either approves the public prosecutor's order or not in forty-eight hours. Otherwise the order will be null and void."

A brief justification of the Article 6 is that the punishment of the crimes mentioned in paragraph 1-3 has been made more effective compared with the punishment before the last amendment. The fine puts responsibilty on the owner and their responsible directors for deliberate action or negligence.

---

[2] The article was completely changed by the Amending Act.
[3] Fine penalties, mentioned paragraphs 1, 2 and 3, were changed to prison, para 4 was completely changed, and paragraph 5 was added by the Amending Act.

If the owner participates in a terror crime, he/she will be punished as a terrorist. In other words, the rule of paragraph 4 is not applied to him/her. He/she is considered a main partner of the crime and will be punished with imprisonment. The amendment to paragraph 4 covers all forms of the media. According to paragraph 5, the decision to close down must be instigated or approved by a judge.

5. An Explanation about Crime Organization

The term 'organization' has recently been accepted as a term in criminal law. The word 'organization' means a group formed for the purpose of committing a crime. This concept is described in Article 6/1 (j) of the TCC:

"Whoever establishes a crime organization, or presides over a crime organization, or participates in a crime organization, or commits a crime on behalf of a crime organization by himself/herself, or together with some others, he/she is considered a member of a crime organization in criminal law."

What constitutes a crime organization and organized crime has been covered in different articles of the new TCC. For instance, Article 220 covers "Establishing an organization for committing crime." This is a kind of general purpose crime. The purpose of the organization is only to commit crime. It lacks terrorist intent. Article 314 of the TCC contains a "special organized crime," obtaining weapons by establishing an organization.

It is very important to determine the basic difference between a group of ordinary criminals and a crime organization. A crime organization has a social structure. 'Organization' is a concrete unity and individuals participate in that structure.

The main designating element in proving a crime organization is to determine whether an inclination to commit crime exists in an organization or not, and whether this inclination continues or not. In other words, there must be an ongoing program to commit crimes with the willing participation of the members of the group for it to be called a crime organization. The type and purpose of crimes committed may also label the group as a terrrorist organization.

The minimum number of participants in a crime organization is tthree, according to international agreements on organized crime. Organized crime is inevitably classified as a kind of continuing crime, so the existence of a crime organization can be seen as a kind of crime.

The number of crime organizations is growing around the world. That is why every democratic country must struggle against these crime organizations while staying within the frame of the law and observing individual rights and individual and social freedoms. A balance should be kept between these two kinds of freedoms and rights, i.e. individual and social ones. Establishing this balance seems sometimes to be very difficult in general practice and in preventing organized crimes in particular. The balance is very often tipped against individual freedom. International solidarity and specializing in preventing organized crime are the best ways to preserve the balance at the international level.

Accordingly, Article 7 of PTA has completely been amended:

"Terror organizations: Article 7[4]: (1) Whoever establishes a terror organization for committing a crime with the purposes determined in Article 1, by using force or violence, or by using or applying coercion, or by terrorizing, or by intimidating, or by threat; or whoever administrates a terror organization, or whoever becomes a member (participant) of this organization, they will be punished according to the judgment of Article 314 of the TCC. Whoever arranges activities of terror organization, he/she will be punished as an administrator of the

---

[4] The article was completely changed by the Amending Act.

organization. (2) Whoever propagates a terror organization, he/she will be punished in prison. Whoever commits this propagation through press and publications, he/she will severely be punished in prison by increasing half of the punishment, as mentioned above. The owners of press or of publication and responsible directors will be punished with judicial fine punishment, if they do not participate in terror crime, in addition to above judgment.... Following deeds and behaviors are punished as crimes, mentioned above in this paragraph;

- Whoever completely or partly covers his/her face to hide his/her identity in favor of the terror organization's meeting, rally or protest: This is now considered propagation of the organization;
- Or whoever carries badges or signs of a terror organization, for the purpose of show himself to be a member of the organization, or expressing support for it, or whoever shouts slogan, or broadcasts its slogans by using electronical means, or wears the organization's uniform, designed with emblems or signs for above mentioned purpose.

If the crimes mentioned in paragraph 2 are committed at some places belonging to an association, a foundation, a political party, or at a building, or a clubhouse, an office or their annexed buildings or at educational buildings, or at student hostels, or at their annexed buildings, all sorts of those crime actions will be punished by doubling the punishment of the crime."

The crimes mentioned above are considered special crimes according to criminal's purpose and intention. Whoever is the founder, manager, or becomes a participant in terror organization or in its activities, he/she will be punished because of these deeds and actions. In addition to that, whoever is a manager, or holds its management in his/her hands, he/she will be supposed the main participant of these crimes, being committed in the limits of organization's activities, and will be punished because of those organized crime actions.

6. Issues

6.1. The Problem of Financing Terror

Article 8, concerning this problem, has entirely been amended for the sake of public needs and benefits. The judgment of the article is as follows:

"Financing Terror: Article 8[4]: (1) Whoever intentionally and willingly supplies funds, or collects monetary funds, knowing those funds will completely or partially be used for committing terror crimes, he/she will be punished as a direct participant of the terror organization. Whether the funds are spent or not, he/she will be punished with the same punishment. (2) The word 'funds', mentioned above, covers all sorts of money, and of means and materials like properties, rights, credits, taxes and other means that could be equated with money. Thus, Turkish lawmakers have enacted a judgment in Article 8 according to international agreement about "Prevention of Financing Terrorism."

Therefore, all sorts of financing possibilities will be confiscated according to Article 54 of the TCC.

6.2. Qualified Positions of Terror Crimes in terms of Commission

This topic is an entirely new judgment, which has accordingly been enacted for public needs and necessity after thirty years of terrorist activity in the country. Some government officials used to misuse their official responsibilities and authority supplied by the state to them. For those reasons, if an official misuses intentionally his/her authority to aid in the commission of organized crime, he/she will be punished more heavily than an ordinary citizen. The text of Article 8/A is as follows:

"Qualified position: Article 8/A[5]: If terror crimes, counted and regulated in this Act, are committed by misusing government supplied influence, it will be punished by having the punishment mentioned in the TCC increased by half in amount."

6.3. The Problem of Jurisprudential Organization's Responsibility in terms of Terrorism

The judgment of Article 8/B is entirely a new one. Some experience about terror organizations has been gained during the last thirty years. One type of eperience is learning about the use of innocent organizations as a "cover" for a crime organization. For this reason, the aim of the enacted Article 8/B is to prevent misuse of organizations and unions. The text is as follows;

"The responsibility of organization: Article 8/B: Whichever crime, being mentioned and included in the PTA, is committed in the framework of an activity of an establishment or of an association, will carry as punishment for the organization "security precautions," being peculiar to them, and mentioned in Article 60 of the TCC. Article 60 includes two types of precautions; (1) Cancellation of given permission, (2) Confiscation of earned revenues.

6.4. Investigation and Prosecution Procedures

This topic has been renewed as a whole in Article 10 of the PTA as follows:

"Investigation and Prosecution procedure: Article 10[5]: Concerning crimes included in the PTA, judgments of Article 250 and 252 of Criminal Trial Act are applied firstly. If there are no rules within those articles, other rules of Criminal Trial Act are applied secondly. However;

    a. Public prosecutor could inform only one relative of a suspect, if there is a danger of negatively affecting the investigation,
    b. A suspect may make use of legal guidance of only one defender while in custody. The right to interview a suspect could be limited within 24 hours, by the decision of a judge, depending on the demand of the public prosecutor, but a suspect may not be interviewed and his/her testimony may not be written down for 24 hours.
    c. While a suspect is interviewed by a policeman, only one defender can be there,
    ç. The register numbers of official interested persons should be written down instead of their open identities in the written report being drawn up by the police.
    d. The right of the defender to see the investigation file can be limited by a judge's decision after the application of the public prosecutor, if this would negatively affect the investigation.
    e. Documents of defender, his files, and interview records with a detainee, can never be examined because of an investigation of crimes mentioned in this PTA coverage. But if the defender mediates between participants of a terror organization and this activity is proved, the public prosecutor may apply to a judge to have an official present at future interviews with the detainee. In addition to this limitation, the judge can examine the documents which are given by either detainee to defender or defender to detainee. The judge decides what may be passed on. Every interested one can plead about the decision to the court.
    f, g. (some exceptions of the basic rule are mentioned at these paragraphs)"

Therefore, upon those exceptions: correspondence and communication of a terror suspect can be electrinically monitored by court order under the direction of a special investigator appointed by the court.

6.5. Prohibition of Changing Main Punishment to Alternative Sanction

Two types of execution systems have been accepted for personalization of punishment in the Turkish criminal execution system; the first is changing main punishment to

---

[5] This article was completely new and was added by the Amending Act.

alternative sanction; the second one is postponing punishment. Both of these are not applied to terror crimes. The text is as follows:

"Prohibition of Changing Main Punishment to Alternative Sanction: Article 13[6]: The prison punishment in the frame of the PTA may never be changed to any kind of alternative punishment or may never be postponed for any time. But this rule may not be applied to a person under 16 years old."

As a result, the prison punishment may not be changed to alternative sanction, or postponed. However, persons under 16 years old will be excepted from these special rules and the general criminal law procedures may be applied to them.

6.6. Reward

A system of rewards for information to cause the collapse of terror organizations, or to allow a member of a terror organization to leave it after they understood it and its aim is the purpose of Article 19. The text of the article is as follows:

"Being Reward: Article 19[6]: Whoever, under the condition that he/she has not participated in committing a terror crime, has helped arrest criminals of terrorist crime, being mentioned in the PTA, or has informed police of their identity or location, they would be rewarded with money. The sum of the reward and payment procedure are declared in regulations of the Interior Ministry."

6.7. Using Force and Weapon against Terrorist

Generally speaking, policemen and other government officials, charged with keeping public order and security, have had to use force against terrorists and organized criminals. The use of force has been limited within some conditions, declared in the PTA. The additional Article 2[7], contains these condition as follows:

"In whatever operations that are executed against terror organizations by government powers, There must first be a warning and an offer of peaceful surrender. After this warning, officials may use force in balance with other side's defenses and resistance. The last degree of using force is directly to use weapons on the target without interruption."

There is no doubt about the difficulty of the above mentioned rule in practice. It is hoped that this rule is not illogically executed. Using weapons on a target without interruption is a very controversial subject. The judge has to investigate this situation in every way possible, whether the above mentioned conditions are obeyed or not.

7. Conclusion

The Prevention of Terrorism Act covers twenty five articles, some of which have been translated above and explained in brief. As it has been seen. the main articles regulate human rights according to European standards in terms of human and civil rights. After becoming a candidate state for the EU, Turkey has to enact or to renew her essential acts as such. Previous Turkish Criminal Law, translated from Italy and enacted in 1926, has completely been changed and a new national TCC put into practice; and previous Turkish Criminal Law Procedure, translated from Germany and enacted in 1928, has also completely been changed and a new national Turkish Criminal Law Procedure put

---

[6] This article was completely new and was added by the Amending Act.
[7] This additional article was completely new and was added by the Amending Act.

into practice. The Amending Act of PTA, Law no: 5532, of 29 June 2006, does not contain and describe a new crime and punishment but modifies several articles of Criminal Act and of Criminal Judgment Act.

Turkish experiences, being gained with preventing terror throughout thirty years, has guided the new amendment act of the PTA. If such measures are not enacted and applied, the unity of the land and nation could be endangered in the very near future. Turkey has lived with and gained experience about the terrorist initiative by organized groups. This is very important for Turkey and for the Turkish people. The original Act of PTA has been amended several times, and the last major amendment has been done to establish parallelism between European standards concerning human rights, and Turkish basic acts concerning human and civil rights, in 2006. The Turkish Parliament did not create and describe any new crime in terms of preventing terror and terrorist groups. It kept its power within the framework of basic and general TCC and within a few acts concerning or defining specific subjects. It never created a new crime in this field, but it only made the punishments of those crimes more severe on one hand, and it brought a new investigating and judging procedure to bear on those crimes on the other hand. The basic legal principles prevailing in criminal law are obeyed. Nobody knows what terrorists will do today or tomorrow. For that reason, a few protective measures, concerning officials in charge of the machinery of justice and of security organizations, were enacted in this amendment. However, we have no more time to mention all those rules and measure here in this paper.

Terrorist Activities in Kyrgyzstan and Precautionary Measures

Kambarali T. KONGANTIEV
Attorney General of Kyrgyz Republic

Abstract. An overview of recent terrorist activities in Kyrgyzstan was provided from the perspective of Kyrgyz law enforcement. In that context the nature of terrorism in the region, and particularly, the compositions and objectives of terrorist groups were discussed. Further analysis led the author to touch upon the current challenges posed by international terrorism to the Central Asian countries in general, and to provide the views for further perspectives on the war on terrorism. Emphasis was placed on the importance of global cooperation in countering terrorism in Central Asia.

Keywords. Terrorism, religious extremism, Kyrgyzstan, law enforcement, Central Asia, Islamic Movement of Uzbekistan (IMU), global security

Introduction

The present paper sheds light on the current situation and approaches of the law enforcement of Kyrgyz Republic toward the most serious threat in modern times, international terrorism and extremism. In this context, this paper covers not only the analysis of activities of law enforcement on the war against terrorism, but also provides temporary views of the specialists and practitioners regarding the sources, conditions and emergence of radicalism in all its appearances. Special emphasis was placed on social roots of terrorism and religious extremism, while describing the influences of social factors on the process of maintenance and vital activity of the fundamentalist militants.

For the example of Kyrgyzstan, its current socio-economic situation, the path of organizational processes of modern extremist groups and their methods of recruitment of new members were tracked. Besides, the current paper presents the practice of law enforcement operational activities towards uncovering, localization and liquidation of militant groups and the variety of social works targeted at uncovering the inhuman and anti-national essence of terrorism. The following chapters include scientific and special works of Russian and Kyrgyz scholars and practitioners dealing with anti-terrorism. There are also a number of examples from recent experiences of special services of the republic.

1. Recent Terrorist Activities in Kyrgyzstan

In contemporary years, the world has been witnessing a rapid rise of terrorist and extremist activity. Acts of terrorists have more often been causing multiple casualties, substantial destruction and material losses. Threats of the 21st century might pose serious obstacles to further economic, social, and political modernization of our countries.

In a number of states of the Commonwealth of Independent States (CIS), terrorist acts and extremist activity bring about substantial concerns, for they pose a real threat to stability and national security. Kyrgyzstan has repeatedly faced the activities of terrorist groups. In 1999-2000 in the South -the Batken valley- armed forces of the republic were involved in local battles against terrorist guerillas moving from Afghanistan and thus prevented them from entering neighboring Uzbekistan.

On May 12, 2006, a group of terrorists attacked a border post located in the Isfana region of the Republic of Tajikistan, seized seventeen automatic guns and one machine gun, and further attacked a border post in the Batken valley of Kyrgyzstan. After that, the terrorists continued their way by car towards the inner parts of our country. As a result of a special operation on elimination of the armed terrorist group, four of them were killed and one was captured. A search for other members of the group is currently going on. The captured criminals possessed a large amount of ammunition, radios, and religious literature.

A joint investigation group of the prosecutor's office, the police, and the department of national security of Batken valley have accomplished the criminal investigation on Hujaev N.J., Rakhmanov M.M., Shadiev M.A., Joroev M.A., and Nishanbaeva D.A., who were accused of the formation of an illegal armed group, brigandage, attempted forceful usurpation of the government, summons for violent alteration of the constitutional structure, terrorism, and murder. Investigation indicates that the citizen of the Republic of Uzbekistan Akhunov R.A. under an alias of 'Bakhtiyor' is one of the active members of the extremist terrorist organization the Islamic Movement of Uzbekistan (IMU), who had been hiding in the territory of Kyrgyz Republic from the prosecution of Uzbekistan's law enforcement for violent crimes. He had set up a criminal group, which included the citizens of Kyrgyzstan: Rakhmanov M.M., Matiev A.B. (alias 'Abdurahman'), Yuldashev A.K. ('Artyk'), Kamilov H.A. ('Atabek'), Abdullajanov A.G. ('Achyl'), Shadiev M.A., Joroev M.A., and Joroev T.K. on the one hand, and on the other, following citizens of Uzbekistan: Sodikov N.K. ('Palvan'), Khujaev N.J. ('Abdurahmon'), Juraev, M.T. ('Sayfullo'), and Zakirdinov N.D. ('Shurik'). At the same time Akhunov R.A., Sodikov H.K., Khujaev N.J., and Juraev M.T. in 1999-2000 had received special training in guerilla camps under the supervision of field commander Hojiev Jumabay, also known as 'Juma Namangani.'

Other members of the group are from Tajikistan: Rakhimov D.R. ('Bilol'), Rakhimov F.R. ('Abdullo'), Shaknobinov A.A. ('Umar'), Rakhmatov A.A. ('Bekcha'), Umarov A.A. ('Ibrahim'), and Boboev A.A. And the following persons are not identified by the investigation: 'Olmas,' 'Bakhram,' 'Holys,' 'Aziz,' 'Ikram,' 'Dilshod,' and 'Ulugbek.' These people appear to be the members of the following religious extremist organizations: Bayat, Hizb ut-Tahrir, extremist terrorist organization IMU, and were hiding on the soils of foreign Central Asian countries from prosecution of law enforcement agencies of Uzbekistan and Tajikistan for committing violent crimes including murder, banditry, terrorism, and the like.

The main goals of this criminal organization were launching religious conflicts, forceful alteration of the existing constitutional base and building an Islamic state (Caliphate), conducting holy war 'jihad' against people of other religions and 'infidel Muslims.' Their activities were perfectly organized, stable, based on hierarchy, had a well-collaborated system of conspiracy and protection from law enforcement, and involved weapons. It is worth noticing that certain members of this organization were involved in recruitment of local inhabitants of Osh, Jalal-Abad, and Batken valleys, and Osh city in pursuit of agitation and propagandizing the ideas, views, and goals of the extremist terrorist organization IMU, Organization for Liberation of Turkestan, and religious extremist organization Hizb ut-Tahrir. Particularly, in a period of time from September 2005 to May 2006 in the villages of Karavan and Kok-Talaa of Kadamjay province they attempted to recruit local inhabitants Akhunbaev Sh. M., Temirbaev T.K., Taylakov M.A., and Shamiev A.J. However, their efforts were rejected by the latter, who appreciated the criminality of their (terrorists') activities.

In the middle of April 2006, members of this criminal organization had continuously traveled to mountainous areas of Kojo-Kayir and Dangi in Mazar village of Kadamjay province in search of a convenient place to hide from law enforcement, and also to store their weaponry, ammunition and food. At the same place they had conducted their militant trainings and reconnaissance of the area.

The affiliation of the above-mentioned persons, the members of criminal organization of the extremist terrorist organizations of IMU, Organization for Liberation of Turkistan, and religious extremist organization of Hizb ut-Tahrir has been fully proved by the testimonies of suspects and witnesses, and evidence - a large collection of apprehended literature, CDs, and official documents obtained from operative services of the Ministry of Interior and the National Security Agency of Kyrgyz Republic, Republic of Uzbekistan, and Tajikistan.

Taking into account that the terrorist groups are commonly composed of representatives of various countries and they act on the soils of a number of countries, the international cooperation is viewed to be of current importance. Religious extremism currently appears to be more salient in our country. The biggest threat is posed by various missionaries, who are infiltrating malicious seeds of religious extremism into the minds of people. Basically, their activities construct an ideological basis for terrorism.

2. Kyrgyz Law Enforcement Response to Terrorism

Withstanding international terrorism and extremism will be possible through concerted measures of the entire global community, but not of only the countries that have been suffering from terrorists and extremists. Undoubtedly, adequate response to this 'evil' requires solid and immediate measures of law enforcement, including prosecution.

On August 6, special divisions of the National Security Agency (NSA) of Kyrgyz Republic conducted the second phase of anti-terrorism operation in South Kyrgyzstan. Previously, on June 14 in Jalal-Abad the special task division 'Alpha' of NSA destroyed a militant group of the IMU, which through the course of several years had been involved in subversive activity in Central Asian countries. This time the location of the operation was Osh city.

The intelligence indicated that three IMU guerillas were located in the city. NSA operatives had no choice but to act immediately. Besides the information about *IMUers'* possession of weapons and ammunition, which was prepared for terrorist acts on our soil, there was well-grounded suspicion about the extremists' intentions to exact revenge on the special service agencies of Kyrgyzstan for the death of their comrades.

Despite the time constraint, special service agencies quickly prepared for the elimination of religious radicals. They, as their fellow terrorists earlier killed in Jalal-Abad, were directly linked to the events of May 12th, when an armed group premeditatedly attacked the Tajik border post of Lyakkan, and in the aftermath conducted a bloody raid in Kadamjai province of Batken valley. Eight Tajik and six Kyrgyz officers were killed by the bandits.

The main objective of the Osh operation was to repel the extremists from dense precincts of the city in order to avoid civilian casualties. After the accomplishment of the first phase, the operatives worked for the apprehension of the culprits. They were driving a Daewoo Nexia. The attempt to stop the car brought no results. The militants not only ignored the order to stop the vehicle but launched gunshots from an automatic weapon. The response fire from the NSA operatives resulted in the death of all three in the vehicle.

Examination of the vehicle revealed the following findings: a shortened Kalashnikov automatic gun with three loaded magazines for it, 266 bullets for the Kalashnikov, four RGD-5 grenades, one F-1 grenade ('the lemon'), one magazine for a Kalashnikov machine gun with weaponry, military binoculars, a road map of Uzbekistan, underground religious extremist literature (printed and on electronic data holders), and forged passports. It is worth noting that some inhabited areas on the Uzbek map were checked with the word 'jihad.'

It is known that the automobile with two militants and one spiritual cleric in it and belonged to Muhammadrafik Kamalov. He was driving at the time of the operation. The press service of the NSA has already spread the information that on May 24, 2006 he was giving his testimony to officers of the Osh valley regional NSA headquarters concerning his tight relationships with earlier killed leaders of armed IMU groups Nazimjan Sadykov and Abdulvasut Matiev, the existence of telephone numbers of other IMU members in his notebook, and illegal propaganda materials of religious-extremist content which included the video of IMU militant trainings and speeches of the ideological inspirer of the *IMUers* Tahir Yuldashev, that were found in his home. At that time Muhammadrafik Kamalov swore to Allah's name, to the Koran, and his own wife that he has no relationship with any terrorists. Now it is hard to give any evaluation of the humane attitude of the NSA officers, who, as we see it, did not take necessary measures regarding the suspect. However, the analysis of foreign trips of the dead show that at that moment there might be many more questions about his address. In barely five years from September 2001 to February 2005, he made 15 flights to Iran, Pakistan, Turkey, UAE and other Islamic countries. This mere fact might not give any clue, but the investigation is aimed to thoroughly examine the purpose of these trips.

The final thing to add is that during the funeral of Muhammadrafik Kamalov, in late evening (contrary to traditional Muslim customs) the citizens supporting Hizb ut-Tahrir's ideas organized a procession on the streets of Kara-Suu bearing the funeral litter on their shoulders with the body of the dead on it. They would scream 'Allah Akbar!' This incident, undoubtedly, impaired the public order in the city. Most of the Kara-Suu inhabitants openly expressed their disdain with an extremely original 'demonstration.'

Of course, one has to fairly appreciate the local authorities. The emotional tension had become too high, so that it was too difficult to take any measures under those circumstances. In fact, would it be necessary? Fighting for the conscience of our citizens will be better at another time and by other means. The dead body of the imam, in turn, was committed to the earth, in contrast to terrorists, whose bodies were not given to their relatives, and the place of their burial remains unknown.

At this moment, the main threats to Kyrgyzstan are terrorism, extremism, and separatism. During the last several years special agencies of our republic managed to substantially damage the capabilities of the IMU, which significantly weakened their extremist manifestations. Of course it would not be possible without contributions of national agencies of the Central Asian countries, and primarily of Kyrgyzstan and Uzbekistan.

It is my view that the resistance of the IMU hasn't been totally crushed, which is indicated by a number of sallies of the terrorists. Particularly, they showed up in Batken, Jalal Abad, and now in Osh city. At the same time, however, there are a number of successful special operations, which resulted in elimination of certain leaders of the IMU. Among them there are such odious individuals as Zakitdinov Nuritdin, Sadykov Nurimjan, etc.

Law enforcement officers continue to seize extremist literature from the *Kyrgyzstanian*, which has recently been widely spread in the Southern part of the republic. Recently, a case of preserving and distributing religious extremist literature was discovered in the North of Kyrgyzstan. Forty-four brochures of propagandist content were found in Kyrgyz-Ata village in the Osh valley. Illegal literature was found in the house of one of the village inhabitants. According to the testimony of the detained, he accepted the books in May from a stranger, who did not hide his membership in an illegal organization, Hizb ut-Tahrir. While handing the brochures over to the villager, the stranger asked him to distribute them among the inhabitants of Kyrgyz-Ata. To what extent that order was successfully executed, and what amount of the literature was spread by the perpetrator so far, remains unknown. According to the reports of law enforcement, this is not a single case of seizing extremist literature in big numbers. Thus, only in one week in one of the settlements of Jalal Abad valley there were found 600 brochures of Hizb ut-Tahrir.

Hizb ut-Tahrir al Islamiyah (Party of Liberation of Islam) was founded by a man famous in Muslim-Arabic milieu, Takuiddin al-Nabhani, a judge of the shariah court in Jerusalem. In 1953 he established a Sunni religious political party, the main ideology of which was the Shariah law, and the objective is to establish a unified Islamic theocratic country, the Caliphate, which would unite all the Muslim countries. In 1997 after Takuiddin Nabhani passed away, Palestinian Abdul Zullum succeeded to the leadership of the party, who considered that the main tool of Hizb ut-Tahrir for building the Caliphate has to be jihad.

In Kazakhstan and in the CIS countries, the party Hizb ut-Tahrir is considered illegal. The recent activities of its members more often directly go to a clash with the criminal legislation of these countries. The most vivid example is the revealed groups of members of Hizb ut-Tahrir in Russia and Uzbekistan, where not only religious literature of extremist orientation but also a solid arsenal of firearms and explosives have been seized. As marked by law enforcement agencies, the age of members of the organization is noticeably getting younger each year, and now among active participants of Hizb ut-Tahrir, it's more often possible to see students and people under thirty.

In the territory of the Kyrgyz Republic, there operate eight of seventeen organizations recognized as terrorist by the Supreme Court of Russia. On August 8, 2006, the Russian Newspaper with reference to the Center of Public Relations of FSB (FSA-Federal Security Agency) of Russia has published a list of about 17 organizations representing the greatest terrorist threat to the safety of Russia, with detailed information on them. They are the Base (Al-Qaeda), the Party of Islamic Liberation (Hizb ut-Tahrir al Islami), the Islamic Group (Djamaat al Islami), the Islamic Party of Turkistan (previously the Islamic Movement of Uzbekistan), the Society of Renascence of an Islamic Heritage (Djamiyat ihya at-Turaz al-Islami), the House of Two Sacred (Al- Hara-Meiyn), Islamic Jihad-Jamaat of Modjaheds, and Djund ash-Sham.

3. Central Asian Countries in the Context of Global Security

The imposition of global security challenges on intra-regional problems, which in full measure appear in the Central Asian region, in the long run can bring about at least two major consequences, which are necessary to consider for the further long term development of the region.

First, there has been a sharply declined 'area of security' for the population of the countries in the region during the recent several years, which finally leads to its massive weakening. Thus, for instance, 4.2 million people have migrated within and outside the region since 1996. Multiple increases of the threat of drugs, organized crime and international terrorism under the conditions of unstable social and economic circumstances facilitate a new wave of migration of the population, which substantially weakens the human intellectual potential of Central Asia.

Central Asia currently deals with an entire complex of socio-economic, national, ideological, and psychological problems capable of facilitating the growth of terrorist and religious-extremist activity for a long time. A particular role in the given problem is attributed to the constantly evolving transit of Afghanistan-made drugs through the territory of Central Asia to the CIS countries and Western Europe. The estimations of representatives of the EU show that today drug trafficking makes about 65% of the total value of illicit drugs entering the illegal drug market of European countries.

The illegal circulation of drugs is gaining more and more an inter-regional and trans-boundary character, taking the form of drug aggression against the new independent states. Transit of Afghani opium through Tajikistan, Kyrgyzstan, and Uzbekistan sharply destabilizes the situation in Central Asia. The deterioration of the socio-economic situation in the region leads to the growth of criminality and radicalization of religious views of the population.

The counterterrorist operation of the international community in Afghanistan, Operation Enduring Freedom, has not touched the plantations of the Afghani peasants, where the growth of the opium poppy continues to be the most profitable business for simple peasants and the field commanders, supervising separate areas of Afghanistan. The illegal drug circulation and the financial assets accumulated here still represent one of the strong sources of international terrorism in Central Asia.

Secondly, throughout many centuries the Central Asian region has had a peripheral value in the global system. The achievement of independence by the countries of the region and their entrance into the international scene as independent actors in the organization of global political, economic, cultural and other communications, in combination with huge amounts of raw and human resources have put the Central Asian region into the category of priority and strategically important areas. In case of an inability of the countries of the region to conduct a coordinated foreign policy, Central Asia may lose that significant position in the world geopolitical and geo-economic system, which it has gained during the last years. This given fact may have a direct reflection on the reception of financial, intellectual, and other investments by the CA countries from more developed countries of the world and authoritative international organizations.

The possibility of failure in the context of the emerging 'global safety landscape' is fraught with danger for the countries of the region (including the Kyrgyz Republic); failure could reduce the role and the position of the states-participants, which are inadequate to this standard, to those of observers from a peripheral zone.

This means that these countries will face substantial limitations in terms of their access to the world's financial, informational, technological, communicational, and other resources required for a wider human and intellectual reproduction as a basis of any viable state. In conditions of globalization and speeding-up of economic, political, cultural, and other processes, it could lead to the virtual exclusion of the Central Asian states from the global community, and the decrease of trust of the population in the state as the basic guarantor and a source of well-being.

This kind of development of the situation can lead to negative consequences, the growth of religious and ethnic intolerance, and prosperity of the international terrorism and all its negative consequences. They, in turn, put under question all achievements of the Central Asian states during the last 15 years of independence, and thus simultaneously demand the allocation of enormous financial assets away from the sphere of development to the issues of combating international terrorism and organized crime.

What kind of way out is seen in the current situation? It would be unfair to state that the Central Asian countries do not undertake anything towards solving the problem of international terrorism and other threats destroying the stability of this region. The evolution of the situation in Afghanistan and frontier areas has proved that sooner or later the countries of Central Asia will face this problem directly. The only question is when and where it will occur.

What is the secret of such an active dissemination of religious extremism? In the opinion of the writer Robert Wiland, the secret of success for Islamic missionaries is the strong discipline, embodied in the detailed program of 'obedience' to God, (the word 'Islam' literally means 'submission to Allah'). People are getting tired of the disorder and their own excessive freedom, which gives them a sense of uselessness. Islam offers the precise focus of worshipping.

V. Ali Polosin, the Adviser of the Chairman of Counsel of Muftis of Russia, has an interesting judgment about the role of Islam in the modern reality. Once, the Byzantine Christian-soldiers had a custom of taking away babies from Turkish women, boiling them, and sprinkling their own right hands with the obtained liquid in order to make their hands invincible. And they found justification for it in the Bible, where it is said: "Not I have brought the world to you, but a sword." Well, so should we now consider the Bible as an extremist book?

The matter is not the religions themselves, but the position they take in a society, or more precisely, to what degree this position is appropriate for an ideological pivot of the revolutionary moods. It is a peculiarity of people to struggle for justice and equality, and for struggling they need a strong spiritual idea. Formerly it was Christianity, which was followed by Marxist doctrines, and now Islam. Why? The answer is, simply because there is a need for an idea which has an active socio-economic-political importance. In other words, the person willing to make this world a better place needs the rules of life dictated from on high. Once, the Christian church used to take this position. But now it has departed from the secular causes, has worked well with the government, and does not participate in social life but is engaged in merely spiritual and ceremonial affairs.

Communism has become obsolete too. But the ideas of Islam, conformable with the words of Mohammed: "All of you are equal, as teeth of a hairbrush," are perfectly disposed to struggle for equality and brotherhood. Islam is a socially-active religion, the religion of revolutionaries. Whether it is used by unscrupulous people is another issue. It is very easy to transform revolutionary ideas into terrorist ones. It is enough to slightly alter the interpretation, and in the name of an ideal, people will start to commit crimes instead of doing feats. Once in the past the same happened to Christianity. There was a time when crusades were arranged in pursuit of capturing new lands. In essence, those were ordinary robberies and murders for profit under the veil of a religious idea.

In that context, extremism is not popular among Muslims, but Islam is popular among extremists. The reason is that it is convenient to them to be covered by its power, which at the same time perverts its ideas. And Muslims themselves are struggling with this misfortune. For example, Saudi Arabia is considered to be the center of extremism. In fact, however, the most popular there is a rigid current of Islam, a fundamentalism, but in no way extremism. So, the antiterrorist operations there tend to occur on a regular basis.

4. Discussion

Factors that help the survival and prosperity of the idea of religious radicalism, in our view, first of all, are the social ones, namely the poverty of many developing countries. Those factors are the main contributors to the reinforcement of radical Islamic extremists and international terrorists. In particular, emissaries of the terrorist organizations tend to recruit new adherents among the miserable of the population, especially the youth. Driven to despair by gloomy poverty, young men willingly enroll in the ranks of Al-Qaeda and other radical movements. For this reason, it is necessary for the world community to draw the attention of rich countries and international donor organizations to systematic and regular assistance in decreasing the level of poverty in developing countries. And at the same time the governments of these countries must address efforts to raising their own economy and decreasing the level of poverty. It is a common global task for all those national and international antiterrorist forces that are interested in the elimination of the social causes of the emergence and distribution of Islamic fundamentalism and radicalism.

Mass media plays an important role in the popularization and attractiveness of Islamic militant groups. Both visual and printed sources, depicting terrorists as fighters for national freedom and rights of the poor, cause a positive reaction among the watchers and readers in many countries. Thus, there is created a halo of martyrs and self-sacrificers for the sake of -allegedly- the ideas of Islam and the people's defense. It appears that international organizations under the aegis of the United Nations, and also public associations of journalists, should give an unequivocal fundamental evaluation of these sorts of publications and urge the mass-media makers to undertake a more responsible and weighted approach to publication of the issues related to the Islamic movement and activities of illegal militant groups. We also consider that it is necessary to direct the efforts of the governments and the international organizations toward the prevention of the financing of terrorist groups, revealing and blocking monetary accounts of similar organizations and their counterparts.

5. Conclusion

We completely support and are at one with the principles of the global counter terrorist strategy on the necessity of convincing people to refuse terrorism or any support for it; on prevention of terrorists from accessing the means of their attacks; prevention of support for terrorism by countries; strengthening capabilities of countries to exterminate terrorism and protect human rights that were ventilated in the report of the UN Secretary General Kofi Annan. We adhere to the resolutions of the UN and of the Counter-terrorism Security Council, particularly, resolutions number 1267 (1999), 1372 (2001), and 1540 (2004), as well as all international agreements of the Kyrgyz Republic concerning countering terrorism and extremism.

In the final analysis, it is desirable to note that today our country actively runs an antiterrorist campaign, for which our armed forces use new methods and forms of work. For example, we have addressed all participants of illegal formations with an appeal to voluntarily give themselves up, and to those who have weapons to hand them over to law enforcement agencies. The first results give us hope. We already have a number of volunteers who have turned away from their further illegal activities based on the ground of religious extremism. On the other hand, a big explanatory work is being carried out among the citizens, and monetary rewards are offered for any information about the residence of terrorists and active supporters of The Islamic party of Turkistan (IPT) and Hizb ut-Tahrir. Our hope is that these measures will bring desired outcomes.

Despite the present serious economic and social hardship, our country, undoubtedly, will stay as a sovereign country capable of effectively struggling with enemies and defending its own interests and maintaining security. Special services of Kyrgyzstan will put maximum efforts on fighting against international terrorism and extremism.

Today as never before there is a necessity for unification of the existing potential and expanding the efforts on the entire scope of tasks that we are facing. In particular, those tasks are the enforcement of law and order, war against transnational criminality, drug trafficking, and international terrorism and extremism. I have confidence that tighter cooperation of law enforcement agencies of the global community, constant information sharing and conducting joint operations will assist in solving those problems.

At the same time, considering the communications branches of the terrorist organizations on an international scale, it is necessary to integrate the efforts of law enforcement agencies on the regional as well as on the global scale. We have all the confidence that today's conference will give a new impulse to the issues of understanding the essence of international terrorism, and will allow us to operate with more coordination in counteraction to all threats posed by the radical organizations, which cause incalculable troubles to mankind and are capable of destroying the fragile world stability, and claiming new victims among innocent people. So, let us unite around the most common and important problem of rescuing our civilization from a real plague of the current century - international terrorism, radicalism, and extremism.

International Cooperation as a Strategy of Fighting and Prevention Terrorism in Georgia

Giuli ALASANIA
International Black Sea University, Georgia

Abstract. Terrorism, information warfare, political violence and gray-area phenomena are becoming burning problems of the international community. Transnational threats -terrorism and organized crime- cut across national boundaries and are beyond the control of individual governments. With the trend toward globalization, the action of fighting terrorism is becoming a global task which requires the international cooperation of different countries and their governments. The paper examines the cooperative actions in Georgia of fighting terrorism as an example to demonstrate the importance of international cooperation and a practical suggestion for accomplishing it.

Keywords. Terrorism, corruption, cooperation, organized crime, security, legislation

Introduction

"Transnational crime will be a defining issue of the 21st century for policymakers - as defining as the Cold War was for the 20th century and colonialism was for the 19th. Terrorists and transnational crime groups will proliferate because these crime groups are major beneficiaries of globalization. They take advantage of increased travel, trade, rapid money movements, telecommunications and computer links, and are well positioned for growth" [1].

The international paradigm for combating terrorism involves the application of all elements of its power and influence: diplomatic, financial, intelligence, law enforcement, and military activities. Georgia faces an immediate threat to its security and integrity: A network based upon an intolerant ideology, advocating disruption of territorial integrity. Georgia is endangered by activities of international organized crime, which include trafficking in narcotics, weapons, persons, and nuclear, biological and chemical materials. The strategic goal of Georgia is to protect, reunify, rehabilitate its territories, regain its integrity and deprive organized crime and terrorism through international cooperation.

The dissolution of the Soviet Union could not abolish its unpleasant legacies, including corruption in independent states, all at once. Georgia was no exception. The collapse of the economy, the civil war, ethnic conflicts and territorial losses were factors that accompanied the independence of Georgia. As a result of stealing money from the national budget and gerrymandering presidential, parliamentary and local elections, the second president of Georgia, Eduard Shevardnadze, and his government completely lost the support of the people and finally were overthrown in November 2003 by the 'Rose Revolution.'

Another step forward to overcoming the problems was the 'Palm Revolution' in Adjara in May 2004. It resulted in the overthrowing of a criminal clan headed by the corrupt and authoritarian leader Aslan Abashidze, who had long ruled there [2]. After a successful Police Operation in Upper Abkhazia (Kodori Gorge), law and order were reestablished in this part of Georgia. The newly elected president of Georgia (in January 2004) Mikheil Saakashvili and his government started reforms in all spheres and as a result, many positive reforms were enacted. In fact, the World Bank, the IMF, and other international financial organizations assessed Georgian Financial Indicators for 2005 as successful. According to the World Bank, Georgia ranked 1st in the world for the intensity of reforms in 2006, moving up from 2nd position in 2005. The 2006 State of the World Liberty Index data indicated that Georgia holds the 58th position among 166 countries.

Among 163 countries, Georgia was ranked 99th in a '2006 Corruption Perception Index (CPI)' issued by the Corruption Watchdog Transparency International on November 6. Georgia was ranked 130th among 159 nations surveyed in a similar report by Transparency International last year [3].

In terms of current changes, the security system also improved in Georgia. The security sector reform comprises law enforcement and defense. Border management includes the EU Special Representative's Office in Georgia, a successful cooperation in the process of Border Management reform. The Border Guard was transformed from a paramilitary force into a police-type agency. The budget of the Border Police increased significantly (from 21 ml in 2005 to 34 ml 2006). The budget of the Border Police has been decentralized to the level of regional units. Moreover, a joint technical scheme of border and customs management has been elaborated. Since the institution of border guards is extremely important and there are no professionals in the field of Border Police, a faculty has been established in the Police Academy.

The process of Security Defense Reform (SDR) development is at an advanced stage. The work here started from organizing documents. Currently all conceptual documents are in place: The National Military Strategy, Threat Assessment; Vision statements of the Minister of Defense and of the Chief of the General Staff have been created. Also, the priorities of the Defense Policy in 2006 have been determined.

New responsibilities demanded structural changes that have been conducted and as a result responsibilities between the Ministry of Defense and General Staff have been clearly divided. From 2004 to 2006, the defense budget significantly increased. The defense budget is now transparent and open to the public. Since 2003, salaries have increased by 113%. All major infrastructures has been renovated or rebuilt. A reformation of all defense structures and management systems according to the NATO recommendation is also under way. Proceeding from these changes, the Land Forces Command has been formed, while the General Staff is in the process of being transformed into the Joint Staff. The new Law on Defense Planning is to be approved. The Planning, Programming and Budgeting System (PPBS) is under development with the support of the ministries of defense of countries such as the Netherlands and Romania.

1. Terrorism in Georgia: The Roots and Social Causes

Despite all of the above mentioned positive changes, there are reasons why the security system in Georgia still fails to be effective in some cases. One is that the presence of organized criminal groups in the Russia-backed breakaway territories of Abkhazia and

South Ossetia create favorable conditions for smuggling, trafficking and even terrorism. According to the Ministry of State Security, corruption has much decreased in the highest echelons of government after the 'Rose Revolution' [4]. However single cases of corruption can still be traced among the custom employees and border guards and the police. It keeps Georgia at risk and necessitates further changes and improvement in legislation, transnational cooperation, providing techniques, equipment, or personnel training and, more important, the restoration of political control over the breakaway territories.

The present paper deals with terrorism in Georgia, its reasons and ways of combating the current disease. The roots and causes of corruption and terrorism emerging in Georgia were basically the same as in other CIS states:

1. The end of the Cold War entailed an integration process. People started easily moving, crossing the borders. All kinds of communication became much more intensive and thus more difficult to control.
2. A transition from one socio-economic system to another, concretely from socialist property to private property and into a market economy was conducted spontaneously. The state institutions and law enforcement bodies were weak; economic, financial, tax, custom, currency and border control did not exist at all or was so inefficient that they had no influence upon the current situation. The economy collapsed and massive unemployment polarized the society.
3. Corruption at the high echelons, and a decrease of social-moral and law-legislative cultures increased internal tension, confrontation, and even engendered the civil war.
4. The escalating role of organized crime in achieving political and economic goals, the location of Georgia at crossroads, the existence of cross-border ethnic ties between Armenians in the Javakheti region, between the Azerbaijani in Red Bridge, between Ossetians in the Tskhinvali region, and Kist-Chechens in the Pankisi Gorge, as well as unresolved ethnic conflicts resulted either in uncontrolled territories (Abkhazia, South Ossetia), or war in the North Caucasus. As a result, refugees, including militants in some areas bordering on Georgia, encouraged close relations between local criminal groups and criminal groups in the other countries or even between law enforcement bodies and governmental structures (or individual officials) in Abkhazia, South Ossetia and other parts of Georgia. Georgia became a part of an international trafficking and smuggling network[1] [5, 6].

2. Legislative Basis: Preventive Measures against Corruption and Organized Crime

For the prevention of transnational organized crime, the 'National Policy against Corruption' was adopted by decree # 550 of the President of Georgia, on June 24, 2005. The main priority of the strategy is to reveal and analyze the reasons for corruption and find ways to eliminate it; to strengthen the principles of accountability and publicity, and to ensure criminals are brought to justice for corruption. The National Policy includes:

- Preventive measures, such as effective human resources management, increased transparency of public measures, publicity of financing political parties, reform

---

[1] The list can be prolonged. Some of these characteristics mentioned for describing the situation in post-Soviet Russia, correspond to post-Soviet Georgia as well.

of General Inspection, empowering the Institute of Ombudsman, improvement of the system of accounting in the institutions of public service;
- The creation of the competitive environment for the business development, including the elimination of administrative barriers;
- Institutional reforms - reforms of court and law enforcement authorities. The strategy provides for the creation of the Council of the Prosecutor General's Office, with the view of contributing to the effective management of the system of the Prosecutor's Office and participating in the appointment of prosecutors and disciplinary proceedings. It also creates the system of witness protection;
- International cooperation and ratification of Conventions;
- Involvement of the society in anti-corruption efforts.

With Decree # 377, dated September 12, 2005, the Prime Minister adopted the action plan for the National Policy against Corruption. The action plan provides for the creation of a special division at the Office of the Prosecutor General of Georgia that will be responsible for the investigation of cases of corruption committed by high-ranking officials.

In 2004-2005, the Office of the Prosecutor General of Georgia initiated the investigation of 129 criminal cases under Article 338 (bribe taking) and of 16 criminal cases under Article 339 (bribe giving) in 2005. Based on the statistical data, it is calculated that in 2003 only 111 criminal cases were initiated regarding power-abuse, while in 2004 this number increased to 329.

According to the information available for the first 5 months of 2005, 102 cases related to the abuse of power were registered. With the data available for 2004 and the first 6 months of 2005, more than 300 officials were brought to criminal responsibility for the abuse of power.

Table 1. Uniform Statistics of the Registered Crime on Terrorism
(Source: Office of Prosecutor General of Georgia)

Year	Criminal Case Registered	Investigated	Passed to the Court	Interrupted Cases
2004	8	5	1	4
2005	4	3	2	1

The natural development and result of corruption in some cases is terrorism. Georgia is not a country where terrorism is as ferocious as it is in the Middle East. However, fighting terrorism is currently one of the priorities for Georgia. A global war in all directions is being waged to achieve this goal: through military, intelligence, law and order, finance, and diplomacy actions [7]. Criminal responsibility for the crime of terrorism is provided for in the Criminal Code of Georgia. Chapter 38 of the Georgian Criminal Code entitled 'Terrorism' is consecrated to the issue. Under Article 323 of the Criminal Code, an act of terrorism is defined as:

"Explosion, setting fire, using weapons or carrying out other actions creating the threat of taking human life, causing significant property damage or other grave consequences and infringing upon public security, strategic, political or economic interests of the state, committed for the purpose of intimidating the population or making influence over state authorities."

As one can see, the definition considers terrorism as a criminal act, committed for the purpose of intimidating or making influence over state authorities. That is, this means that intimidation is a goal of terrorist act and not just a means for achieving the goal. The existing definitions for terrorism interpret this point in different manners [8]. Some scholars consider intimidation as an attribution of terrorism. The definition does not mention incentives for terrorism such as religious, ideological, or political (for instance, the British Code recently acknowledged political motivation together with religious and ideological [9].)

The National Strategy for Combating Terrorism [10] declared by the US says:

"War on Terror is a different kind of war. From the beginning, it has been both a battle of arms and a battle of ideas. Not only do we fight our terrorist enemies on the battlefield, we promote freedom and human dignity as alternatives to the terrorists' perverse vision of oppression and totalitarian rule" (pg. 1).

"Today, the principal terrorist enemy confronting the United States is a transactional movement of extremist organizations, networks, and individuals -and their state and non-state supporters- which have in common that they exploit Islam and use terrorism for ideological ends" (pg. 5).

The Georgian Code considers different kinds of terrorism: technological terrorism, using or threatening to use nuclear, radiological, chemical or bacteriological (biological) weapons, cyber-terrorism which implies obtaining computer data illegally and is characterized by a high level of threat to the public. The latter, even if present, is not frequent in the Georgian reality.

The Criminal Code of Georgia considers as a crime the terrorist act committed against a person because of his/her state or political activities, particularly, an assault on a state official with a political status (Article 325) and an assault on internationally protected persons. The latter provision ensures the compliance of Georgian legislation with the New York Convention on the Prevention and Punishment of Crimes against Internationally Protected Persons, accepted on December 14, 1973.

Article 327 makes it an offence to establish and manage the terrorist organization or participate in the activities of such an organization notwithstanding whether the mentioned organization commits the act of terrorism or not. The crime is one formal nature and will be regarded as completed from the moment of establishing the organization or being involved in its activities. Commission of the act of terrorism by this organization does not fall within the definition of the given crime and needs to be assessed separately.

The Criminal Code of Georgia also provides for other forms of terrorism, such as joining or providing assistance to a terrorist organization of a foreign country or subordinated to foreign control (Article 329) or obtaining control or blocking a strategic or especially important object for terrorist purposes (Article 330).

False notification regarding the act of terrorism is also criminalized under the Criminal Code of Georgia, since the dissemination of even false information on the preparation of the act of terrorism may cause delays in the work of the state authorities and cause significant damage.

Apart from the crimes envisaged by Chapter 38, the Criminal Code of Georgia includes a number of other crimes related to terrorism, such as production, acquisition or sale of weapons of mass destruction (Article 406), ecocide (Article 409), and obtaining control over the air or water craft or railway illegally (Article 227).

Amendments were planned for terrorism-related provisions in Georgian legislation. The package of amendments (including amendments to the Criminal Code of Georgia) drafted by the Ministry of Justice was presented to the Parliament as a legislative initiative of the President. It was adopted in its first hearing. The mentioned draft law provides for introduction of the criminal liability of legal persons for the crimes of terrorism included in Chapter 38 (Articles 323-330) of the Criminal Code of

Georgia. Liquidation or deprivation of the right to pursue activities and fines are provided as sanctions to be applied against persons for the mentioned criminal acts.

Apart from the imposition of criminal liability on persons for terrorism, the package of draft amendments introduced a number of new crimes; including financing of terrorism (Article 331 of the Criminal Code of Georgia). The necessity of criminalizing this offence derives from International Convention on the Suppression of the Financing of Terrorism of 1999 (ratified by the Parliament of Georgia with the Decree # 1486 -11 dated June 7, 2002)[2].

3. Structural Reforms: Management

Currently the Ministry of Internal Affairs (MIA) is mainly responsible for combating terrorism. In 2005 the MIA established the Counterterrorist Center and the Counterintelligence Department. They work in cooperation with local and international civil or military agencies. The first is State Border Guards Department of the Ministry of Internal Affairs, International-Analytical Department of the Ministry of Internal Affairs, and Consular Department of the Ministry of Foreign Affairs of Georgia.

A special unit of six prosecutors and investigators dedicated to terrorism financing and money-laundering cases was created in Prosecutor General's Office. Pursuant to the Law of Georgia on Facilitating the Prevention of Legalization of Illegal Incomes, the financial body, the Financial Monitoring Service, was created in the system of the National Bank of Georgia. It is the leading authority in the field of identification of money laundering (legalization of illegal incomes). It coordinates the activities of financial monitoring bodies and closely cooperates with law enforcement bodies of Georgia and with component agencies of foreign states and international organizations. Carrying out its functions it can request additional (including confidential) information from monitoring bodies, any state or local self-governing bodies and any person having an official capacity.

The Financial Monitoring Service creates the information networks and databases, processes and analyzes the information obtained from the financial monitoring bodies and other sources. The Special Operative Unit Against Money-Laundering at the Ministry of Interior of Georgia is another financial intelligence body that provides the operative services to the Special Service for Criminal Proceedings against the Legislation of Illegal Incomes of the Office of Prosecutor of Georgia.

The Financial Monitoring Service is empowered to conclude the cooperation agreement with relevant bodies of foreign states, concerning the exchange of information in the field of combating the financing of terrorism and legislation of illegal incomes. The Financial Monitoring Service is entitled to send requests to the competent authorities of foreign states and international organizations, concerning the receipt of information connected with the legislation on illegal incomes and terrorism financing and to execute such requests received from the competent bodies of foreign states and international organizations. Since globalization makes it easy for people, goods, and capital to move across borders, problems of financing terrorism must be solved on a global scale and combating it also needs joint efforts by Selina Realuyo [7].

As Stuart Levy, an assistant to the US Minister of Finance states, the investigation of the financial activity of terrorists is successful. "Information is rather reliable. People don't send money without a purpose. If there is information about a transaction, it means there is a reason. This information is concrete and you can check it. One can trace it and use it" [11].

---

[2] Data of the Office of Prosecutor General and Ministry of Justice.

4. Corruption, Smuggling, and Terrorism in Georgia

The fairly widespread view that considers terrorism as a political issue, political violence, is not, however, universally accepted. Nonetheless, the majority, among them the Georgian Criminal Law, accepts that terrorism is not homogenous by its character and the motivations and actions can be very diverse, such as criminal, religious, technological or cyber-terrorism. Luneev [12] pays attention to the casual basis of terrorism, which is diverse, in his opinion. The author indicates political, ideological, national, separatist, ethnographic, religious, psychological, territorial, geographic, social, economic and other incentives. According to the author, terrorist acts can differ in technological forms as well as the environment - terrestrial, air, marine, technological, informative, nuclear, biological, chemical, genetic etc. [12]. The definition accepted by the Georgian criminal code is more state-centric, "infringing significant property damage or other grave consequences" as it is supposed to influence an audience. One can easily explain the significance of interests of a state by a post-Soviet situation in newly emerged independent states where state interests were intertwined with the interests of non-state actors and non-state entities. For a long time officials in the highest echelons abusing power and wrongly using their rights pursued their private interests.

Terrorism in Georgia is frequently closely connected with cross-bordered activities and is therefore international. The majority of scholars think that separating terrorism from international terrorism is not correct [8]. As Beglova argues, "International terrorism is not a kind of terrorism, but a continuation of inner terrorism, it's coming out of borders of the state" [13, pg. 40].

McCarthy asserts that "to combat crime and to combat terrorism are not synonyms, but there are close links between terrorism and crime and especially organized crime" [14]. The revelation of smuggling, as well as the illegal crossing of borders, as a form of organized crime, is of utmost importance for Georgia.

In summer 2004, a scheme of the routes for transferring people as well as money, equipment, poisonous substances and explosive tools used by the international terrorist net (Al-Qaeda) and the so-called Chechen Opposition was drawn.

4.1. The Main Smuggling Flows in Georgia

- Ergneti (uncontrolled territory in South Ossetia, borders Russia);
- Red Bridge (borders Azerbaijan);
- Abkhazia (breakaway republic borders Russia, outlet to sea);
- Adjara (autonomous republic borders Turkey, outlet to sea);
- Poti (Black Sea port);
- Akhaltsikhe (borders Turkey)
- Kazbegi (borders Russia);
- Lagodekhi (borders Azerbaijan);
- Jandara (borders Azerbaijan);
- Ninotsminda (borders Armenia) [15, pg. 13].

Figure 1. Map of Georgia (Source: From the presentation of MIA)

Various goods inflow and outflow by every kind of transport: small containers and boxes loaded in light cars, buses, trucks, and tanks. Russia-backed secessionist regimes in Abkhazia and South Ossetia hinder establishing order and anti-smuggling operations; in some cases this results in military actions between Georgian and Russia-backed secessionist armed forces:

- In Abkhazia:
  o The Abkhaz part of the Georgian-Russian land border (the Psou River passes through Caucasus Mountains to Russia),
  o The Black Sea ports of Gagra, Gudauta, Sukhumi and Ochamchira,
  o The Cease Fire Line (CEL) on the Enguri River in Gali and Zugdidi districts;
- In the Tskhinvali Region:
  o The road through the Roki tunnel from Vladikavkaz (Russia) to Tskhinvali (Russia),
  o The nearby Ergneti market,
  o The roads from Ergneti market to Tbilisi and other areas of Georgia.

The breakaway Abkhazia and Tskhinvali regions bordering Russia were the main illegal partners of Georgia, followed by Turkey. The main importers and dealers of arms and drugs are Russian peacekeepers. According to a field-study, perpetrators over the border in some cases cooperate with the regional administration and the police.

The employees of Sadakhlo (Georgian-Armenian border), Red Bridge (Georgian-Azerbaijani border), Vale (Georgian-Turkish border) and Lagodekhi (Georgian-Azerbaijani and Georgian-Dagestan/Russian border) border checkpoints in Southern Georgia report good relations and cooperation with border guards on the other side, which is reflected in regular meetings and information sharing. However, some obstacles in submitting information to the central department of borders in Sadakhlo, Vale and Lagodekhi checkpoints are explained by the absence of the appropriate equipment. For that reason border guards are forced to send the border crossing information on a floppy disc once per week to Tbilisi. This does not happen on the Red Bridge, as it is equipped with modern technologies [16]. The absence of radioactive detectors as well as that of the railway platform gives rise to serious problems with the Yerevan-Tbilisi train, which is checked only after it goes 7 km into the territory of Georgia.

There is no radioactive detector on the railway passing the Red Bridge. As special research shows, the transit of radioactive materials from Central Asia through Azerbaijan and Georgia is expected and is possible here [16]. The cases of trafficking and attempts to cross the border with falsified documents were frequent on the Turkish-Georgian border, especially through Vale, which has much more simplified procedures than the Sarpi checkpoint. But the situation improved after the liberalization of the visa regime between Turkey and Georgia and important changes in border guarding and the custom system.

According to the information submitted by custom officials, corruption on the Georgian-Turkish border was essentially reduced though it still exists, as there are no technical means for revealing smuggling on the Sarpi custom point. Recently, a radioactive detector was installed and the US partners also donated an optical system that gives possibility to check the vehicles.

The research shows some difficulties in controlling the Batumi and Poti seaports due to the shortage of technical means and also customs employees. There is no radioactive detector in the Batumi seaport, which was installed in Poti by US colleagues in October 2006. The radiological service is present in the Poti seaport, but the control in general is not so good [16].

As a result of the 1999 Chechnya War, Chechen refugees, including militants of various nationalities, invaded the territory of Georgia, specifically the Pankisi Gorge. Training bases created in the Gorge attracted criminals and turned into uncontrolled territories. After the counter terrorist measures undertaken in 2002-2003, the Chechen militants left the Georgian territory. However, for a long time the Georgian territory was actively used as a transit country for different illegal activities [17]. Smuggling of drug and psychotropic materials is another burning problem for Georgia.

Several years ago the route of illegal arms transit through Georgia started from Abkhazia or South Ossetia – with the final destination point in the Pankisi Gorge. Arms came to Abkhazia on Turkish ships or they were bought from Russian militaries in Abkhazia and South Ossetia by organized crime groups and then escorted to the Pankisi Gorge by representatives of law enforcement structures of Georgia who could guarantee safety. As a result of counterterrorist operations of military and civil structures in the Pankisi Gorge, a large amount of arms was collected, training camps were liquidated and persons suspected in international terrorism were arrested. After all that, the Pankisi Gorge was purged of undesirable guests, and was supplied with humanitarian aid, maintenance, and social rehabilitation for refugees.

One can consider the radioactive materials abandoned by Russian troops on the Georgian territory as a danger and a means for potential terrorist attacks. According to recent data there have been 263 detections of radioactive materials in Georgia. If these materials are smuggled, they can be used in terrorist acts. They can also be used for bioterrorism (contaminating environment) [16].

In terms of measures on preventing illegal migration taken by the counter terrorist center in 2005-2006, there were 18 persons who violated the border regulations. Seven of them were deported according to the order of the Minister of Justice for the violation of the visa regime, three were detained for attempts to cross the Georgian border with falsified documents and a suit was initiated. Six of them were detained for crossing borders avoiding border-control checkpoints, one was detained for illegal crossing of land-border and forging documents, and a suit was initiated [17]. Georgia has to continue further improvement of border services.

Georgia is not a country where organized criminal groups are frequent and numerous. As a rule the terrorist acts performed in Georgia are perpetrated by individuals, or by groups organized for vendetta, or by the mixed groups created and orchestrated from Russia. The analysis of terrorist acts in Georgia shows that the political as well as economic reasons are dominant. Other motivation of terrorism in Georgia is not widespread. Even in case of bacteriological acts perpetrators were mainly motivated by economic or political reasons[3].

4.2. The Most Sensational Terrorist Acts in Georgia

- Assassination of Giorgi Chanturia -Leader of the Democratic Party of Georgia- 1994;
- Assassination of Soliko Khabeishvili -Chair of the Eduard Shevardnadze foundation 'For Democracy and Revival'- 1995;
- Assassination of General George Gulua -Chief of Transport Department of the Ministry of Internal Affairs- 1994;
- Two attempts of assassination of former president of Georgia Eduard Shevardnadze in 1995 and 1998;
- Terrorist acts in Zugdidi (1998) and Gori (2005);
- Failed attempt of a terrorist attack against US President George Bush and Georgian President Micheil Saakashvili (2005);
- Explosions of the main and reserve gas pipes supplying Georgia and Armenia as well as the Caucasian High voltage transmission line supplying Georgia with power in 2006;
- The Helicopter of the Minister of Defense Irakli Okruashvili was shot at by the Ossetian militants and was forced to make an emergency landing in 2006;
- Failed attempt of a terrorist attack against the Georgian Interior Minister Vano Merabishvili during his visit in Upper Abhazia in 2006.

Terrorist acts in Gori (regional centre of Georgia), failed attempt against two presidents, and explosions of the main and reserve gas pipelines have drawn more attention because of their scale. All registered terrorist acts in Georgia are of local importance, except the attempt of the terrorist act against Bush and Saakashvili.

In February 1, 2005 a terrorist act was committed near the Regional Police Department in Gori. Three police officers were killed and twenty-five citizens injured. On July 25, the Georgian Interior Minister Vano Merabishvili announced the arrest of three 'terrorists' in the breakaway region of South Ossetia and accused the Russian military of being behind 'several terrorist attacks' in the surrounding territories, including the Gori terrorist attack mentioned above. The Minister also blamed the group for a series of alleged terrorist attacks in Shida Kartli in the fall of 2004, including the explosion of high-voltage power transmission lines in Gori, a railway line in the district of Kaspi, and a radio station that served Baku-Tbilisi-Ceyhan pipeline personnel in Khashuri district.

In his television statement, the Minister claimed that Colonel Anatoly Sysoev of the Russian Staff's Central Intelligence Administration had organized the group of allegedly 1120 Russian-trained saboteurs in 2003. On July 17, 2005 Georgia's Interior Ministry

---

[3] One can compare this with the situation in Russia, where the former Minister of the Internal Affairs thinks that there are no political assassinations in Russia. All are connected with money [18, pg. 171].

conducted a special operation investigation in Avnevi, a Georgian village in South Ossetia, and arrested three residents of Tskhinvali, the capital of South Ossetian, in connection with the attacks: Gia Valiev, Gia Zasiev and Iosif Kochiev. Six more individuals were identified as members of the sabotage group and put on a wanted list. On July 26, the Georgian television broadcasts confessions by two of the suspects. In his statement, Giya Valiyev alleged that Colonel Sysoev recruited him into military intelligence and said that the Russian colonel was in regular communication with Moscow officials and traveled frequently to South Ossetia. Valiev said that he had received S 1.000 after the Gori attack from Sysoev, who then turned to Russia [19]. On October 7, 2002 Georgia along with CIS nine states signed a protocol on the confirmation of a statute concerning the order of organizing and conducting joint counterterrorist measures on the territory of the CIS member states. The latter unfortunately failed to be effective.

During President Bush's visit to Tbilisi in May 2005, Vladimir Arutunian, 27 years old, attempted to assassinate the American and Georgian presidents. Arutunian threw a hand-made grenade into a crowd of thousands of people who were listening to President Bush speaking, with Mr. Saakashvili standing next to him. Fortunately, the grenade failed to explode. Arutunian was arrested near his home in Tbilisi 10 weeks later and sentenced to life imprisonment.

On January 22, the main and reserve gas pipelines that supply Georgia and Armenia exploded 20 minutes apart on the territory of the Russian republic North Ossetia. After several hours, the Kavkasioni high voltage transmission line, which supplies Georgia with power, also exploded. Georgian officials described the explosions as an 'act of vandalism' committed by Russia. Georgian Interior Minister Vano Merabishvili commented on this act: "Last year, Georgia faced several terrorist acts... But we will investigate it all... as it was done previously." Following that declaration, on January 23, Merabishvili asked Russia to extradite two citizens, Anatoly Sisoev and Roman Boyko, to Georgia for allegedly attacking Georgian regional energy facilities in fall 2004 [20].

5. International Cooperation

As it was once again confirmed, in case of Georgia, terrorism is international by character and needs very close and intensive international cooperation. Georgia works with the international community through CIS, the UN, with the EU, OSCE on counter terrorism and homeland security. This cooperation means professional educational programs as well. The US agreed to support Georgia in developing and protecting military infrastructures, and in exchanging experience and techniques.

Since Georgia is on its way to Euro-Atlantic integration it takes definite obligations, facing some challenges. Georgia follows the Individual Partnership Action Plan (IPAP) with NATO 2004-2006. Membership of NATO as well as integration with the EU means taking part in the international fight on terrorism, offering its space and airfields, participation in different campaigns. Georgia participated in supporting the international coalition during the campaign in Afghanistan. Georgian Armed Forces participated in peacekeeping missions (the Balkans, the Persian Gulf). Mr. Howcroft, who was the US Defense Attaché in Tbilisi from 1995 to 1998, stated:

"Georgia is an important ally in the Global War on Terror. In fact, after the US, Georgia has the highest per capita percentage of forces deployed in Iraq. They have two battalions engaged in security missions there, although their entire military is less than 20.000 people" [21].

In fact, 150 Georgian militaries are deployed in the Balkans (Kosovo), 850 in the Persian Gulf (Iraq).

In accordance with the obligations under the UN Convention against Transnational Organized Crime, Georgia entered the following bilateral and multilateral Agreements concerning the international cooperation against transnational organized crime and in particular, money-laundering:

Treaty among the Government of Member States of the Black Sea Economic Cooperation Organization on the Combat against the Crime, Especially its Organized Forms (1998, October 02). Under Article 1 of the treaty, the state parties undertake to cooperate in the fields of prevention, disclosure, and investigation inter alia in the sphere of legislation of income obtained from illegal international economic operations and criminal activities, suspicious economic and bank transactions and violations in the sphere of investment. Under Article 2, the cooperation among state parties may be conducted in the spheres of common interest and mutual assistance in the field of the identifications of suspicious economic and bank transactions including the legislation of illegal incomes.

Under Article 3 of the Treaty among the Governments of Member States of the Black Sea Economic Cooperation Organization on the Combat Against the Crime, Especially its Organized Forms, the State Parties within the limits of domestic law and international obligations should create the necessary conditions in order to carry out the controlled delivery of narcotic drugs, psychotropic substances and the materials necessary for making them. Parties shall also discuss the issue of employing the method of controlled delivery in case of objects that are sold illegally. In accordance with the additional protocol of the Treaty among the Government of Member States of the Black Sea Economic Cooperation, the network of officers responsible for communication is created. The network is created with the end of strengthening the cooperation for the purpose of crime control and the coordination of interaction among the competent bodies contracting states and the establishment of an information exchange network among the law enforcement bodies of member states under the BSEC Agreement, for the purpose of an effective fight on crime and wrongdoing.

Under Article 6(2) of the protocol, all states signatories to this protocol appoint officers responsible for communications and their deputies. These officers carry out the following tasks and fulfill the functions inter alia: transmit to the relevant state the request on cooperation made pursuant to Article 5 of the BSEC Agreement, promote the exchange of legislative documents and practical experience concerning the combat against transnational organized crime, organize the periodic meetings to discuss the tendencies of transnational crime in the region for the purpose of identifying the new forms of cooperation among the law enforcement bodies of BSEC member states. By the BSEC Agreement contracting states cooperate in the sphere of education training and professional development of personnel. Parties also organize the expert meeting to solve special and urgent problems of common interests (Article 2).

Georgia concluded the international agreement with the Republic of Azerbaijan and the Republic of Turkey on the Cooperation in the Combat against Terrorism, Organized Crime and Other Serious Crimes. Under Article 12 of the Agreement the contracting states cooperate by the means of the personal exchange. By the Article 14 (II) of Agreement contracting states exchange inter alia the samples of seized narcotic drugs, psychotropic substances and their precursors. In accordance with Article 19 the state parties will take necessary steps to prevent the legislation of illegal incomes in their countries. They will operate jointly in the process of the creation of methods of combat against the legalization of illegal incomes. They will exchange the information concerning the methods and means of legalization of illegal incomes. This cooperation will be conducted according to criminal acts. According to Article 20 of the same Agreement, the state parties in accordance with their legislative acts and international obligations ensure the controlled delivery of narcotic drugs, psychotropic substances, their precursors, funds, 'black money' and other smuggling goods linked with them. The channels of communication among law enforcement bodies are also established by the Agreement.

The Georgian government has also concluded the bilateral agreement with the Government of the Republic of Latvia on the Joint Combat against Terrorism, Illegal Circulation of Narcotic Drugs and Organized Crime. Under Article 4 (3) of the Agreement contracting states in accordance with the provisions of this treaty and national legislation, cooperate by means of agreed police measures and exchanging the personnel, through the organizational support. For the purpose of rending assistance in the combat against organized crime the parties of the Agreement exchange the specialists, to receive the higher level of working experience and to learn the use of newest criminal techniques, equipment and methods used in the struggle against crime. Under Article 4 (6) of the Agreement between the Government of Georgia and Republic of Latvia the parties provide each other the samples of objects that were obtained from the crime or were employed in the commissions of the crime. Under Article 5 (2) of this agreement the state parties also cooperate by means of exchanging the information on the income generated from the criminal acts. The Agreement creates the direct channel of communication between the competent authorities in states (the Ministries of Interior of contracting states). Under Article 4 (4) state parties exchange information regarding new methods and forms in the sphere of transnational crime.

Another bilateral international agreement concerning the international cooperation in the field of combat against money-laundering is the Agreement between the Governments of Georgia and Romania on the Cooperation in the Sphere of Combat against Terrorism, Organized Crime, Illegal Trade of Narcotic Drugs, Psychotropic Substances, Their Precursors and other Grave Offences. By the Article 1(3) of this Agreement and in accordance with their legislation in force, inter alia in the field of combat against illegal acts in the sphere of economic and financial activities between the nationals of contracting parties or between foreign nationals on the territory of a contracting party, economic relations and service also in the sphere of prevention of the use of banking process for the purpose of trafficking, evading the tax paying, financial or banking fraud and money - laundering, gaining the benefit from these activities. Under Article 2 (2) of the Agreement the state parties agree to send to one another the liaison officers after the fulfillment of juridical procedures in force in their countries. The cooperation in the field of disclosure the false travel documents and visas is also provided in Article 1 (6) (b) of the Agreement.

Under Article 1 (III) (2) of the Agreement between the Government of Georgia and Arab Republic of Egypt in the Sphere of Combat Against Crime the state parties exchange the information concerning the illegal international economic activities such as money-laundering and legislation of the income gained from criminal activities and also exchange the information concerning the similar offences. Pursuant to Article 5 (3) of the Agreement, for the purpose of direct cooperation and carrying out the obligation under this Agreement the state parties convey to one another the list of competent authorities which are empowered to communicate one another and to cooperate (the competent authorities are the Ministries of Interior of each contracting party). By Article 4 (1) of Agreement contracting states share the experience concerning employment of criminal methods and means of crime research. By Article 1 (II) parties also exchange the information concerning falsification of the identification documents.

In accordance with Article 4 (3) of Agreement between the Government of Georgia and Arab Republic of Egypt contracting states exchange the methods and personnel and assist each other in the preparation of police and security forces.

Under the Paragraph 29 of the Memorandum of Mutual Understanding between the Ministry of State Security, Ministry of Interior, Ministry of Tax Incomes and Office of the Prosecutor General of Georgia and Senior Police Officers Associations of the United Kingdom of Great Britain and Northern Ireland, the Queen's prosecutors Office of England and Wales, the Office of Financial and Economic Crime, the Excise and Customs Service of Her Excellency, the National Subdivision of Crime, National Criminal Investigation Service on the Cooperation in Combat Against Grave Crime, Organized Crime, Illegal Circulation of Narcotic Drugs and in Similar Questions of Common Interest, these authorities are empowered to appoint the persons responsible for communication in order to ensure the effective cooperation.

Pursuant to Paragraph 2 (1) of the Memorandum of Mutual Understanding between the Ministry of State Security, Ministry of Interior, Ministry of Tax Incomes and Office of the Prosecutor General of Georgia and Senior Police Officers Associations of the United Kingdom of Great Britain and Northern Ireland, Queen's Prosecutor's Office of England and Wales, the Office of Financial and Economic Crime, National Criminal Investigation Service on the Cooperation in Combat Against Grave Crime, Organized Crime, Illegal Circulation of Narcotic Drugs and in Similar Questions of Common Interest, the parties also cooperate by means of collecting and providing the evidence and objects if this process does not require the employment of coercive measures.

6. Conclusion

Proceeding from the above-mentioned we can conclude that the high level of corruption in post-Soviet Georgia in the recent past was a natural phenomenon, determined by a transition from one system to another. The transition to privatization and market economy going on randomly and spontaneously resulted in the polarization of the society and was followed by increasing crime. Since 'the Rose Revolution' in 2003 the new Georgian government has undertaken reforms on a large scale, comprising law enforcement bodies, border, customs, finance, currency control, economy, legislation and international cooperation. All of this has destroyed the social and legal basis for crime.

However the existence of Russia-backed breakaway uncontrolled territories -Abkhazia and South Ossetia- hinders the process of establishing order in the country. Counter terrorism operations as well as the legislative and management measures carried out by the new Government, openly condemning terrorism destroyed the balance existing before. As the latest terrorist acts revealed, political causes were prevalent here. The economic motivation, even if available, was less involved.

Almost all registered terrorist acts in Georgia are of local importance, however, since Georgia is a part of global democratic community and fighting terrorism is a global issue to improve the situation, international cooperation, support of the international community turned out to be crucial. It is only possible to fight terrorism with joint efforts today.

Taking into consideration the results of the research, the following recommendations have been elaborated:

- Harmonizing counter terrorism legislation with International law and conventions;

- Preparing and adopting the UN Convention against International Terrorism;
- Supporting fast and peaceful solutions of problems in Abkhazia and South Ossetia;
- Recognizing the importance of dissemination of counter terrorism educational programs not only for officials but also for the population, especially in the problem regions;
- Providing check-points on the borders with high-tech equipment and detectors for border-control;
- Providing more efficient cooperation within local and international law enforcement bodies, especially in the exchange of information that is currently done with reluctance in some cases.

References

[1] L.I. Shelley, Terrorism, Transnational Crime and Corruption Center, American University. [Online] Available from: URL: http://www.american.edu/traccc [2006, August 12]
[2] A. Kukhianidze, A. Kupatadze, Smuggling in radioactive materials. Paper is preserved in Georgia (Tbilisi) Office of Transnational Crime and Corruption Center of American University, 2006.
[3] Georgia makes progress in world corruption table. *Civil Georgia* (2006, November 06). [Online] Available from: URL: http://civil.ge/eng/article.php?id=14026 [2006, December 12].
[4] Ministry of State Security of Georgia, Data provided in Tbilisi on 2004, December 11.
[5] V. Kudriavtsev, Social causes of organized crime in Russia. *Journal of Organized Crime and Corruption: Studies, Surveys, Information* **1** (2000), 12-13.
[6] V.E. Petrishev, Terrorism in CIS. *Journal of Organized Crime and Corruption: Studies, Surveys, Information* **2** (2003), 70-85.
[7] S. Realuyo, Creation of counterterrorist financial regime. [Online] Available from: URL: http://usinfo.state.gov/journals/ites/0904/ijer/reealuyo.htm [2006, July 30] (in Russian)
[8] V.P. Emelianov, Problems of responsibility for international terrorism. *Gosudarstvo i Pravo* **1** (2000), 70-77. (*in Russian*)
[9] UK Intelligence Community Online, Countering terrorism: The United Kingdom's Strategy (2006, July). [Online] Available from: URL: http://www.intelligence.gov.uk/publications/documents/countering.pdf [2006, September 03]
[10] National Strategy for Combating Terrorism (2006, September). [Online] Available from: URL: http://hosted.ap.org/specials/interactives/wdc/documents/wh_terror060905.pdf [2006, December 10]
[11] H. Tomas, Financing of terrorism: Views of experts (2005, November 20). [Online] Available from: URL: http://www.voanews.com/russian/archive/2005-11/2005-11-20-voa6.cfm [2006, July 15]
[12] V.V. Luneev, Terrorism and organized crime: National and transnational aspects. *Journal of Organized Crime and Corruption: Studies, Surveys, Information* **2** (2003), 24-27.
[13] N.S. Beglova, Searching solution of a problem. *Economy, Policy and Ideology* **1** (1991) (*in Russian*)
[14] D. McCarthy, Narco-terrorism: International drug trafficking and terrorism - A dangerous mix. Hearing before the Committee on the Judiciary United States Senate (2003, May 20). [Online] Available from: URL: http://www.state.gov/p/inl/rls/rm/21129.htm [2006, June 15]
[15] A. Kukhianidze, A. Kupatadze, R. Gotsiridze, Smuggling through Abkhazia and Tskhinvali Region of Georgia. Tbilisi: Transnational Crime and Corruption Center (TRaCCC), Georgia Office; (2004).
[16] A. Kukhianidze, A. Kupatadze, Smuggling in radioactive materials. Paper in Transnational Crime and Terrorism Center of American University; Tbilisi Office.
[17] G. Lordkipanidze, Counterterrorist Center of Ministry of Internal Affairs (Presentation).
[18] L.Y. Kislinskaya, Survey of Russian press round-up: Organized crime, terrorism and corruption for the first half of 2003. *Journal of Organized Crime, Terrorism and Corruption* **3** (2003).
[19] T. Freese, A Georgian war on terrorism? (2005, February 08). [Online] Available from: URL: http://www.eurasianet.org/departments/insight/articles/eav080205.shtml [2006, August 27]
[20] D. Petriashvili, As Georgia loses gas, rancor at Russia on the rise (2006, January 23). [Online] Available from: URL: www.eurasianet.org/departments/insight/articles/eav012306b.shtml [2006, June 36]
[21] J. Ferrare, Center professors conduct outreach in Georgia, Armenia (2006, June 30). [Online] Available from: URL: http://www.marshallcenter.org/site-graphic/lang-en/page-mc-news-newsbrief/xdocs/mc/news-newsbrief/06-14.htm [2006, September 19]

Macedonia as a Leader in the South-East Europe's Cooperation in the Fight against Organised Crime

Trpe STOJANOVSKI
Ministry of Internal Affairs of the Republic of Macedonia
Police Academy, University of St. Kliment Ohridski

Abstract. Due to the new wave of danger of trans-national crime in a time of globalization and considering that organized crime and terrorism are becoming more prevalent and global, the European states are prepared to leave behind a part of their national sovereignty to establish closer cooperation to address these problems. Otherwise, the states are left out and can not prevent and fight these problems as isolated national governments.

Even though open borders and advanced technology enabled fast development of international trade and global commerce, they have also led to a dramatic increase in the number of criminal groups engaged in activities throughout nations, regions, and continents. These trans-national criminal organizations have acquired huge assets that are further used for other illegal activities. Establishing joint international cooperation for law enforcement institutions based on a powerful legal foundation is the only response to these emerging criminal threats. The international documents and projects relating to the development of regional cooperation in South-East Europe represent an excellent opportunity for efficient cooperation toward the end of organized crime prevention and suppression. Having received country-candidate status for European Union (EU) membership in 2005, the Republic of Macedonia actively contributes to strengthening confidence between the foreign services partners in the fight against crime.

Keywords. Rule of law, human rights, international institutions, international instruments, law enforcement, police, organized crime, terrorism, regional co-operation

Introduction

Organized crime and the terrorism present a huge threat for democracy, the rule of law, human rights and social and economic progress. Previously, Southeast European countries have been especially concerned by organized crime, the trans-national connection of the criminal groups, their sophisticated techniques and methods, and their corruptive behavior.

Faced with a new wave of danger from transnational crime in this globalization and internationalization era, national governments, UN member countries, the Council of Europe, OSCE and other governments, are showing increased preparedness to relinquish some of their national sovereignty in order to cooperate more closely in the prevention of and fight against these threats. Such preparedness is present in all segments of the national systems of criminal justice, namely the public prosecutor offices, courts, police, customs, counter-intelligence services, and specialized units for fight against crime etc.

Even though open borders and the advanced technology have enabled the rapid growth of international trafficking and the global commerce, they have also led to a dramatic increase in the number of criminal groups engaged in activities throughout different countries, regions and continents. These transnational criminal organizations have allocated large amounts of funds that are then used in other illegal activities. The involvement of organized criminal structures in the 2001 conflict in the Republic of Macedonia indicates that this conflict was also financed by illegal means.

In the last ten to fifteen years Southeast European countries, specifically those considered to be Western Balkan, have faced a need to establish stable institutions designed to implement the rule of law and protect human rights. The Stability Pact (1999) was created to improve the cooperation between the countries of Southeast Europe. The third Stability Pact Table refers to the sectors of Justice, Home Affairs and Security. The benefits to the involved countries are evident seven years later even though citizens' expectations regarding economic outcomes were beyond what implementation has delivered.

The regional and international cooperation in the prevention and fight against organized crime is a priority for the involved nations. Creating a powerful joint legislative institution founded in international cooperation of law enforcement institutions is the only answer to these criminal threats. The international criminal organizations worldwide, base their operation on illegal trafficking and smuggling of weapons, drug trafficking, fraud, and money laundering. Recently, these organizations have expanded into human trafficking, especially women and children for the purpose of sexual and economic abuse, and migrant smuggling. This same development can be seen with the criminal organizations operating in Macedonia. In addition, corruption is the common denominator for different types of organized crime.

The international documents and projects relating to the development of regional cooperation in South-East Europe represent an excellent opportunity for efficient cooperation toward the end of organized crime prevention and suppression. Having received country-candidate status for EU membership in 2005, the Republic of Macedonia actively contributes to strengthening confidence between the foreign services partners in the fight against crime. However, in order to have more efficient police cooperation we must overcome the absence of leveled legal suppositions among the countries, relevant education, and experience in this type of cooperation among police institutions. Another main deficiency is insufficient familiarity with international good practice.

1. Challenges with Which the Contemporary Police Organization Is Faced

The police institution has a public character which largely influences the quality of living in the community making it an especially important institution in state administration and fertile for the kind of analysis implied above. At the same time, the police organization offers a challenge as to whether or not it will prepare itself appropriately and have the capacity to intercepting security threats at times when crime is becoming more and more international. Other challenges offered by a police organization involve questions about what its profile will be in the future and the direction police action's center of gravity will take, etc.

When faced with the question of how a police organization will look in the future, it is first necessary to determine the processes that may influence the future of the community. Also, one must consider the ways in which the community will control the police organization; for instance, what will the community expect of it and how much will the community invest in it? The existence of different police organizations based on different social structures, degree of development, culture, tradition, language, racial and national marks, reflects how complicated a discussion on harmonized standards in the police organization can be. Further complicating such a discussion is the fact that those standards are expected rise to a level of a common denominator in international cooperation. It is even more difficult to foresee the processes that should have influence on the organization of the police in the forthcoming period. Therefore, it seems that the most suitable approach is to start from existing police achievements and competencies. For this paper's purposes, reflecting on the police organization, the focus will be as follows:

- the development and application of information technology in the police
- the organization of the police in the area of suppression of crime, especially transnational crime, with the existence of a network of perpetrators
- the police and its relation to the community, and specifically
- civilian control over the police.

Further work on this thesis involves looking at some countries that practice in a decentralized way and encourage personal responsibility. Such practices are the result of a proactive individual approach in the attempt to create a safe environment. One of the steps toward this end is to extract the police from non-police works, such as firefighting and administrative issues related to some parts of the administrative-legal work etc.

2. The Influence on the Information Technology upon the Police Organization

Policing has been always based on the notions of receiving and working with information and fast and accurate action upon it. In this era of intensive technological development, police are faced with the challenge of understanding these processes and implementing them into the methodology of police work while respecting the principle of rule of law and respect of human rights. These processes have a strong influence on the organization, management, development, supervision and control of the police.

We thus come to the conclusion that the initial and basic forms of police work are to arrive at information on time and to use it appropriately. Information collection, processing and storage are important police functions and technology allows for rapid, high quality processing. Other uses of technology are analytical, professional handling (intelligence). However, a very significant issue for the police organization is methodological profiling of the process, the way the users will get the data, data protection etc. This issue gets its credits up when speaking about the need of international exchange of data which need to be received on-time, to be correct and to be protected from unauthorized use.

A serious problem with which the institutions tasked with prevention of and fight against organized crime in Macedonia is the absence of clear regulations and established methodology in terms of data base access and use. A significant step forward was made with the adoption of the Law on Personal Data Protection. The Law on Classified Information, in terms of the way in which it has been interpreted and practiced, in this period creates confusion because it insists on specificity in its implementation in terms of when there is low familiarity and knowledge of the procedure of confidentiality in handling information. It does the same for un-prepared climate in state institutions for consistent implementation of the law, the absence of rulebooks or methodology for this kind of handling etc.

The statistical data bases are a separate issue. Their slowness in being adapted to the global processes in this area, inappropriate software solutions, non-investment in finding usable solutions are the main difficulties that make statistic an unavoidable attribute in the strategies and plans against organized crime. They suffer from small usability as a support of the operative services due to the incompatibility in their exchange with foreign institutions, etc.

3. Challenges Which the Regional Police Cooperation Is Faced with

The voluntary mutual exchange of information both of informative and operative character among the police services from different countries is a key for the development of the police services in Europe. The Schengen[1] experiences shows that the national sovereignty in the EU is reduced in order to enable at least initial, universal standards for joint action of the police services. The search for new form of police cooperation is not just an idea. This is a beginning of a long and not at all easy road. Several projects were already implemented in Western Balkan. The creation of European police structures, even on a temporarily basis, understands joining of the national sovereignty. The threats and the problems with the transnational organized crime, like terrorism, illegal trafficking with drugs, weapons, trafficking in human beings, nuclear pollution, transnational criminal activities related to money laundering, have strong pressure on the deepening of the cooperation of the police organizations. This form of cooperation in the area of suppression of international organized crime understands that the information must be shared among the sovereign police organizations, although there is reservation manifested regarding the division of information and the means which they avail of due to the fact that such an exchange may lead to opening of sensitive internal issue and interests. However, when it is all compared with the destructive danger which may be caused by the international organized crime, many researchers and scientists are unanimous that its control is more important than the changes in the economy and the policy of specific national legislations.

Within the process of security recovering in some countries of the region, for the first time there were multinational police structures established more or less contributing to the strengthening of the national capacities and developing contemporary concept of police organization. Some of the lessons learned are: association within the frameworks of international police forces, without an exception opens the issues on how these forces will be organized, how to create balance between the national and international interests and even more- who will control the work of that police organization. The numerous linguistic, cultural, religious and other differences decrease daily, but they are a reality, which reduce the communication and understanding between the police officers from different countries. The possibility to solve part of the given problems rises in the existence of international training centers and academies.

On the other hand, giving up a part of the national sovereignty presents condition for the international institutions to practice efficient control of the implementation of the international legal obligations for protection and promotion of human rights. Such an approach supports the thesis for information sharing from several police organizations for the purpose of more efficient fight against crime.

---

[1] To the Schengen Agreement, along with the current eight countries, Austria, Belgium, Germany, Italy, Luxemburg, Portugal, France and Netherlands, since March, 25th, 2001, approached Denmark, Norway and Sweden.

Be that as it may, along with the social changes happening rapidly, the picture and image of a country from the beginning of the 21st century becomes more and more vulnerable when the global market and the national policy are in question. This is especially true if it persistently prefers the national sovereignty. In this way, there is a serious danger for a country if it isolate itself from the global European and worldwide processes in terms of an international association opposing transnational organized crime.

The elevation of the international police cooperation to a higher form with active implementation of the police procedure and through the sovereign borders of the foreign countries continues to come across many obstacles. On the other hand, the international criminal organizations which use political, economic, information, administrative borders are well organized circles that thrive and progress. The political and civilized efforts for definitive suppression of organized crime, given that police activities occur in a fragmented or decentralized way are unrealistic and inadequate to breaking into criminal surroundings and disabling criminal activities.

Theoretical analysis shows that the international community may have significantly more success in the prevention, control and suppression of international crime by an individual nation's relinquishing part of its national sovereignty or preferring solely the concept of 'national police' as well as its more specific involvement in systematic, concrete cases at regional level.

4. International Organized Crime as a Factor Influencing the Police Organization

A separate challenge in the area of international police cooperation involves the cases where there should be an exchange of information between police organizations of foreign countries. In a contemporary police organization, one of the oldest and at the same time, one of the most leading institutions in the international police cooperation is INTERPOL. Beyond this organization, the information is exchanged by independent information bodies. Significant role in the creation of network of European police services has EUROPOL (1995) which competence later on has been passed on collection and procession of information and investigations on the territory of the member countries. The setting up of regional organization, SECI (1999), for prevention and fight against cross-border crime confirmed itself as the first successful example for regional cooperation. However, the forms of exchange of information through the existing organizations are with limited permeable power in view of the real needs and challenges imposed by the organized crime and terrorism in the world today. This is conditioned by the limited personnel-technical potential, as well as by the preparedness and the interests of the parties to share the information. The tendencies being noticed in the last few years, speak in favor of the decrease of these limitations and differences, although the road to their definite overcoming is still far away.

The new relations of cooperation of the police organizations require a lot of different forms of communication. The international police cooperation may use the experiences from the joint judiciary cooperation having longer tradition and within which there are different efficient instruments developed. The direct police cooperation which means internationalization of the police procedures is still the exception rather than the rule [1]. The Palermo Convention (2000) affirms the institute 'liaison officer.' From then onwards, this form of police cooperation is being intensively practiced in large number of countries in the world, although the beginnings of this type of cooperation existed before. The experience from this type of cooperation is of exceptional importance. It is seen in the rapid exchange of information, joint approach in planning different activities against criminal organizations, facilitation and simplification of the cooperation, strengthening of the confidence between the police services etc. The Ministry of Internal Affairs of the Republic of Macedonia, implementing the Police Reform Strategy identified the need of sending police attaches in the neighboring countries, but also in the countries being important partners of Macedonia in the prevention and fight against organized crime.

Primary to the need of joint police action on the territory of two or more countries there are great number of obstacles resulting from the differences in the police and criminal-processed legislations. For instance, the basic rule in police actions on the territory of another country is that police officers must respect the laws of the host country. In the Republic of Macedonia some of the police authorizations are provided in an exceptionally restrictive framework. For example, police detention (arrest) and in cases of existence of a reasonable doubt from the corpus of organized crime is possible up to 24 hours, and in France and Australia- up to 4 days, the Netherlands- up to 5 days, England 6 days etc. One of the basic principles in the international police cooperation is that when acting in other countries, the police officers are obliged to respect the national laws, but also the laws of the host country.

5. The Importance of International Documents for Efficient Police Cooperation

The need for more qualitative police cooperation is motivated by the bigger swing of organized crime and its appearing forms. An efficient international police action is unimaginable without coordination of the police organizations in detecting the crime, perpetrators and evidences. The international documents enable for the police cooperation to be more efficient in the prevention and the fight against international crime. The basic idea of the international documents is for all the countries to harmonize their national laws, so that there are no legal uncertainties. This means that the crime perpetrated in one country in the same time will mean a crime according to the laws of another country.

The basic tendency of the contemporary international legal system towards the main forms of organized crime - terrorism, trafficking in narcotic drugs, money laundering and other crimes is to treat them as extraditable crimes [1]. This character of money laundering, as a genuine grievous crime having no obstacles for extradition, is clearly determined by the Vienna Convention (Article 6). The Convention, also, affirms the principle that upon its ratification and in the absence of other bilateral agreements between the countries, it will present sufficient legal foundation for extradition.

It seems that specific contribution with the strengthening of the international cooperation in opposing organized crime is enabled by the adoption of the UN Convention on the fight against transnational organized crime from 2000. This document, unlike the others, in a more comprehensive manner sets the basis for prevention and fight against international, transnational organized crime. The Convention dedicates attention to the mechanisms which are directly involved in the suppression of crime. This is done by promotion of common terms (Article 2) for the terms 'organized criminal group,' 'serious crime,' 'proceeds of crime,' 'confiscation,' 'freezing or confiscation,' and 'controlled delivery'. Likewise, the Convention provides legislative standards for the crimes 'participation in an organized criminal group,' 'money laundering,' 'corruption,' 'obstruction of justice.' The harmonization of these standards with the national legislation is a condition for proper functioning of the Convention. The ratification of the Convention, finalized by all the countries in the region (and Europe) resulted in adoption of laws incriminating the behavior in the mentioned areas.

Also, this document enters more deeply in the precision of international instruments for cooperation in the area of joint legal assistance, extradition, exchange of information and setting up network of institutions for cooperation. The Convention makes a successful attempt at this approach, and also to the treatment of victims of crime, creating suppositions for change in the philosophy of perception of human rights and appropriate representation by the state representatives of the victims, above all in the transition countries. The Convention takes an appropriate approach in terms of witness protection, as a new, legitimate and legally permitted mechanism for the fight against international criminal organizations.

The UN Convention for fight against transnational organized crime known as the Palermo Convention makes a real pioneering step forward in comparison with the other conventions, promoting law enforcement cooperation. The provisions of the Convention referring to police competencies oblige the countries to adopt efficient strengthening and setting up mechanism for establishing channels of cooperation and fast exchange of information in view of money laundering and other crimes covered with the Convention, as well as for cooperation in investigations [1]. The cooperation in investigations covers determination of identity, place of living, the activities of the suspects, movement of proceeds of crime or property gained by illegal actions, providing necessary items for analytical and investigative aims, exchange of information and experts, designating liaison officers, exchange of information on specific means and methods used by organized criminal groups and exchange of information and coordination of the administrative and other measures for the purpose of rapid identification of money laundering. This approach of the Convention emphasizes the irreplaceable significance of the police and other managing bodies as an integral part in building comprehensive. It also emphasizes integrated strategy for the prevention of and fight against transnational crime by harmonizing criminal justice and police (law enforcement) cooperation in an international framework. This is done by harmonizing legislation, methodology of action, and joint participation in the police actions. Previously, this was avoided and neglected, mainly because of the complexity in finding unified steps for acting in this area.

One of the key features of international criminal organizations is their mobility and speed in action. The sole state institution that can stand in their way is the police and other law enforcement services which are active 24 hours/7 days a week. The police can act fast in an event of escape or to perform control at the border crossing points in order to discover suspects and objects and their efficient procession.

The international police cooperation has an irreplaceable role in the prevention and fight against organized crime. This is visible in the undertaking of operative measures and activities when, as a result of criminal investigation, there are special police measures and actions being applied which include use of police authorizations. This is the so-called zone of dynamic police action. The provided evidence and the reasonable doubt for perpetrated criminal acts are being translated into criminal charges submitted to the competent prosecution office for further processing.

In the absence of institutionalized inter-state cooperation in the area of justice and security, unavoidability of communication, starts in fact, with informal and semi-formal police contacts.

The international police cooperation, along with the previous examples is being realized in two other levels. The first one, involves international mutual-legal assistance and helping the judicial authorities in finding witnesses, insights and other actions in the competence of the police. Also, during extradition procedures the collection of evidence is put at the discretion of the court and other bodies implementing the procedure. The second, by many expert estimations, is that the police organization in one country is the unique or the best crisis managing structure of larger scope in the country. The police organization has unique data bases which are very important for resolution of complex criminal cases. However, the police by itself, regardless of its power and capacity is not sufficient when speaking about criminal acts in the area of international crime. The best practices of international police cooperation show that the police may be good transmitter of the requests from foreign police organizations which are in the competence of other institution in the country in order for them to be directed rapidly and correctly and for the answer to arrive as soon as possible.

6. The Convention on Police Cooperation for Southeastern Europe

A significant step forward in making the suppositions for more concrete international police cooperation is the adoption of the Convention for police cooperation for Southeastern Europe in 2006. This document, within the Stability Pact is ownership of eight countries from the region, assisted by Germany, Europol and the Ministry of Internal Affairs of Austria.

The Convention is a document which rose because of the strategic necessity of a joint approach to strengthen the operative cooperation in the fight against transnational crime. Later on, the Convention should enable increased exchange of information between the countries-partners by strengthening of the existing police structures, as well as by establishing additional joint mechanisms for cooperation.

This type of cooperation, based on EU/Schengen standards for regional approach, is part of the joint involvement for increased police cooperation with Europol. The Convention enables the focus of application of the police cooperation to be directed toward:

- increase of the exchange of information (acting upon requests for information)
- preservation of evidence in urgent cases
- regulation of prosecution and other forms of cross-border cooperation
- special measures such as controlled delivery and observation of secret operation
- exchange of liaison officers

For this purpose, the Convention provides unique definitions for the terms such as 'law enforcement,' 'officials,' 'borders,' 'third country,' 'residence permit,' 'personal data,' 'personal data procession,' and 'information.' This is important to be known previously, in order to interpret and plan the regional police activities in due time.

The Convention provides establishing focal point at central level, as an organizational unit (or part of it) through which the exchange of information will go, but also to transfer and support of the information to the competent subject in the institution or in the country. This is probably where the idea on standardizing the police organization came from by establishing Central Police Service, following the example of European police organizations, which an innovation in the organization of the police in Macedonia, established with the project for Macedonian police reform from 2002. The Convention is a result of the joint negotiation of the partner countries in the period from June 2005 to May 2006.

The Convention dedicated significant attention to the part of request for information, identifying the type of the requested information. Initially, the request referred to:

1. identification of car owners and identification of the drivers
2. driver's licenses
3. place of living
4. place of residence
5. telecommunication data
6. identity
7. subject: especially cars and weapons
8. police intelligence and information and data from open sources
9. flash messages on drugs, weapons and explosives and for forfeiting money
10. messages in view of the practical implementation of hot pursuit and controlled delivery
11. determining the will of taking the stand
12. interviews, examinations
13. exchange of information on evidence at scenes of crimes
14. coordination of initiation joint search measures
15. hotels, accommodation

One of the most significant forms of police cooperation, important for the next phases of the criminal-procedural work, is the request to a foreign police on:

- providing security and transfer of evidence in urgent cases
- body search
- transfer of identification material and DNA profiles

The Convention absorbed standards from the best European practice, promotes the good police cooperation in cases of chasing perpetrator of serious criminal act when the search for him/her continues on the territory of the neighboring country (Article 13). The Convention regulates the procedure and actions which need to be completed by police officers who started the action, the type and marking of the service vehicle and their uniform and equipment, up until taking police powers, including person's stopping, search and use of weapons as final resort to protect one's own life. The representatives of the countries preparing the document expressed their readiness to keep these provisions, because of absence of implementation of this type of police cooperation at this moment, and it will be realized when two neighboring countries will agree to that by bilateral agreements.

The center of importance of the Convention is the special police measures most frequently meaning unity in coordination of action, namely:

- controlled delivery
- secret operations
- exchange of information on prosecution (without request)
- surveillance for the purposes of prevention
- chase for the purpose of prevention
- secret operations for crime prevention
- border centers for exchange of experiences, planning meetings or exchange of detainees

The Convention suggests a pro-active approach. When the police organizations have information critical to a foreign police organization, they must transmit it to the appropriate organizations.

In improving regional cooperation, above all, the border cooperation, the Convention, following the EU/Schengen example, suggests technical solutions which will enable joint radio-telecommunication (Article 3) by exchange of equipment between the neighboring police patrols. This phase will last up till introducing unified radio-equipment and frequencies in all European countries and preparation of unique system especially along the borders.

For purposes of cross-border crime prevention, the Convention provides establishing joint centers (Article 29) which are to facilitate the exchange of information and improve the cooperation between the police officers from foreign police organizations. Following the EU/Schengen experiences, the cooperation in the joint centers composes of exchange, analysis, giving information and realization of supportive role in coordination or the cross-border cooperation.

Exchange of liaison officers is an issue identified with the Palermo Convention, and this document (Article 9) enters more deeply in identification of the profile of the liaison officer, his/her competencies and responsibilities. The liaison officer should contribute to faster and safer police cooperation, especially on issues related to the border matter, exchange of information in the area of organized crime, as well as for completing the request for mutual police and judiciary assistance in criminal matters. The liaison officer does not have the authorization to take police actions independently.

Having in mind the political, legal, social, cultural, national, linguistic differences which objectively may influence the quality and efficient implementation of the Convention, it is rightfully identified that the education and exchange of experience will have positive influence on overcoming the difficulties and in the encouragement to implement the provisions of this document. This may be achieved by unified curricula for basic and advanced training by joint seminar, but also with joint participation in cross-border exercises.

7. Conclusion

1. The problems related to the organized crime and terrorism have global (regional) dimension. The answer, likewise, have to be global. This, above all, means harmonization of the legislation, more joint approach in implementation of the law, exchange of police and intelligence information at regional level.
2. The organized crime is a dynamic phenomenon; it constantly adapts to the changeable surroundings and its possibilities.
3. The growing concern for the organized crime in Southeast Europe, as well as the perspectives of these countries to join EU, requires exhaustive analysis of the scope, nature and the characteristics of the organized crime in the region.
4. Understanding organized crime largely depends on the priorities in implementation of law and on the policy against crime, which are determined on the basis of the expected threats. Without comprehensive knowledge of this phenomenon, the authorities will be limited in the efforts to show success against the organized crime.
5. The changes dictated by the market, result in changes in the criminal organizations which consolidate themselves and get their activities closer to

the legal side, trying to legalize the profit and their position in the society. The corruption aiming in higher circles, but to the lower level as well is used as the main tool to influence the political and commercial structures.
6. The organized crime in Southeast Europe is manifested in different forms and involves different criminal activities. Similar to other parts of Europe, more characteristic are: (a) illegal trafficking with drugs, (b) smuggling of persons, (c) trafficking in human beings, (d) deceptions, tax evasion, economic crime.
7. Although, the authorities of the Southeast European countries are aware of the danger of the organized crime and recognize its negative implication, the law enforcement institutions do not have sufficient capacity for systematic collection of intelligence information, their analysis, procession and taking actions. It is encouraging to know that in the Southeast European countries, reforms are underway in the Sector of Justice and Home Affairs. Only unified progress in all of the sectors in the Chapter Justice and Home Affairs can create a front for more equal implementation of international documents.
8. Further improvement and simplification of the bilateral and regional police cooperation by supplementing and additional concretization of the agreements and protocols on cooperation.
9. Ratification and full implementation of international instruments which should enable the Southeast European countries to improve their independence and professionalism of the competent institutions, to make the decision making faster and on time regarding freezing or confiscation of proceeds of crime, adoption of regional cooperation as the *ultima ratio* in their methodology of work. This especially refers to the Police Cooperation Convention in the Southeast Europe (2006), the Convention for mutual legal assistance in criminal matters (CETS 182), the Convention on laundering, search, seizure and confiscation of proceed of crime and financing terrorism (CETS 198) and the Convention in action against trafficking in human beings (CETS 197).
10. Organizing joint training for law enforcement officers from several competent institutions for prevention and suppression of organized crime, as well as joint training and participation in exercises for law enforcement officer from several countries in the region.
11. Creation of national centralized data bases containing information of individuals wanted for participation in organized criminal groups, which under specific circumstance will be available to foreign police officers and prosecutors.
12. Creation of genuine data bases in the area of organized crime which will be exchanged with foreign countries.

References

[1] V. Kambovski, *Organized crime*. Skopje, Macedonia; 2005.
[2] T. Vitlarov, G. Kalajdziev, M. Labovik, T. Stojanovski, *System analysis of the legal framework and cooperation between the competent institutions in the fight against organized crime.* Skopje, Macedonia: Foundation Institute Open Society; 2005.
[3] E. Savona, C. Federica, The contribution of Data Exchange Systems to the fight against organized crime in SEE countries, (Transcrime, Universita Degli Studi Di Trento, Universita Cattolica Del Sacro Cuore); 2004.
[4] Report on the state of affairs with the organized and economic crime in Southeast Europe, Strasbourg. Regional Carpo project, Council of Europe; 2005.

Collaboration in the Field of Prevention to the Organized Crime and Terrorism

Mykola KHASCHEVOI[a] and Olena IVASCHENKO[b]
[a] *General-Major, Ministry of Interior, Ukraine*
[b] *Major, Ministry of Interior, Ukraine*

Abstract. Today the world community, with great concern, observes the process of activation of international terrorism, which consists of the threats and realization of large-scale terrorist attacks that are directed at the distribution of an atmosphere of fear and panic, political and economic instability, and discrediting of the democratic principles of human existence.

The active foreign-policy activity of Ukraine, participation in numerous international actions, including counterterrorist actions as well as the number of external and internal factors coincide with an increase in the probability of terrorist attacks on the territory of the Ukraine.

Keywords. Terrorism, organized crime, international cooperation, Ukraine

Introduction

Today the world community, with great concern, observes the process of activation of international terrorism, which consists of the threats and realization of large-scale terrorist attacks that are directed at the distribution of an atmosphere of fear and panic, political and economic instability, and discrediting of the democratic principles of human existence. Terrorism became one of the biggest threats to national safety of the states and the globe. Globalization processes have brought internationalization, transformation of ideological and institutional base of terrorism, and substantial expansion of its forms and methods.

Attempts to perfect already existent mechanisms of counter-terrorism, develop new effective forms and methods of fight against terrorism, and increase interdepartmental and intergovernmental levels of co-operation on bilateral and multilateral bases are urgent for each of the states.

1. Counteraction to International Terrorism and Extremism

The active foreign-policy activity of our state, participation in numerous international actions, including counterterrorist actions as well as the number of external and internal factors, coincide with an increase in the probability of terrorist attacks and on the territory of the Ukraine.

The analysis of modern progress trends of terrorism shows that internal social processes, which could produce the terrorist manifestations, are steadily displaced to the sphere of international relations and external factors create the real threat of distribution in the Ukraine of this most dangerous socio-political phenomenon.

Working out the strategies and tactics of the fight against terrorism, the Ukraine realizes that threat of distribution of international terrorism is a global threat. By our estimations, in spite of the liquidation of its separate centers in Central Asia and the Near East, as well as the barriers blocking its basic financial sources, the threat of terrorism grows yet and because it takes new shapes and takes on new methods of actions such as use of the latest achievements in science and technology, new possibilities open up in connection with integration processes. This all occurs in a world, by intensification of international contacts that is growing with migration processes and indulgence of control at border-crossing check points.

Even in the situation of absence of information in relation to the real threats to the Ukraine from the side of international terrorist organizations, leaders of the state pay of principle attention to the settlement of questions in relation to forming an effective national counterterrorist system.

The Ukraine acknowledged the fight against terrorism as one of priority in terms of state policy directions and it participates actively in policy making for providing of effective counteraction to the terrorist manifestations.

In accordance with resolutions of Security Council of UN numbered 1267 and 1269 (in 1999), 1333 (in 2000), 1363, 1368 and 1373 (in 2001), 1388, 1390, 1438, 1440, 1450 and 1452 (in 2002), 1455 (in 2003), 1526, 1566 (in 2004), decisions of the International regional summit on fight against terrorism, that took place on 06.11.2001 in Warsaw, Declaration on the issues of fight against terrorism, which is approved by resolution of UN Security Council numbered 1456 (in 2003), and also taking into consideration Declaration on the fight against terrorism (with addition it is the renewed Plan of actions in relation to the strategic aims of European Union in the sphere of fight against terrorism) and Declaration about solidarity in the fight against terrorism, accepted on meeting of European Union (Brussels, 25-26.03.2004), on implementation of commissions of the President of the Ukraine and the Government of the state, as well as the other decisions accepted at international and national levels by Ministry of Internal Affairs of the Ukraine, within its competence, the complex of the organizational and practical measures directed on the fight against terrorism, non-admission of the expansion on territory of the Ukraine of international terrorist and extremist organizations gets along.

During recent years the Ukraine joined all basic international conventions and to the protocols to them) on the fight against terrorism and organized crime, in particular:

1. Convention on Offences and Certain Other Acts Committed on Board Aircraft, signed in Tokyo on 14 September 1963, is ratified by the Decree of Presidium of the Supreme Council of the USSR on 21 December 1987 N 5049-XI;
2. Convention for the Suppression of Unlawful Seizure of Aircraft, signed at the Hague on 16 December 1970 and came into force on 23 March 1972, is ratified by Presidium of the Supreme Council of the USSR on 27 December 1971;
3. Convention for the Suppression of Unlawful Acts against the Safety of Civil Aviation, signed at Montreal on 23 September 1971 (is ratified by the Presidium of the Supreme Council of the USSR on 27 December 1972); with the Protocol on the Suppression of Unlawful Acts of Violence at Airports Serving International Civil Aviation, supplementary to the Convention for the Suppression of Unlawful Acts against the Safety of Civil Aviation (1988);

4. Convention on the Prevention and Punishment of Crimes against Internationally Protected Persons, including Diplomatic Agents, adopted by the General Assembly of the United Nations on 14 December 1973. It is signed by de Ukraine in 1974 and ratified by the Presidium of the Supreme Council of the USSR on 26 December 1975;
5. International Convention against the Taking of Hostages, adopted by the General Assembly of the United Nations on 17 December 1979;
6. Convention for the Suppression of Unlawful Acts against the Safety of Civil Aviation, signed at Montreal on 23 September 1971.
7. Protocol on the Suppression of Unlawful Acts of Violence at Airports Serving International Civil Aviation, supplementary to the Convention for the Suppression of Unlawful Acts against the Safety of Civil Aviation, signed at Montreal on 24 February 1988.
8. Convention for the Suppression of Unlawful Acts against the Safety of Maritime Navigation, done at Rome on 10 March 1988.
9. Protocol for the Suppression of Unlawful Acts against the Safety of Fixed Platforms Located on the Continental Shelf, done at Rome on 10 March 1988.
10. Convention on marking of Plastic Explosives for the Purpose of Detection, signed at Montreal on 1 March 1991.
11. International Convention for the Suppression of Terrorist Bombings, adopted by the General Assembly of the UN on 15 December 1997.
12. International Convention for the Suppression of the Financing of Terrorism, adopted by the General Assembly of the UN on 9 December 1999.
13. UN Convention on the Suppression of Transnational Crime (12 December, 2000, Palermo);
14. European Convention on the Suppression of Terrorism concluded in Strasbourg on 27 January 1977;
15. Program of realization of provisions of Warsaw Convention on Mutual Suppression of Terrorism (the Decree of the Cabinet of Ministers of 14 December, 2001, N 1694);
16. Treaty on Cooperation among the Ministries if Internal Affairs of the States Members of the Commonwealth of Independent States in Combating Terrorism (8 September, 2000);
17. Protocol on Confirmation of Procedure of Organization and Realization of Antiterrorist Acts on the Territory of the States Members of the Commonwealth of Independent States (7 October 2002, Kyshyniv, ratified by the Law of the Ukraine of 7 April 2004 N 1669-IV).

The number of measures carried out as part of the implementation of provisions of international legal instruments, forming of national counterterrorist legislation and organization of the integral state system of counteraction to terrorism.

The Law of the Ukraine 'On the Suppression of Terrorism' of March, 20, 2003 numbered 638-V was passed. It focuses on the protection of person, state and society from terrorism, exposure and removal of reasons and terms which generate it. This Law also determines legal and organizational frameworks of fight against this dangerous phenomenon, and determines authority and duties of organs of executive power, associations of citizens and organizations, public servants and separate citizens in this sphere, as well as the order of co-ordination of their activity, guarantee of legal and social defense of citizens in connection with participation in the fight against terrorism.

In accordance with the Article 1 of the noted Law of the Ukraine,

"Terrorism is the publicly dangerous activity, which consists in conscious, purposeful use of violence by the taking of hostages, arsons, murders, tortures, intimidation of population and organs of power or accomplishing of other encroachments on life or health of in anything not guilty people or threats of accomplishing of criminal acts with the purpose of achievement of criminal purposes."

The Articles 24 and 25 of the noted Law of the Ukraine set up the order of acknowledgement of organization as a terrorist organization and envisage the responsibility for terrorist activity, and also responsibility for the assistance to terrorist activity.

The Article 258 of the Criminal Code of the Ukraine envisages responsibility for act of terrorism and for creation of terrorist organization. According to this article, act of terrorism is;

"Article 258. Act of terrorism:
1. An act of terrorism, that is the use of weapons, explosions, fire or any other actions that exposed human life or health to danger or caused significant pecuniary damage or any other grave consequences, where such actions sought to violate public security, intimidate population, provoke an armed conflict, or international tension, or to exert influence on decisions made or actions taken or not taken by government agencies or local government authorities, officials and officers of such bodies, associations of citizens, legal entities, or to attract attention of the public to certain political, religious or any other convictions of the culprit (terrorist), and also a threat to commit any such acts for the same purposes, - shall be punishable by imprisonment for a term of five to ten years.
2. The same actions, if repeated or committed by a group of persons upon their prior conspiracy, or where these actions caused significant property damage or other grave consequences, - shall be punishable by imprisonment for a term of seven to twelve years.
3. Any such actions as provided for by paragraph 1 or 2 of this Article, where they caused death of people, - shall be punishable by imprisonment for a term of ten to fifteen years, or life imprisonment.
4. Establishing, leading, or participating in a terrorist group or terrorist organization, and also providing logistical, organizational or any other assistance in order to facilitate the establishment or operation of a terrorist group or terrorist organization, - shall be punishable by imprisonment of eight to fifteen years.
5. Any person, other than an organizer or leader, shall be discharged from criminal liability for any action provided for in paragraph 4 of this Article, if he/she has voluntarily reported it to a law enforcement authority and assisted in termination of existence or operations of such terrorist group or organization, or in uncovering criminal offences related to the creation or operation of actions contain no elements of any other offence."

By Decrees of the President of the Ukraine the Anti-crisis center (from November, 5, 2002 numbered 991/2002), which co-ordinates the measures of central organs of executive power and special organs on realization of state policy in the field of overcoming and prevention of crisis situations which are the result of extremist or terrorist manifestations, is formed, as well as the counterterrorist center at security Service of the Ukraine (from December, 11, 1998 numbered 1343/98), which co-ordinates activity of organs of executive power in prevention of terrorist acts in relation to statesmen, critical objects of life-support of population, dangerous objects, to the acts, which threaten to life and health of considerable number of population, and their stopping.

The Ministry of Internal Affairs of the Ukraine in co-operation with other central organs of executive power has developed and organized implementation of Plan of measures on providing of the proper defense of basic objects vulnerable in the terrorist relation, which is ratified by the decree of Cabinet of Ministers of the Ukraine from June, 17, 2004 numbered 383.

With the purpose of raising the level of their skill, acquisition of knowledge and practical skills on hostage release, and relaxation of consequences of terrorist act, the decree of the Cabinet of Ministers of the Ukraine of July, 13, 2004 numbered 921 about 'Organization of raising the level of the skill of public and other servants which are engaged in participation in counterterrorist operations, on the questions of counteraction to the acts of terrorism' has been signed.

By Decree of the Cabinet of Ministers of the Ukraine of July, 28, 2004 numbered 982, 'the Procedure of conducting of social rehabilitation of persons which suffered from terrorist act' is ratified. In addition, by the decision of Cabinet of Ministers of the Ukraine of May, 25, 2006 numbered 751, 'the procedure of forming of list of the persons related to terrorist activity' is ratified.

The drafts of the Law of the Ukraine are developed 'On the fight against extremism' and decrees of Cabinet of Ministers of the Ukraine 'On Statute about the Unique system of prevention, reaction and counteraction to the acts of terrorism, and also measures on minimization of their consequences,' 'On approval of the Government program from prevention of manifestations of biological (bacteriological) terrorism in the Ukraine and providing of activity of laboratory subsections which are included in the system of epidemiology supervision after especially dangerous infections, on 2006-2011 years.' During the development of legislatively-normative acts, the work on implementation to the national legislation of provisions of international Conventions and resolutions of Security Council of UN is carried out; a legislatively-normative base on the questions of counteraction to financing of terrorist activity appears.

The Law of the Ukraine is adopted on December, 1, 2005 numbered 3163-V about 'Making amendments to some laws of the Ukraine in relation to the improvement of the legal base of international cooperation in the field of prevention of financing of terrorism,' which, in particular, supplements the Law of the Ukraine 'About prevention and counteraction of legalization (laundering) of the profits gained in a criminal way' it is supplemented by the Article 12 (prevention and counteraction to financing of terrorism).

For consideration of Supreme Soviet of the Ukraine the project of Law of the Ukraine 'About bringing of changes in some legislative acts of the Ukraine on the issues of prevention of legalization (laundering) of the profits got a criminal way, and financing of terrorism' (numbered 4190 from September, 24, 2003) is supplied.

By a draft of the law, in particular, it is foreseen to amend the Criminal code of the Ukraine by the Article 258 (financing of terrorism).

In accordance with the resolution of the Cabinet of Ministers of the Ukraine of December, 10, 2003 numbered 1896 is created the Unique state informative system in the field of prevention and counteraction to legalization (laundering) of the profits gained in a criminal way, and financing of terrorism.

Adoption of the noted and other legislatively-normative acts will allow counteracting effectively to financing of terrorist activity in accordance with positions of international law.

After the conclusions of UN experts which conducted an estimation of the state of implementation to the national legislation of the Ukraine of international counterterrorist norms, in spite of existence of insignificant gaps in the legislation, the complex of the national measures, directed on comprehensive and complete implementation of positions of the proper Resolutions of Security Council of UN, international conventions, as well as protocols to them and other universal counterterrorist instruments is successfully carried out in the Ukraine. In opinion of experts experience of the Ukraine on these questions can be recommended into consideration of other third countries as model of development of national counterterrorist legislation.

The experience of setting and development of contacts with international counterterrorist organizations, law enforcement authorities and special services of other states on issues of organization and conducting of counterterrorist measures has accumulated. One of important components of this activity is co-operation by participation in the organized and conducted by international and national counterterrorist structures studies, trainings, scientific conferences and exchange by information within the framework of the specialized data bank. In accordance with Resolution of Security Council of UN from September, 28, 2001 numbered 1373 the questions of comprehensive participation of the Ukraine in the European and other international counterterrorist structures are worked over, as well as development and deepening of collaboration with the proper organs of foreign countries.

Jointly with the State Security Service the projects of agreement are developed between Cabinet of Ministers of the Ukraine and Government of United States of America in relation to mutual acknowledgement and application of Lists of persons and organizations, that carry on terrorist activity or relate to it, as well as Agreement between Government of United States of America and Government of the Ukraine in relation to collaboration for prevention of distribution of, its delivery systems and related materials by a sea-lane.

In addition, currently in connection with the decision of NATO about the grant to the countries-partners of access to the manual renewed in 2006 in relation to the system of NATO on the reaction on crises (NATO Crisis Response System Manual) measures on adaptation of the national system of reaction on crisis with the system of countries-members of Alliance are carried out.

Work in relation to providing participation of the Ukraine in international initiatives in the field of non-proliferation of weapons of mass destruction and terrorism suppression proceeds in a practical plan, in particular, Initiatives on safety in the field of non-proliferation, operation of NATO in Mediterranean 'Active efforts,' as well as on forming of counterterrorist constituent of the Black Sea system of safety (BLACKSEAFOR). During 2005, participation in preparation and conducting of three international studies on a counterterrorist subject is accepted - 'Joint assistance-2005' (former name 'Assistex-2'), 'Bohemian Guard 2005' (Czech Republic) and 'Black Sea Border Security Initiative Exercise' (Romania).

In accordance with the Law of the Ukraine 'About the fight against terrorism,' the organs of internal affairs carry out the fight against terrorism by prevention, exposure and stopping of the crimes made with a terrorist purpose, investigation of which delivered by the legislation of the Ukraine to their jurisdiction. In this connection, basic directions of operative and service activity are directed on: improvement of the system of safety and physical guard of basic objects vulnerable in the terrorist relation; maintenance of public safety and law and order on such objects and round them, as well as in the places of mass stay of people; fight against illegal migration and non-admission of penetration on territory of the Ukraine of persons related to terrorist activity; disclosure of grave and especially grave crimes, counteract to the illegal trafficking in weapon, explosive, radio-active substances and other facilities of terror.

Thus, at implementation of Program of counterterrorist measures on 2005-2007 years, ratified by Decree of President of the Ukraine, Programs of collaboration of the states-participants of CIS in the fight against terrorism and other violent manifestations of extremism on 2005-2007 the law enforcement bodies of the Ukraine participated in conducting of number of national operations ('Inhibition,' 'Weapon and explosive,' 'Foreigner,' 'Migrant,' 'Search,' 'Border') and international operations ('Channel,' 'Purple'), as well as intergovernmental measures, directed on non-admission of acts of terrorism, fight against illegal migration, illegal trafficking in weapon, live ammunitions, explosive substances and explosive devices, products of the double setting and others like that.

Jointly with State Security Service (SSC) the tactical and special trainings within the framework of preventive plans of the counterterrorist operations 'Boomerang,' 'Alarm,' and 'Whirlwind,' general command and staff studies on separate diversionary vulnerable objects and tactical and special studies in accordance with the Anti-terrorist Center' plan at SSC are conducted. The organs of internal affairs of the Ukraine also take part in the 'Whirlwind antiterrorist operations' and 'Hireling,' which are conducted by law enforcement authorities of Russia.

The organs of internal affairs carry out the intensified guard of 2.3 thousand of state establishments, objects of life-support and man-caused-dangerous objects (atomic electro stations, oil and complex etc.), 2.9 thousand of objects with firearms and live ammunitions, 14 thousand of places of mass stay of people. The protection of 122 diplomatic and consular establishments of the foreign states is intensified. During 2005, from the trafficking over 3 thousand of units of firearms, 147 thousand of cartridges, 428 grenades, 36 mines, 225 home-made explosive devices, 1 ton 223 kg of explosives is seized. 11 thousand of crimes, related to the trafficking in weapons and explosives, including 84 crimes, committed by the members of organized groups. A 145 thousand of grave and especially grave crimes are disclosed, including 147 crimes related to illegal imprisonment or theft of man, activities of 35 bands and 19 criminal organizations has been stopped.

The permanent monitoring of migratory processes with a purpose of revealing and neutralizing the intentions of terrorist organizations in relation to transference of their activity on the territory of the Ukraine is carried out.

While these purposeful operations are conducted and executed, everyday operatively-official tasks the organs of internal affairs detain a 14 thousand 785 illegal migrants (in 2004 – a 15 thousand 438), including 1 thousand 443 persons who moved as members of 126 groups.

Due to the corresponding measures of law enforcement authorities of the Ukraine, the of criminal situation worsens and moves into the territory of the states-participants of international terrorist and extremist organizations, committing by them illegal actions, including terrorist acts was prevented.

The unstable situation in the world related to the globalization of terrorism, requires the Ukraine to pay primary attention to subsequent development of current legislation, which would be able to incorporate to the international law and contain the prospect of improvement of law-enforcement activity with the purpose of creation of the effective system of measures of fight against the complex of so called 'asymmetric threats,' namely: international terrorism, transnational organized crime, illegal migration, illegal trafficking in weapons and drugs.

2. Legislation of the Ukraine in the Field of Fight against the Organized Crime

According the Law of the Ukraine 'About organizational and legal base of fight against the organized crime' from June, 30, 1993 numbered 3341-O, the organized crime in the Ukraine is the number of crimes, committed by criminal groups.

According to the Part 3 Article 28 of the Criminal Code of the Ukraine of 5 April 2001 N 2341-III:

"A criminal offence shall be held to have been committed by an organized group where several persons (three or more) participated in its preparation or commission, who have previously established a stable association for the purpose of committing of this and other offence (or offences), and have been consolidated by a common plan with assigned roles designed to achieve this plan known to all members of the group."

According to the Part 4 Article 28 of the Criminal Code of the Ukraine:

"A criminal offence shall be held to have been committed by a criminal organization where it was committed by a stable hierarchical association of several persons (three and more), members or structural units of which have organized themselves, upon prior conspiracy, to jointly act for the purpose of directly committing of grave or special grave criminal offences by the members of this organization, or supervising or coordinating criminal activity of other persons, or supporting the activity of this criminal organization and other criminal groups."

Thus, the National legislation of the Ukraine envisages such definitions as to crimes, committed by organized group or criminal organization:

"*an organized criminal group* is a group consist of several persons (three or more) participated in its preparation or commission, who have previously established a stable association for the purpose of committing of this and other offence (or offences), and have been consolidated by a common plan with assigned roles designed to achieve this plan known to all members of the group."

"*The criminal organization* is a stable hierarchical association of several persons (three and more), members or structural units of which have organized themselves, upon prior conspiracy, to jointly act for the purpose of directly committing of grave or special grave criminal offences by the members of this organization, or supervising or coordinating criminal activity of other persons, or supporting the activity of this criminal organization and other criminal groups."

"*The creation of a criminal organization* is the creation of a stable hierarchical association of several persons (three and more) for the purpose of "committing a grave or special grave offence, and also leadership or participation in such organization, or participation of offences committed by such organization, and also the organizing, running or facilitating a meeting (convention) of members of criminal organizations or organized groups for the purpose of development of plans and conditions for joint commission of criminal offences, providing logistical support of criminal activities or coordination of activities of so associated criminal organizations or organized groups."

"*The organizer* is a person who has organized a criminal offence (or criminal offences) or supervised its (their) preparation or commission. The organizer is also a person who has created an organized group or criminal organization, or supervised it, or financed it, or organized the covering up of the criminal activity of an organized group or criminal organization."

3. International Co-operation in the Fight against the Organized Crime

For the purposes of the national policy implementation concerning the international cooperation development in the sphere of organized crime and terrorism combating the Main Department on Organized Crime Combating of the Ministry of Internal Affairs of the Ukraine in the framework of its competence is actively involved in the international cooperation in those spheres with correspondent departments of following organizations: United Nations, Council of Europe, European Union, NATO, OSCE, OECD, CEI, SECI, European and Atlantic Partnership Council, BSEC, IOM, CIS, GUAM (Georgia, Ukraine, Moldova) etc.

In particular, this cooperation is carried out within the framework of Uthe nited Nations Office for Drug Control and Crime Prevention (UNODC), Group of Countries against Corruption (GRECO), FATF, Egmont Group, MONEYVAL, PC-R-EV, as well as the programs TACIS, Octopus, BUMAD, AGIS, AGRO and the projects Millennium, Bridge, Exit etc.

We continue to cooperate actively with Interpol, Europol, Eurojust, SECI, etc. There are some recent practical results of such cooperation:

- Two foreigners have been detained as suspected terrorists who are wanted for committing grave crimes. One of them has been detained in the Odessa region.

He is the citizen of Algeria who, according to the information of the NCB of Interpol in the Ukraine, is the leader of the terrorist organization and is wanted by the law enforcement bodies of Algeria. Another one has been detained in Crimea. He is the citizen of Uzbekistan and has been wanted by its law enforcement bodies for committing grave crimes in the territory of Uzbekistan. He is an active member of the religious extremist organization 'The Islam Party of Turkmenistan.' Both criminals have been transferred to the initiators of their search.

- During the last year, sub-units of the Main Department on Organized Crime Combating of the Ministry of Internal Affairs of the Ukraine in close cooperation with their foreign colleagues detected 53 organized criminal groups and identified more than 200 criminals who were their members. Besides, three transnational criminal organizations, which had been active in the illegal economic activities connected of trafficking of alcohol (Georgia, Moldova, USA, Slovakia) and meat products (Brazil, Holland, Poland, USA, France, Baltic States), payment cards forgery and embezzlement of money of the international payment systems (Belarus, Latvia Poland, Russia, USA) have been revealed.

The analysis of the crimes, which have been committed by the organized criminal group members last year, demonstrate that the major part of them have been committed in the following spheres: smuggling (19), trafficking in human beings, in particular women for sexual exploitation (16), foreign trade (10), drug trafficking (9), illegal labor migration (6), high technologies (2), as well as other (general) crimes (10). Most of them are revealed mutually with the law enforcement organs of Belarus, Moldova, Poland and Hungary.

Citizens of the Commonwealth of Independent States (former USSR republics) mainly commit grave general crimes (banditry, extortions, armed robberies, assassinations, including the ordered murders). Those criminal groups, which consist from the members who have contacts and links with the citizens of the Western and Central Europe, are often specialized in organization of the illegal migration channels for the representatives of the South-Eastern Asia. They also organize illegal labor migration from the Ukraine and are involved in trafficking in human beings (first of all, for their sexual exploitation).

4. Conclusion

We consider that for further development of the international cooperation it is necessary to strengthen direct contacts with the foreign specialized forces on the organized crime combating, to increase the efficiency of the operative and other information exchange, as well as to carry out joint operative and search activities in the framework of the concrete operative and criminal cases.

Initiatives Taken by the Republic of Armenia in the Fight against Terror: Legislative Regulations and Intergovernmental Cooperation with the CIS States

Armen SANOYAN
Ministry of Justice, Republic of Armenia

Abstract. The Republic of Armenia (RA) has been an active member of the global campaign against terrorism. The following article focuses on the national and international legal initiatives that the RA (Republic of Armenia) has introduced to facilitate terrorism prevention and counterterrorism within the RA and the CIS member states.

Keywords. Republic of Armenia, terrorism, counterterrorism, law and terrorism, CIS states

Introduction

Armenia resolutely condemns terrorism and is fully committed to the international struggle against them. With the full understanding of necessity to combat such phenomena, Armenia has offered unreserved assistance to the global coalition, signed the UN and Council of Europe anti-terrorism conventions and offered military and strategic assistance. Armenia has opened its airspace and provided the necessary facilities for the anti-terrorism operations.

1. Legislative Regulations of RA in the Fight against Terrorism

Article 217 of the Criminal Code (thereinafter the Code) of the Republic of Armenia defines 'an act of terrorism' and provides the following sanction criterion: terrorist acts committed by, a single person, by a group of persons through preliminary agreement, or by an organized group; are punishable up to a minimum prison term of 5-10 years and a maximum term of 10-15 years. 'Acts of terrorism' may include, the mere threat of a terrorist act, the use of weapons, the use of weapons of mass destruction, the use of radio active materials, or any other act that may result in mass victimization.

In addition, the Part 7 of the Code prescribes a criminal responsibility not only for the perpetrator of the offense but also for the accomplices thereof (the organizer, the abettor and the helper). It is our opinion, that Article 217 of the new Criminal Code (terrorism) in combination with Part 7 of the same Code provide sufficient legal basis to not only address cases of terrorism but also cases regarding vicarious liability, conspiracy, aid and abetment of such acts (for example providing financial means to terrorists).

Under Article 38 of the Criminal Code the following persons are subject to criminal responsibility:

- The organizer is the person who organized or governed the committal of the crime, as well as, who created an organized crime or criminal cooperation or governed them;
- The abettor is the person who abetted another person to the committal of crime through persuasion, financial incentive, threat or otherwise;
- The helper is the person who assisted to the crime through pieces of advice, instructions, information or provided means, tools, or eliminated obstacles, as well as, the person who had previously promised to hide the criminal, the means and tools of crime, the traces of the crime or the items procured through crime, as well as, the person who had previously promised to acquire or sell such items.

Article 14 of the Code addresses jurisdictional issues by prescribing cases where an offence shall be considered as committed within the territory of the Republic of Armenia, and for which a person is subject to criminal responsibility under the Criminal Code of the RA. In accordance with the second part of the this Article if an offense has commenced, continued or has been completed in the territory of the RA, or the offense has been committed with the aiding and abetting of persons within the territory of RA, although the act itself may have been committed outside of the territory RA, then the said offense will be considered as punishable under the Criminal Code of the RA.

Moreover, Part 3 of Article 14 states that, a person who commits an offense within the territory of the Republic of Armenia or in the other states is criminally subject to the Criminal Code of the RA, if he is called for criminal responsibility in the RA and if the RA International Agreements do not prescribe otherwise.

Article 15 of the Code extends the authority of the Criminal Code of the RA over those person or persons, who have committed an offense outside of Armenia. Under Part 1 of this Article, citizens or residents of the Republic of Armenia, who have committed an offense in a foreign country shall be criminally liable under the criminal code of the RA, provided the act committed is defined as an offense by the legislature of that country and the perpetrator or perpetrators of the offense have not been convicted in that country.

Part 3 of the same article holds foreigners and persons who are not residents or citizens of the RA as criminally responsible under the Criminal Code of the RA, if they have committed:

- an offence, which is prescribed by the RA International Agreements;
- grave offense, or a particular grave offense under Article 19, or a grave offense falling within the definition of terrorism (under Parts 1 and 2 of Article 217), or a grave offense that is against the RA interests and/or the RA citizens' rights and freedoms (under Part 3 of Article 217).

Such criminal liability under the RA criminal code shall only fall upon those foreigners, non citizens and non residents of the RA, who have committed any or all of the above mentioned offenses, and have not been convicted for such actions under the penal code of any other country.

Moreover, Chapter 6 of the Code provides the definition of a completed and unfinished crime and the attempt to commit or perpetrate a crime. The same chapter provides that the attempt to commit or perpetrate a crime shall be punishable under the same article of the general part of the Code, which provides the definition and punishment of the completed offense.

Article 36 of the Code, which introduces the concept of 'voluntary refusal,' provides the following exceptions to this rule:

"Article 36. Voluntary refusal from a crime:
1. Voluntary refusal is the termination by the person of preparation or termination of action (inaction) directly aimed at the committal of crime, when the person realized the possibility of completion of the crime.
2. The person who refused to complete the crime is not subject to criminal liability, unless his actually committed act contains other elements of crime.
3. If the organizer of the crime, the abettor or helper refuses voluntarily, they are not subject to criminal liability, provided this person informed the state bodies or through other means and prevented the completion of the crime by the perpetrator.
4. If the actions mentioned in part 3 of this Article did not prevent the committal of the crime by the perpetrator, then, when sentencing, these actions can serve as circumstances mitigating the liability and the sentence."

Article 6 of the RA Law on Refugees (27, May 1999) prohibits the granting of refugee status in cases where a person:

- before entering the territory of the RA has committed a crime or military crime against peace and humanity;
- before entering to the territory of the RA has committed a non-political crime or a judgment of the International Court against him/her has been issued for committing a crime that violates the objectives and principles of the UN.

At the same time, in accordance with Article 6 of the RA Law on Political Asylum (19 October 2001), a person who has applied for political asylum in the RA will not be granted such asylum, if the competent authorities of the RA prosecute him/her for committed a crime in the territory of or against the RA. Further, under Article 6 a person who is under prosecution for committing a crime in his or her original country of citizenship, can also not be granted political asylum. Moreover, a person who enters or tries to enter Armenia while being prosecuted under any of the multilateral or bilateral agreements, to which RA is a party, is subject to arrest and extradition to the country prosecuting him or her, by the RA authorities. Such extradition can only occur if under these agreements the RA authorities are not authorized to continue or complete the prosecution initiated by the other country. We believe therefore, that the RA laws provide an adequate legal framework, whereby the RA authorities are afforded sufficient opportunities to scrutinize all political asylum cases and screen out all those applicants who have either personally committed crimes or have organized, abetted, or helped the commission of crimes, including terrorism.

With regard to the establishment of a legal infrastructure by the RA legislature that can ensure the circumvention of terrorist and terrorist organization financing within Armenia, the following checks are worth mentioning. Article 926 of the Criminal Code provides that the financial means that customers can dispose in their accounts are not limited, except for the cases provided under law or when the accounts are seized. Also, in accordance with Part 4 of Article 912 of the Code, the rules of the code on banks apply also to credit companies in case of adoption or implementation of the relevant agreement of bank account by the license given by them. Thus, the rules regarding freezing of assets in bank accounts apply not only to regular consumer accounts but also to the bank accounts opened by the credit companies.

According to the Article 3 of RA Law on Credit Companies (22 June 2002), the credit company is a legal entity, which has a license in the order prescribed, and which has a right to implement the following types of activities prescribed by the mentioned Law:

- involving of the loans as an enterprising activity and/or;
- adoption of such a transaction and/or;
- providing of a credits or making other investments.

With the freezing of bank accounts, the RA legislation also provides for the possibility to seize or to confiscate any other property, including financial means of a person committing a crime, if the authority implementing the criminal proceedings makes an adequate decision in accordance with the Chapters 31-32 of the Criminal Procedure Code of the RA.

Article 226 of the Code grants the government investigators the power to seize all or any things and documents, which may have an important bearing on a case. Private citizens, officials, enterprises, companies and organizations, notwithstanding the type of the property, are required under law to produce and deliver any possessions, things or documents that are required by the government investigators. The legal definition 'things' also includes financial or liquid assets that are a result of a crime or which are the proceeds of the realization of the things of crime.

Additionally, financial assets can also be seized in Armenia at the behest of another country, provided such seizure is performed in accordance with the requirements of the international agreements to which the RA is a party to, the RA Criminal Code (Article 226) and the RA Criminal Procedure Code (Chapter 54).

Article 338 of the Criminal Code provides the sanction for terrorist acts exacted against the representative of a foreign country. According to the first part of this article assault, or kidnapping, or deprivation of freedom, of the representative of foreign states or international organizations committed with the purpose of provoking war, or complication of international relations, is punishable with a prison term of 5 to 12 years. Part 2 of the same article provides that the murder of the representative of foreign states or international organizations, committed with the purpose of provoking war, or complication of international relations, is punished with a prison term of 10 years to life.

Article 389 of the Criminal Code, which relates to the international terrorism directly, stipulates the following:

"International terrorism, i.e., organization or implementation of an explosion or arson or other acts in the territory of a foreign state, with the purpose of international complications or provocation of war or destabilization of a foreign state, aimed at the destruction of people, or bodily injuries, destruction or spoilage of facilities, roads and means of transportation, communications, or other assets, is punished with imprisonment for 10-15 years, or for life."

This article acts as a deterrent to all international terrorists, and terrorist organizations that are looking for safe heavens around the globe.

Regarding the issue of extradition, when the extradition of an international terrorist is requested by a country, then Armenia will extradite that person to the given state in accordance with International Treaties of RA, with the exception of cases stipulated by those treaties and those cases, when the person who committed acts of international terrorism in a foreign state is a citizen of RA. Lastly if a terrorist act is committed in Armenia, then that the perpetrator(s) responsible, regardless of his/her citizenship, is held as criminally liable in the RA.

Concerning the liability for terrorism financing, it follows from Article 217 that any person who finances a terrorist act (Article 217) or gives out any moneys for the commitment of terrorism (Article 217) and such financing is fulfilled by a citizen of that state or any other state or non-citizen who is in a foreign State, then such person, in accordance with Article 217, is criminally liable in accordance with Criminal Code of RA. Similarly if a person finances international terrorism, then it will be considered as a criminal act, as Article 389 and part 5 of Article 38 of the Criminal Code of RA.

The Law of the Republic of Armenia on Combating Terrorism and the Law of the Republic of Armenia against Laundering of Illicit Proceeds and Terrorism Financing are also worth mentioning here. The Law of the Republic of Armenia on Combating Terrorism was adopted on March 22, 2005. The mentioned law defines legal and organizational grounds for combating terrorism in the Republic of Armenia and regulates the relations in the course of combating terrorism. In particular the law defines main principles of combating terrorism, bodies involved in combating terrorism, main functions of these bodies, gives the definition to the terrorist act, terrorist activities, anti-terrorist actions and other terms related to those activities.

According to the Article 6 of the Law it is declared that the Republic of Armenia shall cooperate with foreign states, international organizations involved in combating terrorism efforts, on the basis of the international agreements to which the Republic of Armenia is a party.

Under Article 9 of the Law it is stated that state bodies that are combating terrorism under the powers conferred to them by law, are responsible to:

- Develop and implement logistic, administrative, preventive, disciplinary and other measures to detect, prevent, impede and reduce the consequences of terrorist attacks;
- Identify and eliminate the causes and conditions conducive to terrorist actions;
- Create specialized divisions to combat terrorism;
- Participate in preparation of necessary international agreements deemed as required in the war against terror;
- Develop and submit to the Government of the Republic of Armenia recommendations on improvement of legislation of the Republic of Armenia pertaining to combating terrorism.

The Republic of Armenia adopted the Law of the Republic of Armenia against Laundering of Illicit Proceeds and Terrorism Financing on December 14, 2004. This law regulates the matters related to the laundering of illicit proceeds and terrorism financing, specifies the authorities in charge of regulating laundering of illicit proceeds and terrorism financing, as well as the various procedures and terms of cooperation.

In accordance with Article 10 of the Law, the Central Bank is the authorized body in charge of the fight against laundering of illicit proceeds. With an objective to organize the fight against laundering of illicit proceeds and financing of terrorism and to collect and coordinate the information stipulated by this law, a structural sub-division was established in the Central Bank, The Board of the Central Bank appointed the head and members of this sub-division. The sub-division performs a mandatory supervision over the process of information provision, analyzes all the information regarding on suspicious transactions which is provided by the reporting persons and in cases where the illicit laundering of proceeds is or financing of terrorism is established, it informs the prosecution authorities. Transactions of those accounts which are suspected in turnover of illicit proceeds and financing of terrorism are suspended or terminated on the basis of the decision of the Central Bank (Article 18).

According to Article 3 of the mentioned law reporting persons are banks, credit organizations, persons dealing with dealership sales and purchase of currency and extending professional activities of currency sales and purchase, persons dealing with monetary transfers, persons registering the asset rights, pawn-shops, persons verifying transactions in cases and according to the procedure stipulated by law, persons organizing games with prizes and lotteries, casinos, persons providing with insurance activities, as well as other persons and organizations. Article 4 of the law defines that the reporting persons have to undertake measures in accordance with the procedure defined by law and other standard acts to identify and prevent suspicious transactions (deals) by their customers or third party. The reporting persons also have to provide to the Central Bank information about laundering of illicit proceeds and terrorism financing stipulated by this law and other standard acts passed on the basis of it.

Under Article 12 it is stated that the Central Bank and other state authorities shall cooperate with the authorities of foreign states in the fight against laundering of illicit proceeds and financing of terrorism, within the scope of international treaties and in accordance with the procedure defined by the law.

Seizure of accounts which are suspected in turnover of illicit proceeds and financing of terrorism is regulated by Articles 232-234 of the Criminal Procedure Code of the Republic of Armenia. Under this article the proper authorities are granted the power to arrest (seize) in an operational way those monetary means, regardless their origin, which belong to the persons who are connected or are suspected or accused of being connected to terrorism activities. Part 2 of Article 233 defines those competent bodies, on the decree of which the seizure of monetary means is carried out. Those bodies are the investigating body, the investigator or the prosecutor. In order to make the fight against legalization of illicit proceeds and terrorism financing more effective, the amendments have been made in the laws 'On the Central Bank,' 'On Bank Secrecy,' 'On Banks and Bank Activities,' 'On State Registration of Legal Persons,' 'On Notaries' and other legal acts.

2. RA Cooperation in the Fight against Terrorism with Other CIS Member States (History, adopted international treaties, achievements etc.)

The need of unification of efforts of Commonwealth of Independent States, member states and law enforcement authorities in the fight against terrorism has been realized by the heads of Commonwealth states.

The first intergovernmental agreement between the Ministries of Internal Affairs of CIS states in the fight against crime in general was signed on April 24, 1992, and envisaged cooperation in following main directions:

- The fight with the crimes against life, health, freedom, property and dignity of personality;
- The fight with banditry, terrorism and international criminality.

Moreover, the cooperation of Commonwealth states' law enforcement bodies was defined by Intergovernmental Program of joint actions in the fight against organized crime and other forms of dangerous crimes on the territory of CIS adopted between the years 1996 and 1999. The experience of 4 years implementation of that Intergovernmental Program permitted to enlarge essentially the international legal basis for cooperation between the law enforcement agencies of the CIS. In particular, the terms, procedures and extent of cooperation in the fight against criminality and terror have been worked out and adopted, and a number of intergovernmental treaties have been signed.

In spite of the presence of a number of problems in the field of the illicit turnover of arms and explosives, insufficient availability of scientific legal solutions of problems of the fight against political extremism and terrorism and other problems, the CIS states' cooperation against terrorism was elemental in systematically and purposefully laying down a workable legal structure.

As a result of cumulative experience of cooperation in the fight against criminality the CIS Council of State Heads, a Program that was developed to fight international terrorism and other demonstrations of extremism was adopted till the year 2003.

As a whole, the following CIS bodies, take part in developing and adopting the measures in counterterrorism within the territories of the CIS states: Council of State Heads, Council of Government Heads, the Interparlamentary Assembly, Coordinating Council of General Prosecutors, the Council of Ministers of Internal Affairs, The Council of Heads of Security and Special Service bodies, The Council of Frontier Troops Commanders, The Council of Ministers of Defense, Intergovernmental Anti-terrorism Center. Through the establishment of the above mentioned bodies and also by signed intergovernmental and interdepartmental agreements, a basis is created for elaboration of common policies that deal with the threat of terrorism and political extremism within the territories of CIS states. However, that an example of the superior level of CIS states cooperation, the real and concrete implementation of this cooperation can be observed in the intergovernmental and interdepartmental programs that it creates.

The decree of CIS Council of State Heads, adopted on August 26, 2005, approved a Program for further cooperation between CIS member states in the fight against international terrorism and other forcible demonstrations of extremism for the period 2005-2007. The aim of the Program is activation and promotion of the level of cooperation of CIS member states in prevention, revelation, suppression and investigation of acts of terrorism and other demonstrations of extremism. According to the Program, its main aims are:

- Enlargement and strengthening of international legal base of CIS states cooperation in the fight against terrorism;
- Perfection and harmonization of national legislation in the matter of the fight against terrorism and other demonstration of extremism.

Active actions against international terrorism are conducted by the intergovernmental body Anti-terrorism Center of CIS, founded through the decree of the Council of State Heads on June 21, 2000. Anti-terrorism Center is a permanent acting specialized sectoral CIS body which is designated to ensure the coordination of cooperation of CIS member states competent bodies in the field of the fight against international terrorism and other demonstrations of extremism. The general supervision of the functioning Center is carried out by the Council of Heads of Security and Special Service bodies (CHSS). The head of the Center is appointed (removed) by the decree of CIS Heads of States Council by presentation of CHSS chair. CIS anti-terrorism Center executes functions as a kind of intergovernmental interdepartmental headquarters, which coordinates the antiterrorist activity of security bodies, special service and the law enforcement bodies of CIS states.

Such type of practical experience on Commonwealth space permits to define main directions of coordination of efforts in the field of counterterrorism on the national and regional levels. These directions are:

- The participation in elaboration of normative legal base of the coordination of national competent bodies' activity;
- Ensuring of coordination and cooperation between CIS member states in carrying out of common actions in the sphere of the combat against terrorism.
- Informational analytical activity on the basis of complex continuous exchange of legal information between the participants of anti-terrorism activity on CIS space.

The organization of training of specialists within antiterrorist subdivisions and realization of common antiterrorist training.

The participation in providing of a normative legal base for the antiterrorism activities of CIS states' competent bodies became one of priority goals of the Center from the first days of its existence. The adoption of model laws and other normative acts in the mentioned field, undoubtedly, contributes to the difficult processes of forming of national legislation in Commonwealth states on common methodological base.

At present, the Republic of Armenia in its fight against terror is cooperating with the CIS member states within the framework of the Conventions on 'Legal Assistance and Legal Relations in civil, family and criminal matters' signed in Minsk on January 22,1993 and in Kishinev on October 7, 2002, the Treaty on 'Cooperation of CIS member states in the fight against terrorism' signed in Minsk on June 4, 1999 and the Agreement on 'Cooperation of the Ministries of Justice of CIS member states' signed on September 8, 2000, as well as the framework provided by other relevant legal documents.

The Treaty on 'Cooperation of CIS member states in the fight against terrorism' signed in Minsk on June 4, 1999 provides the fundamental principals that shape the basis for the execution of cooperation between Commonwealth states' competent bodies in matters of prevention, revelation, suppression and investigation of terrorist acts. The most distinctive feature of the Treaty is that, it provides the juridical concept of technological terrorism. According to the definition provided by the treaty, technological terrorism is

"utilization or threat of utilization of nuclear, radiological, chemical or bacteriological (biological) arms or their components, pathogenic microorganisms, radio-active and other harmful for people's health substances, including the seizure, destroy of nuclear, chemical and other objects of increased technological and ecological danger, life support systems of cities and other populated areas, if these actions committed with a view of disturbing the public security, frightening of population, rendering of influence on adoption of decisions by authorities, for reaching of political, mercenary or any other aims, and also the attempt of commitment of one of listed crimes with the same aims, the execution of leadership, financing or participation as an instigator, accomplice or abettor of a person, who commits or attempts to commit such a crime."

Each contracting party, in accordance with Article 3 of the Treaty, has to indicate its competent bodies that are responsible for its implementation and which have the right to communicate with each other directly, without the usual intergovernmental procedure.

Cooperation between the competent bodies of the member states is carried out (Article 7) both on the basis of requests of one of the interested parties, or by initiative of the competent body, which supposes that such a cooperation will be of interest to the other party. According to Article 12, Parties on demand or by consent of the interested party, may expedite the representatives of competent bodies, including special antiterrorist units to render methodical, consultative and practical assistance. Articles 12-15 of the Treaty relate to matters of cooperation between Parties in carrying out special actions while rendering methodical and consultative assistance. Thus, On the matter of legal assistance, Republic of Armenia cooperates with CIS states on the basis of the Minsk and Kishinev Conventions on 'Legal Assistance and Legal Relations in civil, family and criminal matters.'

With those CIS states, which have not yet ratified the Kishinev Convention, the Republic of Armenia cooperates on the basis of Minsk Convention. In accordance with Article 6 of the Minsk Convention, Contracting Parties provide to each other legal assistance by executing procedural and other actions, envisaged by legislation of requested Contracting Parties, in particular: remittance of legal or other documents, carrying out searches, confiscation, remittance and issue related to the remittance of material evidence, realization of expertise, interrogation of accused persons, witnesses, experts, institution of criminal pursuit, search and extradition of persons, who committed crimes, recognition and execution of court decisions in civil cases. The Convention regulates the matters, which are related to the extradition of persons, who are on the territory of one of Contracting Parties to the other Party to institute criminal proceedings or to execute sentences. The Convention regulates as well questions which concern the matters of extradition, postponement of extradition, taking into custody for the extradition, temporary extradition and so on.

Article 56 of the Convention envisages that the extradition for the institution of criminal proceedings is executed for such actions, which, in accordance with laws of requesting and requested Contracting Parties, are punishable by a prison sentence of one year or more. The Convention regulates also the matter, which concern the refusal in extradition.

So, it is envisaged that the extradition is not executed, if:

- a person, whose extradition is requested, is a citizen of the requested Contracting Party;
- on obtaining the request, a criminal pursuit, in accordance with the legislation of the requested Contracting Party, cannot be continued or the sentence cannot be executed as a result of expiration of validity period or other legal motivation.

3. Conclusion

Armenian authorities fully support the fight against terrorism while bearing in mind the importance and necessity to protect rights, freedoms and legal interests of the citizens, society and the state, as well as to ensure the existence of legal mechanisms necessary for the stability of the economic system of the Republic of Armenia through setting up a legal mechanisms to combat terrorism.

At present, the need of more coordinated actions between the states for the fight against terrorism and unification of national legislations in that sphere are the most important.

Part 3

Responding to Terrorism

Terrorism as a Social and Criminal Phenomenon: A Complete Model to Deal with Terrorism

Ahmet Sait YAYLA
Professor and Police Major, Turkish National Police Anti-terrorism Department and Turkish Institute for Police Studies

Abstract. This article studies different social aspects of terrorists and terrorist organizations in an effort to better deal with terrorism, especially in the long run. The researcher, who also worked as a Police Captain at Turkish National Police Anti-Terrorism Department, seeks solutions to today's global problem by studying both literature and a Delphi examination of a survey of 1070 imprisoned terrorists. The researcher through his examination of the findings of the data presented that terrorism is a social phenomenon with criminal consequences that needs to be dealt by means of two dimensional approaches. The first is the social dimension of terrorism and the second is the criminal dimension of terrorism. Based on this, the researcher constructed a conceptual model which addresses both of these dimensions under the titles of long-term solutions and short-term solutions.

Keywords. Prevention of terrorism, social dimensions of terrorism, early intervention

Introduction

Terrorism has continued to be a consistent worry for the world for over a century. A terrorist strike sparked the First World War and since then, terrorist movements and incidents have dramatically increased. Terrorism has begun to claim more casualties, the terrorists have become more systematic and their tactics seems to be more complicated as the time passed. Furthermore, the beginning of the twenty-first century was marred with one of the most shocking terrorist attacks of all time when Al-Qaeda hit the World Trade Center and Pentagon, killing over 3,000 people at once which did not stop there and continued with the bombings in Spain, Istanbul, Indonesia, London and many more places.

In response to terrorism, governments fell short of defeating terrorist movements. As a whole, the world seemed incompetent to produce policies, programs or precautions to conquer such a large scale problem. Governments were typically caught unprepared and officials usually tried to deal with terrorism initially by using power or force. This aggressive action was typically motivated by the cries for retribution from the citizens emotionally affected by the destruction caused by terrorists.

In this regard, there is an urgent need to study terrorism in order to produce new tactics and procedures to more effectively fight and prevent terrorist activities. This research studies terrorism in such a way that we start dealing with terrorism and terrorists proactively before it is too late and before they carry out their actions.

1. Terrorism as a Social and Criminal Phenomenon

1.1. Research Questions

The researcher specifically addressed the research questions to be studied below; however, the findings of this research were not limited to the research questions stated. Moreover, different dependent and independent variables studied in this research happened to provide information not only for only specific research questions but also other questions as well. For this reason, the author chose to study findings of the study variable by variable and to draw conclusions from the variables directly instead of studying the research questions one by one. The research questions listed below constitute the framework of this study. With the study of the following questions and findings of this research, the nature of terrorists' sociological and psychological environment can be understood in order deal with the problem of terrorism more efficiently.

- What are the reasons behind terrorism?
- Why does terrorism occur?
- What ideologies provide the framework for terrorist violence?
- Why do some individuals become terrorists and others do not?
- Under what conditions will terrorists end their violence?
- What strategies and tactics do terrorists employ to achieve their goals?
- How terrorist organizations are internally organized?
- How do terrorist organizations perceive their external environment?

1.2. The Data

Two different databases are used in this research. The first data comes from a research of the Turkish National Police (TNP) Central Anti-Terrorism Department which involves a survey of 1,077 imprisoned or arrested terrorists. The results of this study with the statistics were made public through a book named 'Aileye Acik Mektup Projesi Arastirma Raporu' [1]. This survey provides the following information for all of the respondents where appropriate:

- The terrorist organization affiliation
- Age
- Education
    - Uneducated
    - First school or knows how to read and write
    - Middle school
    - High school
    - College drop out
    - College (Bachelor Degree)
    - Doctorate
- Marriage status
- Frequency of arrest or imprisonment

- Duration of punishment of the imprisoned
- The position in the terrorist organization
- How many years they have been affiliated with the organizations
- Health condition
- Communication condition
- Education status of fathers
- Profession of fathers
- Education status of mothers
- Profession of mothers
- Education status of spouses
- Profession of spouses
- Number of siblings
- Social economic status

The second data is constructed from a number of the terrorist testimonies some of which were directly written to the leaders of the DHKP/C terrorist organization. This database is gathered from the reports of terrorists which were directly written to the leadership of terrorist organizations and includes information regarding their background, education, social and economic conditions, family and family members and most importantly the answer for 'Why did they join the terrorist organization?' These reports and statements are available at the TNP archives or court statements and the researchers had access.

1.3. The Method

The 'Delphi Method,' a method of problem solving and decision making, was used in this research. Delphi Method is especially applicable when confronted with complex or confusing problems [2]. The Delphi Method was originally formed by Norman Dalkey and Olaf Helmer at the US Intelligence think tank RAND Corporation when they were conducting a research in 1946 during the cold war. The strategic planning technique of Delphi Method allows researchers to utilize the information, experience, knowledge, expertise and abilities of a broad perspective [3].

It is obvious that the problem of terrorism is so complex that no single solution or study could remedy the global problem of terrorism. There are even many issues and problems in defining terrorism as a definition of a term or a problem should be considered as the first step of solving that problem. Obviously, researchers, international organizations like the UN, and governments could not reach a consensus on a generally accepted definition of terrorism because of the complex issues surrounding terrorism. Therefore, the complexity of terrorism-related issues is so apparent that this complexity clearly justifies the use of the Delphi Method in this research. Additionally, one of the definitions of the Delphi Method credits it by saying that it is especially good to use when confronted with complex or confusing problems.

1.4. Limitations

Like every study, this research has its own limitations. First of all, there is a general limitation on studies about terrorism simply because the authorities tend to consider any information or data regarding terrorism as 'secret,' 'not to be shared with public,' or 'for internal use only.' Also, the authorities are reluctant by nature, even if there is no prohibition on sharing information about terrorism. This is the primary reason why there are so few research studies on terrorism in which large datasets are used. However, the researcher in this study was able to reach a large dataset that involves over one thousand terrorists through his work for the TNP Anti-terrorism Department for years.

One of the important limitations of this study is that the datasets were pre-collected and not original for this study. However, since the researcher was able to reach the original SPSS files and original responses to each question by each terrorist, the SPSS files were rearranged in accordant with this study's goals. Even with this pre-collected data, the datasets were sufficient to address the research questions.

Finally, it is always difficult to generalize the findings of a study to an entire population. This very large dataset used in this research, along with the researcher's own observations over the years during the dealings with different kind of terrorists including interrogations, interviews and anti-terrorist operations, provide strong indicators and factors derived from this research that can be used to control terrorist activities and prevent people from joining to the terrorist organizations. The findings of this research may be exceptionally useful for the country of Turkey because the respondents are from Turkey. Also, the findings should be deemed functional for other countries as well since the concept of terrorism crosses borders and has been an international issue for many years. Moreover, the country of Turkey has been dealing with such terrorism for over 30 years. Consequently, the findings in the following section will be used to build a conceptual model in accordant with the researcher's study.

2. Key Findings

- Terrorists are most likely to be arrested between the ages of twenty and thirty.
- Eight cities in Turkey account for more than half of the terrorists' birth places. This is a significant ratio when the population of those eight cities compared to the general population as those eight cities represent less than six percent of the general population of Turkey.
- Almost all of the terrorists have received some kind of education.
- Over half of the respondents in data were at least high school graduates.
- Sixty percent of the respondents were considered to be in the rank of supporters.
- Being arrested in the first five years of terrorist organization membership is very common as over half of the respondents fit this profile.
- The education levels of mothers are very low. Forty percent of them are illiterate.
- One third of the respondents lacked paternal supervision because their fathers were deceased.
- Over half of the respondents who had siblings had five or more.
- Over seventy percent of the respondents reported an income that was in the lower level group.
- Previous relations with terrorist organizations significantly increase the chance of being a terrorist.
- Most of the terrorists were persuaded to join a terrorist organization by either their relatives or peers.
- Only three percent of the respondents said that they became a member of a terrorist organization because of their ideologies alone.

2.1. Age

Terrorists are most likely to be arrested between the ages of twenty and thirty. Sixty percent of the respondents were between the ages of eighteen and thirty-first at the time of their arrest. Additionally, most of the respondents over the age of thirty-first reported that they were arrested at least one time prior to their latest arrest. Therefore, a vast majority of the respondents were in their early twenties at the time of their first arrest.

2.2. Birth Places

Eight cities in Turkey account for more than half of the terrorists' birth places. This is a significant ratio when the population of those eight cities is compared to the general population of Turkey. Those eight cities represent less than six percent of the general population. Traditionally, these regions have represented a different understanding and interpretation of Islam called 'Alevilik.' Some of the Alevi people in these regions have formed a closed society over the years. For example, customarily the families only accept inter-community marriages. Social bonds and interactions through these communities are very strong and per their customs, they tend to live together. Some terrorist organizations managed to politically manipulate some of these communities in order to gain support. They did this by misrepresenting themselves somewhat different than what they really are.

2.3. Educational

The two most significant factors in this section are that almost all of the terrorists have received some kind of education and that over half of the respondents were at least high school graduates. In Turkey, most of the children go to public schools where the curriculum is prepared by public officials and where the teachers are hired and trained by the National Education Department. Furthermore, attending elementary school for eight years is mandatory by law. Therefore, the government has direct access to all of the children throughout their education for at least eight years. When we take into account the fact that over half of the respondents are at least high school graduates, this means that those students could be reached during their high school years very easily by their teachers or school counselors. There is a significant opportunity for the government to reach out to at risk children and make sure they understand and acknowledge the consequences and affects of their relations with terrorist organizations. Thus, an effective method and policy in the fight against terrorism has to take education into consideration. Such a policy would help reduce the number of new members dramatically, simply because the children would better know and understand what would happen if they joined a terrorist organization. Also, each child would be explicitly taught how their traditions and religions do not allow terrorism. They would also know that terrorism and violence are not socially accepted. At the very least, this policy would better ensure that children would not be unaware of the schemes of terrorist organizations and their purposes.

2.4. Hierarchy in the Terrorist Organization

The research indicated that sixty percent of the respondents were considered as supporters. Supporters are the people who have recently joined the terrorist organization and have not yet carried out any violent activities and who are also being trained and prepared for the next steps in the terrorist hierarchy, namely to be deployed for terrorist activities. Intervention of the government at this stage is extremely important because supporters can be easily saved from the terrorist organizations if they can be reached before they carry out violent activities. These people are usually quite conflicted. On one hand, they do not want to officially join the terrorist organizations because of various reasons: being afraid of imprisonment, fear of being killed, losing ties with their friends or families. Also, they fear that if they do not complete the process of becoming a member, they may be punished by the terrorist organization.

An early intervention or consultation program guaranteeing the safety of departing supporters is needed. The supporter would have to officially agree to stop supporting the terrorist organization and physically cut their connections with whom they are affiliated. The supporter stage is critical because these people are not full-fledged members and still have strong ties to the community. They are still afraid of the law and legal punishments if they continue to be a member of a terrorist organization. However, they may fear the response of the terrorist organization more; in other words, the legal punishment may be perceived as minor compared to the threat of being killed, having a family member killed or kidnapped, or being imprisoned in an undisclosed location. Therefore, the government's position in the retrieval of terrorist supporters must be firm, and it must be understood that the person would be fully protected.

2.5. The Role of First Time Arrest

Being arrested in the first five years of terrorist organization membership is very common as over half of the respondents fit this profile. This variable shows us two significant findings:

1. Almost all of the terrorists get arrested over time including half of them during the first five years after they become a member of a terrorist organization.
2. The government authorities have a possibility to save people from terrorist organizations at their first arrest by making sure they do not interact with the terrorist organizations after they get released.

However, there are three important challenges here.

1. The first is making sure that the first time arrestees who would be eligible for this program had not been involved in any violent activities.
2. The second is being able to enforce the rules of no contact and guaranteeing that each arrestee understands the consequences of returning to the terrorist organization.
3. The third challenge is being able to track them after they are released to make sure they cut off their connections from the terrorist organization and, if needed, to protect them.

Accordingly, there is a need of attitude adjustment in the behaviors of the law enforcement. The law enforcement approach to non-violent newly recruited terrorists or supporters should not be making sure that they are arrested and get the maximum penalty through the judicial system. Instead, law enforcement officials should be able to act as a psychologist in order to extract these people from terrorist organizations. Most of these prisoners are already experiencing the dilemma of leaving the terrorist organization, so the chance of redirecting their lives is great. The worst possible outcome of this policy would be that the released prisoners return to the terrorist organization. However, at least the law enforcement will have this person under close watch and if he starts to interact with the terrorist organization again, it is very easy to re-arrest him and prosecute from being a member of a terrorist organization. Therefore, this approach may be used to build trust in already distressed people and bring them back to the society peacefully.

2.6. Education Level of Mother

The research indicates that the education level of the respondents' mothers is very low. Forty percent of the mothers are illiterate and over forty-five percent had only elementary school education. This variable is not consistent with the actual literacy rate of Turkey; in fact it is extremely high. Nevertheless, this rate will continue to decrease as literacy improves in the country. However, this variable clearly indicates that teenagers whose mothers have not received education are more likely to be manipulated by terrorist organizations when compared to the other youngsters whose mothers have been educated. There is an undeniable relationship between the education mothers receive and being influenced by terrorist propaganda. Even though attending schools for first eight year education is required by the Turkish regulations, it is very clear that it was not the case for some of respondents' mothers. In this regard, we can clearly conclude that there is a strong relationship in being educated and accepting terrorist propaganda especially in the early stages of adolescent life and parenthood.

2.7. Role of Father

One third of the respondents lacked parental supervision because their fathers were not available to them at their childhood. This ratio with the consideration of strong traditional customs regarding family ties and father supervision that exist in Turkish life evidently signifies that father supervision and parental relations have such an important effect in the process of becoming a member of a terrorist organization. Therefore, we can clearly conclude that youth who lack parental supervision, especially paternal supervision, are more likely to become involved with a terrorist organization.

From experience with numerous prisoners, this researcher has seen that fathers can be highly successful in saving their sons or daughters from terrorist organizations if the father can intervene at the right time. On many occasions, parents of teenagers would come to the police department to ask for help for their teens who were exposed to terrorist propaganda and were becoming to get involved with terrorist organizations. The parents were simply asking for help to save their children. From personal observations, those families who made more effort to save their children usually succeeded, especially if they were assisted by the experts in the anti-terrorist units.

2.8. Siblings

The research showed that over half of the respondents had five or more siblings. This finding is very important especially when we take into account the findings of previous variable on parental supervision and the next variable on the effects of socio-economic status of the families in becoming vulnerable to terrorist propaganda. Obviously, the number of the brothers and sisters, in fact number of the dependants in one family, is directly related with the family supervision and wealth simply because as the number of the dependents increase, the share of the family wealth and the time parents allocate for each child decreases accordingly. Ideally, parents would be aware of this fact and take into account their socio-economic situation and their time available for their children while they are making plans for future. As a result, having many children in one family tends to result in poor parental supervision and a smaller share from the family's wealth for each child. This may cause offspring of these families to search for revenue and encounter social environments that could make them very vulnerable to terrorist organizations.

2.9. Family Income

Most of the findings in this research are interrelated, as are family size and family income. Over seventy percent of the respondents reported an income that was considered in the lower level group when compared to the general population. This situation clearly indicates that poor families' kids are more vulnerable and open to terrorist propaganda. It is important to clearly state that being poor does not mean being underprivileged; however, the research markedly shows that over seventy percent of the terrorists in the study indicated that their families had incomes lower than the general population. When this lower income is combined with the number of the brothers and sisters and with the lack of parental supervision, it makes a great impact in the children's life.

2.10. Previous Terrorist Relationships

The research indicates that previous relationships with any terrorist organization between the people in question or between an organization and the person's family members dramatically increase the chance of being accepted in a terrorist organization. This finding indicates that teenagers are more vulnerable to a terrorist propaganda if they or one of their close family members have had previous interactions with any other terrorist organizations. This issue is significant because even a slightly permissive attitude towards a terrorist group within a family can lead other members to join a terrorist organization. This casual relationship must be understood by the government and the public education system. The public, especially students, must understand the dangers of sympathizing with terrorist organizations. Sharing views with a terrorist organization is not a crime but may certainly lead to involvement. Therefore, precautions must be taken to show the public that sympathizing may lead to active involvement therefore violence, which is illegal.

2.11. Peer Effects

Over sixty percent of the terrorists were persuaded to join a terrorist organization by either relatives or peers. Of this sixty percent, friends make up over thirty-five percent indicates that terrorist candidates are more likely to be persuaded to join a terrorist organization either by friends or by one of their relatives. Ideology alone does not seem to be the driving force in attracting members because only three percent of the respondents cited ideology alone as a reason. However, when ideology and other social factors combined with social and psychological pressure of the peers and relatives, it makes a fertile ground for the terrorist to persuade people to join their organizations. In this regard, it is safe to assume that close monitoring of teenagers' social environment may reduce the risk of terrorist influence dramatically. Therefore, there is a need for a program to inform the families and other elements that have control over the children such as school teachers accordingly in an effort to reduce the number of new terrorist. Consequently, such a program will be addressed during the explanation of proposed model to fight against terrorism in the next sections.

3. Regression Analysis Findings and Discussions

In this section, four different tables with a number of dependent and independent variables were studied. Almost all of the findings of the descriptive studies were validated by the following regression analysis where different datasets and variables were cross-examined.

3.1. Relation of Age and the Sentence Received

As the people in the terrorist organizations get older, the amount of sentence they receive increases. This finding represents how terrorist organizations operate. As the terrorists get older, they participate in more terrorist activities to win the trust of their superiors. As a result, they get assigned to positions in the hierarchical pyramid simply because they are well-known by the organization and they are mature enough to assume responsibilities. Naturally, if a terrorist is involved in more terrorist activities and assumes a responsibility in the organization, the duration of the sentence he/she receives increases as a consequence.

3.2. Relation of the Number of the Siblings and the Sentence Received

The more brothers and sisters a terrorist has, the shorter the sentence. This finding seems odd; however, all those in the TNP Anti-Terrorism units can attest to this fact. Terrorist organizations automatically assign their own lawyers for the cases. In most cases, especially if the suspect has newly joined the terrorist organization, terrorist organizations insist that the suspect use their own lawyer. Most of the time, lawyers are instructed to make sure the new members spend some time in the prison so that the terrorist organization makes sure the suspect will not have any hope for the future and they will have him in the prison for a better and more effective training over the time he spends in prison. If the larger families may have more opportunity to help out their arrested person is able to hire his/her own lawyer, the sentence typically shortens. If the siblings are adults, usually at least one has the financial means to assist the arrested family member.

3.3. Relation of the Socio-Economic Status and the Sentence Received

There is a negative significant relationship between the socio-economic status of the terrorists and the amount of sentence they receive. As the socio-economic status of the respondent increases, the duration of the sentence lessens according to the data. This also indicates the importance of family involvement during the trail process. Families with better socio-economic conditions may hire better lawyers to support their children.

3.4. Relation of the Being Married and the Sentence Received

The next finding from regression analysis is about married terrorists. This is less significant because the number of the married terrorists is not very high. Married terrorists tend to receive lower sentences when compared with non-married terrorists. This finding is logical when considering the fact that married terrorists are often more mature and need to consider their wives and children to get a shorter sentence at any cost. Usually, terrorist organizations encourage their members to display aggressive behavior and not to cooperate with the authorities during trail to support their ideology that the courts are not legitimate. Married terrorists do not tend to disrespect courts openly because they know misbehaving during trials may increase their sentence. Therefore, married terrorists may cooperate with the authorities due to their personal responsibilities and ties.

3.5. Relation of the Years Spent in a Terrorist Organization and the Sentence Received

Terrorists who served more years in a terrorist organization are more likely to try to get shorter sentences. This is logical because the more mature people get, the better they understand the facts about the life, and in return, do not act emotionally in difficult situations. Similarly, the terrorists who spent many years in terrorist organizations, and observed the difficulties their friends experienced over the years know exactly what will happen if they do not work together with the authorities. They may try to reduce the sentence they are going to get by cooperating with the authorities. In this researcher's experience, it was observed that a leader of terrorist organization gave a statement over fifty pages regarding his terrorist organization because he understood that it was the end of the road and tried to save himself.

3.6. Relation of the Years Spent in a Terrorist Organization and the Place in Terrorist Hierarchy

Other findings indicate that the more terrorists spent time in a terrorist organization, the higher place in the hierarchy they receive, which is expected. Also similarly, the better education a person receives the higher position in the hierarchy he maintained according to the data. This indicates that terrorist organizations tend to assign leadership to the terrorists with higher education. Similarly, education level of mothers' had positive effect on a terrorist's place in the structural hierarchy. The more the mothers were educated, the higher the position their offspring had in the terrorist hierarchy. Socio-economic status, just like the other variables, has a positive effect on the status of the terrorists.

3.7. Effect of Loosing a Friend or a Relative

One of the most prominent independent variables deals with anyone who had lost a family member during a governmental conflict with a terrorist group. This factor goes far beyond the variable of having a friend or relative involved in a terrorist organization. The emotional ties to the terrorist organizations and the need for retribution against the government are quite significant. Although it is a notable factor, it cannot be easily altered by the governments though.

3.8. Relation of the Social Class and Duration in the Terrorist Organization

The last factor may be one of the most important findings. It showed that as the social class decreased, the duration in the terrorist organization increased. This finding means that terrorist organizations are more likely to retain the members who come from lower socio-economic class over the years. This finding is extremely important and was also supported by previous findings where it was indicated that lower class terrorists receive higher sentences during their trials. In a very similar fashion, another variable on where terrorists were born also supports this finding. Terrorists who were born in a city would stay as a terrorist less than the terrorists who were not born in a city. If we consider that most of the cities have better living conditions when compared to the suburbs and small towns, this finding also supports the finding on lower socio-economic class members of terrorist organization. Therefore, we can easily argue that terrorists are more successful among lower socio-economic class communities and terrorists from these communities tend to remain more active for more time in the terrorist organizations, so they receive more sentences than other socio-economic classes in the community. Consequently, this fact must be considered in a sound prevention program that tries to deal with terrorism. The focus must concentrate on lower socio-economic classes because they provide more than sixty percent of the new members come from this group which also represents of the long-term terrorist members.

4. A Conceptual Model to Fight against Terrorism Based on the Findings of the Study

Terrorism is a social phenomenon with criminal consequences. Terrorist organizations are formed and shaped over time. Terrorists claim that they began to apply violence because they could not find other solutions to overcome their grievances. This justification helps them to survive because those grievances yield some support from public. Unlike regular criminals, they act in groups and they are very well organized. Furthermore, even though there is no doubt that their tactics are illegal, they purport that they are sacrificing themselves for the good of their society and say what they are doing is not crime. All of these facts make dealing with the problem of terrorism special with two dimensional approaches. The first is the social dimension of terrorism and the second is the criminal dimension of terrorism. This model will address both of these dimensions under the titles of long-term solutions and short-term solutions. The long-term solutions deal with the social aspects of terrorism under the title of *Proactive Approach to Terrorism* and the short-term solutions deal with the criminal aspects of terrorism under the title of *The Immediate Fight against Terrorism*.

Traditionally, dealing with the problem of terrorism has been deemed primarily as the job of the law enforcement. The government authorities and public expect the law enforcement or the military in more serious situations, to deal with the terrorists. However, the researcher argues that dealing with the problem of terrorism is not only the job of the law enforcement, but also the job of the whole divisions of the governments and societies because of the undeniable social aspects of terrorism. Law enforcement cannot be completely successful if the other government agencies, governmental, and non-governmental institutions do not assume critical roles in the fight against terrorism.

This model does not argue that the law enforcement was unsuccessful to deal with the problem of terrorism. On the contrary, the law enforcement is successful but as law enforcement continues to apprehend terrorists, the more new terrorists continue to exist. Simply, action creates back reaction and may cause more people to join the terrorist organization. It should be kept in mind that terrorists desire conflict as it was discussed in the second chapter. In one sense, using pure force against terrorism without any social remedy is what the terrorists are looking for and the law enforcement may be helping the terrorists because conflict is obviously what they desire. However, this does not mean that the law enforcement should not do the job that needs to be done. The *social* aspects of this fight should also be carried out so that the fight against terrorism cannot be seen as a conflict.

In this regard, Turkey constitutes a good example. When terrorism started during the 1960s, the public response was that it would die down over the years. On the contrary, since then, Turkey has continued to live with terrorism on an increasing scale sometimes. It has been over forty years now and Turkey still remains a base for terrorists partially. Even though the Turkish law enforcement proved to be quite successful over the years, there are still terrorists in Turkey and they still have support to survive. In one sense, dealing with terrorism is like dealing with drugs. As long as there is demand for drugs, there will be dealers, and the law enforcement will be going after those dealers. Therefore, there is a need to deal with the both sides of this problem by identifying the stakeholders and assigning responsibilities to both sides including the law enforcement to try to eradicate the problem of terrorism as both a long and short term goal.

4.1. The Purpose of the Proposed Model

The researcher is proposing this model mainly because almost all efforts of different countries in the fight against terrorism has focused on the physical fight and measures against terrorism including hardened law enforcement or military response and hardened security measures. Often, authorities fail to ask the question of 'Why does terrorism exist?' and 'How should we deal with the problem of terrorism without alienating ourselves?', instead they usually ask and focus on questions such as 'What to do to stop terrorists physically?' 'How to catch the terrorists?' or 'How they can better secure their people?' While the questions that are not raised do not deal with terrorism effectively, the questions that are usually asked have what the world been doing to deal with terrorism some what ineffectively for years. In order to deal with terrorism and violence efficiently in the long run, a balance between existing and proposed policies must be achieved. Simply, we need to take security measures while we are asking these questions: Why does terrorism exist? How can we eradicate the causes of terrorism? How can we stop people joining terrorist organizations?

4.2. Proactive Approach to Terrorism

For this section, the researcher considers terrorism as a social phenomenon. The main objective is dealing with terrorism as a social problem without using pure force. Different peaceful approaches are essential so that terrorists can be stopped before committing tedious acts. In other words, by finding peaceful approaches to address the roots of terrorism, fewer people will be recruited and fewer victims will suffer. Identifying the underlying problems and grievances in the society must be the first step in the fight against terrorism because terrorists justify their causes and reach the public through societal grievances. Then, there is a need of going after terrorists while the government and other stakeholders cooperatively and eagerly try to reach everybody to convey the real faces of the terrorists and horrible consequences of terrorism making terrorism and violence socially unacceptable and undesirable.

Terrorists are deeply entrenched in nearly every formation of the society and there are clear indications in this research that can be used to prevent or at least to reduce the number of terrorist activities. For example, the research showed that almost all of the subjects were approximately twenty years old when introduced to the terrorist organizations and they all went to school. In fact, over half of them were high school graduates or over high school graduates. The research also showed a negative relationship between the terrorists and their uneducated parents. Similarly, the research clearly indicated the relationship between the terrorists and their socio-economic status. Almost seventy percent had lower socio-economic backgrounds. Also, there are some regions in which the intensity of terrorists are high and these regions need special attention because over half of the terrorists were from those regions. Therefore, there is a need for a model that deals with all these aspects of terrorism so that the atmosphere that yields terrorists to perform their activities can be vanished and the terrorists or future terrorists can be stopped before it is too late.

4.3. The Yayla Model of Proactive Approach to Terrorism

4.3.1. Objectives

1. Address terrorism as a social problem with long-term goals and planning rather instead of using the traditional crime response approach.
2. Make terrorism and violence concepts completely unacceptable in the eyes and minds of the people through planned anti-terrorist public ads that counter and break down terrorists own propaganda.
3. Prevent people from joining the terrorist organizations so that both the potential terrorists and their potential victims can be saved.

4.3.2. Initial Steps

1. Social research on terrorism through the universities and non-governmental organizations that initially focuses on the causes and justifications of recent terrorist activity.
2. Produce a policy based on the above mentioned research and establish a plan to further record and assess the effectiveness of the policy.
3. Use the country's education system to reach out to teenagers and promote awareness to reduce the number of new terrorists.
4. Awareness programs to ensure parents or guardians can be informed from their children's initial involvements with terrorist organizations and providing consultation to be provided by the law enforcement to save their children form the hands of terrorist organizations.

4.3.3. The Following Stakeholders Must Be Involved in the Implementation:

1. Government
2. Law enforcement and intelligence
3. Schools, colleges and teachers
4. Religious figures
5. Families
6. Prominent people (including regional leaders and celebrities)
7. Non-profit or non-governmental organizations
8. The media

4.3.4. Responsibilities of Stakeholders

4.3.4.1. Government
The most important factor of the government is to organize, fund, and implement this program. There is a need for a body or a committee to oversee all of the responsibilities and objectives

of this model (including members from different governmental bodies, universities, private organizations and the media). Because this plan requires cooperation from diverse groups, it is necessary to have a governing committee to promote harmony and appropriate decision making. Such a body should have full authority to plan a long term fight against terrorism and should be directly tied to the head of the state to overcome the bureaucratic difficulties.

The initial task would be to find the real causes of terrorism through scientific research carried out by independent institutions, such as universities and non-profit organizations. The findings of this research should then be studied to figure out the most important causes for terrorism and the rationalizations that the terrorists use to justify themselves. With those in hand, the committee should produce a plan to eradicate the causes and justifications in the long term. Those causes would probably involve many political, socio-economic, and educational aspects. It would require a great deal of time and effort to work on those issues, so long-term planning is a necessity.

One of the other most important initial tasks should involve a massive campaign to make terrorism and violence unacceptable in the society. This task is very essential and it requires changing the concept and approach of people to terrorism in some places that could only be reached over the years with the help of education system, the media, religious figures, non-profit organizations and may be new economical structures over the years. Social change is usually very slow and people are usually reluctant to change. Therefore, we need long term goals here with the help of a continuing struggle to make terrorism socially unacceptable.

4.3.4.2. Educational System

The educational system has a vital importance in this fight as we are talking about change in the conceptions and making the teenagers aware of the real dangers of the terrorism. Therefore, the educational system is a key player in this fight. By having teachers involved and trained appropriately and with necessary changes in the curriculum, the rate of youth terrorist recruitment will be affected. The teachers would assign research and discuss the true face of terrorist violence. There could be consultants in the schools that would help these efforts simply by working with the kids that cannot openly speak to their parents. There may be some text in history or social class curriculums that mention terrorism and why and how the kids should stay away from terrorism. Another important aspect is having the teachers be alert about terrorist activities, especially in the high schools so that the authorities and parents can get involved before it is too late. A third important measure would be after school programs or providing supervision for outside activities so that the teens could not be easily reached by the terrorists. Finally, the colleges are also needed in this fight. The freshman that leaves his/her hometown to go to college is a potential target for the terrorists because they usually try to offer help or find places to stay for the new students in an effort to build loyalty for further involvement in the group. A strong network of the education systems and a clear plan for revised curriculum can be important tools in the long term reduction of terrorism.

4.3.4.3. Law Enforcement and Intelligence

The law enforcement (which will be used to refer to both law enforcement and intelligence agencies) will assume many important tasks on top in addition to their regular responsibilities that will be presented in the next section under the title of short term or initial goals. The most important task of the law enforcement is to act under the rule of law. Any unlawful activities that are carried out by the law enforcement including unnecessary force and misbehaving or exceeding arrest durations will give the terrorists the ultimate justifications they want. Therefore, it is vital the law enforcement operate in accordance with the rules of the government.

The second important task is to avoid unnecessary conflicts with the society. This does not mean to tolerate to unlawful events. On the contrary, this is stated so that the law enforcement can always be aware that the terrorist ideologies encourage conflict with the law enforcement. Once conflict has begun, any alienation between citizens and the governments can be exploited by the terrorists to build support for their side. In this regard, the actions of the law enforcement should be well-planned and the lines must be drawn beforehand so that the law enforcement personnel know the appropriate tactics under difficult and special circumstances. For example, the terrorists use demonstrations for open conflicts with the law enforcement. Then they can provoke the law enforcement to use force in front of the media. Therefore, the law enforcement should be aware of this fact and should be trained on dealing with such situations. Another important measure is releasing the appropriate information to the media and the public about what is happening. With the correct information, the public will not be easily misled. In this regard, there is a need for a well established, working communication channels between the media and the law enforcement.

Intelligence is one of the other vital duties of law enforcement. In addition to the short-term precautions that will be listed in the next section, the law enforcement intelligence should be able to track the movements and interactions of the terrorists so that they can figure out whom the terrorist organizations have targeted for recruitment. This will give the law enforcement the opportunity of early intervention by working with the parents or schools of these potential terrorists before it is too late. In this manner, with sound intelligence, the law enforcement should also provide consultation to the potential terrorists, their families, and the schools in an effort to save them form the hands of the terrorists. Consultation is extremely important because it will allow parents to have a third party intervene when their children are approached by terrorists, and consultation, when done in the early stages of recruitment, has proven highly effective in the anti-terrorist branch of the TNP.

4.3.4.4. Families
Families have significant tasks under this program. First of all, they must be aware of the friendship circle of their children. They must make sure that their children are never approached by the terrorists. This involves pure precaution effort and does not mean that the families or parents should conflict with their children. However, the parents can always assess their children and take steps to reduce the chances of having them involved with terrorist organizations such as: making sure the children have different opportunities to spend their free times like sport activities or some other hobbies or directing them to more secured environments where interaction risks with terrorists are considerably low. This is very important because the research indicates that over sixty-five percent of the terrorists were strongly influenced to join a terrorist organization by a friend or relative. Secondly, the parents have to openly make it clear that terrorism and violence are not tolerable under any circumstances. The children should be aware of possible exposure to terrorist propaganda. Any form of acceptance of terrorism by the parents can shape and may eventually lead to acceptance in the children' minds. Thirdly, the children should be supervised as much as possible in an effort to make it difficult for terrorists to reach them. Another duty of the families is to provide proper opportunities and activities to their children so that they are busy with those activities instead of being idle and looking for something to do. This approach is important because terrorism might be acknowledged as adventure for some youth at the beginning. Finally, if the families become aware of the interaction of their children with a terrorist organization or if they are informed by the authorities that their kids are approached by the terrorist organizations, they should work and cooperate with the authorities to save their children. Sometimes, families may not let

the authorities know about their son or daughter's position just because they are scared that they would be punished under the law. However, if they do not work with the authorities, this may bring worse consequences including the death of their children. Consequently, it is obvious that the families bear many responsibilities with their children and if they are in a community where they might be open to terrorist propaganda, keeping their children out of terrorist activities becomes one of the initial tasks of the families.

4.3.4.5. Religious Figures

Religion is a social factor and force that cannot be ignored or denied. Most of the Turkish people are affiliated with a religion and we are not aware of any religion that accepts terrorism as a tool as it was studied in the previous chapters. However, some people would use religions to inspire different ideologies by interpreting the religions inappropriately. In this regard, the religious figures have very strong power to deny terrorism. The religious figures and institutions have vital roles and duties in denying terrorism and violence and making it unacceptable by stating in various activities of common prayers or through other means so that the people can openly be presented that terrorism is not accepted by their religion. This fact must be presented very well and supported as clearly as possible so that no one has any doubt about it. Also, many religions focus on the youth by providing different classes to teach them their religion. Anti-terrorism propaganda must be one of the initial teachings to make the teenagers understand that terrorism is also not permitted by their religion.

4.3.4.6. Non-profit or Non-governmental Originations and Prominent People in Society (NGOs and Prominent People)

NGOs and prominent people also have vital roles in the fight against terrorism. There may be many different NGOs that can focus on different aspects of this long-term fight against terrorism. The governments clearly need the help of NGOs as they are social institutions and they could easily fill the uncovered areas by the governments or could without difficulty work with their surroundings to help out this fight. The prominent people could also easily help in this manner. For example, a celebrity could openly deny terrorism or talk to the youth about the disastrous consequences of terrorism. Local tribal leaders and respected people within smaller communities could also help shape public opinion and could easily campaign against terrorism. Therefore, the government should use prominent people and NGOs as resources to reduce terrorist activity.

4.3.4.7. The Media

The job of the media is to inform people without showing bias. One of the major tasks of the government is to inform the public about the true face and danger of terrorism. This can only be done through the media. Therefore, the governments need an open and working channel with the media so that they can inform the media appropriately to ensure the people receive accurate information on terrorism. Inaccurate information on terrorism may lead to unnecessary panic in the society or may be used as propaganda or justification by the terrorist organizations. Another important responsibility of the media should be to help the government in the effort to make terrorism and violence unacceptable. For example, editorials from noted writers denouncing terrorism or discussing the negative effect of terrorism on the society would build public support for the government's campaign against terrorism. Another responsibility of the media is not to become a propaganda tool for the terrorists or to seem to side with terrorists. This is very vital because the media can unwillingly help the terrorists to advertise or help the causes of terrorism depending on the slant of a story.

4.4. The Immediate Fight against Terrorism

This part of the model deals with the criminal and security aspects of terrorism. The main focus is to protect the lives of innocent people, property, daily public life, and the feeling of being secure. Law enforcement plays the major role in the immediate fight against terrorism. As studied in the previous chapters, terrorist activities aim to produce a panic in the society mostly by random and unexpected attacks on people or government authorities. Those attacks are used to reduce the trust of people to their law enforcement and to reduce the feeling of security. Feeling safe is essential for human life and terrorists try to win their war by destroying the feeling of security. In this manner, the criminal and security aspects that must be addressed by law enforcement agencies are listed.

4.5. The Yayla Model for the Immediate Fight against Terrorism

4.5.1. Objectives

Protect the lives, property and daily routine of the society through carefully planned security precautions that are as unobtrusive as possible.
   Qualifications:

1. Prevent potential terrorist activities through intelligence and security operations.
2. Provide extra security for potential targets including people and infrastructures.
3. Carry out operations to arrest the terrorists.
4. Ensure the feeling of safety and secure the continuance of the daily routine of the society.
5. Gain knowledge on the potential and tactics of the terrorist organizations.
6. Predict future activities of the terrorist organizations and take preventative and safety measures against them.
7. Inform the public about the true nature of the terrorism and expected terrorist activities.
8. Seek the cooperation of the public in the fight against terrorism.

4.5.2. Specifications

This plan needs a large-scale, coordinated effort between all law enforcement agencies and particularly intelligence and anti-terrorism units. The law enforcement must carry out this plan by having:

1. Proper equipment
    a. Bullet proof vests or bullet proof vehicles
    b. Information systems to reach the terrorists
    c. Information system support in order to archive, share, and reach information
    d. Surveillance equipment
    e. Other required and appropriate equipment as needed and as technology developed
2. Extensive training about the terrorist organizations, their tactics, and characteristics.
3. Special anti-terrorist training (regular law enforcement training does not

provide such kind of instruction.)
4. Education about their responsibilities.
5. Shared information from any appropriate agency to ensure the harmony in the fight against terrorism.
6. Awareness of the fact that each suspect must be treated without abuse and must be considered innocent until convicted.
7. Respect for human life and civil rights.

Fighting terrorism is a very delicate task for the law enforcement. On one side, the law enforcement has to protect the society from any terrorist threats and make sure they take enough measurers to prevent any potential attacks; on the other side, law enforcement should avoid conflict with the society in order to avoid alienating the society through harsh security measures. This serves to build and maintain the support of the public in this fight, which is very essential since the terrorists live in the same society. Therefore, the response to terrorism needs to be extremely well balanced. The measures should be sound enough to stop terrorists or prevent terrorist activities; however, those measures should be implemented properly so that the society remains in support of the government and is less likely to be influenced by terrorist propaganda. In this regard, the following two phase model must be implemented when a country finds itself in a fight with the terrorists. The first part of the model, long-term fight against terrorism, was discussed above and what follows is the initial law enforcement response to terrorism.

The main objective is to protect the lives and property of the society and the government. The law enforcement needs to deal with the criminal aspect of terrorism under this title. There is a need of well organized and inter-communicating agencies that fights against terrorism on top of regular local law enforcement response because dealing with terrorism requires more professionalism and skills than regular police work. However, this does not mean that regular law enforcement does not have any responsibility under this title. There need to be special units that solely focus on terrorism but they also should be in contact with other units as terrorist activities tend to reach into other crimes, like money laundering, smuggling, or drug trafficking and as the other units happen to deal with the terrorists sometimes whether knowingly or unknowingly.

Preventing potential terrorist activities through intelligence and security operations is the main task of the law enforcement. Terrorists plan their activities very well; likewise, the response and operation of the law enforcement must be well planned. Intelligence is essential in the fight against terrorism. The fight against terrorism requires patience and wise action to intercept terrorists. Law enforcement should try to gather as much information on the terrorist organizations as possible through their intelligence and other means such as interrogation or the documents that are acquired during operations. Every piece of information can lead to a broader map and scope of terrorist connections and plans. These facts must be shared so that each piece of the puzzle is properly placed in order to gain an accurate global view of terrorism. If the law enforcement can see the big picture, they can better control terrorists by following their daily routines and can then carry out their operations more quickly. Consequently, the main task of law enforcement is to prevent terrorist activities. There is also a need to inform the public about some of those activities where appropriate to build public trust.

Security is one of the other vital factors of the law enforcement in the fight against terrorism. Terrorists try to convey an image of an unsuccessful government that cannot even protect its citizens to show themselves more powerful than they are actually. The law enforcement as a whole is responsible from security by being well alert to terrorist activities and knowing the potential targets of the terrorists. Moreover, usually terrorists' special targets are known and those targets need more attention and security precautions to deter the terrorists if possible through security measures. Dedicated security precautions should be well planned and the law enforcement should try to avoid interrupting the daily routine of citizens.

Terrorist organizations should never feel safe in the society and they must always feel that there are two options. If a terrorist is become known by the law enforcement, there are two options. The law enforcement is either need to arrest and persuade him to leave the terrorist organization or prosecute him before it is too late or follow him to find out more contacts, unknown terrorists and cells. The first option is an easy task requiring usually a small operation and interrogation. The second task may be more difficult because there is a need of continuing chase. However the case, the law enforcement should continue to carry out operations to reduce the power and activities of the terrorist organization.

Terrorists consider themselves when they spread the feeling of panic and fear and when they interrupt the daily life whether through their activities or through the measures of the governments. In this regard, the law enforcement makes sure that this does not happen. Of course all of the terrorist activities cannot be prevented. However, the public can be assured about the safety measures and the important activities of the law enforcement to keep them safe. This may be gained through well designed communication between the media and the law enforcement. The public needs to know that they are being protected. Also, law enforcement activities should not interrupt daily life if it is not really necessary because this may over alert the public.

Law enforcement should try to learn everything about the terrorist organizations through strategies, tactics, hierarchy and the potential power of the terrorist organizations. Knowing the terrorist organization well enough will enable the law enforcement to adjust its actions more appropriately and will give the power of predicting the future activities of the terrorist organization so that they can take their precautions accordingly. Like in every aspect of the life, knowledge is power and it is more essential if this power or knowledge is associated with the lives of innocent people.

Public support in the fight against terrorism is essential. Modern terrorists blend in the society and try to protect themselves through anonymity. However, sometimes they give out some clues and an alert public may well receive these clues to inform the law enforcement. If the public is aware the facts about terrorism and in support of the government, this may lead to additional information and arrests.

Law enforcement units may need more advanced tools in the against terrorism including special weaponry, armored vehicles, more sophisticated communication systems, or additional information systems that enable the law enforcement to reach the terrorists or to share the data regarding terrorists. Terrorists usually employ the latest technology; whereas the law enforcement may lack some of the latest tools. The law enforcement obviously needs to have the same level of technology in order to be on a level playing field.

The law enforcement needs special training on the terrorist organizations and on their responsibilities. If they do not know their enemies, they cannot fight with it. Additionally, if they do not know how to fight with that enemy, they are still underprivileged simply because fighting terrorism requires additional and different tactics when compared to a regular law enforcement job. Therefore, these qualifications should be offered to the law enforcement in general, and more specific to the units that directly deal with the terrorists. Another important aspect of providing qualifications is having the law enforcement know their responsibilities and rights very well because some situations in the fight against terrorism needs immediate response and the personnel cannot seek immediate advice in such circumstances. Therefore, there is a need to clarify the responsibilities and rights of the law enforcement very clearly and educate the law enforcement on those issues.

Information sharing is the key to success in the fight against terrorism. Different and various operations convey variety of diverse information regarding the terrorist organizations. The law enforcement needs to share this information to see the big picture and to be successful in the fight against terrorism. The law enforcement should be equipped with the appropriate computer and information systems to share this information completely to ensure a harmony and success in the fight against terrorism. Terrorists use different intelligence sources and they successfully combine their knowledge and information to strike the society. If the law enforcement fails to share any information regarding terrorists, they will fail in the fight against terrorism because terrorism is a very well organized activity of groups of people who are located in different parts of the world. Local knowledge and intelligence on terrorist groups would not be enough to defeat and prevent terrorism.

In the fight against terrorism, the law enforcement and public are usually emotional. Everybody wants to find the terrorists as soon as possible and stop terrorism. Sometimes, this emotion may lead people or law enforcement to label some of the suspects as terrorists even when it is too early or before a conviction from a court. This may jeopardize the fight against terrorism and result in unproductive accusations. If may also cause the suspects to accept the label of terrorism and act as a terrorist. Another important aspect in this regard is being respectful to human life and civil rights. It is essential that the law enforcement be respectful to civil rights for a variety of reasons including not to fight a right fight with wrong tools, not to give propaganda and justification tools to the terrorists, not to become criminal under the rule of law and finally not to alienate the public with the amount of the human right violations.

4.6. Discussion of the Models

These models are based the findings in this research and from experience gained through the interaction with terrorists over the years. Force is not a solution or remedy for terrorism. The law enforcement alone can only partially deal with the criminal aspect of terrorism simply because there will be more terrorists that emerge in the place of those arrested. A longer-term proactive fight is necessary in order to deal with not only the criminal behavior but also the causes of terrorism. In the fight against terrorism, action brings reaction. Unfortunately, with the actions of the law enforcement, terrorists may acquire better bases and support for themselves by using the emotions of people. For example, this researcher has met many terrorists who became a terrorist solely because one of their siblings had been arrested. There are many families in Turkey who have all of their children in the prison through this sequence of events. In this regard, unlike organized crime, terrorism cannot be simply stopped by the law enforcement precautions because of the social aspects associated with it. Therefore, the two phase fight against terrorism presented here is to target both criminal and social aspects of terrorism. This is a plan to gain complete control over terrorism in order to have a peaceful society. This may seem idealistic, but this plan has not yet been tried. One should not forget that most citizens want to live a peaceful life and most of the terrorists interrogated say that if they had had another chance, they would not have chosen the life of terror. Additionally, the people that are labeled as terrorists live with in the very societies we live everyday. Neither can we give up from our daily life, nor can we find all of the terrorists and lock them up to save our societies. However, we can at least try to find some solutions to the problem of terrorism to save our children if not ourselves today. Consequently, the researcher is quite confident that a well established long term plan that is implemented throughout a country focusing on the both aspects of dealing with the problem of terrorism will be successful over the years because the terrorists simply will not be able to find justifications for themselves as they used to and the conception on terrorism and violence will change over they years and people will be more reluctant to join terrorist organizations.

5. Conclusion

Without a doubt, terrorism is one of the most significant challenges of the modern world. Today, many countries around the world find themselves in a position where they need to allocate large portions of their budget and police forces in measures against terrorism. However, possibly because of the emotions involved with terrorism, the efforts have mainly responded directly to the physical responses to terrorism. World leaders often failed or ignored to address the possible reasons behind terrorism. There is a tendency of not asking the question of 'Why does terrorism occur?' Instead, the focus is on dealing with the consequences of terrorism and future terrorist threats. While it is essential that the governments need to provide the finest security measures for their societies, at the same time they need to address the reasons behind terrorism. This research, from stated perspective, offers a conceptual model to address both aspects of terrorism for a more complete fight against today's most painful problem.

This research is out of the ordinary because of two reasons. The first is the researcher's background and the second is the richness of the datasets that were used in the research. The researcher not only brought his experience and knowledge that were gained over the years in anti-terrorism departments of TNP, but he also received the support of his coworkers and their experiences along with their ideas in the direction of this research, may be in one sense the support of a national police agency with over 200.000 members. Additionally, the researcher also would like to emphasize the significance of almost fifty year of practices and experience that the TNP gained over the years in the fight against terrorism. Furthermore, the datasets used in this research are quite significant in a way that the numbers of the subjects exceed 1100 and all of the respondents were in fact actual convicted members of terrorist organizations that are recognized as terrorist organizations both by the EU and the US State Department.

The researcher also assumes the findings of this research as scientifically significant because there are clear indications through the data that terrorism can be interrupted by focusing on some factors and dynamics in the societies. The research indicated that there are a number of major issues that needs to be considered in a profound respond to terrorism. The first major finding is the fact that most of the terrorists are between the ages of twenty and thirty and they are usually approached by the terrorists before the ages of twenty through the end of highs schools or the beginning of college years. The second important factor to consider is the fact that all of the terrorists received some kind of education and over half of them were either high school graduates or they started college. Another significant factor was the socio-economic status of the terrorist or their families. Over two thirds of the terrorist were considered to be in low income status. In addition to the low income, the research indicated that some small regions in general accounted for over half of the terrorists which clearly indicated that those regions needed special attention. Finally, the research also indicated that some of the terrorists lacked parental supervision, in particular father supervision. Therefore, those factors can be intervened in a successful anti-terrorism campaign.

As a conclusion, the researcher would like finalize his study by emphasizing the importance a complete approach to the problem of terrorism by considering not only the pure law enforcement approach to terrorism but also the social aspects of terrorism so that the problem of terrorism could be cured over the years.

References

[1] B. Yilmaz, N. Alkan, D. Kolbasi, *Research Report for the Project of Open Letter to the Families of Terrorism Detainees.* Ankara: Turkish National Police Publications; 2002. (*in Turkish*)
[2] F. Hasson, S. Keeney, H. McKenna, Research guidelines for the Delphi survey technique. *Journal of Advanced Nursing* **32/4** (2000, October).
[3] C.E. Sahakian, *The Delphi method.* Skokie: The Corporate Partnering Institute; 1997.

Legal Policing Responses to Terrorist Operations

Farhad MEHDIYEV
Qafqaz University, Azerbaijan

Abstract. This article looks at the following fundamental issues related to the global initiative against terrorism from a European perspective: 1) Problems in definition of terrorism, legal definition of terrorism; 2) Terrorism: its kinds, reasons and aims; 3) Legal policing (policies) regarding terrorist operations; 4) Protection of human rights and anti-terrorist policing (policies).

Keywords. Terrorism, definition of terrorism, human rights and terrorism, counterterrorism, terrorism and sentencing

Introduction

The definition of terrorism is not clear, though it is very important topic [1]. Some scholars think that the problem is that of a legal nature, because terrorism is punishable under law. The lawyer community however is of the opinion that the issue of the definition of terrorism can be better resolved within the political and military domains.

The next problem lies in the difference between 'fight for freedom' and 'terrorism.' During the period of socialist camp, capitalist and socialist parts of separated world supported fighting groups under policy of 'supporting of movements for freedom and democracy.' Despite different level of support to PKK, it has been accepted as a terrorist group by Western society. Interestingly, Modjaheeds in Afghanistan were fighters for freedom in movies like 'Rambo 3' for American citizens; on the other hand, they were regarded as criminals and terrorist in the US camp. Now however, local fighters in Afghanistan are considered as terrorists in the US society.

Many of researchers in this area offer the following criteria: does fighting group use a force against civil population. If 'yes,' then the group is doubtlessly a terrorist group. If an armed group uses violence only against armed forces of the government, such a group is not considered to be a terrorist group by researches. However, when an armed group uses force and violence against the government and administrative bodies, such activity is called 'guerilla activities' by researchers. There is not a unity of opinions on the matter. UN Convention on Prohibition of Financing Terrorism (9/12/1999) provides that killing of any person who does not take active part in military operations is an act of terrorism [2].

1. Academic Consensus on Definition

According to Schmid (cited in [3]),

"Terrorism is an anxiety-inspiring method of repeated violent action, employed by (semi-) clandestine individual, group or state actors, for idiosyncratic, criminal or political reasons, whereby - in contrast to assassination - the direct targets of violence are not the main targets. The immediate human victims of violence are generally chosen randomly (targets of opportunity) or selectively (representative or symbolic targets) from a target population, and serve as message generators. Threat- and violence-based communication processes between terrorist (organization), (imperiled) victims, and main targets are used to manipulate the main target (audience/s), turning it into a target of terror, a target of demands, or a target of attention, depending on whether intimidation, coercion, or propaganda is primarily sought."

Schmid also points that (cited in [3]),

"Terrorism is a method of combat in which random or symbolic victims become targets of violence. Through the previous use of violence or the credible threat of violence, other members of a group are put in a state of chronic fear (terror). The victimization of the target is considered is meant to terrorize observers, which in turn creates an audience beyond the target of terror or the act of terrorism. The purpose of terrorism is either to immobilize the target of terror in order to produce disorientation and/or compliance, or to mobilize secondary targets of demand or targets of attention."

UN short legal definition, also proposed by Schmid; an act of terrorism is the "peacetime equivalent of a war crime." However, legal provisions of countries foresee the terrorist activity and give them certain definitions in criminal codes. And these definitions are in consonance with the commonly accepted meaning of terrorism. For instance, it is mostly accepted that terrorist activity should have political background. But criminal code of Russia (article 205) provides that terrorism is

"Fulfillment of explosion, arson or other actions creating danger of destruction of people, causing significant property damage or approach of other socially dangerous consequences if these actions are accomplished with an aim of public safety infringement, intimidation of the population or influencing decision-making authorities, and also threat of fulfillment of the specified actions in the same purposes."

The US has defined terrorism under the Federal Criminal Code. Chapter 113B of Part I of Title 18 of the United States Code defines terrorism and lists the crimes associated with terrorism [4]. In Section 2331 of Chapter 113b, terrorism is defined as:

"..activities that involve violent... or life-threatening acts... that are a violation of the criminal laws of the United States or of any State and... appear to be intended (i) to intimidate or coerce a civilian population; (ii) to influence the policy of a government by intimidation or coercion; or (iii) to affect the conduct of a government by mass destruction, assassination, or kidnapping; and ...if domestic...(C) occur primarily within the territorial jurisdiction of the United States...if international...(C) occur primarily outside the territorial jurisdiction of the United States..."

In UK Terrorism Act 2000, terrorism is defined like the use or threat is designed to influence the government or to intimidate the public or a section of the public, and the use or threat is made for the purpose of advancing a political, religious or ideological cause and involves or endanger serious damage to life, health or property [5].

It can be observed that in legal definition of terrorism, use of violence should be designed to influence the government or the intimidate public or a section of the public and should be issued for the purpose of advancing a political, religious or ideological cause.

The EU provides a more detailed definition of terrorism [6]. Acts may seriously damage a country or an international organization where committed with the aim of: seriously intimidating a population, or unduly compelling a Government or international organization to perform or abstain from performing any act, or seriously destabilizing or destroying the fundamental political, constitutional, economic or social structures of a country or an international organization; attacks upon a person's life which may cause death; attacks upon the physical integrity of a person; kidnapping or hostage taking; manufacture, possession, acquisition, transport, supply or use of weapons, explosives or of nuclear, biological or chemical weapons, as well as research into, and development of biological and chemical weapons etc.

After comparing these definitions, we can render a basic definition of terrorism both in political and legal scope: terrorism is,

- an activity, which is inspired by ideological, ethnic or religious motivations,
- an activity that contains unlawful (prohibited) use of violence or threat to such use,
- an activity which does not constitute the main goals of group realizing it,
- the main activity of group is not permitted by law,
- terrorist activity threatens the life and property of people,
- this (terrorist) activity is committed against random and innocent victims.

2. Terrorism: Its Kinds, Reasons and Aims

We can distinguish terrorism between ideological, national (ethnic) and religious-based terrorism. Ideological terrorism is mostly related with political, economic and social problems. This classification is useful: it helps us to analyze the reasons of terrorist activities and struggle against it.

Political oppression, religious intolerance and divine revelation are a few of the most common reason cited by terrorist as justifications for their attacks [7]. Thus, protest or retaliation against the prohibition of some activity is the main reason that causes terrorism. Terrorist activity is therefore the protest, or way of fighting against prohibition of the main aims of a social group or persons, who perform the terrorist acts.

As has been stated above, intolerance and prohibition are the main reason behind terrorist attacks. However, on the other hand it is impossible for states and societies to tolerate all kinds of human activities, especially when such activities are against the law or manifest aggression against the government or the society at large. That is why it is very important to maintain balance between prohibition and tolerance. When a group or sub group feels that they cannot reach their goals through the legal system of a certain country, they will surely think about other possible ways achieving them. When such methods include the use of violence or threats against the society at large, the problem of 'terrorism' may arise. The system of prohibition should be stage-by-stage and absorbing. Where possible, this absorbing system should also provide certain concessions. However, such concessions should not contradict to foundations of a democratic society.

Terrorist acts may also be motivated by revenge: historically there have been many terrorist acts motivated by revenge based on either national or religion based grievances. For example, Armenian ASALA or 'Islamic Jihad' has such a background. It is hard to prevent such terrorist acts because it is difficult to satisfy terrorist emotions, especially when these emotions are unjust, like in the ASALA.

In fighting terrorism, there are too many obstacles because of the irrationality of the terrorist activity. Terrorist organizations usually recruit people with aggressive schizophrenic characteristics [8]. It is really difficult to understand and preempt the behavior of terrorists.

What is then, the aim of terrorist activity? The purpose of terrorism is either to immobilize the target of terror in order to produce disorientation and/or compliance, or to mobilize secondary targets of demand or targets of attention (Schmid, 1983 cited in [3]). Also most of researchers accept that terrorist activities are carried out to push governments to take or restrain from some action and decisions, as it is shown above.

3. Legal Policing Issues and Terrorist Operations

There are two vital principals that should be considered regarding legal policing issues in the fight against terror:

- protection of society and its members from terrorist attacks; including prevention of terrorism and decreasing terrorist behavior
- respecting and providing human rights and rules of law

In light of these principles, legal definition of terrorism is important. However, much more important is choosing an appropriate legal regime to be applied in cases when an activity is accepted as a terrorist act. Legal regime to be applied to terrorist activity could be considered from these aspects:

- which conducts and activities should be considered as terrorism;
- preventive measures, their scope and application grounds;
- criminal investigation measures, the level and scope of increasing the authorities of investigation bodies if committed crime is terrorism;
- penalties, kinds of punishment, their effects on threatening against terrorist behavior.

3.1. Which Conduct and Activities Should Be Considered as Terrorism?

The scope of the definition of terrorist acts should be narrow, and should discern between a terrorist act and other social-threatening conducts. For instance, killing of people during terrorist acts is considered to be assassination in legislation of NIS countries. By widening legal definition of terrorist activities you can misuse the legal instruments as punishment with political motives. W. Laqueur [9] has defined terrorism as illegal use of force against innocent people for achievement of political ends, having added that, attempts to formulate frameworks for simple definitions of terrorism are useless, because the term is very inconsistent. Formulating the definition, W.Laqueur acknowledged the presence of the certain problems, as the term "terrorism" has various meanings for various interested parties. From the point of view of security, Laqueur presents the following conclusions: terrorism is a form of the political or criminal violence, directed on change of behavior by means of fear. The given approach does not solve the problem of definition, but at least employees of security services with some discernable characteristics while identifying and dealing with cases of terrorism. The second approach which is very popular in European countries concentrates on the legal aspects of terrorism. The terrorism is understood as use of criminal acts for political interests or as a way of causing political disorder. Thus, the terrorism is defined as infringement of the law and terrorists who violate the law are subject to certain legal measures. The governments of Germany [10] and the US [11] have used approaches that are similar to this model in dealing with issue of terrorism.

Attacks on innocent people should be the main measure in the definition of terrorism. And if an act or the threat of an act of violence is not directed towards innocent people, then the act of violence should be defined differently, for example rioting, assassination of political or public leader, or organization of armed group etc. Attacks on governmental bodies should not be defined as terrorism but might constitute another kind of crime, like diversion (Criminal Code of Russia article 281, Azerbaijan 282). Additionally if the act of terrorism resulted in the death of innocent people or the destruction of property then these should be counted as separate charges along with the charges of terrorism. In the case of NIS countries the act of terrorism is considered as a generic charge which may include murder as well the punishment of which is life imprisonment.

3.2. Which Preventive Measures Should We Apply, What Should Be Their Scope and Application Grounds?

It is clear that protection of society from terrorist acts is impossible without preventive activity of intelligence and security forces. But most of people would not be willing to let the security forces control their e-mail traffic or listen to their telephone conversations.

With development of technological opportunities, it became easier to collect any sort of information. But the current legislation, frequently forbids it, and such collected information is not regarded as admissible evidence. Such extraction of the information, especially when it is for preventive purposes, is considered to be intervention into private life.

It is necessary to recognize, that human life in the society is becoming more and more complex day by day. The legal status of the person constantly replenishes and extends. Organic connections with the state continue to grow. And they grow for the benefit of the state. It is impossible to stop this growth as it is natural. In its turn, it will generate a new wave of discontent. Only time will show whether such discontent will be translated into acts of violence and whether such violent acts shall be labeled as 'terrorism.' It's not a coincidence that the latest law on terrorism in England extends the definition of terrorism to include hacking of a computer network.

We have to regretfully recognize, that this century will bring an increase in terrorist activity and the subsequent reduction of personal freedom of citizens. Reduction of personal freedom will result from the increase in preventive powers of the state bodies.

Thus, the main point of analysis should be 'how should we protect human rights and security of soceity simultaneously?' Legal protection of human rights is a basic rule, but there are exceptions. It is possible to restrict rights and liberties under certain circumstances and conditions. Thus, what are those reasons?

In conditions like war, disaster, epidemic, riot etc. rights and liberties are restricted automatically without official restriction order. For instance, disaster could cause epidemic, epidemic in turn threatens such essential rights like the right to live. For prevention of this threat, the right to free activity can be restricted by applying quarantine. Thus the restriction of one fundamental right is justified when such restriction is enforced to protect a more important and essential right. For protecting of right to live, you can restrict right to protection of property, but you cannot do vice versa. In addition, such criteria like necessity, rationality and proportionality should be taken into consideration. On the other side, these restrictions should be provisional. As soon as necessity disappears, restriction of the rights should be abolished.

Moreover we can analyze this problem from 3 viewpoints: what are reasons for restrictions, what should be level of restrictions, and in which ways should rights be restricted? Although in different countries this subject is settled by distinct regulations, especially in *supranational* human rights law there are certain principles regarding the above-mentioned problem.

The widest criteria in restrictions of human rights are foreseen in European Convention for the Protection of Human Rights and Fundamental Freedoms, which is an inseparable part of national legal systems across Europe[1]. These criterions are interests of public safety (art, 8/2, 9/2, 10/2, 11/2), interests of public order (art 6/1), interests of national security (art.6/1, 8/2, 10/2, 11/2), interests of territorial integrity (art 10/2), protection of health (art . 8/2, 9/2, 10/2, 11/2), protection of morals (art.8/2, 9/2, 10/2, 11/2), protection of the private life (art .6/1), interests of juveniles (art .6/1), interests of fair trial (art.6/1, 10/2), interests of economic well-being of the country (art.8/2), protection of the rights and freedoms of others (art.10/2, 8/2, 9/2, 11/2), protection of the reputation of others (art.10/2), prevention of disorder or crime (art.8/2, 10/2, 11/2), preventing the disclosure of confident information (art.10/2).

The fundamental rights, recognized by the Convention, that could be restricted under counter-terrorism activities, are

1. right to liberty and security,
2. right to life,
3. right to not be exposed to tortures,
4. right to a fear trail,
5. right to respect for family and private life,
6. freedom of thought, conscience and religion
7. freedom of expression
8. freedom of assembly and association.

Thus most of the rights recognized under Convention could be restricted, however restriction of some of them is unlawful, like restriction of the right to not to be exposed to tortures and inhuman treatment. Also peaceful enjoyment of a person's possessions could not be restricted as measures against terrorist activities.

Supranational human rights documents leave the procedural decision like 'how the states should restrict rights on the high contracting parties. The only provisions are 'prescribing by law' and 'necessity in a democratic society.' (art. 6/1, 8/2, 9/2, 10/2, 11/2) [12]. Criterion 'necessity in democratic society' is very indefinite and wide, but European Court of Human Rights has ruled additional measures and standards.

Classic democracies are regimes that provide human rights in the widest scope. Restrictions that breach rights and liberties can not be considered proper practices in a democratic society. Democratic regimes also should be liberal; they should be governed by rule of law and based on personal liberties. From this point of view, along with levels of restrictions, reasons for restrictions, methods, conditions, possibly remedies, should also be taken into consideration when assessing rules of democratic society. We can certainly say that protection of fundamental rights is the matter of public order in the European concept. That is why rights can and should be restricted, only in cases where democracy itself is under threat in a society. In a democratic state, where law is the only hegemonic power, independent of the pursued aim, human rights can not be restricted by the ways that are deemed unsuitable in a democratic regime[2].

Thus, preventive measures in fight against terrorism could essentially restrict the following fundamental right.

---

[1] According to article 148 of Constitution of Azerbaijan, international agreements wherein the Azerbaijan Republic is one of the parties constitute an integral part of legislative system of the Azerbaijan Republic.
[2] The decision of Turkish Constituional Court, E. 85/8, K.86/27, T. 26 November 1986, RG. 14 August 1987 – 19554.

1. right to respect for private life,
2. freedom of thought, conscience and religion
3. freedom of expression
4. freedom of assembly and association.

Preventive measures as intervention in private life is the most problematic in this regard, because generally people have no idea whether such a right has been restricted or not. One can estimate but one cannot completely ascertain whether one's telephone is listened or not. The problem is that in Europe the decision of court cannot be regarded as an injunction to prevent listening of a person's phone number or monitoring his communications. The problem is that investigation bodies can intervene in a person's private life in spite of a without a court order, because it is very easy to change national legislation, which super cedes the decisions of the judge. The important question to consider here is that should the states or state authorized investigating bodies be allowed to randomly listen to a person's telephone communication as a preventive measure? If we care about future of fundamental rights we have to say no. The intervention in private life should be possible only after serious suspicions on a person's personality and actions. Thus, random listening and control over personal communication should be considered as illegal.

Intervention to freedom of thought and religion as preventive measure could be applied only in the context of their expression. If thought and belief of a person do not call for violence, then the expression of such beliefs should be allowed. It is necessary to notice, that the criterion of violence in this regard is only a direct call and appeal to violence. If such a direct call to violence does not exist then the status of personal freedom should be protected by law. In a recent case in England, Muslims who prayed in the boarding area of an air port were not allowed to board the flight. Such kind of preventive measures is absolutely uncalled for. Kicking of a passenger from boarding a flight on the basis that he was saying his prayer is an uncivil and cruel intervention.

Intervention to freedom of assembly and association is an area which is more suitable for restriction and control. One can put forward some mechanism of control and registration of association especially before such associations have been created. These control mechanisms are: information about founders of association, main area of activity of association, headquarters of association, membership of association etc. You can put on some financing and supporting systems for association and control them by this method. Refusal from funding and support would be suspicious and the government can thus strengthen the control.

But we have to accept, that fact that terrorists do not operate under the roof of a particular organization. Terrorists try to function under deep conspiracy. It is more probable, that organization under suspicion indirectly support terrorists. European Convention of Human Rights provides wide measures for such kind of preventive measures.

Taking into account that the terrorist organizations use deep conspiracy in their actions, freedom of assembly is not a proper area of intervention as preventive measure in fight against terrorism. On the contrary, freedom of assembly is the mechanism absorbing social protests in less violent way.

Finally, the authority of the law enforcement agencies to keep a record of where the fire-arms have been bought, by whom, and where the bought firearms shall be transported etc. is undisputed. But in this case terrorists usually deliver the weapon and units of fire from abroad. Therefore, detailed elaboration and complication of a method of purchase of fire-arms is not an effective way in the struggle against terrorism.

The solution could be the acquisition of technical equipment that would allow law enforcement agencies to find out, discover any kind of explosives in the certain radius. Instead of forbidding passengers to take their luggage, it is necessary to be able to check this luggage for the presence dangerous to other substances.

The most important preventive measure however, is the destroying of the roots that cause terrorism. The most effective way in struggle against terrorism, could be increasing educational level of people which can be considered as potential candidates for recruitment into terrorist organizations. But such method of the prevention is only useful in the struggle against nationalist and religious terrorism. Ideological terrorism, like those based on left-political motives should be prevented also by changing social and economical conditions of the society.

3.3. Criminal Investigation Measures Which Should Be Applied after the Terrorist Acts Have Been Committed, Their Level and Scope. Whether It Is Necessary for Us to Increase Powers of Investigation Bodies?

In spite of Fuller (cited in [1]), who outlines one of the primary differences between a war on terrorism versus a war on crime or other social problems as "a terrorist enemy does not enjoy US legal protections (at least fewer constitutional protections)," Connor [13] finds it impossible to agree with this statement. Such kind of approach is not accepted in European culture. The difference between terrorist and ordinary criminal, who slaughtered 15 men, is only that terrorist acts with political motives, while motives of the ordinary criminal could be more severe and brutal. So, there is no ground to treat with terrorist more merciless than a common criminal. Terrorism is merely a kind of crime in national criminal legislation and there are no reasons which would force us to leave general provisions. But by classifying terrorism as felony and especially grave crime, we can investigate terrorist acts under the regime of such crimes.

Criminal investigations and measures against terrorist activities could be analyzed by these aspects: a) grounds for arrest, search and confiscation; b) duration of detention; c) regime of detention; and d) methods of interrogation (with or without lawyer, duration of interrogation).

The grounds for arrest/detention signify as to what actions, facts and a level of suspicion should be considered sufficient for restriction of freedom. Duration of detention signifies the allowed maximum period of detention in pre-court investigation. Regime of detention covers wide area - from right to communicate with outside to an opportunity to play sports during detention. From this point of view, considerations like whether the prisoner should be kept in a single cell, should he/she be allowed to communicate with others, how many hours a week he can walk while in custody, should methods of psychological oppression be applied over arrested person or not, are most important. Guatemala is the vivid example for regime of detention.

Methods of interrogation are closely tied with regime of detention. Detained person could be granted the help of lawyer and physician. Duration and time of interrogations should be established so that it provides efficiency and speed of investigation, but simultaneously would not traverse into the realm of inhuman treatment. For example, in cases where the lives of others can be rescued, interrogation can be carried out at night, or prolonged till the night. However uninterruptible interrogation of the prisoner for 18 hours or more should be considered as inhuman treatment.

Lastly, there is no necessity to provide in the legislation a special mode of investigation for the crimes connected to terrorism. Investigation of terrorism should be carried out under a mode of the grave crimes accomplished by organized group even if the terrorist operated alone.

3.4. Punishment Policing in Fight with Terrorism and Their Effects against Terrorist Behavior.

In criminal law it is commonly accepted that, punishment for a crime has two purposes. Firstly, to punish, correct or deter the offender and secondly, to provide the society at large with a sense of justice and deter potential criminals. Terrorists are mostly unsocial and sick people. So the question is, which purposes should we pursue in punishment of terrorists?

Taking into account a mental condition of terrorists, it would be better if punishment of the terrorist would pursue the purpose of his socialization and correction, more than rendering of bitterness against his criminal act. Society should punish terrorist for the sake of justice, but should not treat the terrorist like he has treated the society. Before the committing of the act of terrorism, the terrorist regards the society as his/her enemy. Sentence should explain to terrorist that he/she is the part of society and never can exist without it. That is why terrorist criminal should serve neither solitary cell sentence nor serve a sentence in the company of other terrorists or murderers. Terrorists should be placed in cells with harmless criminals. In this case measures should be introduced that the terrorists do not inculcate violent beliefs within the other prisoners. For this purpose it is necessary to take into account also physical and intellectual development of prisoners in the cell. Selective courses should be offered to terrorist prisoner. These selective courses should be in different areas, but at the same time such courses should be developed in pursuance of one fundamental purpose - psychological and intellectual reform of the terrorist.

Once the terrorists have completed their prison terms they should not be negatively labeled. Such labeling shall push them back towards terrorism. Terrorists are alienated individuals, and punishment and imprisonment of such persons should not increase but decrease the level of alienation.

4. Conclusion

Acts of terrorism evoke strong anger within the society against the terrorist or the social group to which the terrorist belongs. That is why punishment for an act of terrorism should mollify such emotions and anger. Nowadays, when death penalty is abolished, application of life imprisonment is possible. Life imprisonment should be applied in especially cases where a lot of lives have been lost as a result of the terrorist act. Azerbaijan Criminal Code Article 120.2 provides such a provision.

However, in cases where the prisoner manifests that he of she has improved then that prisoner should granted a premature conditional release. But, the term that has actually been served in prison should not be less than 75 percent of the original sentence. Such kind of application of imprisonment both is severe yet productive and humane.

On the other hand, punishment for terrorism should not strengthen the beliefs of terrorists that the society, against which they acted, is really cruel and deserves destruction. All process of assignment of punishment should be open to general public. It would be very useful, if the imprisoned terrorists from time to time were interviewed by the mass-media.

References

[1] Wikipedia. [Online] Available from: URL: http://en.wikipedia.org/wiki/Definition_of_terrorism [2006, May 10]
[2] UN Convention on Prohibition of Financing Terrorism. [Online] Available from: URL: http://nostalgia.ncstu.ru/content/_docs/pdf/_trudi/_law/f03/22.pdf [2006, December 10] (*in Russian*)
[3] UN Office on Drugs and Crime, Definitions of Terrorism. [Online] Available from: URL: http://www.unodc.org/unodc/terrorism_definitions.html [2006, July 30]
[4] Findlaw, US Code, Title 18. Crimes and criminal procedure. [Online] Available from: URL: http://caselaw.lp.findlaw.com/casecode/uscodes/18/parts/i/chapters/113b/toc.html [2006, August 19]
[5] Terrorism Act 2000. [Online] Available from: URL: http://www.opsi.gov.uk/ACTS/acts2000/00011--b.htm#1 [2006, July 20]
[6] Council Framework Decision of 13 June 2002 on Combating Terrorism. [Online] Available from: URL: http://www.statewatch.org/news/2002/jul/frameterr622en00030007.pdf [2006, September 01]
[7] C. Payne, Reasons behind terrorism (2002, March). [Online] Available from: URL: http://www.globalterrorism101.com/ReasonsBehindTerrorism.html [2006, August 12]
[8] Terrorism: Psychological and political aspects. *Journal of Foreign Psychology* **10** (1998).
[9] W. Laqueur, *The age of terrorism.* Boston: Little, Brown; 1987.
[10] B. Grosscup, *The explosion of terrorism.* Far Hills: New Horizons; 1987.
[11] US Senate, Bills to Authorize Prosecution of Terrorism and Others Who Attack US Government Employees and Citizens Abroad. Hearing before the Subcommittee on Security and Terrorism of the Committee of the Judiciary. Washington, D.C.: United States Senate; 1985.
[12] M.S. Gemalmaz, *Human rights in real documents.* Ankara: Kavram Publications; 1996.
[13] T. Connor, The criminology of terrorism: History, law, definitions, typologies. [Online] Available from: URL: http://faculty.ncwc.edu/toconnor/429/429lect01.htm [2006, September 03]

Organizing to Combat Future Terrorist Threats: Policy and Operational Implications

Stephen SLOAN
*University Professor and Fellow: Office of Global Perspectives,
University of Central Florida, USA*

Abstract. Meeting the threat of terrorism is difficult given the vital demand of addressing current contingencies. However, it is important to place the threat in a broader context to combat a form of violence, armed conflict, and warfare that is a manifestation of changes in the international environment. Moreover, those changes have both organizational and operational implications for individuals and organizations that are responsible for preventing, deterring, and responding to terrorism. This paper addresses the demands placed on those within a growing counterterrorism community who must engage in their own form of innovation to meet an enduring and also growing threat.

Keywords. Terrorism, combating terrorist threats, international environment, organizational environment, information initiative

Introduction

Meeting the current and future threat of terrorism is especially demanding given the vital and understandable demand of addressing current contingencies. However, it is important to place the threat in a broader context to combat a form of violence, armed conflict, and warfare that is a manifestation of changes in the international environment. Furthermore, those changes have both organizational and operational implications for individuals and organizations that are responsible for preventing, deterring, and responding to acts and campaigns of terrorism. This paper addresses the demands placed on those within a growing counterterrorism community who must engage in their own form of innovation to meet an enduring and also growing threat.

1. The International Environment

The arbitrary and very dangerous equilibrium that took the form of 'the balance of nuclear terrorism' during the Cold War has been replaced by the emergence and diffusion of a wide variety of new actors who pose a threat to international, regional, and national security. From 'rogue states,' to criminal enterprises, there are new players who have compounded the lack of predictability and concomitant new dangers that governments at all levels must adjust to in an increasingly ambiguous threat environment.

At the outset, the technology that has led to increased interdependence in the disorderly and unpredictable processes of globalization has played well into the hands of those who are and will continue to engage in terrorism. With the use of the internet, the terrorists and their organizations and sponsors can, on one hand, maintain a level of security in cyberspace for their respective cellular organizations while now having the ability to coordinate campaigns against potential targets through the internet and other innovative forms of communication. Furthermore, they can spread their messages of fear and intimidation and engage in 'armed propaganda' by effectively utilizing the World Wide Web. It is unfortunately true that terrorists have often seized the initiative in using modern technology to inspire, and train a new ever increasing cadre of terrorists while, at the same time, seizing the initiative in their own form of cyber global information operations. Not faced with the constraints of physical and political boundaries, questions of sovereignty, and the clash of different national interests, the modern terrorists have effectively applied the adage of being able to coordinate internationally but act locally.

In contrast, the existing nation-state system with its focus on sovereignty has unfortunately not achieved the degree of cohesion and unity of action that characterizes the ability of those who are now essentially engaging in a war against all. The challenges posed by these terrorists is further exacerbated by the reality that many of them represent new players in the international arena, that are challenging the long tradition of the nation-state that goes back to the structure and tradition of the classic Westphalian model [1]. The international community that often appears to be a community in name only is confronted by the emergence of non-state actors who do not adhere to the traditional edicts of statecraft and diplomacy or the entire corpus of international law.

We now witness the crucial role of non-state actors that have existed for years in the form, for example, of multinational corporations, but now include a whole host of new players which include terrorists who may be sponsored or supported by states but increasingly have the goals and concomitant capability to launch regional and indeed global operations in what can be broadly called a proto-strategy of global warfare. Whether such strategy is defined in terms of the current significant of religious extremists who engage in terrorism, or the emergence of new groups, be they criminal enterprises practicing their own form of extortion, or secular hate groups and cults who also seek to achieve their goals, all are adopting modern technology in the pursuit of their objectives.

Even if they justify their actions based on their own call for traditional values and indeed the call to turn the clock back to an idealized time in the past, these movements and organizations are quite willing to use modern technology ranging from communication to weapons as they seek to 'Go Back to the Future.' However traditionally oriented, they are also very innovative in utilizing a technologically inspired medium in the form of cyber space to engage their adversary with weapons ranging from the classic bomb to their own form of radio controlled weapons - and the innovation will increase in the years to come. Moreover, as the tragic events of 9/11 affirm, the terrorists have used their own form of man-directed intercontinental delivery systems.

2. The Organizational Environment

The combination of modern technology, the emergence of new actors, and privatization of force, which had been the traditional monopoly of states, have enabled the innovative terrorists to develop organizational doctrine and structures that not only do not mirror the traditional nation-state but also traditional military, police, and security forces. The current terrorists are increasingly practicing their own form of asymmetric warfare by converting the strength of their outwardly stronger adversary into weakness and vulnerability. By employing organizations with relatively flat hierarchies, the ability to coordinate through cyberspace but still maintain their security and secrecy, these cyber guerrillas are a major challenge to the cumbersome, large scale, traditional ladder hierarchies that characterize the nation-state and especially armed forces, security, and police establishments that still emphasize a complex layering of top down command and control.

Moreover, the cumbersome nature of these organizations is amplified by the lack of lateral coordination at all levels with other forces and jurisdictional issues and 'turf ballets,' all of which amplify the inability to those who are responsible for countering terrorism to achieve the unity and flexibility of action that has been the hallmark of successful terrorist organizations and their operations. At the very time when there is a need for counterterrorist organizations to develop their own flat organizations, effective networks and the requirements for flexibility and independence of action, governmental response still unfortunately adheres to the view that larger is beautiful, that coordination among larger organizations can somehow permeate and change the organizational cultures and hierarchies of outwardly sister organizations and that 'throwing money at the problem' can defeat a nimble adversary.

Unfortunately, this approach is most clearly seen in the US where the response to those who practice their own forms of 'small wars' was the creation of the enormous cabinet-level Department of Homeland Security with over 22 units and the employment of over 170,000 personnel. The barriers to coordinate such a massive organization and more specifically address immediate requirements on the local level were readily seen not in an event resulting from WMD (Weapons of Mass Destruction) but WMD (Weather of Mass Destruction) that resulted in the wake of Hurricane Katrina in the US [2]. One can only imagine the chaos had New Orleans and the Gulf Cost been subject to a man-induced nuclear, chemical or biological attack rather than a natural disaster. Faced with this sobering reality on not only the national but the regional and in the international arena, there is a requirement to develop the necessary counter- terrorist cadres who have parallel organizations to combat those who have employed small, flat organizations as a means of creating maximum destruction. In effect, such counterterrorism cadres would be following in the tradition of the parallel hierarchies that successfully neutralized governments by offering their own alternatives to governance as a classic aspect of traditional guerrilla warfare [3].

Certainly, the development of such a cadre will also require the need for the development of both formal and informal networks of counterterrorist cadres that can readily share information and act when necessary, whether individually or in unison, to engage in preemptive acts or quickly respond to acts of terrorism.

The development of such a cadre will of course not be easy. Old traditional national parochial loyalties in the form of concerns of security classifications and associated measures will still act as a barrier to the sharing of information. However, it is here where it is essential that the crucial element of trust is vital. If terrorists of all versions can form their own marriages of convenience, governments must move beyond and achieve meaningful operational networks and alliances that are both formal and informal. Admittedly, the inertia to achieve such goals is high but so are the stakes of failure. How many more 9/11's can the international community endure?

Clearly there will be difficulties in reconciling accountability and independence of actions on the part of an international counterterrorist cadre and network. But effective oversight must be achieved whether it is based on trust, mutual interests, or a combination of both of those factors. If the goal of unity is not achieved, the cumbersome bureaucracies that characterize modern nation states will continue to react and react badly to those who have refined with murderous efficiency their ability to engage in asymmetric warfare through their organizational doctrine; they will enable them to achieve not only 'force multiplication' but especially in regards to their acts 'fear multiplication;' a single act can traumatize hundreds of thousands.

3. Taking the Information Initiative

In the long term whatever organizational format or attendant counterterrorist capabilities emerge, there will ultimately be an absolute requirement to seize the communication initiative from those who have used modern communication to justify their cause and recruit members and supporters. The major themes of such an initiative will -in part- require that the governments that seek to counter terrorist information engage in promoting and disseminating the following D's. That is, it is imperative that they: (1) Deglamorize the terrorists - expose them for what they are, murders who in the name of their cause maim and kill civilians. (2) Demystify them primarily through education at all levels, place terrorism in context, explain that it is a form of protracted conflict where the terrorists seek to inculcate fear in the community and by their actions seek to have a government overreact to their actions. Such a process of education is vital if individuals and groups are going to move beyond essentially emotional reaction to the next incident. (3) Delegitimize them - perhaps the most important of all- for the objective is to strip away the justifications for their actions, whether such justification is based on an egregious interpretation of a religion or an ideology. (4) Deter them from engaging in their acts of carnage, whether such deterrence is based on political or military actions or seeking to eliminate the root causes of their actions [4].

It must be stressed that however the international community seeks to take the initiative, such measures will fail if they are based on an attempt imposed from outside policies and values on other people, cultures, and countries. Those leaders and the public in the line of fire in many countries must address the internal conditions that foster terrorism. From community to the nation-state, to regions and globally, the initiative must be taken away from those who have declared their war against all.

4. Conclusion

It must be recognized that there are no silver bullets for combating terrorism, for the international community is dealing with a form of protracted conflict where there are unfortunately no immediate results or decisive outcomes. However, the combination of trust that instills the resolve and capability to develop the organizations and capabilities to seize the initiative against terrorists can and must be achieved as the stakes for failure get higher with each passing day.

References

[1] S. Gorka, Westphalian and Al-Qaeda (2006, March). Speech at NATO Advanced Research Workshop *(Remaking National Security: Radical Approaches to Rethinking National and International Security Constructs in the post-Westphailan Strategic Environment)* organized by the Institute for Transitional Democracy and International Security (ITDIS) and the Slovene Enterprise Institute (SEI).
[2] S. Sloan, WMD: Now weather of mass destruction, (2005). Orlando Sentinel, 2005, September 12.
[3] B.B. Fall, *The two Viet-Nams: A military and political analysis.* New York: Praeger; 1967.
[4] S. Sloan, The four D's in combating terrorism. Unpublished manuscript; 1989.

Intelligence Led Policing as a Framework for Law Enforcement in the 21st Century

Edmund F. McGARRELL
Michigan State University, USA

Abstract. The intent of this paper is to contribute to our understanding of Intelligence Led Model of Policing (ILP). Specifically, we consider the origins of the move to ILP and provide examples of promising practices in policing that we believe highlight the promise of the ILP model. The paper concludes by advocating for a broad conceptualization of ILP that views ILP as an overarching framework for law enforcement that embraces community policing, problem solving policing, a continuous improvement managerial philosophy, and an 'all-crimes' focus.

Keywords. Intelligence Led Model of Policing, problem solving, community policing

Introduction

Recent years have witnessed increasing calls for law enforcement to move toward an Intelligence Led Model of Policing (ILP). Of particular importance are the positions of highly influential commissions in the UK and in the US. In the UK, the National Criminal Intelligence Service developed the National Intelligence Model (NIM) that advocates for intelligence led policing. The NIM has been endorsed by the Association of Chief Police Officers, the Home Office and Her Majesty's Inspectorate of Constabulary [1, 2]. Similarly, the National Criminal Intelligence Sharing Plan (NCISP), a product of the Global Intelligence Working Group, calls for all US law enforcement agencies to develop an ILP model and has been endorsed by the US Department of Justice, the International Association of Chiefs of Police, and every key professional law enforcement association in the US [3, 4, 5]. Clearly there is momentum to move toward an ILP framework. Yet, much like the situation with community policing two decades ago, there remains a lack of clarity about what we mean by ILP, its mission, goals, and objectives, and how such a model should be implemented in law enforcement agencies.

The intent of this paper is to contribute to our understanding of ILP. Specifically, we consider the origins of the move to ILP and provide examples of promising practices in policing that we believe highlight the promise of the ILP model. The paper concludes by advocating for a broad conceptualization of ILP that views ILP as an overarching framework for law enforcement that embraces community policing, problem solving policing, a continuous improvement managerial philosophy, and an 'all-crimes' focus. This position is in contrast to a narrower perspective that views ILP as a more specialized police function targeted at terrorism and the homeland security mission.[1] Resolving the tension between these two perspectives will ultimately be the province of law enforcement and elected officials but the articulation of the two models of ILP may assist in setting common frameworks.

1. Origins of Intelligence Led Policing

Although the National Advisory Commission on Criminal Justice Standards and Goals [7, 8] recommended that all law enforcement in the US develop an intelligence capacity, and that agencies with over 75 personnel should have a full-time intelligence capacity, the concept of intelligence led policing is a more recent development. Within the US, the early momentum toward law enforcement intelligence capacity was slowed by a number of civil rights lawsuits that demonstrated that many law enforcement intelligence units were maintaining files on citizens without corresponding evidence of criminal activity. The concerns about excessive intrusion into the privacy of citizens was given further weight by the findings of the US Senate's Church Commission that focused particularly on the FBI's Counter Intelligence Program known as COINTELPRO. The Church Commission findings also drew a clear distinction between national security intelligence and law enforcement intelligence [5]. The combination of the threat of lawsuits and the critical scrutiny from elected officials at federal, state, and local levels led many law enforcement agencies to drop or minimize their intelligence operations. The exception to this trend tended to be specialized intelligence operations aimed at organized crime, gangs, and narcotics.

The term ILP can be traced to the UK and the Kent and Northumbria Constabularies in particular [2, 3]. The Kent Constabulary formalized a model of problem solving to focus on burglary and motor vehicle theft. Moving beyond reactive responses to specific incidents, officers engaged in systematic analysis of these offenses and found patterns of small numbers of chronic offenders being responsible for large numbers of incidents as well as patterns of repeat victims and target locations. Utilizing this intelligence, a variety of strategic interventions were implemented and the area experienced a significant decline in crime. Similarly, Northumbria reported consistent annual drops in crime following its implementation of an ILP model focused on identifying chronic high-rate offenders [2, 9, 10].

Ratcliffe [10] and Hale, Heaton, and Uglow [2] linked the emergence of ILP to two influential commission reports within the UK. The first, issued by the Audit Commission and titled 'Helping with Enquiries - Tackling Crime Effectively,' called for using analysis as a tool for more effective and efficient policing [11]. The second was issued by Her Majesty's Inspectorate of Constabulary [12] and endorsed ILP and called for information collection and intelligence analysis as key components of modern policing.[2]

As noted above, the concept of ILP was formalized in the UK's National Intelligence Model. Similarly, in the Post 9/11 context, the need for enhanced intelligence capacity was apparent in the National Criminal Intelligence Sharing Plan's endorsement of ILP as the framework for law enforcement within the US [3, 4].

---

[1] A similarly narrow definition of ILP focuses on identifying and targeting high-rate chronic offenders who account for a disproportionate amount of crime (e.g., "7 percent account for 65 percent of all convictions"; see reference in [2] and [6].

[2] Hale, Heaton, and Uglow [2] note the importance of a subsequent HMIC report in 1998 linking ILP, problem-solving and partnerships as keys to crime reduction.

The adoption of ILP does not arise solely from the concern with terrorism but rather builds on major developments in law enforcement that emerged in the last two decades of the 20th century. These include community policing, problem solving policing, and continuous improvement business models. In the next section, we review the connection between these models and ILP. We then look at examples of several 'promising practices' of the implementation of these models that appear to hold promise for the implementation of ILP.

1.1. Community Policing

The community policing movement that has influenced law enforcement practice globally, though with varying levels of meaning, commitment and implementation, sought to reform the professional model of policing, that had relied heavily on technology and motorized patrol, by re-establishing connections between the police and community members. Typically this involved establishing and strengthening relationships with the community, decentralizing police structures, and gearing police services to meet local needs. Carter [5] articulated the platform provided by community oriented policing (COP) for ILP along a series of key dimensions.

First, both COP and ILP are dependent on two-way communications with the public. Police have long relied on citizens for information and this remains true for both street crime and potential terrorist indicators. Indeed, a key community policing strategy in the era of homeland security is to provide the public with information about activities and signs to be aware of as well as explain what to do with information related to potential threats. Second, both COP and ILP are dependent on analysis of information and the transformation of information to actionable intelligence. This is true whether the analysis involves a patrol officer analyzing a series of break-ins or intelligence analysts in a fusion center conducting link analysis to assess terrorist funding. Third, absent ethical decision-making and a commitment to individual rights, both COP and ILP are likely to repeat mistakes that have resulted in significant set-backs for law enforcement. From a community policing perspective, one sees the damage done to the New York City Police Department following the Louima and Diallo incidents, the Los Angeles Police Department following the investigations of the Rampart gang unit [13, 14, 15], or the New South Wales Police Department following scandals in the use of informants [10].

1.2. Problem Solving

As Nick Tilley [1] and Marilyn Peterson [3] noted, ILP also builds on developments associated with problem-oriented policing (POP).[3] Based on the pioneering work of Herman Goldstein [16], the POP model seeks to use analysis of recurring problems the police must manage in order to proactively craft interventions to address the problem. POP also draws upon concepts generated by routine activities theory [17, 18], opportunity theory and situational crime prevention [19]. These theories suggest a focus on the confluence in time or space of likely offenders, suitable targets or victims, and the presence/absence of effective guardians. Crime problems are analyzed according to the crime triangle (Figure 1) with the idea that interventions be designed to minimize the likely confluence of motivated offenders, suitable victims or targets, in

---

[3] Tilley [1] provides a very thoughtful discussion of the similarities and points of departure between ILP and POP.

the absence of effective guardianship. Implementation of POP has often followed the SARA problem-solving model that consists of scanning, analysis, response, and assessment, very similar to the intelligence process advocated by the National Criminal Intelligence Sharing Plan [3, 4, 5].

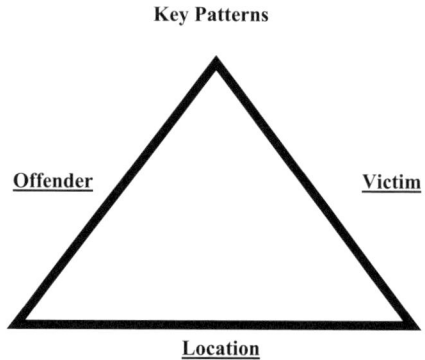

Figure 1. Crime triangle

Research on problem solving has found that although many law enforcement agencies have adopted POP practices, in many agencies there is a tendency to move from the identification of problems through scanning directly to implementation of responses [20]. That is, analysis of the problem is short-changed. Similarly, Cope's [21] study of crime analysis and ILP in two UK police forces found minimal use of analytic products in planning operations. This is not an inherent weakness of the model, but rather of the way it is implemented. Greater infusion of the ILP philosophy within policing could be an important step in strengthening the analytic component of POP.

One development that has emerged through the problem solving movement has been a number of police-research partnerships to promote both the analysis and assessment components of POP. This is reflected in the Problem-Oriented Policing Center developed by Ron Clarke and Graeme Newman (www.pop.org), the Jill Dando Institute in Great Britain, a new police research committee within IACP, and the inclusion of research partnerships in Project Safe Neighborhoods, a national effort within the US to reduce gun crime (www.psn.gov).[4] Clarke [23] has advocated for a new focus within academic programs on 'crime science' that includes analysis at its core and is highly congruent with a problem solving and ILP framework.

1.3. Continuous Improvement Business Models

An additional foundation for ILP is the attempt to apply cutting-edge business practices to public-sector policing. This appears to have been a key impetus within the UK for the adoption of ILP within the National Intelligence Model. Part of a

---

[4] Michigan State University has played a support role for the Department of Justice in PSN by providing training and technical assistance for teams of criminal justice practitioners and researchers and by conducting research on PSN. The model for training and technical assistance is a multi-agency, strategic problem solving approach. PSN included grant support through the 94 US Attorney's Office to allow a local research partner to be part of the problem solving initiative [22].

broader reform movement within the public sector, police officials were held responsible for increasing efficiency and effectiveness through continuous improvement processes [1, 2, 10, 24].[5] According to these models, improved analysis should lead to redeployment of resources and continual assessment.

Within the US, the most well-known application of this business model is the New York Police Department's COMPSTAT program developed during the Giuliani and Bratton administration [25]. Commissioner Bratton shocked many in the law enforcement community by saying that the police were responsible for the level of crime within the city and that the command staff would be held accountable for producing results. The COMPSTAT program involved regular meetings of the command staff, precinct commanders, specialized units, and related officials, whereby crime trends would be analyzed, and commanders would be expected to develop plans to address crime problems. Results were systematically tracked and the failure of district commanders to be aware of crime problems, to not have a thoughtful plan for responding to the problem, and ultimately to not drive down crime rates, was a managerial failure.

At the core, the business practices developed through notions such as total quality management, six sigma, and similar models are based on analysis.[6] Advocates of ILP seek to see analysis become a similar core function of law enforcement.

In the subsequent sections, we consider several manifestations of these concepts that suggest the promise of ILP as a mission-framing model.

2. Models

2.1. COMPSTAT (NYPD and CPD)

As noted above, during the early 1990s, the New York Police Department gained the attention of police leaders and scholars through the implementation of a crime analysis and managerial accountability program known as COMPSTAT ("compare statistics") [25]. Regular meetings of the police command staff, area commanders, special units, and prosecutors were convened to review current crime trends, to develop responses to crime problems, and to hold commanders accountable for the level and trend in crime in their precincts. The dramatic and unexpected decline in crime in New York City that occurred during this period generated significant interest in COMPSTAT. For example, murder declined from over 2,200 in 1990 to under 540 in 2005. Motor vehicle thefts dropped from over 140,000 in 1990 to less than 18,000 in 2005. Total index offenses from over 525,000 to just over 133,000 [27]. Although the link between COMPSTAT and crime reduction has been debated (e.g., [28]), the dramatic decline of crime in New York City throughout the 1990s has led many to a greater acceptance of the value of timely crime analysis and to the idea that the police can influence levels of crime.

The Chicago Police Department (CPD) has developed a similar approach linking crime analysis, rapid deployment of focused resources, and managerial accountability. Within CPD, several COMPSTAT-type meetings occur. Every Friday afternoon, there

---

[5] An example of organizational change resulting from these ideas is the Jacksonville, Florida Sheriff's Department that has a major division known as 'Continuous Improvement' that includes crime analysis and research and development units.

[6] Although written for the broad intelligence community, Kamarck [26] has developed a thoughtful statement on the application of business principles to the collection and management of information.

is a meeting known as the VISE meeting (Violent Incident Strategy Evaluation) that is focused on the top priorities of homicide, gun assaults, and the connections to gangs and drugs. Current crime data, combined with a variety of intelligence products, are used to focus resources on Level 1 and Level 2 violent crime zones. Level 2 priority areas represent the department's top priority areas and receive additional police resources. Level 1 priority areas are also violent crime hotspots and are designated by the 5 police zone commanders as priorities for the particular police district. The VISE meeting is immediately followed by the DOC meeting (Deployment Operations Center). This meeting focuses on the strategies planned and resources needed to deploy to all priority 2 areas. A third COMPSTAT-style meeting occurs less frequently and focuses on other index offenses and less serious crimes.

The VISE and DOC meetings are supported by the Bureau of Strategic Deployment's Deployment Operation Center. The Center acts much like what law enforcement intelligence advocates refer to as a fusion center. All crime incident data, calls for service, field interrogation cards, gang team intelligence and similar information within CPD, as well as information from partnering agencies like the Illinois Department of Correction, ATF, DEA and other federal agencies is sent to the DOC Center. This information is then analyzed, presented at the weekly VISE and DOC meetings, and used to generate intelligence products to support the Level 1 and Level 2 priority areas.

2.2. Project Safe Neighborhoods[7]

Project Safe Neighborhoods (PSN) is a major initiative launched by the US Department of Justice in 2001 with the intent of reducing levels of gun crime. PSN is coordinated through the 94 US Attorney's Offices that cover the nation. The PSN model calls for multi-agency task forces to employ a strategic problem-solving model whereby local gun crime patterns are analyzed, strategies are crafted to respond to these patterns, and ongoing assessment and refinement occurs. PSN built upon the crime analysis and resource deployment approach embodied in COMPSTAT as well as the problem-solving model that was part of Boston's Ceasefire program and later part of DOJ's Strategic Approaches to Community Safety Initiative [22, 29].

2.2.1. Boston Ceasefire

Boston's Ceasefire Program, also referred to as the Boston Gun Project, was a strategic problem solving initiative intended to reduce the high level of youth gun violence in the city. Ceasefire was initiated by a multi-agency working group involving the US Attorney's Office, local prosecutors, the Boston Police Department, probation, youth service workers, and a team of researchers from Harvard's Kennedy School of Government. The problem analysis revealed that youth violence was driven by a relatively small number of chronic offenders involved in networks of known offenders. The strategy that emerged was a deterrence-based model whereby the threat of federal prosecution was directly communicated to these groups of known offenders. Following crack-downs on several of the most violent groups, and ongoing communication through meetings with probationers and parolees connected to these offending networks, youth violence declined dramatically. Indeed, Boston went two and one-half years without a youth homicide and youth gun violence declined by approximately 60 percent [30, 31, 32].

---

[7] These sections are adapted from McGarrell [22]

The Boston Project was characterized by several distinctive features. First, a small working group was convened from multiple agencies and linked to a research team that conducted systematic analysis of the firearms crime problem. Second, the deterrence threat was coupled with attempts to link potential offenders to legitimate services offered by youth service workers, traditional service providers (e.g., jobs, education, drug treatment), and non-traditional providers including the faith community. Third, several distinctive strategies emerged to communicate the deterrence message to potential offenders. These included offender notification meetings and police-probation teams conducting visits to high-risk offenders (Operation Nightlife). Fourth, ATF and the Boston Police Department developed supply-side strategies to disrupt illegal gun markets [33, 34]. Finally, like Project Exile[8], the US Attorney's Office played a key leadership role by convening local-state-federal resources and bringing the threat of federal prosecution to the issue of illegal gun possession and use.

2.2.2. Strategic Approaches to Community Safety Initiative (SACSI)

Building on the Boston project, DOJ developed the Strategic Approaches to Community Safety Initiative (SACSI) in the late 1990s [36, 37, 38]. Federal support was provided to five initial cities (Indianapolis, IN, Memphis, TN, New Haven, CT, Portland, OR, and Winston-Salem, NC) and a second set of cities (Albuquerque, NM, Atlanta, GA, Detroit, MI, St. Louis, MO, and Rochester, NY). The US Attorneys were asked to convene multi-agency working groups. Local research partners were asked to be part of the working groups to assist in problem solving research including problem identification and analysis, development of crime reduction strategies, and assessment of implementation and impact.

SACSI demonstrated the utility of using strategic problem solving to tailor a federal initiative to local contexts that varied considerably across the 10 SACSI sites. It also provided the opportunity for further testing of problem solving approaches and strategies initially developed in Boston's Ceasefire. Thus, for example, a number of SACSI jurisdictions found value in using systematic reviews of homicide incidents and gun assaults to uncover patterns of offenders, victims, locations, and network connections that could then suggest intervention strategies. Many of the SACSI sites implemented offender notification meetings to communicate the deterrence message and offer the opportunity for linkage to legitimate services. The offender notification meetings were coupled with Richmond-style billboards, bus posters, and public service advertisements warning against illegal gun possession and use. Similarly, many of the SACSI sites adapted the Nightlife strategy of pairing police and probation teams to enhance supervision of high-risk offenders and increase the credibility of the deterrence message.

The SACSI process also allowed for cross-site learning among the 10 jurisdictions. As a result, many of these communities developed 'Smart Prosecution' processes whereby federal and local prosecutors, ATF agents and local police, systematically reviewed all gun cases to decide on whether a case could most effectively be prosecuted at the state or federal level. Additionally, the processes helped to identify and fix system gaps that had previously allowed gun cases to fall through the cracks and avoid prosecution. Many of the jurisdictions developed lists of the most violent offenders to increase officer safety, suggest targets for proactive investigation, and prioritize cases for prosecution.

---

[8] Project Exile is also an important foundation of PSN. Established in the Northern District of Virginia to address problems of homicide in Richmond, the program involved a commitment to significantly increased federal prosecution of gun crime offenders coupled with a media campaign to communicate a deterrent message to potential offenders. A recent evaluation concludes that Exile significantly reduced homicide [28]; in contrast see [35].

Several promising findings emerged from SACSI research reports at about the same time that PSN was being developed. For example, Indianapolis experienced significant reductions in homicide and gun violence similar to that witnessed in Boston [39]. Winston-Salem saw continued reductions in youth violence and declines in youth recidivism and Portland experienced a large reduction in drive-by shootings [40, 41]. Additionally, Memphis experienced declines in sexual assault, the target of its SACSI program [42]. Roehl and colleagues' comparison of crime trends in the SACSI cities to comparable cities, suggests that declines in homicide and violent crime were more pronounced in the SACSI sites [37]. Consequently, the multi-agency, strategic problem-solving model, as well as many of these strategic interventions, became components of the PSN initiative, and were supported by training and technical assistance.

The successful interventions involved in COMPSTAT, Ceasefire, and SACSI, suggested that analysis of local crime problems, interventions based on this analysis, and continual assessment and refinement hold significant promise for addressing key crime problems. As noted above, these promising practices were used to help shape the strategic problem solving component of PSN. Although it is too early to provide a national assessment of PSN, a series of reports are being produced by local PSN research partners and a series of case studies are being conducted by the national PSN research team at Michigan State University. Promising signs of gun crime reduction are being witnessed in the initial set of studies from Montgomery, AL, Lowell, MA, Omaha, NE, St. Louis, MO, Chicago, IL, and Mobile, AL (cites). In the following sections, we draw upon several examples from four PSN sites, of very different size communities but that all show how analysis can inform strategic interventions.

2.2.3. High Point, NC

In High Point, local police, local prosecutors, the US Attorney's Office, and federal law enforcement worked with the local PSN research partner, Jim Frabutt as well as with David Kennedy, the researcher involved in Boston's Project Ceasefire. The analysis revealed that High Point's gun violence problem was largely driven by violence associated with two active drug markets. The police developed intelligence portfolios on the groups and individuals associated with the drug markets and undercover operations were implemented. Several key actors in the drug markets, who police believed were involved in a number of violent crime incidents, were arrested and prosecuted federally. The other individuals involved in drug distribution were then ordered to a group meeting along with family members. At the meeting, police and prosecutors presented each individual with a case file that made it clear the police had sufficient evidence to arrest the individual and prosecute federally. However, police and prosecution officials said they would hold the prosecution indefinitely as long as the violence and drug market activity stopped. Similar to Boston, this deterrence message was coupled with the provision of social support services (e.g., job placement, drug treatment, vocational programs). The police and the research partner have monitored pre- and post-crime trends in these neighborhoods where the two drug markets were located and report substantial declines in violent crime.

From an ILP perspective, the key components were the thorough analysis of the source of the violent crime problem, at both strategic (drug market connection) and tactical (specific individuals and groups) levels. This was complemented with detailed intelligence acquired through the undercover operation that provided the intelligence needed to implement the intervention.

2.2.4. Rochester, NY

Rochester, NY is a city of approximately a quarter of a million residents that has suffered from high rates of homicide and gun crime, indeed the highest rates in the state. Beginning in the SACSI program and continued under PSN, the PSN task force has worked with a local researcher, John Klofas, as well as with the analysts in the Rochester Police Department's crime analysis unit.

One of the distinctive features of the Rochester PSN task is the very thorough analysis of gun crime that has informed strategy development. Rochester began by looking at the geographic distribution of homicide and gun crime and discovered that the city's high crime neighborhoods generated risk of victimization for young men at rates 65 times the national average. They then conducted systematic incident reviews [43] where groups of patrol officers, special units officers (gang, narcotics), homicide and major crime investigators, federal law enforcement agents, local and federal prosecutors, and probation and parole officers were brought together to review incident after incident. The incident reviews built on the detailed information that patrol officers and investigators have of cases, with the ability of researchers and analysts to look across cases and uncover the patterns behind the incidents [43, 44].[9] The incident review revealed that homicides in Rochester were largely being generated by drug robberies and disputes. This was useful at a strategic intelligence level and largely confirmed the understandings of street-level officers.

To move deeper into the analysis, the research team decided to conduct focus groups of offenders in the local jail. The intent was to talk with people with real knowledge of both the drug market business as well as knowledge about street disputes. The logic is that going to the source, much like police working with confidential informants, was the most likely way to gain deeper understanding of drug robberies and disputes.

In terms of the drug houses, the focus groups yielded significant insight. Offenders spoke of the life cycle of a crack house and were well aware of the dangers posed by crack houses at different stages of the life cycle. Typically, crack houses open and sell to a fairly tight circle of friends and acquaintances. Over time, however, the word gets out and increasingly business is being done with large numbers of customers and with strangers. On the one hand, this is a sign that business is good and money is to be made. On the other hand, this increased level of activity brings two threats. First, the house may come to the attention of police and be subject to raids and undercover operations. Second, the word may get out to drug robbers that this is a house likely to have significant cash and drugs. It is at this point that the house is considered, 'hot' and subject to either police action or robbery.

The analysis of the drug house situation also revealed that at any given time, there were considerably more drug houses operating in Rochester than the police could possibly respond to with undercover operations. Consequently, the PSN task force decided to utilize an intelligence-led process whereby they would use intelligence to identify 'hot drug houses' and focus their attention on a variety of strategies ranging from traditional drug enforcement to disruption tactics such as knock and talks, probation and parole home visits, positioning a patrol car in front of suspected drug houses and similar tactics designed to either shut down or 'cool off' a hot drug house. It was at this level of identifying specific targets that intelligence moved from strategic to tactical levels.

---

[9] Cope [21] also notes the crucial role of street level officers as a source of information. See also Manning's (1992) findings that much police intelligence resides in the heads of individual officers.

The analysis of disputes revealed additional interesting findings. In contrast to the stereotypical view of street disputes as involving instantaneous eruptions, both the data analysis and the jail focus groups revealed that many of the disputes that resulted in shootings were long standing disputes lasting on average for two weeks and often as long as a month. Further, the jail inmates stated that these disputes were typically well known in the neighborhood. Of particular importance, they mentioned that while disputes were constantly occurring in the neighborhood, consistent with police perceptions, that there were some disputes that were particularly risky. These typically involved disputes with certain chronic violent offenders known to be armed and willing to use a gun to settle disputes.

This strategic intelligence on disputes was used to develop interventions intended to reduce dispute-related shootings and homicides. The PSN task force decided that it needed street-level information from high-violent crime neighborhoods about current disputes, particularly those involving someone believed to be a high-risk individual. Patrol officers working these neighborhoods were encouraged to gather information from local citizens about these disputes. Similarly, gang outreach workers decided to focus their efforts on acquiring information about current disputes that could result in shootings. With this information, the PSN task force could intervene in a variety of ways including knock and talks to inform high-risk individuals that the police were aware of the dispute and would know where to go looking should a shooting occur, probation and parole home visits, and service of outstanding warrants on high-risk individuals involved in disputes. In this way, the intelligence process was intended to move from the strategic to the tactical and operational levels.

2.2.5. Chicago, IL[10]

As noted above, one key component of CPD's move to an ILP model is the adaptation of the COMPSTAT model to analyze current crime patterns and deploy resources to address key problems.[11] Additionally, Chicago has made a very serious effort to address gun crime through its PSN initiative. This involves a multi-agency task force consisting of the US Attorney's Office, the Cook County State's Attorney, CPD, ATF, Illinois Department of Corrections, Cook County Adult Probation, Mayor's Office, City Chicago Corporate Counsel, Chicago Crime Commission, research partners from the University of Chicago, and a large number of community based groups. The task force decided to begin the initiative by focusing on two police districts that historically have had the highest rate of homicide and gun crime in the city. In ILP perspective, strategic intelligence was used to focus resources where they could have the greatest impact.

Further analysis revealed that within these police districts gun violence displayed geographic concentrations and a large portion of the violence was connected to chronic offenders, gangs, and drugs. The interventions developed to address the violence focused on a two-fold strategy similar to that utilized in Boston and the SACSI sites. First, a deterrence message based on the increased likelihood of federal prosecution for felons in possession or using firearms would be delivered, backed up by an increase in federal prosecution. Second, the deterrence message would be coupled with a social support message whereby community resources including vocational training, jobs, substance

---

[10] Greater detail is available in a report by the University of Chicago research partners [45].
[11] Interviews with command staff indicate that the success of the analytical problem solving and focused deployment of resources within Chicago's PSN initiative was one of the reasons the department decided to develop the VISE and DOC meetings and gun crime focus citywide.

abuse treatment, and similar services are made available to probationers and parolees believed to be at risk for involvement in gun crime.

The message is communicated in a variety of ways including billboards throughout the target neighborhoods, but with special attention to offender notification meetings [46]. All parolees returning to the community with any type of prior firearm charge, are asked to attend a meeting that is held weekly whereby a group of parolees and probationers hear this message delivered by representatives of the US Attorney's Office, Cook County State Attorney, parole, CPD, community groups and social service providers. This direct communication is supported by CPD's gun patrols deployed to gun crime hot spots as well as ATF illegal gun supply side interdiction efforts.

The impact of the Chicago PSN initiative appears to be very significant. Citywide homicides declined to historic lows in 2004 and 2005 with the largest decreases occurring in the PSN focus areas. Indeed, the decline in the PSN focus areas was a 37 percent decline in the quarterly homicide rates.

2.2.6. Fort Worth, TX

The Fort Worth Police Department (FWPD) has taken an explicit ILP approach to addressing gun crime in its PSN effort by utilizing the resources available through its Intelligence Unit. Analysts within the Intelligence Unit studied patterns of gun crime and identified geographic patterns that also reflected gang-related violence and the nexus of gangs and drugs. This led to a series of operations targeting specific gangs associated with gun crime. The Intelligence Unit coordinated with a gun crime team operated out of the local ATF office that included both federal agents and FWPD officers assigned to the unit. Undercover operations were initiated that resulted in three successive crackdowns on three major gangs. A large number of arrests, gun and drug seizures, and federal prosecutions followed.

The gang crackdowns, targeted at what were believed to be the most violent groups in the city, were coupled with large monthly offender forums where up to 400 probationers and parolees heard the dual message of federal prosecution for illegal gun crime and social service support. Additionally, consistent with approaches of the Northern District of Texas PSN effort in Dallas, the PSN effort included coordination with the local weed and seed program to focus on community development efforts once the gang operations were completed.

Several additional observations relevant to ILP arose during meetings with local and federal law enforcement officials. First, although focused on local gangs generating gun violence in Fort Worth, the intelligence collection and analysis also resulted in operations focused on the movement of guns to Mexico by groups involved in drug importation to the US. Thus, locally-generated intelligence was being utilized to address international crime patterns. Second, the commander of the Intelligence Unit highlighted the resource challenges for local police departments to implement an "all-crimes" focus within the Intelligence Unit. Although acknowledging the advantages of the all-crimes approach, for example in the gun-drug operation between Mexico and Fort Worth, the commander also expressed the concerns of being able to devote sufficient intelligence unit resources to homeland security threats and to street crime.[12]

---

[12] Similar findings of resource constraints facing local law enforcement were reported in Riley et al. [47].

3. Terrorism Link - Istanbul Example

The examples of the utility of ILP addressed above focus on traditional street crime and gun crime in particular. The question remains of the value that ILP offers for the prevention of terrorist attacks. The arrests following the London subway bombings and the Madrid train bombings suggest that intelligence gathered from multiple sources including surveillance cameras, community informants, and prison officials were instrumental in post-event investigations. Recent arrests of suspected terrorists in the US (Florida) and Canada suggest that intelligence may be able identify terrorist groups and allow for intervention prior to an attack. This is consistent with reports from countries with long experience in combating terrorists such as Great Britain and Israel. In the following section we consider the lessons provided by the investigation by the Turkish National Police (TNP) of a series of bombings in Istanbul.[13] Components of the case have re-affirmed TNP's commitment to intelligence gathering and analysis as a key step in prevention and suggest that terrorist operations are vulnerable to an ILP approach.

In November 2003, a series of coordinated suicide bombings carried out by al-Qaida in Istanbul. The targets represented Israel and the west including two synagogues, an HSBC bank, and the British consulate. The attacks resulted in 68 deaths and over 700 injured. The investigation and arrests that ensued revealed that the network involved in the bombings had trained in Afghanistan. Of particular interest was the interpersonal web that grew from the four suicide bombers as well as the range of materials confiscated in the investigation. Specifically, nearly 300 people were identified who had some knowledge of the planned attack. Of these, 48 were viewed as hard core committed terrorists, leaving approximately 250 community members who were not ideologically committed to al-Qaeda's goals and who had some information that potentially could have been used in preventive action. Similarly, the materials confiscated included items such as 800 pounds of Hexa Methylene Tetramine, 150 pounds of Penta Eritritol-M, and 150 pounds of Sodium Carbonate, all ingredients used for the explosives. Additional items included sticks of dynamite, AK-47 rifles and shotguns, 22 hand radios, forged passports and drivers' licenses, and 89 large detergent barrels. The point was that given all these materials, as well as the number of people in the community with some knowledge or suspicions, that the opportunity existed to acquire intelligence that could be used in a predictive intelligence fashion aimed at prevention.

These findings were reinforced through interviews conducted by TNP officers with detained terrorists. The results suggested that the majority of terrorist members became involved with terrorist organizations through family and friendship networks and were not ideologically committed. Many expressed the desire to leave the terrorist network but feared retribution. Only approximately one-third of those interviewed were assessed to be ideologically committed to extremist views. Consistent with the findings from the investigation, the interviews suggested to the TNP that establishing connections to the community could result in informants and intelligence that could form the basis for predictive intelligence.

---

[13] The author is thankful to the leadership of the Turkish National Police who have provided briefings from the intelligence and anti-terrorism divisions. Particular thanks to Dr. Ahmet Yayla and Majors Samih Teymur and Bilal Sevinc, who are pursuing Ph.D. study at North Texas State University and Michigan State University, respectively, and who provided the data presented herein.

4. Challenges and Key Components

Scholars studying organizational behavior and change have long noted the resistance to change and innovation [48]. Institutional theorists [49] point out that a common form of organizational adaptation is symbolic adoption of the reform but without significant change in structure and service delivery. In the case of ILP, the prediction from an institutional perspective is that many law enforcement agencies will adopt the vestiges of the model, such as creating an intelligence unit, but that the reform will not be adopted throughout the organization and will not significantly influence patrol, investigation and prevention practices. A likely outcome is what Toch and Grant [50] have referred to as an "innovation ghetto" where personnel directly connected to the intelligence unit adopt new practices but in relative isolation from the remainder of the organization.

The obstacles to meaningful adoption of ILP are highlighted in Sheptycki's [44] study of law enforcement intelligence systems. Sheptycki noted a number of organizational pathologies that make the development of effective intelligence systems in the police context a major challenge. Among these is the fragmented organizational structure of law enforcement. This is readily apparent in the US with the decentralized local, state, federal and Tribal structure of law enforcement (even at the federal level over 80 agencies have law enforcement responsibilities), but is true in the UK and many countries. Similar obstacles include police organizational culture that often downplays the value of civilians (crime and intelligence analysts) to police work [21].[14]

Zimmermann's [51] research on the implementation of PSN, including the implementation of research- and analysis-based decision-making, suggests that indeed these obstacles are real but also that there is significant variation in the capacity of law enforcement agencies to adopt such practices and that this capacity varies in predictable ways. Specifically, she finds that PSN task forces with strong leadership, with experience in the use of research and data, and with an adequate technological infrastructure were much more likely to implement research-based decision making and the operational components of PSN.

Effective ties to the community are also likely to be an essential ingredient to ILP. Additionally, the 'all-crimes' approach to ILP as suggested by the National Criminal Intelligence Sharing Plan [4] is likely to create economies of scale when applied to all types of crime and terrorist threats. Recent research on deterrence suggests that ILP is most likely to be effective when implemented in a way that focuses resources on particular crime types and particular threat groups [e.g.,16, 39, 52, 53]. Finally, given the history of abuses of individual privacy rights [5], it is critical that ILP be implemented on the basis of the highest legal and ethical standards if ILP is to be accepted among the public as well as political and judicial levels.

The challenges to implementing ILP are significant but the research reviewed above, although clearly only a starting point, suggests the promise of the integration of intelligence and analysis into police philosophy and operations.

---

[14] Sheptycki [44] identifies 11 "organizational pathologies" hindering intelligence systems.

References

[1] N. Tilley, Problem-oriented policing, intelligence-led policing and the national intelligence model. *Crime Science Short Report Series*. London, Jill Dando Institute of Crime Science; 2003.

[2] C. Hale, R. Heaton, S. Uglow, Uniform styles? Aspects of police centralization in England and Wales. *Policing and Society* **14/4** (2004), 291-312.

[3] Bureau of Justice Assistance, *Intelligence-led policing: The new intelligence architecture*. Washington, DC, US Department of Justice, Bureau of Justice Assistance; 2005.

[4] Bureau of Justice Assistance, *National criminal intelligence sharing plan*. Washington, D.C.: US Department of Justice, Bureau of Justice Assistance; 2005.

[5] D.L. Carter, *Law enforcement intelligence: A guide for state, local, and tribal law enforcement agencies*. Washington, D.C.: US Department of Justice, Office of Community Oriented Policing Services; 2004.

[6] M. R. Wolfgang, R. Figlio, T. Sellin, *Delinquency in a birth cohort*. Chicago: University of Chicago Press; 1972.

[7] National Advisory Commission on Criminal Justice Standards and Goals, *Police*. Washington, D.C.: US Government Printing Office; 1973.

[8] National Advisory Commission on Criminal Justice Standards and Goals, *Report of the task force on organized crime*. Washington, D.C.: US Government Printing Office; 1976.

[9] R. Anderson, Intelligence-led policing: A British perspective. *Intelligence Led Policing: International Perspectives on Policing in the 21st Century*. Lawrenceville: International Association of Law Enforcement Intelligence Analysts; 1997.

[10] J.H. Ratcliffe, Intelligence-led policing and the problems of turning rhetoric into practice. *Policing and Society* **12/1** (2002), 53-66.

[11] A. Commission, *Helping with enquiries: Tackling crime effectively*. London: HMSO; 1993.

[12] Her Majesty's Inspectorate of Constabulary, *Policing with intelligence*. London: Her Majesty's Inspectorate of Constabulary; 1997.

[13] J. Nelson, The Louima decision: Is punishment possible for police brutality? *The Village Voice*. New York City; 2002.

[14] H. MacDonald, Diallo truth, diallo falsehood. *City Journal (Summer)*; 1999.

[15] H. MacDonald, LAPD's gangster cops are gone. *Los Angeles Times*. Los Angeles; 2006.

[16] H. Goldstein, *Problem oriented policing*. Philadelphia: Temple University Press; 1990.

[17] M. Felson, Routine activities and crime prevention in the developing metropolis. *Criminology* **25** (1987), 911-931.

[18] M. Felson, Routine activities, social controls, rational decisions and criminal outcomes. In D. Cornish, R. Clarke, editors. *The reasoning criminal*. New York: Springer-Verlag; 1986.

[19] R.V.G. Clarke, *Situational crime prevention: Successful case studies*. New York: Harrow and Heston; 1997.

[20] D.E. Duffee, B.C. Renauer, J.D. Scott, S. Chermak, E.F. McGarrell, *Measuring community building involving the police*. Final Report submitted to the National Institute of Justice; 2002.

[21] N.Cope, Intelligence led policing or policing led intelligence? *British Journal of Criminology* **44** (2004), 188-203.

[22] E.F. McGarrell, *Strategic problem solving and project safe neighborhoods*. East Lansing: Michigan State University; 2005. [Online] Available from: URL: http://www.cj.msu.edu/%7Eoutreach/psn/Strategic_Problem_Solving_PSN_wp1%5B1%5D.pdf [2006, March 02]

[23] R.V.G. Clarke, Technology, criminology and crime science. *European Journal on Criminal Policy and Research* **10/1** (2004), 55-63.

[24] T. John, M. Maguire, *National intelligence model: Key lessons from early research*. London: Great Britain Home Office Research Development and Statistics Directorate; 2004.

[25] E. Silverman, *NYPD battles crime: Innovative strategies in policing*. Boston: Northeastern University Press; 1999.

[26] E.C. Kamarck, Transforming the intelligence community: Improving the collection and management of information. *Transformation of Organizations Series*. Washington, DC, IBM Center for the Business of Government; 2005.

[27] New York Police Department CompStat Unit, City Wide Crime Statistics (2006). [Online] Available from: URL: http://www.nyc.gov/html/nypd/pdf/chfdept/cscity.pdf [2006, September 30]

[28] R. Rosenfeld, R. Forango, E. Baumer, Did Ceasefire, Compstat, and Exile reduce homicide? *Criminology and Public Policy* **4/3** (2005); 419-450.

[29] US Department of Justice, *Project Safe Neighborhoods: America's network against gun violence*. US Department of Justice, Bureau of Justice Assistance; 2004.

[30] A.A. Braga, D.M. Kennedy, A.M. Piehl, E.J. Waring, Measuring the impact of Operation Ceasefire. *Reducing Gun Violence: The Boston Gun Project's Operation Ceasefire*. Washington, D.C.: National Institute of Justice; 2001.
[31] A.A. Braga, D.M. Kennedy, E.J. Waring, A.M. Piehl, Problem-oriented policing, deterrence, and youth violence: An evaluation of Boston's Operation Ceasefire. *Journal of Research in Crime and Delinquency* **38/3** (2001), 195-225.
[32] D.M. Kennedy, A.A. Braga, A.M. Piehl, Developing and implementing Operation Ceasefire. *Reducing Gun Violence: The Boston Gun Project's Operation Ceasefire*. Washington, D.C.: National Institute of Justice; 2001.
[33] D.M. Kennedy, A.M. Piehl, A.A. Braga, Youth violence in Boston: Gun markets, serious youth offenders, and a use-reduction strategy. *Law and Contemporary Problems* **59** (1996); 147-196.
[34] A.A. Braga, P.J. Cook, D.M. Kennedy, M.H. Moore, The illegal supply of firearms. In M. Tonry, editor. *Crime and justice: An annual review*. Chicago: University of Chicago Press; 2002.
[35] S. Raphael, J. Ludwig, Prison sentence enhancements: The case of Project Exile. In J. Ludwig, P. Cook, editors. *Evaluating gun policy: Effects on crime and violence*. Washington, D.C.: Brookings Institution Press; 2003.
[36] V. Coleman, W.C. Holton Jr., K. Olson, S.C. Robinson, J. Stewart, Using knowledge and teamwork to reduce crime. *National Institute of Justice Journal* (1999, October), 16-23.
[37] J. Roehl, D. Rosenbaum, S. Costello, J. Coldren, A. Schuck, L. Kunard, D. Forde, *Strategic Approaches to Community Safety Initiative (SACSI) in 10 US cities: The building blocks for Project Safe Neighborhoods*. Chicago: University of Illinois at Chicago; 2004.
[38] E. Dalton, Lessons in preventing homicide (2003). [Online] Available from: URL: http://www.cj.msu.edu/~outreach/psn/erins_report_jan_2004.pdf [2005, January 09]
[39] E.F. McGarrell, S. Chermak, J. Wilson, N. Corsaro, Reducing homicide through a 'lever-pulling' strategy. *Justice Quarterly* **23/2** (2006), 214-231.
[40] S.A.L.L Kapsch, *Strategic Approaches to Community Safety Research Team final report*. Final Report submitted to the National Institute of Justice. Portland: Reed College; 2002.
[41] D.L. Easterling, L. Harvey, D. Mac-Thompson, M. Allen, *Evaluation of SACSI in Winston-Salem: Engaging the community in a strategic analysis of youth violence*. Greensboro: University of North Carolina; 2002.
[42] P. Betts, K. Henning, R. Janikowski, L. Klesges, H. Scott, A. Anderson, *Memphis Sexual Assault Project: Final report*. Memphis: University of Memphis; 2003.
[43] J. Klofas, N.K. Hipple, J. McDevitt, T. Bynum, E.F. McGarrell, S.H. Decker, *Crime incident reviews: A Project Safe Neighborhoods Strategic Intervention*. Washington, D.C.: US Department of Justice, Office of Justice Programs; 2006.
[44] J. Sheptycki, Organizational pathologies in police intelligence systems. *European Journal of Criminology* **1/3** (2004), 307-332.
[45] A. Papachristos, T. Meares, J. Fagan, Attention felons: Evaluating Project Safe Neighborhoods in Chicago (2005, November). [Online] Available from: URL: http://ssrn.com/abstract=860685 [2006, August 10]
[46] J. McDevitt, S.H. Decker, N.K. Kroovand, E.F. McGarrell, J. Klofas, T. Bynum, *Offender notification meetings: A project safe neighborhoods strategic intervention*. Washington, D.C.: US Department of Justice, Office of Justice Programs; 2006.
[47] K.J. Riley, G.F. Treverton, J.M. Wilson, L.M. Davis, *State and local intelligence in the war on terrorism*. Santa Monica: Rand Corporation; 2005.
[48] A. Miller, L. Ohlin, R. Coates, *A theory of social reform: Correctional change processing two states*. Cambridge: Ballinger; 1977.
[49] P.J. DiMaggio, W.W. Powell, The iron cage revisited: Institutional isomorphism and collective rationality in organizational fields. In W.W. Powell, P.J. DiMaggio, editors. *The new institutionalism in organizational analysis*. Chicago: University of Chicago Press; 1991, p. 63-82.
[50] H. Toch, J. Grant, *Police as problem-solvers*. New York: Plenum; 1991.
[51] C. Zimmermann, *Federal incentives to address gun violence: A model of success and failure*. Ph.D. dissertation, Michigan State University; 2006.
[52] E.F. McGarrell, S. Chermak, A. Weiss, J. Wilson, Reducing firearms violence through directed police patrol. *Criminology and Public Policy* **1/1** (2001), 119-148.
[53] D. Weisburd, A. Braga, *Policing innovation: Contrasting perspectives*. Cambridge University Press; 2006.

Supply Chains, Illicit Markets, and Terrorism: Understanding Organizations and Strategies

Robyn R. MACE
Michigan State University, USA

Abstract. Illicit goods cross invisible and visible barriers of borders, social regulation and control, and societal norms using largely the same supply chain mechanisms and technologies employed by legitimate organizations. Illicit market participants evade and elude traditional control mechanisms, and, in some cases, capitalize upon systemic gaps or failures to deliver legal or illegal goods in prohibited environments or distribution channels. This paper facilitates an examination of the complexity and common elements of supply chains and organizational environments across functions and international boundaries, and articulates the link between illicit market activities and terrorist organization funding. Insights into constraints and operations of illegal and enforcement activities generate constructive theoretical and research directions for developing intervention and disruption strategies.

Keywords. Supply chains, terrorism, illicit markets, enforcement strategies

Introduction

Illicit products are the ultimate consumables - demanded commodities, despite presumably high costs and risks for sellers and buyers. The profits to be made by a variety of underground economic activities, including intellectual property theft and more unsavory and explicitly prohibited trades, are generous enough inducements enough for investors, manufacturers, transit and related workers to participate; systematic threats and violence may reinforce or supersede monetary and other incentives. Financial opportunities (and concomitant implementation strategies) combined with intense interest in avoiding detection drive illicit market developments.

The global economy has facilitated an enormous market for illicit commodities in unauthorized or underground markets. Increasing global manufacturing and transport of goods generates significant opportunities for illicit marketers to cultivate and distribute their wares, as well as constant challenges for enforcement agencies and responsible companies operating within and across national borders. Additionally, certain activities such as product counterfeiting in particular industries (e.g., pharmaceuticals, automotive parts, and chemicals) can have deadly consequences. 'Commodity crimes' [1] undermine the profits of legitimate enterprises, reduce taxes and tariffs paid, reduce confidence in institutional and governance structures (social trust), and increase the ability of criminal

---

[1] Commodity crimes refer to a range of offenses that target products or their components for theft, alteration, counterfeiting, diversion, piracy, illegal transportation and distribution and that disrupt, disturb, or disconnect intended products from intended uses.

enterprises to organize and operate effectively. Much of the academic literature on funding terrorist operations examines financial transfer and exchange systems and institutions as a mechanism for funding terrorist activities. What is less well known, and potentially of great strategic import to law enforcement and public authorities for harm mitigation, is how illicit markets and commodities support and strengthen organized crime and, apparently increasingly often, terrorist organizations. A consideration of supply chain elements illuminates situational commonalities of licit and illicit markets, and may offer new insights into enforcement strategies and intervention points.

1. Supply Chains and Illicit Commodities

Supply chains[2] are comprised by the same market, structural, and logistical elements, regardless of whether the commodities traded are licit or illicit. Organized crime has long exploited the unregulated markets of prohibited goods, generating and satisfying demands without incumbent responsibilities of legitimate enterprises for public health and welfare via taxation and being subject to criminal or civil regulations. Seized documents and recent prosecutions in the US indicate that terrorist organizations exploit illicit commodity markets and intellectual property (IP) offenses[3] as a method of operational and expense funding [1, 2].

As supply chains have extended globally, production and consumption patterns have shifted and developed; opportunities for illicit activity have been, like legitimate business opportunities, transformed and extended [3, 4]. There are a variety of competencies involved in running a successful and resilient supply chain, including infrastructure, communications, process, and relationship management [5]. Avoiding interruptions to production (due to weather, shortages, or seizures) and border/transit delays, delivering quality product in a timely fashion, and being able to meet distributor and customer demands are all key elements of both successful licit and illicit businesses. In illicit markets, such as financial instrument counterfeiting (printing money) or human trafficking, there are additional challenges related to the necessity and incentives to avoid detection and interdiction, safe and repeated performance or transit of workers, the need for secrecy, and the ability to manage and launder profits.

Much of the 20th century literature on supply chains focused on supply assurance, continuity planning, and access and physical security controls and techniques [7, 8]. In the early 21st century, globalization, the 9/11 attacks, and natural disasters have generated tremendous recognition of and concern about the potentially devastating (disrupting) vulnerabilities inherent or accrued in national infrastructures[4], and the supply chain networks that comprise and support an interconnected and interdependent world economy [6]. These threats include natural disasters and terrorist acts; risk awareness has galvanized government and private sector attention and research on critical infrastructure, continuity,

---

[2] "A *supply chain* is the combination of organizations and service providers that manage the raw material sourcing, manufacturing, and delivery of goods from the sources of the commodities to the ultimate users" [6, pg. 8)
[3] Intellectual property offenses fall into four general categories: Trademark violations include counterfeiting and diversion; Copyright violations generally involve piracy (and frequently relate to software or services); Trade Secrets and Process violations relate to specific and applied information, include research and development; Patent violations involve registered products or processes.
[4] The US Department of Homeland Security has defined 12 critical infrastructures/key resources sectors in the US. As countries privatize elements of infrastructure sectors (e.g., roads, ports, freighters, airports, electricity, services, etc.), the urgency of public-private coordination of vulnerability/threat assessment and mitigation increases.

and recovery issues[5], but has resulted in little focus on analyzing patterns within illicit markets that may undermine consumer safety and confidence and the legitimacy and power of social institutions while simultaneously funding terrorist activities.

Scholars, industrialists, patriots, and citizens all recognize the fundamental tensions between free trade and security [9, 10]. From corporate and public governance standpoints, enhanced border security measures enacted since 9/11 have provided the opportunity (if not the actuality) for more thorough assessment of cargo and product inspection and control; they have also driven technological investment and innovation. The status of the US as both a debtor and increasingly import-dependent may, in the future, present serious challenges to economic stability and public expectations about infrastructure integrity, uninterrupted economic exchanges, and freedom of travel. Good security drives good business.

In a global economy, more consumers with more disposal income create more opportunities to purchase a seeming endless array of essential and discretionary products; this also creates more opportunities for crime [11]. In developing countries, consumer regulatory, government enforcement, and/or consumer education may not be firmly established or effective in managing either border-commodity control or product quality-safety. In developed countries, protection of IP rights is becoming increasingly important across international markets as challenges from counterfeiting, piracy, and diversion undercut profits and growth, brand integrity, consumer confidence, and established business channels.

Numerous examples document threats to public health as a direct or indirect result of illicit market commodities[6]. Confirmed medical reports indicate that counterfeit insulin, meningitis vaccines, and malaria medicines, among others, have resulted millions of illnesses, other unintended consequences, and at least 200,000 deaths worldwide [12]. In the US, several well-publicized cases involve terrorism and counterfeiting and product diversion, including the 1993 World Trade Center bombing [2, 13].

2. Organized Crime: Market Opportunities and Incentives

Before NAFTA and globalization generated a radical shift in the traditional processes and patterns of resource development, manufacturing, and consumption, organized crime was with a few notable exceptions, a localized and regional business. As with legitimate enterprises, however, incentives for illicit market participants changed dramatically as a result of the linking of modern industrial, conventionally developing, and subsistence economies into interdependency. These dramatic changes have been both structural, including innovative, mobile applications of technology and alignment of methods of doing business (between legitimate and illegitimate sectors), and strategic, involving newly motivated alliances between traditionally detached actors and groups [14].

Chief among these motivations is evading as well as undermining governance systems. Corruption of government and private sector employees often accompanies evasive and erosive activities, particularly in governance systems with questionable authority or

---

[5] As many of the same emergency response, incident command and recovery procedures are used in both manmade and weather disasters. This increased attention may have had a diffused benefit of enhanced overall social and institutional preparedness.

[6] Two of the most comprehensive reports on the multi-dimensional impacts of counterfeiting are *Counterfeit Goods and The Public's Health and Safety* [12] and *The Negative Consequences of International Intellectual Property Theft: Economic Harm, Threats to the Public Health and Safety, and Links to Organized Crime and Terrorist Organizations* [2].

legitimacy and in weak economic and enforcement systems or states. Counterfeit identities, espionage, and fraud have long been tools of spy-craft and attempts at state destabilization; it is unsurprising that in the modern era, these practices would converge with available technologies, using industrial methods and processes to undermine political structures.

Participants may choose to participate in illicit markets for a variety of reasons; a significant portion may be forced in certain commodity sectors to participate through coercion (threat of violence) or lack of viable economic alternatives. Incentives for participation vary by market, role, economic conditions, individual abilities and tolerances. IP crimes in particular carry advantages over more overtly morally offensive crimes, such as human or organ trafficking. These include low barriers to entry and investment (with potentially large returns), low profile to law enforcement, low risk or probability of capture and prosecution, and a general attached social and law enforcement perception of no harm/low harm [2, 3, 4].

Experts and practitioners agree that the structures and practices of organized crime and terrorism are evolving [15, 16, 17,18], and are increasingly fluid and dynamic. Electronic communications and travel have revolutionized the ability of people to communicate ideas and organize (legitimate and illegitimate) activities across great distances. Unlike enforcement agencies and private firms, criminal organizations are not constrained in the same manner by state and institutional laws or externally imposed regulations and funding controls. Organized crime and terrorist groups have been more entrepreneurial than law enforcement; they have responded more quickly to changes in technology, markets, regulations (and gaps therein), and the dynamics of skilled and unskilled labor markets. Organized crime and terrorist organizations have become more diffuse (and difficult to identify) as the specialized knowledge and skills of participants are increasingly mobile. Explorations of the swarming characteristics [17] and changing structures and alliances [14, 16, 19] in organized crime and terrorist groups have offered valuable insights into the diffusion of skills and specialized knowledge for purposes of illicit and terrorist activities. Similar attention should be directed towards understanding the role of markets and supply chains in creating viable and sustainable illicit funding opportunities.

New theoretical perspectives and research methods may be necessary to understand the dynamics of organized criminal enterprises and groups as they grow and accommodate mutable economic and business-enforcement conditions, particularly with respect to international transportation of goods and communications/information technology. Integration of population ecology[7] theories with institutional theories[8] may lead to robust exploratory and explanatory multi-disciplinary models of market incentives for organized criminal activities and corresponding enforcement responses using governmental, regulatory, civil/criminal, and corporate data. Particularly salient questions relate the efficacy of regulation and intervention in actual and specific contexts; these studies would be enhanced by comparison across legitimate and illicit organizations and markets. BRICs[9] (Brazil, Russia, India, and China) have garnered specific attention for

---

[7] "Population ecology considers the development, growth, density, and mortality or organizations through 'aggregations of competing and non-interacting organizations' that are related through dependence and common vulnerabilities to external factors [20, pg. 545].
[8] "Institutional theories conceptualize (and measure) organizational development as both a status and process, while focusing on dynamic contexts and factors that stimulate organizational similarities in response to environmental challenges. Similarity, or isomorphism, can be examined using the concepts of institutional pillars (regulative, normative, and cognitive factors) and carriers (structures, cultures, and routines). See reference [21].
[9] Wikipedia (www.wikipedia.org) indicates that the BRICs acronym originated in a 2003 Goldman Sach's report *Dreaming with BRICs: The Path to 2050*, Global Economics Paper 99 by Dominic Wilson and Roopa Purushothaman (October).

their facilitation of various types of IP theft; geopolitical and economic concerns must be integrated into development of research and enforcement strategies.

3. Global Markets and Enforcement Issues

Enforcement agencies operate under institutional constraints, while organized crime and terrorist organizations respond to environmental cues, of which law enforcement is only one. Obstacles to successful international organized crime enforcement include international boundaries and jurisdictional issues, non-existent or ill-defined/ineffective legislation, enforcement priorities and resources, the flexibility and fluidity of criminal enterprises, and, finally, a traditional and perhaps legally prescribed reactive rather than anticipatory approach. One of the most important issues related to illicit trade is corruption; in corrupt environments, these tasks are complicated by facilitating actions of putatively legitimate authorities.

Innovative enforcement methods are needed to systematically undermine the structural opportunities for illicit markets and their external societal costs. Specialized units, cooperative endeavors (working groups, task forces, partnerships), and alignment of systemic intervention tactics and penalties cannot alone address the complicated, transnational issues. Data and market-driven research and intelligence should direct the organization of interdiction points to systemic flaws exploited for criminal profits. Using fire marshals to conduct inspections, rather than traditional and possibly corrupt officials, may be an effective strategy to gain facility access. Confiscating the printing equipment of packaging counterfeiters increases the costs and delays resumption of business. One particularly innovative company undertook (with cooperation from law enforcement) a three year campaign to eradicate counterfeiting of its premium whiskey in Thailand; the efforts involved removal of product from market, identification and inducement of participants into legitimate production, or prosecution [22]. Interestingly, while prohibition generally reduces the ability of the state to manage or control commodity markets (through abdication of the definition and assertion of any regulatory conditions[10]), this example demonstrates that actively regulated prohibition can achieve enforcement strategies.

Continued industrial awareness and enhanced private sector cooperation with law enforcement are necessary components of dismantling and decreasing illicit markets. Expanded partnerships and evolutionary strategies are essential to ameliorate the harms or eliminate related consequences of these markets, including applying profits from commodity crimes into violent activities against citizens and states.

4. Conclusion

Systematic study needs to be undertaken to amass information from legal systems, corporate and public health officials in order to address the various economic, health, and regulatory impacts of illicit markets. A cross-national examination of arrestee commodity networks could make an excellent contribution to understanding the roles, structure, and malleability of illicit commodity networks across transnational boundaries. Interviews with active, arrested, or convicted participants in illicit markets could further enhance

---

[10] While full discussion of range of governance mechanisms and techniques is outside the scope of this paper, this area warrants further investigation, particularly with respect to illicit drug enforcement.

understanding of specific networks, structures, and market management techniques. Comprehensive reports detailing the public health impact and costs[11] of illicit markets could help to focus public awareness and regulatory and enforcement efforts on systematically addressing crimogenic factors and public health threats related to the distributional dynamics of commodities and consumption. Recognizing market-drivers and the mechanical, logistically-driven elements of supply chain processes has potential to offer to law enforcement and the private sector revelatory insights into commonalities, potential intervention points, persistent obstacles, and continually-improving strategies to enhance public safety in multiple contexts.

References

[1] B. Ndaba, N. Kalideen, *Jail alleged fake goods culprits, state urged.* [Online] Available from: URL: http://www.iol.co/za/general/news/newsprint.php?art_id=vn20060 [2006, September 6]
[2] International Anti-Counterfeiting Coalition, *The negative consequences of international intellectual property theft: Economic harm, threats to the public health, and links to organized crime and terrorist organizations.* 2005.
[3] P. Andreas, Transnational crime and economic globalization. In M. Berdal, M. Serrano, editors. *Transnational organized crime and international security: Business as usual?* Boulder: Lynne Rienner Publishers Inc.; 2002. p 37-52.
[4] M. Naim, *Illicit: How smugglers, traffickers, and copycats are hijacking the global economy.* New York: Doubleday; 2005.
[5] D. Closs, S. Cheri, K. Helferich, D. Lynch, R.R. Mace, E.F. McGarrell, D. Voss, J. Whipple, Protecting the supply chain from terrorist threats: A framework for guiding practice. *Business Logistics*. Michigan State University, (2006).
[6] D. Closs, E.F. McGarrell, Enhancing security throughout the supply chain. *Special Report Series*, IBM Center for the Business of Government (2004).
[7] O.K. Helferich, R.L. Cook, *Securing the supply chain*. Chicago: Council of Logistics Management; 2003.
[8] D.J. Bowersox, D.J. Closs, T.P. Stank, *21st Century logistics: Making supply chain integration a reality.* Oak Brook: Council of Logistics Management; 1999.
[9] J. Riley, Border security and the terrorist threat. *Congressional Testimony to US House of Representatives*. Committee on Homeland Security, 2006.
[10] S.E. Flynn, *America the vulnerable.* New York: HarperCollins Publishers; 2004.
[11] M. Felson, *Crime and everyday life.* Thousand Oaks: Pine Forge Press; 1994.
[12] M. Forzley, *Counterfeit goods and the public's health and safety.* Washington, D.C.: International Intellectual Property Institute; 2003.
[13] G. Gordon, N.A. Willox, *Identity fraud: A critical national and global threat.* Utica: Economic Crime Institute; 2003.
[14] P. Williams, Cooperation among criminal organizations. In M. Berdal, M. Serrano, editors. *Transnational organization crime and international security.* Boulder: Lynne Rienner Publishers Inc.; 2002.
[15] O. Al-Hassan, Terrorism, organized crime and drugs: Repercussions for national security [Seminar proceedings]. Seminar organized by Gulf Center for Strategic Studies in Cairo, Egypt; 1997.
[16] B. Hoffman, Terrorism trends and prospects. *The New Terrorism.* Santa Monica: RAND Corporation; 1999.
[17] J. Arquilla, D. Ronfeldt, *Networks and netwar: The future of crime, terror, and militancy.* Santa Monica: RAND Corporation; 2001.
[18] D.C. Rapoport, The four waves of modern terrorism. In A. Cronin, J.M. Ludes, editors. *Attacking terrorism: Elements of a grand strategy.* Washington, D.C.: Georgetown Press; 2004.
[19] P. Andreas, When policies collide: Market reform, market prohibition, and the narcotization of the Mexican economy. In H. Friman, P. Andreas, editors. *The illicit global economy and state power.* Lanham: Rowman & Littlefield Publishers Inc.; 1999.
[20] C. Oliver, The collective strategy framework. *Administrative Science Quarterly* **33** (1988).
[21] W.R. Scott, *Institutions and organizations.* Thousand Oaks: Sage Publications; 1995.
[22] R.T. Green, T. Smith, Executive insights. *Journal of International Marketing* **10**/4 (2002).

---

[11] These costs include hospitalization and treatment, attendant mental illness, drug addition, therapeutic assistance, and health care accrued from the direct and indirect outcomes of illicit activities.

Money Laundering and Financing of Terrorism

Suleyman AYDIN
Turkish National Police Academy

Abstract. It is a cliche to observe that the world became a different place after September 11, 2001, but many things have changed, and the International Money Laundering Counting Abadement and Anti-Terrorist Financing Act of 2001 is part of the new lanscape. The problem of money laundering has attrached the attention of the international community at all levels. Money laundering not only finances crime, it pollutes the international banking system, impedes the international fight against corruption, distorts economies, undermines honest government and threaten international peace and security by being associates with international terrorism. That is, terrorism and its financing pose serious threats to national, regional and international stabilty and economic growth. The international recommendations include making financing terrorism, terrorist acts and terrorist organizations a criminal offence, freezing and confiscating terrorist assets and assisting other countries as much as possible in financing investigations.

Keywords. Money laundering, freeze, confiscate, forfeiture, terrorist asset, financing of terrorism

Introduction

In recent years, and especially since the events of September 11, 2001, worldwide efforts to combat money laundering and the financing of terrorism have assumed heightened important. The terrorist attacks increased the importance of preventing, detecting and suppressing the financing of terrorism and terrorist acts on the part of the international community. Money laundering and the financing of terrorism are global problems that not only threaten security, but also compromise the stability, transparency and efficiency of financial systems, thus undermining economic prosperity.

Terrorist activities are the greatest danger for societies which are based on state systems governed by the rule of law. Terrorism poses a threat to human rights and freedoms while obstructing social and economic development. 'Money laundering' and 'financing terrorism' are the two concepts which have been referred to together in the aftermath of the September 11th attacks. September 11th proved how a terrorist organization could shake the entire planet. This hyper-terror threat was underscored with the attacks in Istanbul, Madrid, and London. The financial capacity of terrorist organizations lies in the very center of the problem; just like mafias, terrorist organizations launder their criminal funds for their operations through international financial transactions.

Today, the total amount of laundered funds is estimated to soar between 1 trillion dollars and 2 trillion [1]. Even the bottom line figure in estimations is three times as big as the national budget of France. Half of this figure is generated from drug smuggling.

A research that was conducted by IMF[1] in 2000 reveals that money laundering worldwide amounts to 2-5% of the world's GNP. Criminal organizations and money laundering groups engage in diverse methods to legitimatize their funds which they employ in order to dominate within the economic and political systems; thus they threaten the independency of the state.

1. Terrorism

Terrorism is a systematized use of terror and violence in order to achieve objectives which are not possible by war and diplomacy, to intimidate and coerce a government or a civilian population committed for realization of a theory, philosophy, or an ideology [2]. Terrorism is a concept with international dimensions and it poses an equal level of threat against all humanity without any discrimination and it exploits the same devastating methods in order to attain various objectives. Furnished with violence and ideological goals, terrorism aims primarily to coerce and suppress the civil population, to impair the state authority, to damage social, political, and state structure, and wishes to pave way to polarization within the society.

'Determining one's own fate' was associated with contemporary terrorism after the World War I. While national movements of independence from hegemonic and colonist powers attained their freedom by violence, the political motivation behind these movements determined in the international arena whether they were terrorist activities or not.

The fact that World War II left behind a colossal cost of material and emotional losses have compelled terrorism to shift to new methods. After 1970s, state-sponsored terrorism has skyrocketed. Some governments have manipulated terrorist organizations for various political reasons.

In the aftermath of the Cold War, a brand new wave of globalization has lifted economic borders between countries, and thus has given birth to new economic dependencies. The Eastern block countries changed their centrally-governed economies with free market economy and they have entered into an integration process with others. Former socialist countries of eastern Europe have had to allow foreign capital, for their new economic proliferation failed to find domestic financial resource. The insufficiency of these countries in fighting organized crime and the process of reconstruction of their economies has set a lucrative ground for terrorist and other criminal organizations. The outcome is a complicated network of organized crime, terrorism, drug dealing, and mafia [3].

As of 1980s money-laundering has come into the agenda of international community, financial circles, and the legal authorities. Laundered funds are being shoveled into criminal activities which bring in additional earnings, and thereby nourishing each other to become a bigger operation; it is cycle of crime-earning chain of activities. This cycle forms the underground economy which devastates social, economic, and democratic structures. It spreads like a virus among unlawful economic activities.

In the new century, terrorism has spread across wide fields, institutionalized, technologically upgraded, and have global influences. Terrorist organizations broadcast via Internet, radio, and TV networks their political message to large audiences; they can raise funds and disseminate their propaganda.

---

[1] IMF - International Monetary Fund (www.imf.org)

It is very challenging today to distinguish pure terrorist activities from other criminal activities. This is mainly due to the fact that terrorists benefit from the same methods a criminal organization exploits in order to access financial resources and to commit their activities; terrorists also cooperate with other criminal organizations and they adopt both criminal and ideological identities side by side. Mutual financing methods dissolve terrorists' economic structures within organized crime organizations. Terrorist groups have access to bigger financial support in recent years than in the past.

2. Financing of Terrorism

Terrorism today requires extensive financial resources with international connections and thus has become a field of commercial activity. Terrorist organizations engage in cooperation with other terrorist organizations in the world without discriminating race or ideology; they organize mutual actions and trafficking. Drug dealing and arms trafficking provide them with financial means to supply weapons. Drug abuse has escalated in the entire world in the last quarter of the twentieth century. Drug dealing, which has a global annual turnover of 500 billion dollars according to the UN, is a significant financial source for terrorist groups. Drug dealing generates high income, it is easy to transport, buyers are plenty, easy to convert into valuable money, and the risk of a previous dealing can be compensated with a latter dealing [1].

Financing is a must for terrorist groups to reach their objectives. A successful terrorist organization is the one with an effective and enduring financial infrastructure. To this end, the organization should research financial sources, devise methods to conceal these funds, and find out a way to supply its needs with these funds [4].

There are a variety of sources from which terrorist groups supply funds. Among these sources and methods are conventional criminal activities, funds from wealthy individuals or institutions, funds supplied by other groups, fees collected from members, racketeering, commercial activities operated by bogus companies, etc. We can categorize these sources as follows: (1) Funds sponsored by some states and organizations - terrorism has been manipulated for many years by powerful states as a foreign policy instrument in order to impair their enemies - (II) Racketeering, usurpation, robbery, forgery, unlawful trading of valuable goods, drug dealing, human trafficking, arms trafficking and diamond smuggling, etc. (III) Establishing legal enterprises and engaging in commercial activities; generating income out of organizational publications; channeling lawfully raised funds and fees into the criminal activities [3].

Terrorist organizations that are active at international level or locally use several of the above-listed methods of financing. Some of the organizations are obliged to use certain financing methods due to region in which they are active or due to their ideologies, whereas other groups can use all of the methods. For instance, Red Army Faction (RAF) in Germany solves its financial problems with bank robbery, however, Red Brigades in Italy did not use this method until 1972 [5]. ETA in Spain obtained some of its funds via robbery, racketeering, and foreign support, whereas the majority of its funds were the ransoms from kidnapped businessmen. IRA has been supported by the Northern Ireland Memorial Fund and donations from the public. Hezbollah in Lebanon have been mainly funded by aid from Iran [6]. Al-Qaeda provides its financial support from donations obtained at foundations, prescribed charity (*zakat*), funds by some businessmen of the Gulf and some princes from the Middle East [7].

An efficient way of funding is raising funds and donations, which are legal. Some members of the organization infiltrate social charity foundations and collect funds under legal appearance. Fees for membership, registration, orientation tours, cultural and social activities, sales of publications, donation of some of the income, etc. form the earnings through such foundations. These funds are later processed for money-laundering.

Terrorist organizations shift to illegal activities like human trafficking, drug dealing, racketeering, arms trafficking, kidnapping, blackmailing, robbery, usurpation, forgery, and money-laundering especially due to high costs of activities, strict measures enacted by financial and legal authorities and after their enterprises are not concealed any more.

Among the methods used for money-laundering and transferring funds to members are wiring money less than declared, using off-shore banks for financial transactions, issuing fake invoices in the name of bogus companies, etc. Developments in monetary systems and technological facilities have forced criminal groups to shift their activities towards countries with less protected economies [8].

Human trafficking and smuggling have become a major problem in recent years. Illegal immigrants are estimated to amount to 30 million. Criminal organizations earn 3.2 billion dollars every year by human smuggling [9]. Millions of people emigrate to other countries and continents for various reasons: conflicts between countries, human rights violations, civil war, natural disasters, famine, need for cheap labor, high income with small risk, desire for a better living, other socio-economic and political reasons. Terrorist organizations use human trafficking for financing their needs. These organizations transfer their uncovered members to other countries using this method. They transport people to other countries due to economic, political, or other reasons in return for a payment; they provide accommodation and employment for them and they later use them for their activities and also exact protection money from them [10].

Terrorist organizations engage in all kinds of forgery: credit card crimes, social charity fraud, counterfeit banknotes and coins, raising funds from the public and calling for aid to humanitarian institutions. Companies, restaurants, cafeterias, and other enterprises established by the organization are other sources of financing. Publishing newspapers, magazines, books, audio- video cassettes, establishing enterprises and cultural centers are also among activities of organizations.

Terrorist organizations have close links with other terrorist groups operating in other countries. Alongside organizing mutual actions, they also cooperate in trafficking arms and drugs [3]. Although they do not get involved in terrorist activities drug dealers and arms traffickers get in touch with terrorist organizations while placing weapons and drugs into the market. The close link between traffickers and terrorists pose a great threat to countries, civil public, and democratic values.

International organizations and institutions have been warning the world against this serious threat. Connections between terrorist groups and international drug traffickers have been noted in many declarations, conventions, and symposiums: the fifth article of the 1993 report by UN Narcotics Control Board; the resolution made by UN General Assembly in 1993 on Terrorism and Human Rights [11]; the ninth article of the Second Pan-European Conference of the Ministers of Transport Declaration announced by Pompidou Group (held in February 1994); the Gokero Declaration announced by the EU Council in 1995; the political declaration draft adopted at the Special Session of the UN General Assembly on the world drug problem in June 1998, New York [12]; and the UN General Assembly resolution in September 28, 2001 [3].

3. The Solution to the Problem

Prevention of money-laundering and punishment of criminals contributes to the prevention of financing of terrorism. If a certain money-laundering case involves great amounts of funds, then it is usually an international case. Money-laundering at international levels usually have a complicated nature, and its investigation requires a multi-dimensional approach and effort in order to reveal their legal, punitive, police, administrative, and financial aspects. As terrorism has become a global threat in the world's agenda, international organizations have developed strategies of fighting financing of terrorism. In the wake of 9/11 attacks, Financial Action Task Force (FATF) met in Washington in October 29-30, 2001, and by accepting 8 special decisions it expanded its range of actions beyond money-laundering to include financing of terrorism. FATF revised its 40 advisory decisions so as to refer to this new threat in June 2003. Members to FATF are supposed to put these decisions into action immediately and cut off financial sources of terrorism.

Recognising the vital importance of taking action to combat the financing of terrorism, the FATF has agreed these recommendations, which, when combined with the FATF Forty Recommendations on money laundering, set out the basic framework to detect, prevent and suppress the financing of terrorism and terrorist acts. FATF Special Recommendations on Terrorist Financing are the following:

3.1. Ratification and Implementation of UN Instruments

Each country should take immediate steps to ratify and to implement fully the 1999 UN International Convention for the Suppression of the Financing of Terrorism. Countries should also immediately implement the UN resolutions relating to the prevention and suppression of the financing of terrorist acts, particularly UN Security Council Resolution 1373 [13].

The first part of recommendation that each country is to take immediate steps to ratify and to implement fully the UN Convention for the Suppression of the Financing of Terrorism in 1999 [13]. This resolution obligates all UN members to:

- Criminalize actions aiming to finance terrorism,
- Deny all forms of support for terrorist grows,
- Suppress the provision of safe haven or support for terrorists, including freezing funds or assets of persons, organizations or entities involved in terrorists acts,
- Prohibit active or passive assistance to terrorists,
- Cooperate with other countries in criminal investigations and sharing information about planned terrorist acts.

3.2. Criminalizing Financing of Terrorism and Associated Money Laundering

Each country should criminalize the financing of terrorism, terrorist acts and terrorist organizations. Countries should ensure that such offences are designated as money laundering predicate offences.

This recommendation requires each country to criminalize the financing of terrorism, terrorist acts and terrorist organizations whether the funds were derived illegally or legally. The legislation should be specific in terms of criminalizing the financing of terrorism. It is not enough to criminalize aiding and abetting or attempting or conspiracy.

3.3. Freezing and Confiscated of Terrorist Assets

Each country should implement measures to freeze without delay funds or other assets of terrorists, those who finance terrorism and terrorist organizations in accordance with the UN resolutions relating to the prevention and suppression of the financing of terrorist acts.

Each country should also adopt and implement measures, including legislative ones, which would enable the competent authorities to seize and confiscate property that is the proceeds of, or used in, or intended or allocated for use in, the financing of terrorism, terrorist acts or terrorist organizations [14].

There are freezing, seizure and forfeiture concepts which may have different meanings in different countries. Freezing means that a compotent authority within a country has the authorization to block or restrain specific funds from being moved or otherwise dispersed. The frozen funds or assets remain the property of the owner and remain under the administration of the financial institution and under the control of existing management.

Seizure means that the component government authority has the authorization to take control of the specified funds or assets. Confiscation or forfeiture means that the component authority has authorization to transfer ownership of the specified funds or assets to the country itself. Countries should take into account the freezing action taken by other countries Resolution 1373 and take such action on the basis of reasonable grounds and belief that designated entity or individual is involved in financing terrorism [15].

3.4. Reporting Suspicious Transactions Related to Terrorism

If financial institutions, or other businesses or entities subject to anti-money laundering obligations, suspect or have reasonable grounds to suspect that funds are linked or related to, or are to be used for terrorism, terrorist acts or by terrorist organizations, they should be required to report promptly their suspicions to the competent authorities.

This recommendation involves reporting under two alternative circumstances: When there is a suspicion that funds are linked to terrorists financing; and where are reasonable grounds to suspect that funds are linked to terrorist financing. The distinction between the two is the certainty that forms the standard for the required reporting of a transaction.

3.5. International Co-operation

Each country should afford another country, on the basis of a treaty, arrangement or other mechanism for mutual legal assistance or information exchange, the greatest possible measure of assistance in connection with criminal, civil enforcement, and administrative investigations, inquiries and proceedings relating to the financing of terrorism, terrorist acts and terrorist organizations. Countries should also take all possible measures to ensure that they do not provide safe havens for individuals charged with the financing of terrorism, terrorist acts or terrorist organizations, and should have procedures in place to extradite, where possible, such individuals [14].

Mutual legal assistance means the authority to provide a full range of legal assistance, including the taking of evidence; the search and seizure of documents or items relevant to criminal proceedings or criminal investigations; and the ability to enforce a foreign restraint, seizure, confiscation or forfeiture order in a criminal matter. Countries should assure that claims of political motivation are not recognized as a ground for refusing requests to extradite persons alleged to be involved in terrorist financing.

3.6. Alternative Remittance

Each country should take measures to ensure that persons or legal entities, including agents, that provide a service for the transmission of money or value, including transmission through an informal money or value transfer system or network, should be licensed or registered and subject to all the FATF Recommendations that apply to banks and non-bank financial institutions. Each country should ensure that persons or legal entities that carry out this service illegally are subject to administrative, civil or criminal sanctions [14].

Formal money remittance or transfer services are often provided by a distinct category of non-bank financing institutions whose funds are moved on behalf of individuals or legal entities through a dedicated network or the regulated banking system. These money transmitters should be subjected to a country's AML/CFT laws and also must be licensed or registered. The goal of recommendation is to assure that countries impose AML and CFT requirements on all forms of money and value transfer system. Most countries are reluctant to regulate to the informal money value transfer system. These systems provide a valuable service to people who can't easily access to the formal financial sector.

3.7. Wire Transfers

Countries should take measures to require financial institutions, including money remitters, to include accurate and meaningful originator information (name, address and account number) on funds transfers and related messages that are sent, and the information should remain with the transfer or related message through the payment chain. Countries should take measures to ensure that financial institutions, including money remitters, conduct enhanced scrutiny of and monitor for suspicious activity funds transfers which do not contain complete originator information (name, address and account number).

The objective of this recommendation is to obtain information on who is sending wire transfers so that funds sent for illegal purposes can be identified along with their senders [14]. The information depends on the nature of the transfer whether it is domestic or international. Cross-border transfers need to be accompanied by the name, account number and address. Taking these information on the wire transfer will enable information about the sender to be obtained much more quickly and easily if there is an international money laundering or terrorist financing investigation. Financial institutions must be able to identify wire transfers that do not show meaningful information.

3.8. Non-Profit Organizations

Countries should review the adequacy of laws and regulations that relate to entities that can be abused for the financing of terrorism. Non-profit organizations are particularly vulnerable, and countries should ensure that they cannot be misused by terrorist organizations posing as legitimate ones,

- To exploit legitimate entities as conduits for terrorist financing, including to avoid asset freezing measures,
- To conceal or obscure the clandestine diversion of funds intended for legitimate purposes to terrorist organizations.

- The aim of recommendation is to prevent non-organizations like charitable, educational, social or fraternal purposes, as well as other legal entities and arrangements, from being misused by terrorists. There are three areas for attention by countries under the recommendation:
- Administration: It is necessary to establish fair clear governance structures and internal accountability. The financial activities of the organizations should be filed in a systematical and simple way.
- Programmatic verification: The organizations should know who receives funds and how they are spent and also take active steps to monitor these things.
- Ensure financial transparency: Account should be published and disbursements of funds must be done through accounts with established financial institutions.

3.9. Cash Couriers

Countries should have measures in place to detect the physical cross-border transportation of currency and bearer negotiable instruments, including a declaration system or other disclosure.

Countries should ensure that their component authorities have the legal authority to stop or restrain currency or bearer negotiable to be related to terrorist financing or money laundering, or that are falsely declared or disclosed.

'The International Convention for the Suppression of the Financing of Terrorism' prepared by UN on December 9, 1999 [13], adopted actions that are aimed at financing terrorist activities as a separate crime, and it came up with new jurisdiction that calls for precautionary action on the commodities suspected to have been used for financing terrorism. Article 18 of the Convention limits banking privacy and holds banks and other financial institutions responsible to specify identification and to report extraordinary and suspected transactions. European authorities also agree to the necessity of a more careful investigation on the privacy rule, suspected accounts and money transfers. Ernst Welteke, the President of German Central Bank (Bundesbank) stated that it does not make sense if the investigations on drug trafficking, terrorism, and tax evasion are obstructed by the privacy rule of the banking sector; he said a true balance between individual and societal matters of security [16]. Countries that are parties to this Convention are expected to enact what they are supposed to do and they should also cooperate with other countries which are parties in order to prevent financing of terrorism.

The third directive regarding money-laundering, adopted by both the European Parliament and the EU, should also be adopted by all countries. Public institutions, banks, and other financial agents should control more strictly international money flow. Civilian and charity organizations should be more transparent in their activities and good care should be given so that funds are not shoveled to wrong people.

Fighting terrorism should be handled comprehensively; however, we still do not have a global definition for terrorism. An extensive global convention against terrorism should be organized to this end. Currently, there are 13 conventions, which are legally binding, on different dimensions of terrorism. All these 13 conventions together with The EU Convention on the Prevention of Terrorist Bombings and The Convention of Financing Terrorism should be approved and supported by all the countries in the world.

Contrary to the money-laundering, one of the challenges in finding out financial sources of terrorism is that all these funds and earnings are always generated from illegal activities. Therefore, it is not always possible to determine and prove the crime.

This is a reality which is related with the nature of financing terrorism, therefore it requires expertise, technical information, and international cooperation.

Punitive fight with money-laundering and forfeiture of illegal funds are the two components of the criminal war strategy that brings about results. This strategy has been identified as 3Fs in the last fifteen years: Finding, Freezing, Forfeiture [1]. It is necessary to take part in the agreements, resolutions and conventions that are adopted by international organizations like the UN, EU, and FATF, and thereby actively participate in the process.

A special attention must be paid to business relations, services and transactions that will take place with the citizens, companies and financial institutions of the countries which do not follow FATF's advices or fail to follow completely and that's why which are included in the Non-Cooperative Countries and Territories (NCCT) list of FATF.

Banks should be utmost careful with the transaction of their customers who are based in offshore centers, free zones, and international financial centers which apply strict banking and privacy principles; such centers provide banking privacy, tax advantages, and legal immunities and therefore they are suitable for keeping funds earned from organized crime and used for financing terrorism [17].

While fighting financing terrorism, information obtained by intelligence units should be shared with various private and state financial institutions. Suspected transaction reports, forfeiture, and other operations should be informed to intelligence units. Suspected funds should be put under surveillance.

The success of terrorist organizations usually depends on foreign support. Success is impossible without foreign support. Domestic supply of food, accommodation, training, and arms is very difficult. Some countries grant right of asylum, give permission to open institutions and publishing activities, allocating camping grounds, providing with training, supplying arms, arsenal, and ammunition, and helping with accommodation, clothes and other logistical needs [18]. As long as terrorist groups are supported by international organizations or states, it will be impossible to put an end to their activities. Governments of the developed or developing countries should stop using terrorist groups for realizing their policies or impairing their enemies. It is inevitable to establish an international approach of collective fighting against terrorism.

Regarding terrorist crimes as 'political crimes' and to providing right of asylum to the criminal is certainly damaging to this international fight. The real problem is the relative character of political component in the definition of terror. The double standard applied in determining the political component is the source of problems.

Following the 9/11 attacks the field of activity has expanded for the NATO. It seems today that no security problem falls out of NATO's realm. Various initiatives, activities and operations in the agenda are mainly a result of the NATO's efforts to meet the new challenges that arose out of the changed strategic circumstances. NATO has transformed from an organization that had focused on a collective defense to the most experienced organization of the world in establishing and preserving peace. Within the process of this shift, NATO's contribution to the fight against the financing of terrorist groups in inevitable.

4. Conclusion

Money-laundering and its integrity with the financial markets are damaging socio-economic values, causing economic crises, and threatening independence of states and democracy.

The fact that economies have gone liberal and communication technologies have developed so fast, have made funds able to travel across the entire world in minutes. While providing a great advantage for legal funds, such technology has also facilitated international transactions of illegal funds. It has become almost impossible for individual countries to fight this crime on their own.

This dramatic result has created a consciousness of collective actions, cooperation and solidarity in order to fight money-laundering. Money-laundering of illegal funds causes deterioration in economies, social life, and the politics, bringing in unbearable financial responsibilities to the public. An effective fight against money-laundering is of necessity for a competitive economy, uncorrupted public administration, strong social structure, and for minimizing terrorism.

In parallel with the rest of the world, terrorism also has global dimensions, and thus it has a wider influence, power, and range greater than any other time in history. Terrorism is a violation of human rights.

Money laundering and financing terrorism have become to be used side by side especially after 9/11 attacks and bombings in London, Madrid, and Istanbul. Terrorist groups launder their funds within international financial transactions just like the mafia. Therefore prevention and punishment of money-laundering will also help prevent terrorist financing. Facilities should be increased for domestic agents like legal authorities, law-enforcement officers, financial intelligence units, and inspective units. Mechanisms for stronger cooperation at international level should be developed.

Like any other organization, terrorist groups are also in need of financial support for survival. They supply funds with various ways. Fighting financing terrorism compels these organizations to develop new methods in order to find new financial sources.

References

[1] E. Ergul, *Kara ekonomi ve aklama suçu*. Ankara: Adalet Kitabevi; 2005. (*in Turkish*)
[2] Turkish National Police. [Online] URL: http://www.egm.gov.tr
[3] T. Uyar, Terörizmin finansmanı noktasında terör örgütlerinin organize suç örgütleri ile ilişkisi, yolsuzluk. In S. Aydın, editor, *Türkiye'de suç ekonomisi ve organize suçlar*. Ankara: Turhan Kitabevi; 2006. p 197-241. (*in Turkish*)
[4] Turkish Ministry of Finance, MASAK-Mali Suclari Arastirma Kurulu. [Online] URL: http://www.masak.gov.tr
[5] A. Steiner, L. Debray, *Kızılordu fraksiyonu*. (translated by R. Cakır). Istanbul: Metis Yayınları; 2000. p 140-148.
[6] M. Erdem, *Hizbullah ve Hamas*. Istanbul: Sarmal Yayınevi; 1999. (*in Turkish*)
[7] J. Burke, *Terörün gölgesi El Kaide*. (translated by E. Kılıç). Istanbul: Everest Yayınları; 2003.
[8] M.J. Winer, *Illicit finance and global conflict*. Fafo Institute for Applied Social Science, 2002. p 78-82.
[9] IOM – International Organization for Migration. [Online] URL: http://www.iom.int/jahia/jsp/index.jsp
[10] N. Alkan, Terörizmin finansmanı. [Online] URL: http:///www.egm.gov.tr [2006, August 13]
[11] UN – United Nations. [Online] URL: http://www.un.org
[12] US Department of State. [Online] URL: http://www.state.gov/
[13] UN Convention for the Suppression of the Financing of Terrorism, (1999). [Online] Available from: URL: http://untreaty.un.org/English/Terrorism/Conv12.pdf [2006, July 20]
[14] FATF – The Financial Action Task Force. [Online] URL: http://www.fatf-gafi.org
[15] E.M. Truman, P. Reuter, *Chasing dirty money: Progress on anti-money laundering*. Washington D.C.: Institute for International Economics; 2004. p 123-132.
[16] Financial Times, 2001, September 24.
[17] S. Aydın, Yolsuzluk, In S. Aydın, editor, *Türkiye'de suç ekonomisi ve organize suçlar*. Ankara: Turhan Kitabevi, 2006. p 121-163. (*in Turkish*)
[18] M.S. Denker, *Uluslararası terör, Türkiye ve PKK*. Istanbul: Boğaziçi Yayınları; 1997. (*in Turkish*)

Local Policing: Using Community Policing Principles as a Tactic in the Time of Terror

Mehmet AFACAN
Northeastern University, USA

Abstract. The level of threat with September 11, 2001 not only heightened public interest, but also disclosed the necessity of new roles for American police in combating terrorism. Because good information comes from everyday sources, the role of local police agencies in homeland security especially in intelligence gathering can not be underestimated. However, thin trust and incomplete information is fragile and may create more harm than help. Preventing such a failure starts with public participation in the decision-making process of the police. With the help of the principles of community policing literature, the American police can benefit from increased police-community relations in dealing with terrorism. This paper is intended to emphasize the crucial value of community policing principles in the daily practices of American policing.

Keywords. Community policing, mutual communication, profiling, disorientation, democratic policing, legitimacy

Introduction

Terrorism is one of the most unpleasant and difficult problems of the whole world. It has been an important term for both security forces and ordinary people. In recent years, terrorist acts reached a level threatening not only the security of a certain country or region but also threatening the global peace of the whole of humanity. Many countries and communities became victims deeply affected by the increased and severe terrorism incidents.

Although terrorism is not a new phenomenon in the world, the American public -even members of law enforcements agencies- were surprised particularly by the terrorist attack of September 11. The US is still living in the aftermath of the saddening 9/11 attacks. While it is time of building relationships between the police and the community, White [1] states that the police are, instead, becoming more militaristic. In the time of 'response to terrorism,' this paper highlights the importance of community policing practices for both local American police and regular citizens in dealing with terrorism when needed. It is desired to emphasize the crucial value of community policing principles in the daily practices of American policing. The principles of community policing such as mutual communication, dialog, reconnection with the public combined with the democratic policing principles are recommended as viable solutions for dealing with terrorist threats as well as necessity for intelligence gathering concerns for local American police. Also, contemporary issues related with the legitimacy and highly discretionary nature of the police is also evaluated. The examination of this topic is limited to local level policing; federal and state level concerns are beyond the scope of this paper.

1. Absence of Visible Enemy: Terrorism

Sheehan and Cordner [2] argue that the basic methods of the traditional model of policing such as motorized patrol, rapid response, and follow-up investigations are limited in answering the fundamental problems of the society in the US (as cited in [3]). In general, nobody has a definite answer about what the ultimate satisfactory level of 'security' in a society is. But, it is inevitable that more perplexing and more sophisticated problems such as terrorism need very careful and detailed consideration. Besides the given statement, it is crucial what kind of methods we are willing to use against terrorism. This is important because the method and tactics used in response to terrorism, to a great extent, will determine the overall success in dealing with terrorism.

Manning [4] defines terrorism as a tactic and a political act that relies on unpredictability; therefore, it cannot be fully anticipated, guarded against, or, in fact, eliminated. Accepting the fact that terrorism is a tactic but not an enemy to be destroyed, then, terrorism itself, in fact, never wins. When the quality of response to terrorism fails, however, failure must be expected consequently. From our perspective, this failure would be failure in the application of community policing and democratic policing principles that weaken efforts in dealing with terrorism. In a similar manner, Lyons [5] cites Barghothi [6] stating that "By itself, terror can accomplish nothing in terms of political goals; it can only aim at obtaining a response that will achieve those goals for it."

2. Terrorism and Disorientation: Community Perspective

Terror is used as a basic instrument to gain political, economic, psychological, and even military objectives. The FBI defines terrorism as "the unlawful use of force or violence against persons or property to intimidate or coerce a government, the civilian population, or any segment thereof, in furtherance of political or social objectives" [7]. Terrorists, using terror as a tool and tactic [4], seek political power as well as absolute control over their target population [8]. Today, terrorism causes intense fear and strong negative feelings among most of its observers, especially among the public, by using one of its key components, 'extreme violence against persons.' Terrorists may develop a strong devotion to their missions and justify them by giving reasons for their actions, even for the killing of innocents. According to the methods and tactics they choose, terrorists intensify the emotional state within the movement and among supporters outside the movement while disorientating and confusing civil authorities. By doing so, they leave only two sharp-edged options for the legal authorities: to become too repressive in response to terrorism or to cause short-term social, economic, and political policies [8]. Picking either option causes infraction of civil liberties and isolation of individuals from their society.

Unlike some other countries in the world, the US is not a homogeneous population. Rather, it is a complex mixture of diverse groups. Every year, immigration to the US and the growth in minority populations in general dramatically changes the face of America. For instance, the US accepts approximately 1 million new immigrants each year. Close to one-third of American children are black, Hispanic, or Asian [9]. With the terror attack of 9/11, increasing suspiciousness based on profiling of potential terrorists not only caused disorientation and confusion of the public, but also damaged police-ethnic minority relations. In addition, these quick and unplanned policies caused unexpected erosions among the members of the community itself.

Disorientation especially may be unavoidable when the victim feels insecure and loses his or her trust in security forces. As one of the unwanted consequences of such confusion and disorientation, 'defense' against terrorists and terrorism comes with the profiling of potential terrorists. Although the success rate is debatable in prevention; nowadays, 'terrorist profiling' is used as one of the key measures of law enforcement in dealing with terrorism [7]. With the attack of September 11, Arab-Americans who are Muslim, between eighteen and twenty-four years of age, and born outside the US simply fit in the 'profile' on suspicion of conducting terrorist activities [7]. Boccabella [10, pg. 31] states that "a very damaging aspect of profiling is the stigmatization of those people belonging to the group being profiled." It is very likely that the new wave of increased suspiciousness presents many puzzled victims with no chance of presenting their own opinion if they do not cooperate.

3. Local Policing: Police Perspective

3.1. Use of Regular Citizens

Dealing with such a special matter called terrorism is not an easy task. Many countries are suffering in the hands of various terrorism threats and unfortunately, there are not many examples of succeeding strategies and tactics against terrorism. It is clear that the attack of September 11, 2001 increased national concern significantly about terrorism in the US. After the attack on America on September 11, many people asked, 'But, what can I do?' While professional law enforcement agencies focused their attention on anticipation of future attacks of terrorists, on the other side, some scholars gave attention to the role of the average citizen in the detection of crime as well as information collection. For instance, after the events of September 11, 2001, the American Truckers Association (ATA) began to organize a national highway watch program, funded by the Federal Motor Carrier Safety Administration, a subdivision of the US Department of Transportation, to train and enlist professional truck drivers to recognize and report incidents on the nation's highways. A similar program was developed for the field of general aviation (GA) that involves more than 650,000 pilots at small airports throughout the country [11].

3.2. Traditional American Policing

The level of threat with September 11, 2001 not only heightened public interest but also disclosed the necessity of new roles for American police in combating terrorism. However, although terrorism is not a new phenomenon in the world, the American public and even members of law enforcement agencies were not prepared for terrorist attacks. This is true especially when we consider most of the terrorists are thoroughly trained to meet law enforcement officers more than any other subjects police officers encountered in the past. Besides, this is a case where police are prepared for this or not [12]. The recently released 9/11 Commission Report includes over forty recommendations for the protection of America from further terrorist assaults. Among the five major recommendations of the report, the major recommendation is 'unity' to improve the performance of the government agencies involved with counterterrorism [13].

Currently, there are four national agencies responsible for counter-terrorism in the US: the Terrorist Threat Integration Center (TTIC), the Counter Terrorism Center, the Department of Defense Intelligence Agency, and the Department of Homeland Security [8]. Since this paper intended to explore the proposed role of local police in combating terrorism in the US, discussions about policing at the national level will be out of our consideration.

After the events of 9/11, local police organizations were willing to do something, but they were confused and had no clear agenda [12]. It needs to be noted that encountering terrorism at the local level across the US seems problematic for several reasons. First of all, American policing is highly diverse and decentralized. Depending on the definition that is used, there are about 21,000 federal, state, and local law enforcement agencies across the US [14]. The traditional decentralized structure of American policing may be one of the reasons for difficulties that limit the ability of coordinated response to domestic antiterrorism efforts [14]. For instance, the existence of some formal plans for responding to large-scale disasters, such as civil disorders, earthquakes, tornados, and the accidental release of hazardous materials is very limited. Also, presented plans simply lack an appropriate evaluation of their effectiveness. Law Enforcement Management and Administrative Survey (LEMAS), for instance, provides periodic information on various special units but includes no data on disaster planning [14].

3.3. American Police Dealing with Terrorism

Second, White [1] expresses that the new and additional wave of crime called 'terrorism' is troublesome for local police departments because of their traditional reactive, response-oriented role and limited ability to deal with more typical sorts of crime (as cited in [7]). A certain amount of local police power has been channeled to assorted forms of homeland security, such as protecting at-risk public spaces, vulnerable sites, dams, power stations and bridges as well as responding to reports of possible attacks [15]. This particularly new and heightened responsibility of local police in dealing with terrorism requires specialized training of local police, the existence of new, rapid policies and programs at both national and local level, a high level of multi-agency cooperation and coordination, and most importantly, increased awareness of local police agencies. However, neither were any of these theoretical and practical establishments present at the time of the attack, nor has any systematic research been established yet as a guide for this new scheme. Still many aspects of so-called 'fighting against terrorism' are vague in terms of winning antiterrorist strategies and tactics in a domestic US context [14].

3.4. Democratic Policing

The police, in general, have various responsibilities and some of these responsibilities are not defined precisely. This is simply because these responsibilities are framed in very vague and incompatible terms. When tools at hand are vague and ill developed [16], understanding and application of justice becomes even more difficult. There are differing responsibilities of police such that selecting the priority of one from the other may cause conflicting results. For example, the answers vary according to the practitioners about what should be done when the responsibility of maintaining order, for instance with 'zero tolerance policing' conflicts with the public demand to give priority to protecting individual liberties. Given this example, the inherent dilemma between the maintenance of order and civil rights becomes more complex with the frequent use of police discretion.

Scholars indicate that the highly discretionary nature of police work increases the difficulty of ensuring the fairness and lawfulness of everyday policing. Use of police discretion when blended with bias and prejudgment may generate one the most unwanted consequences for both police and the public: 'injustice.' Biases and prejudices regarding others are generally based on past experiences and beliefs acquired within one's own culture. However, the job of the police, to interact fairly and objectively with others in a diverse society, requires special care in dealing with cultural differences of others [3]. It is one of the most difficult arts to be 'just'; but, also it is one of the most important components of policing in a democratic country. In fact, the responsibility of a police officer to be 'just' requires a lot more professionalism and training in the legal 'art' of justice. Also, it composes one of the indisputable and necessary parts of police work.

Official police data do not provide insightful and detailed information on police-public interactions in terms of the behaviors of civilians and police officers consequently. The majority of the knowledge comes from researcher-initiated, observational studies [14]. A great deal of scholarly research and contemporary researchers such as Sherman et al. [17], and Tyler [18] assert that when professionals enforce the law impartially and with fairness people are more likely to consent to the law (as cited in [19]). Also, the more people consent to the law, the more likely the police are to be effective in achieving their goals, because when citizens trust the police, they become willing to invest more authority in the police. In other words, while disrespectful treatment decreases compliance, respectful treatment increases it [19]. Therefore, it should be kept in mind that the behavior of the practitioner greatly influences whether people will obey and respect the law [7]. Police, as the most visible face of government, encounter the public frequently in their daily life [14]. For instance, O'Keefe [20] and Whisenand and Ferguson [21] state that police officers spend around 70 percent of their working time in contact with the public (as cited in [3]).

Among various branches of police tasks, especially patrol officers spend the majority of their unassigned time conducting patrolling in their jurisdictions [22], which is known as 'preventive patrol' (cited in [3]). As one of the most visible representatives of law and government in most citizens' lives, the way the police administer the law can significantly influence the strength of that judgment [14]. For instance, police experienced in this advise one another not to arrest men in front of their children, not to humiliate people by having them kneel on the ground, or not to use disrespectful language [19]. But, other than some practical experiences and superficial knowledge, the patrolman, usually the least well-trained and educated, occupies one of the key positions of exercising the greatest amount of discretion on criminal or potentially criminal activities [16]. While many police-public encounters are unproblematic, a significant number of individual citizens come away dissatisfied with how they were treated. For instance, some research as well as public surveys show that there is evidence of racial and ethnic disparities in the assessments of police generally. Regardless of their crime control effectiveness, these disparities and special attention of police create a significant deal of antipathy among the minorities who were over-policed by proactive police tactics [14]. Also, while disparities cause an increase in the gap between local police and minority groups [19], it also lowers the sense of police legitimacy [14].

Notions about crime and justice are related to an individual's view of the world [3]. Similarly, legitimacy of the police can be measured by looking at the hearts and minds of the whole public. Although the term of 'legitimacy,' by definition, is a subjective matter, it is one of the important products of policing [14]. Discussing the level of legitimacy is especially important, because the lack of legitimacy of a police force, on the other hand, indicates the failure to sustain a sense of assurance in their actions by the citizens they serve.

4. Recommendations

4.1. Community Policing

Preventing such a failure, hence, starts with public participation in the decision-making process of the police. This could be done best at the precinct or neighborhood level. In recent years, through efforts to bring together the police with the community, many police and other public safety agencies have adopted the philosophy of community policing. Such efforts, in fact, are essential in building both the legitimacy of the police and participation of the public in an attempt to help the police achieve their law enforcement objectives [14].

With the idea of 'community policing,' police can make a virtue of providing service that is responsive to public priorities by allowing communities to shape police priorities in their neighborhoods. To learn not only individual concerns or city wide mandates but also local neighborhood demands requires both formal and informal consultations with the community. This consultation, especially with the help of police patrol work involving face to face interactions between the public and police officers, in turn, can warrant police actions through their legal authority, professional commitments, and legitimacy of their actions [14].

4.2. Mutual partnership and dialog

To a great extent, the success of community policing depends on winning mutual partnerships of the police with neighborhoods and communities. The existence of such partnerships promotes trust and dialogue, creating a mechanism through which the police become aware of relevant issues and concerns in their community. This dialog can be started with the identification of educational, religious, and business leaders within that community. The police can be the party who create the necessary environment in which the leaders of that particular community and police can work together toward a shared vision. However, the success of establishing such a partnership largely depends on mutual willingness as well as the participants' ability to communicate through a common language [3].

4.3. Communication

The basis of counter intelligence is information, and it is best collected with the help of open communication [13]. However, the local police have a finite number of resources and very limited education in developing effective counterterrorism intelligence. There is evidence that effective and appropriate communication between the police and the public diminishes victim distress and encourages citizen crime prevention activities;

correspondingly, good communication skills increase the possibility of collecting information and obtaining admissions and confessions. On the other hand, the impact of poor communication, standing as a huge barrier between the police and the public, most of the time cannot be erased and cuts mutual communication immediately [3]. For instance, being identified as 'suspicious' causes some minorities to keep family and communal issues within their local community, and not to share with 'others,' especially the police. Similarly, when a distrustful relationship exists, the victim or any encountered citizen may not be eager to provide any information [3]. This especially makes it more difficult, therefore, for officers to collect and secure information [7].

5. Conclusion

The use of regular citizens in information collection and public awareness appears to be a valuable resource for maintaining homeland security [11]. However, the potential risk of segregation and separation of communities must be considered as drawbacks of this process in dealing with terrorism [7]. The heightened role of citizens can become fruitful and viable only with the coordination of professional law enforcement agencies integrated with the promising principles of community policing philosophy.

It is possible to benefit from local police agencies in homeland security, especially in intelligence gathering. The role of local police in intelligence gathering can not be underestimated because good information comes from everyday sources, and intelligence gathering is often nothing more than good police work [12]. However, developing a long-term national program for tracking and evaluating the performance of local police departments' efforts in gathering and handling intelligence on terrorism is needed [14]. Also, efforts towards intelligence gathering, while tactics largely rely on 'suspicion' and 'target profiling' considered as a method against terrorism, can also be a big threat to the integrity and legitimacy of the police. Policing depending on profiling and exclusion would decrease police access to information and public willingness to work with the police [5].

It is impossible to seek a secure society without implementing the principles of democratic policing, such as legitimacy, trust, fairness, and the impartiality of the police. In counterterrorism, it is a well-known fact that thin trust and incomplete information is fragile and may create more harm than help. Without 'trust' and a feeling of 'justice and equality,' there would always be a gap of information that cuts out the most necessary part of 'complete information.' This is of course fairly true in dealing with terrorism. The role of community policing in the prevention of terrorism cannot be underestimated. Citizen-police collaboration helps build trust and sharing of information, an absolute necessity for effective law enforcement. Collaboration based on trust and mutual respect can help balance new police counterterrorism strategies with traditional values associated with liberty and civil rights [3].

Since community policing seeks social order, harmony and quality of life concerns of all citizens, in reality it represents a democratic form of policing. With the lessons drawn from the principles of community policing literature, the American police can benefit from increased police-community relations in dealing with terrorism. Understanding and appreciating individuals and groups within their cultural context would eventually increase and strengthen police-community relationships, create new opportunities for open communication, increase mutual respect [3], and expand the confidence and trust in the police [23].

It is very difficult, if not impossible, to have a real and functioning democracy without safety and security. Whatever the dimension of the terror-based security threat is, the struggle against terrorism must be sustained within the democratic system. Terror must never be a justification for interrupting or abolishing democratic principles [24]. Hence, in democratic societies, the struggle against terrorism should be conducted in careful consideration of certain sensitivities. Thus, the role of local police must be within the framework of universal principles such as 'rule of law,' and 'human rights' in dealing with terrorism [24].

References

[1] J.R. White, *Terrorism: An introduction*. Belmont: Wadsworth Thomson Learning; 2002.
[2] R. Sheehan, G.W. Cordner, *Police administration*. Fifth ed. Cincinnati: Anderson; 2004.
[3] P.J. Ortmeier, *Introduction to law enforcement and criminal justice*. New Jersey: Pearson Education Inc.; 2006.
[4] P.K. Manning, Reflections on risk analysis, screening, and contested rationalities. *Canadian Journal of Criminology and Criminal Justice* **48** (2006), 453-469.
[5] W. Lyons, Partnership, information and public safety: Community policing in a time of terror. *Policing: An International Journal of Police Strategies & Management* **25** (2002), 530-542.
[6] J. Barghothi, International terrorism in historical perspective. In C.B. Fields, R.H. Moore, editors. *Comparative criminal justice: Traditional and non-traditional systems of law and control*. Prospect Heights: Waveland Press; 1996.
[7] M.S. Jackson, *Policing in a diverse society*. Durham: Carolina Academic Press; 2006.
[8] A.F. Eldridge, *Images of conflict*. New York: St. Martin's Press; 1979.
[9] K.J. Peak, *Justice administration: Police, courts and corrections management*. Fourth ed. Upper Saddle River: Pearson Prentice Hall; 2004.
[10] J. Boccabella, Profiling the anti-terrorism act: Dangerous and discriminatory in the fight against terrorism. *Appeal: Review of Current Law and Law Reform* **9** (2003), 17-31.
[11] M.A. Greenberg, *Citizens defending America*. Pittsburgh: University of Pittsburgh Press; 2005.
[12] J.R. White, *Defending the homeland*. Belmont: Thomson Learning Inc.; 2004.
[13] D.A. Kessler, A theoretical critique of the 9/11 Commission report. In: *Istanbul Conference on Democracy & Global Security*; 2005 June 9-11; Istanbul, Turkey. Ankara: Oncu Press, 2006. p 730-740.
[14] W. Skogan, *Fairness and effectiveness in policing the evidence*, National Research Council, Washington, D.C.: National Academies Press; 2004.
[15] W.J. Stuntz, Local policing after terror. *The Yale Law Journal* **111** (2002, June), 2137-2194.
[16] P.K. Manning, J.V. Maanen, Policing: A view from the street. In V.E. Kappeler, editor. *The police and society: Touchstone readings*. Second ed. Illinois: Waveland Press; 1999. p 7-32
[17] L.W. Sherman, National Institute of Justice (U.S.), *Preventing crime: What works, what doesn't, what's promising*. Washington, D.C.: U.S. Dept. of Justice Office of Justice Programs National Institute of Justice; 1998.
[18] T. R. Tyler, *Why people obey the law?* New Haven: Yale University Press; 1990.
[19] D.H. Bayley, *Changing the guard, developing democratic police abroad*. New York: Oxford University Press; 2006,
[20] J. O'Keefe, *Protecting the republic: The education and training of American police officers*. Upper Saddle River: Pearson Prentice Hall; 2004.
[21] P.M. Whisenand, R.F. Ferguson, *The managing of police organizations*. Fifth ed. Upper Saddle River: Pearson Prentice Hall. 2002.
[22] G.L. Kelling, M.H. Moore, From political reform to community: The evolving strategy of police. In J.R. Green, S.D. Mastrofski, editors. *Community policing: Rhetoric or reality*. New York: Praeger; 1991. p 14-15, 22-23.
[23] W.V. Pelfrey, Parallels between community oriented policing and the war on terrorism: Lessons learned. *Criminal Justice Studies* **18** (2005), 335-346.
[24] I. Cerrah, Comparative terrorism in a democratic society: Turkish case. In: *Istanbul Conference on Democracy & Global Security*; 2005 June 9-11; Istanbul, Turkey. Ankara: Oncu Press, 2006. p 656-661.

Local Values and Police

Iskender ORMON UULU
International Ataturk-Alatoo University, Kyrgyzstan

Abstract. As we know, sometimes there are clashes between local people and security forces in many areas in the world. One of the reasons for this may be the security force's failure to understand local values. This situation leads the local people to think that their values are disrespected, which in turn make them resort to violence. As a result, even those who are against terror actions may join ones who advocate violence. For this reason, the security forces must be aware of the local cultures, living standards, and their world view, and they should act accordingly. In this paper we study how the actions of security forces should be oriented in relation to local values.

Keywords. Police, local values, society, culture

Introduction

It is a well known fact that in many parts of the world security forces and civilians might have violent conflicts. Some of them are observed to have been caused by security forces' erroneous attitudes due to their insufficient knowledge of the norms and values of the locals. Local people react, if necessary, violently when they sense violation of their own values. They sometimes seem lined up next to terrorists even if they do not support terrorism. For this reason, security forces have to take the cultural codes of locals into consideration, be aware of the cultural values of those codes, and act accordingly to avoid a clash.

1. Local Values and Police

In fact, the issue requires a holistic perspective. To achieve this, though, is laborious and needs immense coordination. We cannot ignore the fact that security forces and police are officials working in the service of higher authorities as well. They are, too, individuals grown up in a culture of their own. Naturally, they will carry with themselves the characteristics of their own culture when acting upon their duties. Misunderstanding and disorganization can minimize the overall outcome of an action, bringing the effect of a good effort down to next to nothing. We cannot assume that conflicts between the police and civilians would peacefully disappear unless the administrative body of the government, directors of security forces, security forces themselves and the media -news provider of the society- coordinate effectively.

What we are driving at here is the processes police undergo during the period of their socialization and the way these processes function in their identity development phase.

As products of the said processes, security forces -police- should be trained for optimum utility within a society. The socio-cultural and political processes that influence society and the behavioral patterns in a society in terms of interaction with others thus gain more importance. Even though all factors have equal importance in the socialization process, we should be more attentive to the subcultures of police. Indubitably, security forces all have their subcultures. Attended a police academy and working at different departments of the institution, in time, individuals are imbued with a particular culture of their own.

This peculiar condition bestows on the police and security forces in general a distinct vocational subculture and professional ethics. In parallel with these differences, police isolate themselves from the other members of the society and identify themselves with their profession; their reactions to social events, naturally, differ from that of civilians [1]. We distance ourselves from an overall assumption which suggests that the police are guilty when there is a conflict between people and the police or the security forces. The focus of our attention is on what the attitudes and behaviors of police should be in case of a disagreement or a conflict, inasmuch as police are responsible for restoring security. Even if people misbehave, they cannot be claimed to have official responsibility, which does not bring together the liabilities and officers.

It is the society which justifies the existence of the police. However, society leaves any related arrangements to the hands of the State. A police department is a unit of the people, by the people and for the people, established to fight against crime and criminals, and thus to serve the people. This, however, requires continuous and healthy public relations, since the unit itself emerges from the society. Good relations mean cooperation of the people and the police in fighting criminals.

Since the police owe their existence to society, it is their duty, rather than a favor from them, to serve the people according to their expectations. It is highly important that police appear as a 'service' unit to the people, instead of standing as a 'power' against them. A show of 'power' would be counterproductive; the police should act bearing in the mind the fact that it is a unit in the service of people. For this reason, the actions of police must be seen as serving the people; this should be regarded as an obligation rather than a preference. This can only be accomplished if police departments or academic circles identify the perspectives and expectations of people for the police and the police try to produce service correspondingly.

We cannot disregard the local culture, traditions, and beliefs of the people which the police are serving. To prejudge the way people react to certain situations depending on their culture and life style is a difficult task. The evaluation of this by security forces would be quite wrong, since it is the business of anthropologists, ethnologists, historians, sociologists and philosophers. However, security forces can only regard an existing situation as a fact and behave accordingly, rather than determine what is correct and what is not. Otherwise, conflict between the people and the police would be inevitable. In this paper, I will try to draw operational limits for this subject's basic terms. In addition, I will cover the definition of security forces and their duties and how all these reflect on people. Analyzing the expectations of the society and the quality of interaction, I will try to elucidate the relation between police and the people. Finally, I will discuss the position of security forces in our contemporary world. Our findings will lead us to question what the most auspicious police-people relationship should be.

2. Conceptual Explanations

Here, I would like to put down the definitions of some concepts that occasionally occur in the paper. However much concepts used in social sciences have common usages, it is not unusual to employ them for specific reasons. This is necessary both to fully comprehend the paper and to clarify the framework of it.

First of all, I titled the paper as "Local values and Police." However, the word 'police' here refers to security forces in general. While the police are chiefly responsible for the domestic security of the people, police, in this article, may also mean military and peacekeeping corps. Although the police are in charge of maintaining security in a country, in practice, gendarmes and Special Forces might also be in close touch with the people. Other than that, army officials and security forces from second and third countries in Afghanistan, Iraq, and Lebanon are presently employed for the said duty. These also enter into direct relations with the locals and try to convince the people that they are responsible for their security. My study is also directly related to these issues. Local culture here refers to culture of the local people, which the security forces interact with, their life standards, their understanding and values. Indeed, people's behaviors and their reactions are closely linked to their socialization process. Environment, traditions, religion, and social norms are most influential in this process.

Moreover, the term 'subcultures' of security forces is also used in the article. It is never possible to consider the practices of police and security forces independently of their subcultures. Behind the existence of every institution lies always a 'theoretical,' 'philosophic' and 'scientific' reason. People may not be aware of these scientific reasons, which does not necessarily mean that their behaviors do not have their reasons within. So too, the implications of security forces have their unique reasons. During the socialization period of the security forces, the educational and training institutions lay the scientific base for security in the minds of the security forces. This training of theirs also includes in it mass education, which is always more influential than formal education. The subcultures of police and security forces in general are products of this mass education which is provided in time. Then, practices of police do not essentially spring from the formal education they were once exposed to at school. The traditional informal education that goes down through generations in these institutions plays a greater role than their formal education [2, pg. 218].

3. The Aim of Security

We should define first what security is before resolving the aim of it. Security is a state of being safe, especially from outside threats. Any action to disrupt safety in a society is defined as infringement of security. Security is the maintenance of law and order in a society and ensuring the wellbeing of individuals. Security is the feeling of safety and being certain about one's immediate environment.

The topicality of security issue escalates in today's world, which is stirring with everyday conflicts and terrorist actions, culminating with the killings of thousands of innocent civilians. It should be underlined that, above all, security is for the people and it should be so. Security does not refer to the welfare of a privileged part of a society and to their profits, nor is it to bother the lives of people on the pretext of the safety of the state. We should keep in mind that the state is by the people and for the people. If everything is for the people, so should the security be. In the contemporary world, which changes at a head-spinning pace and where it is clearly conceived that no person is superior to another, the concept of security needs to be redefined. In this respect, as we will touch on in the following pages, both the institutions in charge of security and the perspectives upon the society should be provided with a newer understanding for the restoration of more modern paradigms of security. To achieve this, it is important to follow this newer understanding in the socialization process of both the people and the police.

Security forces cannot be regarded as a 'fist' upon the people which they originate from and which they are responsible for serving. Otherwise, the security forces would be an occupation force in the country of its service. There are security units in every country, and the aim of their service is to catch criminals, which continually exist in every nation but in small numbers, and to deter potential criminals in advance. While security forces are 'fighting forces' for a small group of criminals, they should produce 'service' for the rest of the society, which is nearly 99 percent.

4. The Main Function of Security Units and Their Necessity

What is the reason for the existence of security units? The widespread answer for this question is 'to restore the law and order in a society.' As state institutions, police departments, within these security units, have their roots in the last centuries. Security units as yet function by helping people, preventing crime, and, when committed, fighting crime and criminals.

Today's modern world owes its existence and development to two processes: industrialization and nationalism. Industrialization in the last three centuries has also triggered the urbanization process. The population of the cities increased immensely, which also boosted the crime rate in overcrowded, big cities. Thus, police departments and other security units have come into being to meet the need for security and to maintain order in society.

Police and other security units have their reasonable excuses to exist. While police restore the domestic security in a country, the army protects it from the outside threats. Moreover, the state manages the order in society mostly with the help of police. As mentioned earlier, in times of need, the army and peacekeeper corps from other countries might also be employed together with the police. The police, the task of which is to keep the domestic security and peace, are in close touch with the people. While in some countries the police are responsible both in cities and in rural areas, in other countries like the US and Britain, the police are in charge of cities, whereas, in rural areas, gendarmes take control. However, in many developed countries, especially, members of the European Union, gendarmes render the job of domestic security to the police [3, pg. 2].

The basic duties of the police are:

- Maintaining the social order, perpetuation of security in society
- Maintaining the law
- Combating criminals and prevention of crimes
- Monitoring criminals, arresting and handing them to justice, conducting justice according to the law
- Checking and maintaining the order of traffic
- Helping the people

4.1. Maintaining the Social Order and the Perpetuation of Security in Society

Police and security forces are in charge of maintaining the order in society, preventing a possible attack on them, and taking measures accordingly. While maintaining the order, police should not have a passive role, waiting for the crime to take place; rather, they are to prevent a potential crime and dissuade the criminal. This cannot be achieved only by deterrents. On the contrary, in accordance with our modern world, this can be fulfilled by persuasion, earning the love of people rather than their hatred. This enables an approach that is lawful and well-intentioned. In brief, while the police are practicing their job, their actions should have a legal ground, and they should employ limited violence; their actions should be legal and legitimate.

4.2. Maintaining the Law

The police department is responsible for the implementation of law. In case of a violation of law, it is the job of the police to intervene. A state institution, too, may get help from the police departments in case there is a problem in implementing the law. In this aspect, the police can also be defined as the institution responsible for the overall practice of law.

4.3. Combating Criminals and Prevention of Crime

One other function the police are in charge should be the prevention of crime. In many countries, the police attempt to take precautions before the crime takes place. To conduct investigations on location and to take necessary measures both eases the job of police and decreases the crime rate in a society. Combating crime is handled in two ways; preventing crimes by realizing the preventive security services in advance and/or fulfilling the necessary administrative and judicial actions in the aftermath of the crime. While the first one is called proactive policing, the latter is called reactive policing.

4.4. Monitoring Criminals, Arresting and Handing Them to Justice, Conducting Justice According to Law

Another task of police is to hand the suspects or criminals to justice after the crime is committed. According to the definitions above, this is called reactive policing. This understanding of policing is basically to take action after a crime is committed and helping to practice the laws accordingly. Here, the crime is conceived as a problem, disregarding the sociological background of it. Reactive policing is not interested in the reasons for which the crime is committed; for this reason, preventive action also becomes a part of this policing method.

    This understanding mostly exists in countries with authoritative policing. Authoritative policing refers to the maintenance of security only by police and security units without the interference of volunteer and private institutions in a society. In this respect, authoritative policing is witnessed mostly in strong countries with a centralist structure which has a from-above understanding of governance. In addition, as mentioned above, today's developed countries apply both of these policing policies. Firstly, preventive precautions are applied by destroying the places which may possibly be home to crimes. If a crime is committed, then, combating this crime by means of reactive policing is one of the leading tasks of police.

4.5. Helping Society

In our contemporary world, the police are not responsible for combating the crime and the criminals only. Together with this, the police are also in charge of helping out people who are in need. This is both the premises of the regulations of the state, and the expectations of the society. It is very true that the police are first among other state institutions which people resort to for the solution of their problems.

People expect that police should meet their needs when they ask. Police should also help needy people, homeless children, the old, the sick, and all others in need of help. For instance, they help a little child or an old lady to cross the street. Police also help those who are stuck on the roads, hungry people, and the ones left on the streets. In short, police are responsible for helping the people who are in need [3, pg. 4]. This is not only a necessity of modern policing but also a way to earn the love of people and restoring security in society.

4.6. Society and Culture

In this section, after analyzing the concepts of society and culture, I will try to explicate the relation between the two terms. We will witness the way culture and the values of society shape the behaviors of individuals and create reactions. I will try to focus on the careful handling of police and security forces of a society which reacts in a mass psychology and the development of positive relations.

4.7. Culture and Values

When we consider culture and its role in society, we could say many things on the issue. The influence of culture on a particular society is incomparably great with respect to any other factor. Especially when someone is interacting with others, the culture he has acquired thus far is reflected in this. And indeed this is also true about culture. We hope that when we look at this with the definition of culture in mind it will be understood better.

There are different definitions of culture according to different branches. The definition by social scientists is as such in general:

"The total, generally organized way of life, including values, norms, institutions, and artifacts, that is passed on from generation to generation by learning alone" [4].

"All the behavior and related products which men, as members of human society, acquire by means of symbolic interaction..." [4].

"Pertaining to the social and the cultural in human life, the two terms, society and culture, being combined into one so as to call attention to the functional inseparability of these two essential aspects of human existence" [4].

"The patterned behavior resulting from social interaction" [5].

"Culture stems from the development and transmission of human belief in symbols" [6].
"The language system is a series of symbols used to transmit cultural beliefs among members of a society" [6].
"Messages about cultural expectations can be found in the media, government, religious institutions, educational systems, and the like" [6].

"Culture is something that gives a nation character, and can be used to differentiate between countries and something that has been formed in the flow of the history. It is the total of concrete and spiritual values that belongs to that nation." [7].

"Culture is the thing that gives society wholeness and differentiates between societies, something that has been formed in the course of the history, and the whole of the things that is unique to that society both concretely and abstractly." [7].

The religion, which unifies humans in a wholeness making use of its connectiveness, the language, which is the means of communication and a tool for cohesiveness between people, ethics, which is an indication of a complete and valid life, the tradition which brings history to our day, in short, all the values that have been preserved from the root to the body of a society, makes up what we call culture. As such, culture with its own unique essence and color with its own sensitiveness, style of thought and way of expression constitutes a nation's character [8].

When we look at the definitions above, although they differ according to the type of definition, as some pertain to naming of culture, and some to its function, they indicate commonalities. And that commonality is a nation's character which has been summed up with developments and additions over history till the present day. That summation indicates all behavior codes, lifestyles and reaction codes to actions. For example, in the Middle East religion and nationality have very important influence on behavior codes and shaping of the culture. As we every day see on TV or in the news etc., these two factors are very important for culture in these countries. If the security forces or soldiers who are working in these areas do not consider such factors, this may result in violence or other atrocities with important results. For example, in these areas where religion and nationality are very important, the relationship codes between women and men and young and the old, etc., are very different from those in other countries of the world. Also in the Far East countries, there are codes that are unique to these cultures. In India, which is an Asian country and is composed of many different essences and components, it is easy to see these unique characters. For example, the symbolism of a cow, which has different meaning in other cultures, has a holy and untouchable status in Indian culture. And the government and security behavior is shaped according to this fact. But sometimes, due to small discrepancies, even in such places there may occur religious or nationality oriented disputes.

Due to these facts, in societies from Africa to the Far East, culture codes and accordingly behavior codes, and the approach to individuality are very different, and as such the reaction codes to events are very different. This situation, which may be exacerbated by a PR mistake by the security forces, may cause atrocities that may result in violence. Crowd psychology reveals the most backward side that is hidden in the collective psyche in such situations and leads the individual to violence. Gustav Le Bon [9] depicts this in his book "The Crowd."

According to him, in this age the crowd psychology is in a state at which it is very fragile and full of traumas. The two main causes that lay at the root of all these changes are, first, that the religious, political beliefs that are the root of our civilization have been eradicated. Secondly, the new sciences and technology have brought totally new ways of lives and perspectives. Although our old beliefs and the old pillars of our belonging are being demolished one by one, the pressure of the crowds has become a very important force. Due to this reason, the age we are coming into will become the age of the crowds.

Le Bon [9] here also mentions the politicians and governors that make use of this peculiar quality of crowd psychology. He states:

"The real understanding of the crowd psychology is demonstrated not by who manages the crowd, but by the one who can manage not to be dictated by the crowds completely. To say the least, the men who govern the world, the founders of religions and empires, the prophets of all beliefs, famous statesmen, and beside these more humble leaders of groups of people are all very good psychologists who have a very certain knowledge of crowd psychology. Although they may not be aware of this themselves, due to their strong knowledge of the soul of the crowd, they have been able to manage them easily" [9].

Here, a point that we should not forget is that the ones who are using this crowd psychology are not only statesmen, politicians, or legal leaders. Also terrorists can use this knowledge against their rivals in the most ruthless ways. Of course, this is never for the benefit of the state, government, or humanity.

Due to all those reasons, today's police add another dimension to their relationship with the public, and should practice this at maximum. The most important factors that affect human life in our age are scientific and technological improvement and acquiring knowledge. The increasing success of science and technology is greatly affecting the environment that the contemporary man lives in. Keeping current with all these changes requires a high degree of knowledge and job competence. At this juncture, the responsibility of public governors should be education of public servants according to the requirements of our day and age both technically and information-wise.

Changing relationship types within society and expectations getting higher cause the responsibility of the police, who are in a relationship with the public at the first degree, to change greatly. At this point what especially come to the front are the special qualities that the police may have in dealing with and communicating with the public. Today, many countries are especially known for the particular qualities that the staff of their institutions have [10].

Consequently, the duty of the security forces and the police that have primary contact with the public is getting harder and harder each passing day. Today, at the day and age when the borders are even vanishing, and positive science and technique are valued above anything else, there is dire need for an aware and contemporary police force.

The changes in the democratic way of life and public expectations and the fact that this process will gain momentum in the next century make it imperative to constantly educate police forces. It is quite difficult to solve the problems of tomorrow with the techniques of today. For this reason, the police should be educated before duty and also they should be subjected to continuing education while they are employed, and they should be provided opportunities for self development. This will provide development for the country, welfare and security, better communication and cooperation and most importantly a guarantee of the future of the country and will lead to reconciliation with modern values. As such, starting from today, we should take measures to develop and educate the security forces of tomorrow, and we should modify the education programs to accommodate the changing values and conditions that the new age dictates [11].

Today, when scientific and technological developments have reached a mind-boggling speed, it is impossible to think that the social change will be unaffected by this. The ever-changing conditions require the presence of qualified individuals in all areas of life. Today many countries are trying to determine the characteristics of the next century and the dimensions of international relations and what kind of individuals are needed. The competition between countries brings with it the need to develop and go ahead further [12].

Education is a process that enables a process whereby individuals fit in the society in a healthy and appropriate way. The development of human character and behavior is also through education. The fact that many countries are pulling the compulsory education years upwards and trying to provide quality education to its citizens proves the need for education.

Societies are in a constant search for a guarantee for a secure and comfortable future. This results in heightened expectations. Especially, the need for better quality products and services has become the number one issue for some countries. To provide a more secure, democratic, modern, and healthy world for the future generations, we should take some measures starting from today and restructuring should start in many areas, starting with education. Only in such a way is it possible to produce the generation that will meet the needs of the 21st century.

It is a fact that social development accompanies cultural development. As such, the security forces and the police who represent the government should be able to keep step with these changes. With this purpose in mind, both in the process of socialization and as a lifelong project there should be concern for education of police forces that will make an addition to the society that has a modern and new vision.

With this new vision, it should be made certain that there is an awareness of good communication with the public and appreciation of ethical values. The connotation of the word force in security forces should change from power and force to service and persuasion. Of course this will require patience, empathy, and tolerance that are based on a systematic style of socialization. The security forces that are carrying on their duties in a global world that is turning into an information society should take the following points into account in their relationships:

- If it is 'responsibility-irresponsibility' rule it is acting according to, it may cause those that it helps to get irresponsible in the same amount that it is held responsible.
- If it is patient-doctor relationship, it may take the position that it is always the providing party and the public is the receiving end that has physical and psychological problems.
- If it is the student-teacher relationship, then the police may take the position of the one that knows all, with the citizen in the position of the one that knows nothing.
- If it is the 'distancing and getting closer' type relation, while it is continually getting close, it may cause a distancing in other people [13].

In these relation types we indicated here, it is always possible that the two may switch. The police should keep the initiative according to the characteristic of any kind of event, and should have a containing, soothing, and directing attitude. And while they are demonstrating this problem-solving attitude, they should act according to a co-workers principle. To achieve full capacity in their co-workers, superior officers who have a vision should:

- Make the job interesting. According to Frederick Hertzberg [14] "If you want somebody to do a good job, give him a good job."
- Do not hesitate to communicate. That is, if we keep the questioning and information sharing channels open, we will get ideas from our workers about how to save money and time.
- Have them participate in the decision making process. If they take part in this process, their loyalty will increase and this will make it possible to realize new ideas.
- Encourage independence and flexibility. The freedom that will be provided to workers will result in higher performance and more energy.

- Provide them opportunity. The best way of developing co-workers is to provide the opportunity to learn new things and see new places and get experience with them.
- Use simple techniques. The most successful appreciation technique is the simplest one. You don't need a complicated and chic technique to appreciate somebody. The simplest and free-of-exaggeration way is the best.
- Be sincere. If you are not sincere in commending the other party, what you say will not be effective. Each word of praise you say without actually feeling will be nothing but a wrong management tactic [15].

Of course, it is a long and tedious process to create an ideal person, and it is equally long and tedious to make the security force assume a new vision. Apart from what we mention above, the police should approach humanity with humanity above all else. They should demonstrate a human face and approach. This requires a good understanding of the concept of what a human is and acting accordingly. To make them good human beings, they should be provided the ways of being a good human being, they should be educated accordingly, and necessary conditions should be provided. If we direct the police whom we want to have a vision suitable to the information age we are living in towards good, and if we prepare conditions which make it impossible to move towards bad, and if we prepare the conditions where the police can be respected by people and act only within the law, then we will have the right to receive feedback from them [13]. Therefore, as we indicated at the beginning, we are all responsible for the establishment of good relationships between the police and the public.

5. Conclusion

As a conclusion, in today's world, the public's expectations of security forces differentiate day by day. This differentiation is spreading among societies rapidly as a result of the globalizing world's effect on socialized human beings. Human beings have more common points as liberty, individualism, democracy, and equality on the demand side and also the common ideals side. According to Gustave Le Bon's [9] famous book, these demands depend on social physiologist ethics. On the other side, these are the results of norms' and values' ethics that affect the socialization of societies.

In this study, the interaction between the police or the security forces representing the state or government or a known international subject that represents power and local culture as changing living styles of human beings and societies that have unique ideals was examined. It must be mentioned that today security demands of nationalist and religious societies have increased too much, especially in conservative Asia and the Middle East.

Till today, police and the security forces were represented by 'power,' but they must get a new vision.

In order to create this vision, initial and continuous education is essential. The Police must have a service mentality instead of a power mentality. They must give importance to relations with the society. They must learn the culture and values that form the demands and ideals of the society in order to give better service. Of course, it takes time and a process to achieve this.

Beside the things that have been mentioned, the police-people relations must be based on humanitarian bases. For this reason men must know what 'human' and 'the acceptance of people' means. In order to get a 'good man,' education must be given in that way, infrastructure must be prepared in that way, and being a 'good man' must be a motivation. Therefore, in order to have a visional and information society police department, we must motivate them to be good and prepare the infrastructure. When we prepare the legal infrastructure to create a positive relation with people, we can ask for positive feedback from them [13]. As I mentioned, all of us are responsible for creating a positive relation between the police and the society.

Never forget that Bin Laden, the most frightened and dangerous man in today's world, perhaps once was normal, polite and not violence oriented. But some factors during his socialization process made him angry at others slowly. As a result of this anger, he adopted some wrong ideals. He ultimately found himself a part of the most dangerous terrorist group, not just an ordinary part of this most dangerous terrorist group, but the leader of this group, also the most dangerous man of the world.

In any society, norms and cultures of the society must be carefully examined in any part of the world. Knowing each other, tolerance, cooperation, and respect must be the key issues among us. These kinds of conferences are important for those aims. By this way we can know each other, we can share our experience, and we can keep the common trusts of humanity.

References

[1] I. Cerrah, M.B. Eryilmaz, Socialization within the police service and police professional ethics: An examination of legal and ethical consequences of professional socialization. *Turkish Journal of Police Studies* **5/2** (2003).
[2] I. Cerrah, E. Semiz, editors, *Police in the 21st century: Major problems and contemporary approaches.* Ankara: Sibel Press; 2000.
[3] H.H. Cevik, T. Goksu, editors, *State, society, and police in Turkey.* Ankara: Seckin Publishing; 2002.
[4] T.F. Hoult, *Dictionary of modern sociology.* New Jersey: Littlefield, Adams, 1969.
[5] F.E. Merrill, Society and culture: An introduction to sociology. Prentice-Hall; 1957.
[6] R. Boudon, F. Bourricaud, *A critical dictionary of sociology.* University of Chicago Press; 1989.
[7] E. Bilgic, Understanding of national culture. *Turkish Journal of National Culture* **1/1** (1977). 2-3.
[8] F. Halici, Our history, art, and culture. *Turkish Journal of National Culture* **3/2** (1981), 6.
[9] G, Le Bon, *The crowd: A study of the popular mind.* Dover Publications: 2002.
[10] G. Erten, *Police in the 21st century: Major problems and contemporary approaches.* Turkish National Police-Department of Public Order Publications: 1997.
[11] I. Cerrah, Public order police training in Turkey and its impact on police practices. *Security Journal* **9** (1997), 171-176.
[12] M. Tezcan, *Social change and education.* Ankara: University of Ankara, Publication of Pedagogy Faculty - No: 182: 1998.
[13] O. Aytac, *Police vision in the 21st century information age.*
[14] F. Hertzberg, One more time: How do you motivate employees? *Harvard Business Review* **81/1** (2003), 87-96.
[15] K. Devecioglu, *Not individuals but relationships.* (*Book in Turkish*)

Family Case Approach in Understanding and Combating Crime in General and Specifically Terror

Ersin OGUZ
Gynecologist and Obsetrician, Turkey

Abstract. It is an easily predictable fact that the families of criminals and terrorists contribute their tendency to the actions of crime and terrorism. In this study, the importance of children and young population for terrorist organizations is emphasized and it is considered that the childhood and juvenile period are periods under the influence of the family and findings of different disciplines are gathered together. While behavioral sciences data like childhood - crime relation and juvenile period behavior disorders are collected, they have been assessed together with social data like the family situation in setting an example and the position of the family in the society. Medical and social causes resulting in negativities by impairing the family environment are considered and common manners and conducts of the terrorist organizations in using the negativities in the family in gaining members and having them commit actions and the detective data regarding the subject are stated.
 While the effects of the family on persons and the society and the effects of the negativities in the family environment on the person during the periods of joining crime and terror are considered, how the domestic factors affect the society afterwards with regard to crime and terror is emphasized.

Keywords. Family, terror, crime

Introduction

Different methods are used to serve the same cause in preventing terrorism. The most important of these initiatives, aimed somehow to eliminate terror elements, is to prevent persons who will carry out and conduct terror from becoming terrorists. Although preparatory factors like lack of education, economic backwardness, social life, and historical development types are effective on the persons, the importance of the raising process of the individual by the family is one step forward beyond question. If there is no situation at an illness level, criminal tendency in these types of persons can be controlled in the family, during preschool and school periods. It should not be forgotten that the family related negativities will increase the crime and terror tendency ratio in the child.

1. General Concepts

1.1. Definition of the Family

'Why do people found families although they have so many difficulties?' Although the misogamists often use that expression, many characteristics in human nature different from other living creatures lead people to search for emotional satisfaction acquired by sociality, strength, wealth, trust, and solidarity, besides leading them to find partners and breed.

The family concept has differences in respect to social characteristics. Mother, father and the children are the most common elements of the family, and the absence or abundance of these persons does not change the definition of the family; persons being together and sharing common concerns is the material issue. Family ties consist of a very interesting team spirit and dynamics in which emotional characteristics are dominant.

The most important aspect of being a member of the family is to be together without expecting anything in return; problems are inevitable in family organizations based only on self interest. Family relations of persons being happy with the joy of each other, worrying for the troubles of each other, taking pride in the success of each other, are defined as successful family relations. Successful family ties are the indispensable cornerstones of successful societies.

Actually, regarding the family, the matter emphasized all the time is the family being the foundation of the society; however, the family is the society itself. Countries must consist of structurally strong families, and social factors must be combined with a family integrity.

In the most known form of it, mother and father undertake the family task of looking after and protecting children. Sometimes, persons at institutions like schools, work places, military or social welfare associations substitute for the mother and father. While the places where basic human needs like solidarity, love, and affection are met can substitute for the family environment, nuclear families, consisting of mother, father, and the children, are those to be considered of primary importance.

Family is a school. In this school there are lessons on identity and personality. Family is a harbor; one's first sheltering port is the embrace of the mother. That is the place where a person feels most secure. Family is like a military barracks; the individual learns in these barracks how to protect oneself, and who the friends and enemies are. Family environments are those where love and confidence are felt the most intense. The family provides the individual with the opportunities of education and health, personal development and gaining the characteristics to cope with life, and maybe the most important of all: distinguishing who is friend and who is enemy, and many others.

People who do not have a family have problems in satisfying this missing basic need; the important point here is that the society is negatively affected because its members do not have a family concept or suffer deficiencies of homes without ideal family characteristics.

1.2. Healthy Family

For the continuity of a happy family; there are social, emotional and biological requirements. Mutual harmony, following a common way of thinking and living, social and cultural balance are the factors that are indispensable for the peace of the family. When the biological aspect of the person is not considered, most of the time the flaws in the happiness of the family may affect the general society. The biological requirements of being a family may be examined under three groups: healthy spouses, an appropriate environment, and having the desired sexual life. Being a couple, founding a family and the continuity of the family is directly related to keeping these organic characteristics within ideal limits. There is a difference between the continuity of the family and a successful family. If there is no happiness; even if the family institution lasts, negative interactions between the spouses and effects on the children will be unavoidable.

Health problems create negative interactions between family members by means of various mechanisms. First of all, this is the person providing the economic income of the family not being able to meet the needs of the family like sheltering, nutrition, and education due to a health problem. People become more sensitive when their relatives get sick. Most of the time, the idea of not being able to cope with health problems and despair becomes an igniting factor for revolting against authority.

By solving health problems of the family members, life, which is the most important value, is respected, and all family members are affected by that. The most important value to be given to persons is their right to live. Those who are esteemed and feeling themselves valuable will esteem people around them too.

1.3. What is the Family Aspect of Terrorism?

Terror was etymologically used for the first time as intimidating, daunting by the ancient Greek philosopher and historian Xenopon, related to daunting an enemy population at war time. This concept has become a modern phenomenon. Terror expression has started to be used frequently by airplane hijackers in the 1960s and 1970s.

Nowadays, while some people define terror as practicing violence on unarmed people, some accept terrorism as objecting to the state authority. Unfortunately, not having it defined with a single sentence throughout the world prevents a common idea to occur in defining who the terrorists are. Since there are many interests although there is one truth, we encounter unbelievable terrorist activities for interests in today's world.

Although the universal values guide us when determining who the terrorists are, since nobody imputes the word terrorist to themselves, those who commit violent acts and those who have this type of behaviors and actions, even mass murderers, do not call themselves terrorists. In this situation, it results in these activities which they define sometimes as seeking remedy and sometimes as despair to be perceived as heroism by some people while it is perceived as terrorist activity by others.

When the concepts get mixed up, humaneness and respect for life are the topics that will bring a common sense to make a definition to guide all humanity. No kind of inhumane and disrespectful act against the right to live can be considered just.

Since using violence in achieving the purpose will be with the orders and participation of persons and since persons will learn to respect human life first from their families; it cannot be expected that persons who were brought up in families whose members loved, esteemed, and respected each other would tend to crimes including violence. When the structures of societies of all sizes are composed of families built by these love and respect factors, the fact that their personal and social politics will be far from terrorism shows that the family is the first priority factor in terror, even in its definition.

2. Relation between Family Characteristics and Crime and Terror

2.1. Effect of the Family Structure in Tending to Crime

Common aspects of the modern terrorist groups whose family structures have been examined are that they come from separated families, having no father, oppression of father, lack of economy or authority [1]. It is inevitable to have disorder occur in societies without an ideal family concept. There are some factors required for a family in raising an individual. In cases where these factors are not present or they are affected negatively, the probability of the family to raise an individual with good qualities is low.

The most effective factors for criminal tendency in children are separated parents, poverty, broken family, low cultural and educational level, lack of economy, bad and unhealthy residence, consanguineous marriages, migration, and having criminals in the family [2]. When we look at all these factors, we can see the factors impeding a peaceful family structure together.

In a study including the children who are forced to crime and committed crime in a terror region in Turkey, it was found that fathers of 25% of these children and mothers of 65% of these children are illiterates, 27% have 9 or more siblings, 35% have 6-8 siblings, 40% have a monthly income of 150 USD and only 18% have an income more than that suggested for the hunger limits for a family of 4 persons. 70.7% of the children participating in the study stated that they had problems in their families and 72% of them stated that the individuals in the family have problems with communicating with each other. It was revealed that 80% of these children think that the individuals in the family do not fulfill their responsibilities [3]. It was found in another study that 68.8% of the children committing felonies come from crowded families and 56.3% of those come from low socio-economic level families and 56.3% of those providing for the family are unskilled workers [4].

Actually if we think of combating crime and terror as keeping a boat floating, when the buoyancy is not counted it will not be wrong to consider a peaceful family as the backbone of the boat.

2.2. The Effect of the Example Situation of the Family to Crime and Terror

While some of the behaviors learned by observing the family have positive effects on the children, others cause the children to present negative behaviors in the future. Instead of the positive characteristics in the family like helping one another, self sacrifice, and honesty, bad examples like malevolence, self interest, dishonesty, egotism, fake behaviors, violence, humiliation, and deception unavoidably result in negative behaviors of the child in his or her future life. People practicing and planning tyranny, anarchy, savagery and terror who come from families with these types of negative examples is an indicator of this situation.

In the studies of Glueck and Glueck [5], there has been a comparison between the houses of criminal juveniles and of the juveniles in a control group, and it was seen that the houses of the criminals are untidy and neglected, whereas it was observed that the houses of the juveniles with the same income levels are tidy and well kept. Lack of harmony between parents, troubles between fathers and sons, and disciplinary inconsistency are obviously seen in the families of the children committing crimes.

Here it may be misleading to restrict the negativities with lack of economy and education. Educated persons from wealthy families also enter crime and terror when they cannot get positive contributions from their families. Today the requirements of the social life and modern age promise a better life. However, not being able to limit these requirements damages the relations within the family at unbelievable levels. Effort and time spent for material needs like the desire to be wealthier or social needs like having a better career sometimes take all the effort and time that should have been spent for the family. Contrary to expectations, children of wealthy families also search for the satisfaction which they could not find in their families in different places, and sometimes they may even consider organizations prone to violence. The presence of this type of person is an indication of how important emotional satisfaction in the family environment is.

In order to set a positive example, a family has to have education. The primary requirement of having an important influence on a child is to be knowledgeable. This requires the family to have education. Taking mother and father as examples, preschool and school education and social environment are effective in the education process. But even in the process when the persons set an example for their children, their own education process plays the most effective role.

If there is no unity and cooperation within the family, it cannot be expected from that family to be successful and to set an example for their children. Lack of harmony within the family and distances between persons will lead to generations that could not realize the beauties of unity and cooperation. Considering the ease with which some are able to carry out or support actions that impair unity and cooperation and harm their own society or other societies, the example effect of the family in this sense will become indisputable.

The children are affected in their behaviors by whoever they see first, that is, family members. If there is nobody to set an example for the individual when determining his or her characteristics, he or she looks for another way to satisfy this example need. Individuals without a good example can follow the example of persons among their family members or in their environment who have characteristics of education, intellectuality, niceness, and effective speaking [6]. That is why following an example in the family is an important matter in crime and terror cases.

As the child's tendency to commit acts of violence may originate from bad behaviors and experiences in early ages, it is also known that the child can be affected by following the example of criminal persons within the family [7, 8]. By committing crimes and even participating in terror some family members not only do not set a good example but also may set a bad example and affect and misguide the persons around them.

2.3. The Effect of the Family Structure on Group Dynamics and the Way Crime Organizations Approach It

An important factor in acquiring new members for the terrorist organizations is group dynamics. Group means more than one person in interaction. In that sense terrorist groups also affect each other. When persons who are not equipped with sufficient knowledge join a group, they always stay in the position of being influenced. Individuals who do not have or have a weak collective life culture in the family and who were not supported by their parents in terms of self confidence, have problems in joining a group in their school or work lives, and sometimes this plays an important role in joining a terrorist group [9].

The first intelligence terrorist organizations gather for the person they plan to recruit is his or her family structure. Individuals with a team spirit in their families are not suitable for terrorist organizations. That is why they alienate those with strong family ties from their families and an image is formed as if the only fulcrum is the group. If there are persons without warm relations with their families, their hunger for love and attention is used. Negative changes of individuals with strong family ties are observed by their family members and when the juvenile is supported by this natural control mechanism, the group dynamics of the terrorist organizations are broken. As the individuals without such support become alienated from their families, they do not realize the gradual changes in themselves, and they may find themselves in a dangerous situation.

Parents never want their children to be in danger, and almost all the time the children take their parents into consideration. Therefore, there should not be distance between the young and their families. Persons with separated parents or with no family peace may look in the wrong places for the group energy they would take from the family. Sometimes the leaders of the terrorist organizations form a family atmosphere and approach the organization members with a good father identity [10].

The reason why leaders of terrorist organizations are usually called "father" is that they provide the embracing and authoritarian characteristics which real fathers lacked.

3. Importance of the Childhood and Juvenile Period as for Their Effect on Crime and Terror

3.1. Condition of the Children of the World Who Do Not Live in Appropriate Conditions Starting With Their Families

It is not really possible to understand how much the children are affected by terror without empathy. While terrorism is somehow causing children to cry all over the world, it seems like these teardrops will never dry out if this global problem is not remedied. Besides child abuse and being used in crimes, being a direct victim or being harmed indirectly are indications of how little the children are cared about in the world of grown ups. It must be thought how the children who were shot, taken far from their houses, left without anybody, and who do not know what physical and psychological satisfaction is, will affect themselves and also the people around them in the future.

In the world, eight hundred million children are experiencing malnutrition, two million children are forced into prostitution, eighty million children are left alone, one hundred thousand children in Romania are using addictive drugs, and five thousand children are living on the streets just in Rio de Janeiro. A child dies every three seconds from negative conditions that can be prevented, two million children have died in wars in the last two years, twelve million children have been left homeless in these wars, seven million children have become refugees, and there are so many other problems related to children that the world is ashamed of provide information about meeting the physical and emotional needs of the children of the world [11].

Children who are taking part in the front lines in the wars and who even do not know why they are fighting for are used as pawns, and many babies are born and die in wars due to direct or indirect effects of terror. In any case, being a baby or a child gives a human being the right to be innocent. For this reason, all kinds of crime and terror acts against babies and children are unacceptable. In the same manner, since all anti-terror methods impairing the family unity of the children will unjustly treat innocent people, no mistake must be made in the name of anti-terrorism; it should be known that besides innocent people harmed, these generations being raised away from their parents will be pregnant with problems.

3.2. Relation between Childhood Age Groups and Family-Crime-Terror

The childhood period is very important, and it is expected to be a period passed within the family. Not passing this period in desired conditions, which is important in being induced into terror and crime, invites negativities. Although it is effective in all periods of life, since the childhood is the period when persons draw a route for themselves, the effect of the family is quite important in these ages, especially regarding crime and terror. In crimes committed by children in the 11-15 age group, those socially important are the violent crimes. There is no doubt that the most important of these crimes are the attempts against life [12].

When the age groups of terrorists are examined, those between the ages of 11-25 seem to be the target group of the terrorist organizations [13]. Although there are geographical differences for this age group, especially in many places the effect of the family on the individual continues at these ages. A 1996 study by Robins on 524 children with an average age of 13 who had behavioral and psychological adaptation problems in order to emphasize the importance of the childhood regarding crime and terror is remarkable. 66% of these children present adaptation problems in later ages. In a similar study (Mitchell and Rosa 1981), 3210 children have been observed for 15 years, and when they became adults at least half of them participated in several, and 10% of them participated in 8-11 criminal events.

It is a fact that the ratio for the persons who were not sufficiently provided with the conditions to become good individuals and could be affected by persons with negative characteristics will increase. Behavior types and psychological advancements of the child first develop within the family, but another important factor for psychological development is group activities [15]. The most important group activities for the persons at early ages are the group activities that they will attend with their families.

It is known that learned behaviors at early ages affect personal characteristics; in this respect, it is believed that the social environment, especially the family environment, is effective in directing our children who commit crime as a learned behavior to attempt the crime of killing people with its economic and social aspects as well as its psychological aspects [4].

3.3. Psychopathologies, Terror and Family in the Formative Period

In the study carried out by Glueck and Glueck [5] for determining whether a juvenile will tend towards crime or not, by looking at some factors it is possible to expect in advance with 90% probability that the juvenile will commit a crime in his or her life in the future. According to that, the factors are the love and concern of the father, disciplinary sense of the father, and love of the mother, supervision of the mother on her child and the peace and order of the family. All of these factors are related to the family.

This study on simple offences, casts the idea that maybe the juvenile drawn to crimes like terror are mostly forced to terror by family factors. Today some children are completely uncontrolled by their families and are unable to balance freedoms; the individual used to living without control thinks that he or she practices his or her freedoms by violating the lives of others. It is a known fact that children are affected by computer games and TV. In a study conducted in the US, it is emphasized that the crimes shown on the media without being restricted exert a major influence, and families need to be educated in this subject [15].

Children and juveniles inclined to violent acts are defined as repressed, unattended, unsatisfied people trying to solve their family and personal problems in these actions [12]. When the lives of people coming from different families with similar social conditions are examined, some of them become harmful for themselves and for the people around them, while others become just the opposite, which is an indication how much they were affected by their families.

There is a wide variety of reasons why persons have behavior disorders at the ages when the effect of the family is sensed. Personal characteristics and abilities, family structure and family problems of the juvenile, environments where the juvenile and his or her family go, form three main factor groups. These factors are closely related to each other [16]. No one turns towards crime and terror with no reason. Therefore, the factors effective for being pushed to crime must be handled on time and the problems must be remedied in one way or another. The period within the family, which is the period when these factors affect the person, forms the most important time period. Glueck's [5] study on these factors researching the role of the families in crime reveals with scientific data that the family characteristics are definitely preparatory factors. In a study by Delisi and Gatling [17] in 1950, research on persons that will feel safe and be happy in the family environment states that the ratio of persons with an unhappiness and insecurity basis trying to prove themselves by means of violence reaches 75% among those who choose violence.

3.4. Wrong Manners of the Family

Feeling estimable occupies an important position in the life objectives of a human being. Getting the respect deserved in a material or moral manner increases the self esteem and motivation of the person and also protects the person from negativity. The children are the most valuable of all for the parents. It is at least said like that, but many parents prefer their household duties and activities in the sense of economy, career, and their hobbies and comfort to their children. While individuals with economic difficulties bring those forward as reasons for not taking care of their children, wealthy ones state that they could not spend time with their children in order to provide even a better life for their children. The biggest role in forming and losing self confidence in children belongs to the mother and the father. Losing self confidence leads to unhappiness and a desire to somehow recapture happiness.

Individuals want to be with people who esteem them; if the parents do not show that they admire their children, especially in the adolescence period, the risk of participating in groups with crime and terror elements increases. It is known that homicidal crimes come together with participating in gang-like groups when the desire for being admired is very dense. Unbalanced behaviors prepare grounds for unwanted situations. If parents are unable to show their concern and love to their children, if they overprotect or suppress or even disown the child, the child becomes rebellious and aggressive. It is an expected risk for this type of child to be inclined towards violent crimes [13].

The most important social environment space for children is the family. While the family as a concept forms the social environment, the social environment that the head of the family prefers inevitably forms the social environment that the children will live in. It is found that the most effective role in revealing guilt in homicidal crimes belongs to the social environment [18]. Also in the families of the persons with antisocial tendencies, the fathers are inconsistent, insensitive, inconsiderate, and selfish and mothers are like helpless, oppressed victims complaining continuously. Juveniles growing up in such a family see themselves as worthless [16]. The most important problem starts there; the first step for harming others without remorse is a person feeling of no value and therefore easily seeing others as worthless too after a certain period of time.

Not having a father or being afraid of the father is a part of the childhood stories of many terrorists. In the studies carried out by German and Italian researchers in the 1970s, it was found that in their families the terrorists did not have much communication with their fathers [19, 20]. It is known that there have been problems with the father concept in 70% of the terrorists captured. Some did not have fathers, fathers of some did not come home or left the house, and in addition to that, in child crimes, almost all of them had family problems. It can also be seen from that how important it is for the father to remain at home.

Although it is said by the parents that for the self confidence of the child to increase and for the child to improve on his or her own, keeping the tolerance limit too high and leaving the child as free as possible is for his or her own benefit; this statement is usually only a rationalization of irresponsible parents who do not spare time for their children. In one of the studies of Robins, it was seen that although the discipline within the family sometimes restricts the freedoms, 32% of the children raised in families with loose discipline practices and only 9% of the children which were raised in families with discipline present antisocial tendencies.

Also, supportive behaviors of the parents towards their children participating in crime or terror may negatively motivate the children. For example, if the parents are called by a teacher due to discipline problems, but the parents only seem to be upset in the presence of authority but later do not reinforce discipline, the child is liable to interpret this as approval of his misbehavior. Communities in which acts of violence are viewed as heroic deeds give messages to their children like 'steal but do not get caught, beat but do not get beaten,' and parents tell about criminal acts they committed when they were young, 'we have beaten many persons, those were the days, we were almost caught.' These things encourage violence [16].

3.5. Special Importance of the Girl Children

Women playing roles in terrorism, like being live bombs, seem contrary to the physical and psychological structure of women. However, some preparatory factors reveal connections between family, girls, and terror. In many societies, in contrast to the boys, girls continue their most important personal development stages until marriage. Especially if they are not far from their families for education, they are prepared for life as they see it in the family. Although it is relative, when compared to boys, girls are expected to be under the influence of the family much more.

The psychological condition of women who are in less interaction with other people in their lives is more easily affected when compared to that of men. This type of girl is deceived easily, does not use self-protection mechanisms, and does not know about persons with negative characteristics who lead them into crime and terror-related matters more easily than men.

Often seen as a commodity, such a woman naturally desires to be seen as more valuable and will seek various ways to increase her feeling of self-worth. The lack of esteem she receives at home makes her vulnerable to manipulation. A terrorist leader can manipulate her with promises of an active, 'heroic' role in a terrorist act.

Although there are differences between societies, in general another reason why the effect of the family is discussed for the girls more than for the boys is the biological and psychological structures of the girls. Men may carry out more aggressive actions due to their physical and psychological characteristics. While men are harming others with rage and rebellion, girls are inclined towards themselves due to their natures.

That is why suicides are often observed in girls. Another way of rebellion for girls is to escape from their houses and to practice uncontrolled sexual relationships [16].

Introverted girls or those who want to escape from their homes have a separate importance for terror. Girls who want to run away when they do not get sufficient support from the family may become a material of choice for terrorist organizations. While there is no social and legal restriction imposed on natural sexual life above certain age limits, sexual life is sometimes restricted by the laws or social structures of the country. Satisfying the needs of present members by using women for sex and also using the sexuality of women in the name of complimentary love or self-sacrifice while gaining members for the organizations are very well known methods [13].

4. Terrorism and Family Relation with Medical View

4.1. Is Becoming a Terrorist a Hereditary Legacy from the Family?

Each baby carries the characteristics of its parents when it is born. The children are expected to be physically similar to their parents. The actual reason for the similarities in the nature of persons and their parents is not related to genetics but to the persons following the examples around them. We do not have any evidence known regarding anybody who was born as a terrorist. Therefore, it is not a just approach to be prejudiced by suggesting matters like regional characteristics, kinships, religion, language and race, and to mark newborn human beings as if they will be terrorists in the future.

It is known that high testosterone levels make persons more aggressive; not having endorphin and serotonin secretion may create unhappy people. It is also known that neuro-chemical substances may cause seizures with aggression. Although all these may be cases that can be genetically transferred, they may also occur as individual results. Although it is mentioned that tendency to violence by hormonal and genetic causes may be seen in some persons, stating this as genetic tendency to terror is a matter which must be discussed further.

Terrorist actions usually make us ask the question if these people are psychologically sick. If the terror act is carried out due to a psychological illness, the family stories of the persons with psychological disorders become important. Although it is generally said that terrorists are persons who are mentally sick, the common opinion of the researchers on terrorism is that the terrorists do not have psychopathologies. Is there is a common mental illness in terrorists? No such data has been found [21, 22].

Terrorists have not become terrorists by a genetic disease from their parents; they just could not get enough goodness in their maturing period, and later on they were controlled, and they became persons who have committed crimes against humanity either by using others or by being used by others.

Even they are not ill, these persons are in the position of losing the value given to human beings, and unfortunately they cause damage to themselves and to others which cannot result from any illness.

4.2. Importance of Women's and Children's Health for Terrorism

Women's health is relatively more important than that of men for peace in the home. The most important aspect of this is related to bringing up the children. When a mother is healthy, that positively affects the baby starting from the pregnancy. Babies born after a healthy pregnancy period complete their psychological and physical developments rapidly. Breast milk contains various immunity substances that will be important for the babies throughout their whole lives.

A woman's health matters for her family as well as for herself. A healthy woman has more time to give to her child. An unhealthy woman is also unhappy. If she thinks that her bad health is a result of her spouse and her deliveries, she may develop a negative opinion against her spouse and her child. An unhealthy woman may present an attitude of diminishing self confidence to her children and repulsion to her spouse. Women continuously complaining and thus expecting to be cared for may be left alone in the family with a completely opposite reaction. This is a bad example for the children in terms of esteeming people. If the family members followed as an example are a father who does not value even the health of his wife and a mother continuously complaining, the child naturally cannot be happy in that family. In that case, it is observed that especially the hopes of the girls regarding the future are broken. They may try anything to escape the family to avoid that unhappy future.

In some societies there are many women who are always ill due to their life styles, their upbringing, or lack of care. Because health problems bring family members together with a different effect in people with socio-cultural maturity, the happiness caused by unity and cooperation may overcome the sadness from the illness.

Children who could not complete their physical and social developments within certain conditions and who had certain health problems that were not remedied are more likely to be controlled by others when they grow up. While malnutrition negatively affects the physical development of children, damage to mental development is seen more often. Health problems like anemia and hypothyroidism are medical problems that can be easily remedied, but when these problems are not cured, they may negatively affect the mental power of the children in the future. To what extent terrorist organizations prey upon those seen as physically healthy and with low mental capacities is something that should be researched.

4.3. Sexual Health and Its Relation to Terror

We know that children who grow up in a healthy family environment have little tendency towards crime and terror. Since a problematic sexual life between spouses will negatively affect the healthy family structure, it is possible to say that this very special situation between the spouses will absolutely have indirect effects on the general society. When the effect of the happiness of the family on terror is considered, one of the least spoken-about factors of terror compared to its importance is the unhealthy sexual life. Husband and wife relationships where expectations regarding sexual life are not met usually cause the spouses to become alienated from each other. However, sexuality is a beneficial activity which supports the team spirit of the spouses and causes them to obtain physical and mental satisfaction.

Though levels of development in societies reveal different ratios in the solution of sexual problems, solutions are not adequately found for various reasons in general, most of which are related to the idea of protecting the unity and cooperation of the family. Even in countries that are most advanced in health care, doctors seldom ask women questions about their sexual lives [23]. Not having an expert team in such an important matter is one of the important factors [24]. Besides not having enough doctors in the field of sexual questioning and therapy, in many regions the ability to reach specialist and practitioner doctors is very limited. It is also true that patients complicate the solution of sexual problems by not telling their problems. A very low ratio of patients talks about these problems before the doctors ask about them. Socio-economic conditions are effective in expressing and remedying sexual problems [25, 26, 27].

General health problems affect the families. While individual illnesses of the family members are wearisome, problems related to sexuality damage the team spirit, inhibit communication between spouses, and leave a negative effect on the group dynamics of the family regarding terror. This happens either by directly affecting and alienating the spouses or by the consequences of its effects on the negative family environment as the children being raised in that family cannot find the appropriate atmosphere. When this is the case, the sexual life of a couple must be examined at the places where health services are given and the matters causing sexual functioning disorders must be remedied. Especially in regions inclined to terrorism, health personnel must be educated in using appropriate methods and timing for the solution of sexual functioning disorders.

Table 1. Appropriate medical examination times for scanning sexual functioning disorders [28]

Control of past operations	Examinations related to menopause	Pre-pregnancy controls	Infertility
Uterus prolapse	Before hormone treatments	Postnatal controls	Depression
Hysterectomy (Removal of uterus)		Routine annual controls	Chronic diseases
Oophorectomy (Removal of ovary)			

Sexual education and mitigating problems regarding sexuality can only be carried out by professionals. In sexual functioning disorders occurring as both physical and mental problems, in addition to sexual therapists, mental health professionals, neurologists, gynecologists and urologists that are expert in sexuality related subjects are the ones to whom the patients with such conditions can be directed [28].

Sexual life practiced just as heard and sexual stimulus and needs damaging the unity of the family and occurring by the prevalence of the visual media negatively affects the natural process between the spouses.

Abstaining from sex due to fear of pregnancy is a prevalent problem in places with low socioeconomic levels. In societies where the family planning responsibilities are attributed to women, sexuality may become a problem for women. Women who refrain from being examined complicate the diagnosis of many illnesses causing sexual problems. Problems related to sexual life are left unsolvable in different ways. One of those is not being able to give or receive adequate health services for various reasons. The patients are generally easily embarrassed and wait for the doctor to ask a question about the matter and the frequency for the doctors to ask that is rather lower than expected. Even in the US, having high levels of socioeconomic power, only 14% of the women were asked about sexuality in the last 3 years [29]. Doctors must see the problems of each individual as lined dominoes when they are easing the pain of the patient and must try to solve the problems that the patient could not talk about but that will have negative reflections on the persons, their families, and the society by a chain reaction. Lack of specialist doctors and doctors perceiving health problems only as the solution of organic problems of illness (not considering that it will affect the relatives of the patient and the society, as well as the patient) make the job complicated.

5. Conclusion

It is not possible to get a result when terror is considered as regional. If it is not realized that it is a contagious disease, it may be spread to persons and societies at an unexpected time and place.

Since there cannot be terror without the terrorist, it is clear that preventing an individual from becoming a terrorist is one of the most important elements of combating terror.

While being the basic elements of the society adds a separate importance to the families in the position of the cells of our globalizing world, in the micro-plan, the family concept is the very first priority matter that must be handled to determine common action policies not only for the countries but for the world. Within this context, education must not be limited to schools, and the education policies towards the family concept must be revised. It has to be accepted that ideas like getting wealthier or having a better career should come before the idea of living as a happy person may make people unhappy in the short and long term by decreasing the time spent on the family. Constructive aspects of unity and cooperation must be prioritized, starting with the family, for healthy societies.

It is an expected result that the generations observing and learning that love, tolerance, peace, forgiveness, kindness and compassion are practiced as principles in the family environment will stay away from the ideas of violence. If mothers and fathers feel like they are not adequate, they must ensure that their children contact people that will set right examples for them.

Physical health and especially sexual health is very important. It must not be forgotten that it is an element to be considered in combating crime and terror. Physical conditions impeding sexual life, which is required for the happiness of the family, must be removed. While treating cases of family planning, women's illnesses, suitable birth conditions, infections, uterus prolapse, and menopause impeding sexual life, those involved must know that these will reflect in some way on the general peace of the society.

When looking at an organization by considering its group dynamics, it can be understood whether it is a terrorist organization or an interest group or not. The opinions of the organizations or their leaders regarding family, whether they care for the concepts of mother and father, points out whether that organization will use persons for their own benefit or not.

References

[1] S.J. Morgan, *The mind of a terrorist fundamentalist: The psychology of terror cults*. Brussels: Institute Spiritus Vitus; 2001.
[2] N. Uygur, P.C. Geyran, S. Türkcan, *Homicidal behavior in juveniles*. 2nd Child and Adolescent Psychiatry Congress. Istanbul: Congress Papers Book; 1993. (*in Turkish*)
[3] Bianet, Free Communication Web. [Online] Available from: URL: www.bianet.org/2006/07/01_c/1288.htm [2006, July 02]
[4] B. Tuzun, H. Ince, M. Copur, I. Elmas, Homicidal crimes among 11-15 years-old children. *Istanbul University Faculty of Medicine Journal* **61** (1998), 69-73. (*in Turkish*)
[5] S. Glueck, E. Glueck, *Predicting delinquency and crime*. Cambridge: Harvard University Press;1959.
[6] T. Robins, Cults, convents, and charizma: The sociology of new religious movements. *Current Sociology* **36** (1988), 1-25.
[7] M.S. Lundy, B.M. Pfohl, S. Kuperman, Adult criminality among formerly hospitalized child psychiatric patients. *Journal of the American Academy of Child and Adolescent Psychiatry* **32** (1993). 568-577.
[8] H. Yavuzer, *Child and crime*. Istanbul: Remzi Kitabevi; 1994. (*in Turkish*)
[9] S. Akhar, The psycodynamic dimension of terrorism. *Psychiatric Annuals* **29** (1999), 350-355.

[10] M.T. Singer, *Cults in our midst: The hidden menace in our everyday lives*. San Francisco: Jossey-Bass; 1995.
[11] UNICEF Forecasts. [Online] Available from: URL: www.erzurumemniyet.gov.tr/htmlçocukvesuç.asp [2006, June 10]
[12] A. Yörükoğlu, *Family and child in a changing society*. Istanbul: Özgür Yayınları; 1992. (*in Turkish*)
[13] Ankara Police Department, How terrorist organizations recruit youth? [Online] Available from: URL: http://www.ankara.pol.tr/html/guven/teror/g_nasil_kazaniyor.php [2006, August 20]
[14] D.R. Forsyth, *Group dynamics*. Belmont: Wadsworth Publishing; 1999.
[15] A.V. Fulginiti, Violence and children in United States. *American Journal of Disease of the Child* **146** (1992), 671-672.
[16] A. Yörükoğlu, *Adolescent age*. Istanbul: Özgür Yayınları; 1989. (*in Turkish*)
[17] M. Delisi, J. Gatling, Who pays for a life of crime? An empirical assessment of the assorted victimization costs posed by career criminals. *The Justice Professional* **16** (2003), 283-293.
[18] J.P. Shepherd, D.P. Farrington, Preventing crime and violence. *British Medical Journal* **310** (1995), 271-272.
[19] H. Jager, G. Schmidtchen, L. Sülllwold, *Analysen zum terorismus 2: Lebenlaufanalysen*. Darmstadt: Westdeutscher Verlag; 1981.
[20] F. Ferracuti, Psychiatric aspects of Italian left wing and right wing terrorism. Presented at the VII World Cogress of Psychiatry, Vien, Austria, 1983.
[21] J.M. Post, Terrorist psycho-logic: Terrorist behoviar as a product of psychological forces. In W. Reich, editor. *Origins of terrorism: Psychologies, ideologies, theologies, states of mind*. Cambridge: Cambridge University Pres; 1998. p 25-40.
[22] M. Crenshaw, The psychology of terrorism: An agenda for the 21st century. *Political Psychology* **21** (2000), 405-420.
[23] The Pfizer Global Study of Sexual Attitudes and Behaviors. [Online] Available from: URL: http://www.pfizerglobalstudy.com/study/study-results.asp [2006, August 10]
[24] World Health Organization. *The international statistical classification of disease and related health problems*. 10th revision. Geneva: World Health Organization; 1992.
[25] American Association of Retired Persons - AARP, Modern maturity sexuality study. [Online] Available from: URL: http://research.aarp.org/health/mmsexsurvey.pdf [2006, March 05]
[26] A.I. Montejo, G. Llorca, J.A. Izquierdo, et al. Sexual dysfunction secondary to SSRIs: A comparative analysis in 308 patients. *Actas Luso Esp Neurol Psiquiatr Cienc Afines* **26/6** (1996), 311-321.
[27] C. Marwic, Surveys say patients expect little physician help on sex. *The Journal of the American Medical Association* **281** (1999), 2173-2174.
[28] R. Basson, Sexuality and sexual disorders. *Clinical Updates in Women's Health Care* **11** (2003); 1-94.
[29] S. Kingsberg, Just ask! Talking to patients about sexual function. *Sexuality Reproduction and Menopause* **2/4** (2004), 199-203.

Youth and Terrorism

Necati ALKAN and M.Cemil CITAK
Turkish National Police

Abstract. The youth are most vulnerable emotionally during the searching and learning period that the feelings of courage, adventure and emotions that supersede the feelings of shyness, comfort and logic. The terrorist organizations and other harmful movements try to exploit the youth at this particular stage in their life. This article is an attempt to identify the processes and tactics employed by the terrorist organizations to recruit young people. Finally, the methods used by these organizations to mentally and physically new recruits are also explained.

Keywords. Terrorism, terrorist recruitment, youth and terrorism, terrorist training

Introduction

Youth is the most dynamic, most active, most sensitive and also most altruistic groups of the society. Meanwhile, youth is the future and mirror of society that shows us its problems, chaos, crisis, hope, and desperation. For that reason, the young population of the society must be cared for and the problem they may face in the future must be preempted and solved earlier.

The youth are most vulnerable emotionally during the searching and learning period that the feelings of courage, adventure and emotions that supersede the feelings of shyness, comfort and logic. The terrorist organizations and other harmful movements try to exploit the youth at this particular stage in their life. It can be said that the basic human resource of the active terrorist organizations in Turkey is the young population. The use of young militants at hunger strike activities and suicide attacks are the clear evidence of that claim. However, it is necessary to make a clear definition of youth to picture the relation between youth and terrorism.

1. Youth and Terrorism

Youth is the transition period from childhood to maturity in terms of biological, psychological, mental and social development and ripening [1]. The concept of youth is dealt with different approaches in various societies and periods in terms of fixing its description, classification and age segments. Furthermore, there may be different approaches in the same society [2]. For this reason, providing a definite description and fixation of youth that everyone could agree is impossible [3]. Many academics, intellectual, philosopher, and researcher have made studies on youth. Well-known philosopher Plato calls youth, "a spiritual drunkenness" while Aristotle describes young people as "callous creatures." Rousseau was one of the intellectuals, who made a detailed description of the age of youth in his book 'Emile' (1762). The first scientific book about the age of youth was written by Stanley Hall. Hall's two-volume book named 'Adolescence' was published in 1904 [4].

A young person, according to UNESCO's definition, is anyone between the ages of 15 and 20, continuing his education, not earning his living and not living in a separate apartment [3]. Youth, which by definition mediates the of childhood and maturity periods, was defined to exist between the ages of 12 to 24 years in Turkey, before Turkey entered the planned development period. In the Second Planning Period this age range remained unchanged, however in the Third and Fifth Planning Period this range was altered to 14-22 years and 15-25 years, respectively. This range remained unchanged in the Sixth Planning Period [5].

In short, in the framework of these definitions, youth is that segment of society, which usually goes to school, does not work, is sensitive to the problems in the society and is between the ages of 14 and 25 in terms of demography [4]. In this research, the individuals between the ages of 14 and 25 are considered to fall under the category of 'youth.'

2. Ages of Youth in the Terrorist Organizations

2.1. Left Terrorist Organizations

Table 1 shows the age distribution of the militants in the left terrorist organization, according to a research made by Counter Terrorism and Operation Department of Turkish National Police-TNP on 826 left terror organization members' documents by using casual sampling [6].

Table 1. Distribution of the left terrorist organization militants according to their ages

Age group	Number	Percent
14-25	537	65
25-30	139	16,8
After 30	150	18,2

When the average ages of the 826 leftist terrorist organization members is evaluated, it is observed that 65% of the members belonged to the 14-25 years age group, while 16.8% belonged to the 25-30 years age group. Based on this evidence, it can be declared that the left terrorist organizations chiefly use the youth as a potential recruitment resource.

2.2. Right Terrorist Organizations

Below is the age distribution of the members of right terrorist organizations, according to a research made on 200 right terror organization members' documents by Counter Terrorism and Operation Department of TNP, by using casual sampling [7].

Table 2. Distribution of the right terrorist organization militants according to their ages

Age group	Number	Percent
10-14	5	2,5
15-25	145	72,5
26-29	34	17
30-34	12	6
35-65	4	2

When the average ages of 200 right terrorist organization members are compared, it is observed that some 72.5% are in the 15-25 years age group, while 17% are in the 26-29 years age group. Thus, it can be declared that the right terrorist organizations recruit their members from the youth category.

2.3. Terrorist Organization PKK-KONGRA GEL

Table 3 below shows the age distribution of the members in the Kurdistan Workers' Party (PKK/KONGRA GEL), according to a research made on 262 PKK militants by Counter Terrorism and Operation Department of TNP [8].

Table 3. Distribution of the PKK terrorist organization militants according to their ages

Age group	Number	Percent
14-25	141	54
26-37	90	34
38-58	31	12

When the average ages of 262 PKK members are evaluated, it is observed that some 54% are between the ages of 14-25, while 34% are between the ages of 26-37. Once again, it can be declared that the PKK terrorist organization recruit their members from the youth category.

Alkan and Yucel [9] determined the ages of the members of the PKK members by using the information provided in the so-called 'martyrdom album' at the PKK website (www.serxwebun.com/sehitler). Their findings are presented in Table 4 and Table 5.

Table 4. Distribution of the PKK terrorist organization militants according to their ages

Age group	Number	Percent
Ones who did not respond	3	1,3
Smaller than 14	2	0,6
Between ages 14-25	167	77,4
Between ages 26-35	39	18,2
Between ages 36-40	3	1,9
Older than 40	2	0,6

As can be observed from the table, out of a total 216 terrorists, who died in the skirmish with the security forces, some 77% were between the ages of 14-25 years, and 18.2% were between the ages of 26-35. Thus, this new data validates the findings of the previous research.

Table 5. PKK militants' average living periods after they joined the organization

Militants' Living Period Under Organization	Number	Percent
Not certain	4	1,9
Militants dying within 0-2 years	100	46,5
Militants dying within 2-4 years	46	21,3
Militants dying within 4-8 years	46	21,3
Militants living more than 8 years	20	9

The above table shows that some 46.5% of the militants activating under the PKK's armed staff die within 0-2 years, either during the skirmishes against the security forces or by the organization itself. Some 21.3% of them die within 2-4 years and 21.3% die within 4-8 years. According to these results, 90% of the militants associated with the armed staff of the PKK loose their lives within eight years after they join the organization.

3. Factors Facilitating Things for Terrorist Organizations to Influence Youth

Youth formulates the energetic and dynamic section of the society [10]. Youth, in line with these features, has an important role in the social development and formulating the society's current and future condition. It is the means through which the society replenishes its values and culture. According to prior research on the issue, youth is also a very important social force [11].

All the terrorist organizations try to take advantage of youth's 'energy' [12]. Research has shown that the young people who join the terrorist organization are not motivated directly by economic, social, cultural, and psychological reasons, however, since the organizations know how to manipulate social, economical, cultural, and psychological problems and use them as a source of propaganda, the presence of such problem make it easier for these organizations to influence young people.

The problems that make it easier for the terrorist organizations to have influence on youth shall be evaluated under the following titles; 'Social problems of Youth,' 'Psychological Features of Youth,' 'Parents' Attitude and Youth,' 'Human Model Growing within the Turkish Society.'

3.1. Social Problems of Youth

Youth is the common product of the society it lives in. Its identity, personality and conceit take the form of the society's economical, social and cultural conditions. Resultantly, the society's economical, social and cultural structure forms the youth's problems.

The problems faced by the youth in Turkey can be listed as unemployment, education, sheltering, nourishment, health and cultural problems. The extent of the existence of such problem of course differs on an individual level depending upon whether the youth goes to school or not. It is necessary to classify the young people continuing their education as 'high school and university youth,' and the ones who do not continue their education as 'working-non working youth,' 'village-city youth'; and according to the sex differences, 'young girls' and 'young boys.' In the scope of this classification, the problems of youth may in short be defined as;

- Problems of Youth Continuing Education
- Problems Regarding High School Youth
- Problems Regarding University Youth
- Problems of Youth not Going to School

3.2. Psychological Features of Youth

Youth period, according to the developmental psychologists, is defined as the most beautiful, happiest and the strongest period and at the same time the 'crisis' and 'depression' period [13]. The adolescence, which starts with puberty, is the transition period between the childhood and the maturity, as much as it comprises the development and repining in biological, psychological, mental and social terms. This period is evaluated under three subtitles as; puberty, first period of adolescence, and final period of adolescence [14].

The individuals passing through the youth phase leave their childhood behind and enter into the biological and physical transformation and development period. Growth of hands, feet, nose, lengthening of neck, increase in weight, growth of body and facial hair, changes in voice, intensive working of the sweat glands, settling of the body smell, and cartilage formation at the throat are the typical features of this period. Youth also marks the start of girls' menstruation periods, boys' wet dreams [14].

Since growth does not manifest a regular pattern during adolescence period, growth of the various organs may not be proportional and as a result the body of an adolescent may seem disproportional [15]. Usually, the nose, upper teeth and sub-chin become clear at first. The forehead widens and the distance between the eyes grows. The cheekbones appear. The skin looses its smoothness, which is followed by the growth of facial hair. The growth of facial hair is the most important feature in a person's transition from childhood to youth. The face and hair become the limelight of the bachelor profile. A mature expression replaces the childhood's mild expression. The asymmetric outlook of the face ends with the completion of the growth of the organs at the head.

In short, some changes occur unexpectedly during the adolescence period. The disproportionate growth of the body, individual level discriminations and the sudden formation of the sexual characters [15], deeply influence the young person's thoughts, senses and behavior.

According to Onur [14], Razon [16], and Yorukoglu [17], young people during this period,

- Find themselves vulnerable due to the physical transformations and are not self-confident.
- Since their senses can change rapidly, they are quick tempered and may manifest sudden mood swings. For this reason, their reactions cannot be estimated beforehand.
- Since they have an adventurous spirit, their desires are temporary.
- There are many things they would like to do but they are indecisive and impatient and they want immediate solutions to problems because of their impatience. In addition, they tend to give up if an immediate solution to a problem at hand is not available.
- They become selfish. They develop a tendency to question the rules imposed on them and find their rights inadequate.
- They are enthusiastic, daydreamers and idealist. They support their thought with strong belief and acquire a merciless attitude and want to change the social order at once and abolish the inequalities.
- While they cannot accept any animadversion because of being very sensitive, they unnecessarily start to criticize their parents.
- They try to rebel against the all representatives of authority from their parents to the state.

Other than these inconsistent mannerisms, the positive features of young people may be listed as; being energetic and vigorous, having high power of perception and sensitivity, just and tolerant behavior, flexibility, stoutheartedness, frankness, optimism, benevolence, sincere concern about the country's and the world's future and spending true effort on development [14].

Furthermore, each young person does not pass this period at the same level. While some go through this period with great depression, anxieties and fears, some have no problems. Although this period seems negative from the outside, the young people are struggling to develop their own personalities and identities in terms of biophysical growth. Hence, these discrepancies have to be dealt with in a positive manner. As a matter of fact, the depressions, worries and fears countered at this period are followed by calming down and participation in the grown-ups' world.

3.3. Parents' Approach and Youth

The family, which starts to influence the human life before the birth and continues to affect it until the end of life, shapes the person's spiritual development, formation and attitudes, through its economic and social relations. Besides its basic educational function, which passes the society's cultural values from generation to generation, the family is a socializing institution in a child's world in pre-school period [18].

The family, other than a home where a baby is born and grows through the provision of nourishment and shelter, is the place where psychological needs, like security, love, respect, belonging and sharing of the individual are met [19]. Prior research indicates that the parents' attitude and approaches to their children have the most important effect on shaping their positive or negative characters, personalities and identities [15]. Children who develop successfully are the ones who grow with respectful family relations. The successful relations within the family provide the children with a happy, friendly and creative environment. On the other hand, children having adaptation problems are generally the product of unsuccessful mother-father-child relations. These children usually feel a desire for more attention and love. And this hunger for love may be at the root of the child's subsequent development of certain psychological and personality disorders.

In this respect, it may be remarked that a mature person, during the adolescence period, which is the transition from childhood to maturity, may solve the problems easily and overcome this transition phase without countering difficulties due to the affirmative family relations established in the past. A child, that grows up in an environment where there is love and the feeling of confidence and discipline is successfully implemented, is a candidate to be a happy mature person. Such a child can have a proper dialogue with his/her parents, can solve the personal problems easily and continues the friendly relations during the hard adolescence period [18].

The most affective feeling during the youth period is to be saved from the 'authority.' For this reason, although the young people harshly criticize the other people, they cannot stand any criticism and they judge every representative of authority from the parents to the state [20]. On the other hand, the parents in the Turkish society tend to raise their in an overly protective and authoritative environment. Thus, communication problems may develop at this stage between the youth and their parents. Researches reveal that young people mostly complain about not being taken seriously, lack of understanding, strict attitude of parents and to being treated as a child [17]. Since a young person is not treated as a mature person within the family, he/she starts to search for places where he would be valued. Terrorist organizations manipulate the youth at this point in time. They give the love, respect and value these young people desire. At this period, what the young people ask from their parents is not unlimited independence or doing things without others' approval. They want to be respected within the society, be independent to prove themselves, and be trusted and treated as a mature person.

Their impatience proceeds from the effort to be immediately saved from the uncertainty of the youth period [17]. In this scope, parents' most significant duty is to treat their children without judging and criticizing and help them at this critical period.

When we closely analyze the young people that joined the terrorist organizations and the extremist movements, we find that part from economical, social, cultural and psychological problems they also have family related problems. In the researches, especially the young members of the terrorist organizations Hizbullah, the radical Shiite organization located in Lebanon and the PKK, come from big families. These young people, in their testimonies they give to the security forces, say that their families do not show adequate love and respect to them [21].[1] Thus in order to avert young people from joining terrorist organization parent's attitude is very important. There are two important factors in raising children: love and discipline, both to be used at the proper place and proper time by the parents. The absence on any one or both of these factors may affect the child's personality in an adversely.

4. Methods Terrorist Organizations Use to Attract Youth

In a research made on police's official reports, it has been concluded that the majority of the young people who become members of terrorist organizations join these groups without their own will. Even if a young person wants to join a terrorist organization, it would not be possible for that youth to find them, since they carry out their activities with great secrecy. As a matter of fact, a research made on some 1003 members of a terrorist organization, who are currently under arrest for being PKK member, justifies our assignments. According to this research, 71 percent of them stated that they did not seek out the organization rather the terrorist organization members found them [21]. In this respect, the terrorist organizations recruit young people among them by taking advantage of the propaganda techniques and by using 'social' and 'physiological' methods as well. In this part of the research, the 'social' and 'physiological' methods will be identified to be discussed.

4.1. Social Methods

4.1.1. Friend Relations

During the adolescence period, the girls and boys are looking for some people to discuss the changes in their bodies and their physiological conditions. The young people expect these people to love them in any condition and to talk with them on any subject. Such relationships help the adolescent to understand themselves and the world around them [24]. The confidence they gain from such friendship is very important at this period, because

---

[1] KOK A research is made by Social and Strategic Researches Union between the years 1994-1996 on 1003 PKK organization members. The mentioned research was named as 'PKK Terrorist Organization.' According to the results of this research, "a great deal of the arrested terrorists were born in the East Anatolia region's country side. The people's families are extracted from the economical and social development of the country. These young people, between the ages of 18 and 27 represent the marginal side of the society. See also reference in [22] and [23].

such relationships help the adolescent to deal with their problems, which he or she may not have been able to face or succumb alone [15]. Friendships are based on love and thought, communication and interaction. Keeping people around him, who are loving and supportive, would give courage to the young person. Talking with friends about sufferings and discussing their problems with them are the most useful methods to establish healthy relations [2].

Through friendships, young people meet their social and psychological needs like, belonging to a group, love and being loved and to be treated as adult. The effect of the people at the same age is so strong that friends' influence may at times be more than that of the parents and teachers, which may cause negative results [25]. At this period, the young people, who completely trust their friends, may become drug addicts and find themselves in a terrorist organization [26]. The terrorist organizations mostly take advantage of high school, university and district friendships.

The life stories of the militants are full of such examples. Saliha Dagci's story is one of the best examples for this [27].

"Saliha Dagci had come to Istanbul from a small village of Anatolia. She was 23 and she wanted to study. Starting her university education at Istanbul University's Literature Department, Dagci, not knowing how she would destroy her own life, became friends with a PKK fanatic named Ayten, with whom she shared her dormitory room. Dagci's aim was to enlighten the children of her own country by becoming a teacher. However, there was something wrong. Her closest friend Ayten was constantly feeding her PKK propaganda. The things she heard on TV contradicted from the things her friend told her. After listening to Ayten's and her sympathizer friends' lies, Saliha one day decided to join the organization. She was given a code name as 'Hevin-Brivan.' However, after she realized that she had made a terrible mistake but by then it was too late for her and the only escape was death. The group including Saliha fought with the security forces in Erzurum on February 28, 1998. In the fight, which lasted two hours, Saliha who was 27 at the time lost her life. In the diary found on her dead body, the following words were written;

I have missed my family. I wished to be at home, I would lie down beside the hot stove. Then I would drink the soup my mother would prepare. The PKK was told different to me but I have learnt about the despicable behavior at the mountain after I went there. I had never felt so regretful. Who am I, what am I doing with these people? I am so regretful to leave the university. Those two years I have spent at the university were the best days of my life. We had a very happy life at the dormitory. Hatice, Aysun and Saadet, we were going everywhere together. Now they finished school. May be they are all married. God, please forgive me. I am so regretful. I want my diary to be given to my mother if I die. I want her to make it a book and distribute it, so that other people would not make the same mistake I have done. Mother, father, please forgive me. I do not deserve to be your daughter."

4.1.2. Relative Relations

The word relative is defined as "people related to each other with blood or marriage." [28, pg. 63]. In other words, kinship is a relation between people formed through birth, marriage or adoption [4].

Kinship does no longer exist in a certain region due to the various reasons (like migration) in terms of both its members and its functions. While relatives were living in a certain place with solidarity, the traditional families are separated as a result of industrialism and nuclear family gained importance. As a result of this, the wide social institution called kinship, is being separated into small pieces in towns and is slowly being lost [4]. The relative ties in Turkey, from the west to the east and from the towns to the villages, are strong. In line with this, kinship is also strong in shanty houses in big cities.

The terrorist organizations are evaluating and manipulating the relative relations as well. This fact is observable from the following statements made by militants and members of terrorist organizations. A member of an organization tells his experiences in Turkish Workers and Peasant Liberation Army (TKP/ML/TIKKO)[2];

---

[2] For detailed information see TEMUH Head Office, Branch Office of the Struggle Against the Left Terror Archive.

"My uncle was arrested after he was injured in the fight against the security forces in 1992 and sentenced to the life-long imprisonment. Inspired by my uncle, I started to feel sympathy to this organization at the very small age. At first I was only reading about their activities. In the following days, I met with the person responsible for me in this organization. This person made me the sympathizer of the TKP/ML TİKKO."

4.1.3. Social and Cultural Activities

Another method the terrorist organizations use to recruit members is to arrange conditions to meet people by organizing 'social and cultural activities.' The organizations organize a lot of picnics, sportive activities, tea parties, concerts, friend meetings, cultural activities, show movies, interviews and youth camps etc. The organizations openly mention about the methods in their publications [29].

Nesrin Teke's life story published in the New Independent Public Magazine gives an example of how the social and cultural activities are used to recruit members [30, pg. 61]. Talking about how she first met with the representatives of the organization she said;

"I heard from a friend of mine that the Independent Public magazine has an office in Diyarbakir. But I could not believe because of the pictures on the magazine. When I first entered the office, the people inside seemed interesting to me. It may be because of the pictures on the wall."

Among those misguided youth who joined terrorist organizations and lost their lives, Sultan Canik's story presents another example of how terrorist organization entice recruits into joining the organization through social events. Her life story was written by her friends at the 'Yasadigimiz Vatan Magazine.' [31, pg. 21-23]

"Sultan Canik was born in 1969 in Sivas's Hafik province. Like many families in the east, her family had also migrated to Istanbul, the city told to be made of gold. They settled in a shanty house in Ok Meydanı. The father was a worker. He could hardly earn money. For this reason, she could only continue her education up to the primary school. She was a typical house girl before joining the organization. Her family was not a stranger to the organization members because some of her family members were member in the organization.

When she participated to a night arranged by DEMKAD, she was very affected. She met with DEMKAD members. After that night, these people started to visit Sultan's house. After a while she started to go to DEMKAD. Sultan did not speak to anyone in the first days. She was shy but she did not have difficulty in finding friend in DEMKAD. Trained by organization members, Sultan became an active member of the organization.

Sultan was made ready for the duty she was given after the training. She was doing what the organization was telling her to do. Sultan, who was in 1990 at the armed unit of the organization, died on December 10, 1992 in a fight against the security forces."

4.1.4. Using Religious Values

Historical and sociological researches indicate that the sense of religion rose in line with humanity [32]. Religion is defined as, "an institution, which systemizes the super natural powers, various existences defined as sacred and the believing in God and worshipping" [33, pg. 69-70]. On the other hand, religion, according to the Islamic scholars, is "a system of divine laws, which conveys the people of wisdom to the most beautiful and the best through their own will" [34, pg. 11].

There are at present 3,000 religions, 6,000 sects and 12,000 religious orders in the world [33]. Religions, by the researchers, are classified under two categories, 'Celestial Religions,' brought by prophets through revelation and 'Human Religions' detected by the human. In the scope of these principles, Judaism, Christianity and Islam can be exemplified as Celestial Religions and Totemism, Brahmanism, Buddhism as Human Religions.

The concept of religion serves an indispensable function for individuals and societies, which the need to believe in a higher order. Meeting this need by worshipping to the sun, moon, stone, soil, fire, etc., which he defines as supernatural, the human beings started to appease this need more systematically through human religions.

The religion phenomenon also brings with it certain differences in beliefs within the same religion due to the differences between the human beings' life styles, interpretation and perception. In this respect, there are radical understandings and movements that perceive and interpret Islam differently in Turkey. Some of these groups carry out their activities on the basis of thought alone and some actually convert their thoughts into actions.

The terrorist organization like Hizbullah and Islamic Great Raiders Front (IBDA-C), which are active in Turkey, are using the Turkish people's religious feelings as an instrument to recruit them into their group. In this context, the system of Hizbullah is different from the others. Hizbullah's first and basic principle to recruit someone depends on mosques [35, 36, 37].

The Hizbullah militants try to have close relations with the people they find from the streets, schools and bookstores advising them to teach how to read Koran and then the ones, who are deemed fit after a weekly and monthly evaluation, are invited to join the organization [38].

4.1.5. Using the Ethnical Roots

Ethnical group is defined as a common cultural tradition and consciousness of identity in a society [4]. The members of an ethnical group are seen different from the other members of the society in terms of cultural features. This group may have its own religion and language as long as it has a different tradition.

The terrorist organization PKK was established with a Marxist-Leninist ideology and it transformed into an ethnicity based terrorist organization after the collapse of the Soviet Union in 1989 [39]. It started with spreading the propaganda all over the world that Kurds are a different ethnical group. However, the socio-cultural and anthropological researches indicate that the Kurds do not own have different identity from the Turkish people [40].

In order to win supporter for the organization, the PKK uses the thesis that they are the best ethnical group. A member of the PKK stated this fact in his testimony that he has given to the police[3].

"In the fall of 1992, I met with a person called Arif during a wedding party I went in Diyarbakir's Baglar district. We danced together at the wedding and I invited him to my house to drink tea. After a week later, this person called Arif came to my house and said that he was a member of the PKK and proposing me to join him as a 'Kurd.' Since I had sympathy for the PKK, I accepted his proposal without thinking and without any pressure."

4.2. Psychological Methods

The terrorist organizations active in Turkey take advantage from the physiological methods other than the social ones to win hearts of the youth. In using such methods the terrorist organizations concentrate on meeting the meeting the physiological, psychological and social needs of the recruits and potential recruits. The members of the organization change the attitude of the person they have attracted. Through the organization's ideology they penetrate their perception of the world, form a new subconscious, giving them a militant identity and personality. In this respect, the psychological processes used by the organizations to attract new members are listed below.

---

[3] For detailed information see TEMUH Head Office, Branch Office of the Struggle Against the Left Terror Archive

4.2.1. Motivation

The terrorist organizations collect detailed information about the young people they want to find from schools, working places, streets, syndicates, unions, political parties, villages etc [41][4]. Such information made on the person to be attracted is gathered especially about family structure, weaknesses, friends he communicates with, economic level, religious, ethnical and cultural root, and physiological, psychological and social needs.

In a publication of the organization, the reason for why such information is gathered is explained [41, pg. 188],

"Above everything, is the person worth enough to be paid attention? Can he be a police agent trying to show himself good? Can he be a weak person and can he speak to the police? Is he capable of being a revolutionist? What's his way of thinking, what kind of a personality does he have, what kind of a surrounding he comes from? Such questions about the person have to be cleared."

The organizations, after gaining the necessary information about the young people they planned to approach, communicate with them. They also exploit the physiological, psychological and social needs of the youth. The concept of 'motivation' has to be understood in order to understand this issue better.

4.2.1.1. Concept of Motivation

Instinct according to psychologists lay at the base of human and animal behavior. The motives may be well-understood or may not be clear. Wherever we are or whatever we do, there is a chain of instinct or instincts under every behavior [42, 43].

So, what's an instinct? 'Instinct' in psychology, is a general concept comprising of motives. The physiological instincts like hunger, thirst, sexuality are called incentive. The high incentives like reaching success is called the requirement (need). Instincts motivate the organism and direct the organism's behavior to a certain aim. When these two features are seen in the organism's attitude, it can be told that the organism is motivated [42].

In this respect, the concept of motive can be defined as the source that 'pushes the organism to take action.' We look for water when we are thirty, we look for a job when we need money and status and a friend when we need to talk to someone. In short, we take action in line with the motives we have.

4.2.1.2. Terrorist Organizations and Motivation

The terrorist organizations address to the physiological, psychological and social needs of the people, whom they plan to communicate with. In this respect, they can provide the students, who have the problems of finance, dormitory and scholarships with money and job for the unemployed. Also, tea, cinema, theatre, concert and picnic invitations can be the first steps of the dialogue to be established.

An organization addresses this issue in one of its publications [41, pg. 189-191]:

"Giving a book (should not be thick) or a cassette, watching video cassette or a programme together, going to a movie, a play or a concert, taking into consideration the people's interests and tendencies, visiting a museum, taking him to a picnic or sportive activities would develop friendship and communication. The first thing that comes to mind to customize the person to the organization, and progress the communication with him, is to invite him to the cultural centers, magazine, union and syndicate. We should not forget that there are various possibilities."

A young person planned to be included in the organization, is drawn into a group, which accepts him as he is. An individual dragged into an organization can no longer

---

[4] Such expressions take place on this issue in the same publication: "It's the duty of all to supervise the people to achieve sympathizers in all stages of life including the schools, working places, districts, unions, political parties, village etc. and to determine the ones capable of resistance, communicating with them, gaining their confidence and respect, tending them to the revolutionist ideas without scaring" (pg. 189).

act in the way he thinks. This group is the only power that dominates the individual's thoughts, senses and attitudes.

In this respect, just like Maslow defines in his pyramid of needs, the terrorist organizations provide the best conditions to meet the physiological, safety, belongingness and love, esteem and self-actualization of needs of the young person they have recruited. Berrin Bıckılar explains the reasons behind her joining the DHKP/C terrorist organization in her own words as,

"The interest, confidence and value the organization showed me and the contradiction between these approaches and my way of searching form the basis of the reasons for me joining the revolution…" [31, pg. 14]

Sami Demirkan, who surrendered to the security forces after being a member of the PKK for about 3.5 years, tells in his book called 'Trembling Confessions' about what kind of needs the organization gives importance to while attracting young people [44, pg. 222-223];

"…Why the organization was looking for people? It's true at a certain point that the organization was gathering people due to the unemployment in the southeast. Some people were joining the PKK to have an adventure and some really believed that they would formulate a state. The rise of the guerilla romanticism was effective in big cities."

4.2.2. Group Dynamic

The terrorist organization and an extremist movement, in order to be successful at recruiting young people, must have a closed (secret) union and own the power to make its followers a part of the organization [45]. In this regard, the organizations use the brainwashing techniques and change the militants' attitudes in line with the ideologies of the organization and remove his or her personal identity.

The concepts of 'group' and 'group dynamics' have to be defined in order to explain how the terrorist organizations take advantage of the 'group dynamics' to change the attitude and behavior of the young people they attract.

4.2.2.1. Group Norms and System of Values

The group has a supervisory effect on the attitude and the behavior of the member and this is realized by the establishing norms and system of values. As long as the individual's behavior in consonance with the group's values, the group supports the attitude, but when the behavior is against the group's norms, it warns the member and puts pressure on them to change their behavior. By doing so, the individual, within the group, starts to see and understand the incidents based on the group's norms and values. Thus, the individual reality is replaced by the group reality [46].

The concept of values is signified by the "criterion and the thoughts shared by the group and which describe what kind of attitude is right or wrong and which outcomes are desired." Accordingly, the group's values tell about the whole of the views, thoughts, rules and their implementations [46, pg. 87-88].

On the other hand, norms, "in short, can be identified as the rules considered valid in groups" [47, pg. 91]. Thus, a member of a group arranges his attitude and behavior according to the group's system of norms. Norms can be formed as a result of interaction as well as by the group members consciously.

While norms are seen as unwritten common behavior, attitude and beliefs within the natural groups, they usually come out as the legal rules in formal groups [46]. Below are the basic functions of norms: [47]

- Providing the usage of the group's possibilities through the aim by decreasing the in-group bargaining and contradictions and raising the group synergy,

- Determining the common identity of the group and protecting it from the outer world,
- Determining the in-group authority and the distribution of labor.

4.2.2.2. Individual's Act of Compliance to the Group

The 'Act of Compliance,' is defined as, "forming the person's behavior and attitude in accordance to the group's behavior and attitude" [48, pg. 184]. Prior research indicates that the individuals try to comply with the group in order not to be mocked, despised within the group, or excluded from the group. Likewise, the researches indicate that the group rejects the members who do not fit within its structure [49].

The act of compliance is bound to the compliance, identification and assimilation processes. In addition, this attitude is the product of personal and environmental powers [48]. Compliance is the change within the individual's attitude by obeying a legal authority's direct order. The compliance may also be seen as obedience to a person or a group's view. There is the strength or control of the obeyed on the obedient on the basis of the compliance. On the basis of compliance as a result of identifying one with a group, there is the charm and value of the obeyed. The value of the obeyed in the eyes of the obedient continues, but when it disappears, the act of obedience demolishes.

In the act of owning, the person obeys a rule or a view because of believing in its rightness. The thought behind the obedience is believed by the obedient. At the base of the act of obeying, there is 'belief' and acceptance of the truth. As a result, it can be said that obeying the norm or value in line through the compliance, identification and owning processes is advantageous to the person. Such benefits can be divided into following three types: rewards, identification with the group and owning the group values and following the path believed to be right [50].

When a person counters a group decision on which everyone has agreed, he is under pressure to comply. For most of the time, even a single different voice among a group, where people may think differently but are afraid of express their thoughts, may have a great and significant impact. Therefore, the totalitarian regimes and the terrorist organizations do not permit even the expression of different ideas, because a single different voice in the group may encourage the others.

The following social and environmental factors also affect obedience[5]:

- As the membership of the group rises the magnitude of the pressure to comply on individual members also increases.
- The social impact source, in other words, the magnitude of the perceived status and esteems of the person or the group is parallel to the magnitude of the act of obedience occurring in individuals.
- Impact on condition of being face to face and the act of obedience as its outcome are stronger.
- The individual's intelligence level, character, personality and the understanding of independence, influence the act of obedience. People with low self confidence and weak personality comply easily.
- Submitting or compliance may be increased by the pressure proceeding from the conditions on rewarding and threatening. Merely, more outer pressure may kick back and cause a reverse reaction.

---

[5] For detailed information see reference in [49]

4.2.2.3. Functions Group Realizes
Groups while realizing the group level aims, also have to meet its members' physiological, psychological and social needs in order to ensure cohesion and obedience. These may be listed as [51]:

- The group meets the members' primary needs. In this context, it help member to overcome their financial difficulties and find job for the unemployed members.
- The group may provide its members' security against a common or a strong enemy.
- The group satisfies its members' feelings regarding love and esteem making them feel that they are worthy
- The group evokes a sense of belonging in its members.
- It gives ideals, aims and targets to the members. It motives them in achieving these ideals, aims and targets.
- It helps members in self-actualization and it gives responsibilities and duties according to the members' abilities. The member, who cannot achieve the targets alone, may reach them by cooperating with the other members.

4.2.2.4. Group Dynamics and Importance for Terrorist Organizations
The terrorist organizations attract the young people into an illegal group, where the activities are carried out secretly. These organizations change youth's ideas, senses and attitudes through the direction of their own ideologies and they take advantage of 'group dynamics.' The structure and the functioning of the terrorist organization may be shortly explained as;

- The terrorist organizations are the secret organizations operating in 'cell systems.' Thus, the terrorist organizations build a wall between the members and the outer world through the group dynamics. For this reason, the people cannot enter an organization any time they want, because since the organizations carries out activities secretly, they look at the person willing to join by his own free will with suspicion. However, they trust the members, they themselves find and select.
- A young person attracted by an organization cannot part from it by his own will. When he wants to leave, the organizations would never let them go and use physical and psychological torture [52][6].
- Each group in organizations has norms and system of values. Although all the norms and values are not written, there are also written ones.
- An organization group has a collective mind, attitude and behavior [54].[7] Therefore, since the decision mechanism is controlled by the collective mind, the individuals in a terrorist organization do not act in the way they want,

---

[6] The propaganda, the terrorist organization DHKP/C made in its publication for the members giving up death fast is one of the most significant examples. The memories of a university student, who stayed in the terrorist organization PKK for 400 days support our idea. Once a person joins the organization, it becomes very difficult to leave. For this reason, the condition of a person who starts to recognize the ugliness ad contradictions in the organization would be tragic. Also see reference in [53]

[7] The following expressions take place in the same issue: "The organization would create its own individual. It assimilates by collectivizing. It shapes the individual to make him a part of the whole. There is an organic tie between the organization having a collective power union and the individual. It's both an instrument and an aim in the development of the individual. Because an individual without an organization is nothing. He is powerless and hopeless without an organization (pg. 28); "To be organised means to be collective. To be organised and collectivism is two incidents connected to each other. To be organised would be realized at the militants level and to achieve the union of decision and will through the common aim" (pg. 30).

cannot read books they want to read or meet with people they want to see and marry with the person they would like to [55].
- There is no place for individuality in the organizational groups. The group mentality is based on 'we' rather than 'I'. For this purpose, the individuals may be sacrificed for the organization's sake [55].[8]
- There is a solid hierarchical structure in the organizational groups. This structure is built on a cell type group structuring and each militant of the organization knows the people in his own group. The instructions of the organization's leader are conveyed by the people responsible for the group. The information coming from the higher ups are conveyed to the exponents through the mediation of the group leaders as reports [54].
- The organizations are managed under the control of their leaders due to the hierarchic structure. A leader is everything for the organization. The leader is the mother, father, brother, God...For this reason, the leaders have immunity. They cannot be criticized and have the absolute dominance on the organization [56].[9]

These conditions, which exist in most of the organizations, cause the loss of the members' personality and identities [57]. Taking advantage of the group psychology, the terrorist organizations change the individuals' attitudes, system of perceptions and identities through their own ideologies. These individuals, whose brains are washed and spirits are conditioned, are no different from the robots after they enter these organizations. After adopting a 'robotic sub-culture,' the young people can easily kill others or themselves.

4.2.3. Change of Attitude in a Group

The organizations change the attitude of the individuals, who they attract and based upon their respective potential may use them to perform various tasks ranging from hanging posters on the walls, distributing bulletins, and participating to a demonstration, to death fasts, arranging suicide attacks, and killing people etc. However, before the methods employed by the terrorist organizations to change the young people's attitudes can be explained, it is necessary first that the concept of attitude be defined [58].

4.2.3.1. Attitude's Elements

- *Intellectual Elements:* Attitudes are the entity of beliefs and knowledge that a person holds [50]. Attitudes have the power to direct the senses and behavior. The exchange of ideas or a change in environment or acquisition of relevant new information may create changes of attitudes.
- *Sensitive Elements:* Sensitive elements are an expression of the senses (e.g. liking/disliking, loving/not loving) regarding the object of the attitude regarding the object of attitude [58]. The sensitive elements of the attitudes are simpler than the intellectual elements. They signify a pre-tendency toward the positive

---

[8] The following expressions take place in this book; "The revolutionists are the public's property. They do not have a private life. They do not get married and cannot fall in love. Our aim is to realize the revolutions that the Turkish public desires" (pg. 25-26).
[9] Can Deniz, who has activated in PKK for long years tell on the issue: "The terrorist organization leader Abdullah Ocalan could not be criticised because he was like God. The general approach among the militants was like this. Some were scared, some really believed in this, some thought like that due to the feudal judges. This approach was defined in the devotion psychology to the leader" (pg. 53).

or negative reaction. In addition, changing an attitude, regarding which a person is very sensitive, is more difficult [50].
- *Behavioral Element:* It is the individual's tendency to behave in line with his ideas and feelings. Human beings do not always behave in line with their ideas and feelings or they cannot, however, the tendency of behaving according to the ideas and feelings permanently exist [43]. In short, these three elements of attitude are dependent upon each other, and a change in one of them causes a change in the other elements to establish consistency.

4.2.3.2. Formation of Attitudes

Attitudes are acquired afterwards and not from birth. The attitudes of children, from the birth to the adolescence period, are shaped by the parents. As children grow, the parents' effect on them reduces and attitudes take their final shape between the ages of 12 and 30. The period between the ages of 12 and 30, when the attitudes are crystallized, is called critical. Throughout this critical period, three main factors play a role in the formation of the attitude: Friend groups (of the same age), mass communication instruments and other sources [43].

- *Effect of Coevals:* The coevals are an individual's contemporaries in terms of his/her age and education level. The effect of the coevals on the attitudes is seen at the adolescence period when children start to spend more time with their friends than with their parents. The reason for the importance of the coevals in changing or shaping the attitudes of a person is that they, like the individuals regard their parents and teachers etc. as authority figures.
- *Information:* The impact of parents on their children is being reduced day by day as a result of a rapid development in the mass communication instruments like newspapers, magazines, radio-televisions, internet and cinema. Thus, these days the new information gathering sources are more effective than parents in the formation of the young people's attitudes.
- *Education:* Education is the most effective factor in the formation of the attitude. The effect of education on the attitude is as strong as the parents' political and religious beliefs. The effect of education on attitudes increases with the level of education and the new generation have a higher education level than their parents.

4.2.3.3. Change of Attitude in a Group

The terrorist organizations have an absolute authority on the young people, who have been dragged into an illegal group and are unable to leave it. The ones who resist against the group's norms are harshly punished. However, harsh methods of persuasion are not used at the stage where the organization members are attracting and recruiting young people by propagating the ideology of the terrorist organization. The organization starts to attract the young person by first giving him a book, magazine or newspapers, because these publications are the most effective instruments for brainwashing. The print and visual media plays the most important role in the formation of the expectations, values, beliefs, feelings and ideas [59]. Books, newspapers and magazines are the three main factors in the formation of attitudes.

Thus the process of brainwashing is initiated by giving the youth books, newspapers and magazines, and feeding them the thought, which is the primary the element of the attitude. There are also discussions within the group while the militant reads the books[10].

---

[10] The expressions in an organization's publication back our view: "It would not be proper to put standard timing in order to make the individual a sympathizer. Some people can be convinced in a longer period and

As a matter of fact, while these discussions are carried out in a controlled manned by the organization members by raising pre-decided issues and questions and providing preplanned answers. Meanwhile, the person is asked about what he has read. He is taken to the seminars and meetings that have been organized by the organization, and is given new propaganda materials to read.

Meanwhile, the individual is only allowed to read the books, newspapers and magazines provided by the organization and told to believe in the facts, opinions and ideologies provided in these materials [60]. The aim of this is that is to impose upon the individual a single way of thinking. In other words, the individual will acquire a black and white perspective[11]. This black and white way of thinking imbues in the youth a strong sense of differentiation between 'the ones that are sympathetic to the organization's cause' and the 'ones that are not,' or in other words, a strong sense on differentiation between 'friends' and 'enemies.' Especially after 1980 these organizations have used slogans like 'Turkish vs. Kurdish,' 'partisans of the Caliph Ali-Sunni,' 'secular vs. anti-secular,' 'believer vs. non believer' to indoctrinate the youth with their ideologies. The young individual is also charged with the duties like hanging posters on the walls, distributing notices and participating in the public meetings [41].

Even if the young person dragged into an illegal group thinks that their activities are wrong, he cannot object because while listing the features of the group, we had mentioned that there were common values, norms, attitudes and behaviors. It can be told that this psychological process has started to be more effective on the individual.

The terrorist organizations use a warm and sincere attitude to change the young individuals through their own ideologies. It has however been observed that once these people become member of the organization, those who later resist or question the group ideology or actions are met with physical and psychological torture.

4.2.4. Perception

The terrorist organizations not only change the young people's attitude and behavior through their ideologies. At the same time, they penetrate into their perception worlds and make them not to think anything other than the organization's own targets and ideals.

In this respect, the issue on perception has to be explained in details, because the prior condition for a person to take action is to know about the alternative and to perceive this alternative knowledge. For this reason, the individual has to perceive the subject and its concept [50].

4.2.4.1. Factors Effecting Perception
Perception is not the only the function of sensations. It comes out as a result of the interaction of two elements. These may be summarized as follows [50];

- The first group factor comes from the environment. For example, the colors used in an advertisement may effect perception. The differences (discrepancy)

---

some at a shorter time. At this rank, people may be given of our magazines and publications. These publications must be discussed with these people. When a book is given, a date should be set and that book should be discussed after that date. The activities must be evaluated immediately. See reference in [41]

[11] The black and white type of thinking can also be called to be polarized. We are polarized only when the attitudes regarding the events and people are at the pen points.The person, who polarizes a certain event, perceives the incident black or white because there is no the color of grey in polarization. There is the feeling of unity. The polarized people love or hate very much. For further information, see references in [61] and [62].

of the object from the others increase its recognition. Bigness is another feature. Bigger objects are more attractive than the small ones. The factors mentioned above, are usually used by advertisers and propagandists. One of the most important instrument that used by the terrorist organizations propaganda. Thus, the terrorist organizations take advantage of the environmental factors while making propaganda. In addition, culture is one of the most important environmental factors effecting perception. The terrorist organizations, which form a sub-culture require strict adherence to its values from its members.

- The second group factors are individual factors. The needs of the individual, standards of judgment, beliefs, motives, experiences, attitudes, personality and expectations affect perception. This thesis has been presented before in this paper that the terrorist recruiters are trained to judge and meet the individual level need of the youth, which earns them a position of trust. This position of trust of trust is later used by them to mould the youths' perceptions and ideologies.

4.2.5. Acquiring Militant Identity and Personality

The next step after brain washing and the inculcation of the group ideology is evoking the militant identity in the adolescent. The most important aim at this stage is to make the young people a part of the collective organizational identity and personality [63]. In other words, it is to make them the spoke within the organizational wheel.

In order to make the militants ready to kill and die, the terrorist organizations turn them into true believers in the cause and ideology of the organization by first destroying their individual personality and then replacing it with the group identity. Identification with the group identity results in the acquisition of deviant militant beliefs whereby life looses its sanctity and the indoctrinated militant is ready to kill or be killed in the name of ideology.

Tufan Turenc, Hurriyet daily's writer and Managing Editor, stated the following in one of his article [64]:

"A woman (!) activist, who wildly attacked the tulips having no guilt other than showing their beauty around, was the only thing remained from May 1, 1996. A young girl, wearing blue jean, jean waistcoat and the scarf of the organization on her neck, hits the tulips with a stick in her hands. The tulips, which were raised with great difficulties, are scattered all over the place leaving behind only the stems. And the other tulips are waiting for their death sentence. May be the young girl will cut all of their heads. I am süre that young girl also raised, watered and talked to the flowers as a mother (before she became a part of the organization). However, the terror makes people wild. The organizations turn the militants into robots. And that young girl would hit a person in the same way. She is programmed like that. She is only a merciless robot and not a human being."

5. Training of a Militant

5.1. Ideological and Theoretical Education

The terrorist organizations subject the people they have attracted to the ideological education first. According to the organizations' features, certain publications are given to the recruits as the basic education books. The militants, who are sent to the training camps for practical education, are first ideologically-theoretically educated and the theoretical education continues even after the practical education [65].

The organizational education is explained in an organization's publication called the 'Alternative in Life' [66, pg. 27].

"...We have to demolish everything in the past of a militant, who is under training, and give him a new militant perspective decking him out with new measures and principles... In terms of cadre education, the target is to shape them according to the party's militant features and make them ready for practice. Training is the act of shaping the militant to serve a certain aim..."

5.2. Practical Training

The members of an organization, who are ideologically well-trained, are then subjected to basic training necessary for armed- strife. Other than the usage of any kind of weapons that the Organization would provide and the way to arrange an action or assassination, the militants are also trained in the tactics to organize a bomb attack [65]. Lastly, physical training and survival training are also integral part of a militant's training. Gaining physical fitness forms the basis of the practical education.

5.3. Ranks followed in the Training of a Militant

The order mentioned below is followed in training a terrorist [67]:

- Conveying the ideas to an individual, group or society, thus attracting sympathizer,
- Raising the sympathizers' volume of ideas: giving them brochures, newspapers, books, magazines, etc.
- Transportation of the necessary equipment for the action,
- Providing necessary equipment for action,
- Watching during the action,
- Armed-protection during the action,
- Encouraging the militant to join the actions of writing and hanging posters,
- Encouraging the militant to take part in legal activities,
- Encouraging the militant to participate in pirate activities and resistance,
- Encouraging the militant to take part in armed actions,
- Increasing the militants' knowledge in line with these actions.

References

[1] H.Yavuzer, *Child psychology*. Istanbul: Remzi Publications; 1999.
[2] O. Koknel, *Republic youth and their problems*. Istanbul: Cem Publications; 1979.
[3] A.T. Kıslalı, *Student commotions*. Ankara: Bilgi Publications; 1974.
[4] S. Kızılcelik, Y. Erjem, *Annotated sociology dictionary*. Izmir: Saray Bookstore; 1996.
[5] I. Dogan, *Sociology, concepts, and problems*. Istanbul: Sistem Publications; 2000.
[6] Turkish National Police, *Profile of left terrorist organization militants*. Ankara: Counter Terrorism and Operation Department-TEMUH; 1996.
[7] Turkish National Police, *Profile of right terrorist organization militants*. Ankara: Counter Terrorism and Operation Department -TEMUH; 1996.
[8] Turkish National Police, *Profile of PKK terrorist organization militants*. Ankara: Counter Terrorism and Operation Department -TEMUH; 1998.
[9] N. Alkan, A. Yucel, *Profile of PKK terrorist organization militants*. Ankara: Counter Terrorism and Operation Department -TEMUH; 2002.
[10] Z. Bulcas, A. Bulcas, *Adolescence period and stress*. Istanbul: Der Publications; 1979.
[11] F. Gurses, H.B. Gurses, *Youth in the world and in Turkey*. Istanbul: Der Publications; 1979.
[12] M. Karaaslan, Terror and youth. Declarations of Security and Peace in Eastern Anatolia Symposium. Elazıg: Fırat University Publications; 1998.

[13] H. Kırbas, Puberty. [Online] Available from: URL: http://greatestfeelpsikoloji.com [2002, January 10]
[14] B. Onur, *Puberty psychology*. Ankara: Hacettepe Tas Bookstore; 1987.
[15] R.U. Semin, *Youth psychology*. Istanbul: University Literature Faculty Publications; 1984.
[16] N. Razon, *Recognition and guidance of youth*. Youth Year Conferences. Istanbul: Akbank Publications; 1985.
[17] A. Yorukoglu, *Adolescent period*. Istanbul: Ozgur Publications Distributions; 1993.
[18] H. Yavuzer, *Child and crime*. Ankara: Remzi Bookstore; 1993.
[19] E. Kemerlioglu, M. Gunduz, S. Kizilcelik, *Education sociology*. Izmir: Saray Bookstore; l996.
[20] F. Varıs, *Cultural factors affecting the development of adolescent*. Ankara: Ankara University Education Sciences Faculty Publications; 1968.
[21] C. Ozonder, Socio-cultural aspects of terrorism. Security and Peace in Eastern Anatolia Symposium. Elazıg: Fırat Universitesi Publications; 1998.
[22] A. Oksuz, Yearning for family in PKK. *Aksiyon Magazine* **179** (1998).
[23] Turkish Grand Parliament Hizbullah Report. [Online] Available from: URL: http://uk.internations.net/policeteam/ tbmm_hizbullah_raporu.htm [2002, January 7]
[24] A. Kulaksızoglu, *Puberty psychology*. Istanbul: Remzi Bookstore; 2001.
[25] I.S. Kon, *Society and youth*. (Translated by S. Keles). Istanbul: Ar-Tu Press; 1977.
[26] Z. Erdogmus, Reasons of terrorist acts in Turkey. In *International terrorism and youth*. Ankara: MEB; 1987.
[27] T. Bozkurt, O. Yıldırım, Fading lives in terrorism. *Zaman Daily* (01.17.2001).
[28] Turkish Language Institution, *Turkish dictionary*. Ankara: TTK Press; 1998.
[29] H. Deniz, Crisis, its effects on youth and struggle. *Ozgurluk Dunyası* **11** (2001).
[30] From martyries album. *Yeni Ozgur Halk Dergisi* **115** (2001).
[31] Our women. *Yasadıgımız Vatan Dergisi* **82** (2001).
[32] A. Gurtas, *Ataturk and religious education*. Ankara: Diyanet Isler Baskanligi Publications; 2000.
[33] Turkish National Police, Counter Terrorism and Operation Department-TEMUH, Religion, secularism and exploitation. *Polis Dergisi* **17** (1998).
[34] L. Senturk, S. Yazici, *Catechism of Islam*. Ankara: Diyanet Isler Baskanligi Publications; 2001.
[35] E. Demirel, *Hizbullah*. Kultur Sanat Publications; 2001.
[36] H. Cicek, *Which Hizbullah*. Istanbul: Kaynak Publications; 2000.
[37] F. Bulut, M. Farac, *Hizbullah*. Istanbul: Ozan Publication; 1999.
[38] Turkish National Police, *Hizbullah terrorism organization*. Ankara: Counter Terrorism and Operation Department -TEMUH Publications; 2001.
[39] A. Celik, *The psycology of ethnic terrorism*. Ankara: Basbakanlık Publications; l993.
[40] A.H. Cay, *Every aspects of Kurdish file*. Ankara: Turan Culture Union Publications; 1996.
[41] *Gaining sympathiser and training up the cadre*. Istanbul: Yasam Publications; 2000.
[42] D. Cuceloglu, *Human and his behavior*. Istanbul: Remzi Bookstore; 1991.
[43] C.T. Morgan, *Introduction to psychology*. Ankara: Hacettepe University Psycolgy Department Publications; 1989.
[44] S. Demirkıran, *Trembling confessions*. Istanbul: Turan Publication; 1996.
[45] E. Hoffer, *The true believer*. (Translated by E. Gunur). Istanbul: Yuksel Press; 1980.
[46] F. Ulug, *Group processes in education*. Ankara: TODAIE Publications; 1999.
[47] N. Hottacsu, *In-group and inter-group processes*. Ankara: Imge Bookstore; 1998.
[48] M. Silah, *Social psychology*. Ankara: Gazi Bookstore; 2000.
[49] J.L. Freedman, D.O. Sears, J.M. Carlsmith. *Social psychology*. (Translated by A. Donmez), Ankara: Imge; l993.
[50] M. Inceoglu, *Attitude-perception relationship*. Ankara: Imaj Publication; 2000.
[51] E.H. Schein, *Organizational psychology*. (Translated by M. Tosun). Ankara: TODAIE Publications: l978.
[52] Know well these! They betrayed teir comrades! *Yasadıgımız Vatan Magazine* **103** (2001).
[53] O. Unes, *400 days of a university student with PKK*. Erzurum: Bakanlar Media; 1999.
[54] V. Sincar, *On education and organization*. Istanbul: Mem Publications; 2001.
[55] V. Acansoy, *Station*. Ankara: Yeni Forum Publications; 1987
[56] C. Deniz, *The anatomy of my revolutionism and APO - our God*. Ankara: Aksu Printing; 1996.
[57] E.R. Hilgard, R.L. Atkinson, R.C. Atkinson, *Introduction to psychology*. New York: Harcourt Brace: 1979.
[58] S. A. Arkonac, *Social psychology*. Istanbul: Alfa Publications; 1998.
[59] O. Koknel, *Understanding human*. Istanbul: Altın Kitaplar Publication; 1986.
[60] S. Tascı, Freedom of book selection which has been trampled by the hegemony of terrorist organization. In *From craziness to common sense: Confitents are explaining*. Ankara: Yeni Forum Publications; 1987.
[61] K. Ozer, *Managing emotional stress*. Istanbul: Varlık Publications; 1990.
[62] I.M. Blackburn, *Coping with depression* (Translated by N.H. Şahin). Istanbul: Remzi Bookstore; 1992.
[63] Some emphasis about personality transformation III. *Ozgür Halk Dergisi* **119** (2001).
[64] T. Turenc, The young girl destroying the tulips. *Hurriyet Daily* (05.04.1996).
[65] S. Dilmac, *Terrorism problem and Turkey*. Ankara: EGM Publications; 1997.
[66] U. Ekin, On education. *Yasamda Alternatif Dergisi* **1** (1998).
[67] M. Soyvural, *Anatomy of terrorism*. Ankara: Basar Ofset; 1997.

Part 4

Terrorism Emergency Management

An Emerging Concept: 'Terrorism Emergency Management'

Alican KAPTI[a] and Zeki PAMUK[b]
[a] University of North Texas, USA
[b] University of Cincinnati, USA

Abstract. This paper addresses the issue of a new management concept in the public sector, terrorism emergency management. With the increasing threat of terrorism attacks worldwide, traditional emergency management in the public sector is undergoing transformation and how to manage emergency issues brought by terrorism attacks is becoming one of the important issues. After defining the concept of 'terrorism emergency management,' the paper then clarifies the difference between terrorism events and natural disasters in terms of the core managerial task. The paper also suggests reasonable methods to reduce the harm of terrorism by focusing on certain stages of the whole emergency management process.

Keywords. Terrorism, emergency management, disaster

Introduction

Natural disasters are main issues in emergency management science. Various research and strategic management plans about disaster management have been applied to this field for years. The kinds of disasters that people face increased in the 21st century with terrorism because of the change in stability as a global dimension. Environmental and sociological structures of a society may directly and indirectly affect the degree of vulnerability in disasters. The emergency management of terrorist disasters was not an issue in the past. Now, it is a central dilemma in our contemporary world. The improvement of technology and increased social disagreement caused terrorism threats to emerge world-wide. The consequences of the terrorist threats are similar to those of natural disasters. Both events cause death and injury of many living creatures. With the increased threat of terrorism after 9/11, terrorist events have become a focus of the field of emergency management. In this study, we will address why terrorist events should be a part of the emergency management field and we will compare terrorist disasters with natural disasters in terms of effective mitigation, preparedness, response, and recovery stages.

1. The Concept of 'Terrorism Emergency Management'

Considering the catastrophic events occurring in the world, we can assume that the disaster management field has broad borders. Establishing the boundaries of the field is a major problem in emergency management. Not only does the field deal with natural and technological disasters, it also deals with compelling reasons to include public health threats such as acquired immune deficiency syndrome (AIDS), that may affect millions of people; environmental issues such as acid rain, global warming, and deforestation that may result in tremendous economic loss, and astronomical issues as seemingly farfetched as the possibility of large meteor strikes on earth [1]. The field must cover all threats that humankind faces.

When the word 'disaster' is mentioned, it usually brings to mind earthquakes, hurricanes, floods, and droughts. A disaster should be defined on the basis of its human consequences, rather than the phenomenon that causes it. For instance, an earthquake is a natural event, and unless it causes injury or destroys properties, it is not considered as disaster even if it is a very strong earthquake [2]. The main point of the 'disaster' is the physical and psychological destruction of living creatures.

According to Fritz, disaster is "...actual or threatened accidental or uncomfortable events that are concentrated in time and space, in which a society, or a relatively self-sufficient subdivision of society undergoes severe danger, and injures such losses to its members and physical appurtenances that the social structure is disrupted and the fulfillment of all or some of the essential functions of the society, or its division, is prevented" (as cited in [3, pg. 2]). The basic purpose of a terrorist event is to disrupt the social structure of the society by killing, threatening, and destroying. Terrorist disasters always leave messages to the societies causing social disruption.

Quarantelli and Wenger [4] point out that the word 'disaster' is used in everyday speech and scientific discourse to refer to a variety of negatively defined individual and collective stress phenomena. However, while the term in popular parlance continues to be applied to a range of heterogeneous and undesirable activities, conditions, and states, scientists have been attempting to more precisely delimit its meaning. As of yet, there is no full consensus on the concept, but some ideas have won more acceptance than others among social scientists [5].

"Disaster management is essentially a matter of determining priorities, recognition of future problems whose solutions must be implemented well in advance, and delegation of routine support duties so that the focus of attention can constantly be upon a situation as it changes. Disaster management is implementation of a disaster plan with innovations to meet changing needs, and applying proven techniques to meet specific problems such as evacuation, casualty sorting, custody of recovered property, and body recovery" [6, pg. 77].

According to Pussekel [7], "from an historical perspective, natural hazards and wars have been the most long term and disastrous threats to the very existence of humankind" (pg. 10). Also, Hugles [8] indicates that "much has been accomplished since 9/11, but the lessons from Katrina and Rita suggest that many American cities may still not be any more prepared for a devastating terrorist attack than they were for the awesome destructive force of a major hurricane" (pg. 1). Disasters may be more disruptive and destructive when the vulnerability is higher in specific conditions. That is why it is essential that organizations take into consideration all vulnerabilities in their fields [9].

Weichselgartner [10] indicates that the borders and the concept of the disaster are changing in today's world. By increasing the technology and with the transformation of conditions in the world, changes lead to a broader definition of disaster, including terrorist events. In the past, the definition was more likely about natural events while now it is about both natural and artificial. Human creatures became a part of the disasters because of high consequences of the human-related disasters [10].

These concerns led emergency management organizations to cover the terrorist events within their organizational structures. The main reason for this inclusion was the catastrophic terrorist events all over the world. The increasing vulnerability of the terrorist events led the institutions to review their systems and reorganize their structures to combat terrorism. These reformations are more common in the countries affected by terrorism. Through these reformations, terrorist events have become a part of emergency management field and include collaboration with law enforcement agencies in some countries.

2. Natural Disasters vs. Terrorist Events

Mother Nature has no compassion while acting randomly. She damages properties and kills and injures living creatures. Humankind has always wanted to find an absolute solution to natural disasters but could not afford the cost. Thus, disasters have become a part of life and people accept them as reality. This reality leads people to create systems for mitigation, preparation, recovery, and response for the disasters. Among those four stages, mitigation and preparation require taking action before disasters occur while recovery and response relate to the aftermath.

There is no clear distinction between the emergency management field and the law enforcement field in terms of division of labor. Some of the emergency management organizations in the world deal only with natural disasters because terrorist events are not perceived as disasters that relate to the emergency management field. The origin of the terrorist events and natural events is different but their results are more or less identical. This condition may create conflict and ambiguousness among organizations. For instance, the same duties are done by different organizations while combating the results terrorism. That is why a waste of time and budget takes place as a main problem among these institutions.

The consequences of the disasters are generally similar, whereas their sources and backgrounds vary exceptionally. Disasters can be classified as natural, technological, or human-engineered. Natural disasters include floods, earthquakes, hurricanes, tornados, wind, rain, and snowstorms, along with the concomitant fires, structural collapses, and power and energy failures that oftentimes follow the natural disaster. Technological or human-engineered disasters can include terrorism, industrial sabotage, and occurrences that result from human error, such as transportation, accidents, and judgment errors in various work procedures and operations Regardless of a disaster's nature, planning that addresses emergency preparedness and response is essential to minimize the threat to human life, property damage, and business operations [11].

The emergency management processes of terrorism have similar stages as natural disasters, but there are some significant differences. Shaluf, Ahmadun, and Said [12] categorize disasters into three types: natural disasters, man-made socio-technical disasters, and hybrid disasters. They summarize the differences between natural disasters and man-made disasters as follows:

1. Natural disaster is an unplanned and socially disruptive event with sudden and severe disruptive effects,
2. Natural disaster is a single event over which no human has control,
3. The impact of natural disaster is localized to geographical region and specific time period,
4. The consequences of natural disaster are felt at the place and time of occurrence,
5. Man-made disaster (MMD) occurs due to interaction between the complex set of human, organizational, and technological factors and regulatory, infrastructure and preparedness factors,

6. Natural disaster arises suddenly and when occurs, it shocks,
7. MMD is a complex system of interdependent impacts,
8. The impacts of MMD sometimes transcend geographical boundaries and can even have trans-generational effects (TMI, Bhopal, and Chernobyl),
9. The MMD does not always have its worst consequences at the point of occurrence, the worst effects occur long after the event and its causes have been identified, and
10. Socio-technical disaster is characterized by a low probability/high consequences event [12].

Quarantelli compares findings on the similarities and differences between consensus and conflict-type events by illustrating a conceptual distinction between the two [13]. Natural and technological disasters differ from ecological problems on the basis of their sudden and crisis generating nature. He especially comments that a generic approach, which views disasters as social occasions rather than physical happenings, has important implications for the preparing for and managing of such social occurrences. Common sense and traditional views of different disasters are not useful for planning and managing purposes, as disasters do differ along certain socially relevant dimensions. While sources of ecological problems and outcomes are similar to natural and technological disasters, they are, nonetheless, fundamentally different. They differ not only in origin and career, but also in effect. As such, they require different kinds of planning and managing than do the more sudden natural and technological types of disasters.

Emerging as a significant threat against the world, terrorism required countries to renew their policies about emergency management. Historically, the federal disaster assistance policy is intended to facilitate the rebuilding, recovery, and reoccupation of areas destroyed by hurricanes, floods, earthquakes, fires, and other events that occur for relatively brief time periods and do not generally recur. The destruction associated with terrorist attacks, however, could span no longer periods of the time, result in the contamination of residential or commercial neighborhoods with toxic or radiological substances, and require considerable investments of federal and non-federal resources. US President George W. Bush (2002) claims:

"We can not assume that we can prevent all acts of terror and therefore must also prepare to minimize the damage and recover from attacks that do occur.... The consequences of a terrorist attack are wide-ranging and can include: loss of life and health, destruction of families, fear and panic, loss of confidence in government, destruction of property, and disruption of commerce and financial markets. The Department would lead federal efforts to promote recovery from terrorist attacks and natural disasters. The Department would maintain FEMA's procedures for aiding recovery from natural and terrorist disasters" (cited in [14, pg. 15]).

Terrorism is one of the major man-made hazards and disasters that may occur. A list of terrorist disasters may include various kinds of actions that threaten people. According to Waugh [1], technological advancements create hazards and make societies more fragile because they are vulnerable to disruptions of critical systems. In that respect, it is difficult to anticipate all the kinds of disasters that may occur. Mitigating man-made disasters is essentially a function of protecting people from themselves and one another. Individualism is a core American value, and there is a notion ingrained in the American psyche that people should be able to do whatever they wish as long as they do not hurt other people.

The categorization of disasters as 'natural' or 'man made' is ambiguous. People may indirectly cause a natural disaster by deforestation. Some scientists believe that most natural disasters occur because of people's carelessness. There are also increasing risks of social disruption, property loss, and human casualties from acts of random and purposeful violence. Riots, large-scale street and workplace violence, low intensity terrorism, and terrorism involving so-called 'weapons of mass destruction,' and war require efforts of mitigation and preparation just like natural and other man-made hazards. Even rather unsophisticated terrorist groups have the capacity to develop and use nuclear, biological, and chemical weapons and, as demonstrated by the Aum Shrinkyo sarin nerve gas attack on the Tokyo subway system in 1995, the willingness to use them. Cyber terrorism is also a growing threat as society becomes more dependent upon computers. The disruption of computer networks can have devastating effects both in terms of the loss of essential community life support systems and the loss of critical public and private data. There is tremendous potential for mass causalities and billions of dollars in economic losses when government services and private sector operations are disrupted [1].

According to Waugh [1], the trend of the terrorism has changed dramatically during the period between the 1950s and 1980s from moderate violence to the murders of individuals or groups and serious catastrophic events. Today, terrorist organized groups threaten the world's stability with terrorist attacks. During the last decade, terrorist groups have performed sensational terrorist events all over the world. The 9/11 attacks were the most serious attacks, causing countries to review their systems of controlling terrorist actions. The 7/7 London attacks are among the latest terrorist attacks happening in the world. Countries and international organizations must review their strategies for combating terrorism. It is essential that countries have effective strategic plans for combating against and recovering from terrorism threats. Consequently, the emergency management of terrorist attacks has become more dominant in emergency plans after 9/11 attacks.

Terrorism threatens society's and the individual's security needs. The social impact of terrorism may cause long term negative effects on people unless emergency management organizations establish effective management plans for the preparation for and response to terrorist events.

"Part of the answer has to do with the psychological aspects of terrorism. One only has to witness the aftermath of the above-mentioned attacks on New York City and Washington D.C. to understand the sheer terror and grief that results from sensational terrorist attacks. For many, terrorism seems to be a random and senseless form of violence perpetrated by very disturbed people. The idea that one is susceptible to such seemingly uncontrollable and bizarre attacks certainly leads to a heightened sense of anxiety. Another important psychological aspect of terrorism is the terrorist's ideological or political motivation, making terrorism akin to war. These ideological and political aspects may engender a feeling of powerlessness in potential victims similar to the fatalistic resignation seen in soldiers on the battlefield who are just waiting for 'the bullet with their name on it'. These psychological aspects are likely to make people more sensitive to terrorism than they are to the much greater probabilities of traffic accidents or criminal victimization" [15, pg. 10].

The impact of the terrorist disaster may cause different consequences among different societies. Dorsey indicates that the US was affected by the terrorist attacks in Madrid on March 11, 2004 [16]:

Without stepping foot on US soil the terrorists involved in the rail attacks in Spain have placed additional economic and political strains on the American rail industry....Whether direct or indirect, perceived or real, the implications of loss generated in the US rail industry due to the recent attacks overseas have forced both industry and government to reevaluate the status of US rail security and safety. By creating this increased concern and resultant political action, the reaction in the US falls into the parameters of the goals of terrorism. As such, the bombings in Madrid have resulted in a somewhat successful attack against US society and economy (pg. 1-5).

Both the media and the general population express concerns that communities are not prepared when disaster strikes. It is very important to establish effective organizations for all kinds of disasters including terrorism.

3. Understanding Terrorism

It is important to know that the level of mitigation and preparedness for the disasters directly reflect to the loss from the disasters. The more focus on mitigation and preparation, the lower loss of the disasters. Similarly, response and recovery stages are also very important in terms of lower loss from the disasters. Consequently, emergency management systems focus on all four stages. However, effective mitigation and preparedness for natural disasters has become a major concern for people experiencing catastrophic disasters all over the world.

In terms of terrorist events, it is more important for emergency management systems to focus on mitigation and preparedness stages rather than response and recovery stages. Unlike natural disasters, terrorist events are more likely to be prevented because of being related to human behavior. Humans have an ability to prevent terrorist disasters by establishing effective systems, which they can not do for natural disasters. The prevention ability is a result of being able to track terrorist activities before terrorist actions occur and of predicting human behaviors that are vulnerable to terrorism. Tractability of terrorism directly relates to law enforcement actions while prediction of human behaviors relates to social issues. Consequently, mitigation and preparedness for terrorist disasters are very crucial because it is possible to prevent terrorist disasters if emergency management organizations take into consideration the social issues while combating terrorism.

Social scientists indicate the great difficulty of predicting human behaviors. However, it is not impossible. Understanding terrorism will lead to predicting and finding solutions for terrorism. Why does terrorism exist? What are the sources of the terrorism? How can we prevent terrorism? These questions are the main questions that emergency management organizations should take into consideration. However, the focus of the emergency management systems is generally on tractability of terrorism rather than on the origin of the problem. The main evidence for this assumption is that there are few areas in emergency management systems that focus on the social issues of terrorism in. Good education, just social treatment, and recognition of multicultural issues are the main keys to preventing terrorism from occurring. We need to understand and focus on these aspects. Consequently, emergency management systems should structure their organizations not only by considering physical issues but also social issues. In organizational structures, there should be departments dealing with the social issues of the terrorism. We need more terrorism research centers in organizations and institutions.

4. Conclusion

Throughout the years various emergency management systems have been created to deal with disasters effectively. People have been coping with disasters for years by creating efficient emergency management systems. In the past, the emergency management field has only covered natural disasters. The field has mainly focused on occurrences such as earthquakes, hurricanes, tornados, and floods. However, the technological advancements, globalization, and changing social and multicultural dimensions in the 21st century have in some cases, engendered terrorism. Terrorism has become a major problem that people face in the world, causing the loss of life and social values. This condition automatically broadened the concept of disaster. Emerging as serious problem in this century, terrorism is now considered as a topic of emergency management systems in most counties.

The consequences of terrorist events are similar to natural disasters; therefore, terrorist disasters should become a part of the emergency management field world-wide. Although the field of emergency management identifies some differences in aspects of natural and terrorist disasters, the main concept of 'disaster' covers both of them. Effective preparedness and response to terrorist events require cooperation and coordination among organizations. These cooperation and coordination issues are a major focus in emergency management systems. Thus, it can be assumed that terrorism emergency management systems will provide more effective preparation, response, and relief services together, in collaboration with others, than by functioning independently.

Consequently, it is crucial that terrorist disasters be handled by emergency management systems in today's world through the collaboration of emergency management organizations and law enforcement organizations. Some countries, such as the US and UK, have already made adjustments in their emergency management systems by taking into consideration terrorist events. Currently, a terrorist emergency management system is a part of the overall emergency management system in these countries. However, terrorist events are not a part of emergency management systems in most countries. The effective and efficient diffusion of this type of system globally requires further research in this field.

References

[1] W.L. Waugh, *Living with hazards dealing with disasters: An introduction to emergency management.* Armonk: M.E. Sharpe; 2002.
[2] F.C. Cuny, *Disasters and development.* Oxford: Oxford University Press; 1983.
[3] H.W. Fischer, III, *Response to disaster: Facts versus fiction & its perpetuation.* Lanham: University Press of America; 1998.
[4] E.L. Quarantelli, D. Wenger, Disaster: An entry for an Italian dictionary of sociology. University of Delaware - Disaster Research Center (1985). [Online] Available from: URL: http://dspace.udel.edu:8080/dspace/bitstream/19716/473/1/PP97.pdf [2006, September 05]
[5] Z. Pamuk, *The role of police in disaster management: Comparison of natural and man-made disasters.* Master Dissertation, Eastern Kentucky University; 2005.
[6] A.P. Bristow, *Police disaster operations.* Springfield: Thomas Books; 1972.
[7] A.K. Possekel, *Living with the unexpected.* Hamburg: Springer; 1999.
[8] J. Hughes, If we weren't hurricane-ready, what about a terrorist attack? *The Christian Science Monitor* (2005, September 28). [Online] Available from: URL: http://www.csmonitor.com/2005/0928/p09s01-cojh.html [2006, October 11]
[9] D.A. McEntire, Triggering agents, vulnerabilities and disaster reduction: Towards a holistic paradigm. *Disaster Prevention and Management* **10/3** (2001), 189-196.
[10] J. Weichselgartner, Disaster mitigation: The concept of vulnerability revisited. *Disaster Prevention and Management* **10/2** (2001), 85-94.
[11] J.F. Gustin, *Disaster & recovery planning: A guide for facility managers.* Lilburn: Fairmont Press; 2004.
[12] I.M. Shaluf, F. Ahmadun, A.M. Said, A review of disaster and crisis. *Disaster Prevention and Management* **12/1** (2003), 24-32.
[13] E.L. Quarantelli, Technological and natural disasters and ecological problems: Similarities and differences in planning for and managing them. University of Delaware - Disaster Research Center (1993). [Online] Available from: URL: http://www.udel.edu/DRC/preliminary/192.pdf [2006, September 05]
[14] K. Bea, *Federal disaster policies after terrorist strike.* Hauppauge: Nova Science Publishers; 2003.
[15] C.L. Ruby, The definition of terrorism. *Analyses of Social Issues and Public Policy* **2/1** (2002), 9-14.
[16] C. Dorsey, Attacks in Spain impact US trains. *Disaster Recovery Journal* **17/4** (2004).

The Impacts of Catastrophic Events in Large Cities: Considerations for Coping with the Aftermath of Terrorism in Urban Settings

Jack L. ROZDILSKY
Assistant Professor of Emergency Administration and Planning Department of Public Administration, University of North Texas, USA

Abstract. In 2005, the impacts of Hurricane Katrina illustrated what a catastrophe in an urban setting looks like. In the hurricane disaster, authorities had both advanced warnings and some idea of the potential scope of the crisis, yet the dealing with the aftermath of the disaster proved difficult. This paper suggests that due to the unknowns inherent in social hazards (like terrorism) and the complexity of urban systems in a metropolitan area, reaching an acceptable level of preparedness may not be possible. Therefore, any efforts made to enhance the resiliency of the urban system, through sustainable development activities, work towards reducing the potential impacts of catastrophic events in large cities

Keywords. Disaster recovery, resiliency, urban systems, sustainable development

Introduction

As large cities prepare for disasters, terrorism is among the range of threats faced by urban areas. Many cities take an all-hazards approach to emergency management where steps are taken to prepare for hazards of natural, technological, and social origin. Such an approach provides for a balanced method of handling various types of emergencies. However, preparations for disasters also need to consider the unique characteristics of specific hazards. In order to best balance the need for overall disaster preparedness versus specific hazard-orientated preparedness steps, actions taken to create sustainable cities will create the greatest overall societal benefits. This paper summarizes ideas presented at the North Atlantic Treaty Organization's Advanced Research Workshop 'Understanding and Responding to Terrorism' held in Washington D.C. in September 2006. The concepts are based on the presentation, 'The impacts of catastrophic events in large cities: Considerations for coping with the aftermath of terrorism in urban settings.'

The Impacts of Catastrophic Events in Large Cities

Cities function as complex entities. Overlapping, physical, social, economic, and cultural systems provide for a mixture of elements that make cities an attractive place to live. However, these overlapping systems also create a level of complexity that makes it difficult to manage the impacts of a sudden-onset crisis. A recent survey commissioned by the US Department of Homeland Security asked the question whether 75 of the major urban areas of the US had adequate plans in place to deal with catastrophic events. Answers to the survey indicated that 21% of urban areas had no basic response plans, 40% of the cities did not have an adequate evacuation plan, and 40% of the cities did not have adequate mass casualty plans [1].

Evacuation planning is illustrative of this complex issue. Recent experiences in the US have indicated that even when emergency management plans are in place for situations like mass evacuations, various complexities can arise. For the 2005 Hurricane Katrina disaster, in the New Orleans vicinity tens of thousands of persons were able to successfully evacuate using private automobiles. Louisiana Governor Kathleen Blanco estimated that 92% of the 1.3 million persons in the New Orleans vicinity evacuated successfully [2]. However, even with that evacuation rate, thousands of persons without automobiles were stranded in the city. As the impact of the Hurricane resulted in levee breaches, persons who did not evacuate faced dire situations. A recent report by the US Department of Homeland Security has suggested that significant weaknesses in evacuation planning are an area of profound concern [3]. It is interesting to note that the natural disaster of Hurricane Katrina represented a disaster which was known, emergency managers had fairly good estimates concerning the potential magnitude of the event, and there was a prior warning available. Considering the social hazard of urban terrorism, the form of the disaster is unknown, estimates concerning the magnitude of the event are vague, and it is unlikely prior warnings will be available. Therefore, this author suggests that given the range of complexity inherent in cities and the unknown variables of potential urban terrorist attacks, achieving a suitable state of preparedness may be questionable.

However, despite the questions present in preparing for potential terrorist attacks, it is imperative that emergency managers make efforts to attempt to isolate portions of the problem which may be manageable. One way to accomplish this task is to consider the city as a system of interconnected parts. In taking a systems view of a city, the city can be considered as both an organism and as a mechanism [4].

As an organism, cities convert raw material into products and waste, energizing themselves in the process. As a result of the conversion processes, the urban organism seeks to reproduce the conditions necessary for survival. In looking at modern cities of the 21st century, it is also apparent that for cities to survive in their current configurations, they must also act as mechanisms. These mechanisms consist of artificial structures dependent on various forms of physical infrastructure, transportation systems, and the production capability of factories. This mechanism seeks to sustain itself, beyond natural limits, and produce products, or waste, that are alien to natural systems.

In considering how to take steps to better prepare for terrorism, viewing the city as both an organism and a mechanism can be a useful construct. For example, understanding which critical systems are needed to help the city sustain itself beyond natural limits can assist in the task of defining critical infrastructure that needs additional protection. Beyond the immediate-term tasks of hardening critical infrastructure, cities can also consider longer-term mitigation actions like engaging in more sustainable methods of production and consumption. Such actions would reduce the reliance of the urban system's survival on complex and fragile mechanisms that would represent targets of opportunity for a terrorist intent on causing urban chaos. A redundant urban system, working like an organism based on natural processes, would result a greater degree of robustness to shocks caused by terrorist attacks.

Applying the same concepts, community development can also be considered as an anti-terrorism strategy or a defense strategy. As previously mentioned urban areas have overlapping, physical, social, economic, and cultural systems that provide for a mixture of elements that make cities an attractive place to live. However, extremes in the social-economic characteristics of the population within an urban area, such as education, income, health care, etc. can result in a socially fragmented metropolitan area. In such a socially fragmented system, many persons may be living in precarious situations. These precarious situations may involve a lack of adequate health care, lack of transportation, and a lack of income due to lack of decent employment opportunities or educational facilities. In the event of any catastrophic situation, it may be likely that at least for the immediate aftermath of the crisis, persons in the disaster zone may either need to self-evacuate or tend to their own basic needs. Unfortunately, for those persons on the precipice of declining health, with no personal mobility, nor the income disposable income necessary to act in their own best survival interest, their need for immediate services will increase during a disaster. Depending on the extent of the crisis, the emergency management system may not be able to meet this group's basic needs to a satisfactory level. This situation will result in additional chaos and social disorganization. If the intention of a terrorist attack is to bring chaos to an urban area, cities with large social and economic disparities may be especially vulnerable to post-crisis management difficulties. Community development efforts that attempt to bridge the gaps between the rich and poor, and attempt to ensure that all citizens of a city live at an acceptable social-economic standard, will result in a city that has a greater resiliency to urban terrorist attacks. This resiliency will be due to the fact that most persons will be better able to sustain themselves without assistance in the time of chaos immediately following a catastrophic disaster.

Conclusion

In conclusion, the presentation 'The impacts of catastrophic events in large cities: Considerations for coping with the aftermath of terrorism in urban settings' suggested the following strategies for making cities more resilient to catastrophic events such as terrorist attacks. First, taking an all-hazards approach to disaster preparedness would best prepare cities for dealing with all types of disasters, whether they are of natural or human origin. Second, recent experiences in the US with hurricanes have illustrated the complexities apparent in dealing with city-wide catastrophes. Given the range of these urban emergency management problems, the range of complexity inherent in the systems which make up cities, and the unknown variables of potential urban terrorist attacks, being able to achieve a suitable state of urban preparedness may be questionable. Third, this predicament does not imply that urban preparedness is a futile effort; however, it suggests that new approaches may be necessary. One such approach would be to consider a city as both a mechanism and an organism. Such a systems-based approach would allow for portions of the complex problem to be both isolated and addressed.

Fourth, community development should be considered as a defense strategy. In other words, an urban area that has a population of persons who are better able to sustain themselves in the time immediately after a disaster, will be better able to move quickly towards recovery. Recognizing the complexities inherent in urban areas causes one to focus on considering the overall resiliency the city. Actions taken to move the urban area towards a greater degree of sustainability also act to provide for a greater degree of resiliency for all hazards, including terrorism.

References

[1] E. Lipton, Many states are not confident in disaster plans, survey finds. *New York Times* (2006, February 10). p A16.
[2] US Office of the President, The While House. *The federal response to Hurricane Katrina: Lessons learned.* Washington D.C.: The White House; 2006, February. [Online] Available from: URL: http://www.whitehouse.gov/reports/katrina-lessons-learned.pdf [2006, August 10]
[3] US Department of Homeland Security. *Nationwide Plan Review, Phase 2 Report.* Washington D.C.: US Department of Homeland Security; 2006, June 2006. [Online] Available from: URL: http://www.dhs.gov/interweb/assetlibrary/Prep_NationcwidePlanReview.pdf [2006, August 12]
[4] H. Girardet, *The GAIA atlas of cities: New directions for sustainable urban living.* London: Anchor Books; 1992.

Terrorism, Vulnerability and Assessment

Huseyin AKDOGAN
University of North Texas, USA

Abstract. Compared with natural disasters, terrorism attacks are more controllable in terms of reducing their vulnerability with well constructed prevention system and responding system. The paper examines the definitions of terrorism actions and terrorism vulnerability, and then suggests several methods for the public sector to reduce terrorism vulnerability.

Keywords. Terrorism, vulnerability, emergency management

Introduction

Terrorism is classified as man-made disaster by emergency managers. Sarin gas dispersion in Tokyo subways in 1995 showed the possibility of the usage of chemical, biological and nuclear materials by terrorists. However, this attack was not as deadly and destructive as a natural disaster. Six years later in the 9/11 attacks, people witnessed how deadly and destructive a terrorist attack can be; in fact, approximately 3000 people were killed, and billions of dollars were lost. Disasters are defined by some as natural events, but this approach is not broad enough and thus, people are giving it up. For others, like McEntire [1], disasters are being accepted as the interaction of triggering agents and vulnerability. McEntire defines the disaster as a "disruptive and/or deadly and destructive outcome of triggering agents when they interact with, and are exacerbated by, various forms of vulnerability" [1, pg. 190]. Triggering agents and vulnerability are the two components of disasters according to this definition. A volcanic eruption or an earthquake can be a triggering agent which comes from natural environment. Triggering agents can also come from human activities such as terrorism.

The second component, vulnerability, can be defined in various ways. Lewis [2, pg. 4] defines it as the "degree of susceptibility to a natural hazard." Twigg [3] explains the complexity of vulnerability. For him, it is a complex term because many components such as economic, social, demographic, political, and psychological make up dimensions. Those complex dimensions are also valid for man-made disasters. While vulnerability can be reduced or increased by people, and it is related to every hazard including terrorism, triggering agents can not be prevented by people, so the efforts should focus on reducing vulnerability. People should examine their vulnerabilities in order to be prepared for both man-made and natural disasters.

1. Understanding Vulnerability

McEntire stresses the issue of vulnerability because while it can be determined by people, stopping or preventing the triggering agents may not be so easy [1]. While stopping an earthquake is not possible, preventing deaths and injuries can be possible. In fact, some of the times the triggering agents do not kill anybody, but the vulnerabilities cause a lot of deaths. While an earthquake is sometimes not lethal, the structures which people have built can be lethal. A recent example of this situation was witnessed after the 17 August earthquake in Turkey. The earthquake did not kill directly, but weak buildings did.

Salter defines vulnerability as the "susceptibility and resilience of the community and environment to hazards" [4, pg. 53]. In addition to susceptibility and resilience, risk and resistance are the other categories of vulnerability in McEntire's definition; "Vulnerability is the dependant component of disaster that is determined by the degree of risk, susceptibility, resistance, and resilience" [1, pg. 190]. Each of the four categories of vulnerability may affect others and may be affected by others. The relations between them may be inverse or direct. If the resistance of buildings can be strengthened, the risk in an earthquake may be lowered. Therefore, assessing vulnerability is a complex issue. All relations among the categories of vulnerability must be assessed in order to accurately assess the vulnerability [2].

The nature of vulnerability changes according to the types of hazards and the place. Today, Americans are more vulnerable to hurricanes because of quadrupled population and properties along hurricane-prone coastlines. Similarly, increased development and population in floodplains are the causes of flooding vulnerability. An increase in heavy rains during the past fifty years is another accompanying factor needed to be considered when trying to reduce the flooding vulnerability.

The growing population in the drier regions, changes in land and water use, and urbanization make people more vulnerable to drought [5]. Hospitals are another example of vulnerability because of their characteristics. High levels of occupancy, the critical and vital supplies for the patients, essential and important basic facilities like power, clinical gases, and oxygen, are some of those characteristics causing vulnerability. Hazardous materials, heavy objects near patients' beds can also be a vulnerability sources for hospitals [6].

Even the degree of vulnerability can change at the macro level. The level of vulnerability among small or poor countries is different than that of big or developed countries. While poor countries are economically more vulnerable than rich countries, small countries are physically more vulnerable to disaster impacts than big countries.

At each level vulnerability has a direct proportion with dependency; dependency is a real cause of vulnerability [2]. Morrow also mentions the general vulnerable categories of hazards [7]. Poverty, location of buildings, age, school systems are factors in vulnerability. The mentally and physically disordered people, non-educated people, immigrants, tourists, minorities, and women are also vulnerable to disasters. FEMA classifies vulnerability as physical and social [8]. Human, agricultural, and structural are the subheadings of physical vulnerability. Although these classifications are necessary to improve those groups' resistance and resilience, Buckle [9] points out that all groups of people may be vulnerable in different ways, so categorization has to be on the basis of an issue related to the matter of a particular event or type of emergency.

2. Terrorism Vulnerability

The definition of terrorism is a hard issue although it is as old as human kind's communal life. Studies show that terrorism has been defined in numerous ways around the world, for example, the US Army found over 100 terrorism definitions [10]. Terrorism, guerilla warfare, revolutionaries, anarchists, and freedom fighters are words close in meaning and organizations can be named using these words by states according to international relations. Even though there is no unique definition of terrorism, there is an agreement on some certain acts which the international community condemns as terrorist acts, such as targeting civilians to kill, and destroying a lot of people [11].

There is no absolute target for terrorists. The best target for terrorists is the most vulnerable so that they can kill a lot of people in order to shock both the government and citizens. Terrorist attacks are kinds of propaganda tools to show the power of the organization to the government and to terrorize the people. Therefore, the more shocking and lethal the attacks are, the more success for terrorist organizations. Bennet points out the costs of terrorism and says because of this reason terrorists want to be successful in their attacks [12]. A successful attack will serve the propaganda of the organization, the morale of the others and sympathizers, and it will also cause a fear in the society. Terrorists can use this situation to recruit new sympathizers or militants and to collect donations or contributions.

Open societies are more vulnerable to terrorist attacks. Every country has some critical infrastructures which are very important to daily life and vulnerable to terrorist attacks such as transportation, electrical energy, telecommunications, water supply systems, gas and storage and delivery, banking and finance, and government buildings. These infrastructures can be more or less in different states. For example, the US has 171 critical infrastructures according to the Homeland Security Presidential Directive 7 which was issued in December 2003 [13]. The vulnerability of transportation systems has been witnessed in the Tokyo subway attacks, in the 9/11 attacks, in the Madrid train bombings, and recently in the London subway bombings. Not only is the transportation system vulnerable to terrorist attacks, but also it is now a lethal weapon for terrorists. Besides this, Trager and Zagorcheva underline that terrorists can buy and use more destructive weapons [14]. Either they or their sponsor states can buy biological or chemical materials from former Soviet areas, or scientists.

McEntire organizes the reasons for increased vulnerability under six categories which are physical, social, political, economic, and technological reasons [1]. Some of those reasons may be adapted to terrorist vulnerability. Not only does massive and unplanned migration to urban areas increase natural triggering disasters, but it also increases the human triggering disasters. Massive and unplanned migration can also cause criminality. Since the new settlement is probably in a suburb, there will be a sub-culture among the immigrants. In addition to losing parental and cultural control, the effects of the new sub-culture as well as some other effects make the immigrants the source of both criminal and terrorist organizations. The sub-cultures and immigrants are always vulnerable to terrorist recruitments. Marginalization of specific groups and individuals also triggers this effect.

Traditional coping measures help individuals to deal with the tough issues of life. These also tie the individual to the community. Losing traditional coping measures makes a person a stranger to his community, and makes him vulnerable to both terrorist recruitment and other disasters. An absence of personal responsibility means disappointment. Hoffer defines a "disappointed man" as a man who has no ties to society, or to a person [15]. A disappointed man can do anything without hesitating, and without being scared. These kinds of men do not care about the disasters, do not care about living well. Offering a precious identity to him is the strategy of terrorist organizations. This can be being a member of an organization, or being a martyr for a belief. Having an identity and becoming a person means everything for them. A disappointed man can be a suicide bomber easily, because escalating from being nobody to an eternal noble identity is worth dying for.

A divergence in the distribution of wealth is the main focal point that terrorist organizations use to affect people. If a country or a region has a big gap in the distribution of wealth, that place is more vulnerable to terrorist recruitment and terrorist attacks. This can explain the terrorist attacks to the US, as the US is far away from the source of some of the terrorist organizations. Capitalism can be seen as a main reason of inequality in the world, so the symbols of capitalism such as the World Trade Center can be a good target for terrorists.

McEntire says one of the reasons for an increase in the vulnerability is the actions of the response and recovery operations [1]. This statement is also valid for terrorist attacks, especially in bombing attacks. The first responders on the scene and the first arriving officers can augment vulnerability with the panic at the scene shadowing the truths and risks around the scene. Another bomb can explode when the authorities come to the scene. Therefore, reducing the risk at the scene has great importance. On the other hand, the first responder can spoil the evidence which may be the only clue to reach the respondents. Even though saving lives and helping injured people is the first thing to be done on the scene, some small precautions may prevent the loss of evidences.

3. Reducing Terrorism Vulnerability

Although humans are not capable of preventing or controlling natural hazards, it is possible to control the vulnerabilities [1]. This point is important to reduce the disaster vulnerabilities. If the vulnerability can be controlled, everything must be done because the life of a human being is valuable.

Liabilities of vulnerability, risk and susceptibility, must be assessed very carefully in terrorism events. While we work at reducing risk and susceptibility, we must raise resistance and resilience to disasters [16]. To reduce terrorism vulnerability, empathy, education, intelligence, coordination, and technology must be examined very carefully. The characteristics of countries can change, but risk and susceptibility factors can be determined by authorities. The unforeseeable character of terrorist attacks, make terrorism vulnerability very important and complex. Thus, the emergency managers, police and other related departments must think as a terrorist does in order to define the vulnerabilities. Information and perception of the organization and the supporters are needed to empathize. Although empathy is very hard to practice, knowledge about terrorism organizations and terrorists may help.

"Knowledge is power[1]." Increasing knowledge about the occurrence, nearness, and cost of disasters is necessary to reduce the disaster vulnerability. Individuals, public agencies, and communities must be informed with this knowledge to empower them. This information flow can reduce the risk before, during and after the disasters.

---

[1] Francis Bacon (1561 - 1626), English author, courtier, and philosopher [17]

McEntire also suggests that the main concern must be education [18]. Educating people about triggering agents and vulnerabilities can reduce the vulnerabilities. This famous axiom is also central to terrorism vulnerability reduction. Intelligence activities are a branch of this axiom in terrorism. While meteorologists are working on some scientific prediction systems for disasters, intelligence is the best prediction system of terrorism activities. One of the specific efforts to reduce the US vulnerabilities to international terrorism is collecting and analyzing intelligence, counterintelligence, and covert action according to the Presidential Decision Directive 39 [19].

Coordination among the agencies, preparing, responding and recovering to disasters, is vital. Since the vulnerability has a complex structure, the efforts to reduce it must be complex, too. Coordination can make effective all efforts, otherwise all efforts may fail like before 9/11 events. On duty departments about terrorism must share the information and this information must be analyzed, and used.

Technology is improving very fast. Not only are the state authorities using the technology, but also terrorists are using it, too. Thus, the authorities must pursue the improvements in technology and keep their departments up to date. The Geographic Information System (GIS) is useful in vulnerability assessment because of its power for exploring qualitative and quantitative relationships between communities, the environment, systems, and hazards by visualizing situations, and modeling them [4]. GIS is also useful for terrorism events. Integrating social and geographic data through GIS allows us to understand, respond to, and recover from terrorism. Intelligence agencies can also use the GIS system to integrate and visualize their information.

4. Conclusion

Terrorism vulnerability and assessment is somewhat similar to disaster vulnerability. However, there may be some differences because of the triggering agents. In fact, nature is a triggering agent for disasters, while humans are the triggering agent for terrorism. Developing scientific prediction systems can be effective to reduce the disaster vulnerability, but they can not work to reduce terrorism vulnerability. Terrorists can attack seemingly invulnerable structures and, destroy them. However, the vulnerability is also a valid concern for terrorism, so we can control the terrorism vulnerability. Reducing the risk and susceptibility of terrorism can increase the capabilities. Increasing the resistance and resilience can also reduce the liabilities. The focal point of future studies on disasters, both natural and human triggering agent disasters, must be vulnerability because it is controllable by people. Vulnerability is also related to every disaster. Moreover, every individual can play a role in reducing the vulnerability, because people on the street are the first responder to the disasters.

References

[1] D. McEntire, Triggering agents, vulnerabilities and disaster reduction: Towards a holistic paradigm. *Disaster Prevention and Management* **10/3** (2001), 189-196.
[2] J. Lewis, *Development in disaster-prone places*. United Kingdom: The Cromwell Press; 1999.
[3] J. Twigg, M. Bhatt, editors, *Understanding vulnerability*. North Yorkshire: Intermediate Technology Publications; 1998.

[4] J. Salter, Public safety risk management: Assessing the latest national guidelines. *Australian Journal of Emergency Management* **13/4** (1998), 50-53.
[5] SDR - Subcommittee on Disaster Reduction, *Reducing disaster vulnerability through science and technology* (2003, July). [Online] Available from: URL: http://ostp.gov/nstc/html/SDR_Report_ReducingDisasterVulnerability2003.pdf [2006, February 20]
[6] PAHO - Pan American Health Organization, *Principles of disaster mitigation in health facilities*. Washington, D.C.: World Health Organization; 2002.
[7] B.H. Morrow, Identifying and mapping community vulnerability. *Disasters* **23/1** (1999), 1-18.
[8] FEMA: Hazard, vulnerability, and risk analysis. [Online] Available from: URL: www.fema.gov/emiweb/edu/introtoEM.asp [2006, February 20]
[9] P. Buckle, Re-defining community and vulnerability in the context of emergency management. *Australian Journal of Emergency Management* **3** (1998), 21-26.
[10] J. Record, Bounding the global war in terrorism; 2003. [Online] Available from: URL: from http://www.strategicstudiesinstitute.army.mil/pubs/display.cfm?pubID=207 [2006, February 20]
[11] P. Hoffman, Human rights and terrorism. *Human Rights Quarterly* **26** (2004), 932-955.
[12] B. Bennet, Rings of protection: Reducing your vulnerability to a terrorist attack. *Occupational Health & Safety* **73/6** (2004), 52-56.
[13] D. Purdy, Jr., Cybersecurity vulnerabilities. CQ Congressional Testimony (2005, September 15). [Online] Retrieved from LexisNexis Academic universe database [2006, February 20]
[14] R.F. Trager, D.P. Zagorcheva, Deterring terrorism; It can be done. *International Security* **30/3** (2006), 87-123.
[15] E. Hoffer, *The true believers*. Perennial Publications; 1989.
[16] D. McEntire, Why vulnerability matters? *Disaster Prevention and Management* **14/2** (2005), 206-222.
[17] Wikiquote, Knowledge is power. [Online] Available from: URL: http://en.wikiquote.org/wiki/Francis_Bacon [2006, November 09]
[18] D. McEntire, Sustainability or invulnerable development? *Australian Journal of Emergency Management* **4** (2000), 58-61.
[19] Presidential decision directives (1995, June 21). [Online] Available from: URL: http://www.fas.org/irp/offdocs/pdd39.htm [2006, March 20]

Improvisation, Creativity, and the Art of Emergency Management

James KENDRA[a] and Tricia WACHTENDORF[b]
[a] *Department of Public Administration, University of North Texas, USA*
[b] *Department of Sociology and Criminal Justice, University of Delaware, USA*

Abstract. With increasing concerns of the harmful effects brought by disasters, how to improve the efficiency of emergency management is becoming a more important issue faced by public sectors worldwide. Among all the aspects of a disaster, the improvisation of it is the most uncontrollable one that affects the outcome of emergency management. This paper presents the definition of the improvisation, creative ways of handling improvising in disasters and the emergency management experiences summarized from them.

Keywords. Improvisation, creativity, emergency management

1. Improvising in Disaster

Improvisation is a significant feature of every disaster, and Tierney has argued that if an event does not require improvisation, it is probably not a disaster [1]. Improvisation has had something of a checkered history in the emergency management field since its appearance in a disaster response seems to suggest a failure to plan for a particular contingency. Even scholars who have recognized the value of this capacity have tended to subordinate it to planning. Kreps, for example, who has completed some of the most detailed studies of organizational improvisation in disaster, has defined improvisation as organizing "during an event," while preparedness is organizing "before an event" [2, pg. 34]. He has stressed that preparedness and improvisation are the "foundations" of emergency management [2, pg. 31], yet he nevertheless privileges preparedness, especially planning, as the favored element. Drabek, too, emphasizes the need for planning to reduce the incidence of (the inevitably necessary) improvisation [3]. Thus improvisation occupies a somewhat conflicted space in the realm of emergency and crisis management capacities: we plan in detail so that we do not have to improvise, while knowing that we *will* have to improvise.

This paper discusses emerging understandings of improvisation in emergency management and their relationship to planning as well as to other such noted disaster phenomena as emergence, or the appearance of new groups of people organized to meet disaster-related needs. We reconsider the suggestion that improvisation must be positioned with respect to planning in such a way that it seems to be the weak link, or an indication of some failure or dysfunction. We argue that improvisation is a distinct capacity that individuals and groups employ, and that while planning encompasses the normative "what ought to be done," improvisation encompasses the emergent and actual "what needs to be done." The public policy scholar Michael McGuire has suggested that "plans are hypotheses" about a projected future condition. Since real conditions are likely to differ, adjustment to plans will always be necessary. Weick has drawn on jazz as a model and lens for understanding improvisation in organizational settings [4]. Jazz musicians are not censured for their improvisations, nor are they criticized for not composing their scores in advance. Rather, their extemporaneous compositions are celebrated -that is what jazz *is*, and a successful jazz performance is the end result of training, knowledge, practice, and experimentation. Similarly, improvisational comedy and theater are regarded as high expressions of a stage performer's art. This does not mean that these performers do not practice or build repertoires of material that they can draw upon in given circumstances. On the contrary, they work to build their knowledge across a range of fields, and it is this knowledge that provides the elements for each improvisational outcome. Improvisation plays an equally important role in emergency management, where training, practice, and knowledge of both the field and the community serve as repertoires of material emergency managers can draw upon in the ambiguous and dynamic conditions of a disaster where not every need has been anticipated or accounted for [5, 6].

Scholars and practitioners often define emergency management as both an art and a science [7], an understanding that applies to other professions where people interact with the natural environment. For example in medicine, a specialty routinely also described as art and science, the environment is the highly localized one of a patient's body; in navigation and aviation the environment is the natural one of ocean basins, the atmosphere, land forms, weather, and climate. But in emergency management, the setting is even more complex, consisting not only of the earth's processes but also humanity's industrial activity and the distribution of people and their complex social and economic systems, systems that are imperfectly understood even in normal times yet whose ramifications extend into, and even create, the situations we colloquially call disasters.

For the emergency manager, the science extends from the natural and social sciences that provide the foundations for understanding the causes and distribution of hazard. The earth and atmospheric sciences tell us about geologic and climatic processes, while the social sciences tell us about people's understanding of and response to those processes. Moreover, they provide insight into the social systems that either lead to exposure to the forces of nature, or that lead to mismanagement of our industrial systems resulting in systems failures, hazardous releases, and environmental degradations.

But more can be said about the science of emergency management, for though it involves applications of principles from various disciplines, its practice is a particular kind of science, one that leaves behind standard methods and well-defined procedures of its foundational disciplines to become something more rooted in interpretation, judgment, and the negotiation of ambiguity. Funtowicz and Ravetz have identified various forms of scientific practice [8]. They distinguish between Kuhnian "normal science" where scholars work within established norms and sets of procedures, and "post-normal science," characterized by problems both with high uncertainties and high decision stakes, where issues are often ill-defined, proper methods unclear, data mixed or incomplete, and social and political considerations intermixed. Environmental challenges such as global warming are "post normal," for example. Funtowicz and Ravetz also identified a middle ground of moderately high decision stakes and moderately high uncertainty, a conceptual zone requiring the application of professional craftsmanship, as is required in the various engineering disciplines [8].

These are also the characteristics of emergencies, where the precise unfolding of circumstances is unknown. As in other disciplines, the art is in the application of knowledge in irregular circumstances, where we encounter the genuine evolving of actual events, not an idealized type. "Science deals with regularities in our experience; art deals with singularities" [9, pg. 60]. Singularities are the elements of disaster not predicted in advance. Weick, in reviewing recent management theory, noted that all management is improvisation to some extent [4]. If that observation is valid for organizations in commercial enterprises where decision making scenarios that are often described as 'dynamic' are ponderous as compared to crisis management time scales, then surely improvisation would seem to be elemental in emergency management, too. Given this, we suggest that improvisation is a high expression of an emergency manager's art.

2. Concepts of Improvisation

Scholars have defined improvisation variously. Moorman and Miner [10] identified some two dozen different definitions from a number of fields, and they also noted that a number of concepts are related to improvisation, such as creativity. Weick provided an often-cited definition [4, pg. 546-547]:

"Considered as a noun, an improvisation is a transformation of some original model. Considered as a verb, improvisation is composing in real time that begins with embellishments of a simple model, but increasingly feeds on these embellishments themselves to move father from the original melody and closer to a new composition. Whether treated as a noun or a verb, improvisation is guided activity whose guidance comes from elapsed patterns discovered retrospectively."

Miner, Bassoff, and Moorman have defined improvisation as "the deliberate and substantive fusion of the design and execution of a novel production" [11, pg. 314]. In other words, theorists place an emphasis on time, and all stress the simultaneous or near-simultaneous conception and implementation of action, as in the playing of a note in jazz or the introduction of a product design element or process in manufacturing. Miner, Bassoff, and Moorman have further identified several distinct improvisational products [11]. These include "artifactual improvisations," where the outcome is a tool or object; "behavioral improvisations," where the outcome is a new process of set of actions; and "interpretive improvisations", where the product is a new way of understanding needs, obligations, or conditions. They note that while much writing about improvisation in the management literature takes a generally positive stance, outcomes are not always favorable, and moreover organizations do not always learn from their improvisations, gain methods or maintain insights with any longevity.

Adopting a different approach, we have postulated a 3-element typology of improvisational types, based on the emergence of improvisational activity with respect to an existing plan, model for action, or standard procedure [5, 6, 12]. In *reproductive improvisation,* improvisers recreate an existing capacity; in *adaptive improvisation,* they amend an existing capacity to match changing demands, producing a new system, and in *creative improvisation* they create an entirely new capacity in the absence of an existing model. All of these forms occur under tight time constraints and with pressing demands for action.

Public officials, especially those accustomed to highly controlled and regimented organizational structures, tend to be discomfited by the prospect of improvisation in their environs, since improvisation suggests not only novel, untested, and perhaps unexpected actions, but also actions that may be taken unbeknownst to other participants in an emergency response. The result of such autonomous activity is likely to be confusion, waste, and poor delivery of emergency management services. Indeed, for some officials, and even for some scholars, the image of improvisation is of independent, disconnected, and chaotic activity -the kind of activity that emergency plans, and management structures such as the Incident Command System, were developed to prevent. Such images are, at best, a caricature of improvisation and at worst reinforce the perception that improvising is an also-ran to detailed planning. Improvisation, if it is truly a set of individualistic acts, can go badly and yield the malfunctional outcome feared by emergency managers and other officials. However, group improvisations, the emergent products of collective problem-solving activity, can be highly effective responses to unusual situations and novel demands.

3. Examples

Other works explore in detail the numerous examples of improvisation during the World Trade Center response [5, 6, 12, 13]. We review some of them here to illustrate the important role improvisation plays in disaster management. On the morning of September 11, 2001, Office of Emergency Management (OEM) officials were at their emergency operations center (EOC) preparing for a bio-terrorism exercise. The EOC and OEM offices were located at 7 World Trade Center, adjacent to the Twin Towers. This state-of-the-art facility was constructed in the late 1990s and was both equipped with sophisticated monitoring equipment and designed in such a way -in multi-agency work pods comprised of specific organizational representatives- to maximize coordination between the numerous agencies that would need to respond to various emergency support functions. The integrity of the EOC was compromised shortly after the Twin Towers were attacked and the building collapsed later that afternoon.

With no back-up facility in place, OEM staff and city agency representatives needed to quickly improvise a new site of central coordination. Eventually that day, a temporary site was established in the police academy library, and within several days the operations were shifted to a large shipping pier along the Hudson River (the intended site for the next day's bio-terrorism drill). The initial goal was clear: improvise in such a way as to closely reproduce the 7 World Trade Center EOC. The original EOC would have proven a formidable site from which to launch a response of this kind. Even at the temporary library site, agency representatives began situating themselves to mirror the work pods that were in place at 7 World Trade Center. In other words, improvisation manifested itself so as to employ substitutes in an effort to replicate the original facility.

There were alternative courses of action. The involved agency representatives could have decided that reestablishing an EOC was not necessary or would place too high a demand on their time during a still evolving crisis. Another possible option would have been to improvise an entirely different way of coordinating agencies, perhaps around differently conceived functions, focused on the locations of the response activities (e.g. warehouse, the Staten Island debris sorting site, sections of the impact zone), or around jurisdictional levels (federal, state, local, non-profit, private sector). Nevertheless, the original facility as well as its layout representing the way organizations should coordinate their roles was understood as appropriate. As a result, reproductive improvisation was undertaken.

At the same time, improvisation is not static. Assessment and reassessment of needs in real time often accompanies improvised action as the environment presents new demands on organizational actors. Even after the EOC was reestablished to reproduce the original, additional improvisations that could best be characterized according to the three-fold typology as adaptive were implemented. For example, over time adaptations were made to the original layout -and thus to operational functioning between organizations- as new demands emerged. Members of the New York State National Guard acting under the auspices of the New York State Emergency Management Office (SEMO) played a critical role in the logistics work pod. Yet SEMO's extensive role in logistics grew even greater as the response unfolded over the first few weeks. The size of SEMO's section accordingly expanded until the organization rearranged the furniture to cordon off a work sub-pod of its own.

This redesignation of space is not as insignificant as some may suggest. It represents a greater improvisation of role and task assumption by SEMO as a greater understanding of needs emerged. The interpretation of needs by organizational actors led them to conclude that it was no longer appropriate to mirror the original facility just as the original level of involvement by SEMO in logistics was no longer appropriate.

In a like manner, the overwhelming involvement of local agencies and volunteers as well as the widespread convergence of people and organizations from across the country to help with the response generated a demand for adaptive improvisations with respect to credentialing. The standard operating procedure of relying on agency badges for entry into areas associated with the response efforts was inadequate to limit the number of personnel and volunteers from entering secured areas. Indeed, the emerging response network included key participants with much needed expertise, but who were either unaffiliated with a recognized agency, associated with an agency from outside the traditional response network, or affiliated with an organization from outside the greater New York metropolitan area. At the same time, allowing every city worker with an agency badge to have site access would have been equally unmanageable. A new credentialing system consequently had to be adapted from the original protocol. Then, as response locations changed, as badges needed to be accounted for, as access needed to be tightened -for example, for safety reasons at Ground Zero- and as more sophisticated credentialing equipment became available, adaptations were made to the badges themselves. Even as a new credentialing system was improvised, those in charge of site security found that additional adaptations were needed to account for new circumstances or unintended consequences of the new badges themselves.

The waterborne evacuation of Lower Manhattan is an exemplar of creative improvisation. During that event, several hundred thousand people were evacuated in a spontaneous fleet of assorted vessels: towboats, dinner cruise boats, tour boats, yachts, and other craft converged on Manhattan and shuttled evacuees to Staten Island, Brooklyn, or various points in New Jersey. Upon disembarking people, the boats carried supplies and rescue workers into the city, an operation which for some vessels lasted several days. There was no pre-planning for this kind of event, although the Coast Guard personnel who coordinated -and it is important to stress coordinated, rather than directed- this event drew on elements of search and rescue and crisis management plans that presupposed a much smaller incident. Instead, participants in the evacuation and supply lift operation responded to cues within their environment based on their own repertoire of knowledge and experience to determine that a response was necessary. Such cues included sightings of individuals gathering at the waterfront as well as sightings of and radio transmissions from other vessels. Their repertoire included an understanding of the harbor, knowledge of the commuter population that comprised the daily population of Lower Manhattan, training in spills or search and rescue operations, and an occupational ethos of rescue, albeit one typically associated with rescue-at-sea operations. This form of improvisation does not develop in a vacuum and still draws upon a repertoire of skills and knowledge; nevertheless this activity was creative in that it did not emanate from an original plan.

4. Improvising and Coordinating

We should be clear when we discuss improvisation that we're not talking about everyone "doing his own thing" simply hoping that, as the theater owner says in *Shakespeare in Love*, "it all turns out well." Certainly there is room for individual initiative and innovation. For a particular set of necessary tasks, tools and methods can be assembled from available materials. Such improvisations, enacted at a local level and at a restricted scale, are not likely to disrupt action in a larger response milieu. But improvisations that are likely to ramify throughout organizational space present a different set of challenges. Here decisions and actions can influence the conduct of other actors, perhaps by drawing away resources of personnel or equipment, or by shifting the conditions of the operational environment that someone else depends on.

It is this outcome -an anarchical collapse of organization- that emergency planners fear most in improvisational settings and for which operational protocols such as the Incident Command System were developed to avoid. Yet the Incident Command System has its faults. Buck, Trainor, and Aguirre [14] noted that ICS functions best in situations that are familiar, where participants have worked together before, and that are of a limited scope. It is less effective, according to their findings, in situations that are new, surprising, or massive [14] -in other words, where its promised benefits are most urgent! This suggests that there is something about making ICS work that is not inherent in its design, but rather that there is something that organizations bring into the mix (otherwise it would always work). Bigley and Roberts found that members of incident command systems indeed did improvise some aspects of it to help them in particular situations [15], a finding that again suggests that responders have an "extra-ICS" set of capacities that they draw on in an emergency but which ICS allows them to focus and which, also, *supports* ICS, too.

Our work on improvisation supports this broad proposition -in particular, that the individual and organizational properties that make ICS 'work' can allow organizations to cooperate effectively outside the ICS regime and might in fact be the starting point for a larger organizational development. Stated differently, the same qualities that make ICS work can allow other kinds of organization to be effective, as well. For example, in the waterborne evacuation, the participants were familiar with each other. They had worked together before, and they were familiar with the resources and with the maritime operating environment. In this event, a loose-fitting organization evolved with a very flat hierarchy that emerged around coordination and traffic control of vessels and the establishment of three main evacuee marshalling points ashore in Manhattan. A bus company joined the operation on the New Jersey side, transporting the disembarked evacuees to mass transit points. Participants in this operation became participants by identifying and filling needs; organizing around tasks and geography; and providing information and allowing the persistence of organizational autonomy.

Moreover, this operation occurred almost completely disconnected from the response operations at the WTC site. It was a separate entity, with no intersection with the shoreside emergency management function regarding sharing or drawing away resources. In fact, these vessels brought *in* personnel, equipment, and fuel, functioning in a modular organizational structure that carried out collectively-defined tasks in support of overall response goals.

But, though this event was improvised it was not anarchical. Some participants referred to 'chaos,' and in reviewing certain photographs and video of the event it certainly appears, at least superficially, to be extremely hectic. But there is other information to bear in mind when considering whether 'anarchy' was involved, or something else. There were no significant injuries or vessel mishaps of any substance during the evacuation. Boat operators negotiated with each other for access to docking space, or simply stood off and waited their turn. Several participants reported that the usual competitive maneuvering did not occur between captains.

5. What We Should Be Doing

The utility of community organizations, and community-based participation, should not be underestimated even in terrorist-attack scenarios. While we lately hear considerable discussion of the need for 'command and control,' the desired outcome of this -the coordinated use of resources- is achievable through many types of organizational structures, some of which are likely to be far more appropriate in civil contexts where command-and-control has little resonance. Instead, preparedness activities should involve considerable outreach into communities.

We need to be identifying resources in advance, and we need to allow our collective imaginations to roam over the range of skills and assets that are out there. If there are obstacles to a particular application of a certain resource, those should be identified and examined to see if they might be reasonably set aside in a compelling emergency. Our work in the World Trade Center disaster uncovered numerous such 'workarounds' of greater or lesser scope -for example, boats carried passengers in excess of their certified capacities, or carried passengers with no certificate to do so.

5.1. Identifying Resources

Where do such resources exist? They exist everywhere in our communities. To take the WTC attack as an example, we have said elsewhere that New York City contained every skill needed to handle the disaster [13]. But it is important to bear in mind that those skills and capacities were not all in the formal, pre-established emergency response organizations. Some of those skills were in other organizations in the city government. For instance, as has been documented elsewhere [5, 6, 16] the city's Department of Design and Construction had had no previous disaster management experience, yet emerged as the lead agency for the long 'unbuilding' of the Trade Center. The Department of Health had no statutory authority for the environmental health aspects of the response, yet they took on that role. The private sector provided personnel, materials, and expertise, as in the construction trades. Restaurants supplied food [17], while community based organizations from the service, advocacy, and faith communities provided support and comfort. The speed at which OEM was able to reestablish the EOC after it was destroyed was in no small part due to the tremendous resources at its fingertips and its knowledge of those resources. Expanding the lease on the shipping pier from a day-long exercise to occupation of several months and transforming the site into the necessary facility required a flexibility to conceive of that space in non-traditional ways. Without having an open mind to envision resources in new ways, or without having an organizational culture to allow for that envisioning, improvisation is improbable. Without having an understanding of the resources available to begin with, improvisation becomes impossible.

5.2. Usefulness of Plans

As with any art, the skill of improvisation cannot be taught by assigning a script or working through a check-list of steps. Its principles, however, can be taught and the knack of improvisation can be developed through practice and exercise. To the extent that acts of improvisation depend on attributes of creativity, improvisation can be enhanced by removing organizational impediments to creative thinking [18] and by creating an organizational culture that values improvisation. Again, we do not suggest that plans or planning should be discarded, only that plans should be seen as guides, and planning should be seen as rehearsing for later improvisation. Simply inviting representatives of organizations and agencies to meet regularly can be a useful activity, to build acquaintances, to share information, and to develop norms of mutual interaction. Drabek argued that "the capacity to improvise is greatest when the pre-disaster response network has been nurtured and integrated" [3, pg. 11]. The extent to which plans do account for circumstances that arise in a disaster in fact can facilitate the process of improvisation. That is, when certain elements of the response are not disrupted or are encompassed in prior planning, responders can direct their attention to the unanticipated elements of the disaster and improvise with a more concentrated focus. It is not a matter of abandoning planning for improvisation, nor is it a matter of planning with the goal of eliminating the need for improvisation. Rather, planning and improvisation are important aspects of any effective disaster response and are best considered as complementary.

6. Future of Improvising

Thus far we have been concerned with a practical or instrumental outcome of tolerance for, even celebration of, improvisation. But we can argue for a more theoretical significance for an institutionalized appreciation for improvisation: that it provides leverage for putting management -contemporary, updated, current conceptions of management- into emergency management, at least with regard to the response phase, the phase that is least amenable to standard management practices familiar in routinely-functioning organizations and situations. As noted earlier, Weick asserted that all management is improvisation to some extent [4]. Thus, as a common reference point, improvisation can provide a connection between emergency management and 'regular' management. Such a connection would be important in the further development and grounding of the emergency management field.

Weick, in the 40th anniversary issue of *Administrative Science Quarterly*, reflected on the challenges facing organizational scientists -challenges that included encroachments by the competing discipline of economics, and by a shift in the legitimacy of knowledge production away from universities and toward the business sector [19]. Weick developed his argument by allegory, highlighting the failure of firefighters at Mann Gulch and South Canyon to "drop their tools." Burdened by their heavy equipment, they could not run fast enough and perished in advancing wildfires. For Weick, those tools emerged as central to the firefighters' identities *as* firefighters, and the inability to discard them was the physical manifestation of an individual and organizational incapacity to make new sense of a shifting situation. The tools were a kind of existential compass that oriented them to a certain view of themselves and their relationship to that place, though its features shifted around them. Weick thought that organization researchers now faced a similar crisis of situational awareness, which demanded an ability and a willingness to drop old tools of research methods and paradigmatic understanding.

An inverse situation is possible -the need for a discipline to *pick up* its tools [20]. Emergency managers often talk about the 'hands on' nature of their work, especially to distinguish it from research and academia. But the phrase is at best metaphorical, referring to engagement with real events, because emergency managers do not really use 'tools' in the sense conferred by the phrase. First responders, rescue workers, and heavy equipment operators use tools. However, the principal tools of emergency managers are intellectual and conceptual, involving relationships of people, things, and places [21, 22, 23].

While it is easy to see the intellectual heritage of the emergency management field, it is less easy to find a unifying theme for its practice, since emergency management encompasses an enormous array of activities taking place at many temporal scales and at multiple organizational levels. Indeed, much of what emergency managers do does not involve emergencies, but rather involves reducing the likelihood of emergency (mitigation) or preparing to respond to one (preparedness) [22]. These activities involve management as generally understood. In a recent essay for example, Pine discusses how management theory applies to emergency management, identifying a number of management principles that relate to recognized emergency management activities [23]. These principles include long-term and strategic management approaches, sustainability, diversity, systems theory, and flexible thinking and flexible structures. He stresses the need for "improving the management in emergency management." Our assessment is generally congruent with Pine's comments on the intersection of management theory with emergency management, and that the emergency management discipline shares certain analogous historical trajectories, as in both fields' borrowing of themes and practices from other disciplines. However, although the applicability of management theory to emergency management can be seen, application of management principles is more by the accident of situational necessity than by conscious effort to incorporate management theories. As a consequence much insight is lost, and there is a tendency to see emergency management as a separate kind of management, where ordinary rules don't apply. But people are people whether the milieu is corporate or crisis, and there is no good reason to suppose that the social relationships of organizations in emergency are going to be different from the relationships that function in other situations. In fact, the guiding idea at the founding of the disasters field was the opposite: that disasters were an opportunity to examine social relationships in a compressed time interval [24, pg. 654], an idea that depended on the congruence of these relationships in both crisis and normal times. It might be more accurate to argue for the need for "putting the management into emergency management" because although we can see the relevance of management science and the appearance of social phenomena that occur in other settings explicit management applications are sketchy at best in emergency scenarios.

There is one exception to this observation about the sketchiness of management theory in emergency management, and that is the near-universal approval of the Incident Command System, which was developed according to the management principles that were ascendant in the early to mid-1970s [25]. These principles have, however, been superseded in many applications, especially those focusing on rapidly-changing environments [26]. Thus management theory's most significant and enduring impact is in a largely obsolete organizational scheme [27].

If we are going to put the management into emergency management, what should it look like? While it is beyond the scope of this paper to offer a complete mapping of management principles to emergency settings (a task begun by [23]), we argue that creativity and improvisation are good candidates for comprising an orienting theme or set of concepts for emergency management in the response phase. If we take the view that disasters are social events, as Dombrowsky [28] and others have argued, involving disrupted social structure, as in Fritz's definition [24, pg. 655], we can see that emergency managers manage social relationships to correct those disruptions. They do this by rapidly recombining resources, skills, and experience, capitalizing on agreements, expectations, and norms.

Either for improving the management in the field, or for putting it in, an updated approach is needed. Pine suggests the need for "more dynamic organizational structures" that are responsive to changing needs, especially given the open system character of emergency management operations [23]. Emergencies are the most open of open systems; much of the management, when an emergency is involved, is of fleeting and transient things. Individual and organizational participants come and go, so that emergency managers are really managing a shifting pastiche of relationships and arrangements. They are managing, or trying to manage, interactions of social and physical systems, not in the comparatively stable situation of a factory or a firm, but in the changing circumstances of environmental turbulence.

Harrald asserts that characteristics of both "agility and discipline" are needed so that organizations can maintain their coherence while at the same time respond to surprising conditions [29]. Plans and structures that allow for easy modification facilitate both the shared operational concepts and mutable procedures needed in crisis, but practice together, as in a jazz band or theater ensemble, is need to fine-tune the artistry of response. We would argue for a scientific basis of emergency management that emphasizes management, not emergency, but it should be the management of dynamism, of ambiguity, and of change. Only improvisational skills can provide the necessary capacity for this spirited approach to crisis.

7. Acknowledgement

Funds for portions of this research were provided by Multidisciplinary Center for Earthquake and Engineering Research (MCEER) New Technologies in Emergency Management, No. 00-

10-81 and Measures of Resilience No. 99-32-01; the National Science Foundation; the Public Entity Risk Institute No. 2001-70 (Kathleen Tierney, Principal Investigator); National Science Foundation No. 0603561 and 0510188 (James Kendra and Tricia Wachtendorf, Principal Investigators) and the University of Delaware Research Foundation (Tricia Wachtendorf, Principal Investigator). We are grateful to the South Street Seaport Museum (Mr. Jeffrey Remling, Collections Director), for access to interviews with participants in the waterborne operations. Funding to the museum for these interviews was provided by the National Endowment for the Humanities, and the interviews were conducted by David Tarnow.

References

[1] K.J. Tierney, Lessons learned from research on group and organizational responses to disasters. Paper presented at Countering Terrorism: Lessons Learned from Natural and Technological Disasters. Academy of Sciences (2002, February 28-March 1).
[2] G. Kreps, Organizing for emergency management. In T.E. Drabek, G.J. Hoetmer, editors. *Emergency management: Principles and practice for local government.* International City Management Association; 1991. p 30-54.
[3] T.E. Drabek, Coordinating disaster response: A strategic perspective. Paper presented at the Western Social Science Association Meeting, Reno, Nevada (2001, April).
[4] K.E. Weick, Improvisation as a mindset for organizational analysis. *Organization Science* **9** (1998), 543-555.
[5] T. Wachtendorf, Improvising 9/11 organizational improvisation following the World Trade Center disaster (Doctoral dissertation). Newark: University of Delaware, Department of Sociology and Criminal Justice; 2004.
[6] T. Wachtendorf, J. Kendra, Improvising disaster in the City of Jazz: Organizational response to Hurricane Katrina. [Online] Available from: URL: http://understandingkatrina.ssrc.org/Wachtendorf_Kendra/ [2006, May 11]
[7] C. Rubin, Emergency management in the 21st century: Dealing with Al Qaeda, Tom Ridge, and Julie Gerberding. Working Paper 108. Natural Hazards Research and Applications Information Center. University of Colorado: Boulder; 2004.
[8] S. Funtowicz, J.R. Ravetz, Three types of risk assessment and the emergence of post-normal science. In S. Krimsky, D. Golding, editors. *Social theories of risk.* Westport: Praeger; 1998. p 251-273.
[9] A.M. Weinberg, Science and its limits: The regulator's dilemma. *Issues in Science and Technology* **2/1** (1985), 59-72.
[10] C. Moorman, A.S. Miner, Organizational improvisation and organizational memory. *The Academy of Management Review* **23** (1998), 698-723.
[11] A. Miner, P. Bassoff, C. Moorman, Organizational improvisation and learning: A field study. *Administrative Science Quarterly* **46** (2001), 304-337.
[12] J.M. Kendra, T. Wachtendorf, Community innovation. In H. Rodriguez, E.L. Quarantelli, R. Dynes, editors. *Handbook of disaster research.* New York: Springer; 2006. p 316-334.
[13] J. Kendra, T. Wachtendorf, Elements of resilience after the World Trade Center disaster: Reconstituting New York City's Emergency Operations Center. *Disasters* **27/1** (2003), 37-53.
[14] D. Buck, J. Trainor, B. Aguirre, A critical evaluation of the Incident Command System and NIMS. *Journal of Homeland Security and Emergency Management* **3/3** (2006).
[15] G.A. Bigley, K.H. Roberts, The Incident Command System: High-reliability organizing for complex and volatile task environments. *Academy of Management Review* **44** (2001), 1281-1299.
[16] W. Langewiesche, *American ground: Unbuilding the World Trade Center.* New York: North Point Press; 2002.
[17] J. Kendra, T. Wachtendorf, Reconsidering convergence and converger legitimacy in response to the World Trade Center disaster. *Research in Social Problems and Public Policy* **11** (2003), 97-122.
[18] J. Kendra, T. Wachtendorf, Creativity in emergency response to the World Trade Center disaster. In Natural Hazards Research and Applications Information Center, Public Entity Risk Institute, and Institute for Civil Infrastructure Systems. *Beyond September 11th: An account of post-disaster research,* No. 39. Special Publication. Boulder: Natural Hazards Research and Applications Information Center, University of Colorado; 2003. p 121-146.
[19] K.E. Weick, Drop your tools: An allegory for organizational studies. *Administrative Science Quarterly* **41/2** (1996), 301-313.

[20] D. Beunzaand, D. Stark, A desk on the 20th floor: Survival and sense-making in a trading room. Working Paper Series, Center on Organizational Innovation, Columbia University; 2003. [Online] Available from: URL: http://www.coi.columbia.edu/pdf/beunza_stark_d20.pdf [2006, October 25]
[21] E.L. Quarantelli, Ten criteria for evaluating the management of community disasters. *Disasters* **21** (1997), 39-56.
[22] D. McEntire, What should we call what we do: Comprehensive vulnerability management. 8th Annual Emergency Management Higher Education Conference National Emergency Training Center Emmitsburg, Maryland (2005).
[23] J. Pine, The contributions of management theory and practice to emergency management. In D. McEntire, editor. *Disciplines and disasters*. Emmitsburg: Federal Emergency Management Agency; 2006.
[24] C.E. Fritz, Disasters. In R.K. Merton, R.A. Nisbet, editors. *Contemporary social problems: An introduction to the sociology of deviant behavior and social disorganization*. Riverside: Univ. of California Press; 1961. p 651-694.
[25] L.R. Irwin, The Incident Command System (ICS). In E.A.D. Heide, editor. *Disaster response: Principles of preparation and coordination*. Unpaginated online edition; 1989. [Online] Available from: URL: http://orgmail2.coe-dmha.org/dr/Download.htm [2006, November 11]
[26] R.L. Daft, *Organization theory and design*. Mason: Southwestern; 2004.
[27] W. Waugh, Mechanisms for collaboration in emergency management: ICS, NIMS, and the problem with command and control. 2006 Collaborative Public Management Conference, Syracuse University Greenberg House, Washington, D.C. (2006, September 28-30).
[28] W.R. Dombrowsky, Again and again: Is a disaster what we call a 'disaster'? *International Journal of Mass Emergencies and Disasters* **13/3** (1995), 241-254.
[29] J.R Harrald, Agility and discipline: Critical success factors for disaster response. *Annals of the American Academy of Political and Social Science* **604** (2006), 256-272.

Coordinated Response to Man-made and Natural Disasters

Naim KAPUCU
*Assistant Professor, Department of Public Administration,
University of Central Florida, USA*

Abstract. This paper addresses the problem of inter-organizational coordination in response to extreme events. Extreme events require coordinated action among multiple actors across many jurisdictions under conditions of urgent stress, heavy demand, and tight time constraints. Inter-organizational coordination depends upon the technical structure and performance of the information systems that support decision making among the participating organizations. Interactions among human managers, computers, and organizations under suddenly altered conditions of operation are complex and not well understood. Yet, coordinating response operations to extreme events is an extraordinarily complex task for public agencies. This paper analyzes the interactions among public, private, and nonprofit organizations that evolved in response to the September 11, 2001 attacks, examining the relationships among organizations in terms of timely access to information and types of supporting infrastructure.

Keywords. Inter-organizational networks, social capital, network organizations, public value, extreme events, emergency management

Introduction

Public management increasingly takes place in settings of networked actors who necessarily rely on each other. Building networks of effective action is a very difficult task. It is particularly difficult in dynamic environments of disasters. The appropriate design, role, and application of these interacting mechanisms - including their relations to each other, and the appropriate relationships among organizations across sectors and jurisdictions are not well understood. As Chisholm [1] argues, contrary to contemporary principles of public administration, we should actively resist the temptation to consolidate and centralize our public organizations. Rather, we should carefully match organizational design with observed types and levels of interdependence, since organizational systems that on the surface appear to be tightly linked webs of interdependence on closer examination often prove decomposable into relatively simpler subsystems that may be coordinated through decentralized, informal organizational arrangements.

This paper explores the process of emerging inter-organizational networks in response to the World Trade Center (WTC) disaster and addresses the following questions:

- How did inter-organizational networks evolve in response to the September 11, 2001 terrorist attacks to the WTC in New York City?
- What primary organizations were involved in response to the attacks?

- How can inter-organizational coordination be better organized to function more effectively under emergency conditions?

This paper focuses on the manner in which emergency management and crisis-relevant organizations in the City of New York coordinated with other responding organizations and jurisdictions to develop multi-organizational strategies for managing the WTC disaster.

1. Conceptual Background

This section provides the theoretical foundations for the study of inter-organizational networks in emergencies by surveying the literature from general organizational theory to the theory of systems in emergencies. These theories together provide insights for understanding interactions among organizations, and they help explain successful inter-organizational network in emergencies. The paper uses the theoretical framework primarily drawn from dynamic network theory, complex adaptive systems theory, and social capital theory [2, 3, 4, 5, 6, 7, 8].

1.1. Social Basis for Networks in Emergencies

Inter-organizational network refers to any intentionally collaborative relationship between two or more organizations which joins resources to identify and subsequently pursue a joint approach to solving societal problems. Multilateral collaborations, public-private and public-nonprofit partnerships are just some examples of this phenomenon. Inter-organizational networks can also be perceived as a social exchange involving commitment of knowledge, skills, and emotions by leaders and staff of participating organizations. From an organizational standpoint, organizational network entails the commitment of organizational resources to an initiative involving two or more entities that come together and act on recognition that they cannot accomplish their missions alone [9].

Since inter-organizational networks are based on a recognition of key inter-dependencies across sectors and organizations, and thus on the need for inter-organizational collaboration to solve emergent problems, they also require effective mobilization and utilization of many available community resources, public as well as private. Given the voluntary nature of networks, their effectiveness depends, for the most part, on the willingness of an array of individuals across organizations to participate in and contribute to the success of the collaborative endeavor. The value of effective collaborative relationships as well as the complexities and challenges they present have been recognized by many researchers, and they continue to be a frequent subject of scholarly and practitioner-oriented literature [9, 10, 11, 12, 13].

Social capital has been applied in a variety of contexts to explain the ability of communities to solve the problems of collective action, ranging from the provision of public education, to the maintenance of effective and smooth-functioning government institutions, as well as the exercise of informal control over criminal behavior. Social capital, in this study, is conceived as an incentive for inter-organizational networks and collective behavior in emergencies. In the public sector, issues involving the creation of 'public value' across organizational boundaries have gained more importance since 9/11, both in terms of information-sharing and in terms of collective action across different sectors (public and nonprofit), including units at different levels of government (federal, regional, state, county, and city).

1.2. Inter-organizational Networks

A network is group of actors who, on a voluntary basis, exchange information and undertake joint activities and who organize themselves in such a way that their individual autonomy remains intact. In this definition, the important points are that the relationship must be voluntary and that belonging to the network does not affect the autonomy and independence of the members. Networks are based on mutuality and multi-directional information exchange and resource sharing. Inter-organizational network describes a certain kind of communication capacity that facilitates efficient communications among organizations. This means that there is some element of trust in the relationship so that post-transaction adjustments to meet the parties' needs and interests can be quickly addressed with minimal inter-organizational resistance.

Cleveland [14] predicts that organizations are moving toward a more horizontal style of management in which leadership is shared and decisions are often made on the basis of expertise rather than positions.

"The organizations that get things done will no longer be hierarchical pyramids with most of the real control at the top. They will be systems -interlaced webs of tension in which control is loose, power diffused, and centers of decision plural… Because organizations will be more horizontal, the way they are governed is likely to be more collegial, consensual, and consultative. The bigger the problems to be tackled, the more real power is diffused and the larger the number of persons who can exercise it -if they work at it" [14, pg. 13].

Ackoff [15] points out that many important current problems are "messes" that actually involve sets of interconnected problems. The multifaceted nature of these complex problems makes them extremely difficult to conceptualize and analyze, and which are immune to simple solutions [1]. This complexity and interdependence often requires extensive collaboration among different types and various levels of organizations. Forming and developing inter-organizational networks represents a response to this complexity and interdependence. Milward [16] uses "hollow state" to characterize what he regards as the increasingly networked character of public management. Despite the evidence that networks are very important for public administration, much of the discussion of this subject has been vague [17, 18]. Helpful starts have been made in other fields. In particular, sociologists and public choice specialists have developed rich conceptualizations regarding networks [19, 20, 21]. Network perspective gained significant attention in explaining the intergovernmental networks [22, 23]. Berry et al. [24] seek to provide research insights to the study of public management networks.

1.3. Inter-organizational Networks in Response to Extreme Events

Extreme events are occurrences that are notable, rare, unique, and profound, in terms of their impacts, effects, or outcomes. When extreme events occur at the interface between natural, social and human systems, they are often called "disasters" [25]. The September 11, 2001 terrorist attack is an example of an extreme event with significant impact upon humanity. All members of the community were affected, and no single organization could have managed the response alone. The initial conditions in which the incidents occurred shaped distinctively the emergence of the response systems in New York City. At the World Trade Center, the physical devastation was catastrophic. The attacks caused not only the collapse of the 110-story twin towers, with an estimated 20,000 people in the buildings at the time of the attacks, but also the complete or partial loss of five smaller buildings in the immediate area, and heavy damage to twelve other buildings in the roughly six-square-block area in which the towers were located. In addition, the electrical power generation and distribution system for lower Manhattan was destroyed; the water distribution system, dependent upon electricity for pumping water, was disabled; gas pipelines were heavily damaged; and the telephone and telecommunications services were seriously disrupted [26].

Extreme events trigger greater density of communication and interaction among organizations. Trustworthiness and social capital can, especially, play an important role in extreme events within which there is no clear policy or guidelines available to the participant organizations and individuals. Organizational networks facilitate the rapid dissemination of information among members and reduce the asymmetries of information that can otherwise discourage profitable transactions. Social capital improves access to resources among network members and allows members to solve collective action problems more easily with less fear of defection and free riding.

The capacity of a society to understand and manage emergencies depends on its ability to understand, anticipate, prepare for, and respond to them. Aaron Wildawsky describes resilience as "the capacity to cope with unexpected dangers after they have become manifest, learning to bounce back" [27, pg. 77]. Communities responding to disasters are seen as coping collectively with shared pain, loss, and disruption and as temporarily suspending ongoing conflicts and disagreements in the interest of meeting urgent needs and beginning the recovery process. Resilient communities are characterized by reduced failure, measured in terms of lives lost, damage, and negative social and economic impacts, and reduced time to recovery - that is, more rapid restoration of the social systems and institutions to their normal, pre-disaster levels of functioning.

The previous sections provided the theoretical foundations for the study of inter-organizational networks and developed a conceptual framework for understanding inter-organizational networks in dynamic environments of extreme events. Studying an extreme event independent of its context provides incomplete knowledge. Extreme events reflect not just actions, but interactions. Such complexities add greater challenge to the understanding and anticipation of extreme events and their consequences. Disseminating useable knowledge through an organization and improving the ability to create value across organizational boundaries are especially important in emergencies.

Organizations can contribute to resilience in a society by incorporation with other emergency response organizations based on trust and by integrating volunteers into emergency response operations as appropriate. Based on the inter-organizational networks conceptual framework in dynamic context discussed above, this paper assumes the following: Extreme events will likely lead to greater density of communication among organizations and less centralized networks; as organizations increase their interactions, they have greater opportunity to share information and resources; to the extent that organizations share information and resources, they can increase coordination; and as organizations improve their coordination, victims in impacted areas will be served better by integrating volunteers into emergency operations as appropriate.

Figure 1 illustrates the actual inter-organizational networks from the FEMA New York situation reports data. The nonprofit organizations represented were Salvation Army, Jacoby Medical Center, Church of Scientology, Veterinary Medical Assistance Team (VMAT), Southern Baptist Kitchens, City Harvest, Adventist Disaster Services, New York City Volunteer Organizations Active in Disasters (NYC VOAD), New York City Volunteer Network, New York City Bar Association, and Volunteer Agencies (VOLAG). The private organizations represented were the following organizations from FEMA situation reports: Consolidated Edison, NY Stock Exchange, Prime Power, John Deere, MapInfo Corporation, and United Parcel Service.

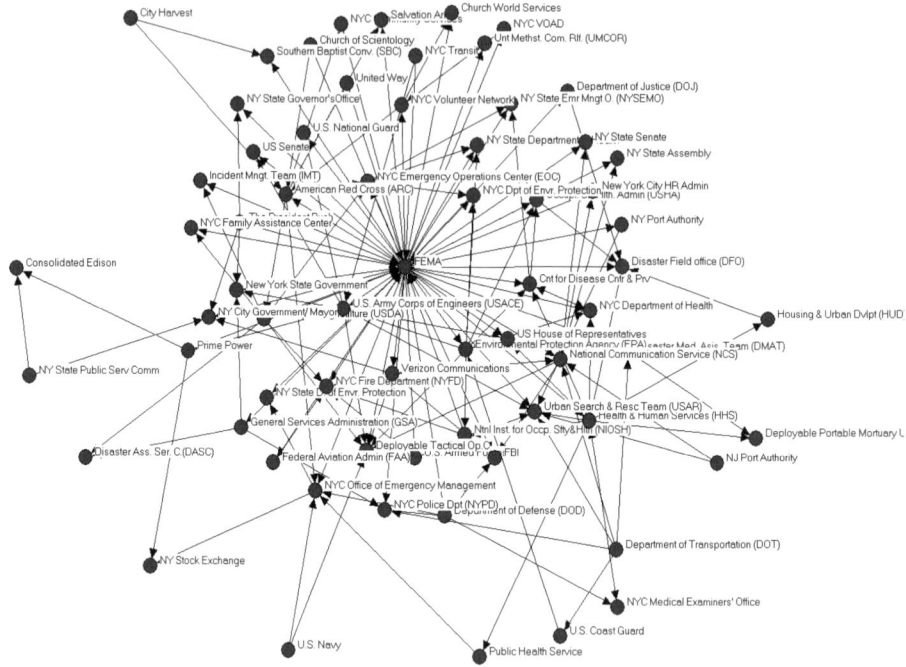

Figure 1. Inter-organizational network
(Source: Situation Reports, Federal Emergency Management Agency, 2001, September 11- October 4)

In Figure 1, there are a limited number of actors (67), and all of them are 'connected.' But, clearly not every possible connection is present. There appear to be some differences among the actors in how connected they are. If we compare FEMA and New York City Emergency Operation Center (NYCEMO) with HUD and GSA for example, we can easily see the difference. FEMA and NYCEMO are in the center of the activities. On the other hand, HUD and GSA are not well connected to other organizations. We can also see that some actors' connections are likely to be reciprocated in this network but some others are not.

2. Inter-organizational Networks in Response to the WTC Attacks in 2001

Several organizations responded to the WTC disasters are seen as coping with "shared risk." The terrorist bombing at the WTC site in 1993 had promoted officials to devote considerable time to emergency preparedness in New York City. These activities yielded benefits in the cities' response operations after 9/11. The coordinated response by several hundred organizations and individuals, with very little direct oversight by any single organization, was established within hours after the attack.

As demonstrated in Figure 1, organizations realized that the recovery task, if it was to be performed fast enough to prevent further disaster from occurring, lay well beyond their capabilities as individual organizations. Because many of the organizations, (but not all), involved in the recovery effort had previously exchanged information and resources with each other, they made use of [3] lines of communication, information resources, and social networks that were already established. Good planning prior to disasters and trust among the organizations prior to disasters helped inter-organizational networks work in disaster response operations.

As a result of already established networks, the resilience of the community response to the WTC disaster was effective. Even though the facility that constituted the central node in the City's emergency management coordination system, the Emergency Operations Center (EOC) at 7 World Trade Center, had to be evacuated following the attack and collapsed in late afternoon on September 11. Both the management and the conduct of emergency response activities continued uninterrupted through the most intense phase of the crisis starting immediately after the attacks. Having lost a technology-rich, state-of-the art facility, experiencing very significant communications disruptions, and facing a massive tragedy unforeseen even in their worst-case plans, some response organizations in New York City, showed resiliency to mobilize and coordinate resources of public and private agencies.

Inadequate communication patterns such as disjointed information flows prohibit formation of inter-organizational networks. Communication can determine the success or failure of a disaster response [28]. The effective flow of information across organizational boundaries is critical for an organization's ability remain effective in dynamic environments. Communications that result in more accurate public perceptions of risk are comprised of multiple communications, arranged in a programmatic format, that take a variety of communication variables or factors into account [29]. If responders are not in contact with each other (as was the case between fire and police departments in New York City), and if information (whether a report or instruction) does not flow properly, it is hard to envision a successful disaster response.

The rescuers' ability to save themselves and others was hobbled by technical difficulties and management lapses that have been part of the emergency response culture in New York City and other regions for years. When the firefighters needed to communicate, their radio system failed, just as it had in those same buildings eight years earlier, during the response to the 1993 bombing at the trade center. No other agency lost communications on 9/11 to such devastating effect, as the Fire Department. Throughout the crisis, the two largest emergency departments, Police and Fire, barely spoke to coordinate strategy or to share intelligence about building conditions. During those final minutes, most firefighters inside the north tower did not know the other building had crumbled, and how urgent it was for them to get out. Others were awaiting orders in the lobby. Still others were evacuating the disabled and the frightened [26]. Lack of prior established networks prior to disasters and poor relationships or no relationships prior to disasters can lead to non-functioning networks in disaster response operations.

3. Conclusion

The paper examined the inter-organizational networks to achieve public service goals in emergencies. The study used the WTC disaster which was a high-impact disaster that cut across geographical jurisdictions and functional lines too large to be handled by the local organizations. The study demonstrated complex inter-organizational networks composed of public, private, and nonprofit organizations. The complex inter-organization networks cannot be accomplished without an existing trust between government agencies at all levels and between the private and nonprofit organizations. It is very important for success of a disaster response operation that organizations must develop working relationships before any disaster occurs. Otherwise it will be very difficult to know the contact people in each organization and develop working relationships in highly stressful environments of disasters.

In order to foster linkages and the trust that would enable accelerating inter-organizational network coordination in emergency management response operations, first public emergency management agencies should provide incentives and information to promote inter-organizational networks. Second, greater decentralization within emergency management would allow for greater responsiveness without loss of control. Finally, the key enabler to strengthening networks may be the use of organizational social capital from the voluntary and private sector organizations.

References

[1] R.F. Chisholm, *Developing network organizations: Learning from practice and theory.* New York: Addison-Wesley; 1998.
[2] J. Scott, *Social network analysis.* Thousand Oak: SAGE Publications; 2000.
[3] R. Axelrod, M.D. Cohen, *Harnessing complexity: Organizational implications of a scientific frontier.* New York: Free Press; 1999.
[4] K.M. Carley, On the evolution of social and organizational networks. In S.B. Andrews, D. Knoke, editors. *Networks in and around organizations.* Special Issue of Research in the Sociology of Organizations (Volume 16). Stamford: JAI Press, Inc.; 1999. p 3-30.
[5] J. Holland, *Hidden order: How adaptation builds complexity.* Reading: Addison Wesley Publishing, Company; 1995.
[6] S. Wasserman, K. Faust, *Social network analysis: Methods and applications.* New York and Cambridge: Cambridge University Press; 1994.
[7] N. Nohria, R. Eccles, editors, *Networks and organizations.* Cambridge: Harvard Business School Press; 1992.
[8] J. Coleman, *Foundations of social theory.* Cambridge: Belknap, Harvard University Press; 1990.
[9] B. Gray, *Collaborating: Finding common ground for multiparty problems.* San Francisco: Jossey-Bass; 1989.
[10] P.J. Robertson, Inter-organizational relationships: Key issues for integrated services. In J. McCroskey, S.D. Einbinder, editors. *Communities and universities: Remaking professional and interprofessional education for the next century.* Westport: Greenwood Publishing Group; 1998. p 67-87.
[11] R.M. Kanter, Collaborative advantage: The art of alliances. *Harvard Business Review* **72/4** (1994), 96-108.
[12] W.W. Powell, Neither market nor hierarchy: Network form of organization. In B.M. Staw, L.L. Cummings, editors. *Research in organizational behavior* (Volume 12). Greenwich: JAI Press; 1990. p 295-336.
[13] J.D. Thompson, *Organizations in action: Social science bases of administrative theory.* New York: McGraw Hill Book Company; 1967.
[14] H. Cleveland, *The future executive.* New York: Harper Collins; 1972.
[15] R.L. Ackoff, *Redesigning the future: A systems approach to societal problems.* New York: Wiley; 1974.
[16] H.B. Milward, editor, Symposium on 'The Hollow State: Capacity, Control and Performance in Inter-organizational Settings.' *Journal of Public Administration Research and Theory* **6** (1996), 193-313.
[17] G.L. Wamsley, R.N. Bacher, C.T. Goodsell, P.S. Kronenberg, *Refounding public administration.* Newbury Park: Sage Publications; 1990.
[18] K.G. Provan, H.B. Milward, Do networks really work? A framework for evaluating public-sector organizational networks. *Public Administration Review* **61/4** (2001), 414-423.
[19] H.T. Miller, Post-progressive public administration: Lessons from policy networks. *Public Administration Review* **54** (1994), 378-385.
[20] K.S. Cook, J.M. Whitmeyer, Two approaches to social structure: Exchange theory and network analysis. *Annual Review of Sociology* **18** (1992), 109-127.
[21] E. Ostrom, *Governing the commons: The evolution of institutions for collective action.* Cambridge: Cambridge University Press; 1990.
[22] L.J. O'Toole, Jr., K. Meier, Public management in intergovernmental networks: Matching structural networks and managerial networking. *Journal of Public Administration Research and Theory* **14/4** (2004), 469-495.
[23] R. Agranoff, M. McGuire, Another look at bargaining and negotiating in intergovernmental management. *Journal of Public Administration Research and Theory* **14/4** (2004), 495-512.

[24] F.S. Berry, R.S. Brower, O.S. Choi, W.X. Goa, H. Jang, M. Kwon, J. Word, Three traditions of network research: What the public management research agenda can learn from other research communities. *Public Administration Review* **64/5** (2004), 539-552.
[25] E.L. Quarantelli, R.R. Dynes, *Disasters: Theory and research.* Beverly Hills: Sage; 1977.
[26] The 9/11 Commission Report, *Final report of the National Commission on terrorist attacks upon the United States.* New York: W.W. Norton & Company; 2004.
[27] A. Wildavsky, *Searching for safety.* New Brunswick: Transaction Publishers; 1971.
[28] J. Levinson, H. Granot, *Transportation disaster response handbook.* New York: Academic Press; 2002.
[29] C. Fitzpatrick, D.S. Mileti, Public risk communication. In R.R. Dynes, K.J. Tierney, editors. *Disasters, collective behavior, and social organizations.* Newark: University of Delaware Press; 1994.

Reassessing FEMA and its Role in Preparing the Nation: Recommendations to Respond Effectively to Disasters

Sıddık EKICI and David A. McENTIRE
University of North Texas, USA

Abstract. In this paper we evaluate the emergence and the role of the Federal Emergency Management Agency (FEMA) in preparing the America to respond effectively to disasters. We see FEMA's constant changing focus based on the developments of homeland security as a problem. We first review the creation and evolution of FEMA and expose the tension between the civil defense and natural hazards perspectives. We acknowledge the growing threat of terrorism and evaluate its impact on emergency management policy. We then examine the mistakes made during the response to Hurricane Katrina and conclude with recommendations for the future. We suggest that FEMA should remain prepared to deal with any kind of disaster.

Keywords. FEMA, disaster, mitigation, emergency management, Department of Homeland Security, terrorism

Introduction

Human beings have been dealing with emergency situations since the beginning of time. Regardless of whether these responses to disasters were undertaken consciously or unconsciously in the past, they are today certainly matters that are addressed by experts in a more professional manner. Nevertheless, mistakes continue to be made and there are several opportunities to improve emergency management. This is true even in countries such as the US, which have had a great deal of experience with disasters.

In the following paper we discuss the emergence and the shifting focus of FEMA over time. We first examine the creation and evolution of FEMA as well as the impact of terrorism and 9/11. We then explore some of the significant mistakes associated with Hurricane Katrina and conclude with recommendations for the future. Our central argument is that FEMA requires a more stable theoretical framework or policy guide - one that is not easily influenced by changes in the political landscape or by the most publicized and recent disaster.

1. Emergency Management and the Historical Context of FEMA

Emergency management is responsible for dealing with disasters, which Donahue and Tuohy define as [1, pg. 2]:

"devastating, natural accidental, or willful events that suddenly result in severe negative economical consequences for the populations they affect, often including physical injury, loss of life, property damage and physical and emotional hardship, destruction of physical infrastructure, and failure of administrative and operational systems."

Emergency management is therefore concerned about natural disasters such as (but not limited to) floods, earthquakes, hurricanes, storm surges, tornadoes, tsunamis, volcanic eruptions, extreme heat, hailstorms and land subsidence. In addition, emergency management addresses technological disasters such as hazardous material incidents and nuclear accidents as well as terrorism involving weapons of mass destruction [2]. The goal of emergency management is to intervene in a disaster, avoid disasters, or handle all types of operations before, during or after a disaster [1]. For this reason, Haddow and Bullock [2, pg.1] assert that emergency management deals "with risk and risk avoidance," and is seen as a vital role of the government during emergency situations. Although the cities, counties and states are required by the constitution to meet public needs regarding health and safety issues, the US federal government has the obligation to support states when they get overwhelmed as a result of the aforementioned situations [2].

The federal government first became involved in local disasters when a Congressional Act was passed in 1803 to provide financial support to a New Hampshire town which was recovering from its losses caused by a severe fire. Over time, further measures were taken at the national level to deal with disasters. For instance, in the 1930s, the Reconstruction Finance Corporation and the Bureau of Public Roads were authorized to provide loans for those that experienced disasters. Also during this period, the Flood Control Act of 1934 entitled the Army Corps to develop flood prevention projects [2]. However, federal involvement in emergency management witnessed a dramatic increase during the civil defense era and after major natural disasters. This resulted in the creation of the Federal Emergency Management Agency (FEMA), several management challenges, and greater support for the nascent organization.

1.1. Emphasis on Civil Defense

After World War II, the main risk facing the US was presumed to be nuclear war with communists in the Soviet Union. During this era of emergency management, the national focus was on civil defense programs. Many local civil defense structures were formed in this period, and the directors of these agencies were the first recognized emergency managers in the US. Eventually, the Federal Civil Defense Administration (FCDA) was authorized to support the local civil defense authorities, and an office of the FCDA, the office of Defense Mobilization, was opened in the Department of Defense (DOD) to stockpile and mobilize equipment during war time. By 1958 the two offices got merged under the name *Office of Civil and Defense Mobilization* [2]. The central goal was to prepare targeted communities for evacuation in case nuclear war broke out. Emergency management was, in some respects, synonymous with civil defense.

1.2. Recognition of Natural Disasters and Mitigation

The 1950s and the early 1960s were also times when the US faced some severe hurricanes and earthquakes. Funds were allocated to affected states and the Kennedy administration decided to create an Emergency Preparedness Office in the White House in 1961. Additional natural disasters occurred which led to the passage of the National Flood Insurance Act in 1968. The National Flood Insurance Act of 1968 created the National Flood Insurance Program (NFIP). Congressman Hale Boggs of Louisiana played a key role in the passage of the act. He recommended that the nation confront risk before disasters strike. This was the first time that mitigation was formally stated in disaster legislation.

Hurricane Camilla's destruction in 1969 on the coasts of Louisiana, Alabama, Mississippi, and Hurricane Agnes' devastating damage on the Florida coasts encouraged the government to consider additional ways to decrease the losses to the citizens and the expenditures of the national government in fighting disasters. As a result, the Nixon government proposed the mandatory purchase of flood insurance to all homeowners [2].

1.3. The Creation and Management of FEMA

The 1970s witnessed an even greater role for emergency management functions in US federal agencies. Among the agencies assigned with tasks related to emergency management were the Department of Commerce, the General Services Administration, the Treasury Department, the Nuclear Regulatory Commission, and the Department of Housing and Urban Planning (HUD). Considering the wide range of risks (now to include industrial accidents) and ever growing tasks to be completed in emergency management, there were more than 100 federal agencies involved in disasters. This led to overlapping tasks and programs, and confusion over roles and responsibilities [2].

In 1979, President Jimmy Carter created FEMA during his attempt at restructuring the federal government. The newly established entity had two main goals. First, the agency would direct and coordinate disaster relief and hazard mitigation nationwide. The second goal was preparing for nuclear attacks and national security matters which were already carried out by many other agencies. Under the legislation, the FEMA Director was authorized to report directly to the US President [3].

When President Carter lost his second bid for election, the Reagan administration emphasized the second goal and neglected the first one. FEMA was preoccupied with nuclear defense and national security issues while all other disasters remained ignored [3]. Because of this priority, half of FEMA's budget was to prepare the nation for a massive nuclear attack [4]. Other problems began to plague the recently created disaster agency.

Managing FEMA was a challenging task since it was pieced together from many government agencies and assigned numerous monumental tasks. This complexity is revealed when one considers that it had to respond to 23 oversight committees and subcommittees in Congress. Although FEMA did not face any significant natural disaster in the early 1980s, its new Director Louis O. Guiffrida (the President's former advisor), resigned during a grand jury investigation into allegations of fraud and corruption. President Reagan then appointed General Julius Becton as the Director of FEMA. Although Becton initially continued emphasizing the same priorities as Guiffrida had, he later shifted to other issues. He noted that earthquakes, hurricanes, and flood programs were listed at the bottom of a list of 20 of FEMA's major programs. Senator Gore likewise noted that FEMA's priorities were misplaced, and he suggested that FEMA should work more cooperatively with its federal, state and local counterparts on natural hazards [2].

The years between 1989 and 1992 only added to FEMA's troubled history. It faced management, budget and morale problems, and was in conflict with many of its federal and state level partners. Moreover, FEMA showed poor performance in responding to Hurricane Hugo that caused "$15 billion damage and 85 deaths" [2, pg. 9], and to the Loma Prieta earthquake in the Bay area of California. Many claimed that FEMA failed to respond effectively because it spent its last decade focusing on nuclear attacks. A few years later, FEMA experienced another serious test from Hurricane Andrew and failed even more miserably than was it had with Hugo or Loma Prieta. From the perspective of legislators and the public, FEMA was incapable of performing its essential duties [2].

1.4. Ascendance of National Emergency Management

After these troubled years, FEMA was reinvented and reinvigorated with the appointment of James Lee Witt as the Director of FEMA in 1993 [3]. He was nominated by President Clinton and happened to be the first FEMA Director with prior emergency management experience. Witt's knowledge and outstanding management skills helped FEMA to focus on mitigation and risk avoidance as well as the application of modern technologies to improve service delivery in disasters. Although his leadership was soon to be tested by sizable hazards, FEMA responded in a professional manner to the Midwest Floods in 1993 and this drew needed attention to post-disaster recovery operations. FEMA later launched a program called Project Impact with the aim of building disaster-resistant communities. Project Impact encouraged cities and counties to identify risks and develop projects to eliminate them. The project introduced emergency management and mitigation applications in a wide range of settlements. Project-Impact made FEMA a globally recognized organization in emergency management [2]. FEMA's success under Director Witt continued for several years and the significance of emergency management was recognized when President Clinton elevated Witt as a member of his cabinet [2].

2. The Emergence of Terrorism

While the Witt revolution was taking place, a new and unrecognized threat began to emerge in the US. The bombings of both the World Trade Center in 1993 and the Murrah Federal Building in Oklahoma City in 1995 opened a new era for FEMA and slowly began to alter the nature of emergency management. Officials and the public began to question whether the nation was prepared for terrorist incidents. This movement picked up speed when President Bush was elected and especially after the terrorist attacks on 9/11.

2.1. A Growing Threat

After George W. Bush took office, he appointed Joe Albaugh to become the new Director of FEMA. Albaugh's lack of emergency management experience did not seem to be an issue due to his close relationship with President Bush [2]. As soon as Albaugh was approved by Congress, he and President Bush terminated Project-Impact [3], arguing that it was ineffective and a waste of money. They also re-established the

Office of National Preparedness which had been abolished by Witt in 1992, and worked on a Federal Response Plan annex to respond to terrorist attacks [2].

FEMA was now expected to be a lead federal agency under this new planning document. Although terrorism fell into the "all-hazards approach championed by emergency management" [2, pg. 11], FEMA really viewed terrorism matters as requiring more resources and newer technologies to enable the successful responses to the potential use of weapons of mass destruction. The new threats seemed to require a reformation in the current emergency management organization.

2.2. The Impact of 9/11

Although a shift in emphasis was clearly underway, it was the world-shocking attacks that propelled further and even more significant changes in the structure and functions of FEMA. On September 11, 2001, multiple terrorist cells hijacked planes and attempted to use them as weapons of mass destruction. In 3 of the 4 cases the hijackers were successful. All planes were lost in the attacks, and the Pentagon was partially damaged and both towers of the World Trade Center collapsed (along with many others in the vicinity). Around 3,000 individuals perished [5], hundreds were injured, and the economy was severely affected. The nation was quickly awakened to its own sense of vulnerability.

Immediately after the September 11, 2001 terrorist attacks the Federal Response Plan was activated and response operations were initiated in New York and Virginia [2]. As the nation began to heal and recovery activities were underway, the military was ordered to hunt down those responsible and bring them to justice. Troops were sent to Afghanistan and later to Iraq. The nation seemed to be directing all of its attention to thwarting terrorists before they could strike again. Significant changes were taking place in emergency management in the US as well.

Recognizing the growing threat of terrorism, President Bush and Director Albaugh demanded that FEMA focus on terrorism rather than hazard mitigation and disaster relief. They attempted to cut the federal contribution for large-scale natural disasters by 33%, but the Congress prevented that from happening [3]. They created an Office of Homeland Security in the White House and gave it responsibility over counter-terrorism efforts.

In the meantime, Senator Joseph Lieberman and some other Democrats pushed for the establishment of the Department of Homeland Security (DHS) [3]. The Homeland Security Act of 2002 created DHS to protect the nation from terrorist attacks. Bush integrated many agencies with tasks related to national security under the umbrella of DHS to better coordinate and strengthen counter-terrorism efforts [6]. The most sweeping reform of government in the last 50 years resulted in the placement of FEMA under DHS, and caused it to lose its direct link to the President. In time, the Office of Domestic Preparedness was pulled out of FEMA as well.

While additional funding and publicity was given to FEMA, the vast majority of efforts went to thwart terrorism. The all-hazards approach existed in name only, and mitigation and preparedness were important only to the extent that they dealt with potential terrorist disasters. The focus on terrorism was magnified by numerous pieces of legislation in the years after 9/11. Making matters worse, FEMA employees became increasingly disgruntled with such changes and the apparent lack of leadership of Joe Albaugh. Several left the agency, thereby adding insult to an already beleaguered organization. Michael Brown was then appointed to lead FEMA. Unfortunately, his experience in disasters was also limited (at least initially). The nation appeared to be consumed with terrorism and homeland security. This was most visible in the new National Response Plan, which downplayed other types of disasters and added multiple layers of bureaucracy to the country's emergency management system. All other concerns, including the status of FEMA and probability for major natural disasters, took a back seat.

3. Mistakes after Hurricane Katrina

As can be seen, FEMA's natural disaster capabilities were seriously eroded because of the exclusive emphasis on homeland security. Only Hurricane Katrina would cause policy makers to rethink their priorities after 9/11. Unfortunately, by this time, it would be too late.

Hurricane Katrina made landfall in New Orleans on August 29, 2005 in a scenario that strikingly resembled the Hurricane Pam exercise a year earlier. The storm caught people off guard and Lake Ponchartrain overflowed over its poorly maintained retaining walls into the low lying areas of the Big Easy. Approximately 2,500 people died as a result of the flooding. Wind and water damages were estimated at well over $100 billion. The lack of mitigation for this widely anticipated hazard is only overshadowed by the ineffective response that followed.

The response to Katrina exhibited problems that are common to many disasters. For instance, New Orleans was not able to receive aid initially from the federal government because fax machines did not function after the disaster [1]. Also, volunteers such as physicians could not help victims because they were not licensed in the state of Louisiana.

In addition, many of the problems made evident during the response were created by local and state governments. New Orleans failed to use busses to evacuate those people without access to transportation. The state government seemed to have no clue about the impact and did not frame or sign requests for assistance as had been the case with Hurricane Andrew in 1992 [4].

Not all of the challenges were routine or can be blamed on government officials at these levels, however. Even though FEMA was present in New Orleans much quicker than in Miami after Hurricane Andrew, the days after Katrina struck witnessed a plethora of problems created by the federal government. Many of these were ironically a result of the policies pertaining to homeland security. For instance, the evacuations by air were slowed down because the post 9/11 procedures required long searches and detailed security screenings. The intensive security checks held many canned goods back to make sure there were no explosives in them, which delayed or cancelled their delivery to Katrina victims. In addition, DHS and the federal government came up with overlapping operations and unclear plans in responding Hurricane Katrina, and the officers deployed by the federal government to the disaster area lacked field experience [1]. The net result was confusion, delay, and wasted resources. The ineffective response also resulted in unnecessary deaths and suffering as well as a great deal of blame. The federal response to Katrina did not show any acceptable performance at all. According to many, the response by FEMA was seen as a total collapse [3].

3.1. Explanations for FEMA's Failure

Although organizations under stress experience "prosaic" organizational failures [3, pg. 1], FEMA had several more fundamental issues. The failures are best explained in terms of overstated priorities, misguided budgeting, ineffective structural arrangements, and poor managerial performance. Others see the failure as part of a much broader challenge facing governments today.

First, it is now believed that the federal government had focused too much on terrorism. By giving excessive attention to the adverse consequences of terrorism, the President and his advisors had ignored the more likely probability of natural disasters. This had a devastating impact on FEMA's ability to mitigate and react to Hurricane Katrina.

Second, it is asserted that the budgeting process was skewed in favor of terrorism and homeland security. Although FEMA's income had increased since President Bush took office, the amount of funds allocated for natural disasters dramatically decreased so that expenditures for counter-terrorism could be boosted. Around three of four grants are now spent on counterterrorism. Funding for mitigation and emergency management performance grants (the lifeblood of local and state emergency management activities) were cut substantially. This increased our nation's vulnerability to events like Hurricane Katrina [3].

Third, the structural arrangements of FEMA under DHS are regarded to be detrimental and ineffective. In prior years, the Director of FEMA was closely tied to the President. More recently, the FEMA Director has to go through the DHS to reach the President which causes delays in relief operations and responding to disasters [3]. Also, FEMA's new guidelines under the National Response Plan have resulted in additional bureaucratic complexity. FEMA does not have enough flexibility to deal with major disaster response and recovery operations.

Fourth, poor managerial performance is regarded by many to be a key feature of the culture in DHS. The Bush administration has around 15% more political appointees than previous administrations. The assertion is that inexperienced political appointees such as Albaugh and Brown replaced experienced professionals. The outcome was incoherent policy and ineffective implementation [3].

Finally, the changes taking place in government also had an adverse impact on all public administrators. After 9/11, public administrators are facing more challenging and complex administrative problems [7]. The incident drew attention to America's long lasting governance, public services and financial challenges. Simply put, there is more to be done than the current system is able to meet. In terms of emergency management, the tragedy of 9/11 indicated the need to be better prepared for unexpected and expected disasters. Federal, state and local agencies as well as business groups, and individual citizens now feel the need to cooperate and coordinate more to strengthen disaster preparedness [6].

Because of these problems, many have suggested that FEMA should be abolished and replaced with a more effective organization [8]. In essence, legislators are toying with the idea of renaming FEMA. Many believe the new disaster response should remain under DHS, but have closer ties to the President. It is also recommended that the new organization have responsibilities in dealing with both natural disasters and terrorism. Additional human and material resources would be given to the organization to help it meet its monumental challenges.

4. Conclusion

Some scholars such as Donahue and Tuohy state that the problems in emergency management merely lie with resource management, evacuation, situational awareness, communication, and coordination [1, pg. 5]. This is certainly evident when disasters occur. To their list we include another factor that is more prevalent and even more important when policies are made - especially when they are in reaction to major disasters or when there are periods with fewer or less severe disasters. What we believe is of utmost importance is maintaining 'stability in focus and determination' on all kinds of disasters, rather than shifting attention to other issues depending on occurring or non-occurring events.

We argue that some important lessons must be incorporated into US disaster policy from the devastation and desperation of Hurricane Katrina. Donahue and Tuohy's suggestions on learning from mistakes could shed some light on how we should learn from prior mistakes [1]. They advocate evaluating the incident (e.g., finding out what happened and why?), identifying lessons (what were the strengths and the weaknesses of those involved?), and third, reacting accordingly the experience (e.g., clearly determining what should be understood and what changes are required to perform better in the future).

In the context of Katrina, the federal government needs to realize that FEMA's focus should be on all kinds of disasters. This implies that we need to be in an "all time prepared status" for any type of event and not just terrorist attacks or not just natural hazards. We must rethink priorities, budget allotments, and organizational arrangements. Furthermore, we must avoid managerial mistakes, and bring balance to the high demands and constraints placed on government today. Here we understand the importance of the federal government and FEMA. As Wise and Nader point out, only the federal government is in the position to respond to large scale operations such as 9/11 [9]. We can now include Hurricane Katrina or Rita or any other potential disaster that exceeds the control of local or state governments. Since FEMA is the leading organization in large scale disaster related operations, it must be on alert at all times for any risk and be capable of dealing with sizable disasters.

References

[1] A.K. Donahue, R.V. Tuohy, Lessons we don't learn: A study of the lessons of disasters, why repeat them, and how we can learn them. *Homeland Security Affairs* **2/2** (2006). 28 pages. [Online] Available from: URL: http://www.hsaj.org/pages/volume2/issue2/pdfs/2.2.4.pdf [2006, August 25]
[2] G.D. Haddow, J.A. Bullock, *Introduction to emergency management*. Burlington: Elsevier Inc.; 2003.
[3] C. Perrow, Using organizations: The case of FEMA. *Homeland Security Affairs* **1/2** (2005). 10 pages. [Online] Available from: URL: http://www.hsaj.org/pages/volume1/issue2/pdfs/1.2.4.pdf [2006, August 26]
[4] F. Daniel, The FEMA phoenix. *Washington Monthly* **27(7/8)** (1995). Retrieved on August 23, 2006 from Business Source Complete Database.
[5] S. Barr, Security won out over workers, study says (2006, July 25). [Online] Available from: URL: http://ww.washingtonpost.com/wp-dyn/content.article/2006/07/24AR2006072401089.htm [2006, August 15]
[6] D.M. Walker, 9/11: The implications for public-sector management. *Public Administration Review* **62/4** (2002), 94-97.
[7] M.W. Spicer, The war on terrorism and the administration of the American state. *Public Administration Review* **62/4** (2002), 63-68.
[8] *USA Today*. Senate is right: FEMA must go. P.7. (2006, July).
[9] C.R. Wise, R. Nader, Organizing the Federal System for Homeland Security: Problems, issues, and dilemmas. *Public Administration Review* **62/4** (2002), 44-57.

Responding to Terrorist Attacks within the Labyrinth of Independent Governments: Collaborating and Quarrelling

Abraham BENAVIDES and Sebahattin GULTEKIN
University of North Texas, USA

Abstract. How to respond effectively and efficiently to emergencies resulting from the terrorist attacks is an important issue that the public sector needs to reconsider. With the increasing complexity of emergency management, the old response system is facing reorganization and integration. The paper provides a definition of terrorism and its damage to communities. It also explains/outlines the current emergency response model. After identifying problems existing in the current model, the paper offers two other response plans as the inspiration to enhancing mitigation and collaboration of the systems.

Keywords. Terrorism, emergency management, FEMA, DHS, collaboration

Introduction

The field of emergency management in the last few years has become more complicated. On the one hand, it continues to deal with traditional natural and man made disasters. On the other, it has had to absorb emergencies brought about because of politically charged terrorist attacks. Although some believe that responding to emergencies, regardless of their origin, can be done by any agency equipped for this purpose; recent changes to the Department of Homeland Security (DHS) in the US would indicate otherwise. The basic change made to DHS was the reorganization of the Federal Emergency Management Agency (FEMA). In essence, the legislation restored the basic components of emergency management: preparedness, mitigation, response, and recovery. It charged FEMA with the responsibility for dealing with the consequences of all types of vulnerabilities. Additionally, another key component was elevating the status of the Administrator of FEMA within DHS and designating this person to be the chief advisor to the President on disasters.

Fundamentally, FEMA was given more authority to act in response to disasters, whereas previously, under DHS, FEMA was hampered and relegated to a second class status not allowing it to fulfill its original mission. It appeared that the focus on terrorism in DHS clouded the response role of FEMA. These changes can be directly tied to Hurricane Katrina in the fall of 2005. The lack of any coordinated response to this disaster, at all levels of government, showed the inadequacies and proved that FEMA needed to be reorganized in terms of its relationship to DHS. The result was more autonomy and enhanced collaboration. Wamsley and Schroeder [1] note that after Hurricane Andrew in 1992 more emphasis was placed on emergency management as a policy subsystem. In other words, as with Katrina, it took a disaster to bring about changes in a rigid bureaucracy.

The complexity of disasters today, combined with insufficient preparation and the insecurity of not knowing how or when to respond to unpredictable terrorist attacks, makes the job of responding to emergencies a difficult challenge. Just as the relationship between DHS and FEMA has changed, so too is there a need for change in the relationship between FEMA and other levels of government. Primarily the change that needs to occur is less quarreling about whose responsibility it is to respond to various incidents and more collaboration in the response phase of any disaster. Kweit and Kweit [2, pg. 1] argue that intergovernmental response "can be successful if those who respond to the disaster interact in a collaborative network". They go on to consider how collaborative networks can be created and they evaluate some of the recommendations from the report entitled *The Federal Response to Hurricane Katrina*.

Additionally, Schneider [3] develops an explanation for why some governmental responses are successful and others are not. She states that:

"In the aftermath of virtually every disaster situation, a "gap" exists between the emergent norms that guide the social interactions and the bureaucratic norms that dominate governmental activity. When this gap is large, the relief effort is likely to be viewed as a failure; when the gap is small, the effort proceeds smoothly, and government operations are perceived to be successful. Thus the gap is the primary determinant of public perceptions about the success or failure of governmental relief efforts."

The purpose of this article is to add another voice to the growing number of scholars that propose and promote better collaboration within levels of government to more appropriately respond to disasters. To this end we first define terrorism and the devastating effects that it has on communities. Next we examine emergency responses and list key components of the response model. At this point, we list various problems that exist with coordinating response plans. We discuss federalism and how some of the traditions embedded in this form of governance actually hinder collaboration and a joint response plan. Finally, we talk about the National Incident Management System and the National Response Plan as programs that have been instituted to mitigate the coordination problem and promote a collaborative system.

1. What is Terrorism?

Terror events have been increasing for several decades and the 9/11 attacks in New York and Washington highlighted the gravity of the situation. Subsequent attacks in many cities of the world including Bali, Madrid, London, Diyarbakir, and Istanbul confirm that terrorism is not isolated to just one country or group of people but is it a worldwide phenomenon. Terrorism is a new type of war in which the enemy hides among the civilian population and even attacks its own people to make a political statement. Gone are the days of easy identification of the enemy. The enemy is among us. For much of the 21st century, it is likely that terrorism will be on the agenda of policy makers and world leaders. There will still be state conflicts in the traditional sense in which identification of an enemy can be concluded by national boundaries. However, many nations will choose to fight wars using unidentified soldiers and attack innocent civilians to terrorize other nations into compliance with their demands.

With the occurrence of the September 11 attacks, the term, 'terrorism' has been seen overwhelmingly in the media and among politicians and governmental officials all across the world. However, there is no consensus about what terrorism is, how to define it, or even what actions constitute terrorism; the term terrorism is a very controversial concept.

Even the UN Security Council failed to define terrorism [4]. Research shows that according to many scholars, one man's terrorist is another man's freedom fighter [5].

After the 9/11 attacks, the US government declared a war on terrorism. However, what was meant by that has not been clear [6]. Since the term itself is debatable, constructing a very large anti-terrorism coalition becomes problematic and challenging. Therefore, a widely acceptable definition of terrorism is crucial to combating it. Notably, Ganor asserts that an objective and widely acceptable definition of terrorism is possible if the definition is based on international laws and principles [5]. He then defines terrorism as "the deliberate use or the threat to use violence against civilians in order to gain political, ideological, and religious aims" [5, pg. 288].

Terrorism can also simply be defined as a form of violence [7] although there are many more detailed definitions. According to the US Federal Bureau of Investigation (FBI) [8] for example, terrorism is "the unlawful use of force or violence against persons or property to intimidate or coerce a government, the civilian population, or any segment thereof, in furtherance of political or social objectives" [8]. Legislatures have also defined terrorism. In America, the US House of Representatives Permanent Select Committee states that terrorism is "the illegitimate premeditated violence or threat of violence by subnational groups against persons of property with the intent to coerce a government by instilling fear amongst the populace" [9]. In Great Britain, terrorism, in the Prevention of Terrorism Act of 1974, is defined as any violent action to gain political results [6].

Other scholars have also attempted to define terrorism. Dolgova [10, pg. 61], for instance, states that terrorism is "a kind of violence in which physical and psychological violence against innocent victims is used to back up demands made on a third party." Rodin [11, pg. 755] expands the definition by emphasizing that terrorism should be characterized as "the deliberate, negligent, or reckless use of force against noncombatants, by state or nonstate actors for ideological ends and in the absence of a substantively just legal process". This addition of state terrorism is troubling to some, yet a reality in the 21st century.

In terms of types or classes of terrorism, the FBI states that there are two types of terrorism based on objectives, targets, and origin: domestic terrorism and international terrorism [8]. According to Grob-Fitzgibbon [6], there are four types of terrorism: national terrorism which is used to define those who act within national boundaries; revolutionary terrorism that aims to change forms of governments; reactionary terrorism which is the reverse of revolutionary terrorism and works to protect the form of government; and religious terrorism which applies to violence for religious purposes.

It is obvious that a great variety of different characteristics exist in terms of defining terrorism. Consequently, it should be noted, as historian Richard Drake pointed out, "no definition of terrorism can possibly cover all the various forms of state and individual or group violence that have appeared throughout history" [cited in 6, pg. 235]. What is certain, however, is that terrorism is growing in popularity and intensity and nation states will need to learn to respond to various threats to its citizens.

2. Response

In emergency management, the elements that describe the field are mitigation, preparedness, response, and recovery. According to McEntire [12], mitigation refers to disaster prevention and loss reduction; preparedness implies efforts to increase readiness for a disaster; response is the activity in the immediate aftermath of the disaster to protect life and property; and recovery is concerned with returning the affected community to a pre-disaster status or, preferably to an improved situation. These broad areas have a number of subfields such as communications, planning, technology, coordination, and command. For our purposes here the main area we shall discuss is response.

The response phase is aimed at taking action to effectively contain and resolve an emergency. During this stage, the emergency management plans that have been carefully developed are operationalized. There are a number of steps that are taken in addition to activating the plan. We offer six:

1. The deployment of resources is one of the key events that occur. A variety of resources are brought into play that directly addresses the needs of the emergency. If resources are insufficient at that local level, municipalities can tap state and federal resources to meet the needs of the local emergency.
2. The activation a communication plan is essential in conducting an appropriate response. These plans are diverse and can range from local contingency plans to plans that involve other levels of government. It is essential that communication systems are compatible so that individuals and software can speak the same language. Many response plans have unified commands or incident command systems that address interoperability of equipment and messages to the media for wide dissemination.
3. The arrival of the first responders, for whom it is essential that a good relationship exists with the community partners. They must be aware of the particular potential disasters in their specific community. Collaboration between these groups is essential if a successful response is to be achieved.
4. The mobilization of volunteers is an essential part of any response activity. Governmental staff, students, churches, volunteer organizations, service organizations and other groups that could be mobilized should be contacted in advance to secure cooperation. Where appropriate, commitments should be reached with organizations that will render assistance.
5. The creation/implementation of a workable decision-making model in the response phase is crucial to life and property. Local municipalities should have a workable model in place that will allow for flexibility and change. Rigid bureaucracy-type structures are at times inappropriate for responding to disasters because they fail to adapt to the circumstances at hand. There are a number of decision making techniques that would be appropriate for response situations.
6. The acceleration of the recovery plan. One of the final aspects of the response phase is to make a smooth transition between the two phases of response and recover. It must be one obvious to the trained professionals yet seamless to the victims of the tragedy. To better serve the community, it is recommended that overlap in response and recovery be a part of the overall implementation of the emergency management plan.

3. The Problems

A number of problems can be identified in responding to terrorist attacks and other disasters. These range from types of government, such as a federalist system, a lack of preparation, differing types of software and data bases, lack of information sharing, organizational culture, language differences, technical jargon, entrenched assumptions about emergencies, the difficulty of coordinating multiple units with diverse training, general misinformation, and secrecy in paramilitary organizations. Waugh [13] argues that law enforcement agencies "are legendary for their secrecy. They are closed systems that seldom are inclined to involve outside agencies in their efforts and, indeed, on occasion, do not easily share information among their own offices" (pg. 378). He goes on to say that centralized decision processes easily move information from the bottom up but have difficulty getting information from the top down, which can impede information flow and thus some investigations. One of his main conjectures is that other types of organizations may be more beneficial to responding to terrorism or natural disasters because of the way communication and organizational culture impact that organization. Closed systems could overlook other agencies that have critical resources to assist in the response.

Although local governments are the first responders, at times they are left out of the conversation about responding to incidents in their communities. Patricia A. Dalton, Director, Strategic Issues, US General Accounting Office in testimony to the US House of Representatives cautioned that "achieving national preparedness and response goals hinges on the federal government's ability to form effective partnerships with non federal entities. Therefore federal initiatives should be conceived as national not federal in nature. Decision makers have to balance the national interest of prevention and preparedness with the unique needs and interests of local communities" [quoted in 14, pg. 7]. In other words, responding to incidents involves more than just federal, state, and local governments. Instead it involves national, federal state and local governments plus non profit organizations, nongovernmental organizations, churches, schools, the private sector, and any and all interested in assisting in the response. Krane [15] further expounds upon this issue of division of labor between the levels/groups by saying: "perhaps the most important intergovernmental issue is the classic question of the appropriate division of responsibility among the federal, state, and local governments. Similarly this division will have to be determined within each state. Tensions between state and local officials as well as intrastate feuds among local officials have surfaced and are likely to increase in frequency rather than decrease" (pg. 8-9). He goes on to quote Kettl who also weighed in on the matter of intergovernmental relations and said:

"Homeland security is primarily an issue of coordination, but coordination is fundamentally a problem in intergovernmental relations and federalism. Left to its own devises federalism is not likely to respond effectively. It's going to require some innovative strategies for coming at this problem. The consequences for doing so could very well prove to be dangerous - even catastrophic - so the urgency for attacking this problem is huge" [16].

In essence, the problem is that the nature of the federalist system creates independent governments that in many instances have no reason to collaborate unless it is advantageous for them. What they need to realize is what is in it for them is the security of the people they serve.

4. Federalism

Federalism is constitutional sovereignty divided between a central governing authority and constituent political units, such as states or provinces. In the US, there is one federal government with 50 states and a number of local municipalities. The 10th amendment to the US Constitution recognizes and reserves substantial powers for the states. Throughout the history of the US, a number of incidents have caused the line to blur between federal government powers and state powers. Therefore, for federalism to exist at least two of the following elements must be in place. There must be two general levels of government, each deriving power directly from the people. These governments can act directly on the people within their jurisdiction without permission from any other authority. They must be protected by a constitution from being destroyed by the other power and are supreme in the powers assigned to them. Finally, power and functions should be divided between governments and the individuals in this system should have dual citizenship in both governments.

Federalism by nature implies a decentralized system of independent governments. For homeland security purposes this poses a great challenge. According to the 2002 Census of Governments, in the US there are over 87,525 local governments, many with their own police and fire departments. These units of governments can be broken down as 19,429 municipal governments, 16,504 towns or township governments, 3,034 county governments, 13,506 school districts, and 35,052 special district governments. The over 800,000 police officers can be an advantage and a disadvantage to national security. By comparison, the FBI only has around 12,000 agents; there are a total of 75,000 federal agents. Additionally, there are over 1 million firefighters and 155,000 nationally registered emergency medical technicians. For this reason Homeland Security Presidential Directive 5 [17] states clearly:

"The Federal Government recognizes the roles and responsibilities of state and local authorities in domestic incident management. Initial responsibility for managing domestic incidents generally falls on state and local authorities. The Federal Government will assist state and local authorities when their resources are overwhelmed, or when Federal interests are involved."

Thacher [18] looks at this difficulty by first stating that, "any activity performed by nations can be performed by cities, so local governments can easily be enlisted in the service of national goals" (pg. 636). He draws from Peterson [19] and from Grodzins [20] to show that "policy functions can be distributed somewhat arbitrarily among local, state, and national governments" [18]. However, he does note that this perspective of loose distribution of labor fails to account for the "distinctive limits within which local governments operate" [18]. He goes on to support the writings of Peterson by saying:

If a policy mainly benefits jurisdictions other than the one that bears its burdens, it is unlikely that any local government will pursue it; indeed it would generally be inappropriate for a local government to do so because local governments should mainly serve local interests. That obvious fact has important implications for the local role in homeland security because there is often a geographic mismatch between the costs and the benefits of anti-terrorism activities [18, pg. 637].

This can be an issue with local governments because they have in the past and continue to this day to receive a number of unfunded mandates form the US federal governments. However, in terms of equipment for combating terrorism and disasters the federal government in these past years has been very generous in distributing money to states who in turn have allocated these funds to local municipalities.

It has been the practice in the US federal system when local level response has exceeded capabilities that state and federal government level responders are brought onto the scene to augment the local needs. Waugh and Sylves argue that

"emergency managers are well practiced in coordinating their work in multijurisdictional operations. There are lessons to be learned from that system, and the first among them is that emergency management is a bottom-up process. Capacity building has to begin at the level of the first responders who will be responsible for dealing with crisis and their consequences until support arrives. The second lesson is in how multiorganizational, multisector, and intergovernmental operations are coordinated" [13, pg. 147].

Wise [21] also discusses the issues surrounding organizational matters at DHS and suggests that the best organizational structure would be one that is less hierarchical. He notes that "direct command-and-control approaches may even be counter productive because they often encourage resentment and resistance, while collaboration encourages commitment and cooperation" (pg. 142). Wise points out that a "network approach" would probably be more effective in responding and organizing a response to disasters.

Another study by Kincaid and Cole [22] concluded that the American Society for Public Administration scholars "do not believe the terrorist attacks will have a significant impact on US federalism and intergovernmental relations" (pg. 182). They feel that more cooperation and "exchange of information between federal, state, and local officials in the area of disaster relief and emergency preparedness will be the case" (pg. 183). They go on to say that "terrorism has not killed federalism or rendered it a quaint luxury of quiet times; instead 'continuity in crises' perhaps best summarizes their overall views" (pg. 191). In summary, despite the problems with federalism, the system is not broken. What it lacks is a better understanding of what it is and how it works and that the various levels of government can collaborate to enhance the response phase to emergencies.

5. The National Response Plan

The federalist system in the US has sparked the necessity to have some type of national response plan in place to address the needs of various levels of governments in times of disasters. Nevertheless, as Staten [23, pg. 2] indicated that well before 9/11 and hurricane Katrina "local agencies should be aware of the possibility that the assistance of some federal agencies may not be forthcoming for as long as 24 hours, and that they should plan to manage any incident until the arrival of outside agencies". Today the federal government response time has increased from three days to three to six days for full response mode. Katrina and other disasters clearly show that a crucial element of any national response plan is local preparation and self sufficiency. When a natural or man made disaster occurs there are thousands of organizations and people that are willing to help. Waugh [24, pg. 376] points out that these groups and people "bring their resources to bear to provide emergency medical care, search and rescue, emergency shelter and feeding, pet rescue, counseling and so on. These groups all have varying levels of competency and are essential elements in our national emergency management system."

As mentioned earlier, response and collaboration to disasters are not always as smooth as the participants would like them to be. However, a National Response Plan (NRP) is intended to help alleviate some of that confusion. Its major premise is that local governments are the first responders to disasters and that if these first responders are overwhelmed that the next level of government the state should step in to assist. All states in the US have departments of emergency management, although called by different names, in addition to access to the National Guard. If these resources are not sufficient to adequately respond to the disaster the governor of each can make a formal request to the President of the US for a presidential disaster declaration.

Haddow and Bullock [25, pg. 77] describe this process in the following way:

"A request is prepared by state officials in cooperation with regional staff from FEMA. The governor's request is analyzed first by the FEMA regional office and then forwarded to FEMA headquarters in Washington D.C. FEMA headquarter staff review and evaluate the governor's request and forward their analysis and recommendation to the President. The President considers FEMA's recommendation and then makes a decision to grant the declaration or to turn it down. If the President grants a major disaster declaration FEMA activates the National Response Plan (NRP) and proceeds to directs 32 federal agencies and departments including the American Red Cross in support of state and local officials to respond to and recover from the disaster event."

One of the benefits of the NRP is that it makes available to local communities the resource of the federal government. These resources can be water, food, emergency generators, counseling, shelters, meals, and transportation. In the long run, the federal government can secure grants, loans; rebuild roads, tax relief, legal services, and job placement. The NRP goals are "to make the response and recovery aspects of out nation's readiness system as efficient and effective as possible, a cooperative national effort is essential, one with a unified approach to incident management and with the ultimate goal of a significant reduction in our nation's vulnerability over time" [26].

Although the NRP concept was in place at the time that hurricane Katrina hit the city of New Orleans, its implementation was less than successful. Much has been learned since that time and significant changes have been made to avoid some of the pitfalls that typified the federal government's response during Katrina. All levels of government share in the blame, from the local level in its evacuation procedures and failure to correctly assess the situation, to the state level for failing to request a presidential disaster declaration, to the federal government for responding too slowly when it was clear that the state and local levels failed to take corrective action. It is interesting to note that the New Orleans mayor-council form of government failed in its response while council-manager forms of government - with a professionally trained city manager - were much more successful in their response to this disaster. More research should be conducted to see if the form of government and its structure have a direct impact of emergency response.

6. The National Incident Management System

In an effort to mitigate some of the problems of coordination and miscommunication, the US federal government through the Homeland Security Presidential Directive 5 [17] initiated a request to develop a system that would ensure that the various levels of American government in the would have the capacity to be able to work together by standardizing a number of procedures across the country. This system would be called the National Incident Management System (NIMS) and would be a comprehensive national approach to disasters. The Department of Homeland Security defines NIMS "as a core set of doctrines, concepts, principles, terminology, and organizational processes that are applicable to all hazardous situations." NIMS has six broad components:

1. Command and Management
2. Preparedness
3. Resource Management
4. Communication and Information Management
5. Supporting Technologies
6. Ongoing Management and Maintenance

According to Anderson, Compton, and Mason [27, pg. 4] it is "applicable to all levels of government, federal, state, local, and tribal, as well as many private and nongovernmental organizations." NIMS uses the concept of incident command to standardize responses [23]. DHS defines an Incident Command System (ICS) as a "management system designed to enable effective and efficient domestic incident management by integrating a combination of facilities, equipment, personnel, procedures, and communications operating within a common organizational structure" [28]. Anderson, Compton, and Mason go on to say that ICS are "organizationally structured to facilitate the activities in five major functional areas: command, operations, planning, logistics, finance, and administration" [27, pg. 4].

It should also be pointed out that most local governments have an Emergency Operations Center (EOC) these facilities help coordinate major disasters. Compton [29, pg. 9] says that the purpose of the EOC is "to establish a central location from which government, at any level, can provide interagency coordination and executive decision making for managing a major response and recovery effort while providing other essential services simultaneously."

Just as the US has instituted a NRP and NIMS as forms to increase collaboration, we can look to other countries for similar examples of successes and failures. One case in point is the collaboration that exists in the emergency management system in the country of Turkey. As does the US, Turkey has had a similar problem with cooperation and responding to disasters. Although Turkey has not been able to eliminate terrorism and its difficulty with the PKK have caused many deaths; it does have a system in place in which collaboration is taking place and other countries can look to Turkey as an example.

7. Case Study: Emergency Management in Turkey

Turkey has a central administrative structure. It is divided into provinces according to criteria including geographical conditions, economic situations, and public needs. Provinces are also divided into smaller districts. Provinces and districts are administered according to the principle of devolution of powers. In this sense, it should be noted that local administrations are inseparable elements of central government. Therefore, although not a federalist system, Turkey still suffers from some of the same drawbacks of such a system.

The Ministry of Public Works and Settlement has the authority and responsibility for the coordination of preparedness for disasters among central governmental organizations. Correspondingly, General Directorate of Civil Defense, which functions under the Ministry of Internal Affairs, has responsibility to coordinate and prepare governmental organizations. In addition, after the 1999 Marmara Earthquake, Turkish Emergency Management Directorate was founded to play parallel roles. Hence, it can be said that Turkish Emergency Management system has a kind of tripartite structure. However, it is noteworthy that though the above organizations are supposed to plan and prepare for earthquakes they have almost no enforcement to use in order to make a successful disaster management plan. Moreover, there are a number of boards that are established after disasters such as Prime Ministry Crisis Management Center and Central Disasters Coordination Board.

At the local level, local administrative bodies are in charge. Following any kind of disaster, the top local administrator, the appointed governor, and district authorities including mayors are given extraordinary entitlements to respond to disasters effectively and at a local scale. These local administrations depend on the central government. Local administrations can form unions with the permission of the Cabinet to respond to disasters and meet the needs of those who have exprienced earthquakes or any type of disaster. Figure 1 shows a sample preparedness scheme of a local administration.

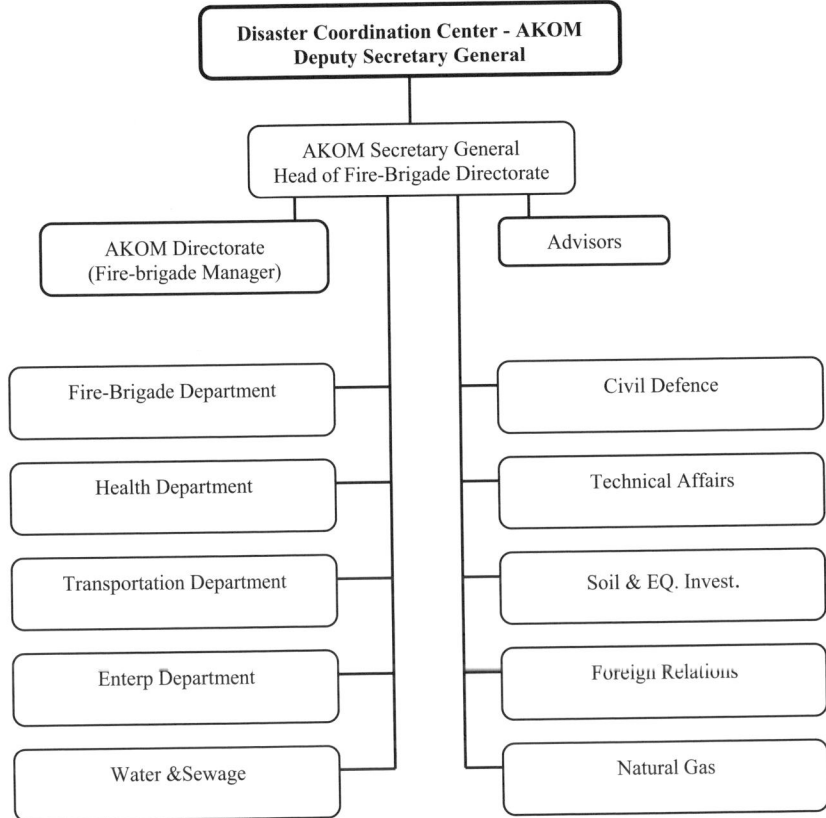

Figure 1. A local disaster preparedness scheme (Istanbul) (Adapted from [30] pg. 18)

Emergency issues are a part of life in Turkey largely because of earthquakes that occur relatively frequently. It is expected that countries such as Turkey develop very effective and well-prepared emergency management systems. However, Turkey, in many instances, has not responded to emergency issues successfully. For example, the General Directorate of Civil Defense plays a central role in emergency management in Turkey. However, it has a very limited capacity which was observed during the response phase of 1999 Marmara Earthquake. Similarly, the Turkish Red Crescent has been subjected to severe criticism due to its incompetence in the 1999 Marmara Earthquake. Non-governmental organizations, on the other hand, act more effectively and successfully in terms of disaster response. The AKUT (Search and Rescue Team) was so extremely successful in the Marmara Earthquake that the government sent it to Greece to help the Greeks immediately after the earthquake in their country [31]. Nevertheless, there is no a formal connection between the executive and non-governmental organizations in terms of disaster-response. In this sense, lack of communication before disasters makes it more difficult to prepare for and respond to disasters effectively and efficiently. The connection happens haphazardly in times of disasters.

It is also noteworthy that Turkish Armed Forces have a major role in the response phase of disaster management. The Armed Forces, with around 600,000 soldiers, is a very large and effective body for disaster-response. Many past disasters showed that the Army is very important in disaster management, especially in the response process. Nonetheless, there is a communication problem between local administrative bodies and the Armed Forces. Due to the nature of the occupation of the Army, it lacks a connection with local administrators. This results in problems with the practice of response.

Politicians and the government have played a central role in disaster management, especially in the disaster-response phase and in the allocation of national resources. Some politicians are more interested in political grandstanding [32]. In the short run, governments distribute many resources and provide the necessities of injured people. However, many problems are ignored or given inadequate attention during the recovery phase as the media and public attention lose their focus on a particular disaster. In short, coordination in terms of disaster management in Turkey is a very problematic issue. It has been discussed publicly since the 1999 Marmara Earthquake. However, the majority in the country believes that an effective collaboration is needed, especially in preparedness and response stages of the disaster management cycle. Therefore in summary, Turkey is a prime candidate, as is the US, in finding systems that use collaborative methods to respond to disasters. Only in this manner will the communication problems be resolved.

8. Conclusion

The world today needs to face the fact that terrorism is part of the new world dynamic and learning to respond to terrorism and other disasters are an essential part of government responsibility in an emergency management system. Gokhan Aydiner, Director of Turkish National Police, put it best when he said "… terrorism has no religion, no nationality, and no geography. No matter how sound the legal basis the nations might have, we should always bear in mind that intelligence sharing, cooperation and sincere joint initiatives are the sound pillars of the combat against terrorism" [33, pg. 6] Collaboration, networking, or any other term that cycles in the management vocabulary that congers up this same meaning, should be the modus operandi of local governments as they combat the evil that is terrorism. By working together the various levels of governments will be able to protect their people.

References

[1] G. Wamsley, A. Schroeder, Escalating in a quagmire: The changing dynamics of the emergency management policy subsystem. *Public Administration Review* **56/3** (1996), 235-244.
[2] M.G. Kweit, R.W. Kweit, A tale of two disasters. *The Journal of Federalism* **36/3** (2006), 375-393.
[3] S.K. Schneider, Governmental response to disasters: The conflict between bureaucratic procedures and emergent norms. *Public Administration Review* **52/2** (1992), 135-145.
[4] B. Saul, Definition of 'terrorism' in the UN Security Council: 1985-2004. *Chinese Journal of International Law* **4/1** (2005), 141-166.
[5] B. Ganor, Defining terrorism: Is one man's terrorist another man's freedom fighter? *Police Practice and Research* **3/4** (2002), 287-304.
[6] B. Grob-Fitzgibbon, What is terrorism? Redefining a phenomenon in time of war. *Peace & Change* **30/2** (2005), 231-246.
[7] J. Waldron, Terrorism and the uses of terror. *The Journal of Ethics* **8** (2004), 5-35.
[8] Federal Bureau of Investigation, Domestic terrorism problem. [Online] Available from: URL: http://baltimore.fbi.gov/domter.htm [2006, October 01]
[9] A. Schmid, Terrorism: The definitional problem. *Case Western Reserve Journal of International Law* **36** (2004), 103-147.

[10] A.I. Dolgova, Theoretical problems of terrorism and the struggle against it. *Statutes and Decisions* **40/5** (2004), 57-70.
[11] D. Rodin, Terrorism without intention. *Ethics* **114** (2004), 752-771.
[12] D. McEntire, *Disaster response and recovery: Strategies and tactics for resilience*. John Wiley & Sons Inc.; 2006.
[13] W.L. Waugh, Jr., R.T. Sylves, Organizing the war on terror. *Public Administration Review* **62/5** (2002), 145-153.
[14] D. Krane, The state of American federalism, 2001-2002: Resilience in response to crisis. *Publius* **32/4** (2002), 1-28.
[15] D. Krane, The state of American federalism, 2002-2003: Division replaces unity. *Publius* **33/3** (2003), 1-44.
[16] D. Kettl, Speakers Remarks - *The role of "home" in Homeland Security - The federalism challenge: The challenge for state and local government*. Albany: Rockefeller Institute of Government, Symposium Series No. 2; 2003.
[17] The White House, Homeland Security Presidential Directive/HSPD-5. [Online] Available from: URL: http://www.whitehouse.gov/news/releases/2003/02/20030228-9.html [2006, August 28]
[18] D. Thacher, The local role in Homeland Security. *Law and Society Review* **39/3** (2005), 635-676.
[19] P. Peterson, *City limits*. Chicago: University of Chicago Press; 1998.
[20] M. Grodzins, *The American system*. Chicago: Rand McNally; 1996.
[21] C.R. Wise, Organizing for Homeland Security. *Public Administration Review* **62/2** (2002), 131-144.
[22] J. Kincaid, R. Cole, Issues of federalism in response to terrorism. *Public Administration Review* **62/5** (2002), 181-192.
[23] C.L. Staten, *Emergency response to chemical/biological terrorist incidents*. Emergency Response and Research Institute; 1997.
[24] W.L. Waugh, Jr., Terrorism, Homeland Security and the National Emergency Management Network. *Public Organization Review* **3/4** (2003), 373-385.
[25] G. Haddow, J.A. Bullock, *Introduction to emergency management*. Elsevier Press; 2006.
[26] Department of Homeland Security, *Initial national response plan*. [Online] Available from: URL: http://www.nemaweb.org/docs/national_response_plan.pdf [2006, August 10]
[27] A.I. Anderson, D. Campton, T. Mason, Managing in a dangerous world: The National Incident Management System. *Engineering Management Journal* **16/4** (2004), 3-9.
[28] Department of Homeland Security, Emergencies and disasters: Planning and prevention (2004). [Online] Available from: URL: http://www.dhs.gov/dhspublic/display?theme=14&content=3697 [2006, July 15]
[29] D. Compton, Unifying and integrating command of major emergency incidents. Conference Presentation. Salt Lake City. As quoted in [27].
[30] The Pacific Disaster Center – PDC, Istanbul, Turkey: Disaster risk management profile (2005, October). [Online] Available from: URL: http://emi.pdc.org/cities/CP-Istanbul-09-05.pdf#search=%22Disaster%20risk%20management%20profile%22 [2006, October 02]
[31] A. Ozerdem, S. Barakat, After the Marmara earthquake: Lessons for avoiding short cuts to disasters. *Third World Quarterly* **21/3** (2000), 425-439.
[32] M. Balamir, Painful steps of progress from crisis planning to contingency planning: Changes for disaster preparedness in Turkey. *Journal of Contingencies and Crisis Management* **10/1** (2002), 39-49.
[33] G. Aydiner, Terrorism in the world and in Turkey. In: *Istanbul Conference on Democracy & Global Security*; 2005 June 9-11; Istanbul, Turkey. Ankara: Oncu Press, 2006. p 1-6.

Public Archetypes in U.S. Counter-Bioterrorist Policy

Monica SCHOCH-SPANA
Senior Associate, Center for Biosecurity of the University of Pittsburgh Medical Center

Abstract. 'How will the public react to a biological attack?' is a fundamental question underpinning US policy and practice in the realm of terrorism preparedness and response. This essay chronicles the major trends over the last decade or so in authorities' operating assumptions about mass behaviors in the context of bioterrorism and other extreme events; such assumptions are driven in part by unquestioned common sense notions and by historic events and scholarly critiques that have catalyzed new ways of thinking. Accompanying this catalog of public archetypes is the discussion of the conceptual and empirical limits to each model, as well as recommended approaches. Admittedly cursory, this typology nonetheless helps to reveal that policy-makers, by adopting one notional public over another, are tacitly endorsing some forms of governance -that is, the relationship between the governed and the governing- over others. Decision-makers from the US and NATO member states thus may benefit from a self-conscious audit of the premises regarding mass behaviors that currently underwrite counter-terrorist policies and their implementation.

Keywords. Public archetype, counter-bio terror policy, self-reliant stockpilers, volunteers, survivors

1. Envisioning the Public in the Bioterrorist Context

1.1. Panicky Mob

Prior to 2001 when catastrophic terrorism was a serious but postulated danger, US officials frequently conceived public reactions to a biological event as part and parcel of the crisis: the 'worried well' who would pour into hospitals and hinder health care workers' ability to treat 'real' victims. The perpetrator, the pathogen, and the public were all forces that seemed to demand containment by authorities [1]. Playing one-dimensional roles in hypothetical scenarios and tabletop exercises, members of the public usually surfaced as mass casualties or hysteria-driven mobs who would self-evacuate affected areas or resort to violence to gain access to scarce, potentially life saving antibiotics and vaccines [2]. Such typecasting arguably was seen as necessary to prepare planners and responders for the 'worst case,' and to devise contingency plans for managing the public so that the professionals could perform their respective missions.

According to extensive social research into disasters, however, people rarely fall apart and put themselves first [3, 4, 5, 6, 7]. This finding contradicts what people tend to say on surveys that ask them how they *think* they will behave when disaster hits. In reality, people may feel fearful, anxious and capable of doing just about anything to protect their loved ones. They may be irritable with politicians and safety professionals and ignore their advice when it is irrelevant to their situation. But, contrary to the scary stories authorities tell each other, panic is the exception. Ordinary people emerge as innovative problem-solvers who are responsive to the needs of others around them.

Adaptive, pro-social responses have been documented by researchers over several decades in countless disasters, and these findings have been bolstered by reports of the reasoned and often altruistic responses of those directly affected in the 9/11 attacks and the July 7, 2005 London bombings [8, 9]. Moreover, regular people are not merely disaster victims who must rely on trained responders for protection. Studies show that the majority of people rescued are saved by non-professionals who happen to be in the immediate vicinity. Of the 50 people saved from the rubble of the 1989 Loma Prieta earthquake in California, 49 were rescued by a group of 8 Mexican construction workers who have long since been forgotten in the larger US cultural narrative of the heroic efforts by trained search-and-rescue professionals [10].

The overriding notion of the 'problem public' to be managed precludes careful consideration of, and planning for ways to solicit the cooperation of affected populations. Emphasis instead is on crowd control, not enhancing the people's ability to cope with a public health emergency. Unfortunately, this way of thinking continues to linger today: in the pandemic influenza context, for example, the medical director for the Department of Homeland Security has expressed concern over the potential for "insurrection" and the President in October of 2005 advocated military-enforced quarantines [11].

1.2. Anxious Audience

Prevailing approaches among decision-makers and professional responders toward the public have, however, shifted in great measure from an emphasis on containing disorder to communicating information in the bioterrorist context. The complex realities of the September 11th and anthrax letter attacks helped refine many authorities' understanding of the public not simply as a problem to be managed, but as a constituency to be served: anxious people understandably in need of good information about what the danger was and what to do about it.

Communications failures on the part of authorities during the serial tragedies of 2001 spurred recognition of the essential role of public outreach in managing the effects of a bioattack. Following the anthrax crisis, US federal health authorities thus identified "risk communication and health information dissemination" as 1 of 7 priority areas in their guidance and financial support to upgrade the ability of state and local health departments to respond to bioterrorism (almost $3 billion in the period FY2001-04). Critical reflection on responses to the 2001 terrorist attacks spurred the release of many helpful analyses and guidebooks for officials regarding successful communications with the media and the larger public [12, 13, 14, 15]. Practitioner and policy-maker interest in public communication remains high: typically, 2 of the top 5 articles that are downloaded each month from the journal, *Biosecurity and Bioterrorism*, have a focus on communication [16].

As 2001 demonstrated, open and informative relationships among citizens, government, and public health and safety authorities are fundamental to the nation's ability to cope with unconventional terrorism. US leaders and professional responders should be lauded for embracing effective crisis and risk communications as remedies for a potentially anxious, skeptical, and/or resistant public. Powerful cultural and technological forces (e.g., computerization, media proliferation, the internet, e-mail), however, make it too easy to think of social life merely in terms of information exchange. Authorities, thus, should be careful not to approach improved communications as the 'quick fix' for the more complex, underlying tensions that can precede and/or emerge during bioattacks or other health crises.

'Public communications,' 'risk communications,' and the like have unfortunately become codes words with which to skirt the sociopolitical complexities associated with community responses to terrorist crises, especially those that involve bioweapons. When authorities say that they want better communication with the public, what they tend to mean is public 'buy in,' public compliance, and understanding -possibly even absolution- when tough choices arise for officials such as how to distribute scarce resources in an emergency. When members of the public indicate that they want better communication from officials, what they are asking for is inclusion, consideration, and mutual respect as 'peer' decision-makers; expert guidance on which they can act; and proof that their needs have justly been considered by people in authority.

1.3. Self-Reliant Stockpilers

Interpreted as an anxious audience, citizens are expected to remain alert to uncertain and evolving events, awaiting instructions about what to do from officials who are adept at risk communication. A complement or alternate to this model is the self-reliant individual and his/her household [17, 18, 19, 20]. In this approach, members of the public ready themselves for disaster by preparing contingency plans for their families, including a communications strategy to keep each other informed of personal location and well-being. Officials also consider it prudent for members of the public to stockpile enough food, water, and other essentials to be self-sufficient until help arrives or the crisis resolves -72 hours being the general rule of thumb. Another recommended act of self-reliance is becoming familiar with the special challenges posed by unconventional terrorist attacks that involve chemical, radiological, nuclear or biological agents.

Reasonable arguments support the notion of a public equipped to make do on its own. Self-study of unconventional attacks may reduce the shock value of otherwise novel and insidious hazards such as radiological, chemical and biological weapons. Family plans for emergencies target a practical and meaningful solution to one of the most emotionally wrenching qualities of an extreme event -worry and uncertainty about the welfare of loved ones. Compiling an emergency kit that includes flashlight, radio, fresh batteries, non-perishable foods, maintenance medications, and other 'basics' is a do-able, human-scaled project that -depending upon the circumstances- can have real material value, but it also brings intangibles like personal safety and security into being. Lastly, from the perspective of disaster response professionals, every self-sufficient individual and household lightens the burden of having to protect an entire population, focusing limited resources on the most needy.

Family communication plans, emergency kits, and self-study of threat agents are sensible preparedness activities, but with notable limitations. Capable institutions and professionals -including those that make up the health care and public health systems- are still necessary to handle the needs of large numbers of people. In a bioattack, it certainly helps for private citizens to be informed and alert to specific symptoms, but if doctors and health authorities do not know the next best steps or have not jointly planned community-wide contingency plans, a community's well-being may still be in jeopardy. And, even if members of the public knows better, they may put off seeing a physician if they have no health insurance and are behind on the rent or the utility bill.

Public self-reliance is not an equal opportunity policy, as a review of present US pandemic flu plans suggests [21]. The recommendation, for instance, that citizens keep "supplies of materials at home, as recommended by authorities, to support essential needs of the household for several days if necessary" and to stay home for up-to-10 "snow days" ignores economic realities in the US. Many poor and working class Americans can barely get by on a day-to-day basis, let alone stockpile their larder for what is, for most, a theoretical danger. In addition, asking hourly employees to miss 10 days of work as part of a flu furlough creates a real fiscal crisis for their households.

1.4. Assembled Volunteers

American residents are on the receiving end of much thoughtful advice about individual and household preparedness for a variety of hazards, as noted previously. The extent to which citizens have acted on this advice, however, is not what disaster planners and educators would hope. Some Americans have moved beyond disaster preparedness, however, as a private act like stockpiling to a public good by volunteering their time in a variety of national and local programs. Government sponsored programs include the Citizens Corps and its constituent volunteer programs such as the Medical Reserve Corps and the Community Emergency Response Teams [22]. Non-governmental programs include the Red Cross and Voluntary Organizations Active in Disaster.

Community-oriented groups are also acting on behalf of the public good for disasters. The National Organization on Disability, the American Association for Retired Persons, and the Red Cross recently joined the DHS in preparing brochures that provide seniors and disabled persons preparedness tips directly relevant to their circumstances [23]. Collaborating Agencies Responding to Disasters (CARD) emerged in the aftermath of the Loma Prieta earthquake and the Oakland Hills firestorm as the publicly-minded mechanism to train, unite, and coordinate Alameda County service providers as a safety net for people with little or no ability to address their own preparedness, response and recovery needs such as seniors, children, the disabled, the homeless, non-English speakers, and low income families [24].

'Disaster-ready' households and voluntary associations are significant achievements in terms of civic engagement in a pressing public policy issue. But important gaps remain. First, notions of citizen and community preparedness play an important rhetorical role in homeland security. Yet, their symbolic significance is not matched by a commensurate level of public funding, judging from a proxy index such the inconsistent and diminishing operating budget for the Citizen Corps [22]. More importantly, the prevailing emphasis on equipping individual households (i.e., the private sphere) to weather a disaster and on volunteering in the event of a disaster -both absolutely essential goods- helps make it easier for citizens to rescind on another kind of public-spirited obligation: paying closer attention to the politics of disasters, a characteristically uncomfortable position for most US residents.

1.5. Resilient Survivors

The image of resilient individuals and communities has recently emerged to counter officials' lingering expectations of mass psychopathology and anti-social behaviors following an unconventional terrorist attack. Social and behavioral research into disaster and trauma-related phenomena call into question those public policies that fail both to recognize and to nurture the public's adaptive responses to extreme events. Many psychological researchers agree that resilience, and not psychopathology, is the likely community outcome following a traumatic event -including an act of terrorism [25, 26], and have issued a call for further understanding into community cohesion and post-traumatic growth [27]. Sociologists studying a range of disaster situations, including terrorist attacks, have similarly chronicled the creative problem-solving, voluntarism, and adaptive behaviors of people in extreme circumstances [2, 3, 8].

Resilience -a concept used in disparate fields from materials science and engineering to psychology and sociology- denotes both strength and flexibility, and represents the capacity to "bounce back" after some kind of shock to the system [28, 29]. Present interest in resilience among mental health professionals is part of a larger disciplinary shift away from a singular focus on psychopathology and mental disorders, to broader emphasis on psychological well-being and its contributing factors. Both the sociological and psychology literature on recovery from terrorist attacks (and other extreme events) note the presence of strong social bonds and 'caring communities' as protective factors that permit individuals and groups to cope better with jarring, tragic circumstances [30]. Other contributing factors include opportunities to exercise personal and collective efficacy; broad understanding of structure, roles and responsibilities; resources including physical capital and human resources; support, nurturance and broad interested in the needs of community members; critical reflection and skill building; and communication [29].

Reframing the public from a panic-stricken mob to a band of hearty survivors is a positive development and more realistic in terms of the empirical record. Two cautions are worth making, however. First, *in extremis*, the resilience model may unwittingly support a public policy of government non-interference. If people and communities more-or-less rebound from large-scale tragedy, the thinking could go, perhaps officials need not concern themselves with actively cultivating supportive mechanisms. As some leading disaster experts have recently warned: "The suggestion of psychological resilience and recovery does not obviate the need to develop mental health prevention strategies and support systems as part of the infrastructure of preparedness" [26]. Second, a policy focus on generalized resilience could obscure the vulnerabilities of specific individuals and groups of people. As numerous studies have documented, disasters are not equal opportunity events; the most vulnerable members of society often bear the brunt of damages, whether lost lives or livelihoods [3, 31, 32].

2. Reframing Policy Discussions about Bioterror and the Public: The Partner Model

Currently, circulating notions about the public in the bioterrorist context range from the helpless and hysterical to the hearty and humanitarian-minded. Various implicit and explicit roles are also imagined for government: riot control, credible communication, volunteer mobilization, and laissez faire. The following section considers a final kind of public-namely, a full partner with government in preparedness, response, and recovery- around which the Center for Biosecurity of the University of Pittsburgh Medical Center has convened two Working Groups to help reframe bioterror policy discussions.

2.1. Governance Dilemmas

In 2003-2004, the *Working Group on 'Governance Dilemmas' in Bioterrorism Response* met to distill public communications guidance for mayors, governors, health officers and other top US officials [33]. Governing successfully during large, fast-moving, lethal epidemics, the Working Group maintained, requires a dynamic collaboration among members of a community and the community's leaders. In their deliberations, the members recognized that the increasing emphasis upon communications was a positive development within biodefense. Still needed, however, was more robust discussion among leaders, and between authorities and communities-at-large, about what an optimal societal response to a biological attack looks like.

Whether so-called natural or deliberate in origin, a large outbreak poses unique 'governance dilemmas.' Leaders and their communities must tend to immediate life-and-death matters such as caring for the sick, must ward off socially corrosive effects like ostracism of the afflicted, and must stem dramatic economic effects for victims and affected locales alike. Conflicts of interest, priority, and purpose can emerge in pursuit of these goals. The Working Group prepared a set of analytic templates for decision-makers faced with these difficult situations to prepare them to safeguard the public's trust and cooperation during a response to an infectious disease threat.

2.1.1. What Defines Successful Response to an Epidemic or Biological Attack?

Five strategic goals distinguish an effective response in the 21st century. An informed and involved public, along with guidance and material support from respected leaders, can help achieve these aims:

- Limit death and suffering through proper preventive, curative, and supportive care; tend to the greater vulnerability of children, the frail elderly, and the physically compromised.
- Defend civil liberties by using the least restrictive interventions to contain an infectious agent that causes communicable disease.
- Preserve economic stability, managing the financial blow to victims as well as the near- and long-term losses of hard-hit industries, cities, and neighborhoods.
- Discourage scapegoating, hate crimes, and the stigmatization of specific people or places as 'contaminated' or unhealthy.
- Bolster the ability of individuals and the larger community to rebound from unpredictable and traumatic events; provide mental health support to those who need it.

2.1.2. What Competing Goals May Arise in an Epidemic, and How Might They Be Averted?

Large-scale outbreaks are complex events that provoke fear and contradictory impulses. Because an epidemic's impact-illness, death, lost livelihood, disrupted commerce-is troubling to consider, leaders and the larger public may deny that a problem exists, or intervene too quickly without regard to the negative effects of their actions. Once acknowledged, an epidemic exerts immense political and social pressure for swift, decisive, visible response, more so in the case of a deliberate epidemic. Apparent and sometimes genuine conflicts among strategic goals can arise. The most common dilemmas facing past leaders have been balancing disease control imperatives with those of individual liberty, economic stability, and stigma prevention (Table 1).

Table 1. Recommendations for handling potential conflicts between strategic response goals

Stop disease that spreads person-to-person while upholding individual freedoms	Make response plans public before a crisis occurs; a well-informed population is more likely to cooperate with advice for reducing the spread of disease.
	Sketch out the 'big picture'; make concrete the fact that personal actions can affect the safety of others -for example, remind people that staying home from work or keeping children out of school when they are ill protects others from getting sick.
	Use disease controls that respect ideals of autonomy, self-determination, and equality -public cooperation limits illness and death; public resistance does not.
	Provide goods and services that help people comply with health orders -for example, set up vaccination clinics in locations accessible to people without cars.
	Restrict civil liberties, if necessary, *only* in a transparent and equitable way.
Protect the economy while using disease controls that disrupt commerce	Be mindful of the goal of long-term financial recovery when controlling disease; do not react based solely on the desire to avert short-term economic loss.
	Recognize public trust as precious 'capital' that grows the economy -for example, if people see their health as your top priority, confidence in your efforts to safeguard the economy will follow.
	Account for the less visible and more scattered monetary impacts when making epidemic control decisions (e.g., costs of victims' healthcare; economic toll of stigma).
Restore social bonds when people feel at the mercy of a mysterious disease	Express empathy for people's fears about getting sick from others; follow up with meaningful medical details that allow people to gauge personal risk accurately.
	Demonstrate compassion toward victims of disease; explain to the community-at-large the social costs of avoiding people out of fear, rather than out of actual danger.
	Direct law enforcement to deal appropriately with hate crimes in the event prevention fails.
	Coordinate volunteers, relief groups, and civic organizations in humanitarian response, with extra focus on assisting the most vulnerable -for example, children, the frail elderly, and disabled people of all ages.

2.1.3. What Situations Splinter the Social Trust Necessary to Cope with Health Crises, and How Might They Be Defused?

Mutual confidence and obligation among decision-makers, citizens and their leaders, and community members are the basis for achieving any and all strategic goals. Breaches of social trust, however, are a common predicament for leaders during outbreaks and are likely to arise during a bioattack (Table 2). Conditions that confound social trust involve preconceptions about 'the government,' 'the public,' or 'the media'; the social and economic fault lines that are exacerbated by disease and dread of it; and questions about the morally defensible use of communal resources in times of crisis.

Table 2. Principles and actions for addressing social trust predicaments

Prevent unproductive fear, denial, or skepticism on the part of the public when delivering crisis updates	Share what you know. Do not withhold information because you think people will panic. Creative coping is the norm; panic is the exception.
	Hold press briefings early and often to reach the public. Answering questions is not a distraction from managing the crisis; it *is* managing the crisis.
	Confirm that local health agencies and medical facilities are prepared to handle an onslaught of questions from concerned individuals, in person and by phone.
	Convey basic health facts clearly and quickly so that people have peace of mind that they are safe or so that they seek out care, if need be; similarly, brief healthcare and emergency workers so they have a realistic understanding about job safety.
	View rumors as a normal sign of people's need to make sense of vague or disturbing events. Refine your outreach efforts; the current ones may not be working.
Earn confidence in the use of scarce resources despite existing social and economic gaps	Account for income disparities in response plans; anticipate the need for free or low-cost prevention and treatment.
	Make planning transparent so that the public sees that access to life-saving resources is based on medical need and not on wealth or favored status.
	Be open about eligibility criteria for goods and services, especially when tough choices arise unexpectedly -for example, which botulism attack victims will receive the limited antitoxin that exists.
	Show thorough preparations to protect vulnerable populations like children and the frail elderly, thus bolstering *everyone's* sense of security.
Maintain credibility when decisions must be made before all the facts are in	Advise the community at the outset if crisis conditions are evolving or could be prolonged.
	Offer more detail rather than less, even when the unknowns outnumber what is known; resist the urge to reassure for reassurance sake alone.
	Be frank about any uncertainty regarding "facts"; describe plans to fill in knowledge gaps.
	Vary your means of reaching the public. Mix high-tech outreach (internet, cable, network, print, radio, cell phone, automated hotlines) with contact through grassroots leaders.

2.2. Community Engagement

During the second half of 2006, the *Working Group on Citizen Engagement in Health Emergency Planning* convened around how to secure the active role of citizens and civil society institutions alongside response professionals, private enterprise, and government agencies in preparing for, responding to, and recovering from an extreme health event. The civic infrastructure-that vibrant whole comprised of citizens' collective wisdom and capacity to problem-solve and innovate; voluntary associations (both virtual and face-to-face) that arise from shared interests and/or a public good; and non-governmental organizations that look out for the well-being of various groups -is essential to managing a mass health emergency and other large-scale disasters, yet policy and practice rarely articulate well with this critical resource.

The civic infrastructure -rather than the lone citizen, individual household, or undifferentiated masses- provides a very specific target for leaders to incorporate into disaster policy-making and implementation. In the pre-event period, it can help set policy priorities, inform value-laden policy decisions, and function as a 'multifrequency' communications network that can reach dispersed and diverse populations. In addition, it can provide operational and tactical support during the crisis and recovery periods. Leaders have a range of techniques through which to mobilize elements of the civic infrastructure in (and for) disasters. Public participation methods are the most under-utilized despite indicators from research and practical experience that this tactic, in contrast to mass communications, may help leaders tackle some of the more intractable problems posed by extreme events.

Leaders typically rely upon three broad approaches when seeking to involve the citizenry in a pressing issue of public importance [34][1]. Operating in a 'communication' mode, an official or agency conveys information to members of the public in one-way fashion, often with the intent of educating and informing the populace. Public feedback is not required or specifically sought out. Alternately, leaders may assume a 'consultation' posture, soliciting opinions through surveys, polls, focus groups, and advisory panels. The public's opinions, criticisms, and constructive advice comprise only one factor among others for a policy maker's consideration. In contrast, 'engagement,' the third approach, constitutes a two-way flow of information between authorities and citizens, where dialogue helps foster a more nuanced understanding of a complex issue, and where the goal is to work together to conceive and implement a policy solution.

In this modality, leaders expressly seek out the counsel of citizens and consciously share decision-making power, to more or less degrees, depending upon the context. Citizens, in turn, draw upon and exercise collective power through open deliberation. Ideally, these conversations help them to glean views of a problem that reach beyond their immediate circumstances and to learn how to make appropriate demands upon government (that is, act as a public) and what government may need from them to meet those requests [38]. This last and most robust form of public involvement has yet to be incorporated into public health preparedness. It is nonetheless very promising in terms of developing socially acceptable approaches to the distribution of scarce, life-saving medical resources and practically feasible strategies to care for large numbers of sick people when the health care system is inundated.

3. Conclusion

The panic-stricken mob, on-edge audience, self-sufficient stockpiler, committed volunteer, resilient survivor, and preparedness partner are the prevalent conceptualizations of the public in the bioterror context that have circulated in the US over the past decade or so. Some of the frameworks have empirical evidence from the social and behavioral sciences to back them up, while others (namely, the helpless and hysterical masses) exist only in fantasy despite their emphasis in some policy-making circles. Decision-makers from the US and NATO member states may benefit from a self-conscious audit of the premises regarding mass behaviors that currently underwrite counter-terrorist policies and their implementation. In addition, they should consciously explore the promising partnership model.

---

[1] This analysis relies upon Rowe and Frewer's (2005) characterization of public involvement activities in terms of the distinctive information flows that constitute communication, consultation and participation [34]. Readers are referred to the original analysis for additional gradations within each of these categories. Alternative modeling of the public involvement continuum is also available [35, 36, 37].

References

[1] M. Schoch-Spana, Bioterrorism: US public health and a secular apocalypse. *Anthropology Today* **20/5** (2004), 8-13.
[2] M. Schoch-Spana, Educating, informing, and mobilizing the public. In B.S. Levy, V.W. Sidel, editors. *Terrorism and public health.* New York: Oxford University Press; 2003. p 118-135.
[3] Committee on Disaster Research in the Social Sciences, *Facing hazards and disasters: Understanding human dimensions.* Washington, D.C.: The National Academies Press; 2006.
[4] R.R. Dynes, K.J. Tierney, editors, *Disasters, collective behavior and social organization.* Newark: University of Delaware Press; 1994.
[5] L. Clarke, Panic: Myth or reality? *Contexts* **1/3** (2002), 21-26.
[6] E.L. Quarantelli, The sociology of panic. In N.J. Smelser, P.B. Baltes, editors. *International encyclopedia of the social and behavioral sciences.* New York: Pergamon Press; 2001. p 11020-11030.
[7] H.W. Fischer, *Response to disaster: Fact versus fiction and its perpetuation.* Lanham: University Press of America; 1994.
[8] B. Sheppard, G.J. Rubin, J.K. Wardman, S. Wessely, Terrorism and dispelling the myth of a panic prone public. *Journal of Public Health Policy* **27** (2006), 219-245.
[9] T. Glass, M. Schoch-Spana, Bioterrorism and the people: How to vaccinate a city against panic. *Clinical Infectious Diseases* **34** (2002), 217-223.
[10] T. Glass, Citizens' information needs in responding to disaster. Workshop remarks. Computer Science and Telecommunications Board of the NAS/National Research Council, Washington, D.C. (2005, July 19).
[11] Bush suggests military-enforced quarantines for avian flu, CIDRAP NEWS (2005, October 4). [Online] Available from: URL: http://www.cidrap.umn.edu/cidrap/content/influenza/panflu/news/oct0405bush.html [2006, August 10]
[12] US Department of Health and Human Services. *Communicating in a crisis: Risk communication Guidelines for Public Officials.* Washington, D.C.: Department of Health and Human Services; 2002.
[13] B. Fischhoff, Assessing and communicating the risks of terrorism. In A.H. Teich, S.D. Nelson, S.J. Lita, editors. *Science and technology in a vulnerable world.* Washington, D.C.: American Association for the Advancement of Science; 2002. p 51-64.
[14] N. Ethiel, editor, *Terrorism: Informing the public.* Chicago: McCormick Tribune Foundation; 2002.
[15] Centers for Disease Control and Prevention. *Crisis and emergency risk communication.* Atlanta: CDC; 2002.
[16] F. Jackie, managing editor, *Biosecurity and bioterrorism.* [Personal Communication]
[17] American Red Cross, *Be prepared: American Red Cross preparedness information.* [Online] Available from: URL: http://www.redcross.org/services/disaster/0,1082,0_500_,00.html [2006, October 15]
[18] A.J. Dory, *Civil security: Americans and the challenge of Homeland Security.* Washington, D.C.: Center for Strategic and International Studies; 2003, September.
[19] US Department of Homeland Security, Ready: Prepare, plan, stay informed. [Online] Available from: URL: http://www.ready.gov/ [2006, October 15]
[20] L.E. Davis, T. LaTourrette, D.E. Mosher, et al., *Individual preparedness and response to chemical, radiological, nuclear, and biological terrorist attacks.* Santa Monica: RAND Public Safety and Justice; 2003.
[21] US Department of Health and Human Services, *HHS Pandemic Influenza Plan* (2005, November). [Online] Available from: URL: http://www.hhs.gov/pandemicflu/plan/pdf/HHSPandemicInfluenzaPlan.pdf [2006, July 18]
[22] M. Schoch-Spana, D. Chamberlain, C. Franco, et al., Disease, disaster, and democracy: The public's stake in health emergency planning. *Biosecurity & Bioterrorism* **4/3** (2006), 313-319.
[23] American Association for Retired Persons. *AARP offers tips to help older Americans prepare for emergencies.* News release (2006, September 6). [Online] Available from: URL: http://www.aarp.org/research/press-center/presscurrentnews/preparing_for_emergencies.html [2006, October 17]
[24] Collaborating Agencies Responding to Disasters. [Online] Available from: URL: http://www.firstvictims.org/whoweare.html [2006, October 17]
[25] J. Hamblen, L.B. Slone, *What are the traumatic stress effects of terrorism? A National Center for PTSD fact sheet.* [Online] Available from: URL: http://www.ncptsd.va.gov/facts/disasters/fs_terrorism.html [2006, November 20]
[26] B. Pfefferbaum, R.L. Pfefferbaum, E.H. Christiansen, et al., Comparing stress responses to terrorism in residents of two communities over time. *Brief Treatment and Crisis Intervention* **6/2** (2006), 137-143.
[27] A.S. Butler, A.M. Panzer, L.R. Goldfrank, editors. *Preparing for the psychological consequences of terrorism: A public health strategy.* Washington, D.C.: The National Academies Press; 2003.
[28] M. Bruneau, S.E. Chang, R.T. Eguchi, et al., A framework to quantitatively assess and enhance the seismic resilience of communities. *Earthquake Spectra* **19/4** (2003), 733-753.

[29] F.H. Norris, B. Pfefferbuam, Community resilience. Presentation at the Annual Research Symposium of the National Consortium for the Study of Terrorism and Responses to Terrorism. University of Maryland, College Park (2006, June 28).
[30] S. Steury, S. Spencer, G.W. Parkinson, The social context of recovery. *Psychiatry* **67/2** (2004), 158-163.
[31] A. Fothergill, E. Maestas, J.D. Darlington, Race, ethnicity and disasters in the United States: A review of the literature. *Disasters* **23/2** (1999), 156-173.
[32] A. Fothergill, L.A. Peek, Poverty and disaster in the United States: A review of recent sociological findings. *Natural Hazards* **32/1** (2004), 89-110.
[33] The Working Group on 'Governance Dilemmas' in Bioterrorism Response, Leading during bioattacks and epidemics with the public's trust and help. *Biosecurity and Bioterrorism* **2/1** (2004), 25-40.
[34] G. Rowe, L.J. Frewer, A typology of public engagement mechanisms. *Science, Technology, & Human Values* **30/2** (2005), 251-290.
[35] Health Canada, Corporate Consultation Secretariat, Health Policy and Communications Branch, *Health Canada policy toolkit for public involvement in decision making*. Ottawa: Minister of Public Works and Government Services Canada; 2000.
[36] S.R. Arnstein, A ladder of citizen participation. *Journal of American Institute of Planners* **35** (1969), 216-224.
[37] T. Webler, The craft and theory of public participation: A dialectical process. *Journal of Risk Research* **2/1** (1999), 55-71.
[38] A.J. Perrin, *Citizen speak: The democratic imagination in American life*. Chicago: Chicago University Press; 2006.

The Disaster Management Perspective of the November 20, 2003 Events in Istanbul, Turkey

Derin N. URAL
*Associate Professor of Civil Engineering, and Founding Director,
Center of Excellence for Disaster Management, Istanbul Technical University, Turkey*

Abstract. This paper presents findings, from a disaster management perspective, from two terrorist events that occurred in Istanbul, Turkey on November 20, 2003. Man-made and natural disasters have to be examined from the disaster management perspective, in order to improve current management systems. The two attacks occurred at the General Consulate of Great Britain in Beyoglu and at the General Directorate of the HSBC Bank in Levent, on November 20, 2003. The response and recovery stages following these blasts are described. A comparison with the event that occurred in Oklahoma City is also presented. The similarities and differences are outlined. One can see that countries can learn from each other, and disaster management systems can be improved with continued cooperation and understanding.

Keywords. Disaster management, response, recovery, terrorist event, Istanbul, Oklahoma

Introduction

A precursor to the November 20th events was the events that occurred at the Neve Shalom Synagogue in Kuledibi and the Beth Israel Synagogue in Sisli at 9:30 a.m. on November 15, 2003. The attacks were initiated by explosive-laden vans in front of the two synagogues. The attacks took place on a day of worship, which led to larger losses and damage.

The second group of attacks occurred at the General Consulate of the United Kingdom in Beyoglu, and the Headquarters of the HSBC Bank, situated in Levent, on November 20, 2003. The Headquarters of the HSBC Bank was attacked at approximately 11:00 a.m. while the building was at close to full capacity.

In the four events described above, there were a total of 53 casualties, including the British General Consul. The total number of injured was 718.

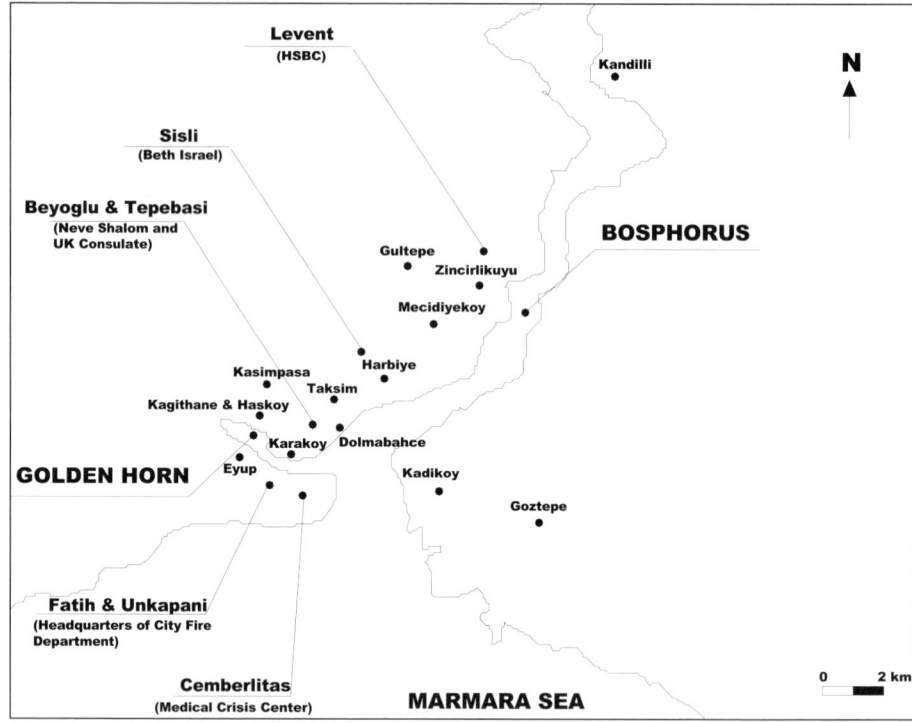

Figure 1. Map of Istanbul, and location of events

1. The Disaster Management Perspective of November 20, 2003 Events

The four phases of disaster management are assessed for the November 20th events. The role of preparedness, mitigation, the response efforts, and recovery [1,2] are given in the sections below.

1.1. Preparedness

The private sector, as well as the local government of Istanbul [3, 4, 5, 6, 7] has disaster plans, and it has carried out exercises for their employees at varying levels, in preparation for a major disaster. The preparedness level of the HSBC Headquarters was exceptional. The preparedness was described by the General Manager of the Bank in Istanbul in an interview:

"There was no panic among staff and clients who were in the Headquarters Building, just after the attack. This was due to the fact that we have trainings and different evacuation plans. We do training 2 to 3 times a year as if there was a disaster. Moreover, we have other buildings in the city, and affected staff was transported to those locations to continue their work. Surely, employees have not been working during the same shift. Managers of departments have called in just enough personnel daily."

The local government had a plan in place in Istanbul and as presented in Table 1, there were available and organized resources in the three districts where the attacks occurred: Besiktas, Beyoglu, and Sisli.

Table 1. Preparedness: Resources in Istanbul

Service Field	Besiktas (HSBC)	Beyoglu (Neve Shalom and UK Consulate)	Sisli (Beth Israel)	Istanbul TOTAL
Staging Areas	13	19	18	416
Helicopter Pads	12	12	5	250
1st Degree Roads with Parking Prohibition	25	42	29	562
2nd Degree Under Control Roads with Parking Prohibition	14	20	19	751
3rd Degree Inter-City Roads with Parking Prohibition	52	18	19	1 383
Medical Facilities	6	12	28	220
Management Facilities	20	49	26	541
Educational Facilities	34	41	57	1 146
ISKI Facilities (Istanbul Clean Water and Sewer Systems Directorate)	1	-	2	29
TEAS Facilities (Turkish Electricity Co.)	1	-	-	16
AKTAS Facilities (Municipal Electricity Company)	-	-	-	7
BEDAS Facilities (Municipal Electricity Company)	-	-	-	5
IGDAS (Istanbul Natural Gas Directorate)	18	8	16	90
Turkish Telecommunication Facilities	2	-	-	26
Military Facilities	15	26	2	124
IDO (Istanbul Hydrofoil) Piers	1	2	-	12
TDI (Turkish Naval Trans. Co.) Piers	1	5	-	44
Sea Ports for Disasters	1	1	-	42
Cemeteries	4	8	6	83
Fire Department Facilities	1	1	1	29

1.2. Mitigation

Mitigation efforts were made at both locations prior to the events [8, 9, 10, 11]. One mitigation shortcoming could be the fact that the English diplomats were working in a temporary building of the Consulate compound that was part of the main gate, situated closer to and easier to access from the main street. Moreover, the UK Consulate in Istanbul is situated in a heavily populated district of the city. As the Istanbul visa office is the second busiest visa office of the UK, the Consulate remains in the heart of the city. The 200 year history of the UK Consulate Building includes three significant fires. In addition, the visa office of the Consulate was attacked in April 2003, 6 months prior to the November attacks.

Drills made by local responders also assisted in the mitigation strategies of the city. Table 2 depicts the rapid response times of firefighters to the call for assistance [12, 13, 14].

Table 2. Call times to firefighters and their access times

Event	Fire Squad	Call Time	Arrival Time
Neve Salom Synagogue November 15, 2003	Beyoglu, all teams	09:25	09:33
	Fatih, all teams	09:34	09:43
	Sisli, one vehicle	09:52	10:02
Beth Israel Synagogue November 15, 2003	Beyoglu, 2 vehicles	09:25	09:32
	Besiktas, all teams	09:35	09:50
	Sisli, all teams	09:32	09:45
UK Consulate November 20, 2003	Beyoglu, all teams	11:06	11:12
	Fatih, all teams	11:06	11:17
	Sisli, one vehicle	11:12	11:25
	Fatih, light truck	15:00	-
HSBC Headquarters November 20, 2003	Besiktas, all teams	10:56	11:10
	Seyrantepe, 2 vehicles	11:00	11:12
	Sisli, all teams	10:57	11:15
	Istinye, all teams	11:15	11:32

1.3. Response

The November 20th events response efforts are discussed here. In addition, the events caused traffic congestion in Levent, the heart of commerce in Istanbul. The Buyukdere Street (the street in front of the HSBC Headquarters) was re-opened to traffic 10 hours after the event, in one direction, as the other remained closed. Moreover, during all 4 events, many vital roads of the city were closed to traffic for long periods of time. Those roads are listed below;

- Bosphorus Bridge Zincirlikuyu access road (1 km to HSBC Headquarters) TEM Highway Zincirlikuyu direction
- E-5 Highway Zincirlikuyu access road (1.5 km to HSBC Headquarters)
- Taksim-Tarlabasi direction (near the UK Consulate Compound and Neve Shalom Synagogue)
- Unkapani Bridge Taksim direction (near the UK Consulate Compound and Neve Shalom Synagogue)

As problems increased with city traffic on November 20, the EOC of the Greater Municipality of Istanbul announced alternate routes [15]. Precautionary measures taken during the reponse efforts included the following:

- HSBC Bank announced at 15:00 that they stopped banking operations in Turkey for one day.
- Turkish Airlines announced shortly after Synagogue attacks that precaution and alarm degree for pilots was increased one level.
- Izmir (the third largest coastal city of Turkey) City Police sent many police and patrols to strategic points including HSBC Branches. Those who work in US facilities were sent home. US Hospital, Turkish - US Common Defense Facility (TUSLOG) and the US Base supermarket were temporarily closed.
- Vehicles passing in front of the US Consulate, UK Consulate and Ministry of Foreign Affairs in the capital were stopped and checked.
- Security precautions were increased in Parliament of the Republic of Turkey in Ankara.

- British Airways closed their offices, except the Ataturk Airport, Istanbul branch on November 20.
- The city police closed Istiklal Street (near the UK Consulate Compound) for vehicles and for pedestrians.
- The White House in Washington DC was evacuated on November 20, as one plane reportedly left its route.
- Bursa (the fourth largest city of Turkey) City Police held an emergency meeting and increased precautions throughout the city.

1.4. Recovery

The recovery stage of the November 20th events unfolded through various public and private support mechanisms. The local government was in charge of assessing the levels of damage sustained and categorizing the damage as light, moderate, or heavy. Businesses and residences in each category were entitled to a different range of assistance. The total assistance donated by the Governership to these victims was 4.3 million USD. All privately insured entities were reimbursed for their damage.

Those businesses with need of additional support were given the choice to obtain a 24 month loan, with a low interest rate of 1% from VakifBank. The Istanbul Chamber of Commerce announced it would assist the 100 businesses that sustained losses. In addition, to support the victims of the attacks, the Turkish Society of Psychology called its members to volunteer their services. Closure to the events was reached when the Turkish Police arrested those involved in the attacks within 60 days of the event.

2. The April 19, 1995 Oklahoma City Event and November 20, 2003 Istanbul Events: Response Comparison

The events that occurred in Oklahoma City and Istanbul share many similarities, and also have important differences. In the following tables, these events are summarized for various response categories [16, 17, 18, 19].

Table 3. Event

Oklahoma City	Istanbul
Approximately 2200 kg AN-FO was used during the attack	1800 kg was used in the HSBC headquarter attack, and 1500 kg was used in the UK Consulate attack
Citizens up to 90 km from event reported hearing or feeling the blast shock wave	Citizens up to 30-40 km from attack, in the Asian part of the city, reported hearing or feeling the blast shock wave
Structures within a 10 block radius from event sustained window/glass damage	Structures within a 3 block radius from HSBC event sustained window/glass damage. The UK Consulate environs consist of narrow streets, and damage reports were not clear.

Table 4. Damage sustained

Oklahoma City	Istanbul
9 buildings were heavily damaged	Following the 4 attacks, 259 buildings had sustained window damage, 43 buildings were slightly damaged, 18 buildings were moderately damaged, and 9 buildings were heavily damaged.
There were 86 buried vehicles	28 buried vehicles at the UK Consulate, 18 at Neve Shalom Synagogue, and 21 buried/damaged cars at Beth Israel Synagogue.

Table 5. Emergency medical services

Oklahoma City	Istanbul
20 minutes after the event, all hospitals in the area officially called for help. 5 hospitals of 9 in the area were as close as 2 km to the scene.	The first minutes after the events, hospitals near area were shifted to plan 'A'. According to that plan, medical personnel were called back from their homes to the hospitals. 24 private and state hospitals in the area responded.
The first medical team that arrived at the scene couldn't communicate with the fire department due to the large number of injuries and the chaos.	First teams that arrived at the scene were medical services. These were able to communicate with other responders.
Hundreds of doctors and nurses assisted following the event, in 15 hospitals. Due to a shortage in blood stocks, a blood drive was initiated. The blood stock was recovered within 3 hours.	Doctors and nurses assisted following the event in 24 hospitals. The blood supplies were adequate.
Prior to the event, 16 of the 35 ambulances were stationed throughout the city. By mutual aid, the number of ambulances assisting increased to 65 in 1.5 hours. In the first minutes, some private vehicles were used to carry injuries, rather than ambulances.	During both group of attacks, 26 of 54 ambulances of *the Government Emergency Service* reached the scenes within 15 minutes. During the day, the total number of ambulances assisting reached 50.

Table 6. Search and rescue following events

Oklahoma	Istanbul
Response and recovery of debris, and site investigations took 17 days.	During the 4 events, the average total working days were: Fire Department 3 days, Civil Defense 2 days, NGO Search and Rescue Teams 1 day, Police Department 10 days at the UK Consulate, 4 days at HSBC headquarters, 5 days at synagogues. Unlike Oklahoma, there was no structural collapse.
Mutual aid agreements led to support from neighboring cities.	There was some support between province establishments, i.e Fatih and Beyoglu, and Sisli and Besiktas. There is no mutual aid agreement between them; however, they are under the same authority of the Governorship of the City.
Urban Search and Rescue (USAR), Arizona Task Force 1, Phoenix, California Task Force 7, Sacramento teams participated in search and rescue operations with the call of FEMA.	Search and rescue operations were conducted by Civil Defense, Fire Department and NGO Search and Rescue teams.
Although Fire Department rushed 70 workers with heavy machines as a precaution, human labor was preferred rather than machine force.	Heavy machines were not allowed to operate at scenes until all injured and bodies were found and recovered.

Eight establishments participated in response operations: the Fire Department, Police, State Police, FBI, EOC, State EOC, Medical Works Directorate and Public Works.	Eight establishments participated in response operations under the control of the City Governor. Under the coordination of City EOC; the Civil Defense, City Medical Works Directorate, Crime Scene Investigations Directorate, Police Teams, Greater Municipality of Istanbul and dependent establishments, Province Municipalities, Public Works teams, and State Head Court of Republic (DGM) conducted all response operations.
A team of architects and civil engineers evaluated the building plans, and decided on how the injured would be rescued and where they might be.	A team of architects and civil engineers from the Public Works Directorate and the Greater Municipality of Istanbul searched affected structures in order to classify damage sustained.

Table 7. Communication

Oklahoma	Istanbul
911 telephone lines were blocked due to overloaded calls, immediately after television channels reported the event	Calls were not from citizens to officials, but from officials to officials. However, because of the communication traffic between citizens, local telephone and GSM lines were blocked.
There were communication problems between officials due to wireless systems. Responders tried to reach hospitals with runners. In order to overcome communication problems, two private communication companies provided free cell phones to responders.	There were no communication problems between responders; however, Turk Telecom network was blocked locally. During the second group of attacks, with the efforts of Turk Telecomm and private companies, these problems were resolved in 2 hours.

Table 8. Role of the media

Oklahoma	Istanbul
Immediately after the event, the media affected the responders due to contradicting news stories.	Immediately following the two groups of events, the media gave incorrect news about explosions in other provinces of Istanbul. News created panic among the public.
Responders applied some additional precautions to keep the media safe and away from the site. A press area was designated for the media.	Following the explosions, some media staff illegally entered the site with live electricity cables and natural gas odor. Later, they were kept away from the scene; no formal location was arranged for them to work in.
Media was informed regularly. Only verified information was given to the media. Police, FBI, Fire Department and the Public Works organized press conferences regularly.	Media was not informed regularly by press conferences. Because of the lack of flow of information, the media tried to get information from other sources leading to incorrect news.
Many volunteers came to the scene within the first hour to help; however, this led to chaos.	Following the initial chaos, similar to Oklahoma, only expert NGO volunteers were allowed to work on the scene.

3. Conclusion

The disaster management perspective of the November 20, 2003 events is presented, along with an academic comparison of the response efforts and capabilities with the April 19, 1995, Oklahoma City event. The response based on the level of damage is presented for the emergency medical services, search and rescue, communications, and the role of the media. The response efforts to the two events had varying successes, shortcomings, and challenges.

Countries can learn from each other, through their various disaster management techniques, and mechanisms. A successful response lies in the preparation of a comprehensive plan, execution of the plan, and effective management of resources. The April 19, 1995, Oklahoma City event and the November 20, 2003, Istanbul events, had various degrees of success in terms of response efforts. Both cities had plans in place, mitigation strategies, resources for response, and policies for recovery. These two response efforts in urban areas are exemplary cases to better prepare for future disasters.

References

[1] Center of Excellence for Disaster Management, *Basics of disaster management.* Istanbul: Istanbul Technical University Publications; 2001. *(in Turkish)*
[2] *Principles of emergency management course,* Federal Emergency Management Institute Course, Washington D.C., US.
[3] Great Municipality of Istanbul, *Urgent access and action plan for emergencies and disasters.* Istanbul: Transportation Planning Directorate; 2000, February. *(in Turkish)*
[4] D. Spaide, Talking about terror with kids. [Online] Available from: URL: http://www.soulrise.com/common/terror.htm [2006, August 20]
[5] Center of Excellence for Disaster Management, *Relationship with press and public during emergencies and disasters.* Istanbul: Istanbul Technical University Publications; 2001. *(in Turkish)*
[6] B. Akaltan, *Turkish media and disaster preparedness.* Masters Thesis, Istanbul Technical University, Center of Excellence for Disaster Management; 2003, December.
[7] R.W. Ritchie, *Emergency procedures for the small business and shop: A guide and disaster plan framework.* Springfield, Oregon: Ritchie Unlimited Publications; 1995.
[8] FEMA 426, *Reference manual to mitigate potential terrorism attacks against buildings.* Washington, D.C.: Federal Emergency Management Agency, Mitigation Directorate; 2003.
[9] K. Sengupta, Diplomats exposed by security failures. *The Independent* 2003, November 22.
[10] FEMA 427, *Primer for design of commercial buildings to mitigate terrorist attacks.* Washington, D.C.: Federal Emergency Management Agency, Mitigation Directorate; 2003, December.
[11] FEMA 331, *Protecting business operations, second report on costs and benefits of natural hazard mitigation.* Washington, D.C.: Federal Emergency Management Agency, Mitigation Directorate; 1998, August.
[12] Center of Excellence for Disaster Management, *Mitigation strategies for disaster managers.* Istanbul: Istanbul Technical University Publications; 2001. *(in Turkish)*
[13] Center of Excellence for Disaster Management, *Proceedings of international workshop on the restructuring of Turkish Fire Brigades under the light of international experiences.* Istanbul: Istanbul Technical University Publications; 2001. *(in Turkish)*
[14] Center of Excellence for Disaster Management, *Emergency management operations.* Istanbul: Istanbul Technical University Publications; 2001. *(in Turkish)*
[15] Center of Excellence for Disaster Management, *Incident command system.* Istanbul: Istanbul Technical University Publications; 2001. *(in Turkish)*
[16] US Department of State, *Significant terrorist incidents, 1961-2001: A brief chronology.* Office of the Historian Bureau of Public Affairs; 2003.
[17] T. Wahle, G. Beatty, *Emergency management guide for business & industry.* Prepared under FEMA Contract EMW-90-C-3348.
[18] B.A. Jackson, D.J. Peterson, J.T. Bartis, T. Tourrette, I. Brahmakulam, A. Houser, J. Sollinger, *Protecting emergency responders: Lessons learned from terrorist attacks.* RAND Science and Technology Policy Institute, Conference Proceedings; 2002.
[19] The City of Oklahoma City Document Management Team, *Alfred P. Murrah Federal Building bombing: Final report.* Oklahoma: Oklahoma City Fire Department Publications; 1996, July.

Building Trust among Community Stakeholders

Sudha ARLIKATTI[a], Michael K. LINDELL[b] and Carla S. PRATER[c]
[a] *Assistant Professor, University of North Texas, USA*
[b] *Professor, Texas A&M University, USA*
[c] *Associate Director, Texas A&M University, USA*

Abstract. Risk communication, consensus building, and protective action research literature have long argued that promoting trust among community stakeholders is beneficial in increasing risk perception and encouraging the adoption of risk reduction measures, thereby increasing disaster resilience. However, in recent years with the new command-and-control oriented Department of Homeland Security in place in the US, the values of transparency, cooperation, and collaboration, which are key to trust building, seem to be relegated to a secondary role. This paper reviews findings from empirical studies exploring the effects of trust on stakeholders risk perception and hazard adjustments adoption (pre-impact actions to reduce danger to persons and property). The findings point to the fact that perceived trust in our peer group (family, employers, and friends) stakeholders rather than our political group (local, state and federal government) stakeholders is key to the adoption of risk reduction measures. The paper concludes with suggestions on how emergency managers and policy makers can help build collaboration among community stakeholders thereby increasing knowledge and trustworthiness among peer groups. This will in turn help achieve the goals of risk communication and disaster resilience against multiple threats including natural, technological and terrorist.

Keywords. Trust, community stakeholders, risk communication, disaster resilience, collaboration

Introduction

The world that we live in today does not allow us simply to 'hope for the best.' Unfortunately we must be 'prepared for the worst!' The history of emergency management has evolved with changes in threats generated by advances in technology, demands on the environment created by changing settlement patterns, and increases in terrorist activities. For many years, emergency management in the US was framed in terms of the Cold War confrontation with the Soviet Union. In the 1980s and 1990s a shift in framing from civil defense to *Comprehensive Emergency Management* occurred, which promoted an increased emphasis on natural hazards and technological accidents. The attack on the World Trade Center on 11 September 2001 caused the federal government to reframe emergency management in terms of terrorism, coining the phrase 'Homeland Security' to describe the new frame of reference. Response generated lessons from emergency management endeavors of organizations and communities continue to point to the importance of trust among community stakeholders. However, in recent years with the new command-and-control oriented Department of Homeland Security in place the values of transparency, cooperation, and collaboration, which are key to building trust, seem to be relegated to a secondary role.

The purpose of this paper is to briefly review the conceptual basis of trust as a component of the process of amplification/attenuation of risk, the bases of power that affect consensus building among policy stakeholders, and the adoption of risk reduction measures by households. It concludes by emphasizing the importance of trust among peer groups (employer, friends, family) in affecting risk perception, hazard adjustment adoption (pre-impact actions to reduce danger to persons and property), and building disaster resilience to multiple threats.

1. Community Stakeholders

We use the term 'community' in a general sense, as a unified body of individuals or people living in the same place under the same laws, and 'stakeholders' as people who have or think they have a personal interest in the outcome of a policy or share in an undertaking. Consequently we recognize all citizens as being 'emergency management stakeholders' as they are affected directly or indirectly by the decisions made (or not made) by emergency managers or policy makers in the community. Although this is true, it is not very helpful because stakeholders differ in the ways they are affected by emergency management policies and, even more importantly, they differ in the times at which they are affected, and the magnitude of the effects the policies have on them. Hence it is important to understand the differences among these stakeholders. Community stakeholders having an interest in the emergency management process can be broadly divided into three different categories -social, economic, and political groups.

Lindell et al. [1] held that the adoption of household hazard adjustments (pre-impact actions to reduce danger to persons and property) is linked to extremes in the physical environment and societal/community stakeholders by three dyadic relationships as illustrated in Figure 1. Risk of disaster impact defines the relationship between environmental extremes and societal stakeholders; cost defines the relationship between these stakeholders and hazard adjustments; and efficacy (i.e., the degree to which adjustments reduce risks) defines the relationship between hazard adjustments and environmental extremes.

1.1. Social Groups

Social groups include households, friends, employers, news media, non-profit, non-governmental organizations, and religious institutions. It is sometimes said that local government is the foundation for emergency management but, in fact, the basic organizational unit for emergency management is the household [2]. Households adopt risk reducing or protective measures (hazard adjustments), households evacuate, and households suffer economic losses. All households, no matter their size or level of resources, have an interest in the emergency management policies developed and implemented in their communities. While we recognize that the choices households make are constrained by socioeconomic conditions, it is nevertheless true that households affect the vulnerability of a substantial amount of financial assets (in aggregate) by choosing to live in hazard prone areas and when they do so, choosing whether or not to adopt pre-impact hazard adjustments. Peers (family and friends) are sources of information and social comparison [3]. Employers affect household members' safety through hazard adjustments that protect employees in the workplace. The news media comprise an important social group because they can put environmental hazards on the public agenda and educate those who do not have direct experiences with disasters [4]. Finally, non-profits and non-governmental organizations, including religious organizations, can provide information and resources to households seeking to reduce their exposure to hazards.

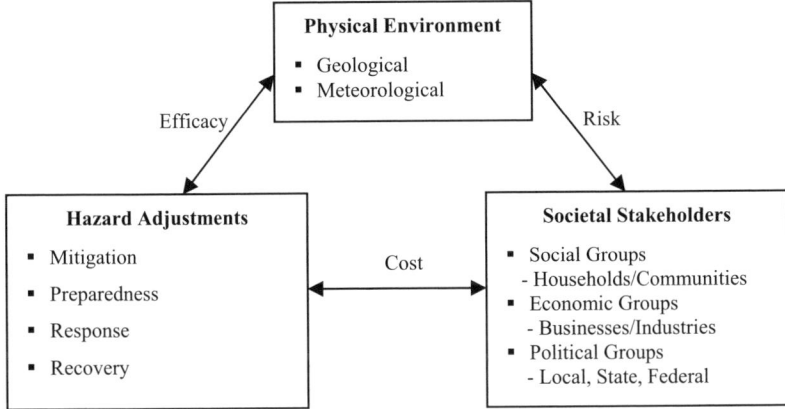

Figure 1. Interrelationships among environmental extremes, societal stakeholders, and hazard adjustments

1.2. Economic Groups

As households are the basic units in the hierarchy of social stakeholders, so too are individual businesses the fundamental units in the hierarchy of economic stakeholders. Businesses are important stakeholders because they are part of the societal flow of goods and services. Destruction, damage, or even interruption of business activities can have significant adverse effects on the local economy and, in smaller countries, on the regional or even national economy. Business owners are in control of their resources in the same way as householders and, thus, can make the same sort of choices about how to react to hazards. Unlike households -which rarely exceed more than a half-dozen persons in number- businesses range in size from 'small mom-and-pops' that are the same size as families to large multinational corporations employing tens or even hundreds of thousands of people.

1.3. Political Groups

Finally, there are various types of governmental stakeholders including the local, state and federal government. Beginning at the base, we have the lowest level of organization, the municipality (i.e., town or city) and, just above this, the county. These jurisdictions have varying levels of power from one state to another in each country because of differences in the powers granted to political subdivisions. In the US, much emergency management policy is set at the state level, and the federal level has traditionally been seen as a supporter of local and state efforts. Political stakeholders include authorities such as federal, state, and local government agencies that have extensive resources of knowledge and capital. These jurisdictions bear legal responsibility for protecting the health and safety of residents within their jurisdictions, but vary in their sizes and level of resources available.

2. Stakeholders and Power

The previous section noted that stakeholders vary in the types and amounts of resources they bring to the emergency management process. One of the greatest differences is in the power different stakeholders have to influence other stakeholders' behavior, and thus alter emergency management policy. More specifically, organizational theorists have described six types or bases of power -reward, coercive, legitimate, expert, referent, and information power [5, 6]. These different forms of power can be distinguished on the basis of social dependence and the need for surveillance to maintain the target's desired behavior. The most familiar bases of power (reward and coercive) are the principal bases of regulatory approaches and are most commonly associated with governmental actors, but Raven [7] noted these require continuing surveillance to assure that rewards are received only for compliance and punishment regularly follows noncompliance. Unfortunately, state mandates are hampered by a lack of formal reporting or review by state officials, and limited or no penalties for failing to enforce their provisions [8, 9]. Consequently, there is a need to better understand the ways in which households can be influenced by bases of power other than those used by governmental actors. Legitimate, expert, and referent power do not depend so heavily on surveillance, but their exercise depends on the social relationship between the parties in the transaction. Legitimate power most frequently comes from a formal social relationship (a city mayor has such power), expert power derives from the possession of socially valued knowledge, and referent power is based on the targets' identification with the power holder. Finally, information power involves the introduction or withholding of useful information that may not rise to the level of understanding an expert has yet is valid, novel and relevant [10]. Peers may have such information power about hazards and methods of mitigating or preparing for them.

The existence of these multiple bases of power should make it clear that power operates in the upward (i.e., households to local government to states to federal government) as well as in the downward direction. Thus, households and businesses can exert upward influence through lawsuits, boycotts, public ridicule, and voter pressure that allows them to actively resist other stakeholders' actions. This balance of power is the consequence of the federal political structure of the US coupled with a market economy which produces a complex policy environment that is fragmented vertically (between different levels of government) and horizontally (between the private and public sectors, and within the latter, among agencies within a given community). Planning and consensus building literature have also indicated that power differentials among stakeholders lead to positive and negative tensions [11, 12] affecting stakeholder relationships and the policy evaluation and implementation stages.

3. Expected Benefits of Trust

Although trustworthiness clearly is an important stakeholder attribute, it is difficult to make specific predictions about differences in stakeholders' perceived trustworthiness because the most relevant research on trust in institutions has examined only a few of the stakeholders that are relevant to household hazard adjustment adoption. For example, the Gallup Organization [13] reported that only a minority had a "great deal/quite a lot" of confidence in newspapers (33%) and TV news (35%); the other institutions included big business (22%), police (61%), the Presidency (55%), and Congress (29%). Furthermore, scholars have attributed the failure of risk control efforts to lack of trust, transparency, and openness [14], and have sought to add general requirements of a democratic society such as social trust [15] to the risk amplification process through which an understanding of risk is developed and disseminated in a community. Trust also generates an increased probability of changing the attitudes of others [16]. Following this line of thought, Frewer [17] has contended the role of public trust in institutions plays an important role in social amplification of risk and therefore merits further empirical investigation. French and Raven's [5] conception of referent power suggests addressing the trustworthiness of different stakeholders. This is reinforced by Kasperson et al.'s [18] social amplification/ attenuation of risk framework, which seeks to explain why "risk events with minor physical consequences often elicit strong public concern and produce extraordinarily severe social impacts" (pg. 177) (see also [14]).

The planning and consensus building onion model (Figure 2) presented by Godschalk, et al. [11] implies that trust will be highest in stakeholders that are closest to the respondents (peers) and lowest in the stakeholders that are the most remote from the respondents (federal government). According to this line of reasoning, the higher similarity in values between respondents and peers, one of the major bases of interpersonal attraction [19], would be expected to lead peers to communicate more honestly about seismic hazards and be perceived as more trustworthy [20]. However, peers might be perceived to be more variable in trustworthiness and this variability would decrease the mean rating. By contrast, an alternative line of reasoning suggests government and news media are likely to be trusted more than peers because of *role-based trust* that is "predicated on knowledge that specific person occupies a particular role in the organization rather than specific knowledge about the person's capabilities, dispositions, motives, and intentions" [21, pg. 578].

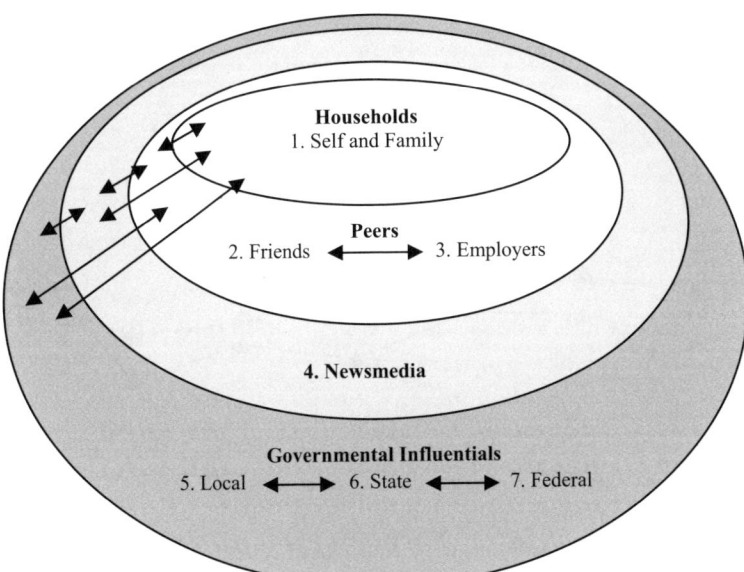

Figure 2. Stakeholder interactions related to adoption of hazard adjustments
(Adapted from Godschalk et al. [11])

Survey results from a study by Arlikatti, Lindell, and Prater [22] on self-reported adoption of 16 seismic protective actions by residents in areas of high and medium seismic risks are shown in Figure 3. Results from this randomly sampled longitudinal panel of 232 residents from 6 cities showed that the mean ratings for perceived trustworthiness and hazard knowledge were consistently high for the state and local governments, media and self/family and consistently low for employers and friends in both years of our survey. However, there was a seeming paradox when it came to significant correlations predicting protective action decision making. Perceived knowledge, trustworthiness and responsibility of their peers (employer, friends and self/family) -not of governmental influentials and news media- correlated significantly with respondents' self reported hazard adjustments adoption. Results from the 1997 panel data revealed significant ($p < .01$) correlations of hazard adjustments adoption with peer group knowledge (average $r = 0.31$), peer group trustworthiness (average $r = 0.31$), and peer group responsibility (average $r = 0.18$). The panel responses from 1999 revealed similar results.

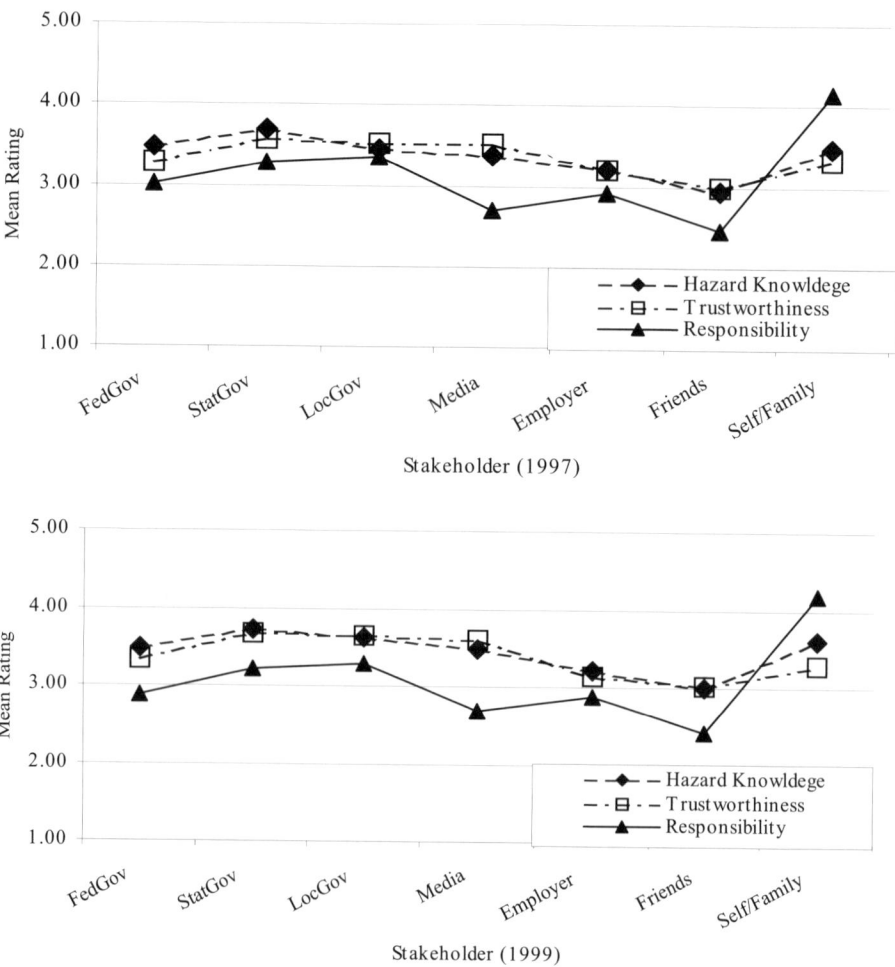

Figure 3. Mean ratings of perceived hazard knowledge, trustworthiness, and protection responsibility across seven stakeholders in 1997 and 1999 - Seismic hazard adjustment adoption decision making

There were statistically significant ($p < .01$) correlations of hazard adjustment adoptions with peer group knowledge (average $r = 0.28$), employer trustworthiness ($r = 0.20$), self/family trustworthiness ($r = 0.21$), and self/family responsibility ($r = 0.23$) ratings.

Thus, even though peers are presumed to know less (and be less trustworthy) than the authorities and media, they have more influence on respondents' risk perceptions and adoption of hazard adjustments. This implies that, to increase people's adoption of protective measures, one could try to increase peers' perceived hazard knowledge and trustworthiness. One way to achieve this objective would be to increase their knowledge through a hazard awareness program. Alternatively, peers might actually have high levels of hazard knowledge, but this would not be obvious unless they engage in discussions or behaviors that reveal their knowledge. Thus, it might be that increasing the accuracy of people's beliefs about their peers' hazard knowledge would increase their levels of trustworthiness and hazard adjustment adoption.

4. Conclusion

Whatever the frame of reference, be it civil defense, comprehensive emergency management, or the war on terror, emergency managers and disaster researchers need to familiarize themselves with the different types of stakeholders in their communities. Decisions about the level of preparedness for each individual household are made at the household level and emergency managers can support good mitigation and preparedness practices by undertaking public education efforts and enhancing local government support for organizations like Community Emergency Response Teams (CERTs).

Focusing on an all hazards approach to increasing risk perception and risk communication is the key to this endeavor [23]. Some of the ways in which we can encourage dialogue between community stakeholders are elaborated below.

1. One of the most obvious gaps in the picture of stakeholders is the lack of broad-based support groups for individual householders analogous to the Neighborhood Watch programs that exist across the country. CERTs and other similarly designated groups are neighborhood emergency response and/or assistance teams that share a common origin and many other characteristics [24]. They should be encouraged and supported by local fire departments and other governmental organizations with emergency management responsibilities. As CERTs become institutionalized they can serve as support groups and interest aggregators, transferring information about householder needs up to the government as well as information about how to deal with hazards down to householders.
2. Private sector groups like non-governmental, non-profit, and community based organizations, businesses, and religious organizations that reach out to larger peer groups should be integrated in the early stages of risk communication in order to ensure their resources are fully utilized without unnecessary duplication of effort and competition. They can serve the same information dissemination and interest aggregation functions as CERTs.
3. Large scale environmental organizations like the Sierra Club and the World Watch Institute that are key sources of information and support interdisciplinary environmental research on both the national and global scales have not been involved with local emergency management agencies. These alliances need to be

forged at the local government level so that citizens can learn from best practices, or lessons learned from across the globe, helping them look at the bigger picture of sustainable communities instead of being limited to the micro-level. Such linkages between the environmental and hazards communities could go a long way to raising the importance of hazards on the local agenda.

4. With rapid restoration of basic services being the key to post disaster recovery efforts it is important to encourage businesses at the local level to understand the importance of their linkages to suppliers, customers and employers as well as their dependence on a functioning infrastructure system [25]. This linkage was fostered by the 'Partnership model' that was promoted by FEMAs Project Impact Initiative that many cities began experimenting with during the 1990s. Federal funding should be restored so that the Project Impact Model can once again spread to cities around the country. It is a valuable method for emergency managers to develop a more trusting, transparent and cooperative relationship with local business communities. Ultimately the key to disaster resilience is to continue to work on improving risk communication and ensuring that all the stakeholders in the community work in unison.

References

[1] M.K. Lindell, D. Alesch, P.A. Bolton, M.R. Greene, L.A. Larson, R. Lopes, P.J. May, J.P. Mulilis, S. Nathe, J.M. Nigg, R. Palm, P. Pate, R.W. Perry, J. Pine, K. Tubbesing, D.J. Whitney, Adoption and implementation of hazard adjustments. *International Journal of Mass Emergencies and Disasters* Special Issue **15** (1997), 327-453.
[2] M.K. Lindell, C.S. Prater, R.W. Perry, *Fundamentals of emergency management.* Emmitsburg: Federal Emergency Management Agency, Emergency Management Institute; 2006. [Online] Available from: URL: http://www.training.fema.gov/EMIWeb/edu/fem.asp [2006, November 10]
[3] J.C. Turner, *Social influence.* Pacific Grove: Brooks/Cole; 1991.
[4] C.S. Prater, M.K. Lindell, Politics of hazard mitigation. *Natural Hazards Review* **1** (2000), 73-82.
[5] J.P. French, B.H. Raven, The bases of social power. In D. Cartwright, editor. *Studies in social power.* Ann Arbor: Institute for Social Research; 1959. p 150-167.
[6] B.H. Raven, Social influence and power. In I.D. Steiner, M. Fishbein, editors. *Current studies in social psychology.* New York: Holt, Rinehart and Winston; 1965. p 371-382.
[7] B.H. Raven, The bases of power: Origins and recent developments. *Journal of Social Issues* **49** (1993), 227-251.
[8] R.J. Burby, S.P. French, A.C. Nelson, Plans, code enforcement, and damage reduction: Evidence from the Northridge earthquake. *Earthquake Spectra* **14** (1998), 59-74.
[9] A.C. Nelson, S.P. French, Plan quality and mitigating damage from natural disasters: A case study of the Northridge earthquake with planning policy considerations. *Journal of the American Planning Association* **68** (2002), 194-207.
[10] E. Burnstein, A. Vinokur, Persuasive argumentation and social comparison as determinants of attitude polarization. *Journal of Experimental Social Psychology* **13** (1997), 315-332.
[11] D. Godschalk, D. Parham, D. Porter, W. Potapchuk, S. Schukraft, *Pulling together: A planning and development consensus building manual.* Washington, D.C.: Urban Land Institute; 1994.
[12] S.D. Brody, D.R. Godschalk, R.J. Burby, Mandating citizen participation in plan making. *Journal of the American Planning Association* **69** (2003), 245-266.
[13] Gallup Organization, Trust in institutions. The Gallup Poll Tuesday briefing (2003, June 9-10), 32-38.
[14] J.X. Kasperson, R.E. Kasperson, N. Pidgeon, P. Slovic, The social amplification of risk: Assessing fifteen years of research and theory. In N. Pidgeon, R.E. Kasperson, P. Slovic, editors. *The social amplification of risk.* New York: Cambridge University Press; 2003. p 13-46.
[15] G. Cvetkovich, R.E. Lofstedt, *Social trust and the management of risk.* London: Earthscan; 1999.
[16] A. Maass, R.D. Clark, Internalization versus compliance: Differential processes underlying minority influence and conformity. *European Journal of Social Psychology* **13** (1983), 197-215.

[17] L.J. Frewer, Trust, transparency, and social context: Implications for social amplification of risk. In N. Pidgeon, R.E. Kasperson, P. Slovic, editors. *The social amplification of risk.* New York: Cambridge University Press; 2003. p 123-137.
[18] R.E. Kasperson, O. Renn, P. Slovic, A.S. Brown, J. Emel, R. Goble, J.X. Kasperson, S. Natick, The social amplification of risk: A conceptual framework. *Risk Analysis* **8** (1998), 178-187.
[19] E. Berscheid, Interpersonal attraction. In G. Lindzey, E. Aronson, editors. *The handbook of social psychology* (Volume 2). New York: Random House; 1985. p 413-484.
[20] W.J. McGuire, Attitudes and attitude change. In G. Lindzey, E. Aronson, editors. *The handbook of social psychology.* New York: Random House; 1985. p 233-346.
[21] R.M. Kramer, Trust and distrust in organizations: Emerging perspectives, enduring questions. *Annual Review of Psychology* **50** (1999), 569-598.
[22] S. Arlikatti, M. Lindell, C. Prater, *Perceived stakeholder role relationships and adoption of seismic hazard adjustments.* College Station: Texas A&M University, Hazard Reduction & Recovery Center; 2006.
[23] M.K. Lindell, R.W. Perry, *Behavioral foundations of community emergency planning.* Washington, D.C.: Hemisphere Press; 1992.
[24] D.A. Simpson, Community Emergency Response Training (CERTs): A recent history and review. *Natural Hazards Review* **2** (2001), 54-63.
[25] M.K. Lindell, C.S. Prater, Assessing community impacts of natural disasters. *Natural Hazards Review* **4** (2003), 176-185.

Part 5

Closing Remarks

Closing Remarks

Mathieu DEFLEM
University of South Carolina, USA

The following four issues were central in the presentations and discussions at the workshop sessions on counter-terrorism policing and cooperation.

1. Objectives of Counter-Terrorism

In terms of the objectives of counter-terrorism policing, a critical issue remains the manifold definitions of terrorism that exist. Related problems are the extent to which terrorism is considered a political violation or, conversely, a crime. The connection with religion is problematic as well. Depending on how the problem of terrorism is defined, different nations respond differently. To some extent these responses across the world may nonetheless exhibit certain similarities, so that there is a factual harmonization of legal systems across different nations. Thus, while not every nation defines terrorism in the same way, it is also true that there are certain similarities. Arguably, also, these similarities have increased in more recent times and they may additional increase in the future.

2. National Police Responses

With respect to the police response to terrorism, a central characteristic of the policing of any form of criminal activity is that the police response is always of a primarily local character. And even though terrorism is a distinctly international crime, especially under present conditions of globalization, police forces by definition have limited jurisdictional competency.

However, there is also a process of standardization of counter-terrorism policing strategies and an increasing interconnectedness of police across nations in matters of terrorism. First, the police response to terrorism in countries where terrorism is very central problem (e.g., Turkey, Israel, USA since 9/11) may serve as a model for similar police operations in other nations. Second, there are also local police operations against terrorism in nations where the terrorism problem is less directly relevant. In such nations, the training of terrorist organizations or the use of financial institutions for terrorist means may pose a peculiar problem. In this sense, many more nations than ever before have a local response in relation to counter-terrorism.

3. Methods of Counter-Terrorism Policing

Among the two most important components that have been discussed in the panels on the policing of terrorism are the methods in the fight against terrorism, particularly from international point of view. At least three methods have been given centrality in international cooperation efforts against terrorist activities:

3.1. Information Sharing

The exchange of information about terrorist activities and organizations among police organizations in different nations and between police organizations at the national and international is an extremely important component to establish effective counter-terrorism policing. Sometimes, this information exchange even takes place across types of organization (inter-agency cooperation) as terrorism is in some nations primarily a police responsibility, whereas in other nations it is handled by intelligence agencies.

3.2. The Role of Technology

The technological emphasis in counter-terrorism policing stems in part from the fact that terrorist organizations rely heavily on advanced technologies. The increasing use of the internet, cell phones, and various kinds of information storage and distribution systems has increased the importance of technology. Relatedly, of special importance are the counter-terrorism strategies aimed at the financial infrastructure of terrorist organizations.

3.3. The Rise of Intelligence Policing

Modern law enforcement is much more focused on intelligence-led police strategies. For example, Europol places a strong emphasis on the analysis of information. Local police agencies in many nations, likewise, rely on intelligence, for instance to collect information about events taking place in communities that are suspected to be more likely to have people potentially contributing to terrorist organizations.

4. Cooperation

A final important component in the policing of terrorism is cooperation, including both international cooperation between police organizations across nations as well as inter-agency cooperation. For effective cooperation to take a place, whether it is at a limited bilateral level or in multilateral organizations, there must be a good rapport established on a personal level. In that respect, a meeting such as this workshop plays an important role as well. Whether institutions and formal policies are in place to facilitate cooperation or not, cooperation practices are always engaged by people, bringing a central personal component to cooperation.

With respect to the form, cooperation can vary from bilateral cooperation for specific cases, involving the police of only two nations, to participation in large multilateral organizations, such as Interpol. Typically, police agencies find ways to deal with these various models without there being any kind of overlap or conflict. The most appropriate models are used in terms of the specific needs that arise.

In terms of international cooperation, there is also a growing need for international police training. Nations that have a long history with terrorism can be more supportive towards those nations where terrorism is relatively new problem. In this sense, some of the expertise and experience of the police in some nations can be used to the benefit of the police in other nations where the focus on terrorism is more recent.

Finally, it is important to recognize that, corresponding to the theme of our conference, terrorism is indeed a multi-dimensional issue. Terrorism is not just a crime that is in need of a law enforcement response. Terrorism is also a disaster, a hazardous event that produces a lot of victims. This means that it is also in need of an emergency response. The complexity of terrorism thus requires more advanced models of interagency cooperation across agencies with different functions (police, emergency, and so on). This is an important problem that needs to be addressed.

Author Index

Afacan, M.	252	Lindell, M.K.	383
Akdogan, H.	318	Mace, R.R.	236
Akgul, A.	84	Marenin, O.	84
Alasania, G.	138	McEntire, D.A.	344
Alkan, N.	285	McGarrell, E.F.	221
Arlikatti, S.	383	Mehdiyev, F.	207
Aydin, S.	242	Oguz, E.	271
Benavides, A.	352	Ormon Uulu, I.	260
Cinoglu, H.	99	Pamuk, Z.	307
Citak, M.C.	285	Prater, C.S.	383
Deflem, M.	v, 17, 395	Ratzel, M.-P.	11
Demir, S.	26	Roth, M.P.	42
Durmaz, H.	v, 66	Rozdilsky, J.L.	314
Ekici, S.	344	Safak, A.	117
Gultekin, K.	99	Sanoyan, A.	173
Gultekin, R.	99	Schoch-Spana, M.	364
Gultekin, S.	352	Sever, M.	42
Gurer, C.	26	Sloan, S.	217
Hurst, J.	3	Stojanovski, T.	153
Ivaschenko, O.	164	Teymur, S.	99
Kapti, A.	307	Ural, D.N.	375
Kapucu, N.	336	Wachtendorf, T.	324
Kazimli, E.	111	Yasar, M.M.	56
Kendra, J.	324	Yayla, A.S.	185
Khaschevoi, M.	164	Zengin, S.	56, 99
Kongantiev, K.T.	129